Lecture Notes in Computer Science   10921

Commenced Publication in 1973
Founding and Former Series Editors:
Gerhard Goos, Juris Hartmanis, and Jan van Leeuwen

More information about this series at http://www.springer.com/series/7409

Norbert Streitz · Shin'ichi Konomi (Eds.)

Distributed, Ambient and Pervasive Interactions

Understanding Humans

6th International Conference, DAPI 2018
Held as Part of HCI International 2018
Las Vegas, NV, USA, July 15–20, 2018
Proceedings, Part I

 Springer

Editors
Norbert Streitz (iD)
Smart Future Initiative
Frankfurt am Main
Germany

Shin'ichi Konomi
Learning Analytics Center
Kyushu University
Fukuoka
Japan

ISSN 0302-9743   ISSN 1611-3349   (electronic)
Lecture Notes in Computer Science
ISBN 978-3-319-91124-3   ISBN 978-3-319-91125-0   (eBook)
https://doi.org/10.1007/978-3-319-91125-0

Library of Congress Control Number: 2018942173

LNCS Sublibrary: SL3 – Information Systems and Applications, incl. Internet/Web, and HCI

This Springer imprint is published by the registered company Springer International Publishing AG
part of Springer Nature
The registered company address is: Gewerbestrasse 11, 6330 Cham, Switzerland

Foreword

The 20th International Conference on Human-Computer Interaction, HCI International 2018, was held in Las Vegas, NV, USA, during July 15–20, 2018. The event incorporated the 14 conferences/thematic areas listed on the following page.

A total of 4,373 individuals from academia, research institutes, industry, and governmental agencies from 76 countries submitted contributions, and 1,170 papers and 195 posters have been included in the proceedings. These contributions address the latest research and development efforts and highlight the human aspects of design and use of computing systems. The contributions thoroughly cover the entire field of human-computer interaction, addressing major advances in knowledge and effective use of computers in a variety of application areas. The volumes constituting the full set of the conference proceedings are listed in the following pages.

I would like to thank the program board chairs and the members of the program boards of all thematic areas and affiliated conferences for their contribution to the highest scientific quality and the overall success of the HCI International 2018 conference.

This conference would not have been possible without the continuous and unwavering support and advice of the founder, Conference General Chair Emeritus and Conference Scientific Advisor Prof. Gavriel Salvendy. For his outstanding efforts, I would like to express my appreciation to the communications chair and editor of *HCI International News*, Dr. Abbas Moallem.

July 2018   Constantine Stephanidis

HCI International 2018 Thematic Areas and Affiliated Conferences

Thematic areas:

- Human-Computer Interaction (HCI 2018)
- Human Interface and the Management of Information (HIMI 2018)

Affiliated conferences:

- 15th International Conference on Engineering Psychology and Cognitive Ergonomics (EPCE 2018)
- 12th International Conference on Universal Access in Human-Computer Interaction (UAHCI 2018)
- 10th International Conference on Virtual, Augmented, and Mixed Reality (VAMR 2018)
- 10th International Conference on Cross-Cultural Design (CCD 2018)
- 10th International Conference on Social Computing and Social Media (SCSM 2018)
- 12th International Conference on Augmented Cognition (AC 2018)
- 9th International Conference on Digital Human Modeling and Applications in Health, Safety, Ergonomics, and Risk Management (DHM 2018)
- 7th International Conference on Design, User Experience, and Usability (DUXU 2018)
- 6th International Conference on Distributed, Ambient, and Pervasive Interactions (DAPI 2018)
- 5th International Conference on HCI in Business, Government, and Organizations (HCIBGO)
- 5th International Conference on Learning and Collaboration Technologies (LCT 2018)
- 4th International Conference on Human Aspects of IT for the Aged Population (ITAP 2018)

Conference Proceedings Volumes Full List

1. LNCS 10901, Human-Computer Interaction: Theories, Methods, and Human Issues (Part I), edited by Masaaki Kurosu
2. LNCS 10902, Human-Computer Interaction: Interaction in Context (Part II), edited by Masaaki Kurosu
3. LNCS 10903, Human-Computer Interaction: Interaction Technologies (Part III), edited by Masaaki Kurosu
4. LNCS 10904, Human Interface and the Management of Information: Interaction, Visualization, and Analytics (Part I), edited by Sakae Yamamoto and Hirohiko Mori
5. LNCS 10905, Human Interface and the Management of Information: Information in Applications and Services (Part II), edited by Sakae Yamamoto and Hirohiko Mori
6. LNAI 10906, Engineering Psychology and Cognitive Ergonomics, edited by Don Harris
7. LNCS 10907, Universal Access in Human-Computer Interaction: Methods, Technologies, and Users (Part I), edited by Margherita Antona and Constantine Stephanidis
8. LNCS 10908, Universal Access in Human-Computer Interaction: Virtual, Augmented, and Intelligent Environments (Part II), edited by Margherita Antona and Constantine Stephanidis
9. LNCS 10909, Virtual, Augmented and Mixed Reality: Interaction, Navigation, Visualization, Embodiment, and Simulation (Part I), edited by Jessie Y. C. Chen and Gino Fragomeni
10. LNCS 10910, Virtual, Augmented and Mixed Reality: Applications in Health, Cultural Heritage, and Industry (Part II), edited by Jessie Y. C. Chen and Gino Fragomeni
11. LNCS 10911, Cross-Cultural Design: Methods, Tools, and Users (Part I), edited by Pei-Luen Patrick Rau
12. LNCS 10912, Cross-Cultural Design: Applications in Cultural Heritage, Creativity, and Social Development (Part II), edited by Pei-Luen Patrick Rau
13. LNCS 10913, Social Computing and Social Media: User Experience and Behavior (Part I), edited by Gabriele Meiselwitz
14. LNCS 10914, Social Computing and Social Media: Technologies and Analytics (Part II), edited by Gabriele Meiselwitz
15. LNAI 10915, Augmented Cognition: Intelligent Technologies (Part I), edited by Dylan D. Schmorrow and Cali M. Fidopiastis
16. LNAI 10916, Augmented Cognition: Users and Contexts (Part II), edited by Dylan D. Schmorrow and Cali M. Fidopiastis
17. LNCS 10917, Digital Human Modeling and Applications in Health, Safety, Ergonomics, and Risk Management, edited by Vincent G. Duffy
18. LNCS 10918, Design, User Experience, and Usability: Theory and Practice (Part I), edited by Aaron Marcus and Wentao Wang

19. LNCS 10919, Design, User Experience, and Usability: Designing Interactions (Part II), edited by Aaron Marcus and Wentao Wang
20. LNCS 10920, Design, User Experience, and Usability: Users, Contexts, and Case Studies (Part III), edited by Aaron Marcus and Wentao Wang
21. LNCS 10921, Distributed, Ambient, and Pervasive Interactions: Understanding Humans (Part I), edited by Norbert Streitz and Shin'ichi Konomi
22. LNCS 10922, Distributed, Ambient, and Pervasive Interactions: Technologies and Contexts (Part II), edited by Norbert Streitz and Shin'ichi Konomi
23. LNCS 10923, HCI in Business, Government, and Organizations, edited by Fiona Fui-Hoon Nah and Bo Sophia Xiao
24. LNCS 10924, Learning and Collaboration Technologies: Design, Development and Technological Innovation (Part I), edited by Panayiotis Zaphiris and Andri Ioannou
25. LNCS 10925, Learning and Collaboration Technologies: Learning and Teaching (Part II), edited by Panayiotis Zaphiris and Andri Ioannou
26. LNCS 10926, Human Aspects of IT for the Aged Population: Acceptance, Communication, and Participation (Part I), edited by Jia Zhou and Gavriel Salvendy
27. LNCS 10927, Human Aspects of IT for the Aged Population: Applications in Health, Assistance, and Entertainment (Part II), edited by Jia Zhou and Gavriel Salvendy
28. CCIS 850, HCI International 2018 Posters Extended Abstracts (Part I), edited by Constantine Stephanidis
29. CCIS 851, HCI International 2018 Posters Extended Abstracts (Part II), edited by Constantine Stephanidis
30. CCIS 852, HCI International 2018 Posters Extended Abstracts (Part III), edited by Constantine Stephanidis

http://2018.hci.international/proceedings

6th International Conference on Distributed, Ambient, and Pervasive Interactions

Program Board Chair(s): Norbert Streitz, *Germany* and Shin'ichi Konomi, *Japan*

The full list with the Program Board Chairs and the members of the Program Boards of all thematic areas and affiliated conferences is available online at:

http://www.hci.international/board-members-2018.php

HCI International 2019

The 21st International Conference on Human-Computer Interaction, HCI International 2019, will be held jointly with the affiliated conferences in Orlando, FL, USA, at Walt Disney World Swan and Dolphin Resort, July 26–31, 2019. It will cover a broad spectrum of themes related to Human-Computer Interaction, including theoretical issues, methods, tools, processes, and case studies in HCI design, as well as novel interaction techniques, interfaces, and applications. The proceedings will be published by Springer. More information will be available on the conference website: http://2019.hci.international/.

General Chair
Prof. Constantine Stephanidis
University of Crete and ICS-FORTH
Heraklion, Crete, Greece
E-mail: general_chair@hcii2019.org

http://2019.hci.international/

Contents – Part I

Internet of Things and Smart Cities

Contents – Part II

Human Activity and Context Understanding

Human Enhancement in Intelligent Environments

Affect and Humour in Intelligent Environments

Designing and Developing Intelligent
Environment

Design Towards AI-Powered Workplace of the Future

Yujia Cao[✉][iD], Jiri Vasek, and Matej Dusik

Konica Minolta Laboratory Europe, Brno, Czech Republic
{yujia.cao,jiri.vasek,matej.dusik}@konicaminolta.cz

Abstract. The advances of technology have profoundly improved the way people live and work. However, accompanying fast-paced technological development is information overload, which can minimise our capacity for cognitive processing and our ability to make quality decisions. We conducted extensive user research to identify needs and problems of contemporary office workers. Based on the insights of these real needs, the concept of a system called Cognitive Hub has been developed which supports an activity-based new metaphor for work, user state adaptation, smart enterprise search, smart transformation between physical and digital contents and multimodal interaction. Konica Minolta is thus developing Cognitive Hub as a platform that will serve as a nexus for users' information flows within the digital workplace. Cognitive Hub will also provide AI-based services to improve work experience and the well-being of office workers. A demonstrator was created to show the concept in action and illustrate its benefits and value for users.

Keywords: Digital workplace · Artificial intelligence · User-centred design
User state inference · Multimodal interaction

1 Introduction

We live in an era of unprecedented change. The world's population is expected to reach 7.6 billion in 2020, and the number of connected devices is expected to grow to between 20 and 30 billion by the same year as the Internet of Things (IoT) continues to mature. We are observing an exponential increase in available data and ubiquitous information that together are already causing information overload. This overloading can minimise our capacity for cognitive processing and our ability to make quality decisions. It is apparent that we have entered an era in which new human necessities are emerging: we strive to reduce the time spent searching for and memorising reliable information; we struggle with the risks associated with the security of digital information; and we battle to manage a plethora of unforeseen events and adapt to fast-paced changes around us. Artificial intelligence (AI) can provide the answer to many of these needs by offering a system of technologies that can automate information flows and help us to better identify relevant digital contents, make informed decisions and to take advantage of enhanced cognition in a broader sense [17].

© Springer International Publishing AG, part of Springer Nature 2018
N. Streitz and S. Konomi (Eds.): DAPI 2018, LNCS 10921, pp. 3–20, 2018.
https://doi.org/10.1007/978-3-319-91125-0_1

Konica Minolta Laboratory Europe is embracing the AI challenges with a focus on the context where most of our skills reside: the workplace. Our proposed solution is a platform called Cognitive Hub. It is expected to become a nexus for users' information flows within the digital workplace and provide augmented-intelligence-based services to improve the work experience and more importantly the overall well-being of office workers. The concept of Cognitive Hub is built upon extensive user research of current problems and needs in the workplace (see Sect. 2), so that it is meaningful and valuable to the users. The concept delivers benefits through features including: supporting a personalised activity-based approach to work; smart enterprise search; user state adaptation; and smart transformation between digital and physical contents and multimodal interaction (see Sect. 3). Cognitive Hub is powered by various cutting-edge AI/HCI (human computer interaction) technologies including: semantic understanding of data, smart data categorisation, machine learning, computer vision, speech recognition, natural language understanding, gaze recognition and multimodal fusion. Section 4 presents a demonstrator that shows the concept of Cognitive Hub in action with a defined set of interaction scenarios.

2 Needs of Contemporary Office Worker

Following a user-centred design approach, a combination of methods has been employed including desk research, design thinking workshops, and interviews with end-users to identify problems and needs in the current workplace. The interview questionnaire consisted of 51 questions that spread over 8 topics, including: task management, time management, information management, team collaboration, communication, productivity, work load, work satisfaction and work-life balance. The interview was conducted with 19 participants in 6 European countries. The participants had varied job positions such as: management, researcher, logistics, accountant, salesman, customer support and IT administrator. The analysis of the interviews revealed that there were 8 categories of needs, described below, that were tightly interconnected and centred around the concept of well-being (see Fig. 1).

The Need to Help with Task Management. Tasks originate from different sources, some are structured (e.g., Microsoft Project) and some are unstructured (e.g., e-mail and chat conversations). People invest significant effort in maintaining an overview of their tasks. Besides relying on memory, people use various methods and tools for tracking their tasks from paper notes and task management systems, to indicating outstanding tasks such as marking emails as 'unread'. People also spend a lot of time performing administrative tasks. When it comes to prioritisation, tasks are typically given priority based on time urgency. This means that workers execute tasks which are urgent, but not necessarily the most important. The link between tasks and their goals/purposes is generally missing or not obviously apparent to workers.

The Need to Have an Integrated Overview of Information. The information that people receive or need to remember comes from multiple sources (e.g., e-mails, passwords, chat conversations, newsletters and web page updates), which makes it difficult

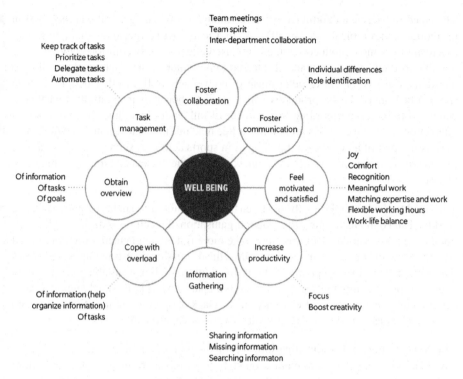

Team meetings
Team spirit
Inter-department collaboration

Keep track of tasks
Prioritize tasks
Delegate tasks
Automate tasks

Individual differences
Role identification

Foster
collaboration

Task
management

Foster
communication

Joy
Comfort
Recognition
Meaningful work
Matching expertise and work
Flexible working hours
Work-life balance

Of information
Of tasks
Of goals

Obtain
overview

WELL BEING

Feel
motivated
and satisfied

Cope with
overload

Increase
productivity

Information
Gathering

Of information (help
organize information)
Of tasks

Focus
Boost creativity

Sharing information
Missing information
Searching informaton

Fig. 1. Needs of office workers

to monitor, organise and integrate. Vast amounts can remain unprocessed. This means that even information which might be relevant for a particular person can remain unnoticed. The organisation of information is often managed via multiple folders (i.e., organisation schemes) which causes duplication of information and ultimately makes the whole information system hard to maintain.

The Need to Cope with Overload. Employees are overloaded with information, as there are too many sources of information to process or remember, including documents, e-mails and passwords. They find it difficult to organise, process and follow, thus missing out on the integration of all those sources. Sometimes there are too many tasks that need to be completed by the same deadline, which then results in people working overtime.

The Need to Help with Information Gathering. There is a lack of transparency in companies concerning knowledge about what other teams, colleagues or departments are working on, and this can make companies inefficient. The process of gathering information is difficult and when information is missing it causes delays. To compensate, employees ask other colleagues and managers to obtain information about contacts, processes and files. Searching for information also takes a lot of time as there are too many sources, inferior quality data (e.g., data that has not been updated) and people need to remember where the relevant and correct information is stored.

The Need to Increase Productivity. Even though people are generally at their best in the morning, they typically do 'small' tasks first so as not to forget about them, however, as a result their most productive time is not used effectively. In addition, they are often not able to focus due to unplanned interruptions, 'quick' tasks such as responding to questions, e-mails, or background noise or conversations from other people in open space office areas. To be productive they need to boost their creativity and this is perceived to increase according to a number of influences including: increased social interactions (e.g., discussions around the coffee machine); in heterogeneous work activities; being part of a great team; taking part in sports activities such as yoga; or having a dynamic environment (e.g., a café, a break room or the presence of music in the workplace).

The Need to Foster Collaboration. Even though collaboration helps people to balance workload and build team spirit, the proper organisation of meetings is difficult. Meetings often have poor agendas, lack structure, take more time than planned, or are organised with more people invited than required. Often the discussion diverts to unplanned topics that sometimes is due to a poor facilitator. In addition, finding a suitable meeting room with appropriate equipment at a time that suits all participants is also challenging. Cross-department collaboration is often tricky due to a lack of open communication, a plethora of 'own agendas', and the different goals of various departments.

The Need to Foster Communication. Problems with communication are caused by individual differences in communication style (e.g., misinterpretation of information) or different levels of language knowledge (e.g., lack of comprehension of information). Unclear role identification means that sometimes people don't know to whom they should address a request because there is a lack of information about other people's responsibilities or skills.

The Need to Feel Motivated and be Satisfied. Joy comes from social interactions and a comfortable office environment. Satisfaction with one's work comes from multiple sources including: recognition of work, professional growth, doing meaningful work, being able to utilise skills in which one excels, not having too much routine work, flexible work hours and a healthy work-life balance. People struggle with not having their desired work-life balance. Work is given higher priority over private activities so that, for example, checking work e-mails at home to prevent surprises is an all too common activity for many workers.

In summary, the well-being of an office worker is to a large extent reflected in the way work is conducted, not only within the work environment and through social interactions, but also through efficiency, effectiveness, productivity, creativity, motivation and satisfaction.

3   Cognitive Hub Concept

Taking into account the needs and requirements reviewed in Sect. 2, Konica Minolta proposes a platform called Cognitive Hub that will become a nexus for user's information flows within the digital workplace and provide augmented-intelligence-based services to improve work experience and workers' well-being [16]. Cognitive Hub delivers benefits and values to users from the following aspects: it supports a new metaphor of work that goes beyond the desktop metaphor; it is able to detect user's emotional and cognitive states to offer corrective actions or infer user preferences; it applies semantic technology to construct a digital knowledge base about a user, to deliver a personalised experience; it supports seamless transformation between digital and physical information contents; and it allows novel means of multimodal interaction (e.g. voice, touch, gaze, gesture interaction) which is expected to be more natural, flexible, efficient and robust. This section introduces each of these aspects in more detail.

3.1   A New Metaphor of Work

A large proportion of workers' problems and needs that have been identified were related to information management. People have problems to cope with an information overload and to maintain an overview of this information that is coming from many different sources. As a consequence, it is often hard to keep track of everything they need to work on and to prioritise effectively. These problems are partially caused by the desktop metaphor which has dominated the way computers work for more than half a century [15]. Fundamentally the desktop metaphor is file-centric; it treats the computer monitor as if it is the user's desktop upon which objects such as files and applications can be placed into folder systems. To work on one task people often need to manually retrieve files from multiple folders and switch between multiple applications. In the era of information overload, the desktop metaphor is clearly no longer the best means to support the work of contemporary office workers.

Inspired by the 'lifestream' concept [15], Cognitive Hub goes beyond the desktop metaphor to offer an activity-centric metaphor of work. As shown in Fig. 2, the activity-centric metaphor supports 3 levels of work: namely strategic, tactical and operational work. It is proposed here that all people, no matter what job positions they occupy, conduct their work within these 3 levels and dynamically switch between them. However, without any supporting tools, most people are unaware of the levels and they switch between them without making a conscious decision. Cognitive Hub aims to provide a visualised tool to support people in better managing their work tasks at these 3 different levels as described in more detail below.

Strategic Work. This level is about strategically managing the 'purpose and meaning of work'. Users can define and manage their personal goals. Goals should include those work-related objectives that are typically provided by the employer, such as successfully completing a project, or increasing sales by 10%. In addition, users can also define goals to reflect their private targets and interest, such as career growth, learning a new language, keeping fit, etc. Achieving these private goals will increase the overall satisfaction and motivation in life and in turn improve work performance. A user can also set priorities amongst his/her goals. The importance of strategic work is to provide a link between what users do (tasks/activities) and what users want to achieve (goals). This way users are less likely to 'lose the purpose of work' or 'not know what to focus

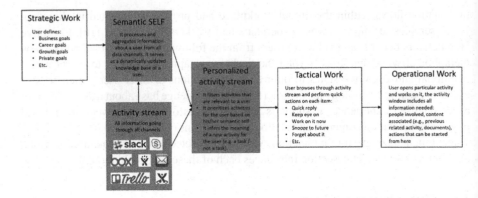

Fig. 2. The activity-centric metaphor of work

on'. Moreover, personal goals are one of the inputs to a Semantic SELF (semantic enrichment and linking framework) that is used for personalising and prioritising activities for a user.

Semantic SELF. Every user has his/her own profile, preference and a unique method of communicating and organising his/her personal enterprise environment. Semantic SELF is a dynamically updated knowledge database of a user, including all the information that can be retrieved from the digital system or inferred from the user's behaviour through the use of the digital system (see Fig. 3). Goals defined by the user are also a part of the input to a Semantic SELF.

Personalised Activity Stream. In workplace, information typically flows through multiple channels including: emails or instant messaging (e.g. MS Outlook, Skype, Slack, etc.); task management (e.g. JIRA, MS Project, etc.); and shared storage systems (MS Sharepoint, Box, Google drive, etc.). Currently, people need to monitor all these channels separately to keep track of everything that they need to do. In the Semantic SELF concept, information from all channels are integrated into one single stream. Then semantic technology is applied to each item within the stream to infer what the user needs to do upon receiving that piece of information. In such an approach the incoming information stream is transformed into an activity stream. For example, if a user receives an email with the subject 'presentation', body text 'Please review it by this Friday' and a MS PowerPoint file as an attachment, the associated activity item would have a title 'Review presentation' and a due-date of 'this Friday'.

The activity stream is personalised for each user based on his/her Semantic SELF. Personalisation includes two aspects: firstly, activity items are prioritised based on the user's goal setting and other preferences; and secondly, a task inference on the same piece of information is performed for each related user separately. For example, a meeting organiser sends out meeting minutes to all invited participants; these minutes contain action items for several people. In this case, each recipient of the meeting minutes would receive an activity item with a personalised title that reflects his/her specific task.

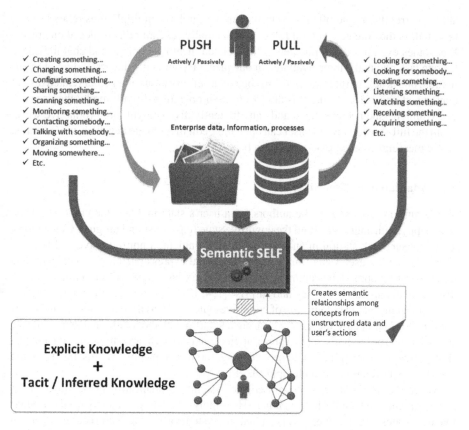

Fig. 3. Semantic SELF

Tactical Work. Once a personalised activity stream is generated, the tactical work level is entered when the user browses through the stream and performs quick actions on each item, such as to make a quick reply, set to snooze for later, or disregard the item. According to the conclusion of the present study people prefer to solve first 'small tasks' at the start of their workday. This way they reduce the number of pending tasks significantly after a small amount of time. Then they can better concentrate on 'big tasks' that take longer time to complete and also require more continuous concentration. Tactical work in the concept presented here supports users to efficiently solve 'small tasks' and plan for 'big tasks'. In addition, a link is proposed here between strategical work and tactical work, so that defined goals can be used as activity filters. The user is then able to see only those activities related to a particular goal.

Operational Work. Operational work is required to spend a longer period of time (e.g. 1–2 h) to continuously work on one 'big task'. An activity item can be extended to a full-screen mode, in which users can see all of the digital contents associated with this activity, including related previous activities (e.g. meetings), communications (e.g. emails, chats), other people involved, documents, images, videos, etc. As mentioned above, currently people often need to manually search for multiple files related to one task, unless they create a central folder and manually save all related files at one place. It becomes even more complicated to link related meetings, emails and chat messages for one task and make them available in one place. By semantic understanding of information, one is able to infer relationships between activity items and gather related digital contents at one place. Using this approach in an operational work mode, the user has everything he/she needs at hand and can efficiently dive straight into productive work. From the full-screen view, the user can open files, edit files, create new files, write emails, create meetings or even plan a business trip.

3.2 Adaptation to User State

The definition proposed by the authors for a user's state includes the emotional state (e.g. happy, sad, angry, etc.) and the cognitive state (e.g. stress and fatigue). Considering a single-user work station in an open office environment, a non-intrusive and feasible way to detect the user's emotion is to analyse facial expressions based on camera data input. Existing approaches commonly detect the six basic types of emotions – anger, disgust, fear, happiness, sadness and surprise [1, 4, 13]. An eye-tracker is a non-intrusive sensor that can enable recognition of cognitive states, such as arousal, fatigue, and overload [8, 20, 31]. In case the user is wearing a smart wristband, emotional and cognitive states can also be recognised from physiological signals like heart rate, skin conductance, skin temperature, etc. [10, 26]. In private office rooms and meeting rooms, the user state can also be detected via speech input [3, 28].

When the user's state is recognised the system can adapt to it in two manners: a timely manner and a long-term manner. The timely adaptation is mostly used for negative user states (e.g. fatigue, anger) so that the system can propose corrective actions to improve the user state. For example, when fatigue is detected the system can propose to have a break or add more blue-spectral content into the ambient lighting that may help the user to remain vigilant and concentrating [27] (illustrated in Fig. 4). The long-term adaptation is mostly used for positive user states where the system then learns what makes the user happy over a longer period of time and registers this information as a personal preference. An example is illustrated in Fig. 5, where the system detects the task preference of a user and shares it with her team. In addition to the emotional and cognitive states, user preference can also be derived from the mouse and keyboard inputs (how a user interacts with the system, their personal style of work, etc.) and semantic analysis of this and other user-related information.

Fig. 4. Adaptation to detected user fatigue

Fig. 5. Adaptation to detected user task preference

3.3 Smart Enterprise Search

One of the most prominent findings in the present user study (see Sect. 2) is that searching for the right information can be difficult and frustrating in the workplace. This result stands in line with various recent statists on enterprise search [9]: 'workers took up to 8 searches to find the right document and information'; 'employees spend approx. 1.8 h every day—9.3 h per week on average—searching and gathering information'. Or to put it another way, a business hires 5 employees but only 4 effectively contribute and the 5th is away searching for answers and is unable to generate value for the company. While Google and many others have provided high-quality internet search tools for everyone, enterprise search is still left 'in the dark' [25]. Cognitive Hub will provide a smart enterprise search engine to tackle this problem. Enterprise search should cover all resources within an organisation including: emails, all contents on the intranet, employee profiles, meeting rooms, software, licenses, hardware equipment, devices, etc. For each employee, enterprise search should also cover personal files on his/her local drive.

When it comes to searching for documents, which is perhaps the most common search use case in the workplace, the smart enterprise search is content-based but not file-based. Content-based search is enabled by document content extraction technology such as Tika [6], Rockhopper and Magellan (both developed within Konica Minolta). These technologies all index contents within a document including: titles, headings, body text, paragraphs, images and layout structure (the position of all of its contents). Using elastic content-based search, the smart enterprise search engine is capable of searching by several different attributes including: keyword; images; positions of specific contents; functional type (e.g. presentation, contract, invoice, etc.); related dates (creation, modification); related persons (e.g. the originator of the email); and by similarity (e.g. a document which looks like another document).

In case users are unsatisfied with search results after the first attempt, smart enterprise search provides a way to show users how queries are understood by the search engine and how users can adjust the query. As shown in Fig. 6, a search interpretation panel can be extended from the search query field. Users can review the understanding and correct any mistake. They can also specify more information to narrow down the search, for example by entering, 'Peter emailed it to me last week' (people: Petr, time: last week, source: email). This search interpretation panel is especially beneficial when users provide voice queries in natural language, because the natural language understanding technology is still far from being perfect, which is not entirely surprising given that even humans misunderstand each other from time to time.

3.4 Smart Transformation Between Physical and Digital Contents

Despite the observation that more and more paper documents have been migrated to digital versions and that more and more tasks have been being digitalised, recent statistics have shown that office printing volume is still slightly increasing [22, 29]. Based on various research literature [5, 11, 21], paper documents, books and learning materials have advantages that their electronic counterparts are currently not able to offer. In addition, one can observe that many people still carry around paper notebooks to

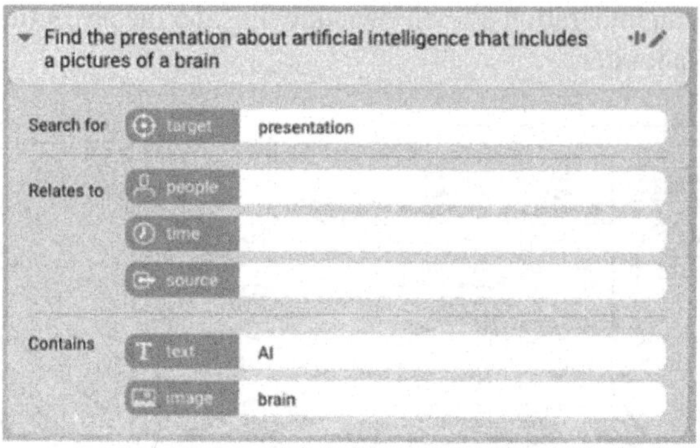

Fig. 6. The search interpretation panel

meetings and that Post-It is still a popular type of office supply. There are reasons to believe that paper documents and associated notes are not going to disappear from the office environment in the immediate future. However, the current workplace provides minimal support on transforming information between physical and digital forms. Printers and scanners typically only make a one-to-one exact transformation without understating the information content.

Cognitive Hub strives to provide a cyber-physical system that allows for smart transformation between digital and physical contents. This requires a device that has a projector, a camera with scanning function and integrated computer vision and machine learning capability. One example product that provides such functionality is offered by Lampix [18]. The following use cases demonstrate some of the features that are required to perform the physical to digital content transformation:

1. Digitising hand-written notes with smart understanding of contents. Assume that a user has a paper note that contains different types of contents, such as text, drawing, flow charts, etc. When the user digitises this note different contents are recognised and imported as separate objects so that the user can deal with them separately later on.
2. Digitising highlighted text in printed documents. A user has read a printed document and highlighted some text with a marker. He is able to digitise only the highlighted text but not the whole document.
3. Search for the digital version of a printed contents. When a user puts a printed document under the camera he can search for the digital version of the document. He can then point to an object on a page (e.g. a chart) and search for the digital version of this object. He can also, for example, point to a photograph of a person and receive more information about this person.
4. Search for keywords on printed document. If a printed document is lengthy and text-heavy, a user can search for a keyword and have it highlighted on the page, for example using an illumination projection system.
5. Paper-based collaborative work. Two people work at different locations can remotely collaborate using the paper medium. As illustrated in Fig. 7, the two people are working on a diagram. They see the same combination drawing on their own

paper which is an integration of their own drawing and the projection of the drawing from their collaborator.

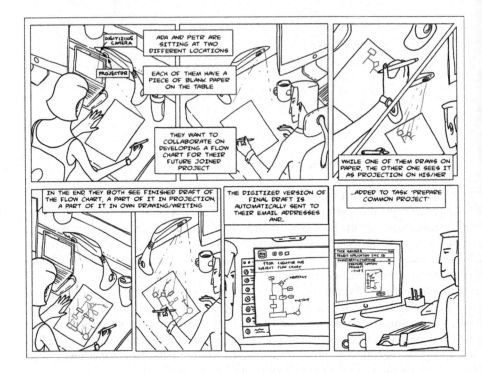

Fig. 7. Remote collaborated work on paper

3.5 Multimodal Interaction

The traditional keyboard and mouse are the earliest developed input modalities for human-computer interaction. After the turn of the century, novel modalities such as touch, voice, gesture and gaze have made their way to applications in several domains including consumer electronics, automotive, gaming, advertising, manufacturing, entertainment, etc. [14]. However, in the office environment, human-computer interaction is still solely based on the keyboard, mouse (or trackpad) and the conventional windows-icons-menus-pointers (WIMP) interfaces.

A Cognitive Hub workstation will be well equipped to support voice, touch, gaze interaction and multimodal interaction. Multimodal interaction means that multiple modalities are available at all times, so that users can freely choose modalities based on task characteristics, environment and their personal preference. They can choose different modalities for different tasks or even switch modalities between different steps within a single task. As illustrated in Fig. 8, a user wants to send a scan to Petr. He used voice command in the first step because it saved him many clicks on the display, then he switched to touch at the second step because it was much faster than describing which Petr to be selected verbally.

Fig. 8. Example of multimodal interaction.

Another valuable attribute that multimodal interaction should deliver is to combine two modalities into one input. Usually one modality is used to determine the object (e.g., looking at a window) and then the second modality identifies the action/command (e.g., speaking the word, "close"). In this case, each modality alone doesn't provide sufficient information about the user's intent. Cognitive Hub workstation will support gaze combined with voice input, gesture combined with voice input and touch combined with voice input. The voice modality provides actions/commands whilst other modalities specify the objects.

Multimodal interaction presents a paradigm shift from the conventional WIMP towards providing users with a more natural interaction and greater expressive power, flexibility, efficiency and robustness [23]. Multimodal interaction is **natural**, because human-to-human interaction is invariably multimodal. Humans tend to interact in a highly multimodal manner, especially in situations when they are frustrated, in tension, or under high workload [2, 12]. Multimodal interaction provides the user with **flexibility** in 'how' to conduct a task. Flexibility in executing the task eliminates potential conflicts of resources as described in the literature [30], because the user can flexibly adapt the response to the context. It is expected that by offering the flexibility in 'how' to conduct a task, the user will find a personalised way of conducting the task that would remain stable [24]. Multimodal interaction is expected to improve **efficiency** of both the short-term memory (i.e., operational/working memory) and procedural memory [7, 19] because a more natural interaction requires less hierarchy and less abstraction. Considering multimodal interaction is natural for humans, the person can focus on 'what' to do rather than on 'how' to do it. The procedural memory responsible for how to do a certain task is then less loaded. Not requiring the user to remember multiple artificial steps (i.e., sub-tasks) within a process also results in increased free capacity of their working memory. As a consequence, the user is able to perform the task more quickly by having direct access to functions with less hierarchy and less abstraction. Building on the benefits described above, multimodal interaction then also improves the **robustness** of the interaction by reducing the occurrence of errors. Errors are more infrequent because task execution contains less steps, it can be completed more quickly and in a more personalised manner.

4   Proof of Concept Demonstrator

Cognitive Hub is still at a research and development stage within Konica Minolta. To illustrate the concept further a demonstrator has been designed that can immerse a user within a set of pre-defined interaction scenarios.

4.1   UI Design

The UI design supports the activity-centric metaphor of work (see Sect. 3.1). As shown in Fig. 9, the interface contains 4 panels. The 'Goals' panel on the left supports the strategic work. Users can add, describe, edit and delete goals. The 'Activities' panel in the centre is where the personalised activity stream is displayed. The most important ones (identified by Semantic SELF) are displayed at the top followed by the rest. Users can filter activities by selecting a goal so that only activities related to this goal are displayed. Each activity item contains an inferred task as its title, the due-date (if specified), sender, sending channel and related goal(s). A set of action icons appears on an item once the mouse hovers on it so that users can book time for it now, snooze it for later, or disregard it. When users click on an item it expands to show the original incoming information and users can perform short tasks such as making a quick reply, accepting a meeting request, etc. For operational work each item can be opened to a full-screen view where users can find all associated activities, people and digital contents. Contents can be created, opened and edited directly from the full-screen view. Actions such as creating meetings, writing emails and chat can also be directly performed from the full-screen view. Cognitive Hub will provide the functionalities described above to support 'quick tasks'; for more complex tasks it will connect to external applications and services including: text editors, instant messaging, financial tools, trip booking services, etc.

At the top of the interface, a timeline of the day shows all planned meetings within that day. This helps users to select appropriate tasks based on the time available until the next meeting. Users can also drag and drop an activity item on to the timeline to block time for it. On the right side of the screen, there is an 'Assistant' panel. This serves as a location for search functions and smart Q&A with a virtual assistant.

Fig. 9. User interface of Cognitive Hub PoC demonstrator

4.2 Hardware Setup

As shown in Fig. 10, the demonstration is equipped with a standard computer monitor, a keyboard, a mouse, a camera (for emotion detection), two microphones (for voice interaction and face orientation detection, an eye tracker (for gaze interaction) and a Lampix device.

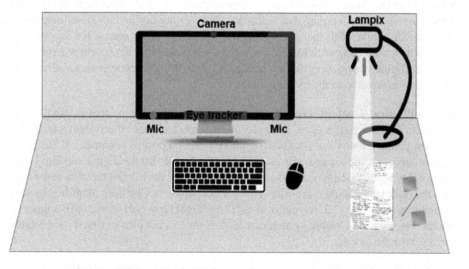

Fig. 10. Hardware setup of the Cognitive Hub PoC demonstration

4.3 Scenarios

Smart Q&A. At the beginning of a work day (which is envisaged as the start of the demonstration scenario), users can ask the assistant to provide a summary of what is new in their activity stream. They can ask questions related to their goals, activities and meetings. They can also ask for suggestions on which activity to work on first. Questions can be typed in the assistant panel or provided by voice. The assistant responds by voice and text.

Interaction with Activities. The activity stream in the demo includes 10 executable tasks. Users can scan through the activity stream and perform tactical work, such as to reply to an email, reply to a chat message, disregard an item, create a meeting, accept a meeting request, snooze an activity until next week, plan a fitness session, plan a business trip, etc.

Multimodal Interaction. In addition to keyboard and mouse, the demonstration also supports voice input, gaze input (based on Tobii eye-tracker [32]) and touch input on a smart surface (based on Lampix [18]). Voice modality can be used for all functionalities, including activity control, Q&A, search and the Lampix control. Keyboard and mouse can be used for all functionalities except the Lampix control. Gaze is not considered as a stand-alone modality in this demo so that gaze always needs to be used in combination with voice. For example, users can look at an activity item and say, "delete" or, "extend" or, "snooze." For the interaction using Lampix, voice and touch are interchangeable so that users can freely choose their preference.

Smart Search. Smart search in this demonstration supports document search and person search, by both typing and voice. Sample user queries include: find the presentation on Cognitive Hub that shows a picture of dirty hands; search for the meeting minutes from a meeting with Michal last week; I am looking for the brochure explaining the term 'digital cortex' near the beginning; or I need the article/paper about gaze interface that was emailed to me by Jane Smart.

Digital-Physical Content Transformation. The Lampix device that is used in this demo allows users to place, for example, a business card under the system and save it as a new contact. Users can ask for a digital version of a printed document. If the document contains multiple pages any page can be used to obtain the digital version. Users can point to a photograph of a person under the Lampix device and create a new email with the right email address pre-filled (the correct person having been identified by face recognition technology). Users can also ask to highlight keywords on printed documents. Interaction with the Lampix system can be performed via voice or touch on the table surface near the device.

Emotion Detection. The emotion detection solution uses camera input and a facial expression recognition SDK by Affectiva [1]. This solution identifies six basic emotions plus neutral faces. Emotion detection runs constantly in the background. When negative emotions such as anger and sadness are detected, the system may propose some corrective actions. For example, if a user expresses dissatisfaction with a search result, the system may ask, "It seems that you were unhappy with the search results, should I adjust search parameters?" At the same time the search interpretation panel (Fig. 6) is extended for the user to review and make changes. At the very end of the demonstration, the system presents an overview of the user's emotion journey throughout the demo and shows statistics for each type of emotion (e.g. 40% neutral, 30% happy, 10% anger, etc.).

5 Conclusion

This paper presented the concept of a platform called Cognitive Hub, which aims to provide AI-powered services and features to improve the work experience and overall well-being of office workers. A demonstrator was developed to show the concept in action and illustrate its benefits and value. As a future step it is planned to conduct a study with a wide range of users who will experience the demonstrator and provide valuable feedback on the concept. The results of this future study will inform the authors on the necessary refinements of the Cognitive Hub concept. In parallel to this all technological enablers described above will continue to be developed and matured. Konica Minolta is working towards the launch of Cognitive Hub in the horizon of the next 2–3 years.

References

1. Affectiva. https://www.affectiva.com/. Accessed 26 Jan 2018
2. Alibali, M.W., Kita, S., Young, A.J.: Gesture and the process of speech production: we think, therefore we gesture. Lang. Cogn. Process. **15**, 593–613 (2000)
3. Anagnostopoulos, C.N., Iliou, T., Giannoukos, I.: Features and classifiers for emotion recognition from speech: a survey from 2000 to 2011. Artif. Intell. Rev. **43**(2), 155–177 (2015)
4. Anil, J., Suresh, L.P.: Literature survey on face and face expression recognition. In: Proceedings of the International Conference on Circuit, Power and Computing Technologies, ICCPCT, pp. 1–6. IEEE (2016)
5. Mangen, A., Walgermo, B.R., Brønnick, K.: Reading linear texts on paper versus computer screen: effects on reading comprehension. Int. J. Educ. Res. **58**, 61–68 (2013)
6. Apache Tika - a content analysis toolkit. https://tika.apache.org/. Accessed 30 Jan 2018
7. Bernsen, N.O.: Multimodality theory. In: Tzovaras, D. (ed.) Multimodal User Interfaces: From Signals to Interaction. SCT, pp. 5–29. Springer, Heidelberg (2008). https://doi.org/10.1007/978-3-540-78345-9_2
8. Chen, S., Epps, J.: Automatic classification of eye activity for cognitive load measurement with emotion interference. Comput. Methods Prog. Biomed. **110**(2), 111–124 (2013)
9. Cottrill Research: Various Survey Statistics: Workers Spend Too Much Time Searching For Information. https://www.cottrillresearch.com/various-survey-statistics-workers-spend-too-much-time-searching-for-information/. Accessed 30 Jan 2018
10. Feel. https://www.myfeel.co/. Accessed 26 Jan 2018
11. Ferris, J.: The Reading Brain in the Digital Age: The Science of Paper versus Screens. Scientific American (2014)

12. Goldin-Meadow, S., Nusbaum, H., Kelly, S.D., Wagner, S.: Explaining math: gesturing lightens the load. Psychol. Sci. **12**, 516–522 (2001)
13. Happy, S.L., Routray, A.: Automatic facial expression recognition using features of salient facial patches. IEEE Trans. Affect. Comput. **6**(1), 1–12 (2015)
14. Jessica, G., Aditya, K.: Artificial Intelligence Use Cases – 215 Use Case Descriptions, Examples, and Market Sizing and Forecasts Across Enterprise, Consumer, and Government Markets. Tractica (2017)
15. Kaptelinin, V., Mary, C.: Beyond the Desktop Metaphor: Designing Integrated Digital Work Environments. The MIT Press, Cambridge (2007)
16. Konica Minolta: Cognitive Hub: the operating system for the workplace of the future. White paper in Artificial Intelligence series (2017)
17. Konica Minolta: The future of work. White paper in Artificial Intelligence series (2017)
18. Lampix. https://www.lampix.co/. Accessed 30 Jan 2018
19. Maragos, P., Gros, P., Katsamanis, A., Papandreou, G.: Cross-modal integration for performance improving in multimedia: a review. In: Maragos, P., Potamianos, A., Gros, P. (eds.) Multimodal Processing and Interaction. MMSA, vol. 33, pp. 1–46. Springer, Boston (2008). https://doi.org/10.1007/978-0-387-76316-3_1
20. Marshall, S.P.: Identifying cognitive state from eye metrics. Aviat. Space Environ. Med. **78**(5), B165–B175 (2007)
21. Myrberg, C., Wiberg, N.: Screen vs. paper: what is the difference for reading and learning? Insights **28**(2), 49–54 (2015)
22. Neville, W.: Office Printing Statistics 2017. https://www.lasersresource.com/blog/office-printing-statistics. Lasers Resource. Accessed 30 Jan 2018
23. Oviatt, S.: Ten myths of multimodal interaction. Commun. ACM **42**(11), 74–81 (1999)
24. Potamianos, A., Perakakis, M.: Human-computer interfaces to multimedia content: a review. In: Maragos, P., Potamianos, A., Gros, P. (eds.) Multimodal Processing and Interaction: Audio, Video, Text. MMSA, vol. 33, pp. 50–89. Springer, Boston (2008). https://doi.org/10.1007/978-0-387-76316-3_2
25. Susan, F., Chris, S.: The high cost of not finding information. ICD white paper (2001)
26. Verma, G.K., Tiwary, U.S.: Multimodal fusion framework: a multiresolution approach for emotion classification and recognition from physiological signals. NeuroImage **102**, 162–172 (2014)
27. Viola, U., James, L.M., Schlangen, L.J., Dijk, D.-J.: Blue-enriched white light in the workplace improves self-reported alertness, performance and sleep quality. Scand. J. Work Environ. Health **34**, 297–306 (2008)
28. Weninger, F., Wöllmer, M., Schuller, B.: Emotion recognition in naturalistic speech and language – a survey. Emot. Recognit.: Pattern Anal. Approach 237–267 (2015)
29. West, M.: Is Office Printing Increasing or Declining?. https://www.printaudit.com/printaudit-blog/premier/is-office-printing-increasing-or-declining-answer-yes. Print Audit. Accessed 30 Jan 2018
30. Wickens, C.D.: Multiple resources and performance prediction. Theoret. Issues Ergon. Sci. **3**(2), 159–177 (2002)
31. Zhang, F., Su, J., Geng, L., Xiao, Z.: Driver fatigue detection based on eye state recognition. In: Machine International Conference on Vision and Information Technology, CMVIT, pp. 105–110. IEEE (2017)
32. Tobii eye tracker. https://www.tobii.com/

A Comparative Testing on Performance of Blockchain and Relational Database: Foundation for Applying Smart Technology into Current Business Systems

Si Chen, Jinyu Zhang, Rui Shi$^{(\boxtimes)}$, Jiaqi Yan, and Qing Ke

Nanjing University, Nanjing 210023, Jiangsu, China
{si.chen, zhjinyu, jiaqiyan, keqing}@nju.edu.cn,
141070049@smail.nju.edu.cn

Abstract. Blockchain technologies have been developing very fast recently. Ethereum, as the second generation of blockchain, can support smart contracts with various functions. Blockchain, combined with IoT technologies like RFID, can bring more security into IoT systems. It has been noted that just storing hash values, addresses and transaction records cannot meet the needs of various blockchain applications. Thus, how to test capacity of reading/writing data for blockchain and further make comparisons with the traditional relational databases needs to be paid attention. Although there has been some research on testing and analyzing the performance of blockchains, few studies focus on analyzing blockchains and relational databases. This test was conducted to analyze the capacities of reading/writing data and processing/recording transactions of blockchains and relational databases. Ethereum and MySQL are chosen as the representatives of blockchain and relational databases. This test has three aims: (1) getting the detailed data of the blockchain's capacity of processing transactions; (2) identifying the bottleneck or potential bottleneck in blockchain systems; (3) putting forward a testing method and testing indexes which are reasonable, practical and compatible with the current development situations of blockchain systems. With the results data, it was concluded that the maximum data volume in single transaction on blockchain network was about 1/10 of MySQL. As for the time spent in processing single transaction, the blockchain network was 80–2000 times as much as MySQL. Thus, it's recommended to store little-size data into blockchain. For more detailed testing, these indexes and testing method can be referenced.

Keywords: Blockchain · Relational database · Performance testing
Ethereum · MySQL

1 Introduction

Recently, blockchain has attracted lots of attention and interests from both academia and various industries. The original idea of Bitcoin is put forward by Nakamoto in 2008 [1]. And since then, blockchain, as the underlying technology framework, has been studied and developed greatly [2]. Blockchain has no standard technical definition. And it is

© Springer International Publishing AG, part of Springer Nature 2018
N. Streitz and S. Konomi (Eds.): DAPI 2018, LNCS 10921, pp. 21–34, 2018.
https://doi.org/10.1007/978-3-319-91125-0_2

usually a loose 'umbrella' term used by people in various fields when referring to systems which are similar to bitcoin and its ledger in some respects [3]. Blockchain has three main characteristics, (1) decentralized, (2) recording transactions by some consensus mechanism and (3) tamper-resistant. With these characteristics, blockchain has been honored with 'trust machine' [4]. It's because blockchain provides a practical technical solution to the problem of lack of trust in business world and our society.

Usually, Bitcoin has been considered as the original implementation of blockchain. Bitcoin supports electronic cash transactions peer to peer in its system. And Ethereum, as the second generation of blockchain, supports smart contracts to be deployed and executed on it [5]. With smart contracts, Ethereum blockchain is able to support many functions besides electronic cash transactions, such as digital identity, electronic voting, string data processing and so on. Smart contracts are computer programs deployed on blockchains, which can execute automatically under some specific conditions [6]. In the perspective of data reading and writing, Bitcoin can just read and store numeric values and strings with fixed length. This limitation is constrained to the design of Bitcoin: a design of a peer to peer electronic cash transaction system. Therefore, Ethereum has widely extended the functions of blockchain. In order to support various functions, Ethereum allows data to be read and written in various length. Apart from Ethereum, Hyperledger Fabric project also supports smart contracts [7]. Specifically, Fabric is designed for blockchain applications in industries and there are amount of data with different length in various industries.

IoT technology can connect things in various industries and empower smart industries. And blockchain provide a probability of a secure IoT world. The problem of data security limits the wider applications of IoT technology in industries. However, based on blockchain, smart contracts can be used to implement digital identity and access control of IoT data. Azaria et al. applied blockchain into medical data access and permission management [8]. Li et al. exploited consortium blockchain technology and proposed a secure energy trading system in industrial IoT [9]. Besides academia, there exists examples of such application in industries. IBM and Samsung announced ADEPT Project, which uses blockchain, specifically Ethereum, to build a decentralized and secure IoT [10]. In ADEPT project, blockchain technology can bring trust into supply chain management and help improve their manufacture security and service quality. Microsoft and ConsenSys announced EBaaS Project to offer Ethereum Blockchain as a Service (BaaS) on Microsoft Azure [11]. By offering such BaaS, Microsoft and Consensys can empower a number of developers and companies to develop and deploy blockchain-based applications and systems, which will bring trust and security into their business and profits to Microsoft and Consensys. And Deloitte opened its own BaaS platform named Rubix [12]. Such BaaS projects will empower industries to applying blockchain into their own business more quickly and conveniently. And blockchain binds with IoT more closely.

One big obstacle and challenge for blockchain deployment in different industries is that blockchain system cannot process data in an acceptable way now. A practical solution is to combine blockchain with current relational databases to provide speed-accepted service for users. Blockchain applications are usually combined with electronic cash and financial systems, medical data, digital assets transaction systems and supply chain management systems [8, 13–15]. If all these systems need to implement all the functions that blockchain provides, the capabilities to read and write the data with various length are required. Especially in supply chains, an amount of real-time industrial is generated during the process of manufacturing, logistics and retailing. For example, there are thousands of components in a car and in a supply chain quality management system for the production of cars, how to process such a lot of real-time quality data for these thousands of components is crucial. Therefore, there is a need to test the capabilities of reading and writing data in blockchain and make comparisons between blockchain and mainstream relational databases. Furthermore, considering the differences of capabilities of reading and writing data between blockchain and relational databases, a combination of above two ways may be a practical solution to applying blockchain technologies in various industries. Based on this solution, how to make the distribution of blockchain and relational databases so as to obtain the best balance between efficiency and security, is a realistic question. Thus, it is meaningful to offer a testing framework to compare their own ability of reading and writing data. With such a testing framework, blockchain systems developers are able to carry out necessary test accordingly. And after getting the exact test result, they can make the decision about how to combine the two methods of storing data to reach the balance of efficiency and security.

2   Literature Review

With the rapid development of blockchain technology, investigations on testing various blockchain have been made. However, these studies have mainly focused on just testing blockchains or comparing different blockchains. Dinh et al. has put forward a framework for analyzing private blockchains, called Blockbench [16]. They choose three representative private blockchains as the sample. Private blockchain is such a blockchain that all nodes are authenticated in some way, for example, some specific initial parameters in Ethereum private blockchain or some membership service in Fabric. Data is shared and synchronized among the authenticated nodes in private blockchain. So, private blockchain is not open to the public. It's not like Bitcoin, in which system everyone can participant in or withdraw freely and can access data with no right control. Dinh et al. pointed out that recent private blockchains have made improvement on their consensus mechanism. Considering that the traditional PoW consensus mechanism uses an amount of computational resources to ensure the security, which results in a waste of computational resource and electricity, they have adopted PBFT algorithms or developed their own variants to improve the performance of the consensus mechanism instead of PoW. Dinh et al. divided private blockchains into three layers: consensus layer, data model layer and execution layer. They first measure the overall performance indexes of the three private blockchain, which indexes are throughput, latency scalability and fault-tolerance. Then test perform micro-test on the above three layers. The testing results demonstrate that there exist big performance among these private blockchains, and that these private blockchains are still far from replacing the current database systems to support various applications.

In September 2017, European central bank and Bank of Japan published their joint research project report on testing of blockchain, which project is called Stella [17]. The

Stella project's test object is the blockchain application in the area of financial market infrastructure. Stella project used smart contracts to implement the business logic of transactions and executed these smart contacts in both a virtualized and restricted in-house test environment and cloud computing environment. It concluded that the blockchain based solutions could meet the performance needs in a real-time gross settlement system. Although favorable results had been reached, they still suggested that it's too earlier to conclude that blockchain technologies could be used in realistic production.

Croman et al. studied the performance of bitcoin regarding to the scalability of decentralized blockchains, including maximum throughput, latency, bootstrap time and cost per confirmed transaction [18]. They concluded that a basic rethinking of technical approaches is required to advance current blockchains. Gervais et al. studied the proof of work (PoW) blockchains' security and performance and their influence on each other. They put forward a framework, in which they can capture the current PoW blockchains and develop variants to compare the tradeoffs between their security and performance [19]. Aniello et al. put forward a method of prototype evaluation based on the implementation of their previous work on architect of blockchain-based redo logs [20]. Their prototype adopts a specific consensus algorithm based on a three-phase commit protocol [21]. Their analysis focused on the throughput, stability and latency of two operations, get operation and set operation. Suankaewmanee et al. designed an application of mobile blockchain [22]. And their performance analysis focused on memory utilization, PoW process and chain verification process. They set different numbers of transactions contained in one block and observe the different execution time and energy consumption correspondingly. Spasovski and Eklund conducted testing to analyze performance and scalability of PoS (Proof of Stake) blockchain [23]. They designed and implemented blockchain-based and non-blockchain-based groupware communication applications for comparison testing. Their analysis focused on response time, throughput and network topology. Although their work compared blockchain-based and non-blockchain-based applications, they still focused on the overall performance instead of just data reading and writing module. Walker et al. put forward a platform for trans active IoT blockchain applications repeatable testing [24]. This platform focused on the execution time of various manipulations including miners create, blockchain make, distribute to miners and so on.

As for testing on relational databases, a number of works have been done. Vicknair et al. compared a graph database and a relational database before [27]. They adopted Neo4j as the representative for graph databases and MySQL for relational databases. In their paper, the evaluation was divided into objective measures, execution time for example, and subjective measures including maturity/level of support, ease of programming, flexibility and security. They constructed twelve MySQL databases and twelve Neo4j databases and each database stored a directed acyclic graph (DAG) consisting of some number of nodes and edges. Then they used SQL queries and manipulation sentences to test the capacity of these two kinds of databases. They concluded that both systems performed acceptably and graph database Neo4j performed better than relational database MySQL in structural type queries and full-text character searches and relational database works more efficiently than graph databases in numeric queries. Jing et al. made a comparison between Lucene and relational database [28]. They prepared a test data set and executed queries separately in unindexed relational database and Lucene. An operation audit log was used as the original data source for their performance tests. And the result data was analyzed in aspects of exact query, wildcard query, influence of results set size, combinational query and performance influence of record complexity. Chays et al. put forward a set of tools named AGENDA (A test GENerator for Database Applications) for testing database applications [29]. AGENDA is written for PostgreSQL and can parse a schema, generate a programmatically identifiable database state from that schema, generate test cases, and test the resulting state and output from executing those test cases. While many studies have been done to test blockchain's and relational databases' performance and functions separately, there are just few work on comparing blockchain with relational databases. Regarding to the importance of comparing them mentioned in Sect. 1, we're offering a framework for comparing their capacities of reading and writing data.

3 Testing Design

For this testing, we chose Ethereum to stand for blockchains and MySQL database for relational databases. As for such arrangement, we have three standards to depend on. The first is whether the objects tested are functionally complete or not. Ethereum is Turing-Complete and can support smart contracts to implement various functions and executions [16]. And MySQL can be used to store various kinds of data. Both are functionally complete. The second standard is that objects for testing should be used or adopted widely in their own fields. Ethereum is one of the most mainstream blockchains and has been supporting one of the largest public blockchains since 2014. Also, Ethereum is open source and often adopted to power various private blockchains. There are nearly 900 decentralized apps built on Ethereum now. As for MySQL database, it is the second most popular databases among hundreds of databases according to DB-engines ranking, only a little less popular than Oracle databases [25]. The last standard is that open source is more suitable than not open source. This is out of the needs to know its inner implementation for the research and testing in our next step. And thanks for the work of Blockbench, we could just pick one blockchain for comparison testing without loss of reliability.

Ethereum blockchain based systems' core part can be divided into three layers: data layer, consensus layer, smart contract layer. Data layer is responsible for data storing, direct reading and writing. This layer consists of each node's local database keeping a copy from blockchain. Actually, the reading and writing at data layer is just the same as these same manipulations in traditional databases. Consensus layer is usually responsible for synchronizing blocks and reaching consensus among authenticated nodes to record transactions. Comparing to centralized databases, blockchain systems can spend more time because of the consensus layer recording transactions. Consensus layer may perhaps become the bottleneck of system's performance. Another potential bottleneck is smart contract layer. This layer may perform complex computation tasks, which can also result to the increasing of time spent. However, smart contract just implements the business logic the same as in a centralized system. Reasonably, this part should not be the main point to test. Figure 1 shows the manipulation relations between the general four layers. Users send a transaction request from the application layer to the smart contract layer. After executing some tasks, the smart contract layer will send new transaction to the consensus layer. With reaching the consensus about this new transaction, the consensus layer will admit and record this new transaction and store it into block in the data layer. To sum up, we should focus on the testing for consensus layer's performance. With this in mind, we need to design such smart contracts that are as simple as they can to lower the effect on the testing of consensus layer.

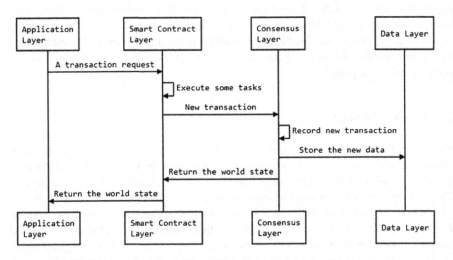

Fig. 1. Figure of manipulation relations between the general four layers.

To assess the ability of reading and writing data, these three main perspectives are necessary to consider: the ability of reaction, throughput and loading capacity. These indexes are also key to a successful service provided by blockchain based systems. For the purpose of exactness, the above indexes were divided into nine more specific and observable indexes (Table 1):

Table 1. Table of the nine specific and observable indexes.

Number	Indexes
T01	The average reaction time of transactions
T02	The longest reaction time of transactions
T03	The rate of successful transactions
T04	The amount of transactions processed per second
T05	The amount of transactions processed in unit time
T06	The most time-consuming module in each transaction
T07	The biggest volume of data processed in each transaction
T08	The execution time of each transaction
T09	Throughput

4 Testing Implementation

A six-nodes private blockchain has been prepared for the test, which was initialized with our own parameters in genesis.json file. The detailed information about our testing machines is as below (Table 2):

Table 2. Table of detailed information of the machines for testing.

Machine number	Operating system	CPU	Disk	Memory
1	Win 10	i7-6700HQ 2.60 GHz 4 cores	M2S3138E-128GM-B	8G
2	Mac OS	2.9 GHz Intel Core i5	APPLE SSD AP0256J	8G
3	Win 10	i5-4210H 2.9 GHZ 4 cores	128G SSD	8G
4	Win 10	i5-4210U 1.70 GHz 4 cores	250G SSD	4G
5	Ubuntu 16.0.4	AMD A8-4500M APU with Radeon (tm) HD Graphics	WDC WD10JPV X-00JC3T 0 (1T)	8G
6	Win 7	i7-5500U 2.40 Gz 4 cores	1 TB/5400 rotation per minute	8G
7	Win 10	i5-4210H 2.9 GHZ 4 cores	1 TB/5400 rotation per minute	8G

The Ethereum applications (or called Dapps, Decentralized applications) development and testing framework Truffle was adopted to perform this testing [26]. Dapps are applications based on blockchain like Ethereum. Dapps consist mainly of smart contracts and other interactive modules. They use smart contracts to read data from blockchain and execute many kinds of tasks like transactions, voting, analyzing and so on. And what we want to test is the capacity of reading and writing data of blockchain. The smart contracts for the test use can be viewed as a very simple Dapps with few other modules. Thus, the Truffle development and testing framework can be used to undertake such tasks in this testing: deploying smart contracts onto blockchain, providing a testing framework to write the testing programs and providing small tools to improve the efficiency of testing.

Based on the testing indexes and analysis on layers in blockchain based systems, two smart contracts were used. The first smart contract Transaction.sol can initialize an account with fixed number of altcoin (represented by numeric value). Transaction.sol can also send some number of altcoin to other accounts and query the balance that some specific account still has. Transaction.sol can cover the indexes from T01 to T08. The second smart contract KvStorage.sol can just put or get some value into or out from our private blockchains, which covers the indexes from T07 to T09. Then two test scripts were used to deploy these two smart contracts and execute the manipulations of

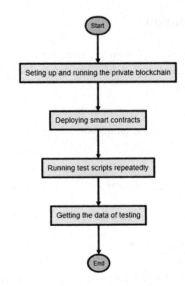

Fig. 2. Figure of the workflow of this testing.

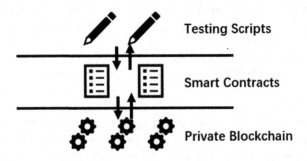

Fig. 3. Figure of the manipulation relationship between testing scripts, smart contracts and private blockchain.

putting data, getting data and sending altcoins to other accounts repeatedly. When testing, a increasing pressure policy was adopted, and the seven kinds of data volume are 128 B, 256 B, 512 B, 1 KB, 2 KB, 3 KB and 6 KB.

The outline of testing on private blockchain part is as follows. A private blockchain of six-nodes was set up firstly. Then the two smart contracts, Transaction.sol and KvStorage.sol, were deployed onto this blockchain. After deploying, the test scripts were executed by some of these seven machines/nodes to get the testing data for analysis (Figs. 2 and 3).

As for MySQL part, a Python script was written to manipulate reading and writing data from and into MySQL database. A Python package named pymysql was imported to implement these functions. Similar to Ethereum part, seven kinds of data volume which are 128 B, 256 B, 512 B, 1 KB, 2 KB, 3 KB and 6 KB were used to test MySQL's performance under the same indexes.

5 Results Evaluation

The testing result data varies among different machines. Considering that the comparison results vary from machines, and the simple average is not enough to stand for the common situations, machine No. 2 was chosen as the standard machine because of its highest complex performance among all the testing machines. The reason is that in the real industrial environment, computing machines' performance is usually higher than these seven portable computers. It's reasonable to choose the machine No. 2 as the standard (Tables 3 and 4).

Table 3. Table of testing results data of the indexes T07, T08 and T09 of MySQL database.

Number	Index	Results
T01	The average reaction time of transactions	125.08 ms
T02	The longest reaction time of transactions	322 ms
T03	The rate of successful transactions	100%
T04	The amount of transactions processed per second	8.00 times
T05	The amount of transactions processed in unit time	8.00 times/s
T06	The most time-consuming module in each transaction	Write/read data: 76.4%
T07	The biggest volume of data processed in each transaction	6,688 bytes
T08	The execution time of each transaction	Refer to Fig. 4
T09	Throughput	Refer to Fig. 6
Number	Index	Results
T07	The biggest volume of data processed in each transaction	65,535 bytes
T08	The execution time of each transaction	Refer to Fig. 5
T09	Throughput	Refer to Fig. 7

Table 4. Table of the comparison between the result data of the index T07 of the private blockchain and MySQL database.

Testing objects	The biggest volume of data processed in each transaction
Private blockchain	6,688 bytes
MySQL database	65,535 bytes

From the table above, it's obvious that the private blockchain's biggest volume of data processed in each transaction, which is 6,688 bytes, is far less than that of MySQL database, which is 65,535 bytes because of the limitation of data type varchar in MySQL. This implies that this six-nodes private blockchain is not suitable to store too large volume of data in a system, or that would lower the performance of the whole system. Considering such a fact, it's natural to choose to store just some hash values into blockchain systems. In the next step, a more specific and reasonable arrangement would be made with the results data. The T06 index's result shows that the potential bottleneck of this private blockchain can be the module responsible for reading and writing data, which consumes about 76.4% of the testing time.

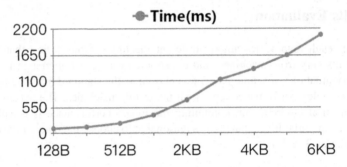

Fig. 4. Figure of relationship between data volume and time for reading/writing per transaction of the six-nodes private blockchain.

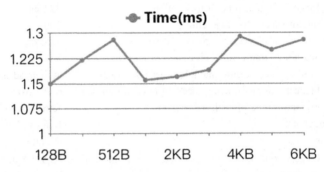

Fig. 5. Figure of relationship between data volume and time for reading/writing per transaction of MySQL database.

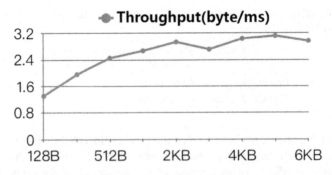

Fig. 6. Figure of relationship between throughput and data volume per transaction of the six-nodes private blockchain.

With the growing data volume of one transaction, the time consumed increase. The used time and data volume are in an exponential-like relationship. Notice that there are six nodes in this private blockchain, the exponential-like relationship may be a result of the number of nodes. This needs more accurate testing to verify (Table 5).

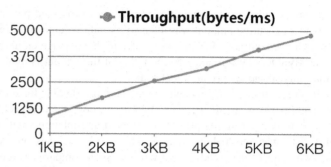

Fig. 7. Figure of relationship between throughput and data volume per transaction of the MySQL database.

Table 5. Table of the comparison between the result data of the index T09 of the private blockchain and MySQL database.

Testing objects	Throughput
Private blockchain	Varies with different data volume and around 3 bytes/ms
MySQL database	Linearly related to data volume

Table 6. Table of the comparison between the result data of the index T08 of the private blockchain and MySQL database.

Testing objects	The execution time of each transaction
Private blockchain	Varies with different data volume, less than 2027 ms
MySQL database	1.22 ms in average

When the data volume keeps increasing and is more than some threshold, here it is 2 KB, the throughput of the private blockchain keeps relatively fixed. Comparing to the six-nodes private blockchain, MySQL shows more high performance with far more bigger data volume to process and linear-like relationship with time consumed (Table 6).

As for the execution time of each transaction, this six-nodes private blockchain spends more time on bigger volume of data, reaching 2027 ms with 6 KB of data. However, the time MySQL spends on different volume has no apparent relation to the data volume. And on machine No. 2, it's average time of reading and writing is 1.22 ms. The time used for reading and writing data which this private blockchain spends is more than 1660 times as long as that of MySQL (Table 7).

Table 7. Table of the comparison between the result data of the index T04 of the private blockchain and MySQL database.

Testing objects	The amount of transactions processed per second
Private blockchain	Varies with different data volume, more than 0.49 times
MySQL database	819.67 times in average

Another important index is the amount of transactions processed per second. The private blockchain's execution amount was affected by data volume and can be low to 0.49 per second. On the contrast, MySQL has a much higher average number of 819.67 per second. And MySQL's performance on the index of throughput is more than 1000 times better than this six-nodes private blockchain.

These results imply that private blockchain may be more suitable for some modules which is not data-intensive in the systems. In this section, three aspects and nine indexes were used to comparing the private blockchain and relational databases. And detailed results data was reached by testing. This work provides an example for comparing the two ways of data reading and writing. Such comparisons are necessary for deciding how to combine blockchain technology and centralized databases in a practical way to gain a balance. And more complex tests are needed for more detailed evaluation between the two ways.

6   Discussion

Although blockchain is an emerging technology filed, and it can bring trust into business world and human society. Successful real-world business use cases based on blockchain are still rare. One big obstacle and challenge for blockchain deployment in different industries is that blockchain system cannot process data in an acceptable way up to now. Thus, a pure-blockchain system may come across failure in real-world business systems and applications. A practical solution to apply blockchain technology into various industries is to combine the two different ways of reading and writing data in systems. Then it's necessary to divide the whole system into data-intensive modules and non-data-intensive modules. The data-intensive modules can be built on relational databases for the high requirement of data reading and writing. And the non-data-intensive modules can be built on blockchain. Another practical solution is to reorganize their business system's architecture. The system can be divided into trust-related part and non-trust-related part. The part regarding trust and security should be simplified in data volume, using hash values for example, to meet the blockchain's data reading and writing performance. So, they can make use of blockchain technology to secure their business. And the part not related to trust and security can store more detailed information and be built on relational databases. With the testing results data and business requirements, a reasonable solution would be reached to obtain the best balance between performance and security.

Reviewing on the above testing, there are three points to improve in the future research. Firstly, the smart contracts are not fine enough to testing each layer's performance. To design blockchain based systems, more exact data is needed. Secondly, a tool named testrpc provided by Truffle framework was used in the testing. This tool will fasten the reaction time of this private blockchain. In the future testing research, such tools should be excluded for a more accurate result. Another important point is that blockchain-based systems and centralized systems are not only different in architecture, but also in the business processing mechanism. More complex tests are needed to evaluate the comprehensive performance of the two types of systems in various industries.

7 Conclusion

Blockchain technology will bring trust, security and decentralization into current business systems and applications. However, the performance of blockchain limits its better application in various industries. Because of blockchain's low capacity of reading and writing data compared to current relational databases, based on pure-blockchain's business systems and applications' speed of processing business cannot be accepted. This is surely a big challenge for blockchain deployment in various industries and our society, where cost trust can be reduced by blockchain technology. If a real-world business system which combine blockchain technology and current relational databases can provide acceptable service for users, it will be a solution for this challenge. A practical solution may be combining blockchain with relational databases to implement industrial functions. IoT technology can connect different kinds of things in real world and bring smart functions into our life and industries. And blockchain will bring security and decentralization. The method and indexes used in this paper provide a foundation for applying blockchain into current IoT systems. With testing data, decisions can be made reasonably about how the design better architecture including blockchain and relational databases, reaching better balance between security and performance. In other words, the method and indexes here will provide testing data to reduce the limit of blockchain's performance and can make contributions to more applications in various industries and IoT world, in a way of combining blockchain with relational databases.

Acknowledgement. This work was supported by Natural Science Foundation of China (NSFC No. 71701091) and the Chinese Ministry of Education Project of Humanities and Social Science (No. 17YJC870020).

References

1. Nakamoto, S.: Bitcoin: a peer-to-peer electronic cash system (2008). Consulted
2. Romano, D., Schmid, G.: Beyond Bitcoin: a critical look at blockchain-based systems. Cryptography **1**(2), 15 (2017)
3. Narayanan, A., Clark, J.: Bitcoin's academic pedigree. Commun. ACM **60**(12), 36–45 (2017)
4. Katz, D.M., Bommarito, M., Zelner, J.: The trust machine. The Economist, October 2015. https://www.economist.com/news/leaders/21677198-technology-behind-bitcoin-could-transf orm-how-economy-works-trust-machine. Accessed 28 Dec 2017
5. Ethereum Project Homepage. https://www.ethereum.org/. Accessed 28 Dec 2017
6. Buterin, V.: A next-generation smart contract and decentralized application platform. White paper (2014). http://www.the-blockchain.com/docs/Ethereum_white_paper-a_next_generatsi on_smart_contract_and_decentralized_application_platform-vitalik-buterin.pdf. Accessed 28 Dec 2017
7. Fabric Project Homepage. https://www.hyperledger.org/projects/fabric. Accessed 28 Dec 2017
8. Azaria, A., Ekblaw, A., Vieira, T., et al.: MedRec: using blockchain for medical data access and permission management. In: International Conference on Open and Big Data, pp. 25–30. IEEE (2016)

9. Li, Z., Kang, J., Yu, R., et al.: Consortium blockchain for secure energy trading in Industrial Internet of Things. IEEE Trans. Ind. Inf. **PP**(99), 1 (2017)
10. IBM and Samsung: IBM ADEPT Practitioner Perspective - Pre Publication Draft. https://zh. scribd.com/doc/252917347/IBM-ADEPT-Practictioner-Perspective-Pre-Publication-Draft-7-Jan-2015. Accessed 28 Dec 2017
11. Gray, M.: Ethereum Blockchain as a Service now on Azure. https://azure.microsoft.com/en-us/blog/ethereum-blockchain-as-a-service-now-on-azure/. Accessed 28 Dec 2017
12. Deloitte's Blockchain Service Homepage. https://www2.deloitte.com/ca/en/pages/techno logy/solutions/deloitte-digital-blockchain.html. Accessed 28 Dec 2017
13. Tian, F.: An agri-food supply chain traceability system for China based on RFID & blockchain technology. In: International Conference on Service Systems and Service Management, pp. 1–6. IEEE, June 2016
14. Xia, Q., Sifah, E., Smahi, A., et al.: BBDS: blockchain-based data sharing for electronic medical records in cloud environments. Information **8**(2), 44 (2017)
15. Corda Project Homapage. https://www.corda.net/. Accessed 28 Dec 2017
16. Dinh, T.T.A., Wang, J., Chen, G., et al.: BLOCKBENCH: a framework for analyzing private blockchains (2017). https://arxiv.org/abs/1703.04057. Accessed 28 Dec 2017
17. Stella Project Report by European Central Bank and Bank of Japan. https://www.ecb.europa. eu/pub/pdf/other/ecb.stella_project_report_september_2017.pdf. Accessed 28 Dec 2017
18. Croman, K., et al.: On scaling decentralized blockchains. In: Clark, J., Meiklejohn, S., Ryan, P.Y.A., Wallach, D., Brenner, M., Rohloff, K. (eds.) FC 2016. LNCS, vol. 9604, pp. 106–125. Springer, Heidelberg (2016). https://doi.org/10.1007/978-3-662-53357-4_8
19. Gervais, A., Karame, G.O., Glykantzis, V., et al.: On the security and performance of proof of work blockchains. In: ACM SIGSAC Conference on Computer and Communications Security, pp. 3–16. ACM (2016)
20. Aniello, L., Baldoni, R., Gaetani, E., et al.: A prototype evaluation of a tamper-resistant high performance blockchain-based transaction log for a distributed database. In: European Dependable Computing Conference (2017)
21. Skeen, D., Stonebraker, M.: A formal model of crash recovery in a distributed system. IEEE Press (1983)
22. Suankaewmanee, K., Hoang, D.T., Niyato, D., Sawadsitang, S., Wang, P., Han, Z.: Performance analysis and application of mobile blockchain. arXiv preprint arXiv:1712. 03659, 11 December 2017
23. Spasovski, J., Eklund, P.: Proof of stake blockchain: performance and scalability for groupware communications. In: The International Conference on Management of Digital Ecosystems (2017)
24. Walker, M.A., Dubey, A., Laszka, A., et al.: PlaTIBART: a platform for transactive IoT blockchain applications with repeatable testing (2017)
25. DB-Engines Databases Ranking. https://db-engines.com/en/ranking. Accessed 28 Dec 2017
26. Truffle Framework Homepage. http://truffleframework.com/. Accessed 28 Dec 2017
27. Vicknair, C., Macias, M., Zhao, Z., et al.: A comparison of a graph database and a relational database: a data provenance perspective. In: Southeast Regional Conference, Oxford, MS, USA, pp. 1–6. DBLP, April 2010
28. Jing, Y., Zhang, C., Wang, X.: An empirical study on performance comparison of lucene and relational database. In: International Conference on Communication Software and Networks, pp. 336–340. IEEE (2009)
29. Chays, D., Deng, Y., Frankl, P.G., et al.: An AGENDA for testing relational database applications. Softw. Test. Verif. Reliab. **14**(1), 17–44 (2010)

Hybrid Connected Spaces: Mediating User Activities in Physical and Digital Space

Carla Farina, Sotirios D. Kotsopoulos[✉], and Federico Casalegno

Mobile Experience Lab, Massachusetts Institute of Technology,
20 Ames Street, Cambridge, MA 02139, USA
skots@mit.edu

Abstract. The ever connected, almost symbiotic bond between physical and digital domain gives birth to new contexts of use and behavior. Designing a building, conceiving its interior or exterior arrangement, is no longer an issue that can be resolved solely in the physical domain. It calls for the integration of a digital, immaterial dimension introducing new variables and expertise. The fields of Human Computer Interaction, Human Building Interaction and Architecture, designate new environments that appear to be a middle ground between the physical and digital domain. In these new Hybrid Spaces the traditional utilitarian features of space are different, the users act differently, and have reformed expectations. In this paper we question if space can guide, inform, and educate the users to improve usability. To answer this question two projects carried out by the Mobile Experience Lab are presented: the Atlas Service Center at the Massachusetts Institute of Technology, and the Connected Sustainable Home in Trento, north Italy. Motivation for this research was our interest in reconsidering the nature of everyday work and live environments and activities in a way that integrates the latest technological advancements. Hybrid Connected Spaces represent the potential of an original type of symbiotic physical and digital domain that enables new enactments to take place.

Keywords: Interactive architecture · Media architecture
Human-building interaction · User-center design

1 Introduction

The integration of the physical and the digital domain gives birth to a new type of architectural space, the Hybrid Connected Space, which operates in active and reactive modes. This article presents the design and development of two examples of hybrid space that offer different levels of interaction in two different fields. More specifically we present a space for public service, the Atlas Service Center at the Massachusetts Institute of Technology (Fig. 1a), and a domestic living space, the Connected Sustainable Home in Trento, Italy (Fig. 1b).

This presentation provides an overview of the design process of Hybrid Spaces, and discusses the adopted means and ends. More importantly it explains how design, which has always been the dominion of physical and material expertise, is now driven to

© Springer International Publishing AG, part of Springer Nature 2018
N. Streitz and S. Konomi (Eds.): DAPI 2018, LNCS 10921, pp. 35–55, 2018.
https://doi.org/10.1007/978-3-319-91125-0_3

Fig. 1. (a) The vision of the MIT Atlas Service Center. (b) The connected sustainable home, in Trento, north Italy. Exterior and interior views

integrate digital features that demand different skills. The characterization "hybrid" is given because the presented projects involve fusion of physical and digital methods. Hybrid Spaces are distinguished by their enhanced potential to be interactive, connected, and able to meet the user expectations in the digital age.

Motivation for the two projects was our interest in reconsidering the nature of everyday spatial contexts, such like the services and domestic environment, in a way that seamlessly integrates the technological advancements of today. The presented examples are part of a discourse that signifies cross-disciplinary collaboration between Human Computer Interaction, Human Building Interaction and Architecture. The adopted approach is to design new spatial experiences in response to the demands of the new emerging contexts of digital media and technological phenomena.

2   Background

In the era of the digital communication, referred also as Collaborative Social Media Age [1], the evolution of live-work environments is rapid. A virtual overlay generates a new dimension that is typically referred as the 4D-space [2]. The introduction of intangible media augments the experience of the users that act in the physical space. Both private and public environments become increasingly sensitive to the undertakings of wider contexts of individuals and communities. This development is triggered by the exponential growth of Information and Communication Technologies (ICT) and the demand for communication and sharing at all layers of private and public life. Everyday actions change as they are carried out via constantly evolving devices, which have become many in number and indispensable in importance, so that they are comparable to "digital prostheses". These prosthesis devices enable individuals to connect to the virtual domain, to enhance their actions, and to accentuate their social presence. Through connectivity individuals accomplish many tasks: from the exchange of information, to the management of household items and bank accounts, to business meetings, and more.

Tasks that can be accomplished through prosthesis devices, such as smartphones, computers, webcams do no longer require predefined physical environments with specific formal or material identity.

Accordingly, there is no longer need of a traditionally designed physical space to perform such tasks. Human activity becomes "de-contextualized" from physical place and the physical space is losing its functional specificity [3]. Hence, buildings no longer determine a place for a designated activity in the traditional sense, i.e. living (in the house), working (in the office), selling (in the store), and so on.

Buildings are also transformed by the integration of new technologies into their physical components. Vertical and horizontal surfaces, fixtures and building equipment, acquire interactive capabilities through the integration of electronics, such as wireless sensors, actuators, dynamic automation with embedded microprocessors, smart materials etc. [4]. Buildings obtain new aesthetic appearance and performance through man-to-machine, or machine-to-machine communication. They have the capacity to communicate what they are, where they are, what happens in them, and how to achieve the optimal usability, or energy consumption overtime.

3   The Design Challenge - Hybrid Interactive Space

Physical architecture has evolved in three stages: First, a built structure was characterized by the static presence and passive performance of its physical mass, and its sole objective was to cover and protect; Second, a built structure acquired the capacity to react to user's actions: the user could trigger changes by mechanical or electronic means, such as lighting, sound, or temperature change; Third, ICT technologies, enabled the creation of a reactive performance that is able to track human behavior, predict it, and even suggest it. The increased potential for interaction instigated changes in the form of buildings, by introducing new elements, processes, and experiences [3].

The process to create physical places where the physical and digital domains meet is a mediation procedure that establishes the presence of the user within the virtual dimension. Designers redefine their role as mediators of the virtual dimension, and express it in a language of physical form [5]. However, built space does not simply serve as a container of new technologies. It becomes an expressive and functional tool enhancing the user activities, and a human-scale interface with multiple purposes. All its parts contribute to the interactions of the user. The materials, the lighting systems, the built components, the windows, the walls and floors, the interior fixtures, the furniture etc., implanted with smart technologies, give birth to hybrid architecture. The challenge to obtain built environments in which the reactive performance is coupled with predictive capability leads to establishing a new symbiotic relationship between man and architectural space.

4 The Mobile Experience Lab Research and Vision

The aim of Mobile Experience Lab is to join space, users and technology to generate experiences that belong in this new dimension. Another important aim of the lab is to reinvent and create new relationships between people, information and places. Along these lines, studying how human organize and build their live-work and leisure environments can contribute in improving user experience and interaction.

The projects serve various human activities and have common principles.

1. User Centric Environments: A human centric approach to design. The approach of the laboratory places the users and their needs at the center of the three key elements: space/user/technology. Technology and space are tailored to the needs, desires, and aptitudes of the end users, and are at the heart of the ideation process.
2. Interactive Connected Environment. The spaces that we studied are characterized by the extensive presence of information-communication and mobile technologies. The existence of such technologies into the built environment affects usability and the user's lifestyle, modifies the traditional utilitarian character of physical space, and improves peoples lives through the careful design of new meaningful experiences. Along these lines the built environments are not only structured, but also equipped to enable the user to carry out various activities. The user receives advice and is enabled to achieve better integration within a global system of sustainable choices.
3. Multidisciplinary approach (and collaborative culture). The lab adopts a holistic approach to innovation to synthesize the different design variables: spatial, cultural, social and technological, as these emerge during the design process.
4. Multisensory and multidimensional design tools. Interactive and interconnected spaces are designed, emphasizing their capability to link individuals, space and communities and to respond to user behavior. This approach aims to an alternative mode of physical environments.

This paper presents two projects, offering different levels of interaction in two different functional fields. More specifically it presents the public service environment of the Atlas Service Center at MIT and the domestic environment of the Connected Sustainable Home.

5   Atlas Service Center – MIT. An Interactive Gateway to MIT

5.1   Project Genesis and Objectives

The Atlas Service Center was designed in 2015, with the aim to implement a completely renewed vision of the MIT Student Center. The relocation of the Center into a larger space within the campus, and its unification with other offices, offered the opportunity to overcome the functional and spatial restrictions of the pre-existing Center. It offered a chance to design something completely new, reinventing both the experience of the space and the user activities. The challenge has been to rethink the services through an innovative architecture (Fig. 2).

Fig. 2. The vision of the new Atlas Center. View of the interactive map and the digital Kiosk

The goal was to design a new space that represents the values and the spirit of MIT, characterized by innovation, research, and intellectual dynamism, and to create an iconic gateway to the Institute. Under this perspective the starting point of the project was to rethink the characteristics of the physical architecture and user experience, to provide better service, and to strengthen community ties. Along these lines, we simplified and speed up many services by making them more transparent and by eliminating waiting times; we proposed a new scheme of spatial organization to manage discontinuous streams of users to optimize the use of space, and we crafted a sense of place with iconographic value.

The underlying philosophy guiding this project was to optimize the use information communication technologies in enhancing utility and improving service performance. The interaction between user, devices, and space provided the basis for turning the Atlas Center into a social meeting hub. The new Atlas Center was envisioned as a hub for experiencing new media that connect the visitors to the campus, a point for sharing information, and providing service to the community. The digital interaction was designed in parallel to the physical space and the social interaction. The role of information communication technologies was pivotal in promoting social interaction and communication between individuals. Ultimate challenge was to design a service space that would support the user, enable him to understand and carry out multiple tasks in shorter time, and provide an immersive experience by endorsing social connectivity. We called this space a "hybrid space", a space that exists in symbiosis with the user.

5.2 Working Methodology: From Brainstorming to Body-Storming

Controlling the numerous variables, affecting the physical, functional and virtual levels of the design, demanded a multidisciplinary approach and the adoption of multi-communicational tools and methods.

The design process was organized in several stages that determined the nature and the features of the *Hybrid Space*. Each stage enabled dialogue and collaboration among different specialists.

In the initial phase of the Ethnographic Research, interviews and meetings identified the needs and desires of the Atlas staff and its users, and the deficiencies of the existing Atlas Center. The information gathered at this stage, enabled the formation of use scenarios describing the ideal workplace, in which the quality of service and the communication between staff and visitors would be improved.

The use scenarios and their needs were synthesized in a brainstorming session to map the user needs (Fig. 3). The Brainstorming Experience Map was the starting point of the preliminary design phase that aimed to develop multiple design layouts.

Fig. 3. The brainstorming process. Mapping out the user experience and all the necessary programmatic requirements. With many moving parts and various needs this required multiple meetings with specialists of various backgrounds.

In the preliminary design phase the preferred scenarios were visualized and set in the physical space. Building elements and physical components were designed and prototyped in physical scale, paths and actions were outlined, and various technologies responding to the needs of the plans were sought. The functional needs shaped the spatial arrangement and determined its requirements.

Four key characteristics of the design solution are explained next in further detail.

(a) Open Plan and Open View. The administrative activities grouped in the same space – specifically more than 18 of services and activities – demanded a space characterized by functional transparency and flux that makes the services visible and accessible. This led to the proposal of an open and dynamic plan with transparent dividers and direct visual contact between public and operators.

(b) Multifunctional Space. The need to manage a large number of users, students, staff and visitors, with discontinuous flows during the different seasons of the year, was met by a multifunctional spatial system. The use of mobile walls and multifunctional elements for discontinuous use of particular services allows for flexible change of use and transformation based on demand.

(c) Network of Digital Systems. Systems connected to the physical space speed up and simplify the services by eliminating the waiting time. It has been envisaged implementation of Mobile Integration and Hands-Free Authentication Systems, like the Hermes System, in combination with a system of Digital Kiosks. The Kiosks are physical entity that characterizes the design and the dynamic circulation of individuals in space.

(d) Interactive Tools. A touch-sensitive tangible map and an interactive media-wall were proposed as interactive media interfaces. They are incorporated into the space to enforce the socialization and connection between users.

After identifying the key design elements, functionality and interaction were sketched and modeled with the aid of analogue and digital tools. The sketching and design phase allowed various ideas to take visual manifestation. Digital and physical models were developed to enable the accomplishment of the various functional tasks. From sketches and ideas (Fig. 4) five alternative design layouts were developed. The design ideas were initially developed and tested with graphic methods and tools: from two-dimensional plans, and 3-dimensional drawings, to physical models and 3D printing (Fig. 5).

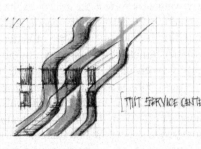

Fig. 4. Sketching. After receiving the design brief, visiting the service center, and going through the interviews the team started sketching the first design schemes. A dynamic space that promoted movement in zones was key priority.

Fig. 5. Rapid prototyping. Testing ideas trough rendering, modeling, and 3D printing

The layouts (Fig. 6) were also represented by the means of graphs capturing spatial and functional solutions according to alternative design strategies from the most conservative to the most innovative one.

Fig. 6. Presentation and discussion of the design layouts.

After generating alternative design layouts (Fig. 7) where the functional requirements were fulfilled, and the form of the physical elements was taken into account, the next step was to test the user's experience and ability to navigate. It was clear that perception, understanding, and quality of experience within space, as well as its usability, are non-measurable qualities with traditional tools. To evaluate the spatial experience not only through vision but also through a multi-sensory process, various tests were invented involving multiple users in a process of co-design.

An important stage of the project was the *body-storming* process, where users had the chance to dive into a simulated real-world environment comprised of physical scale models of the design. Through the real-size prototype (Fig. 8) the users had the chance to experience what he had imagined. The body-storming phase provided a way to test and evaluate user experience and to receive feedback in order to improve it. The design was built in all its key features, without aesthetic and formal details, to test the distribution of the activities and services and to verify the degree of transparency, accessibility and satisfaction of the user. Feedback was obtained through questionnaires on space usage and general impressions. After this series of tests the design of the Atlas Center was re-described, and the vision was refined.

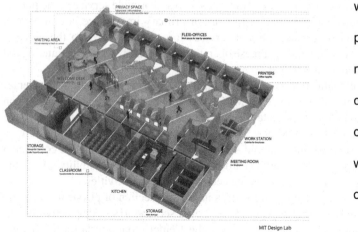

waiting area

privacy space

media wall

counters

digital kiosk

welcome desk

orientation room

Fig. 7. The final design layout. Functional and design elements were defined. User experience, digital interaction and concept of the physical space were formulated to be tested in the bodystorming phase.

Fig. 8. Full-scale light-weight foam prototype of the service center. Participants joined from IS&T, architecture & planning, DSL, HR, parking & transportation, administration, SHASS, medical, DUE, RLE, IMES, and mobile experience lab.

5.3 Design Vision - Physical and Digital Space

The new Atlas Center aims to operate as a visually open, dynamic environment. It is characterized by the combination of traditional private office spaces and transformable multifunctional areas that can be used for meetings and other activities. Transition spaces that are designed to encourage physical and virtual interaction connect all these spaces into a whole. The transition spaces play the role of a unifying link between the meeting and virtual interaction areas. All spaces are equipped with glass partitions, dynamic lighting, and digital devices. The result is a Hybrid Space where physical and digital means complement each other. Meeting, interaction and connectivity are some of the main features of the space as a whole. Traditional ways to provide service to the public, where human contact and physical gesture are of primary importance, are integrated with "invisible" digital services. Digital services inform and speed up the process, enabling the visitor to begin some of these operations remotely before even entering the physical environment of the Center.

A hands free authentication system in physical space is applied to the Atlas Center area. Hermes System [6] developed by MEL team, makes use of credentials stored on the users smartphone to authenticate them when they enter the physical space of the Atlas Center, or are in close proximity. By using this system it is possible for visitors to have access to all services and to avoid delays. Several interactions can be completed remotely: for example, order a new ID card or student pass. This possibility affects the use of the space so that more space can be dedicated to other activities.

The designated area of the Digital Kiosks involves a section of physical space that is dedicated to digital operations. Digital Kiosks offer services to speed up activities and reduce waiting times. They enable to access the Center's online platform, compile modules, and use some services without the need of assistance by an operator.

A touch-sensitive Tangible Map [7], three-dimensional interactive university map (Fig. 9) provides an interactive navigation experience by offering information on buildings, schools, and events, and enabling to store information on the user's smartphone. The main space includes an Interactive Media Wall. It is a digital showcase on University and community news and events, connecting the users with the student community. It is a combination of real-time general information, and more detailed task specific information. It can also be interactive, and the large surface subdivided into modular screens can present a single image or multiple images side by side.

Fig. 9. The mockup of interactive 3D campus map. The tangible map allows access to data related to the MIT buildings by touching a sculptural interface

The design of the digital devices is complemented by the design of the physical space that is equipped with accommodating areas, such as the Welcome Desk, the exhibition area and seats designed to foster human interaction. The Welcome Desk maintains a "human" dimension to guide and assist the visitor in the services.

5.4   Interaction Types

The digital systems and mobile apps combined with the physical components of the space enable different levels, types, and flows of interaction, namely internal interaction, and interaction with the community.

Physical interaction is confined within the Atlas Center and happens between visitors and the Atlas operators. Digital Kiosks exist for this purpose (Fig. 11). The Digital Kiosks allow visitors to book specific services, but also consult and download the available digital modules of the Atlas Center. Placed within the main area, the Digital Kiosks obtain central value as architectural and interface elements. A similar function is carried out by the Welcome Desk, which is designed as a welcoming module involving the presence of tablets and floating operators (Fig. 10).

Fig. 10. Rendering of the Welcome Desk. The Welcome Desk becomes a smart way to optimize the traffic flow inside the space.

Fig. 11. Rendering of the gallery of Digital Kiosk. The installed system permits bluetooth authentication - automatic login if within 1 m.

Design provides form and locality to solutions that are given in response to functional needs. Specialists who deal with abstract, intangible problems often provide these solutions. A designer has to bring the components into human scale and arrange them in physical space. The Atlas Service Center shows that multiple activities and services can be arranged into an overall spatial experience that is both functional and delightful, with a technological aspect that strongly favors human communication.

The reference to a Piazza comes naturally into mind, because it the Atlas Center works as a meeting place for individuals, community and services. The possibility of connectivity is emphasized and stimulated by physical and virtual means.

Within this new methodological framework it is possible to identify the new role and duties of the designer. The architect or interior designer has the role of a mediator, collecting and organizing the user needs, and ultimately situating them within physical space.

The interaction with the MIT community becomes possible through two design elements: the Media Wall (Fig. 12) and the Digital Map (Fig. 13). The Media Wall displays information related to MIT services and news, as well as events related to the student community. The Media Wall also visualizes MIT's history and innovation pickups, supports connectivity within the campus, displays announcements and enables the visualization of tutorials. The Digital Map offers an interactive navigation experience related to the buildings of the campus. Both the Media Wall and the Digital Map are installed in physical space and are expressed by iconic architectural elements. Therefore the space of the Atlas Center becomes a meeting area of communication providing services and showcasing various campus activities. It is a digital Piazza, where physical and virtual dimension are integrated, and physical social interaction and virtual connectivity are complemented.

Fig. 12. The mock up of the Media Wall, during the body-storming process.

Fig. 13. Visualization of the interactive map. Mock up of the interactive map, during the body-storming process.

6 The Connected Sustainable Home: A Tutor for the Inhabitants

The Connected Sustainable Home is a prototype home, designed and built in full scale by the Mobile Experience Laboratory in northern Italy. This research project was part of a research-collaboration, the Green Home Alliance, between the MIT Mobile Experience Lab and the Foundation Bruno Kessler, in Trento, Italy. The research was extended from 2009 to 2012 when the prototype was installed and tested in Trento, in the campus of the Foundation Bruno Kessler (Fig. 14).

Fig. 14. The connected sustainable home. Left: exterior view of the prototype installed in the campus of the foundation Bruno Kessler, in Trento northern Italy.

The design concept of the connected sustainable home follows a holistic approach, where passive and dynamic systems are integrated in the same structure to yield a unique living experience. This prototype house unit was designed to integrate three layers of innovative technologies: a building material system using advanced digital fabrication, a computational system employing AI methods of building control, and an energy production system from renewables [8]. A network of sensors and actuators and an intelligent control system were integrated in the modular building structure made out of local wood, while the sustainable energy system was designed to provide the necessary power. The fusion of these three layers of innovation resulted into a new domestic living experience: connecting the occupants to the community, enforcing sustainable use of the available energy resources, and helping the users to achieve better levels of comfort in non-intrusive, non obstructive ways.

The process of designing the connected sustainable home was a test bed for exploring how home living space can interface with its inhabitants and how domestic living experience can be affected by the patterns of user behavior and local culture [9]. Main objectives were to improve the quality of life, reduce energy consumption, and encourage environmentally responsible ways of living without undermining cultural identity. Interfacing with the house systems becomes possible through monitoring of the daily activities. These actions range from lighting up a light fixture, to opening a window, or going to bed. The intelligent control system of the house adapts the house states to serve these behaviors. Based on these behavioral patterns the control also suggests alternative ways to save energy and optimize comfort.

There are several innovative aspects related to the design of the connected home prototype [10, 11]. In this paper we focus on user interaction. A direct way to attest the interactive features of the home is through the operation of its dynamic south façade. The Dynamic Façade is made up of electro-active windows that modify their position (open-closed) and tinting levels (obscure-clear) based on different inputs provided by the activities of the residents, and the climatic conditions [12]. Each windowpane involves an overlay of two electro-active materials. The first, electrochromic layer enables precise adjustment of the incoming sunlight and heat. The second, poly-dispersed liquid crystal (PDLC) film, is used to control privacy and provides an advanced alternative to the traditional systems of blinds, or louvered grilles. The next Fig. 15 presents the basic state combinations of activated windowpanes, namely: a. the PDLC layer is active and the electrochromic layer is inactive; b. both the PDLC and the elec-trochromic layers are active; c. both the PDLC and the electrochromic layers are inactive; d. the PDLC layer is inactive and the electrochromic layer is active; e. an exterior view of a window with both the PDLC and the electrochromic layers active.

a.   *b.*   *c.*   *d.*

e.

Fig. 15. Basic combinations of window states: frames *a, b, c, d* are window views from the house interior, while frame *e* is a view of a fully tinted window from the house exterior.

Three missions of interface design were identified and challenged in particular: interfacing between interior and exterior; interfacing between private and public, and supporting individual expression.

6.1   Interfacing Between Interior and Exterior

Interfacing between interior and exterior aims at overcoming the extreme conditions and the variability of the local climate. During the process of mediation between interior and exterior, energy is consumed. The Dynamic Façade provides a flexible apparatus that modulates sunlight penetration, incoming heat and natural ventilation at the house inte-rior. These features rely on the integration of electro-active materials, sensing, actuation, and control capabilities. The efficiency of the façade rests on the capacity to monitor and modify the solar transmission of individual windowpanes in real time. Simulation methods were used to project the façade performance in the local climate conditions (Fig. 16). The autonomous control system performs real time simulation, compiles the available data related to the seasonal levels of sunlight, heat, humidity etc. and feedback from sensors, to adjust the states of the electro-active materials as needed to optimize the long-term house performance and thermal [13], and visual comfort [14].

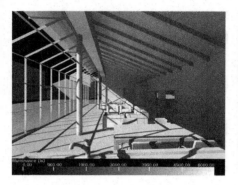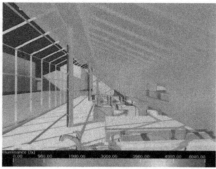

Fig. 16. Solar radiation simulation indicating the angle and intensity of the incoming sunlight in the prototype, on June 21, at 1 PM, in Trento, N. Italy

In the autonomous mode the façade adapts its state based on the desired conditions without requiring supervision or input by the inhabitants. Hence, in the summer the windowpanes are adjusted to reduce the heating effect of incident solar irradiance, and in the winter, to expose the interior to the warm winter sun. Although autonomous functioning is based on an algorithmically calculated action plan, aiming at long-term goals, the façade is also engaged into synchronous interactions with the inhabitants. A parallel, responsive mode permits the adaptation of the façade if an optimization setting is overwritten by a short-term action. For example, if a resident opens many windows in a hot summer day the system would respond to the change of interior temperature by reconfiguring the façade settings (e.g., changing sunlight modulation pattern) to balance the heat loss.

6.2 Interfacing Between Private and Public

While servicing the adjustment of sunlight, heat and view the façade also determines the association between the private interior and the public exterior. As Lyndon and Moore [15] point out, the history of architecture could be approached as a struggle between the membrane and the frame: "Between solidly opaque and flexibly open, based partly on materials available, but more fundamentally on how definitively inside is separated from outside". The modern, inoperable curtain wall is a contemporary expression of definitive separation between inside and outside. Inoperable curtain walls are energy intensive since they require support by artificial lighting and air-conditioning systems, they restrain user behavior and they neglect the urban context. The Dynamic Façade was envisioned as an interactive, automated alternative [16]. Its varying configurations affect privacy and transform how the prototype is perceived from the public street. Without prescribed states the façade functions as a programmable matrix of apertures, allowing the users to determine dynamically how to engage with the street and the neighbors (Fig. 17).

Fig. 17. Left: artist's rendition of the Dynamic Façade's response to human gestures. Right: the actual implementation of the Dynamic Façade in Trento north Italy.

6.3   Supporting Individual Expression

At any moment numerous façade configurations meet the efficiency requirements. This allows satisfying performance and individual preference related to privacy, visibility, comfort and view. The façade becomes a medium of self-expression mirroring the dispositions of the residents to the urban landscape (Fig. 21). The variety of façade configurations was approached as a visual language, and it was mapped through the conventions of a generative grammar producing a large number of patterns based jointly on properties of symmetry and performance [14]. In this way, comfortable interior conditions are maintained while a range of distinct patterns is formed. The reconfiguration of the façade can also happen in response to the presence of a passer-by or to specific gestures that are tracked by the embedded network of sensors. The interactive mode allows the façade to react to gestures, events and conditions like the sunrise or sunset, etc. (Fig. 18). On the transparent façade a patch of PDLC cells can conceal a moving person from the public view, while leaving the rest of the façade transparent.

Fig. 18. The Dynamic Façade responding to sunrise at waking time.

7   Autonomous Control

The values of the house microclimate, such as temperature, humidity, natural light, etc., are monitored and energy consumption is controlled by the autonomous control. This system was developed by the Mobile Experience Laboratory and the Model-Based Embedded and Robotic Systems (MERS) group of MIT. The goal was to develop an intelligent control able to respond to user needs, optimize energy consumption and comfort without direct user input. The autonomous control [17] engages a wireless network of sensors (WSN) that is suitably distributed in the walls, ceiling and window frames of the house. The sensors capture data relevant to user behavior and energy consumption, while an HTTP server enables the exchange of information between the control and all the systems of the house (Fig. 19).

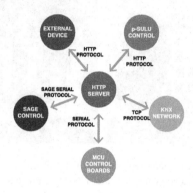

Fig. 19. Diagram of the implemented communication apparatus of the connected home.

The p-Sulu system (Probabilistic Sulu) is a risk sensitive model-based plan executive that controls the home's systems. It combines feedback from sensors, statistic information compiled by a weather station, and environmental data, to evaluate performance in real time. By combining these data with schedules, long-term goals, and preferences, p-Sulu evaluates the risks and predicts the future behaviors to produce a chance constraint qualitative plan executive. This plan is specified as a sequence of state and time constraints (Fig. 20). The control operates to satisfy these constraints while tracking the actual conditions and performing rescheduling as needed.

The intelligent house control p-Sulu takes a threefold approach to optimize comfort: Firstly, it minimizes the use of artificial lighting, heating and cooling by managing the incoming sunlight and heat; Secondly, it exploits the high thermal capacity of the envelope to store solar heat; And thirdly, it helps the residents to choose energy-saving behaviors. A key innovation behind p-Sulu is that it is able to leverage flexibility in a resident's schedule to achieve reduction in energy consumption.

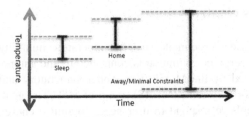

Fig. 20. Simplified diagram of a chance-constrained state plan. The control "drives" the operation of all systems within an upper (red) and a lower (blue) boundary of constraints. (Color figure online)

Fig. 21. Left: day view of the Dynamic Façade with all the electrochromic windows tinted. Right: night view of the Dynamic Façade with the pattern "MIT" formed by the windows.

Finally, the intelligent control informs and empowers the occupants to adjust their behavior to lower energy consumption. The information provided by the intelligent control educates the users and enables them to become more aware regarding the environmental impact of their habits. The house encourages the users to progressively adopt environmentally friendlier practices and at the same time progressively adapts to better serve their needs. By tracking the patterns of use the intelligent control enables an increasingly more effective long-term management of the available resources, while optimizing user comfort. We can therefore say that the dynamic living environment of the connected sustainable home acts as an assistant and a tutor. In the end the users remain always free to follow or overwrite the recommendations of the intelligent control with their behavior.

8   Conclusions

The trajectories of two design projects were described. The first resulted to a new scenario of user experiences for the Atlas Service Center at MIT; the second to a full-scale prototype for a Connected Sustainable Home. The two projects demonstrated possibilities of novel experiences through the integration of dynamic digital systems in physical space. It was also examined how the transformations in user behavior caused by digital media leads to new user expectations and to a need for reconsidering spatial organization. Multi-functionality, connectivity, interaction and symbiosis between users in space, have been supported in both projects. The physical-spatial features of architecture are enhanced by the means of Information Communication Technologies that activate new spatial dynamics. Radical changes take place in the contexts of the design process, performance prediction, and user experience, leading to the generation of new families of physical artifacts. The process of designing becomes more transparent and open-ended to incorporate new technical expertise. Technological change and new tools play important role in the course of ideation. Designers adopt new sets of creative constraints and aim at new objectives. Still, they have always to mediate the needs of the user and to synthesize the technological complexity into a human centric experience, in physical space. Along these lines, the built environment turns into a dynamic interface. At best this interface places the individual at the center of interaction, as the main actor within various contexts. Multiple new territories of exploration open up to design research, like the optimization of energy efficiency and comfort, the integration of intelligent building systems in various social and cultural contexts, the improvement and simplification of services, and the introduction of new aesthetic values and symbolic connotations to the built environment.

In the context of working and service environments the design proposal for the Atlas Center shows that user interaction can acquire greater efficiency and invigorating social character. Services can be simplified and a new type of physical/digital interaction can be developed. The integration of Information Communication Technologies in physical space and the critical aspects of space distribution, augment the functionality of the built space and improve user experience by making the interactions simpler and more transparent.

In the context of domestic living, rethinking the problem of optimizing energy performance and user comfort through responsive living environments leads to more efficient management of the available resources and better quality of life. Educating the users through preventive, symbiotic architectural systems, like these of the connected home, simplifies human-machine interaction, and transforms the home-living experience. Long term monitoring of the patterns of use by intelligent domestic systems can lead to improvements in the well being of the inhabitants.

Interdisciplinary approach, collaborative design processes, multi-communication design tools come to the definition of hybrid environments applicable to all human living contexts, from domestic, to working and social.

Acknowledgments. Acknowledgement is due to all the MIT Mobile Experience Lab members involved in the Atlas Center and the Connected Sustainable Home. The Connected Sustainable Home research was conducted within the Green Home Alliance between the MIT Mobile Experience Lab and the Fondazione Bruno Kessler, in Trento, Italy.

References

1. Van Berkel, B., Piber, A., Lodi, F.: Designing with the immaterial. In: Proceedings of the 2nd Media Architecture Biennale Conference, MAB 2014, Aarthus, Denmark, World Cities, p. 84 (2014)
2. Bullivant, L.: 4dspace: Interactive Architecture, 1st edn. Academy Press, Cambridge (2005)
3. Alavi, H.S., Lalanne, D., Nembrini, J., Churchill, E., Kirk, D., Moncur, W.: Future of human-building interaction. In: Proceedings of the 2016 CHI Conference Extended Abstracts on Human Factors in Computing Systems, CHI 2016, pp. 3408–3414. Association for Computing Machinery, New York (2016)
4. Velicov, K., Thün, G.: Responsive building envelopes: characteristics and evolving paradigms (Chap. 1.3). In: Trubiano, F. (ed.) Design and Construction of High-Performance Homes: Building Envelopes, Renewable Energies and Integrated Practice, pp. 75–91. Routledge, London (2012)
5. Aish, F., Davis, A., O'Malley, M., Papalexopoulos V., Foster + Partners: Designing the infrastructure of human building interaction. In: Proceedings of the CHI Conference Extended Abstracts of Future of Human-Building Interaction a CHI Workshop, CHI 2016, San Jose, CA, USA, 7 May 2016
6. Chilana, K., Casalegno, F.: Hermes: hands-free authentication in physical spaces. In: Tryfonas, T. (ed.) HAS 2016. LNCS, vol. 9750, pp. 15–24. Springer, Cham (2016). https://doi.org/10.1007/978-3-319-39381-0_2
7. Walker, W., Sung, H., Ong, C.K., Casalegno, F.: Exploring spatial meaning with tangible map. In: 6th ACM International Symposium on Pervasive Displays Proceedings, 07–09 June, Lugano, Switzerland (2017). Article No. 6
8. Kotsopoulos, S.D., Farina, C., Casalegno, F.: The three autonomous architectures of a connected sustainable residential unit. In: Energy Procedia, International Conference on Applied Energy (ICAE 2014), vol. 61, pp. 1496–1500 (2014)
9. Scagnetti, G., Casalegno, F.: Social sustainability in design: the window as an interface for social interaction. In: Rau, P.L.P. (ed.) CCD 2014. LNCS, vol. 8528, pp. 321–330. Springer, Cham (2014). https://doi.org/10.1007/978-3-319-07308-8_31
10. Kotsopoulos, S.D., Casalegno, F., Hsiung, B., Graybill, W.: A prototype hut for the post-digital age. In: Proceedings of the 30th International Conference on Education and research in Computer Aided Architectural Design in Europe (ECAADE 2012), 12–14 September 2012, Prague, Czech Republic, pp. 307–316 (2012)
11. Kotsopoulos, S.D., Farina, C., Casalegno, F., Briani, A., Simeone, P., Bindinelli, R., Pasetto, G.: A building system for connected sustainability. In: Proceedings of the 14th World Conference on Timber Engineering 2012 (WCTE 2012), University of Auckland - New Zealand Timber Design Society, 16–19 July 2012, Auckland, New Zealand, pp. 271–279 (2012)
12. Kotsopoulos, S.D., Casalegno, F., Ono, M., Graybill, W.: Windowpanes become smart: how responsive materials and intelligent control will revolutionize the architecture of buildings. In: Proceedings of the First International Conference on Smart Systems, Devices and Technologies (SMART 2012), 27 May–1 June 2012, Stuttgart, Germany, pp. 112–118 (2012)
13. Kotsopoulos, S.D., Cuenin, A., Telhan, O., Casalegno, F.: Personalizing thermal comfort in a prototype indoor space. In: Proceedings of the Eighth International Conference on Simulation in Architecture, SIMUL 2013, 27 October–1 November, Venice, Italy, pp. 178–186 (2013)
14. Kotsopoulos, S.D., Cara, G., Graybill, W., Casalegno, F.: The dynamic façade pattern grammar. Environ. Plann. B: Plann. Des. 41(4), 690–716 (2014)

15. Lyndon, D., Moore, C.W.: Chambers for a Memory Palace. The MIT Press, Cambridge (1996)
16. Kotsopoulos, S.D., Farina, C., Casalegno, F.: Designing an interactive architectural element for a responsive prototype house. In: Proceedings of the XVI Conference of the Society of Digital Graphics (SIGRADI 2012), Fortaleza, Brazil, pp. 369–372 (2012)
17. Kotsopoulos, S.D., Casalegno, F., Ono, M., Graybill, W.: Managing variable transmittance windowpanes with model-based autonomous control. J. Civil Eng. Archit. **7**(5), 507–523 (2013). Serial No. 66

A Novel Interaction Design Approach for Accessing Daily Casual Information Through a Virtual Creature

Kota Gushima, Hina Akasaki, and Tatsuo Nakajima(✉)

Department of Computer Science and Engineering,
Waseda University, Tokyo, Japan
{gushi,h.akasaki,tatsuo}@dcl.cs.waseda.ac.jp

Abstract. The Ambient Bot that we have developed makes it possible to access information by eye contact with virtual creatures in an augmented reality environment. By using Ambient Bot, information can be accessed without using complex operations from smartphones. In this paper, we focus on how that access of information consists of a pull-based interaction method and a push-based interaction method and show the feasibility of both interaction methods in Ambient Bot. In the pull-based interaction method that was adopted by the original Ambient Bot, multiple virtual creatures float around a user. Since each creature provides a different piece of information, it is possible for a user to easily access multiple types of content simply by making eye contact with each creature. On the other hand, in the push-based interaction method, a virtual creature predicts appropriate pieces of information that a user wants and actively notifies the user of that information. Our aim is mainly to investigate the design spaces for the push-based interaction method in Ambient Bot. In addition, we also investigate whether the push-based interaction method in Ambient Bot can be used to offer serendipitous information that will help people come up with new ideas when they receive diverse, interesting stimuli.

Keywords: Augmented reality · Virtual creature · Eye contact
Notification · Head-mounted display · Interaction modality

1 Introduction

Information becomes an important factor in making our everyday lives efficient and also comfortable by augmenting human behavior with access to this information. Accessing digital information has become easier because of the spread of mobile devices. In the latter half of the 1990s, mobile phones in Japan became more widespread, and in the 2000s, mobile phone penetration exceeded 50% [12]. In addition, in 1999, NTT Docomo started a service called "i-mode" that could connect to the Internet from a mobile phone. At that point, the mobile phone began to play an essential role in accessing digital information in the real world. After Apple iPhone appeared in 2007, mobile phones became more like generic digital devices than just voice phones. As a result, people now have access to information through a mobile phone anytime and anywhere.

© Springer International Publishing AG, part of Springer Nature 2018
N. Streitz and S. Konomi (Eds.): DAPI 2018, LNCS 10921, pp. 56–70, 2018.
https://doi.org/10.1007/978-3-319-91125-0_4

People usually need to activate the device and to open a target application in order to access the information provided by mobile devices. Currently, this process is standard procedure; however, that process is changing through the progress of augmented reality (AR) technologies. In particular, the concept of Mixed Reality (MR), which Microsoft HoloLens[1] uses, seamlessly incorporates digital objects into people's real lives. If a wearable smart glass that Google Glass[2] tried to produce is widely available, people will be able to utilize digital content more easily by wearing the glasses. In addition, contact lens type AR devices are currently being developed [7]. With the progress of such devices, people will be able to interact with digital content in their everyday lives more seamlessly. Current mobile phones may change to other forms and play different roles. Moreover, the mobile phone may disappear from our casual daily activities in the near future, as e-mails are replaced with casual social communication tools like Slack[3].

In this paper, we investigate an interaction method for accessing digital information more ambiently in an age when smart glass is becoming widely used. Now, people can interact with digital information without holding a device, so they can acquire information more naturally and with less effort. We discuss accessing information by implementing and evaluating interaction methods in Ambient Bot. In past information systems before the AR era, information was typically shown on a display, and artificial interactions were made using devices such as a keyboard and mouse not typically used in daily reality space. However, Ambient Bot is designed to access information more naturally by using eye contact to replicate human nonverbal communication. The approach that utilizes non-verbal communication may fill a gap between the artificial digital world and the real physical world. If the digital world feels more realistic, information technology can spread more widely. As a result, an information system will help people navigate easily and acquire more useful knowledge with natural interaction.

The structure of this paper is as follows: In Sect. 2, we show an overview of Ambient Bot. Section 3 introduces the basic design of two kinds of interaction methods (the pull-based and push-based interaction methods) for accessing information. In Sect. 4, we will present the design of the push-based interaction method and its evaluation in Ambient Bot. In Sect. 5, we investigate the feasibility of using Ambient Bot to provide serendipitous information. In Sect. 6, we present other work related to this study, and finally, we summarize this paper in Sect. 7.

2 An Overview of Ambient Bot

Ambient Bot offers an agent that ambiently exists around a user to provide information that he/she wants to know by using AR technologies without interfering with their current activities in his/her everyday life. The aim of Ambient Bot is to offer implicit

---

[1] https://www.microsoft.com/hololens.
[2] https://x.company/glass/.
[3] https://slack.com/.

and low-cost interaction that makes it easy to access necessary information even when users are going about their everyday lives, for example, when people are in public places such as stations or walking down the streets.

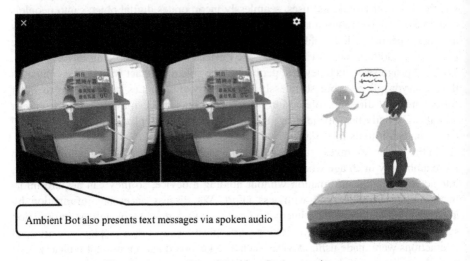

Fig. 1. A screenshot of Ambient Bot presenting news

Ambient Bot allows users to access information when needed by simply making eye contact with virtual creatures that are always floating around them. Eye contact does not enable complicated interaction with accessing information but can initiate implicit and natural interaction without explicit interaction, such as using a controller device. A creature shows and speaks a content article in a translucent window in the real world to provide information to the user, as shown in Fig. 1. Ambient Bot requires people to wear a lightweight head-mounted display (HMD) that shows the real world through a camera attached to the HMD, where they can see a virtual creature in the real world with augmented reality technologies. While there is no eye contact, the creature automatically moves to a position that does not interfere with the user's view, so he or she is not strongly conscious of the existence of the creature. In the current version of Ambient Bot, we chose a floating creature similar to a jellyfish, as shown in Fig. 1. Since animated characters are popular in animations and games, especially for young people, this approach is not unnatural for them as a means to access information.

The original Ambient Bot described in [2, 5] supports only the pull-based interaction method that will be defined in the next section.

3   Designing the Interaction Modality

In this section, we describe the interaction modalities that are used in recent digital services. Then, we define the push-based and pull-based interaction method and show how the methods are used in Ambient Bot by presenting a scenario.

3.1   Interaction Modality

Digital services need to offer interaction methods to access those services and need to design appropriate input and output modalities for those interaction methods. For example, in a modern GUI environment, a user manually uses a mouse and a keyboard as inputs for a service, and the service presents information as the output through a display device. Due to the progress of information technologies, their modalities are diversifying and we can now consider other options. In particular, new input modalities like tangible devices, sounds, gestures, and eye gaze have also appeared. In contrast, the output modalities have not significantly changed, and mainly visual and audio methods are used for presenting information. Although tactile and olfaction senses have appeared to enhance people's user experiences, we do not consider those approaches in this paper because those technologies are not mature enough to be used as general information access.

Table 1. Input and output modalities

Output Input		Vision	Audio
Manipulation	Keyboard	PC	
	Touch	Tablet, Smartphone	
Sensing	Gesture		
	Voice	Smartphone	SmartSpeaker
	Gaze	Ambient Bot	Ambient Bot

Table 1 shows the categorizations of input and output modalities. The current digital services use any modalities belonging to these categories. For example, the standard interaction of a smartphone mainly uses the touch - vision modality. In recent years, voice input has become popular because speech recognition technologies have progressed rapidly. As a result, smart speakers such as Google Home[4] and Amazon Echo[5] have appeared and began to be used widely. The smart speakers typically use the voice - audio modality. This discussion is also necessary for AR technologies, which have become popular recently. In this paper, we discuss how Ambient Bot can support the push-based interaction method. Ambient Bot adopts AR technologies to access information so that investigating the design space of input and output modalities in Ambient Bot offers useful insights to choose appropriate modalities in the AR environment in the future.

3.2   Pull-Based and Push-Based Interaction Methods

We consider two methods for people to access information; the pull-based interaction method and the push-based interaction method. In the pull-based interaction method, a

---

[4] https://store.google.com/product/google_home.

[5] https://www.amazon.com/Amazon-Echo-Bluetooth-Speaker-with-WiFi-Alexa/dp/B00X4WHP5E.

user actively accesses information that he/she wants to know. In the push-based interaction method, information is actively provided to a user and the user can passively access the information. The push-based interaction method includes not only notifications but also accidentally receiving information. For example, people may acquire knowledge about new furniture via advertisements when they walk down the street. Such interaction is also classified as push-based interaction because people acquire the information passively from the outside world, and they may not expect to receive the information.

These two methods may be used separately or combined. For example, watching a weather forecast application is close to a pure pull-based interaction because a user usually has a clear intent to access the information. On the other hand, an SNS (Social Networking Service) has features of both pull-based and push-based interactions. When watching the timeline of an SNS, the purpose of accessing the SNS information is ambiguous; however, a user is willing to acquire various pieces of information published by followers of the SNS. From the above discussions, information access cannot simply be divided into pull-based and push-based interaction methods, but it becomes a spectrum corresponding to what information a user needs to receive concretely.

Recently, push-based notifications on smartphones were studied [3] and an ambient notification method using an eyeglass device was reported [4]. In this paper, our focus is to investigate the design space to use interaction modalities in the push-based and pull-based interaction methods in future AR environments.

3.3 Scenario Demonstration

The section introduces a scenario for explaining the pull-based and push-based interaction methods using Ambient Bot. Figure 2 shows how the two interaction methods are used in Ambient Bot.

"Satoshi is 27 years old. He works at an IT company in Tokyo. His parents' house is in Kyoto, and now he lives by himself.

One day in October, he woke up at 6 am as usual. He went to the washroom to wash his face and put on a pair of glasses. His glasses use smart glass, a tool that provides various pieces of information, and it made an explosive hit several years ago. Smartphones are still significantly popular as most people use smart glasses and smartphones in combination. Although the smart glass is excellent as a display, input methods are poor. For this reason, a smartphone is used for work requiring detailed input. When he wore the smart glasses, multiple virtual creatures floated in the real world. This application is called Ambient Bot, and he can receive several notifications, such as news and weather forecasts, through these creatures. He made eye contact with the creature that conveys the weather forecast. The creature said, "Today's temperature is 16°. It will be a bit cooler than yesterday." He thought, "Then, I'm going to wear my sweater."

He went to his work place by a train. He had decided to watch the news on the train every day. On this day, there was a feature about venture companies, and he thought that working at a venture company would be a tough job. However, he thought that a venture company may not be a bad place to work if there is time to go fishing on the weekends.

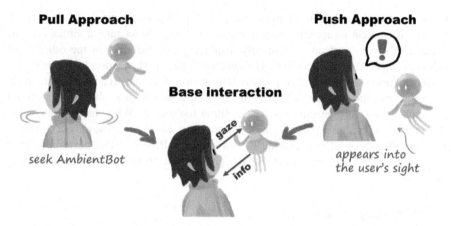

Fig. 2. The pull-based and push-based interaction method in Ambient Bot

Satoshi arrived at work and started working. While he is concentrating on his work, Ambient Bot is not used. During his work that morning, he discovered a bug in the system he had developed last week and he worked on fixing it. He could not finish the bug fix, and it was time for his lunch break. When he finished his lunch and drank a coffee, Ambient Bot suddenly came into his sight. It was a creature who provided information that someone recommended. That creature gave a summary of a company manager's interview. The manager said "When you are confronted with a problem, you don't notice your surroundings". Satoshi realized that he was in that situation right now. After he returned to work, he discovered that the bug was not a problem in his development but that the problem was caused by another department.

The problem was solved, and he left the office. When he was going home as usual, the Ambient Bot creature fell into his sight. The creature tells him, "You are going to the gym at 20 o'clock today." He was busy with work, so he forgot that he had decided to go to the gym that day. Because the next station was the transfer station to the line that goes toward the gym, he changed trains at that station and went to the gym."

4   Design and Implementation of the Push-Based Interaction Method in Ambient Bot

In this section, we show the design and implementation of the push-based interaction method in Ambient Bot. We also investigate the feasibility through user study. As described in Sect. 2, the pull-based interaction method in Ambient Bot is explained and evaluated in detail in [2].

4.1   Design for the Push-Based Interaction Method in Ambient Bot

This section investigates how Ambient Bot provides information in the axis of visual and auditory cues. Since Ambient Bot aims to provide information naturally without increasing a user's cognitive overload, we need to find proper ambient information delivery methods for the AR environment. Therefore, the visual cue designed to notify the user of ambient information is delivered by deliberately locating a virtual creature in the user's view instead of explicitly displaying information. On the other hand, auditory cues need to be considered to ensure ambientness when a user hears the sound.

When Ambient Bot wants to provide information, a virtual creature appears in the real space, but the position is almost the edge of a user's view; thus, the creature's appearance does not consume his/her cognition too much[6]. When he/she makes eye contact with the creature, provides information. Then, the creature moves out of his/her sight and disappears after providing the information. Based on this basic interaction design, we would like to investigate the design space for presenting visual and auditory cues.

4.2　A Prototype System

The prototype system, as shown in Fig. 3, was implemented on Microsoft HoloLens (see footnote 1), which is a platform that offers MR user experiences by enhancing the previous version of Ambient Bot [2, 5]. Microsoft HoloLens offers an HMD to superimpose virtual information onto the real world. For discussing visual cues, we compare two types of cues to indicate that Ambient Bot has information to share: the first one is whether or not to show a notification icon above the creature, and the second one is to indicate what types of content the creature provides to a user.

Also, we prepared six sounds for the auditory cues. Three sounds are traditional, inorganic, and electric sounds, and the other three are sounds the creature seems to naturally generate, where Sound 1 is a comical sound that becomes treble gradually; Sound 2 is a short electronic metallophone sound whose musical scale is C; Sound 3 is

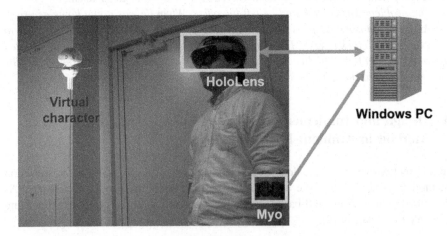

Fig. 3. Overview of the push-based interaction

---

[6] In the original Ambient Bot, a user cannot see a creature until he/she wants to make eye contact with the creature.

also a short electronic metallophone sound, but it is a chord composed of C, E and G; Sound 4 consists of three short marimba sounds; Sound 5 is like the friction sound of paper; and Sound 6 consists of a double-short electronic sound that becomes treble drastically. A user hears these sounds when the creature appears in the real space. The user can also configure the device to receive information without the auditory cue. The content is read via the creature's voice, and the user can choose whether to display the content on the message window or not.

In addition, we added a gesture recognition function to this version of Ambient Bot. When accessing information through Ambient Bot, making eye contact with a creature is a good approach since a user intends to access the information by his/her own intention. However, when the information is actively presented to a user, the user may be currently doing another task. Therefore, it might be uncomfortable for the user to be interrupted to watch the creature and determine whether the information is currently relevant to him/her. Once the user makes eye contact with, the creature continues to read the content article by voice until the end. Thus, we added a function to cancel speaking in the middle of reading. We decided to use Myo[7], which is a wearable gesture recognition device. This device makes it possible to use the shake of a user's hand as an input to Ambient Bot, for example, wave in, wave out, double tap, fist and so on are used as current gestures. An important issue in the basic design philosophy of Ambient Bot is that the interaction should be ambient and natural, and a user can use Ambient Bot in various public spaces without annoyance. A user can stop the creature's reading with a double tap gesture with his/her fingers. In addition, the user can cancel receiving the information by fist gesture if he/she feels that the information is not of interest to him/her.

4.3   User Study

A user study was conducted using nine participants (8 males and 1 female, average age: 22.7). Figure 4 shows screenshots of how Ambient Bot works in each step. In this user study, participants chose their preferred display modes for three typical content types: newsflashes, e-mails and the user's schedule. For each type of content, the participants selected the configuration of sound cues, whether a notification icon is presented or not, and whether a message window is presented or not. The message window presents content, and the content may be read by the creature's voice.

In this user study, we interviewed the participants and asked them why they chose the configurations. Table 2 shows the configurations selected by the participants in the user study. For the types of sound cues, eight participants chose to use a sound cue before information is presented. Only participant D selected no sound cue when a newsflash was presented. All participants claimed that selecting sound cues depends on the taste of each individual, and a treble sound was not used by most participants for indicating there is interesting content. Since all participants chose to use auditory cues, presenting a creature in their sights is not enough of a cue to indicate that there is interesting content for them. However, participant D answered "*I do not need to*

---

[7] https://www.myo.com/.

configure a sound for newsflash because the content may not be necessary for me." In addition, participant D also said, "*In the AR environment, using electronic sound cues is unnatural. I felt the sound from my mobile phone is natural because I implicitly understood that the sound is in cyber space, but the AR environment is closer to the real world, so I'd like to be notified with a more natural sound that exists seamlessly in reality.*" In this user study, the participants felt inconvenienced because the auditory cues that we prepared were mostly electronic sounds.

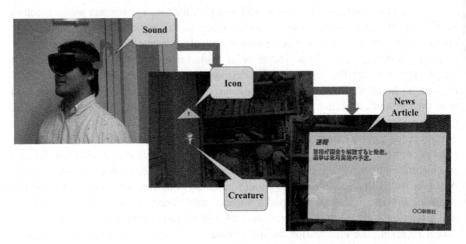

Fig. 4. Screenshots showing how the push-based Ambient Bot works

The message window selected depended on the type of content. Of course, some participants always turned the window on, but other participants changed the configuration to display the message window according to the content. The reason provided for turning the message window on was mostly because they may miss listening to content via voice only, and the reason for turning it off was because the content in the message window does not matter if participants missed listening or not.

For e-mail content, all participants turned on the message window. From the interviews, they did not want to miss the email content. In addition, several participants said they do not need a function to read e-mails via a voice because e-mails are usually read by a user's eye, and not listened to by a voice. The result of the interviews shows that the participants felt the modality used for existing services should be used even in novel services when traditional content is shown to a user.

The icon was turned on by most participants, except participant C. Several participants said, "*The icon was turned on in order that Ambient Bot informed what information would be presented.*" Participant C selected to display the icon only when the message window was not displayed. He commented in the interview "*When the message window comes out, I can read the message quickly; thus, I can fully understand what content it is. In the case of only voice, the icon is displayed soon to see what content it is.*" Hence, we understood through the interviews that all participants wanted to know at the beginning what type of content Ambient Bot wanted to present.

Table 2. The results of the push-based interaction method

participant		a	b	c	d	e	f	g	h	i
newsflash	sound type	4	2	2	none	6	6	3	2	6
	message window	off	on	off	on	on	on	on	on	on
	Icon	on	on	on	on	on	on	off	on	on
mail	sound type	4	3	5	5	2	3	4	5	4
	message window	on	on	on	on	on	on	on	on	on
	Icon	on	on	off	on	on	on	on	on	on
schedule	sound type	4	4	4	5	1	2	2	4	2
	message window	on	on	off	on	off	on	on	off	on
	Icon	on	on	off	on	on	on	on	on	on

4.4   Analyzing the Results of the User Study

In order to investigate the methods for providing a user with interesting content, we conducted a user study using visual and auditory cues. As a result of the user study, both the sound and the icon were used in most cases for existing content. Participants preferred to use icons because they could identify what type of content Ambient Bot has before obtaining the actual content. The icon was also adopted because it does not disturb the participants' views. The results indicate that combining the sound and the icon is effective at making users aware that there is content available. A user can predict what content is available by listening to an auditory cue before receiving the actual content. Similarly, a user can determine what types of content are available by looking at the icon.

The results of the interviews suggested that the modality of information cues should be designed according to the existing services' modalities. For example, participants B, C, and E said, "*Reading e-mails via voice is unnatural.*" Because e-mails are usually read by a user's eye, it is rare to listen to them by voice, so they felt that was strange. Therefore, the modality to offer information cues should keep the traditional style as much as possible. In the case of newsflashes, participants A and C wanted the content to be presented only via a voice. In particular, participant C commented "*Hearing newsflash is like listening to a radio.*" Because newsflashes are originally delivered by voice, we consider listening to that content by sound only as natural for most participants.

Although the message window offers an advantage to reliably grasp the content quickly, the message window in the AR environment may disturb a user's view, which gives the user an uncomfortable feeling. For example, participants A and B pointed out "*The message window may interfere with my daily activities.*" So, we need to carefully design how to present a message window. On the other hand, participants A, F, G and I commented "*The auditory cue does not interfere with everyday life, although there is a risk of missing informed content*"; thus, the designer needs to pay attention to the tradeoff.

Finally, we asked participants about interaction using gestures. All participants said "*The interaction method was good.*" In particular, participant B reported "*When using the pull-based interaction method in Ambient Bot, I felt that the system controls my eye sight because I need to keep my eye sight on virtual creatures, but in this case, I could autonomously control the system by myself, so I like the push-based interaction method better.*" In addition, participants E and G answered, "*Using gestures is better than using gazes when being notified of content.*" It was also suggested that "*The interaction via gestures using Myo was easier for them than the eye contact-based interaction.*" In this case, Ambient Bot may not require using creatures in the push-based interaction method. On the other hand, in the interviews, participants B and E commented "*I preferred that a creature bows after the creature finishes speaking.*" We guess that these participants felt that the creature behaved like a human. The human-like behavior motivates a user to use Ambient Bot, so in the future, we need to compare a notification with only a gesture without creatures to one with creatures without gestures.

5   Evoking Serendipity Through the Push-Based Interaction Method in Ambient Bot

In addition to providing interesting information, as described in the previous sections, we believe that Ambient Bot can trigger people's serendipity through the push-based interaction method. People can come up with new ideas and learn lessons by receiving various stimuli from the outside world. This is usually called serendipitous information [10].

We conducted another user study to investigate whether the push-based interaction method in Ambient Bot can be used to deliver serendipitous information to users. Therefore, another type of content was chosen for this user study. As an example of promoting serendipity, we chose Nietzsche's words as the serendipitous information, and the participants configured the sound type, the message window, and the notification icon just like in the previous user study.

In the interviews, in addition to the reasons why participants chose their configurations, we asked three questions using a seven-step Likert scale, "*Have you experienced serendipity?*", "*Can Ambient Bot randomly offer information to increase serendipity?*" and "*Can an Ambient Bot that takes into account personal preferences raise serendipity?*" In this Ambient Bot, a user can handle several types of inputs using Myo. Therefore, the gestures can tell Ambient Bot whether the content provided by Ambient Bot satisfied a user's preferences or not.

Table 3 shows the results of the user study. Compared with the previous user study, three participants chose the configuration not to display the icon. There is no tendency toward the preferences on the sound and message window. The serendipity experienced by individuals is diversified; however, most participants answered positively that there is a possibility to raise their serendipity. For example, participant D said "*I think that the score is 7, but it depends on the personality of a user. People who have curiosity on a variety of issues will come across the serendipity whether there is this system or not. People who are hard to come across the serendipity think that the serendipity will not happen much even with this system.*"

In this case, a number of participants who did not use the icon and the sound to be notified about new content increased in comparison with the previous test. This result means that the participants may intentionally reduce notification factors to receive serendipitous content compared with the approach shown in the previous section. Participant H said *"Since serendipitous information is not a notification, I need neither icons nor sounds. It is appropriate for me to have the information by chance when I have a break."* Participant I commented *"I felt that I should not be strongly aware that the information is presented because it is not necessary to strongly pay attention."* Likewise, participant G said, *"I did not like to attach the icon to the content because I do not mind missing the content."* Therefore, we recognized that there are some cases in which it is inappropriate to use sounds and icons for content that a user does not mind missing.

Table 3. The results of the push-based interaction method for delivering serendipity

participant	a	b	c	d	e	f	g	h	i
sound	4	2	2	none	5	5	6	none	5
message window	off	on	on	on	on	on	on	off	on
Icon	on	on	off	on	off	on	on	off	on
Have you experienced serendipity?	3	7	3	7	2	5	3	5	6
Can Ambient Bot provide random information realize serendipity?	4	7	5	1	5	3	5	5	1
Can Ambient Bot reflecting personal preferences realize serendipity?	5	7	6	1	5	6	5	6	7

The serendipity offered by Ambient Bot was favorably accepted by most participants. They thought serendipity would increase more for the push-based notifications that are based on a user's personal preferences. However, participant I commented *"I do not need virtual creatures that deliver information that I'm not interested in."* On the other hand, participants B and D said *"I think that it is not good for my serendipity that the scope of the information is narrowed down from the personalization to a user's preferences. Incorporating surprises through the unexpected information leads to more serendipity."* The information source for increasing serendipity strongly depends on a user's personality. For example, Facebook allows us to choose various information sources according to our preferences, and the feeds that appear in our timelines become serendipitous information for us. Thus, it may be a better approach that a user chooses the categories of information and then information in those categories is randomly shown.

6 Related Work

HoloLens, Microsoft's HMD, has recently attracted people to develop new services in a variety of fields. Microsoft HoloLens is able to deliver a MR user experience [1], allowing people to interact with virtual objects and entities within real-world settings.

MR enables designers to develop new types of advanced services that incorporate virtuality into the real world. The software platform that accompanies the Microsoft HoloLens hardware makes it easy to develop MR applications without requiring advanced skills. Various visions of possible novel services have already been presented. Incorporating virtuality in the real space offers opportunities for developing new types of advanced services [8, 9]. Practical examples have been shown in various fields such as education[8], games[9], medical care[10], the space industry[11] and the manufacturing industry[12].

In past research, a concept named Pervasive Ambient Mirrors reflects people's current situations to influence their behavior [11]. In [6], slow technologies enable daily objects to ambiently represent some currently useful information for a user. These past approaches allow a user to receive information ambiently, but the interaction does not make our life richer beyond merely functionalism. For example, strengthening sociality in technologies is desirable especially for Japanese young adults who are living in a collectivism society [14]. Many of them want to attach intimate accessories on their personal technological products, such as mobile phones. In addition, a user sometimes does not notice information because of the abstract representation [6]. We need to investigate an alternative approach to ambiently offer information, but the information should be delivered to a user in a more social and intimate manner [9]. The approach will become an important aspect for making our society truly mindful through the rapid progress of future information technologies like the Internet of Things (IoT) and advanced artificial intelligence technologies because the technologies will make our daily life more and more efficient, but a sense of fulfillment in our life may be lost.

Recently, in particular, for Japanese young adults, the boundary between fictionality and their usual daily real life becomes more and more ambiguous [9, 14]. In their pop-culture-based lifestyles, fictionality is already becoming an alternative reality, and they like to enjoy the social relationship with virtual creatures in the hybrid world [13]. For example, a jellyfish is natural and intimate for them because it is a popular agent in one of the most popular Japanese animations that represents our near-future high-tech society. Thus, technologies used in animations and video games are plausible for them if they appear in our present daily life.

7   Conclusion

In this paper, we discussed the push-based interaction method in Ambient Bot, which interacts with a virtual creature via eye contact. By using eye contact, we determined that the preferred content delivery methods are comparable to existing methods of accessing applications. We focused on the fact that information access can be divided

---

[8] https://www.youtube.com/watch?v=7Xv8A9vqeBw.

[9] https://www.youtube.com/watch?v=29xnzxgCx6I.

[10] https://www.youtube.com/watch?v=SKpKlh1-en0.

[11] https://www.youtube.com/watch?v=ZOWQp0-Bkkw.

[12] https://www.youtube.com/watch?v=5HV3fcTvZk0.

into the pull-based and the push-based interaction method and discussed the design space of each method in Ambient Bot. The results of using the push-based interaction method in Ambient Bot indicated that the notification sound or icon should be first presented for notifying a user that there is useful information before providing the actual content. However, the approach has a limitation because listening for a sound cue or watching a notification icon can lead to a user's cognitive overload even if the load is trivial. In our approach, we also tried to use Myo to notify a user that there is useful content, and the approach was highly appreciated by participants in the user study. The results of the interviews in the user study also indicated that frequently making eye contact has annoyed users. In addition, we showed the feasibility of using a push-based interaction method to offer serendipitous information to a user.

References

1. Accenture Technology: Mixed reality brings real benefits to enterprises. https://www. accenture.com/us-en/insight-real-benefits-mixed-reality-brings-enterprise. Accessed 17 May
2. Akasaki, H., Gushima, K., Nakajima, T.: Providing daily casual information through eye contact with emotional creatures. In: Proceedings of the 6th International Conference on Distributed, Ambient and Pervasive Interactions (2018)
3. Costanza, E., Inverso, S.A., Pavlov, E., et al.: Eye-q: Eyeglass peripheral display for subtle intimate notifications. In: Anonymous Proceedings of the 8th Conference on Human-computer Interaction with Mobile Devices and Services, Helsinki, Finland, pp. 211–218. ACM, New York (2006)
4. Elslander, J., Tanaka, K.: A notification-centric mobile interaction survey and framework. In: Jatowt, A., Lim, E.-P., Ding, Y., Miura, A., Tezuka, T., Dias, G., Tanaka, K., Flanagin, A., Dai, B.T. (eds.) SocInfo 2013. LNCS, vol. 8238, pp. 443–456. Springer, Cham (2013). https://doi.org/10.1007/978-3-319-03260-3_38
5. Gushima, K., Akasaki, H., Nakajima, T.: Ambient Bot: delivering daily casual information through eye contact with an intimate virtual creature. In: Proceedings of the 21st International Academic Mindtrek Conference, pp. 231–234 (2017)
6. Hallnäs, L., Redström, J.: Slow technology – designing for reflection. Pers. Ubiquit. Comput. 5(3), 201–212 (2001)
7. Ho, H., Saeedi, E., Kim, S.S., Shen, T.T., Parviz, B.A.: Contact lens with integrated inorganic semiconductor services. In: Micro Electro Mechanical Systems, vol. 21, no. 1, pp. 403–406. IEEE (2008)
8. Ishizawa, F., Nakajima, T.: Alternative reality: an augmented daily urban world inserting virtual scenes temporally. In: García, C.R., Caballero-Gil, P., Burmester, M., Quesada-Arencibia, A. (eds.) UCAmI 2016. LNCS, vol. 10069, pp. 353–364. Springer, Cham (2016). https://doi.org/10.1007/978-3-319-48746-5_36
9. Ishizawa, F., Sakamoto, M., Nakajima, T.: Extracting intermediate-level design knowledge for speculating digital–physical hybrid alternate reality experiences. Multimed. Tools Appl. 42 p. (2018). https://doi.org/10.1007/s11042-017-5595-8
10. Liu, Y., Alexandrova, T., Hirade, S., Nakajima, T.: Facilitating natural flow of information among "taste-based" groups. In: Proceeding CHI EA 2013 CHI 2013 Extended Abstracts on Human Factors in Computing Systems, pp. 871–876 (2013)

11. Nakajima, T., Lehdonvirta, V.: Designing motivation using persuasive ambient mirrors. Pers. Ubiquit. Comput. **17**(1), 107–126 (2013)
12. NTTCom Research: Shinkasuru keitaidenwa (2007). http://research.nttcoms.com/database/data/000603/. Accessed 23 Jan 2018. (in Japanese)
13. Sakamoto, M., Nakajima, T., Alexandrova, T.: Enhancing values through virtuality for intelligent artifacts that influence human attitude and behavior. Multimed. Tools Appl. **74**(24), 11537–11568 (2015)
14. Sakamoto, M., Nakajima, T., Akioka, S.: Gamifying collective human behavior with gameful digital rhetoric. Multimed. Tools Appl. **76**(10), 12539–12581 (2017)

Automatic Generation of Human-Computer Interfaces from BACnet Descriptions

Lawrence Henschen[✉], Julia Lee, and Ries Guthmann

Northwestern University, Evanston, IL 60208, USA
henschen@eecs.northwestern.edu, j-leeh@comcast.net,
s2t9k3@u.northwestern.edu

Abstract. We present a methodology by which interfaces can be generated for application areas that have standards for definition of systems within that application area. The methodology includes organizational rules that describe the general nature of information for the application area, operational rules that describe the way users interact with that data, and optional user preference rule by which users can tailor the interface for a more meaningful experience. We show that by developing multiple sets of operational and user preference rules our approach can provide for universal access. We demonstrate the methodology for applications defined by BACNet, a standard for defining building control and monitoring systems and which can be used to also define general Internet of Things systems. We provide a brief description of BACNet objects and show how the application area leads to organizational, operational, and user preference rules for BACNet systems. We also illustrate the approach applied to a second application area to show the generality of the method.

Keywords: User interfaces · Automatic interface generation · Universal access
BACNet

1 Introduction

The Internet of Things (IoT) is the next revolution in computing. Although many of the envisioned IoT applications are meant to be totally autonomous, many other IoT applications will involve a significant amount of human interaction. The breadth of application areas is incredibly large – health, assisted living, automation, agriculture, smart buildings and cities, just to name a few. Still, IoT nodes across this vast array of applications have great similarities. Many user interfaces for IoT have been developed for specific applications, for example [1, 2]. However, it will be grossly inefficient to have to develop user interfaces for each new IoT application from scratch. Moreover, various network interfaces, such as REST [3], focus on network structure and/or the command aspect of interacting with sensor nodes and do not address the issue of robust and usable user interfaces. There are some proprietary IoT development systems [4, 5], but these do not have all the features needed for robust development and, of course, are proprietary. Our recent work has focused on the development of a rule-based method for automatically generating a user interface from the descriptions of the underlying objects

© Springer International Publishing AG, part of Springer Nature 2018
N. Streitz and S. Konomi (Eds.): DAPI 2018, LNCS 10921, pp. 71–84, 2018.
https://doi.org/10.1007/978-3-319-91125-0_5

in the application – nodes, sensors, controls, hierarchical objects, etc. Moreover, by varying the rule sets interfaces for a variety of users with special needs (visually impaired, manually impaired, etc.) can be generated. Such a methodology will make the development of user interfaces for IoT applications efficient and simple and at the same time provide for universal access to IoT applications.

In [6] we proposed the use of mark-up languages to describe IoT nodes with sensors and actuators. While this approach holds the promise of being a general method for use in literally any application, it does have a drawback that is quite serious for many IoT applications. Messages containing marked up text are orders of magnitude larger than messages coded in carefully designed bit/byte packed representations. For applications in which the nodes are battery operated, the size of marked-up messages may preclude their use, especially when wireless communication is used. Unfortunately, a bit/byte packed representation for one application will not be usable by other applications, thus precluding the development of a generic methodology for automatic generation of user interfaces across many applications.

In this paper we propose the use of a generic approach for automatically designing interfaces for broad application areas. We show how the presence of formal standards facilitates the generation of rules that determined how to automatically construct the interface for particular application in the chosen broad area. We illustrate this approach with a particular application area, building control, using the formal representation system BACNet [7, 8]. BACNet is both robust in its representational power and formally defined in such a way that good user interfaces can be generated automatically. Its message format is much simpler than xml-based formats, so it solves the issue of energy loss due to large messages while still being formally defined and generic. We begin with a classification of rules about generating interfaces. We then present a brief overview of BACNet and the reasons why it is a good choice for this work. We then list the main features of BACNet that must be used for the user interface. We show sample rules for generating user interface details from BACNet descriptions and show examples of the use of such rules. We also include a discussion of how alternate sets of rules can be used to increase universal accessibility. We show the generality of our approach by applying our methods to a second application area. We close with a restatement of the general approach and why it is important for both IoT and HCI. We also indicate areas of future work.

2   Rules for Generating Interfaces

In our approach we use three sets of rules for generating interfaces – organizational rules, operational rules, and user preference rules. Organizational rules are based on the nature of the application and its data. They describe the general way in which the data in the application area should be presented and the general ways in which a user could interact with the system. We emphasize that these rules depend on the application area only, and they are at a high and very general level. For example, as described in detail in Sect. 5, BACNet objects have several different kinds of properties, and in our example we make use of that general feature about BACNet objects to specify how information should be organized for rendering. Operational rules describe the ways in which a user actually interacts with the system. Operational rules are further partitioned into output rules (how information is rendered) and input rules (how the user enters information). The main motivation for this portioning will be given in Sect. 5.3. Operational rules are based on the organizational rules but can be tailored for particular user groups, such as visually impaired users or users with impaired dexterity. This allows a system using our approach to provide universal accessibility for the chosen application area. Finally, we allow for an optional set of user preference rules. These rules allow individual users to adjust the operational aspects of the interface. Details of these three sets of rules will be illustrated in Sect. 5.

3   Why Use BACNet?

BACNet [7, 8] is a standard for representing the structure and components of embedded systems, which are the foundation of the IoT. It provides for the definition of objects which can sense or control their environment, objects that can process data that is collected by the sensing objects, objects that define the scheduling of tasks, and many others as indicated in the list in the next section. These are exactly the components that make up most embedded systems. It was originally introduced as a way of defining control systems for buildings, and it is used widely in that application [9]. However, because of its generality and completeness it is also being used in many other applications and may well become a standard tool in the development of IoT applications.

BACNet is formally defined with a standards organization [7] that maintains the standard and provides for future development and expansion. Even in its present state BACNet is more complete than other tools, such as Bluemix [4] and Kaa [5]. Moreover, the standard itself provides for both future expansion and user-defined extensions. (Of course, user-defined extensions may require user-developed interfaces on top of the automatically generated interface that we describe in this paper, but that is a reasonable expectation. However, as explained in Sect. 4.2, if done carefully the method we propose can incorporate the extensions without further programming). BACNet is a generic representation methodology used to describe the elements of a system but does not require the use of proprietary systems or software, as is the case for systems like Bluemix and ones provided by other large companies. Finally, we note that Bluemix and other such systems at present do not offer interfaces for users with special needs, such as visually impaired users or physically impaired users. A key feature of our approach is that providing for universal accessibility is straightforward.

In addition to the features mentioned in the preceding paragraph, BACNet has two other key features that allow for the kind of automatic user interface generation we seek. First, in any system defined by BACNet the host computer maintains a model of the objects in the system. The host computer is typically the one through which the human user will interact with the system, so the HCI portal has complete information about all the objects that need to be rendered. Moreover, the BACNet host must provide access to the information about the objects. Thus, the interface system simply requests information when it needs and issues writes when the user wants some property of the system changed. Second, there are a limited set of object types and these are well defined. There is a modest set of features that are universal to all BACNet objects, and for each BACNet type there is a modest set of features for objects of that particular type. Thus a system that can generate renderings for this limited set of objects is relatively easy to develop and implement.

To summarize, BACNet is a formally defined and standardized representational system that handles all the features found in embedded systems and IoT "things". It is of modest size. In any application it would likely run on the same computer used for the user interface. It is likely to become widely used in the IoT field. For these reasons, BACNet is a good choice to use as the basis for automatically generated user interfaces for IoT applications. The availability of such a system means that any IoT application immediately has an acceptable user interface as soon as the system itself has been defined in BACNet.

4   Overview of Main BACNet Features

In this section we describe the main features of BACNet that would be used to generate the user interface. Space precludes describing all of the features that would be used for a robust user interface or mentioning BACNet features that are not relevant to the user interface. The interested reader is referred to [8] for a good overview of BACNet objects and other features and to [7] for the formal definition of the standard. In this paper we focus on the main features used in the generation of user interfaces and on ones that illustrate the principles of the method we are proposing. Most of the material in this section is taken directly from [8].

4.1   BACNet Objects

The major elements of BACNet systems are defined as BACNet objects. There is a top-level "object" type, and there are more special types derived from the base object type. A BACNet object may contain other BACNet objects, providing for definition of hierarchical systems. The following is the list of all BACNet object types.

- Basic object types.
  - Device
  - Analog input
  - Analog output
  - Analog value
  - Binary input
  - Binary output
  - Binary value
  - Multi-state input
  - Multi-state output
  - Multi-state value
  - File

- Process-related object types
  - Averaging
  - Loop
  - Program
- Control-related object types
  - Command
  - Load control
- Meter-related object types
  - Accumulator
  - Pulse converter
- Collection-related object types
  - Group
  - Global group
  - Structured view
- Schedule-related object types
  - Calendar
  - Schedule
- Notification-related object types
  - Event enrollment
  - Notification class
  - Notification forwarder
  - Alert enrollment
- Logging object types
  - Trend log
  - Trend log multiple
  - Event log
- Safety and security object types
  - Life safety point
  - Life safety zone
  - Network security
- Physical access control system object types
  - Access point
  - Access zone
  - Access door
  - Access user
  - Access rights
  - Access credential
  - Credential data input
- Simple value object types
  - Character string value
  - Large analog value
  - Bit string value
  - Integer value
  - Positive integer value
  - Octet string value

- Date value
- Time value
- Date/Time value
- Date pattern value
- Time pattern value
- Date/Time pattern value
- Lighting control object type
  - Channel
  - Lighting output

4.2 Object Properties

Every BACNet object type has a set of associated properties. The BACNet standard specifies that each property has three attributes – property identifier, property datatype, and conformance code. The property identifier is a string describing what that property represents, for example "Present_value" or "Units". The property datatype is a string identifying a primitive datatype, such as INTEGER or REAL or CHARACTERSTRING, or one of the BACNet constructed data types, such BACNetAddress. The conformance code is one of "R" (the property is required and can be read by using the BACNet built-in services), "W" (the property is required and can be both read and written through BACNet services), or "O" (the property is optional). The latter is included mainly to accommodate proprietary extensions to the BACNet standard. The interface system simply uses the BACNet services to obtain the information for all the BACNet objects in that system and to change values of those properties that are writeable.

The following set of properties is common to all BACNet objects:

- Object_identifier – contains the BACNet object type plus the instance number
- Object_name
- Object_type
- Property_list – the list of all properties associated with this object
- Description – an optional property that is a string describing the objects use, purpose, or other aspect
- Profile_name – an optional property that allows extensions to the standard BACNet feature set (typically for proprietary extensions)

Individual object types have additional properties. For example, object types having a value field might also have a "UNITS" property. Objects that sense the environment might have an "EVENT_STATE" property. Many object types have a "STATUS_FLAGS" property. The Analog_Input_Object type, for example, has 29 properties in addition to the six properties mentioned above common to all objects, and the Device object type has fifty additional properties. Although at first glance this might seem like a lot, the rendering mechanism is still quite simple – use BACNet services to obtain the properties and their current values and then render. Whether there are six or thirty-five has no bearing on the complexity of the rendering algorithm.

An important property that occurs in some of the object types, in particular in the Device object type, is the "Object_List" property. For a given object A this property is a list of the objects that are inside A. For example, a sensor node might have several sensing devices (i.e., input objects) and possibly even an actuator device (i.e., an output object). The "Object_List" allows the description of this hierarchical structure. In the interface then, the "Object_List" would allow the user to zoom in to examine or control the internal objects.

We present portions of the property lists for a few sample object types in preparation for the next section. Space precludes showing the entire lists. We only show enough so that the reader will better understand and appreciate the rules used to automatically generate the user interface. The following properties are, of course, in addition to the six mentioned above that occur in all BACNet objects. For the purposes of generating the interface it is not important to understand the meaning of each property, although we have chosen ones whose meaning should be fairly obvious. Similarly, it is not important to understand the specifics of each data type, only to know that each type is well-defined in the standard and thus can be rendered with suitable software.

Sample Properties of the Analog Output Object Type

Property	Datatype
PRESENT_VALUE	REAL
EVENT_DETECTION_ENABLE	BOOLEAN
UNITS	BACNetEngineeringUnits
MIN_PRES_VALUE	REAL
RESOLUTION	REAL
EVENT_MESSAGE_TEXTS	BACNetArray of CharacterString
...	

Sample Properties of the Scheduling Object Type

Property	Datatype
PRESENT_VALUE	any primitive datatype
LIST_OF_OBJECT_PROPERTY_REFERENCES	BACNetDeviceObjectPropertyReference list
WEEKLY_SCHEDULE	BACNetArray[7] of BACNetDailySchedule
EXCEPTION_SCHEDULE	BACNetArray of BACNetSpecialEvents
...	

Sample Properties of the Program Object Type

Property	Datatype
PROGRAM_STATE	BACNetProgramState
INSTANCE_OF	CharacterString
Ref1	proprietary
Ref2	proprietary
...	

The analog output object type illustrates the ability of BACNet to model the standard kinds of "things" in an IoT application. The scheduling object type is an example of the ability to model time-dependent aspects of applications. The program object type illustrates one way that proprietary extensions can be made to BACNet in ways that are compatible with the standard and facilitate the incorporation of such proprietary extensions into the automatically generated interface. All of the properties are BACNet standard properties except the Refi properties of the program object type. Most of the properties are self-explanatory. For the program object type, the INSTANCE_OF property is a string giving the name of the (proprietary) function to be called, and the Refi properties are non-BACNet properties that represent the arguments that are to be passed to that function. These examples are sufficient to illustrate almost all the aspects needed for user interfaces to BACNet systems, as will be illustrated in the next section.

5   A Sample Generic User Interface that Can Be Automatically Generated

In this section we present an example of a user interface that can be generated automatically from any BACNet description and describe some of the rules that would be used in the automatic generation process. As noted in Sect. 5, the use of rules for the generation of the interface means that many other renderings are possible, including especially interfaces for users with special needs. Our choice here is only for illustration and is not necessarily the best for all purposes.

5.1   Organization of the Sample Interface

All BACNet objects have the six common properties. Each object type has its own set of additional properties. Some of these properties can be considered as parameters of individual objects, and these properties would typically not be changeable. For example, a particular analog output device would have fixed minimum and maximum output values, such as 0–5 V. Other properties can be changed. For example, the output of an output device should be controllable through the interface so that the user can make that device change its output value. Finally, some properties only become relevant or get values when an event occurs resulting in some kind of notification or alarm.

This suggests a visual interface with four panels. One panel contains the properties common to all BACNet objects. We decide not to display the property list because the properties will be shown in the other panels. A second panel contains parameter information for the object. A third panel contains information about the current value or status of the object. A fourth panel would show information relevant to events occurring in the object or events occurring in the system that affect that object. Such events include scheduled notifications, alerts, and error conditions. The fourth panel might be shown only when a relevant event has actually occurred; appearing would draw attention to the occurrence of the event, similar to the way a pop-up window draws the attention of a user. Learnability, usability, and other important features of good human-computer interfaces are enhanced by this common rendering. No matter what kind of object is being displayed, the user knows where to look to find the four different kinds of information. Figure 1 shows a sample rendering for an analog output device. The plus in front of "Event messages:" indicates a list that can be expanded. Figure 2 shows the same object with an event that occurred in a different object, a temperature sensor in the same room, that is relevant for this analog output object.

Object name: Office fan control	Current value: 2.87 volts
Object ID: M472fan	(147/256)
Object type: Analog output	Event detection: enabled
Description: Fan speed for fan	
in	
room M472.	

| Minimum value: 0 |
| Maximum value: 5 |
| Units: volts |
| Resolution: 256 steps |
| +Event messages: |
| ... |

Fig. 1. Sample rendering of an analog output device showing the three main panels.

5.2 Rules for Generating Our Interface

As described in Sect. 2, we organize the rules for automatically generating the interface into three sets - interface configuration rules, operational rules, and user preference rules. Again, because of space restrictions we only present examples of the rules.

Recall, configuration rules are rules based on the nature of the application area and its data and provide the general specification of how the user will interact with the system. In our case this set contains the rule about rendering information in panels. Further, for each BACNet object type there is a rule specifying placement of the information about objects of that type into particular panels and the format for displaying

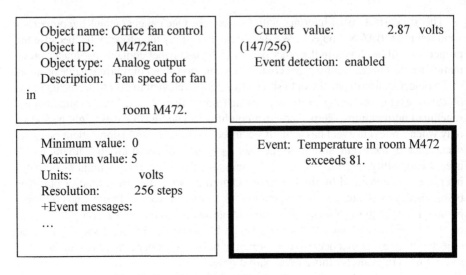

Fig. 2. Sample rendering showing the events panel.

that information. The decision whether or not to make the fourth panel permanently rendered or displayed only when appropriate events actually occur falls into the configuration class.

Operational rules determine the behavior of the interface when users are actually using it. We further divide this class of rules into those dealing with outputs from the interface and those dealing with inputs to the interface. Examples of operational rules for output include expanding/contracting composite values depending on whether the user has clicked the corresponding ± symbol. An example of an operational input rule is to allow the user to click on a ± symbol. Another input rule, one that is particularly important for embedded systems and IoT applications, is to allow users to highlight object output values (such as the fan speed in the example in Sect. 5.1) and type in a new value. BACNet objects can contain other BACNet objects, and the "Object_List" property holds the list of object identifiers of these contained objects. Clicking on an object identifier will cause the referenced object to be rendered. There are a variety of operational rules for how a multiplicity of objects should be handled. For example, the objects being rendered can be stored in stack-like fashion. When a user clicks on an object reference in one object, say A, that object is saved on a stack, and the new object is rendered. When the user has finished with the currently rendered object, the object on the top of the stack is again rendered. Such a rule allows a user to explore the structure of the IoT system by digging into the nested structure of the objects. Of course, there may be other rules for handling such situations.

Of particular importance are operational rules that specify how the interface is to interact with the underlying IoT system. In our example these rules would specify how the information to be rendered is obtained and what is to be done when the user inputs values that are supposedly changeable in the underlying system. For BACNet interfaces these are quite simple. The BACNet standard specifies that BACNet services are to be provided by which properties and their values can be retrieved for any object in the system (BACNet read services) and property values that are changeable can be written with new values (BACNet write services). This is a key and critical feature for automatically generating BACNet interfaces. It is not necessary to read and parse the BACNet specification of the underlying IoT system, which could be in xml or even computer code. All the interaction can be handled through BACNet services, which are standard in all BACNet systems.

As noted, BACNet read and write services allow access to properties of all objects in a given IoT application, even objects that are not standard in BACNet. Venders who incorporate extensions should provide such access services to compliment the BACNet built-in services. If the vender has mapped the user-accessible features of the extension into properties of any associated objects, then our system can still automatically generate the interface even for the extensions. Consider the Program Object Type illustrated in Sect. 4.2. The *Refi* properties are not in the BACNet standard. However, according the BACNet standard the vendor providing such a function as an extension should also provide means to read and write those properties. Now, from the point of view of automatically generating the interface, our system simply reads the list of properties and their related values and allows the user to write new values for writeable properties. We may decide as part of the configuration to generate a fifth panel for proprietary properties. Finally, if the value typed by the user into the interface for a writeable property is simply passed through to the object and the parsing of such (for example translating a string into a real number) is handled on the vender side, then literally no extra work is required for the interface generation.

Although not strictly necessary, the inclusion of rules that allow users to set preferences for some interface features provides for a more flexible and user-friendly experience. In the case of our BACNet interface, we allow users to specify how certain values are rendered. For example, in the BACNet context binary values can represent 0 and 1, ON and OFF, ACTIVE and NOT_ACTIVE, and a variety of other meanings. Analog values could be rendered as numbers within a range, slide bars, meters, and a variety of other ways. Each individual object can have its own representation different from other objects, even objects within the same object type. For example, a user viewing a binary input object representing a door would likely want to see the values as OPEN and CLOSED, while the two values for a binary input object representing a light should be rendered as ON and OFF. Allowing the user to specify renderings other than the default rendering provides for a richer and more meaningful interaction experience by making the rendering of each individual object match more closely to the user's real-world concept of that object. Note that extensions to the standard may suggest additional user preference rules.

5.3   Alternate Rule Sets and Universal Access

It is easy to see that by changing the operational and user preference rule sets the system can be made to generate different kinds of interfaces, in particular interfaces for users with special needs. We illustrate this idea for a few cases.

A visually impaired user would likely prefer voice output. Some BACNet object types have relatively few properties so that reading all the properties and their values is acceptable. Others have too many to make reading the entire set of information useful. A configuration rule would determine which objects fall into which category. For those in the second category, additional configuration rules would determine the mechanism for a user to get the information that was not rendered at the time the object was first presented. The partition into panels still applies, but the initial rendering of an object would read the information to the user instead of display it on a screen. The operational rules, then, might be to speak the common properties (name, ID, description) and their values for every object and inform the user that information about the configuration (panel 2) and current values (panel 3) are available on request. The amount of information about the current values associated with an object is relatively small for all object types, so the interface could simply read the material that would be printed in panel 3 for a visual interface. If the user requests configuration information, the interface can read out the list of properties and ask which one(s) the user wants to hear about. Properties with composite values (such as date or a list) would have the name of the property read and then be expanded only if the user requested. User preference rules would include ones used in the visual interface, the difference being that the values would be rendered by voice instead of screen display. For example, the user would hear that a door was OPEN and a fan was OFF. However, there would be rules specifically for visually impaired users, such as selecting between a terse mode and a verbose mode.

By altering the operational rule sets interfaces can be obtained for many different classes of users – visually impaired users who are still good with keyboards, visually impaired users who also need voice input, users with normal vision but no manual dexterity, etc. Separating the operational rules into output rules and input rules makes the goal of universal access, i.e. access by individuals of all kinds and with all kinds of special needs, much easier to attain. We propose the development of a variety of default classes such as "general default", "visually impaired", "physically impaired (can't use hands to enter data)", etc. that automatically change rendering and user input to match individual users. Following the principle of user-centered design, these rule sets would be developed by studying the needs of different classes of users working in the specific environment of the Internet of Things in such applications as building control, sensor networks, etc. For example, users with normal vision would likely not object to the automatic display of the information in panel 2, even when this information was somewhat lengthy; sighted users just focus their eyes on the parts of the screen in which they are interested. Visually impaired users, on the other hand, would likely object to a long list of object parameter information being read. Studies could reveal information about how visually impaired users actually use such information and appropriate rules for rendering it developed for those users.

5.4   Application of the Method to Another Area

Finally, we illustrate our method in a different application area, namely transportation systems. These could include taxi companies, bus companies, delivery services, and many other similar activities.

For this general application area there would be two kinds of organizational categories – a map and a list of vehicles. This suggests an organizational rule that specifies the rendering of a map plus the vehicles that are located within the map. Vehicles might partition into three sets – vehicles that are in service but currently busy, vehicles that are in service but available for assignment, and vehicles that are currently not in service. Location of the vehicles must be included in the interface as well as the ability to dig into the details of particular vehicle and to send messages to individual vehicles. There would be no obvious separate panels, as was the case for the BACNet interface. The reader can easily imagine other general characteristics of transportation systems.

Operational rules for a sighted user with normal manual dexterity might include the display of the map and the locations of the vehicles. The three different kinds of vehicles could be distinguished by using colors or shapes, a choice that could be left for user preference. Location would be indicated by position on the map. Clicking on a vehicle would open up the details of that vehicle and provide text box for typing messages to be sent to that vehicle. There might be zoom-in and zoom-out buttons for the user to focus on smaller or larger areas.

Operational rules for a visually impaired user who does not use a keyboard for input would be different. Rather than display a visual map, the coordinates of the four corners might be read out to the user or possibly a name associated with the area of focus on the map. Rendering of the vehicles within the area of focus might be done by first speaking the numbers of vehicles in each class and then letting the user issue a voice command requesting more information, such as location, about one or more of those classes. A user might request the IDs of the vehicles and then request the details about a particular one, again by voice input. The idea, as with the BACNet example, is that a careful study of how visually impaired users would want to interact with the system will suggest a suitable set of operational rules for that class of users.

Unfortunately, there is no standards organization for defining transportation systems, as there was for the building control industry. Therefore, many of the issues involved with the interface interacting with the system itself will not be handled automatically. This shows the importance of having such standards and, by the way, suggests that industries would profit from the development of such standards.

6   Conclusion

We have described a system that can generate user interfaces for any standard BACNet-defined application system. It is anticipated that BACNet will become widely used for implementing Internet of Things applications. A system like we described would therefore have a major impact on the development of the IoT because engineers who develop IoT applications will have an immediate user interface and will not have to devote additional time and effort beyond the design of the BACNet application itself. Moreover, developers will not be forced into using commercial or proprietary systems for their IoT applications in order to avoid having to spend time and money on the interface; they will get the interface automatically. We also illustrated that our approach is general and can be applied to other application areas besides building control.

We made two major contributions to the HCI community. First, we have suggested that in areas of endeavor for which formal standards exist for defining applications those formal standards be used to implement an interface system that will automatically generate a user interface for any application defined in that standard. Second, we have demonstrated that a rule-based approach to the implementation of such an interface system can be used to achieve universal access in that area of endeavor, in some cases even in the absence of such standards.

Several key features of BACNet made it suitable for our approach. As noted already, BACNet has a standards organization and a formal definition. BACNet allows for non-standard extensions, but these extensions can be made in a way that complies with the formal definition of BACNet and, thus, is amenable to automatic interface generation like we have described. BACNet objects are simple enough so that information about them can be rendered through both visual and audio outputs and inputs to the interface can be accepted by keyboard or voice or any of several other ways. Thus, it is relatively easy to achieve universal access for BACNet applications through the use of multiple rule sets. None of this is possible for general web pages. There are no standards, and even if there were the amount of information on typical pages is way more than can be easily rendered through non-visual means such as reading.

Future work includes, first, the design of a representation system for defining the rule sets. This would allow for universal access without the need to hand code a particular style of interface, as we have done for the demonstration system. Independent of that, ethnographic studies need to be done to determine the best way to render and interact with users with special needs, after which appropriate rule sets can be developed for those classes of users.

References

1. Kosnik, D., Henschen, L.: A Web-enabled data management interface for health monitoring of civil infrastructure. In: Proceedings of the 15th HCII International Conference, vol. 2, pp. 107–113 (2013)
2. Keller, I., Lehmann, A., Franke, M., Schlegel, T.: Towards an interaction concept for efficient control of cyber-physical systems. In: Shumaker, R., Lackey, S. (eds.) VAMR 2014. LNCS, vol. 8525, pp. 149–158. Springer, Cham (2014). https://doi.org/10.1007/978-3-319-07458-0_15
3. Wikipedia. https://en.wikipedia.org/wiki/Representational_state_transfer. Accessed 04 Feb 2018
4. IBM Developer Works. https://www.ibm.com/developerworks/cloud/library/cl-bluemix foundry/index.html. Accessed 04 Feb 2018
5. Kaa Project Home Page. http://www.kaaproject.org. Accessed 04 Feb 2018
6. Henschen, L., Lee, J.: Human-computer interfaces for sensor/actuator networks. In: Kurosu, M. (ed.) HCI 2016. LNCS, vol. 9732, pp. 379–387. Springer, Cham (2016). https://doi.org/10.1007/978-3-319-39516-6_36
7. BACNet Home Page. http://www.bacnet.org/. Accessed 04 Feb 2018
8. Newman, H.: BACNet: The Global Standard for Building Automation and Control Networks. Momentum Press, New York (2013)
9. Schachinger, D., Stampfel, C., Kastner, W.: Interoperable integration of building automation systems using RESTful BACnet Web services. In: IECON 2015 – 41st Annual Conference of the IEEE Industrial Electronics Society, pp. 003899–003904 (2105)

The AR Strip: A City Incorporated Augmented Reality Educational Curriculum

Si Jung Kim[1(✉)], Su Jin Park[2], Yunhwan Jeong[1], Jehoshua Josue[1], and Mary Valdez[1]

[1] University of Nevada, Las Vegas, Las Vegas, NV 89154, USA
si.kim@unlv.edu
[2] Sogang University, Seoul, South Korea

Abstract. This study introduces an exploratory study about a city-based educational curriculum based on augmented reality (AR), called the AR Strip. The AR Strip is an outdoor active learning platform for the purpose of teaching and learning of STEM (Science, Technology, Engineering, and Math) as well as history and culture associated with the Las Vegas Strip. The project consists of three major components: a creation of metadata of the Las Vegas Strip, a marker less approach as an outdoor AR, and a city-based live actionable curriculum development. A user study conducted in two places, New York New York and Luxor Hotels on the Las Vegas Strip revealed that the proposed AR Strip has a potential to extend the learning of STEM, history, and culture as an active, live learning tool. It also demonstrated that a city can be an active live interactive learning environment by incorporating the technology of augmented reality.

Keywords: Augmented reality · Education · STEM · City · Las Vegas

1 Introduction

Las Vegas is a unique city in the State of Nevada where around 46 million people visit every year. The Strip is a 6.8 km street in length on the South Las Vegas Boulevard in Las Vegas, where world famous hotels and attractions are clustered together under unique themes that comprise of cultural, historical and science facts. The city itself is a giant level of theme park that provides diverse aspects of learning components. This motivated us to conduct the study of utilizing augmented reality (AR) technology with educational contents associated with facilities on the Strip as a live learning environment called, the Augmented Reality Strip (The AR Strip). The AR Strip is intended to examine a possibility for the educational utilization of science, technology, engineering, and mathematics (STEM) as well as cultural and historical information of the Las Vegas Strip through AR.

As a specific approach of the AR Strip, we first conducted an initial literature review to see if there are similar concepts and how AR influences learning and teaching in the domain of outdoor. We found similar concepts and examples described as follows. There was an educational entertainment concerned with virtual learning environment based on virtual reality that experimented with the educational applicability of augmented reality [1]. Gabbard et al. investigated the legibility of outdoor AR [2]. Kato introduced an

© Springer International Publishing AG, part of Springer Nature 2018
N. Streitz and S. Konomi (Eds.): DAPI 2018, LNCS 10921, pp. 85–90, 2018.
https://doi.org/10.1007/978-3-319-91125-0_6

augmented reality city-planning system as an outdoor AR experiment [3]. Schmalstieg suggested an AR museum guide, where visitors browsed multiple photos and animations using an AR based mobile system [4]. AR has been utilized as an assistive materials and interface in teaching and learning of STEM education [5] and also AR was a crucial role in constructing a fun-based education called edutainment [6]. It is shown that the above-mentioned augmented reality of educational approaches provides positive possibilities.

2   The AR STRIP Curriculum

In regard to create an initial AR Strip curriculum that helps people learn STEM plus history and culture associated with the Las Vegas Strip. Two hotels on the Strip, New York New York and Luxor, were chosen as a test site for the proposed AR Strip. These two hotels are shown in Fig. 1. The reason for selecting these two places was that each hotel has ample historical, cultural and science aspects of learning components.

Fig. 1. Two AR strip places- New York New York (Left) and Luxor (Right)

Within the two hotels, a total of six spots were identified as the study place. Each hotel had three study spots. For example, in New York New York hotel, we identified science and history related educational content and associated them with the roller coaster and the Statue of Liberty. As for the second place, Luxor Hotel, we identified cultural, historical, and science facts that are associated with an obelisk, a sphinx and a pyramid found either inside or outside the hotel. The contents were reviewed by a subject matter expert in the school of education at the University of Nevada, Las Vegas. Table 1 shows the six study spots, where potential users experienced the learning of cultural, historical, or science learning using the AR Strip app.

3   Experimental Design

The experimental design of the study was a within-subjects design, where participants experienced all the six study places in two different hotels described in Table 1. Anyone over 18 years old was eligible to participate in the study.

Table 1. Six spots of The AR strip

	Place	Category	Learning object
Study site #1	New York New York	Science	Roller coaster (kinetic energy)
		Science	Roller coaster (acceleration)
		History	Statue of Liberty (history)
Study site #2	Luxor	History	Sphinx (history)
		Science	Pyramid (volume)
		Science	Obelisk (circumference)

With regards to the AR Strip app prototype that provided participants with the learning content of each study place, it was implemented using Unity with iOS. Each study content included text and audio as well as it superimposed the content as 2D/3D visual, which appeared on a mobile device when a participant arrived at each study place. Figure 2 shows the snapshots of the app that we displayed the AR Strip content at the two study places.

(a) Augmentation of the Statue of Liberty (b) Augmentation of the Sphinx

Fig. 2. Visualization of the AR strip content based on GPS

A pre- and post-surveys were administrated before and after the experiment. We asked their previous experience with AR before the study on the pre-survey and then we asked their experience with the AR Strip after the study on the post-survey. Each survey included a section where participants rated their experience with AR technology on a 10-point scale where 1 is the worst rating and 10 being the best rating.

We anonymized participants identity by using numbers. We also used the numbers when we counterbalanced the order of the six study sites so that we minimized the order effect that maybe caused by the order of the stimuli. We assigned even-numbered participants for New York New York Hotel to start with and assigned odd-numbered participants for Luxor Hotel to start with.

4   Results and Discussion

A total of seven people participated in the initial user study. Their age ranged from 31 to 45 years old.

4.1   Pre-survey

The first thing we found from the pre-survey is that all the participants wanted to know more about the Las Vegas Strip. These include hotel information, history of the town and hotels, and attractions of Las Vegas. No one was interested in science related facts that are associated with the Las Vegas Strip.

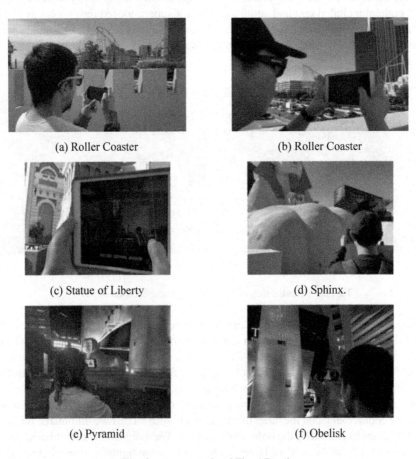

(a) Roller Coaster   (b) Roller Coaster

(c) Statue of Liberty   (d) Sphinx.

(e) Pyramid   (f) Obelisk

Fig. 3. A user study of The AR strip

Four participants (57%) already knew the concept of AR and they had a chance to experience with it with their mobile phone. All the participants thought that there are certain cultural, historical, or science aspects of information that is associated with the

Las Vegas Strip that they can learn. Five (71%) participants had a positive thought that AR would help them facilitate the learning of either cultural, historical, or science learning on the Strip.

4.2 Post-survey

The AR Strip experience took place in six locations as shown in Fig. 3. Their overall experience of the AR Strip was positive because all the participants rated their experience with the AR Strip app over 5 points with a median of 7. They also gave the AR Strip app a was positive rating since the median value was 7.

Six participants (86%) answered that the AR app would help obtain information of the Strip. For questions, if the AR app helped them understand the cultural, historical, and science facts associated with the six places easier, six participants (86%) answered it was helpful. The median value is 8. It was shown that learning the cultural, historical and science aspects of the Las Vegas Strip using the AR Strip was rated positively, meaning that the AR Strip was helpful for their learning.

We received several comments from the participants. The majority of them were about the visualization of the contents. The graphics that we superimposed on the App were not good enough to attract and engage them to the learning of each subject. One participant commented that the volume of the audio was low. Another participant asked to include more examples of history associated with the six places. The participant wanted to see more graphics as well. Another comment that we received was about the user interface. Two participants commented that the user interface on the App was not easy and needs to be improved.

5   Conclusions and Future Works

This study introduced the AR Strip, a city and augmented reality based learning platform, designed to facilitate the learning of cultural, historical, and science facts associated with the Las Vegas facilities. Based on the user study, the AR Strip seems has a potential to extend the learning of STEM (Science, Technology, Engineering, and Math) knowledge as an active, live learning educational curriculum as a city-based learning curriculum.

As an extension of the current study, we will improve the functionality of the AR Strip app along with the AR Strip curriculum in the three categories, STEM, history and culture. We planned to conduct a formal user study with more diverse sample participants.

Acknowledgment. We thank all the participants who participated in a user testing. We also thank all the DEX (Digital Experience) Lab members who provided insight and expertise that greatly assisted the research.

References

Pan, Z., Cheok, A., Yang, H., Zhu, J., Shi, J.: Virtual reality and mixed reality for virtual learning environments. Comput. Graph. **30**(1), 20–28 (2006)

Gabbard, J., Swan, J.E., Hix, D., Kim, S., Fitch, G.: Active text drawing styles for outdoor augmented reality: a user-based study and design implications (2007)

Kato, H., Tachibana, K., Tanabe, M., Nakajima, T., Fukuda, Y.: A city-planning system based on augmented reality with a tangible interface (2003)

Schmalstieg, D., Wagner, D.: A handheld augmented reality museum guide (2005)

Hobbs, M., Holley, D.: Using augmented reality to engage STEM students with an authentic curriculum. EAI Endorsed Trans. E-Learn. **3**(11), 1–7 (2016)

Antognozzi, M., Bottino, A., De Santi, A., Locatelli, M., Lera, V., Cook, D.P.: Re-living Las Vegas: a multi-user, mixed reality edutainment environment based on the enhancement of original archival materials (2009)

Evaluating User Experience in Smart Home Contexts: A Methodological Framework

Peter Mechant[(✉)] [iD], Anissa All[iD], and Lieven De Marez[iD]

imec-mict-Ghent University, 9000 Ghent, Belgium
peter.mechant@ugent.be

Abstract. Similar to the concept of 'smart city', the phrase 'smart home' is being adopted by many businesses and stakeholders as a priority which recognizes the growing importance of digital technologies in the home context. However, few targeted methodologies exist that take into account the dynamic and interactive aspects of this environment when studying user experience. To date, the multi-disciplinary field of user experience studies, which investigates individuals perception about using a particular product, system or service, lacks a methodological and conceptual framework to study these smart homes that are connected to the internet and to a rapidly increasing amount of both sensors and actuators.

The goal of this paper is to create a framework to explore how technology enables and constrains agency and engagement in smart homes or spaces. Our methodological framework is grounded in the concepts of interactivity and affordances. We will propose a framework that takes the operational, structural features of a smart home (expressed in structural affordances) into account as well as the functional, subjective perception and usage of these features by people (expressed in functional affordances).

Keywords: Smart home · Affordance · User experience

1 Introduction

Smart Home technologies are increasingly on sale and are forecasted to reach a value of more than 40 billion U.S. dollars by 2020 (Statista 2017), to grow over 50 billion U.S. dollars by 2022 (Zion 2017), or even with 138 billion U.S. dollars by 2023 (M&M 2017). Despite the rising popularity of smart homes, few concepts or frameworks are available that provide guidelines to study and comprehend these smart spaces. Existing research on smart homes has focused on the technological challenges involved in delivering smart domestic environments (Cook 2012) without too much consideration to smart home users at all (Wilson et al. 2015). An user-centric vision is currently missing from a field being overwhelmingly 'pushed' by technology developers. Hence, literature in social sciences and communication studies lacks generic frameworks that enable the investigation of the many ways in which smart spaces have implications for the daily lives of their inhabitants or of the diverse ways people interact and communicate with and within these smart spaces.

© Springer International Publishing AG, part of Springer Nature 2018
N. Streitz and S. Konomi (Eds.): DAPI 2018, LNCS 10921, pp. 91–102, 2018.
https://doi.org/10.1007/978-3-319-91125-0_7

In this paper we propose a theoretical framework that addresses this gap. We illustrates it's applicability by discussing 'interactivity' in smart spaces. We will use the concept affordance as it offers a way to consider smart spaces independently of 'under-socialized' technological-determinist perspectives that argue that technology shapes interactivity or 'over-socialized' (social) constructivist perspectives that argue that technology is a purely cultural construct. Moreover, while most theories on structure and agency, neglect how structure is actually perceived by people, the notion of affordances enables us to take perception connoted aspects into account as well. Also, the concept underlines that affordances are not mere action possibilities but that they can also invite behavior (see e.g. Hogan 2009; Withagen et al. 2012). Our effort tries to broaden the concept of affordances in order to understand human use and interaction in smart spaces or homes.

This paper is structured as follows. First, smart homes are briefly discussed. Next, the concept affordance is theoretically unpacked. We briefly sketch the history of the concept, provide affordance typologies from literature and propose a working definition. Third, we develop a theoretical framework for the study of smart spaces that uses affordances as a central concept and takes a structural perspective (focusing on the object of interactivity) as well as a functional perspective (focusing on the goal of interactivity). Fourth, in the last part of this paper we discuss and review the value and usefulness of the developed framework.

2   Smart Spaces and Homes

Smart spaces support services that actively involve surrounding digital devices and Internet services (Korzun et al. 2015). As such, a smart home is a physical embodiment of such a system in which software uses sensors to perceive and reason about the state of the home and its residents (Cook et al. 2013). These smart home technologies comprise sensors, monitors, interfaces, appliances and devices networked together to enable automation as well as localized and remote control of the home (Cook 2012).

While a smart space is usually thought of as a meeting place where people come together to collaborate, to share knowledge, and engage in shared activities (Frey et al. 2013), the primary objectives of a smart home are to increase home automation, facilitate energy management, and reduce environmental emissions. (Saad al-sumaiti et al. 2014).

As the term 'smart homes' is often used as a generic descriptor for the introduction of enhanced monitoring and control functionality into homes (Hargreaves and Wilson 2017), we will adopt in this paper the definition provided by Aldrich (2003, p. 17): "(…) a residence equipped with computing and information technology which anticipates and responds to the needs of the occupants, working to promote their comfort, convenience, security and entertainment through the management of technology within the home and connections to the world beyond".

In the literature on smart homes, the domestic environment is often simply the 'taken for granted' backdrop within which technology will be used (Richardson 2009). However, ethnographic and sociological research on the use of ICTs in homes shows these domestic environments are important as they are actively divided by their occupants into functionally and interpretively distinct places (Hargreaves and Wilson 2017). Domestic environments are shared and contested places in which different occupants have sometimes different understandings, preferences, responsibilities and emotional associations (Nyborg 2015).

This paper will present a framework that provides guidelines to study and comprehend such domestic environments taking a user-centric as well as functional viewpoint that considers the home as an informant allowing active control or automation.

3 Affordances

3.1 History of the Phrase Affordance

The term affordance captures relationships between an organism and its environment that allows or inhibits certain actions (Koles and Nagy 2014; Ziglari 2008). Affordances point to the relationship between properties of the environment and the possibilities for action it allows. They highlight the fact that social and cultural artifacts and actions are situated, that they take place using technologies that can be designed, that are controlled and owned. Today, many interpretations of the concept 'affordance' exists and the exact meaning of the term continues to be subject of ongoing debate.

The term affordance was originally proposed in the field of ecological psychology by Gibson (1977). Gibson argues that animals and people initially do not perceive the (physical) properties of objects, but rather what objects offer or afford them: "what we perceive when we look at objects are their affordances, not their qualities" (1986, p. 134). In this sense, the affordances of a home or space refer to those objective and subjective entities that this particular setting can offer its users and surrounding systems (Gibson 1986). They are "what [a tool] offers ... what it provides or furnishes, either for good or ill" (Gibson 1986, p. 127). Scholars from other disciplines have used the term to refer to certain "actionable properties between an object and an actor" (Zhang 2008).

Another view on technology affordances was created by Norman (1988), who focused on the perceived and actual properties of the thing that determine just how the thing could possibly be used. Norman, who applied the concept to everyday artifacts, illustrates the latter with the example of vertical door handles that afford pulling, while flat horizontal door plates afford pushing. Norman adds an important caveat, arguing that affordances are the result of a mental (cognitive) interpretation based on the knowledge and experience of the individual applied to his/her perception. Perceived affordances tell the user what actions are possible and how they should be implemented (Norman 1988).

For Gaver (1991), affordances are independent of perception; they exist whether the perceiver cares about them or not, whether they are perceived or not, whether there is perceptual information available for them or not. Thus it is useful to distinguish affordances from the perceptual information about them. Most examples of affordances refer to perceptible affordances in which there is perceptual information available for an existing affordance. When no information is available, the affordance is hidden (and needs to be inferred from other evidence). When information suggests an affordance that actually is not there; a false affordance exists on which people may mistakenly try to act. When no information about an affordance can be perceived and the affordance does not exist, people will usually not think of a given action.

3.2 Typologies of Affordances

Various typologies of affordances have been created in literature. Creating typologies is a useful approach to better understand a concept as it is a research strategy that raises the level of abstraction and highlights similarities and differences while at the same time requiring exclusivity; i.e. an affordance will be classified in the best fitting category even if it has some features of other affordance types as well. Some of the most interesting typologies include those created by Trepte (2015), Reid and Reid (2010), Hartson (2003), Hogan (2009) and Kaptelinin and Nardi (2012).

Cold and Warm Affordances
Trepte (2015) distinguishes two kinds of social media affordances: 'warm' affordances that invite us to comment, upload, tag and 'cold' affordances that imply agreements about privacy, terms and conditions of use (legal architecture), data ownership, … Communicating in social media spaces thus means experiencing warm affordances (e.g. sharing content) under conditions of cold affordances and as such accepting that all is shared with an (unknown) company that sells or exploits personal information.

Interpersonal and Conversational Affordances
In their study of SMS-culture, Reid and Reid (2010) distinguish between 'interpersonal' en 'conversational' affordances. Interpersonal affordances link up to Goffman's notion of expressive control (1959) and enable self-conscious impression management during a 'social action' (performance). Most online platforms feature different interpersonal affordances that allow such 'expressive control'. The second type distinguished by Reid and Reid (2010) are conversational affordances that determine the extent to which extended interactive exchange of information is possible.

Cognitive, Physical, Sensory, and Functional Affordances
Hartson (2003) describes four complementary types of affordance. Cognitive affordances are design features that help, aid, support, facilitate or enable thinking about something while physical affordances enable doing something. Functional affordances stress the goal a physical affordance can realize and help the user in doing something while sensory affordances provide design features that help, support or enable the user in sensing something.

Informational, Relational, Temporal and Spatial Affordances
Neil Hogan (2009) proposes a typology of social affordances with four specific groups: the social affordances of time, space, relations, and information. Informational social affordances help users to grasp the social setting; they are the socially relevant content of the interaction, and are most closely aligned with cultural signs, values and symbols. Relational social affordances also provide information but are oriented towards other participants rather than the content of the interaction or context. Temporal social

affordances provide perceptual cues about temporality while spatial social affordances convey the properties of space or distance in online spaces that permit or inhibit social interaction.

Instrumental Technology and Auxiliary Technological Affordances
Kaptelinin and Nardi (2012) distinguish between instrumental technology and auxiliary technological affordances. Auxiliary affordances include for example aggregation affordances or maintenance affordances, enabling carrying out maintenance routines and troubleshooting. Instrumental affordances comprise two components; the handling affordance (possibilities for interacting with the technology) and the effecter affordance (possibilities to make an effect on an object using the technology).

3.3 Affordances Working Definition

As our brief literature review shows, the exact meaning of the term affordance continues to be a subject of ongoing debate and many of the interpretations of the concept are incompatible with the original vision of Gibson (Kaptelinin and Nardi 2012). While we can question the use of affordances because of the ambiguity between the absolute 'real' affordances and 'perceived' affordances described in Norman's definition, from a middle ground perspective, affordances can provide a useful lens for studying technologies and the many ways in which smart spaces have implications for interacting and communicating within these digital spaces.

In order to examine the 'physics' of such spaces the properties of the home can be directly related to the actions it affords. Moreover, affordances are defined to both the environment and the interacting organism (the smart home 'user') and in such a way provide or complement insight in computer mediated spaces. As we understand affordances as contextualized in ongoing activities and arising out of interaction between actor and environment or system, we define an affordance as 'what one system provides to another system', in specific, as 'what a smart home provides to its inhabitants or its visitors'. An affordance thus also encompasses the perceived functional significance certain smart home technology for an individual.

4 Towards a Two Folded Affordance Framework

4.1 Structural Approach: User, Media and Home Affordances

In order to transcend the particularities of any technology or its features we first take a structural approach, defining smart contexts by enumerating its affordances and by considering its infrastructure or architecture. As such, we focus on the object of interactivity, describing the home in objective, structural terms as a space that affords (inter)action towards users, documents or media, and the smart home itself.

In general terms, the phrase 'interactivity' describes an active relationship between two things. Three traditions of interactivity research are identified: human-to-human, human-to-documents and human-to-system interaction (McMillan 2006), focusing respectively on human communication, on how people interact with content or media and, on how people interact with the system, computer or any type of technology. From within these traditions, interactivity refers to the features of a medium or technology (its potential for interaction in general) and to the extent that people will use these features or affordances.

Smart spaces assemble a cohesive set of structural affordances, providing us with knowledge about the performative infrastructure that smart spaces supply to inhabitants or visitors. Based on the aforementioned distinction we posit three types of structural affordances; (i) user affordances encompass smart home features that are targeted at other smart home users or people, enabling communication, collaboration or networking, (ii) document or media affordances refer to features that enable smart home users to interact with content, (iii) home affordances provide features for interaction between users and the smart home. Taking into account this last type of structural affordance acknowledges that smart homes as intelligent and context-aware learning systems, do not remove the need for any active user involvement despite the fact that they (try to) automate functions according to users' revealed habits. As smart homes offer integrated affordances and boundaries for their inhabitants or visitors, insight in how these structural affordances are used is essential to analyze how agency and engagement is expressed.

Clearly, structural affordances point well beyond their technical functions to the values and goals of the designers and owners of the home. They envision a certain set of relations and hence externalize the 'politics' of the platform (Gillespie 2010) or home, spelling out and proposing - more or less forcefully - certain sets of relations. As affordances are the things that we recognize rather than the technological smart home components that we infer, they offer a key and under recognized link in a theory of structure and agency (Hogan 2009). Thus, insight in the structural affordances present in a smart home, provides us with knowledge about the performative infrastructure that the home supplies to its users, visitors or inhabitants. Some examples of these structural affordances of smart homes include e.g. technology such as an in-house phone and communication system enabling communication (user affordance), technology to play, stop etc. media content (document or media affordance), or technologies that enable smart home users to raise the temperature, dim the lights etc. (home affordances).

4.2 Implementing the Structural Research Approach

In order to analyze a specific smart home or space from a perspective that takes these structural affordances into account two methods could be applied.

The first is rather straightforward and boils down to listing the different technologies that the smart home provides or affords and logging their usage. As users interacting in contemporary smart homes operate in what could be termed as 'digital enclosures' or as spaces "where every action and transaction generates information about itself" (Andrejevic 2007, p. 2) it is mainly a technological challenge to ensure that everything is captured, mined and instrumentalized.

The second method, the walkthrough method, encompasses an approach that provides insight in the object-oriented character of structural affordances. This design evaluation methodology, initially designed to provide a new tool for assessing the usability of a system, and assigning causes to usability problems, entails a systematic review process "in which the author of a particular aspect of a design presents his or her proposed design solution to a group of peers" (Polson et al. 1992, p. 742). Implementing the aforementioned structural research approach would thus mean that the smart home architect and the providers of the smart home technologies (or a group of external reviewers) step through the available smart home functions considering the behavior of the interface from an object-oriented perspective and assign the home functions to either one of the three structural affordances categories (user, document or media, and home affordances). This inventory exercise should end up with a detailed and fine-grained list of technologies that are embedded in the house and that facilitate human interaction or interaction with media content or the house itself.

4.3   Functional Approach: Inter-action, Intra-action and Outer-action Affordances

We also need a perspective that describes how smart home inhabitants or visitors engage and interact with the structural affordances mentioned above. Hence, we posit a functional approach or perspective that describes the smart home in subjective, functional terms as a space that affords its user certain (inter)action goals. We suggest to add a set of functional affordances to the methodological framework, namely inter-action, intra-action and outer-action affordances.

Inter-action affordances point to the use of affordances for communication. They reflect the use of structural affordances from a 'process' viewpoint; as a type of information exchange between two or more people. They enable conversations and are thus 'social' affordances. Intra-action affordances enable interaction from a person to himself/herself. As the individual receiving the message is (due to time separation) in a different state from the moment when the message was issued, the message is likely to contain something 'new' and hence, valuable to the receiver. Intra-action does not describe a mental or cognitive process but the process of external representation of a mental process. In that sense, intra-action affordances can also be called 'personal' affordances. Outer-action affordances support communicative processes outside of information exchange, in which people reach out to others in patently social ways to enable information exchange. These affordances enable negotiations about availability, assist in finding ways to establish connections, and support the progress of an interaction. Outer-action affordances scaffold information exchange (Nardi et al. 2000); they are 'context' affordances.

Some examples of these functional affordances of smart homes include e.g. using technology such as an in-house phone and communication system to communicate with other inhabitants (inter-action affordance), using technology to store a memo or the specifics of a future event in a calendar (intra-action affordance), or using technologies that enable smart home users to have insight in the presence or absence of inhabitants (outer-action affordances, see Fig. 1).

Fig. 1. The Eta Clock, a Kickstarter project that works with a smartphone app to show the locations of house members as an example of a technology providing outer-action affordances (https://www.kickstarter.com/projects/2111232964/the-eta-clock-a-community-location-device).

4.4   Implementing the Functional Research Approach

Similar to applying the structural approach two methods could be applied in order to take a functional affordances perspective.

The first uses the aforementioned list of different technologies that the smart home provides and the logs of their usage and provides this as feedback to the smart home users, asking them to consider systematically the mental operations in the use of the smart home, such as goal formation.

As a matter of fact, this could serve as a pre-cursor for a walkthrough approach in which smart home inhabitants or visitors step through the available smart home functions considering the behavior of the interface from an goal-oriented perspective and assign the home functions to either one of the three functional affordances categories (inter-, intra-, and outer-action affordances). This second inventory exercise should then end up with a detailed and fine-grained list that describes the smart home in subjective, functional terms as a space that affords its inhabitants certain (inter)action goals.

4.5   The Framework

The combination of the structural and functional affordances approach sketched above creates a twofold analytical lens or research framework (see Fig. 2) that can be used to describe interactivity in smart homes, in objective, structural terms as well as in subjective, functional terms. Structural affordances help us to describe the home as a space of object-oriented user, document or media and home affordances. The functional affordances describe the home as a space of perceived inter-action (social), intra-action (personal) and outer-action (context) affordances. This twofold framework for interactivity in smart spaces thus takes into account structure and agency, synthesizing both the structural properties of the smart home as well as the ways that inhabitants or visitors perceive and interact with these capabilities.

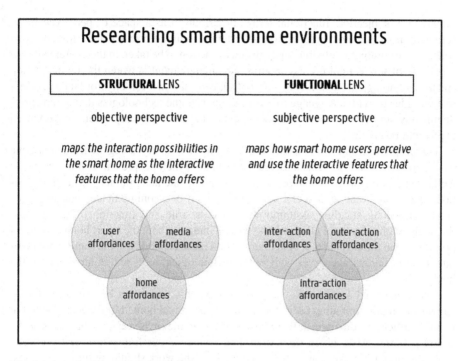

Fig. 2. A methodological framework for researching user experience in smart home contexts

People will often resort to user affordances (as social affordances) to setup conversations with others, they will use media affordances (as personal affordances) to interact with the available content (e.g. in smart home media systems), and they will often use home affordances (as context affordances) to interact with the smart home. Juxtaposing structural and functional affordances shows that structural user affordances can be linked to functional inter-action or 'social' affordances; structural document or media affordances to functional intra-action or 'personal' affordances; and structural home affordances to functional outer-action or 'context' affordances. Figure 2 summarizes the components of our twofold research framework for the analysis of interactivity in smart homes.

Positioning these two perspectives next to each other provides insight in the domestication process of technology (Silverstone and Haddon 1996) and in the appropriation phase in specific as it provides a language to describe how a technology is welcomed into the household and is granted a physical and discursive place, while its use is given a place within existing routines.

5 Discussion and Conclusion

In this paper we considered a smart home's structural affordances, in user, document or media and home affordances. Our analytic framework also made it possible to talk about the home in subjective, functional terms, describing it as a space of perceived inter-action, intra-action and outer-action affordances. Our affordance lens forced us to consider the symbiotic relationship between the action to be taken in the context and the capability of the technology. By treating the entanglement between the human action and the technological capability as a unit of analysis, the two-folded affordance perspec-tive provides us with a language to examine smart home technologies that avoids priv-ileging any single component of a sociotechnical system over any other component in explaining behavior.

Our proposed framework has two important merits. Firstly, using the framework one can interpret a smart home as a medium 'through' which people can communicate, as well as a medium 'with' which people can communicate and interact. As such, it posi-tions the smart home as a social actor with whom one communicates and interacts, challenging long standing assumptions about the role and function of technology. Secondly, with our twofold framework, we can integrate both the smart home structural properties and the ways that people interact with these capabilities; the framework takes into account human agency as well as the technological tools and components of the home.

The conceptual framework we developed in this paper can be criticized for its vagueness in differentiating user, document or media and home affordances. Indeed, it is often difficult to distinguish them based solely on the involved information or inter-action patterns. Also, given the explorative nature of our framework and proposed research approach, a path towards validating the framework should be further explored in order to unearth conceptual, methodological and procedural shortcomings.

Despite these limitations, we believe that the developed framework can function as a steppingstone for more extensive and qualitative research into the many ways in which smart spaces have implications for the creation, use, and experience of digital media content and into the diverse ways people and communities interact and communicate within these spaces.

References

Saad al-sumaiti, A., Ahmed, M.H., Salama, M.M.A.: Smart home activities: a literature review. Electr. Power Compon. Syst. **42**(3–4), 294–305 (2014). https://doi.org/10.1080/15325008.2013.832439

Aldrich, F.K.: Smart homes: past, present and future. In: Harper, R. (ed.) Inside the smart home, pp. 17–39. Springer, London (2003). https://doi.org/10.1007/1-85233-854-7_2

Andrejevic, M.: iSpy: Surveillance and Power in the Interactive Era. The University Press of Kansas, Lawrence (2007)

Cook, D.J.: How smart is your home? Science **335**(6076), 1579–1581 (2012)

Cook, D.J., Crandall, A.S., Thomas, B.L., Krishnan, N.C.: CASAS: a smart home in a box. Computer **46**(7), 62–69 (2013). https://doi.org/10.1109/MC.2012.328

Frey, J., Bird, C., Willoughby, C.: Human aspects of smart spaces for knowledge. In: Howlett, R.J., Gabrys, B., Musial-Gabrys, K., Roach, J. (eds.) Innovation through Knowledge Transfer 2012. Smart Innovation, Systems and Technologies, vol. 18, pp. 19–29. Springer, Heidelberg (2013). https://doi.org/10.1007/978-3-642-34219-6_3

Gaver, W.: Technology affordances. In: CHI 1991, pp. 17–24. ACM (1991)

Gibson, J.J.: The theory of affordances. In: Shaw, R., Bransford, J. (eds.) Perceiving, Acting, and Knowing: Toward an Ecological Psychology, pp. 67–82. Lawrence Erlbaum, Hillsdale (1977)

Gibson, J.J.: The Ecological Approach to Visual Perception. Lawrence Erlbaum, London (1986)

Gillespie, T.: The politics of "platforms". New Media Soc. **12**(3), 347–364 (2010). https://doi.org/10.1177/1461444809342738

Goffman, E.: The Presentation of Self in Everyday Life. Penguin, Harmondsworth (1959)

Hargreaves, T., Wilson, C.: Smart Homes and Their Users, pp. 1–14. Springer, Heidelberg (2017). https://doi.org/10.1007/978-3-319-68018-7

Hartson, H.R.: Cognitive, physical, sensory, and functional affordances in interaction design. Behav. Inf. Technol. **22**(5), 315–338 (2003)

Hogan, B.J.: Networking in everyday life. Graduate Department of Sociology. University of Toronto, Toronto (2009). http://individual.utoronto.ca/berniehogan/Hogan_NIEL_10-29-2008_FINAL.pdf

Kaptelinin, V., Nardi, B.: Affordances of HCI; toward a mediated action perspective. In: Höök, K. (ed.) CHI 2012, pp. 967–976. ACM, Austin (2012). http://dl.acm.org/citation.cfm?id=2208541&dl=ACM&coll=DL&CFID=370918149&CFTOKEN=79438039

Koles, B., Nagy, P.: Virtual worlds as digital workplaces: conceptualizing the affordances of virtual worlds to expand the social and professional spheres in organizations. Organ. Psychol. Rev. **4**(2), 175–195 (2014). https://doi.org/10.1177/2041386613507074

Korzun, D.G., Kashevnik, A.M., Balandin, S.I., Smirnov, A.V.: The Smart-M3 platform: experience of smart space application development for internet of things. In: Balandin, S., Andreev, S., Koucheryavy, Y. (eds.) ruSMART 2015. LNCS, vol. 9247, pp. 56–67. Springer, Cham (2015). https://doi.org/10.1007/978-3-319-23126-6_6

M&M. Smart home market by product, software & service, and geography—global forecast to 2023 (2017)

McMillan, S.J.: Exploring models of interactivity from multiple research traditions: users, documents and systems. In: Lievrouw, L., Livingstone, S. (eds.) The Handbook of New Media, pp. 205–229. Sage, London (2006)

Nardi, B.A., Whittaker, S., Bradner, E.: Interaction and outeraction: instant messaging in action. In: Kellogg, W.A., Whittaker, S. (eds.) Conference on Computer Supported Cooperative Work. ACM Press, Philadelphia (2000). http://delivery.acm.org/10.1145/360000/358975/p79-nardi.pdf?key1=358975&key2=4747714621&coll=GUIDE&dl=GUIDE&CFID=74313543&CFTOKE N=73171065

Norman, D.: The Psychology of Everyday Things. Basic Books, New York (1988)

Nyborg, S.: Pilot users and their families: inventing flexible practices in the smart grid. Sci. Technol. Stud. **28**(3), 54–80 (2015)

Polson, P.G., Lewis, C., Rieman, J., Wharton, C.: Cognitive walkthroughs: a method for theory-based evaluation of user interfaces. Int. J. Man-Mach. Stud. **36**, 741–773 (1992)

Reid, F., Reid, D.: The expressive and conversational affordances of mobile messaging. Behav. Inf. Technol. **29**(1), 3–22 (2010)

Richardson, H.J.: A "smart house" is not a home: the domestication of ICTs. Inf. Syst. Front. **11**, 599–608 (2009)

Silverstone, R., Haddon, L.: Design and domestication of information and communication technologies: technical change and everyday life. In: Mansell, R., Silverstone, R. (eds.) Communication by Design, pp. 44–75. Oxford University Press, Oxford (1996)

Statista. Smart home - Statistics & Facts (2017)

Trepte, S.: Social media, privacy, and self-disclosure: the turbulence caused by social media's affordances. Soc. Media + Soc. (1–2) (2015). https://doi.org/10.1177/2056305115578681

Wilson, C., Hargreaves, T., Hauxwell-Baldwin, R.: Smart homes and their users: a systematic analysis and key challenges. Pers. Ubiquit. Comput. **19**(2), 463–476 (2015)

Withagen, R., de Poel, H.J., Araújo, D., Pepping, G.-J.: Affordances can invite behavior: reconsidering the relationship between affordances and agency. New Ideas Psychol. **30**(2), 250–258 (2012)

Zhang, P.: Motivational affordances: Reasons for ICT design and use. Commun. ACM **51**, 145–147 (2008)

Ziglari, L.: Affordance and second language acquisition. Eur. J. Sci. Res. **23**(3), 373–379 (2008)

Zion. Smart Home Market: Global Industry Perspective, Comprehensive Analysis and Forecast, 2016–2022. Zion Market Research, Sarasota (2017)

Planning Placement of Distributed Sensor Nodes to Achieve Efficient Measurement

Yuichi Nakamura[✉], Masaki Ito, and Kaoru Sezaki

Institute of Industrial Science, The University of Tokyo,
Komaba 4-6-1, Meguro, Tokyo, Japan
y-nakamura@mcl.iis.u-tokyo.ac.jp

Abstract. This paper proposes a method to plan a placement of multiple sensors distributed in a certain area to enable an efficient measurement in terms of the confidence of the interpolation of measured data using kriging. We considered a system where we have some sensors that can move and are distributed in a certain area and a static scaler filed of interest such as a map of temperature in a certain city. We propose a method to plan the placement for the next time step using the value measured until that time by calculating the gradient of kriging variance. For the sake of evaluation of this method, we conducted a simulation of two-step measurement where a scaler filed is created and some sensor nodes are virtually placed. Here, the interpolation with the data from sensor node placement with the proposed method showed better accuracy than that from randomly placed sensors.

Keywords: Active sensing · Mobile sensing · Kriging

1 Introduction

Smartphones have become very common these days and the percentage of the smart phone holders in Japan has risen from 14.6% to 56.8% in 5 years [1]. Due to the advancement in semiconductor and other related technologies, smartphones today are equipped with more various types of sensors and it can be interpreted that there are an increasing number of sensors connected to the Internet in cities. Consequently, mobile sensing, which is a technique to make use of them, has drawn much attention.

Mobile sensing is useful to conduct a measurement of a data in a wide area in a low cost. For example, when one tries to create a heat map of the temperature in one city, in case of mobile sensing, the cost required is less than conventional fixed sensors because s/he doesn't have to implement all the sensors but has to collect sensor data from smartphone holders.

In this paper, the focus has been set to a sensing system, or broader class of measurement using mobile sensors, which of course includes smartphones. For example, if garbage collecting trucks are equipped with sensors, that would provide with virtually exhaustive coverage of the city [2]. Automobiles can move faster than a human being and so it is expected that they can ensure broader coverage per sensor.

Although the data acquired from a sensing system can be useful as mentioned above in an example of mobile sensing, such data have to be processed in order for the user to utilize

© Springer International Publishing AG, part of Springer Nature 2018
N. Streitz and S. Konomi (Eds.): DAPI 2018, LNCS 10921, pp. 103–113, 2018.
https://doi.org/10.1007/978-3-319-91125-0_8

because the raw data acquired is merely a collect of measured values in discrete points. For example, if a temperature measurement is conducted, it is not such discrete data, but a heat map of temperature that is of use. In other words, a sensing system requires spatial interpolation, or spatially completing the estimated values at unvisited points.

In spatial interpolation, the accuracy has dependency on the placement of sensors. As is intuitively understood, measuring values at two points close would give lower accuracy of spatial interpolation than at two points apart. Therefore, we propose a placement optimization strategy of sensors in a sensor system. In our proposal, we use a technique called kriging for spatial interpolation and kriging variance for the placement strategy.

The rest of the paper is organized as follows. Section 2 describes the background to this paper; Sect. 3 introduces the problem settings of this study; Sect. 4 gives details of the proposed method; Sect. 5 shows the simulation that we did; Sect. 6 shows the prototyping and the direction of future research; and Sect. 7 is the conclusions.

2   Related Works

Sensing system or especially mobile sensing has attracted a lot of attention and it is an active area of study and development. As mentioned above, previous research has demonstrated some actual implementation of such system and the method of spatial interpolation, but optimal sensors placement strategies are limited.

The sensor system is implemented for a broad area. In [2], garbage collecting trucks in Fujisawa City, Japan are equipped with sensors such as a GPS sensor, thermometer, barometer and so on. Unlike private vehicles, those trucks go around the city in such a route that covers the entire road. Through actual implementation, they checked that most area of the city can be sensed at least once every garbage-collecting day. In [3], they used pictures taken by a camera installed on automobiles to detect damage on the road. In [4], the acoustic noise level of entire Setagaya City, which is about 60 km^2, has been sensed in 6 h by 40 people. In [5], the participants walked around city with a mobile radiation detector.

For this kind of measurement, interpolation is important. The authors of [6] used a technique named consensus filter. In consensus filter, for each point that sensor nodes did not visit, the value is estimated by waited sum of the values at neighboring visited points. This method is useful for relatively densely sensed situation but not for sparsely measured case. There are also studies that introduces methods using other background data. In [7], they spatially interpolated the temperature data taking into account other geographical knowledge such as the altitude. In [8], they only used 12 sensors to measure AQI, or air quality index, in the entire LA. Combined with contextual data of geography of each points from OpenStreetMap and used the measured data for learning, their estimation was better than conventional IDW, or inversed distance weight, in cross validation.

There are several works of active sensing with sensing robots such as [9]. They proposed a route optimization for a sensing robot. Here, mutual information of the measurement and interpolation is used to determine the trajectory of a sensing robot. In this work, the focus is set on the case of only one sensing node.

As we have listed above, there are a wide variety of application of sensing system and also a number of interpolation methods but few works have covered the strategy of placing sensors, especially multiple sensors. In this paper, we propose a method to interpolate measured data from multiple sensor nodes and plan the placement of them in the next step to achieve the most optimal placement in terms of the accuracy of the interpolation.

3   Problem Settings

In this paper, we propose a method to plan an optimal sensor placement method to a situation as follows:

One would like to map a value of interest in a certain area, such as temperature in Tokyo. For that purpose, multiple movable sensors are deployed in the area. Each sensor conducts the measurement at the same time and send the data to a server. Then each of them moves to the next sensing position, instructed by the server, and measure the value there again.

Here we assumed the scaler field of the true value of the vale of interest do not change between the time of the first measurement and the second. This is because even though the scaler field does change in the time length, in one step of the move the time is short and the change is negligible in the real scenario. In the real use, the measurement will be conducted sequentially beyond the second time but in this paper, two steps of measurement are discussed for simplicity.

4   Method

4.1   Kriging

Kriging is a geostatical method to interpolate data using spatial autocorrelation. For a system where sensor nodes i $(i = 1, \ldots, N)$ are deployed in r_i the field and measurement $z(r_i)$ is conducted, semivariance, or the spatial autocorrelation of z is defined as

$$\gamma(h) = \frac{1}{2n} \sum_{i=1}^{n} \left[z(r_i + h) - z(r_i) \right]. \tag{1}$$

For actual data, since the measured value at an arbitrary point is not always available, semivariance cannot be calculated for all h. It is why variogram, or a plot of $\gamma(h)$ versus h, only for known points. By fitting variogram with certain function, we can get the estimated semivariance for arbitrary h. There are several common functions used to fit variogram, such as spherical model, exponential model and so on. In this paper, we used the exponential model in this case, which is represented as follows:

$$\hat{\gamma}(h) = p \left[1 - \left(1 - \frac{3h}{r} \right) e^{-\frac{3h}{r}} \right] + n \tag{2}$$

where r is called range and p is called sill and n is called nugget; those three parameters are determined by the fitting.

After getting the estimation of semivariance, we now use this to conduct the interpolation. In kriging, the value is interpolated through weighted sum

$$\hat{z}(r) = \sum_{i=1}^{N} \lambda_i \, z(r_i) \tag{3}$$

where the weights λ_i are bound to the normalization

$$\sum_{i=1}^{N} \lambda_i = 1. \tag{4}$$

In order to minimize the estimation error, which is a sum of the gap squared between the estimated value and the weights at each visited point, are determined using semivariance, in such a way as minimizing

$$\sum_{i=1}^{N} \lambda_i \, \hat{\gamma}(r_i - r_j) + \phi = \hat{\gamma}(r_j - r), \quad \forall j. \tag{5}$$

4.2 Kriging Variance Gradient

Then the kriging variance, or the variance of the estimated value, is expressed as:

$$\hat{\sigma}_e^2(r_0) := \sum_{i=1}^{N} \hat{\lambda}_i \gamma(r_i - r_0) + \phi. \tag{6}$$

From the method above we can obtain the kriging variance at all points including unvisited ones as well as estimated value there. In order for each sensor nodes to move towards the direction so that the next measurement would be the most optimal with regard to minimizing the error for the whole area, we also calculated the gradient $G(r)$ of the kriging variance:

$$G(r) = \nabla\left[\hat{\sigma}_e^2(r)\right]. \tag{7}$$

4.3 Placement Determination

It is most optimal to move the sensor nodes towards the direction where the kriging variance is the highest. We used the gradient to find such a direction. Therefore, we determined the placement of the sensor i for the next time step $t + \Delta t$ using the gradient vector $G(r)$ at time t as follows:

$$r_i(t + \Delta t) = r_i(t) + \Delta r \frac{G(r)}{|G(r)|} \tag{8}$$

where in each step each sensor node moves for the distance Δr.

5   Simulation

In order to test the validation of the above method, a simulation was conducted and the mean squared error of estimated values at all points in the area was compared with the random determination.

5.1   Setting of the Simulation

In the simulation, we made a certain scaler field, which is the true value in this simulation, in the area of interest and interpolated the measured values at five sensor nodes. The simulation was conducted in the following settings.

The area of interest has been formed as 40×40 square, filled with 0.5×0.5 meshes. The five sensors were deployed in the sensing area, or the grey area in Fig. 1, so that it is not located on the edge of the 40×40 square, where gradient of kriging variance is not well-defined.

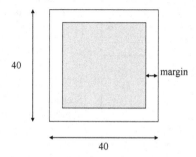

Fig. 1.   The field of simulation is 40×40 including the margin.

The scaler field we prepared was a sum of three different Gaussian with different means μ's and covariance matrices Σ's as:

$$z(r) = \sum_{i=1}^{3} \frac{1}{2\pi |\Sigma_i|^{\frac{1}{2}}} \exp\left[-\frac{1}{2}(r - \mu_i)^{\mathrm{T}} \Sigma_i^{-1} (r - \mu_i)\right]. \tag{9}$$

which is shown in Fig. 2.

In the simulation, first we deployed five sensors at random in the sensing area and made a measurement (step 1). We then kriged the measured values to obtain the map of the value in the entire field and also the kriging variance map (Fig. 3).

5.2   Method

Now we have the kriging variance field and so we used that to determine the placement of the sensor nodes for Step 2. We set two different scenarios.

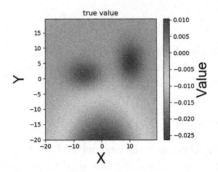

Fig. 2. We made 2-D scaler field by summing three different Gaussians.

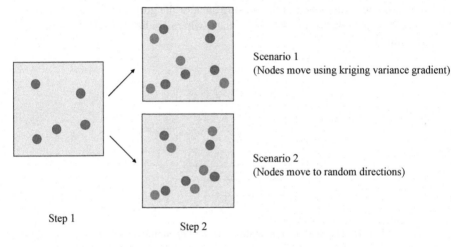

Scenario 1
(Nodes move using kriging variance gradient)

Scenario 2
(Nodes move to random directions)

Step 1

Step 2

Fig. 3. In Step 1, we deployed five sensors randomly. In Step 2, we simulated two different scenarios: in Scenario 1, the sensors were moved using kriging variance gradient; in Scenario 2, they were moved to random directions. In Step 2, both data from 5 initial points and 5 new points were used in the kriging.

Scenario 1. It is most optimal to move the sensor nodes towards the direction where the kriging variance gradient is the highest in all the directions. Therefore, we determined the placement of the sensor i for the next time step as follows:

$$r_i(t + \Delta t) = r_i(t) + \Delta r \frac{\nabla V(r)}{|\nabla V(r)|} \quad (10)$$

where Δr is the step of the movement.

Practically, in this simulation the kriging was done for discrete grid points. Therefore variance calculated only for discretely distributed points and the gradient is not actually calculated through differentiation but computed using second-order accurate central differences with certain sampling distances. Since the resulting gradient has a dependency on sampling distance d_{sample}, we compared the results for different d_{sample}.

Scenario 2. For comparison, we also simulated the case where the nodes are moved to a random direction. For this the position of the same sensor node at the next time step is expressed as:

$$r_i(t + \Delta t) = r_i(t) + \Delta r \begin{pmatrix} \cos \theta \\ \sin \theta \end{pmatrix}$$ (11)

Here, θ is a random value between 0 and 2π (Fig. 4).

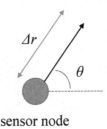

sensor node

Fig. 4. Each sensor node moves by Δr in the direction θ.

5.3 Evaluation

For the evaluation of these methods, we calculated the sum of error squared at each grid point of the entire area of interest, namely,

$$\text{Error} = \sum_j \left[z(r_j) - \hat{z}(r_j) \right]^2$$ (12)

where $z(r_j)$ and $\hat{z}(r_j)$ are the true value and the interpolated value at the grid point j, respectively and the summation is done through all the grid points.

In order to examine the effect of Δr, we executed the simulation for different Δr. Also, as mentioned above, scenario 2 was performed for different d_{sample}.

In other words, for each initial random sensor deployment (step 2), (1) scenario 1 was performed for different Δr's and (2) scenario 2 was performed for different Δr's and different d_{sample}'s.

We calculated the error for each scenario with different parameters for 1000 different initial placement of sensors in Step 1. For each error in Scenario 1 was compared with the error in the corresponding simulation in Scenario 2 with regard to Δr and we counted the number of cases where error in scenario 1 is greater than that in scenario 2 out of 1000 simulations for each Δr and d_{sample}.

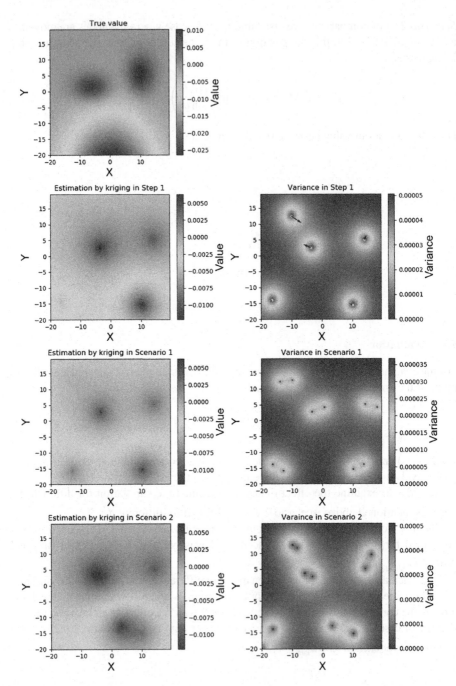

Fig. 5. An example of the simulation results. The left figure of the top row is the true value. The second row show is the kriged result (left) and kriging variance with the positions of sensor nodes (yellow dots) and the gradient (arrows). The third row shows the results of Step 2 in Scenario 1 and the forth that in Scenario 2. (Color figure online)

5.4 Results

Figure 5 shows the true value and the result of kriging at each step. Figures on the left column are the true value or interpolation result of different steps, the true value on the top figure, Step 1 on the second, Step 2 in Scenario 1 on the third, Step 2 in Scenario 2 at the bottom. On the right column are the kriging variance.

Figure 6 shows the result of the comparison of the error in Scenarios 1 and 2. The x axis indicates Δr and y axis d_{sample}. The color bar shows the ratio of the cases where Scenario 1 gives less error than 2, over 1000 simulations. The resulting figure indicates that for certain Δr and d_{sample}, Scenario 1 gives more accurate kriging results than Scenario 2 in more than 50% of the cases. Given 100 trials have been done, if the ratio from the result is greater than 51.6%, the actual ratio will be more than half, with 95% confidence. Therefore, the fact that there are cases that the ratio is over 51.6% shows that this proposed method gave significantly better results than random decision.

The ratio is higher especially when Δr is smaller and d_{sample} is greater.

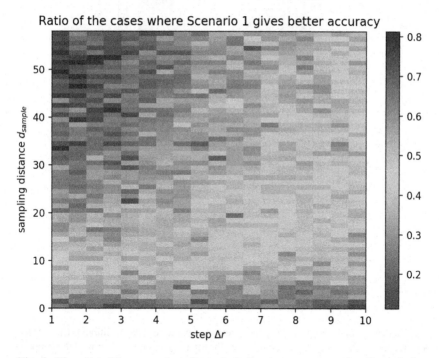

Fig. 6. The ratio of the cases where Scenario 1 gives better accuracy than Scenario 2.

6 Prototype

We also utilized the proposed method to actual measured data from the previous work [10]. Here, some portable devices were prepared and used to make measurement around Shibuya City, Tokyo. They are equipped with multiple sensors including thermometer, hygrometer and air quality sensors such as O_3, CO, NO_2, PM2.5. The devices were made compactly so that human beings can hold while walking. Participants of the experiments were asked to walk around the city carrying one of those. 12 people took part in the experiment and those series of data were collected.

Among those data, the atmospheric temperature was picked and kriged. The results of the kriging and the variance are shown in Fig. 6. Here, with the proposed method, as shown by arrows, the next suggested movement of sensors was successfully calculated (Fig. 7).

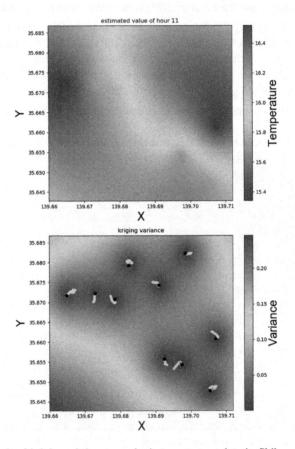

Fig. 7. The result of kriging of the atmospheric temperature data in Shibuya City, Tokyo in 11:00–11:10am on Nov. 14, 2016. The figure on the top is the interpolated map of the temperature and the one below is the kriging variance with gradient shown by arrows. The yellow line in the figure below is the trajectory of each sensor node. (Color figure online)

7   Conclusion

In this paper, we proposed a method of sensor placement in a multiple distributed sensor system in order to achieve better accuracy of interpolation using kriging. Then we demonstrated the method in a simulation and compared with moves with randomly determined direction for validation. As a result, the proposed method was proven to give better accuracy of interpolation in a certain situation, that is, small move step and relatively long sampling distance. We also used actual data from a prototype of a multiple distributed sensor system to execute the proposed method to plan the next step of movement.

As future work, we have three tasks. First one is to extend this method to multiple steps. In this paper we merely focused on two-step measurement. For real usage, it is vital to plan the best trajectory beyond the next move, where it is important not to move different sensors to the same place. This could be realized by introducing a two-body repulsive power among sensors. Second, we have to think about the time dependency of the scaler field of interest. In the simulation above we set a fixed scaler field with regard to time but in the actual world, most values that are measured is not time-invariant. For the last but not least, the method should be carried out for actual sensor placement and movement. By using the prototype mentioned above, it can be achieved.

References

1. 総務省: 情報通信白書. 日経印刷, Tokyo (2017)
2. Chen, Y., Nakazawa, J., Yonezawa, T., Kawasaki, T., Tokuda, H.: An empirical study on coverage-ensured automotive sensing using door-to-door garbage collecting trucks. In: Proceedings of the 2nd International Workshop Smart - SmartCities 2016, pp. 1–6 (2016)
3. Kawasaki, T., et al.: A method for detecting damage of traffic marks by half celestial camera attached to cars. In: Proceedings of the 12th EAI International Conference on Mobile and Ubiquitous Systems: Computing, Networking and Services (2015)
4. Sezaki, K.: 都市をセンシングする. 生産研究, **65**(3), 691–697 (2013)
5. Sullivan, C.J.: Radioactive source localization in urban environments with sensor networks and the Internet of Things. In: 2016 IEEE International Conference on Multisensor Fusion and Integration for Intelligent Systems (MFI), pp. 384–388 (2016)
6. Xiao, L., Boyd, S., Lall, S.: A scheme for robust distributed sensor fusion based on average consensus. In: Fourth International Symposium on Information Processing in Sensor Networks, IPSN 2005, pp. 63–70 (2005)
7. Holden, Z.A., et al.: Development of high-resolution (250 m) historical daily gridded air temperature data using reanalysis and distributed sensor networks for the US Northern Rocky Mountains. Int. J. Climatol. **36**(10), 3620–3632 (2016)
8. Lin, Y., Pan, F., Habre, R.: Mining public datasets for modeling intra-city PM 2.5 concentrations at a fine spatial resolution. In: SIGSPATIAL 2017 (2017)
9. Le Ny, J., Pappas, G.J.: On trajectory optimization for active sensing in Gaussian process models. In: Proceedings of the 48th IEEE Conference Decision Control Held Jointly with 2009 28th Chinese Control Conference, pp. 6286–6292 (2009)
10. Suzuki, T., Ito, M., Sezaki, K.: Evaluating estimation methods of reconstruction accuracy of negative surveys using field survey data of air pollution. IEICE Technical report, vol. 116, no. 488, pp. 85–87 (2017)

Flavor Explore: Rapid Prototyping and Evaluation of User Interfaces

Shi Qiu[1(✉)], Liangyi Du[2], Ting Han[2], and Jun Hu[1]

[1] Department of Industrial Design, Eindhoven University of Technology,
Eindhoven, The Netherlands
{SQIU,J.Hu}@tue.nl
[2] Department of Design, Shanghai Jiao Tong University, Shanghai, China
duliangyi@mail.sjtu.edu.cn, hanting@sjtu.edu.cn

Abstract. Expert-evaluation methods, such as cognitive walkthrough and heuristic evaluation, are widely used in user experience studies due to the reason that it can identify usability problems early and fast and find areas for improvements. In this paper, we present evaluation of Flavor Explore, a high-fidelity prototype, aiming at searching for delicious food and nearby restaurants. A task-based evaluation was conducted to evaluate primary search tasks of the prototype, which included five experts with the background in interaction design and two potential users. Twenty two usability problems were then identified. The findings were helpful for improving the design and for further research.

Keywords: Expert evaluation · Rapid prototyping · Heuristic Evaluation
Cognitive Walkthrough · Usability problems

1 Introduction

Rapid prototyping and expert evaluation are important methods in the development of interactive systems. In the process of rapid prototyping, designers often use sketches, wireframes and interactive prototypes to visualize the concepts. Designers iteratively develop the high-fidelity prototypes to simulate user interface is often helpful and represent the final product. At this point, it makes sense to have experts identify usability problems with these prototypes before exposing to users. In a rapid process of developing systems such as web and mobile applications, expert evaluation may be the only method available before these system go online [1]. There are many forms of expert evaluation, including Cognitive Walkthrough [2, 3], Guidelines Review [4], Consistency Inspection [5] and Heuristic Evaluation [6–8]. Among these methodologies, Cognitive Walkthrough (CW) and Heuristic Evaluation (HE) are widely used in industry. In practice, sometimes a hybrid approach is adopted that combines CW and HE together in a task-based evaluation. In this paper, we present Flavor Explore, a high-fidelity prototype, aiming at searching delicious food and nearby restaurants. After implementation of the prototype, a task-based evaluation which combines CW and HE was adopted to evaluate primary search tasks. The procedure includes these steps: (1) define the target users and their purpose by use scenarios; (2) define three primary search

© Springer International Publishing AG, part of Springer Nature 2018
N. Streitz and S. Konomi (Eds.): DAPI 2018, LNCS 10921, pp. 114–123, 2018.
https://doi.org/10.1007/978-3-319-91125-0_9

tasks they will attempt; (3) walk through each task step-by-step; (4) look and identify usability problems on a set of heuristics; (5) explain where in the user interface the problem is, how severe it is and possible design improvements. Five experts with background in interaction design and two potential users followed this procedure to complete the evaluation. Twenty two usability problems were then identified.

2 Prototype

Brainstorming sessions were conducted based on SET factor analysis ((Social trends (S), Economic forces (E), and Technological advances (T)). We tried to find out design opportunities for conceptualization. This approach, focusing on the product concept and quickly finding out its market opportunity, is widely used in innovative industrial product development [9]. Based on the brain storming results, we positioned our design opportunity on creating a mobile application named Flavor Explore, aiming at users to search for delicious food and nearby restaurants.

2.1 Persona and Scenarios

We clarified and visualized our concept of Flavor Explore by using persona and scenarios, which were developed at early stages of the concept design. Instead of considering user behavior and experience through formal analysis and modeling of well-specified tasks, scenario-based design is a relatively lightweight method for envisioning future use possibilities [10]. Here we identify three typical scenarios of Flavor Explore in our design: searching for restaurants (Fig. 1(a)), recommending dinner menu (Fig. 1(b)) and suggestions for nutrition (Fig. 1(c)).

Fig. 1. Three typical scenarios of Flavor Explore: (a) searching for restaurants, (b) recommending dinner menu, and (c) suggestions for nutrition.

Persona
Emilia is a housewife and her son is a high school student, who has dinner at home with Emilia almost every day. Emilia likes travelling and tasting delicious food in her leisure time. She also concerns about a balanced diet and wants to keep fit.

Scenario 1: Searching for Restaurants
Emilia goes to Hong Kong for her holiday. When she first goes shopping in Mong Kok, she feels tired and hungry. She wants to find a restaurant with local special food. There are many kinds of restaurants on both sides of the street and she cannot decide which one is her favorite. She wants to know nearby restaurants conveniently. In the street, she takes out her mobile phone and starts the camera. From the interface of the camera, she can see information of the nearby restaurants on semi-transparent layers floating in the real-street scene. She checks recommendations and decides to go to Rose Restaurant. In the restaurant, she is interested in a snack looks like dumplings and she wants to know more about it. She takes a photo of it and starts searching. Then she finds its name is *shaomai*, a traditional Chinese food which is worth trying. In this scenario, Emilia uses AR (Augmented Reality) Search, a concept search that based on Augmented Reality technology on mobile photos [11], to find out information of the nearby restaurants. She also uses Image Search to know the name of the snack.

Scenario 2: Recommend Dinner Menu
Emilia is about to prepare dinner at home. She talks with her son by phone and she asks him: "what do you want to have for the dinner?" Her son says: "This week we have three times to take beef with tomatoes. Maybe we can try something different…" Emilia accepts her son's idea and starts flavor Explore to search some recommended cookbooks. In this scenario, Emilia finds out new cookbooks through "Top Recommendations" in Flavor Explore.

Scenario 3: Suggestions for Nutrition
Emilia is now 45 years old. She is no longer slim and not satisfied with her body shape. She wants to lose weight and keeps fit. She tries to keep a balanced diet with lower calories. When she searches for new cookbooks in Flavor Explore, she used "Sort by Calories" to find out most healthy cookbook. In this scenario, Emilia finds out healthy cookbooks through "Sort by Calories" in Flavor Explore.

Based on the scenarios, we proposed three features of Flavor Explore as follows:

1. *Comprehensive search* Combine text, image and AR search to help the user find out food and restaurants.
2. *Top Recommendations* Recommend new and popular cookbooks to the user.
3. *Healthy cookbooks* Use "Sort by Calories" to find cookbooks with lower calories.

2.2 Rapid Prototyping

Sketches of the interface wireframes were created based on three features of Flavor Explore. The wireframe is a visual guide that represents the skeletal framework of an interface. It often lacks color or graphics and primarily focus on the functionality, behavior and priority of content [12, 13]. We were fast to draw the wireframes on a piece of paper and to clarify elements of the user interfaces (Fig. 2(1)). The paper-version wireframes provides a rapid way to visualize design ideas in an early stage. It helps to organize ideas and modify the design concept in an iterative design process. In order to make the prototype more interactive, we used Axture[1] to create an interactive HTML prototype. The axure prototype is shown in Fig. 2(2). The final high-fidelity prototype was created by Adobe Flash Catalyst[2] (Fig. 2(3)). The high-quality images of the user interface in PSD format could be imported into Adobe Flash Catalyst conveniently.

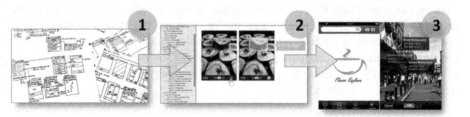

Fig. 2. (1) Wireframes of user interfaces, (2) the interactive HTML prototype created with axure, and (3) high-fidelity prototype created with Adobe Flash Catalyst.

3 Evaluation

Five experts from two online companies and two potential users were invited to evaluate the prototype. The evaluation scope was limited to three search tasks: Image Search, AR Search and Text Search which were completed in the high-fidelity prototype. The task flow of three search tasks is shown in Fig. 3.

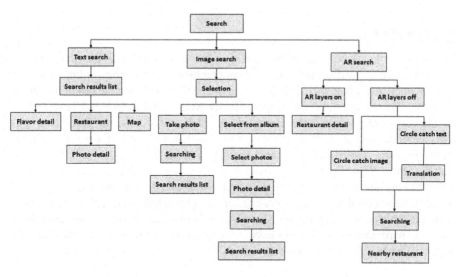

Fig. 3. Task flow of three search tasks in Flavor Explore

---

[1] http://www.axure.com/.
[2] http://www.adobe.com/hu/products/flashcatalyst.html.

3.1 Participants

Five usability experts participated, four of which were female. All of them had higher education qualifications and they had experience in evaluating average five mobile application projects. They were professional interaction designers and user researchers from online companies. Four were from Baidu (Chinese online company, primarily providing search engine services) and the other from Dianping (Chinese online company, primarily providing merchant information and consumer reviews). Two female users were invited to participate in evaluation. They were postgraduate students from School of Design, Hong Kong Polytechnic University. Both had sufficient experiences in using smart phones.

3.2 Setup

Two users participated in the evaluation in Hong Kong Polytechnic University in Hong Kong and five experts conducted the evaluation in online companies in Chinese mainland. Two users used a computer that installed the prototype previously. For the experts, we sent them the high-fidelity prototype with instructions by email before the test. The prototype was asked to be installed on their computers, which was more convenient for testing. The experts could choose to evaluate the prototype at home or at the office, where they should ensure surroundings as quiet as possible. Four experts evaluated at the office and one did it at home. They were asked to record a video with sound during evaluation. The video images contained the whole evaluation setting and partially the expert.

3.3 Procedure

Evaluation took 20–30 min. Table 1 shows the procedure. The pre-questionnaire included questions pertaining to users' demographics and their domain knowledge of smart phones. After that, the participant read the instruction to run the prototype on the computer. There were three search tasks (Image Search, AR Search and Text Search) for the participant to complete. Before doing each search task, the participant was provided with a use scenario and then decided which search method was most suitable for that scenario. The example scenario was: "*Assume you are on a journey abroad and look for 'Rose Restaurant' in the street. Try to find out remark stars of this restaurant.*" During the search task, the participant was asked to follow the think-aloud protocol. She needed to simply verbalize her thoughts when moving through the user interface. After completing the task, she was asked to evaluate it. After completing three tasks, the participant was asked to answer the question "*which search method do you prefer to choose? Please explain the reasons.*"

Table 1. The procedure of the test

No.	Procedure
(i)	The participant (only experts) downloads and installs the prototype on a computer
(ii)	The participant answers pre-questionnaire
(iii)	The participant conducts three search tasks in a sequence. After completing each task, participant answers a short questionnaire
(iv)	The participant answers an open question after completing three tasks

3.4 Measurements

Six evaluative principles were chosen from a categorization of heuristics and guidelines with twenty types [14]. These principles were easy to use, predict next step, clear icon metaphor, have no mistakes, same logical, and have feedbacks. After completing each task, participants were asked to give the weight to six principles and evaluated the task based on a seven-point scale from "strongly disagree" to "strongly agree". The weight of each principle ranged from zero to one. Zero means never care while one means very care. For two users, the researcher explained the meaning of evaluative principles, weight and the seven-point scale to them and ensured that they could well understand before the test.

4   Results

Quantitative analysis was based on the result of the seven-point scale and divided into two categories: experts and potential users. The average score of experts in Image Search, AR Search and Text Search were 4.782, 2.132 and 4.942. Three experts were unable to finish AR Search: two experts used Text Search to complete the task which aimed to use AR Search and the other one just clicked the "Explore" tab. AR Search was scored lower than other two searches, which indicated potential usability problems. The average score of users in Image Search, AR Search and Text Search were 3.415, 0 and 7. Both of them did not complete AR Search and one of them did not complete Image Search. They finished Text Search without any difficulties, and the average score of Text Search was the highest one among three methods.

Twenty two usability problems were identified by experts and they also proposed suggestions for improvements accordingly. Two users almost kept silent during the evaluation and did not "think aloud". Usability problems identified by experts were ranked by frequency based on the video analysis. As shown in Fig. 4, the usability problems of search result page (No. I-5) were reported for 8 times, while restaurant detail page (No. D-3) for 6 times. Other pages were reported less than 3 times. Table 2 illustrates the categorization of example usability problems and design proposals for improvements. For the open question, we collected experts' comments about the preferable search method. Three experts proposed the search method was chosen based on the requirement of different scenarios. The example was *"my preferred search method depends on different scenarios of searching. For example: if I want to find a restaurant for lunch in a journey, I will probably choose AR Search. The reason is that I have no clear goal at that time. If the name of the restaurant is very clear and not nearby, key words search will be more suitable."* One expert preferred Test Search and the reason was *"I prefer Text Search, because the keyword is very accurate. I cannot trust image search for the reason that some photos are difficult to recognize."* Other two experts preferred AR Search and Image Search. The reasons were: *"my favorite search method is AR Search which looks novel and joyful." "I will prefer Image Search, because I do not need to type anything and only need to take a photo. Then the search starts quickly, quite convenient for me."*

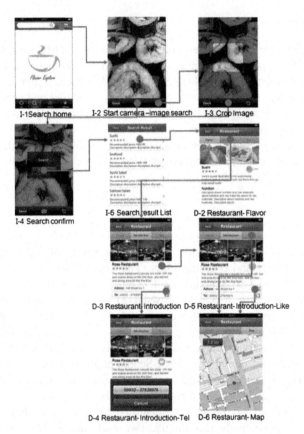

Fig. 4. The flow of the user interfaces

Table 2. Categorization of example usability problems and proposals of improvements

Page no.	Examples of usability problems	Suggestions of improvements
No. I-5 search result	The search result page does not have any pictures	The search result should contain pictures to help the user to make a decision
	The search result page has no ranking remarks, so it cannot helps to decide which restaurant is most recommended	Add ranking remarks in search result page
	Input "Rose Restaurant" in Text Search, the search result has no restaurant information and all about food information	Give user a hint in the search box. For example: please input food name
	The search result page has problems to provide more options to the user and filter the search results	Provide different ordering rules to filter the results. For example: to provide ordering according to distance, price, taste and remarks
No. D-3 restaurant detail	Click the telephone number without any response	Increase clickable area rather than click a small icon
	The wording "Like" is not consistent with "My Favorite"	"My Favorite" changes to "Like"
	Unknown about the information of restaurant environment	Provide the information of restaurant environment
	The icon of "Like" is a heart shape and the icon of "Favorite" is a five-pointed star. They are not consistent in visual language	Make the icon of "Like" and "Favorite" consistent
	Difficult to find out telephone number of the restaurant and no response to click the item	Click the item to activate the phone app
No. A-1 AR search	AR virtual layers cannot provide discount information	Provide discount information on virtual layers
	The switch of the AR layers is confusing. Why need to close AR layers?	Provide a hint to the user to explain the function of AR switch

5   Discussion

5.1   Differences Between Experts and Potential Users

Comparing the experts to the users in average scores of search tasks, experts' scores tend to be more moderate. The average scores of the users have a tendency of a dramatically difference between AR Search ($M_{AR} = 0$) and Text Search ($M_{TS} = 7$). The experts are proficient to complete search tasks and seldom influenced by the usability problems. They tend to evaluate more objectively. They are more patient and give helpful suggestions during the evaluation. However, the users are easily influenced by usability problems. If they cannot complete the task, they tend to give up quickly. So the final score of the search task drop down dramatically. They are more sensitive to usability problems and even possibly exaggerate the severity of the problem compared with experts. In other words, a small usability problem for experts may become a big one for the end users. This phenomenon may be influenced by limited numbers of potential users. In this study, only two potential users were involved. If more potential users participate in the test, the result may be different.

5.2 Usability Problems and Modifications of AR Search

The design of AR Search causes some usability problems. From the video observations, we find one expert and one user try several times to click the "Explore" tab when they did the task of AR Search. It may indicate the wording "Explore" is more relevant to their knowledge of AR Search. The function of "Explore" in this prototype is to be based on LBS (local based service) technology, to provide the information of nearby restaurants to users. The interaction shares some similarities with AR Search. AR Search could be also a kind of "Explore": when a user walks in the street, she can start her camera and check nearby restaurant information in semi-transparent layers. Therefore, we move the "AR" button from "Search" tab to "Explore" tab in the new design. The wording of "AR" is an abbreviation of Augmented Reality. It makes participants feel confused and it might be not necessary for them to know the exact meaning of AR. In the new design, AR button is located on the "Explore" tab and named "layer" which vividly explains its visual appearance. The text "layer" can also use the icon instead.

5.3 Limitations

Considering time and cost, the prototype was evaluated on the computers rather than mobile phones. Usability problems caused by the smaller screen might be neglected. In our future work, we will implement the prototype on mobile phones and conduct the evaluation accordingly. All participants are interaction and user experience designers. They might share the similar ways of thinking. In our future work, we will involve participants with different backgrounds. In this study, we only invited two users. The comparable results between users and experts might not be convincing and we need to recruit more users in the future study.

6   Conclusion

In this paper, we presented the evaluation of a mobile application of Flavor Explore. The implementation of the prototype was an agile procedure. We made the search task available first in the prototype and conducted the evaluation. The prototype was far from perfect, but aiming at shortening the time of development and trying to identify the usability problems in an early stage. In order to find out usability problems, we conducted a task-based evaluation for primary search tasks. Five experts and two users were invited to this study. Users tended to be more sensitive to usability problems. AR Search had some usability problems and we proposed the design improvements based on the suggestions from evaluation.

Acknowledgements. This research is supported by the China Scholarship Council and facilitated by Eindhoven University of Technology. We also thank the support from Tina, Yangzi Li, Xueting Xie in Hong Kong Polytechnic University, Shuang Shi, Ying Chen, Fuhong Han and Jing Li from Baidu as well as Xuejiao Li from Dianping.

References

1. Petrie, H., Power, C.: What do users really care about?: a comparison of usability problems found by users and experts on highly interactive websites. In: Proceedings of the SIGCHI Conference on Human Factors in Computing Systems, pp. 2107–2116 (2012)
2. Lewis, C., Polson, P.G., Wharton, C., Rieman, J.: Testing a walkthrough methodology for theory-based design of walk-up-and-use interfaces. In: Proceedings of the SIGCHI Conference on Human Factors in Computing Systems, pp. 235–242 (1990)
3. Lewis, C., Wharton, C.: Cognitive walkthroughs. In: Handbook of Human-Computer Interaction, vol. 2, pp. 717–732 (1997)
4. Dix, A.: Human-computer interaction. In: Liu, L., Özsu, M.T. (eds.) Encyclopedia of Database Systems. Springer, Heidelberg (2009). https://doi.org/10.1007/978-0-387-39940-9_192
5. Lazar, J., Feng, J.H., Hochheiser, H.: Research Methods in Human-Computer Interaction. Wiley, Hoboken (2010)
6. Molich, R., Nielsen, J.: Improving a human-computer dialogue. Commun. ACM **33**(3), 338–348 (1990)
7. Nielsen, J.: Usability Engineering. Elsevier, Amsterdam (1994)
8. Nielsen, J., Molich, R.: Heuristic evaluation of user interfaces. In: Proceedings of the SIGCHI Conference on Human Factors in Computing Systems, pp. 249–256 (1990)
9. Cagan, J., Vogel, C.M.: Creating Breakthrough Products: Innovation from Product Planning to Program Approval. Ft Press, Upper Saddle River (2002)
10. Rosson, M.B., Carroll, J.M.: Scenario based design. In: Human-Computer Interaction, Boca Raton, FL, pp. 145–162 (2009)
11. Höllerer, T., Feiner, S.: Mobile augmented reality. In: Telegeoinformatics: Location-Based Computing and Services, vol. 21. Taylor and Francis Books Ltd., London (2004)
12. Brown, D.M.: Communicating Design: Developing Web Site Documentation for Design and Planning. New Riders, San Francisco (2010)
13. Garrett, J.J.: The Elements of User Experience: User-Centered Design for the Web and Beyond. Pearson Education, London (2010)
14. Weinschenk, S., Barker, D.T.: Designing Effective Speech Interfaces. Wiley, Hoboken (2000)

HCI Design for People with Visual Disability in Social Interaction

Shi Qiu[1(✉)], Ting Han[2], Hirotaka Osawa[3], Matthias Rauterberg[1], and Jun Hu[1]

[1] Department of Industrial Design, Eindhoven University of Technology,
Eindhoven, The Netherlands
{SQIU,G.W.M.Rauterberg,J.Hu}@tue.nl
[2] Department of Design, Shanghai Jiao Tong University, Shanghai, China
hanting@sjtu.edu.cn
[3] Faculty of Engineering, Information and Systems, University of Tsukuba, Tsukuba, Japan
osawa@iit.tsukuba.ac.jp

Abstract. In the Human Computer Interaction (HCI) field, it has been a long tradition of concern of accessing computer systems by people with visual impairments. It is important to develop high quality user interfaces, accessible, usable, and desirable for these people. In this paper, we first report a preliminary background review about HCI design for people with visual disability. The review of the problems in social interaction the blind people may encounter, are also presented. Further, we narrow down our research scope and focus on gaze and eye contact, which have important social meaning in face-to-face communication. We then identify our research objective that is to design gaze simulation for people with visual impairments. Finally, we report the prototypes of our research project and the progress made so far.

Keywords: Social interaction · Eye contact · Visual impairments
Face-to-face communication

1 Introduction

According to the information from the World Health Organization (WHO) in 2014, there are 285 million people estimated to be visually impaired worldwide: 39 million are blind and 246 have low vision [1]. The loss of vision often indicates loss of independence, lack of communication and human contact, which increase the limitations in mobility and social interaction. In the Human Computer Interaction (HCI) field, it has been a long tradition of concern of accessing computer systems by people with visual impairments [2]. In web design, they meet the problems include the issue of screen design, the font size, color, patterns in screen background that make the text difficult to read and too many graphics. These features designed to be attractive to the sighted user, may make website inaccessible to a visually impaired user [3]. It is important to develop high quality user interfaces, accessible and usable by blind people with different skills, requirements and preferences, in a variety of contexts of use, and through a variety of different technologies [4]. In recent days, access for blind and visually impaired users

© Springer International Publishing AG, part of Springer Nature 2018
N. Streitz and S. Konomi (Eds.): DAPI 2018, LNCS 10921, pp. 124–134, 2018.
https://doi.org/10.1007/978-3-319-91125-0_10

to computer systems is gradually improving. Some of the obstacles that impeded blind people to have access to computer systems are solved by using screen reader software, voice synthesis, speech recognition, Braille and tactile displays etc. [5].

2   HCI Design for Blind People

In this section, a preliminary background review about HCI design for blind people is presented. We conducted this review for the general understanding of the current assistive technologies and applications for blind people in HCI field. A search on Google Scholar was conducted in March. 2014, using the following key terms: "HCI design", "assistive technology", "accessibility", and "blind people". This search returned 46 results, on which we carried out ancestor and descendent search trying to identify related papers introducing assistive technologies for people with visual impairments. Based on the abstracts, eventually 15 papers [6–20] were selected. We use hearing and touch senses (two of the five senses of human), to categorize and report relevant assistive applications based on the user interfaces. There are two categories: (a) the auditory assistive systems to help blind people in navigation, social networking, photography, and others. [6–13]; (b) help blind people in the areas of tactile navigation, Braille, and touch graphics [14–20]. We paid particular attention to three perspectives of these papers: motivation, system implementation, and evaluation.

2.1   Auditory Assistive Systems

Papers in this category report on the auditory assistive systems to help blind people in navigation, social networking, photography, and others. Table 1 summarizes auditory assistive systems reviewed in this section.

Table 1. Auditory assistive systems.

Function	Application	Evaluation
Auditory navigation	Cross watch [6]	Usability evaluation (N = 2)
	Travel aid [7]	Usability evaluation (N = 4)
Social networking	Facebook [8]	Usability evaluation (N = 15)
	Vizwiz social [9]	Field experiment (N = 23)
Photography	Easy snap [10]	Usability evaluation (N = 6)
	Portrait frame [10]	Usability evaluation (N = 15)
Others	Conversation [11]	No evaluation
	Mathematics [12]	Usability evaluation (N = 5)
	Museum guide [13]	No evaluation
	Shopping products [13]	No evaluation

Auditory Navigation
Urban intersections are dangerous for the blind people's travel. They need to enter the crosswalk in the right direction and avoid walking outside of it, which becomes a difficult

task for them. In order to solve this problem, a "Crosswatch" system was developed by Ivanchenko et al. [6], using computer vision to provide information about the location and orientation of the crosswalks to the blind users. When a blind user holds a camera phone to walk through the intersection, the system can detect the crosswalks and send an audio tone to her immediately. In the usability evaluation, two blind participants demonstrated the feasibility of the system by comparing two experimental conditions: the system with and without audio feedback. They were better able to use the "Crosswatch" system provided the audio feedback.

Dunai et al. [7] developed a system as a travel aid for the blind users. It consists of two stereo cameras mounted in a helmet and a portable computer for processing the environmental information (Fig. 1). The system can detect the static and dynamic objects from surroundings and transform them into acoustical signals. Four totally blind participants participated in the user experiment to evaluate the usability of this system. Two experimental settings were proposed: the first was blind participants asked to stay in a static position, and the second was to follow the moving object. Experimental results demonstrated that the blind participants were able to control and navigate the system in both familiar and unfamiliar environments. Better results were obtained when the subject was static and the objects were moving around in the area within a diameter of 30 cm.

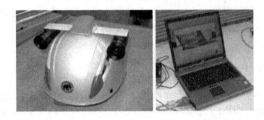

Fig. 1. Real-time assistance prototype [7].

Social Networking
The increasing awareness and concern for accessibility has motivated HCI researchers and developers to claim that mobile user interface should be simpler and more accessible to blind users used screen readers. However, it is reported that blind users still have difficulties to access Facebook and seldom empirical data demonstrate this problem. In response to this, Wentz and Lazar [8] collected empirical data from fifteen blind participants, who participated in the evaluation of "Facebook Desktop" and "Facebook Mobile". Five usability tasks were compared between "Facebook Desktop" and "Facebook Mobile" (e.g. opening and logging into a Facebook account and uploading a picture to a Facebook account). The results indicated that although the user interface of "Facebook Mobile" was missing some features and not consisted with the user interface of "Facebook Desktop", it was more usable than "Facebook Desktop".

Generally, the blind people seek information by the assistance of their family members or friends. If they ask visual questions to their social networks, they can increase the feelings of independence and security. Based on this research motivation, Brady et al. [9] implemented VizWiz Social, an iPhone app, to enable blind users to ask questions to either the crowd or friends. Twenty three blind participants participated in the field experiment to identify the potentiality of using VizWiz Social. The comments from the participants indicated that they were reluctant to bother their social networks with questions, possibly due to the reason that they were not willing to give an impression of being helpless.

Photography

Based on an online survey with 118 blind people, Jayant et al. [10] demonstrated that blind people took photographs for the same reasons as sighted people (e.g. record important events and share experiences). Based on these findings, Jayant et al. [10] introduced an application namely EasySnap, to provide audio feedback to help blind users take pictures of objects and people. Six blind participants participated in the usability test to explore the effectiveness of EasySnap. Most of them agreed that Easy-Snap helped their photography and found it was easy to use.

Furthermore, a group portrait application namely PortraitFramer was designed based on the Android platform [10]. The blind user can be told how many faces are in the camera's sight (Fig. 2). Fifteen blind and low-vision participants participated in an in-depth study and demonstrated that they could understand how to successfully use the application in a short time.

(a) Original Photo   (b) With Framing Boxes   (c) High Contrast Faces

Fig. 2. Steps of PortraitFramer application: (a) Photo taken; (b) Faces found; (c) Announces the number of faces [10].

Others

Nishimoto and Watanabe [11] implemented a lunch delivery web system for blind people. To decrease their mental workload for selection, researchers observed the effective communication for ordering from the menu between two blind people. Based on the analysis of their dialogue, a prototype system was developed, which consists of three steps by speech: rough selection, selection of favorites, and final selection.

Bernareggi and Brigatti [12] introduced a speech input technique to enable the blind users to write mathematical documents. The system was tested by five blind participants and each of them was asked to complete four tasks of inserting mathematical expressions. All tasks were completed by typing on a keyboard and later by speech input. The results demonstrated that the execution time for speech input was faster than typing with complex short-cut keys.

A barcode-based system was implemented to help blind users identify objects in the environment [13]. The QR code (two-dimensional barcode) is affixed to the object that the blind user wants to know more information about. A camera phone with QR reader software decodes the barcode to a URL and directs the phone's browser to get an audio file from the website, containing a verbal description of the object. Two potential scenarios were identified to get benefits from the system: museum and shopping, where it could provide auditory guide for blind people.

2.2 Tactile Assistive Systems

In this category, the papers report on tactile assistive systems that help blind people in the areas of tactile navigation, Braille, and touch graphics. Table 2 summarizes tactile assistive systems reviewed in this section.

Table 2. Tactile assistive systems.

Function	Application	Evaluation
Tactile navigation	Vibrotactile helmet [14]	No evaluation
	Virtual environment [15]	Usability evaluation (N = 5)
Braille	Braille window system [16]	Usability evaluation (N = 8)
	V-Braille [17]	No evaluation
Touch graphics	System of tactile photo/portrait [18]	No evaluation
	Haptic gray scale image [19]	Usability evaluation by 20 blind and blindfolded participants
	Fingertip Guiding Manipulator [20]	Usability evaluation by 18 blindfolded and 2 blind participants

Tactile Navigation
To avoid for blind people's collision, and for workers in low-light environments, Mann et al. [14] presented a navigation system, using a range camera and an array of vibration actuators built into a helmet (Fig. 3). The blind person wears the Kinect range camera on the helmet and the camera can be kept in motion rather than stationary. Six vibration actuators of the helmet are positioned along that person's forehead to provide the corresponding haptic feedbacks. From varying degrees of the haptic feedbacks from the vibration actuators, the blind user can clearly understand the depth in the surroundings.

Spatial information is not accessible for blind people, so some learning tools are provided as a preparation for navigation before going out to the real environment. In response to this research context, Huang [15] presented a learning tool of simulating a real-world environment by using 3D virtual simulation technology, to assist blind people to access non-visual spatial information. A 3D virtual environment in Stockholm was simulated by haptic and audio cues for the experimental study. Five blind participants explored the building in 3D virtual environment to find different locations. The qualitative analysis of the experiment indicated that the virtual environment with both haptic and audio cues was easiest to learn, then the condition with haptic and the last one was the condition with audio.

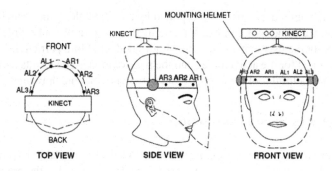

Fig. 3. Kinect range camera and six vibration actuators on a helmet [14].

Braille

Recent window systems present lavish information in a graphic layout. Thus, the text-only access of a standard Braille device is no longer sufficient to enable the blind people to access the window systems. Prescher et al. [16] presented a two-dimension Braille Window System (BWS) based on a tactile display. This tactile display consists of a pin-matrix of six separate regions, to enable the blind person to receive different types of information simultaneously. The primary region among six can be shown in text- or graphics-based manners through four different views. In user experiment, eight blind participants aimed at examining the intuitiveness of operating BWS, and the usability of the system. They confirmed the concept of the Braille windows, regions and views and demonstrated that it provided an efficient way for the interaction.

Braille devices play an important role to enable blind people to access information from the computer systems. Völkel et al. [17] implemented a Braille pin-matrix device, which allows presenting tactile graphics on a matrix of 60 times 120 pins. The pin-matrix device is made up of vertical Braille modules and each of them is equipped with a separate sensor and a separate actuator electronic, capable of detecting multiple points of contact.

Graphics

Although face photos/portraits information is very important in emotional lives, such information is almost inaccessible to blind people. Li et al. [18] proposed a prototypical system namely TactileFace, aiming at enabling blind people to access facial images by automatically creating the corresponding tactile graphics. Two important features were introduced for the desired TactileFace system: (1) Blind people were capable of accessing the system independently; (2) Tactile facial images could be created by the system in a real time.

Nikolakis et al. [19] proposed to develop an interactive system, converting gray images into the haptic representation. Twenty blind and blindfolded participants evaluated the system and the results demonstrated that they could distinguish dark and light areas in the gray images and understand the simple shapes.

Yusoh et al. [20] developed a haptic graphic system, aiming at helping blind people create mental images of line drawings. The system is made of a fingertip guiding manipulator (FGM) with two-mode functions: the passive mode and the active mode. In the active mode, the blind user's fingertip is pulled by the FGM along line drawings. In the passive mode, the blind user can freely move the fingertip in the only direction of the line drawings. In the user experiment, the blindfolded and blind participants evaluated the time consumed for the active mode and the passive mode. The results demonstrated that FGM was a helpful tool for teaching and perceiving the line drawings.

3   Problems in Social Interaction

In the literature review, we gain the overview knowledge of available HCI designs for blind people. Many useful devices and systems are created to solve the practical problems that blind people encounter in their daily lives. However, HCI designs which aim to solve problems in social interaction for blind people are seldom mentioned. In face-to-face communication, blind people are more introverted, submissive, and less confident due to the sighted control. They have the poor social adaption [21]. The impatience, discomfort, or intolerance of the sighted is the other important factor in determining the level of the involvement for the blind person [22].

Kemp [23] investigated social interaction of blind people by controlled, experimental methods. In the experiment, 30 blind and 30 sighted participants were formed into three groups: 10 blind-blind pairs, 10 blind-sighted pairs, and 10 sighted-sighted pairs. Each pair was videotaped while participating in 15-min discussion sessions. Subsequent ratings were made on such dimensions as style, synchrony, and content of interchanges. The impression formation questionnaire was adopted before and after discussions on the accuracy, confidence, and quality of impression.

Several differences were found between blind and sighted people's social behaviors. For example, frequency of interruptions in blind pairs was twice as great as sighted pairs. Blind participants tended to report feelings less confident in their responses. Fewer physical gestures were observed in blind participants. Blind participants turned toward their conversation partner less often than did the sighted.

In social skills training with visually impaired people, particular interest has been the improvement of eye contact [22]. The basis for these effort has been social psychology studies, which documented the significance of visual cues in social communication [24, 25]. Lack of eye contact may cause sighted people to feel that they are not fully in communication [24]. In training, the blind person was asked to simply "look" in the direction towards a sighted person who is talking to her. However, gaze signals among sighted people are far from a simple and unnatural "look". For example, a sighted speaker consciously or unconsciously uses gaze or eye contact to communicate with the conversation partner in face-to-face communication. Through the conversation partner's eyes, she can sense interest, engagement, happiness etc.

4   Research Implementation

Based on the social problem of blind people, we narrow down our research scope and focus on gaze and eye contact, which have important social meaning in face-to-face communication. Our research objective is to design an assistive system, which can simulate natural gaze for the blind person, to improve the conversation quality between the sighted and blind people in face-to-face communication.

The system is expected to have three primary functions (Fig. 4):

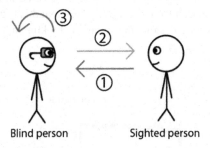

Blind person   Sighted person

Fig. 4. Three functions of gaze simulation between blind and sighted people: (1) Feel eye gaze; (2) Send "eye gaze"; (3) Feel eye contact.

Feel eye gaze: By converting the gaze (visual cues) to corresponding tactile signals, the blind person can perceive eye gaze from the sighted in face-to-face communication.

Send "eye gaze": A wearable glasses device is proposed to simulate the natural "eye gaze" for the blind person as a visual reaction to the sighted interlocutor.

Feel eye contact: After simulating natural gaze for the blind person, more precise eye-to-eye communication (eye contact) can be established between the sighted and blind people. The blind person can feel corresponding tactile signals when the "eye contact" happens.

Early in our research project, a qualitative study was conducted on nonverbal signals (gaze, facial expressions, body gestures etc.) for blind people in face-to-face communication and problems they had due to the lack of visual signals [25]. Based on the literature review and preliminary investigations, the research scope was narrowed down and focused on gaze signals. A conceptual design of E-Gaze glasses was proposed, aiming at creating gaze communication between the sighted and blind people in face-to-face conversations. Twenty totally blind and low vision participants were interviewed to evaluate and envision four design features of the E-Gaze [25].

In order to make gaze signals accessible to the blind person, we developed a prototype, namely Tactile Band. The tactile feedback enabled the blind person to feel attention (gaze signals) from the sighted and tried to enhance the level of engagement in face-to-face communication [26]. To simulate natural gaze for blind people, we implemented a working prototype, E-Gaze glasses, an assistive device based on eye tracking. E-Gaze established the "eye contact" between the sighted and blind people in face-to-face conversations [27]. We refined gaze behaviors of the E-Gaze and designed a gaze model that combined the eye-contact mechanism with a turn-taking strategy, which linked the eye gaze animation with the conversation flow. We further proposed an experimental design to test the E-Gaze and hypothesize that the model-driven gaze simulation can enhance the conversation quality between the sighted and blind people in the face-to-face communication [28].

In our latest E-Gaze system, we let the blind person wear both E-Gaze glasses and Tactile Wristband in the experiment, not only to enable the blind person to feel the "eye contact" from the sighted, but also to send the "e-gaze" to the sighted in a dyadic conversation. If the gaze signal from the sighted is detected to hit the eye area of the blind person, a slight vibration from the Tactile Wristband is triggered by the vibration motor. So the blind person knows that the sighted is looking at her. The overview of E-Gaze system is shown in Fig. 5.

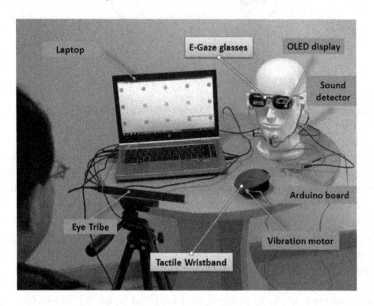

Fig. 5. The overview of the E-Gaze system.

5   Conclusion

In this paper, a preliminary background review about HCI design for blind people is presented. We conduct this review for the general understanding of the current assistive technologies and applications for blind people in the HCI field. Many useful devices and systems are created to solve the practical problems that blind people meet in their daily lives, but the important parts are missing: problems in social interaction, especially in face-to-face communication. The review of social problems for blind people is also presented: due to lack of gaze communication, blind people are more introverted, submissive, and less confident in face-to-face communication with sighted people. Based on the literature review and the primary study, our research objective is to design gaze simulation for people with visual impairments. Finally, we present the iterative prototypes of gaze simulation for blind people in face-to-face communication and report the implementations so far.

Acknowledgments. We thank our colleagues at the Systemic Change research group in Eindhoven University of Technology who offer suggestions and ideas for this project. This research is supported by the China Scholarship Council.

References

1. World Health Organization. Visual impairment and blindness (2014). http://www.who.int/mediacentre/factsheets/fs282/en/. Accessed August 2014
2. Muller, M.J., Wharton, C., McIver Jr., W.J., Laux, L.: Toward an HCI research and practice agenda based on human needs and social responsibility. In: Proceedings of the ACM SIGCHI Conference on Human Factors in Computing Systems, pp. 155–161 (1997)
3. Oppenheim, C., Selby, K.: Access to information on the World Wide Web for blind and visually impaired people. Aslib Proc. **51**(10), 335–345 (1999)
4. Stephanidis, C.: User interfaces for all: new perspectives into human-computer interaction. User Interfaces All-Concepts Methods Tools **1**, 3–17 (2001)
5. Iglesias, R., Casado, S., Gutierrez, T., Barbero, J.I., Avizzano, C.A., Marcheschi, S., Bergamasco, M.: Computer graphics access for blind people through a haptic and audio virtual environment. In: The 3rd IEEE International Workshop on Haptic, Audio and Visual Environments and Their Applications, HAVE 2004, Proceedings, pp. 13–18 (2004)
6. Ivanchenko, V., Coughlan, J., Shen, H.: Crosswatch: a camera phone system for orienting visually impaired pedestrians at traffic intersections. In: Miesenberger, K., Klaus, J., Zagler, W., Karshmer, A. (eds.) ICCHP 2008. LNCS, vol. 5105, pp. 1122–1128. Springer, Heidelberg (2008). https://doi.org/10.1007/978-3-540-70540-6_168
7. Dunai, L., Fajarnes, G.P., Praderas, V.S., Garcia, B.D., Lengua, I.L.: Real-time assistance prototype—a new navigation aid for blind people. In: IECON 2010-36th Annual Conference on IEEE Industrial Electronics Society, pp. 1173–1178 (2010)
8. Wentz, B., Lazar, J.: Are separate interfaces inherently unequal?: an evaluation with blind users of the usability of two interfaces for a social networking platform. In: Proceedings of the 2011 iConference, pp. 91–97 (2011)
9. Brady, E.L., Zhong, Y., Morris, M.R., Bigham, J.P.: Investigating the appropriateness of social network question asking as a resource for blind users. In: Proceedings of the 2013 Conference on Computer Supported Cooperative Work, pp. 1225–1236 (2013)
10. Jayant, C., Ji, H., White, S., Bigham, J.P.: Supporting blind photography. In: The Proceedings of the 13th International ACM SIGACCESS Conference on Computers and Accessibility, pp. 203–210 (2011)
11. Nishimoto, T., Watanabe, T.: An analysis of human-to-human dialogs and its application to assist visually-impaired people. In: Miesenberger, K., Klaus, J., Zagler, W., Karshmer, A. (eds.) ICCHP 2008. LNCS, vol. 5105, pp. 809–812. Springer, Heidelberg (2008). https://doi.org/10.1007/978-3-540-70540-6_120
12. Bernareggi, C., Brigatti, V.: Writing mathematics by speech: a case study for visually impaired. In: Miesenberger, K., Klaus, J., Zagler, W., Karshmer, A. (eds.) ICCHP 2008. LNCS, vol. 5105, pp. 879–882. Springer, Heidelberg (2008). https://doi.org/10.1007/978-3-540-70540-6_131
13. Al-Khalifa, H.S.: Utilizing QR code and mobile phones for blinds and visually impaired people. In: Miesenberger, K., Klaus, J., Zagler, W., Karshmer, A. (eds.) ICCHP 2008. LNCS, vol. 5105, pp. 1065–1069. Springer, Heidelberg (2008). https://doi.org/10.1007/978-3-540-70540-6_159

14. Mann, S., Huang, J., Janzen, R., Lo, R., Rampersad, V., Chen, A., Doha, T.: Blind navigation with a wearable range camera and vibrotactile helmet. In: Proceedings of the 19th ACM International Conference on Multimedia, pp. 1325–1328 (2011)
15. Huang, Y.Y.: Exploration in 3D virtual worlds with haptic-audio support for nonvisual spatial recognition. Hum.-Comput. Interact. **332**, 269–272 (2010)
16. Prescher, D., Weber, G., Spindler, M.: A tactile windowing system for blind users. In: Proceedings of the 12th International ACM SIGACCESS Conference on Computers and Accessibility, pp. 91–98 (2010)
17. Völkel, T., Weber, G., Baumann, U.: Tactile graphics revised: the novel BrailleDis 9000 pin-matrix device with multitouch input. In: Miesenberger, K., Klaus, J., Zagler, W., Karshmer, A. (eds.) ICCHP 2008. LNCS, vol. 5105, pp. 835–842. Springer, Heidelberg (2008). https://doi.org/10.1007/978-3-540-70540-6_124
18. Li, N., Wang, Z., Yuriar, J., Li, B.: TactileFace: a system for enabling access to face photos by visually-impaired people. In: Proceedings of the 16th International Conference on Intelligent User Interfaces, pp. 445–446 (2011)
19. Nikolakis, G., Moustakas, K., Tzovaras, D., Strintzis, M.G.: Haptic representation of images for the blind and the visually impaired. In: Proceedings of the 11th International Conference on Human-Computer Interaction (2005)
20. Yusoh, S.M.N.S., Nomura, Y., Kokubo, N., Sugiura, T., Matsui, H., Kato, N.: Dual mode fingertip guiding manipulator for blind persons enabling passive/active line-drawing explorations. In: Miesenberger, K., Klaus, J., Zagler, W., Karshmer, A. (eds.) ICCHP 2008. LNCS, vol. 5105, pp. 851–858. Springer, Heidelberg (2008). https://doi.org/10.1007/978-3-540-70540-6_126
21. Petrucci, D.: The blind child and his adjustment. New Outlook Blind **47**, 240–246 (1953)
22. Van Hasselt, V.B.: Social adaptation in the blind. Clin. Psychol. Rev. **3**(1), 87–102 (1983)
23. Kemp, N.J.: Social interaction in the blind. Int. J. Rehabil. Res. **3**(1), 87–88 (1980)
24. Argyle, M., Dean, J.: Eye-contact, distance and affiliation. Sociometry **28**, 289–304 (1965)
25. Qiu, S., Hu, J., Rauterberg, M.: Nonverbal signals for face-to-face communication between the blind and the sighted. In: Proceedings of International Conference on Enabling Access for Persons with Visual Impairment (ICEAVPI 2015), pp. 157–165 (2015)
26. Qiu, S., Rauterberg, M., Hu, J.: Designing and evaluating a wearable device for accessing gaze signals from the sighted. In: Antona, M., Stephanidis, C. (eds.) UAHCI 2016. LNCS, vol. 9737, pp. 454–464. Springer, Cham (2016). https://doi.org/10.1007/978-3-319-40250-5_43
27. Qiu, S., Anas, S.A., Osawa, H., Rauterberg, M., Hu, J.: E-gaze glasses: simulating natural gazes for blind people. In: Proceedings of the TEI 2016: Tenth International Conference on Tangible, Embedded, and Embodied Interaction, pp. 563–569 (2016)
28. Qiu, S., Anas, S.A., Osawa, H., Rauterberg, M., Hu, J.: Model-driven gaze simulation for the blind person in face-to-face communication. In: Proceedings of the 4th International Conference on Human-Agent Interaction, pp. 59–62 (2016)

On Interdependent Metabolic Structures: The Case of Cyborg Garden

Zenovia Toloudi[1](✉) and Spyridon Ampanavos[2]

[1] Dartmouth College, Hanover, NH 03755, USA
zenovia@gmail.com
[2] Harvard University, Cambridge, MA 02139, USA
sampanavos@gsd.harvard.edu

Abstract. This paper revisits the concept of metabolic architecture by introducing the pair of plants and ambient computing, constructing a stage between automation and interaction. By acknowledging a technophilic present, the paper proposes ambient computing to control the metabolic architecture, but together with a vulnerable component, that of plants. This way it develops an interdependent system among technology, people, space, and plants. Assuming that in the future, the role of plants (and potentially people) will depend on computers, the automatic process requires to be thought together with vulnerability and unpredictability, so it is more humane. In this system, there is no redundancy, plants and ambient computing are predominant aspects of the design. The plants paired with ambient computing constitute a mediator for future *technoecologies* operating both through automation/control and people's care/interaction. The paper explores this position through a project, which is a provocative statement on ecology, *Photodotes V: Cyborg Garden* (2015).

Keywords: Affective computing · Cyborg · Light art · Interaction design
Installation art · Sensory architecture · Metabolic architecture

1 Introduction

1.1 Metabolic Structures

Metabolic architecture is a design strategy engaging with "the living" and aiming to create impact in the daily lives, quality of space, and well-being of those who experience it [1]. Metabolic architecture deals with material transformations caused by either growth or decay of organic matter, or it relates to immaterial transformations caused by environmental or artificial stimuli. Through these processes, metabolism within architecture becomes an apparatus that produces constant changes in form, space, and in user perception. The ever-changing patterns of immaterial forces, may relate to weather conditions, it may be about movement of people, or movement of light and sound. Time involves the idea of replenishment; that the work is always new. Space comes into existence during the time the work moves or is moved. Such architecture becomes a machine that produces effects as well as time-sensitive and ephemeral spaces, which affect

© Springer International Publishing AG, part of Springer Nature 2018
N. Streitz and S. Konomi (Eds.): DAPI 2018, LNCS 10921, pp. 135–145, 2018.
https://doi.org/10.1007/978-3-319-91125-0_11

feelings, emotions, and senses, and can inspire people to stop rushing, wonder, reflect, and also connect. This approach is extensively presented in the chapter "Architecture and Living Matter(s): From Art/Architectural Installations to Metabolic Aesthetics," published in The Routledge Companion to Biology in Art and Architecture [1]. There is a number of speculative yet tangible examples, materializing these ideas, such as *Photodotes* installations series, which have started in 2011. The *Photodotes* series of installations emphasize how light's relation to energy and survival affects human well-being. They consist of elements of mixed materials that display light emission while being light-wired to natural and artificial lights. They often combine hydroponics and fiberoptic cables illustrating how light accelerates the growth of living organisms, such as edible plants. These projects are experiments in space. They act as architectural interventions, also as visual commentaries and/or spatial statements. They intentionally interrupt peoples' routines through the creation of a spatial interplay, a series of phenomena, triggering viewers' curiosity, instigating multiple senses, beyond the visual promoting therefore an architecture in which audiences can participate in and react to (Fig. 1).

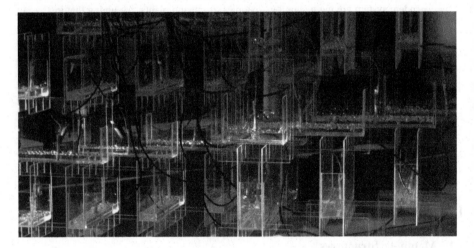

Fig. 1. Photodotes III: Plug-N-Plant (2013). Project by Zenovia Toloudi/Studio Z. Photograph by Zenovia Toloudi.

1.2 Interdependency

Installation art has by definition the viewer as an integral component of the work - without them, the work does not exist [2]. But the degree of this integration, as well as the dynamics involved in it, vary. In most cases there is a common desire leaning towards automation, independency, performance, and spectacle. But in other cases where artists/architects have been working with the immaterial, and the temporal, one can examine how the creators have been re-producing temporal phenomena, what are the elements, the overall ambiance, the level of nuance, what triggers the change, etc. In addition how these creators have imagined the role of humans in the construction of this experience:

how they have set up the experience, as automated, reactive, experiential, or interdependent.

The pioneer artists Otto Piene and Hans Haacke created and worked with machines that produce immaterial patterns and display flows of energy [3]. In case of Otto Pienne *Lichtballett* (1961) the creation of ever-changing rhythms and patterns of light moving in space, metabolic architecture is experienced in darkness and silence through projections, reflections, illuminations, and glows that evolve and flow into energy, infinity, imagination, and memory. Piene himself referred to the silent aspect of the work, as a reaction to loud sounds produced by the war [4]. The project has been automated in terms of the light patterns production. But to fully experience this dimension of healing, one would need to even had a kind of bad/loud past experience to heal from.

Hans Haacke blurred the boundaries between the artificial and natural, the mechanical and living. Haacke has been interested in systems and created works to intentionally show how things interrelate. The elements of his work have often been light, air, grass paired with machines that keep them "alive." This machinic nature of many of his projects would shape the intangible, immaterial elements of space. Caroline Jones, in her essay Artist/System argues, that contemporary artists, like Olafur Eliasson, combine or even appropriate systems art by Haacke (which had no relation to human subjects at the time they were produced) with "perceptual investigations." What is interesting here is that similar works in aesthetics and form, produced with few decades apart, they appear for a different purpose, having the exact opposite intentions (machines and automation versus humans and perception) [5].

1.3   The Vulnerability of Plants

To reinforce the presence of the immaterial and the metabolic in architecture, the *Photodotes* installations have been using plants both as matter and as systems of energy.

From other contemporary works that integrate plants there are two interesting ones by Sean Lally/WEATHERS and Jeremijenko [1]. In these, structure and living matter coexist and coevolve over time. Sean Lally/WEATHERS used multiple plants in *Amplification* (2006–2007), a project which explored the material energies and fluid dynamics in design materials [6]. In *Amplification* the plants are paired with a series of "facilitators," such as tracers of humidity, fans, and lighting, which produced microclimates from heat, water vapor, condensation and air particulates; and therefore the plants offered variability in bloom, growth size, color, scent, and filtration of light. In this case, the immaterial aspects of the environment, such as temperature, humidity, scent, color, and light, materialized through the physiology of the plants. The plants were essentially sensors that capture the subtle changes of the environment and display them.

Engineer and artist Natalie Jeremijenko (1966–) similarly gives shape to the living by setting in relief the vulnerability of plants through public engagement in the ongoing art project, *Tree Logic* (1999–), at MASS MoCA [7]. The plants (inverted and suspended live trees) coexist within a forthright infrastructural system, designed with a metal armature, to support their "unnatural" evolution. By inverting the trees and showcasing their growth based on gravitropic and phototropic forces, Jeremijenko has set up a public experiment that reveals the vulnerability and adaptability of the plants.

In these works, the emphasis has been to use the plants, neither as after-the-fact additions to the left over/surrounding space of architecture/building, nor as decorative elements. But to make them instead integral components of the composition, equal at least, if not the most important elements. The plants in *Photodotes*, being organisms, function in multiple levels which have been explained thoroughly in other essays [1, 8, 9]. But in this paper, the investigation of plants lies on the fact that by being vulnerable and unpredictable they make the system as interdependent, and therefore the new environment as more humane.

Position. This paper revisits the concept of metabolic architecture by introducing the pair of plants and ambient computing, constructing a stage between automation and interaction. By acknowledging a technophilic present, the paper proposes ambient computing to control the metabolic architecture, but together with a vulnerable component, that of plants. This way it develops an interdependent system among technology, people, space, and plants. Assuming that in the future, the role of plants (and potentially people) will depend on computers, the automatic process requires to be thought together with vulnerability and unpredictability, so it is more humane. In this system, there is no redundancy, plants and ambient computing are predominant aspects of the design. The plants paired with ambient computing constitute a mediator for future *technoecologies* operating both through automation/control and people's care/interaction. The paper explores this position through a project, which is a provocative statement on ecology, *Photodotes V: Cyborg Garden* (2015) (Fig. 2).

Fig. 2. Photodotes V: Cyborg Garden (2015). Project by Zenovia Toloudi/Studio Z. Interaction Design: Spyridon Ampanavos. Photograph by Dimitris Papanikolaou.

2   The Case

2.1   About Cyborg Garden

Photodotes V: Cyborg Garden (2015), a hanging garden in large garage space, which included plants, plastic containers, waters, and fiberoptic cables, allowed plants and artificial lights to coexist and coevolve based on people's movements. As visitors approached the installation, the light spectrum changed to enrich the energy provided to the plants' roots while illuminating the garage's dark space. The installation made viewers aware of the diversity of light we encounter in life: the lack of light, homogenous light in interior spaces, and over-lighted spaces.

Cyborg Garden was an isolated laboratory space for endangered organisms, which resembled a natural museum display of species threatened by extinction. Each plant was fed with light via an individual fiberoptic cable. The thick (transparent) fiberoptic cables brought intense light, subjecting each organism to the scrutiny of external observation by people. *Cyborg Garden* relied only on artificial light (other *Photodotes* explored natural light too) to explore a spectrum of wavelengths and colors that are orchestrated by people's movements and interactions. The rationale behind the variation in light was to play out the extremes of homogenous and extremely bright artificial light in sealed environments, and to counter this with a diversity of light that more closely approximates natural light (Fig. 3).

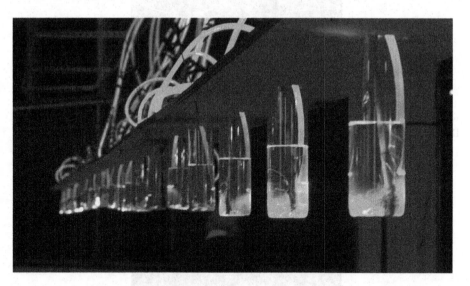

Fig. 3. Photodotes V: Cyborg Garden (2015). Project by Zenovia Toloudi/Studio Z. Interaction Design: Spyridon Ampanavos. Photograph by Saurabh Mhatre.

2.2   On Capsules and Cyborgs

Architect Kurokawa, one the founders of the Metabolism movement, wrote in 1969 that the "capsule is cyborg architecture" [10]. The aesthetics of cyborgs are often associated with automation and technology, wiring and connectivity, as well as machines, appliances and apparatuses [9]. Kurokawa had defined the cyborg as an organism that is partly automated, based on feedback and automated processes, which usually appear in science fiction as half man, half machine. Kurokawa considered the capsule as the ultimate form of prefabricated building, having emancipated itself from the land to become the immediate extension of the moving self, similarly to cars or the traditional Japanese *kago* [11]. In Japanese Metabolism, the capsule is small in size. It is linked to historical elements in architecture, such as the teahouse. The capsule is a tool, a machine for living. Through Philip Galanter's theory of 'complexism', the capsule can refer to modular(ity), embodiment, protective vulnerability, voyeurism, unpredictability, complexity, immateriality and ephemerality [12]. By highlighting the capsule's potential for complexism, the *Capsule as Cyborg Bioarchitecture* essay illustrates how Kurokawa's statement can be reiterated to "capsule as cyborg bioarchitecture" [9] (Figs. 4 and 5).

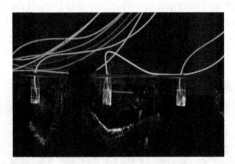

Fig. 4. Photodotes V: Cyborg Garden (2015). Project by Zenovia Toloudi/Studio Z. Interaction Design: Spyridon Ampanavos. Photograph by Dimitris Papanikolaou.

Fig. 5. Photodotes V: Cyborg Garden (2015). Project by Zenovia Toloudi/Studio Z. Interaction Design: Spyridon Ampanavos. Photograph by Dimitris Papanikolaou.

These capsules have high capacity for autonomy, yet unpredictable to some extent in that they materialize the vulnerable self. The wiring of the plants with light energy, along with their capacity to be self-sufficient (e.g., bamboos used as auto-trophs to produce their own food), establishes an automated process. As the bamboo nourishes itself by way of root systems, the units become self-sufficient. Fungus and contamination cause certain plants to die, revealing the vulnerability and unpredict-ability of life. Such fragile situations aspire for protection and surveillance. Enclosed in transparent capsules, these objects are vitrines for surveillance and voyeurism [1] (Fig. 6).

Fig. 6. Photodotes V: Cyborg Garden (2015). Project by Zenovia Toloudi/Studio Z. Interaction Design: Spyridon Ampanavos. Photograph by Dimitris Papanikolaou.

Therefore, the role of the user is integral to plants' existence, as humans, tech-nology, and plants become one interdependent system: the users co-author the event as custodians taking care of the plants, or as performer-spectators offerring the light energy and nutrition through movements and interactions. Depending on human interaction, the plants either flourish or die. Such an unpleasant encounter with their vulnerability cultivates empathy. In *Cyborg Garden*, the plants' presence docu-mented the ever-changing light through their growth and evolution. The metabolic materialized in the interdependent relationship between users and structures [1] (Fig. 7).

Fig. 7. Photodotes V: Cyborg Garden (2015). Project by Zenovia Toloudi/Studio Z. Interaction Design: Spyridon Ampanavos. Photograph by Dimitris Papanikolaou.

3   Ambient Computing

3.1   Lights and Interaction

On the interaction level, the installation is a system of plants, lights, and humans. The visitors become part of the system by directly affecting the amount of light that the plants receive.

Sensing. The presence of the visitors is monitored by an array of proximity sensors. The system uses five Parallax Ping Ultrasonic Range Sensors placed in equal distances along the whole length of the hanging garden. The sensors correspond to five sections, each containing four plants. In this way we gather data describing the presence of people around each of the five groups of plants.

Acting (Lights). Each plant receives light from a 3 W RGB LED source through a fiberoptic cable. In total there are twenty plants, with twenty fiber optic cables, and twenty RGB LEDs.

Control. The LED lights are controlled by an Arduino Mega. In order to receive full color information, each LED requires three signals, which totals to sixty outgoing signals from the Arduino. To make this possible, we daisy-chained eight shift registers (74HC595), regulating external power to sixty channels with a simple transistor configuration for each signal.

For ease of development and convenience of deployment, the ultrasonic sensors are connected to a separate Arduino Uno. The two micro controllers are connected through serial port communication.

Behavior. The information from the sensors is translated to an attention metric, with regard to proximity and duration of the human presence. In a busy physical environment like that of the deployment, the interaction mostly takes place through movement of crowds and less of individuals, which makes the information from the five sensors enough to closely approximate the human presence. The sensor's data are interpolated to achieve a smooth transition between the corresponding areas.

The system responds to attention by changing the amount and the color of the lights. Higher attention will trigger brighter light. The most intense interaction - i.e. when attention exceeds a predefined threshold - triggers an "explosion" effect: a very intense light around the center of attention, that propagates to the whole garden in the form of a wave, gradually fading out.

4   Discussion

4.1   Dual Vulnerability

This paper explained the role of dual vulnerability when inserted in a hybrid design, such as the *Cyborg Garden* installation. The installation became the interface to instigate this duality: people to take care of the plants and plants to take care of people. The hybrid character of the work, which included: contrasting high and low tech materials; the playful component of light interactivity; the spectacular wiring (emphasizing the feeding through light and transferring of energy); the performative aspect for viewers through their body and facial movements it is what eventually activated the actions, thoughts, and relationships.

During the event, people interacted with the plants, but also with each other. Also, the encapsulated plants triggered their curiosity. They asked questions about the feeding, the life cycle. And the imagined other techno-ecological life-cycles for these organisms. At the same time the plants were there to remind people the need to be connected to natural and/or varied light, to be aware about their body rhythms, routines, a better lifestyle.

4.2   On Future Technoecologies

Hughes claimed that in the future, machines will be more like people, and people will be more like machines [13]. This statement can spark questions about how future architecture will be shaped based on automation? And what would the future gardens look like?

Cyborg Garden framed the need for design based on living bio-rhythms. The plants paired with ambient computing constitute the mediators, between energy and us, activators of our emotions. By visualizing real-time, in a bold way, the transferring of energy to our bodies, the installation educates us (or enforces us) to take care of the plants, to take care of ourselves, to activate our feelings, and emotions (Fig. 8).

Fig. 8. Photodotes V: Cyborg Garden (2015). Project by Zenovia Toloudi/Studio Z. Interaction Design: Spyridon Ampanavos. Photograph by Dimitris Papanikolaou.

References

1. Toloudi, Z.: Architecture and living matter(s): From Art/Architectural installations to metabolic aesthetics. In: Terranova, C., Tromble, M. (eds.) The Routledge Companion to Biology in Art and Architecture, pp. 197–217. Routledge Press, London (2016)
2. Bishop, C.: Installation Art: A Critical History. Tate Publishing, London (2014)
3. Toloudi, Z.: Natural and artificial light as energy: experiments in space. In: Proceedings of ACSA 101: New Constellations, New Ecologies, pp. 219–225. ASCA Press, Washington (2013)
4. Piene, O.: Lichtballett, Hans Haacke 1967: Artist Talks, MIT List Visual Arts Center website. listart.mit.edu. https://listart.mit.edu/files/audio/Piene_Haacke_102011.mp3. Accessed 13 Dec 2011
5. Jones, C.A.: Artist/system. In: Dutta, A. (ed.) A second modernism: MIT, architecture, and the 'Techno-Social' moment, pp. 506–549. MIT Press, Cambridge (2013)
6. Lally, S.: Potential energies. In: Lally, S., Jessica Young, J. (eds.) Softspace: from a representation of form to a simulation of space, pp. 33–37. Routledge, Abingdon (2007)
7. Jeremijenko, N.: Tree logic, massmoca.org. http://massmoca.org/event/natalie-jeremijenko/. Accessed 21 December 2015
8. Toloudi, Z.: Ordinary Lilli-pot Gardens: Rendezvous in Tokyo. In: Gil, I. (ed.) MAS Context: Ordinary, vol. 23, pp. 130–147. MAS Studio, Chicago (2014)

9. Toloudi, Z.: The capsule as cyborg bioarchitecture. Technoetic Arts: J. Specul. Res. **14**(1+2), 95–104 (2016)
10. Kurokawa, K.: Metabolism in Architecture. Studio Vista, London (1977)
11. Bijutsukan, M.: Metabolism, the City of the Future: Dreams and Visions of Reconstruction in Postwar and Present-day Japan. Mori Art Museum, Tokyo (2011)
12. Galanter, P.: Complexism and the role of evolutionary art. In: Romero, J., Machado, P. (eds.) The Art of Artificial Evolution: A Handbook on Evolutionary Art and Music, pp. 311–332. Springer, New York (2007). https://doi.org/10.1007/978-3-540-72877-1_15
13. Hughes, J.H.: Citizen Cyborg: Why Democratic Societies Must Respond to the Redesigned Human of the Future. Westview Press, Boulder (2004)

VisHair: A Wearable Fashion Hair Lighting Interaction System

Cheng Yao[1](✉) (iD), Bing Li[1], Fangtian Ying[2], Ting Zhang[3], and Yijun Zhao[4]

[1] College of Computer Science and Technology, Zhejiang University, Hangzhou, China
{yaoch,happyice19870112}@zju.edu.cn
[2] Hubei University of Technology, Wuhan, China
yingft@gmail.com
[3] International Design Institute, Zhejiang University, Hangzhou, China
zhangting5@zju.edu.cn
[4] School of Computer Software Technology, Zhejiang University, Ningbo, China
8635966@qq.com

Abstract. From Apple Watch to Nike HpyerAdapt, wearables and fashion are combining more and more tight. To meet the increasing demands of novel and useful interactive fashion wearables, we design and present VisHair, a head mounted fashion lighting interaction system based on wearable technology which is upgraded from LightingHair. The system mainly discuss how light media emerges in our daily fashion life and the new possibilities brought with interaction and visualization. We build the VisHair system with LED, optical fiber, Arduino with sensors, and mobile APP software. And tests were organized in 3 scenarios (according to 3 level of functions) of self-awareness, arousal awareness and social interaction to see how environment and interactions can provide aesthetic support in personal headwear. However, there're limitations of the system, but the feedback from users are positive and many are willing to see VisHair in market.

Keywords: Interactive aesthetic · Wearable media · Intelligent lighting · Entertainment

1 Introduction

Across different countries and cultures, hair decoration plays a great role in embellishing human beings, not only for beauty, but also for social status indication and religious practices. As the evolution of history and technology, different kinds of material have been taken used to decorate people's hair and outlook. We believe that bringing digital and intelligence elements into personal hair decoration can fresh not only the aesthetic expression of our identity and behavior, but also enrich the functions of hair decoration.

VisHair is a lighting interactive system towards personal fashion based on wearable technology. It mainly discusses how light media emerges in our daily fashion life and the new possibilities brought with interaction, visualization and intelligence. Based on LED system, different light texture and color were carried out and discussed.

© Springer International Publishing AG, part of Springer Nature 2018
N. Streitz and S. Konomi (Eds.): DAPI 2018, LNCS 10921, pp. 146–155, 2018.
https://doi.org/10.1007/978-3-319-91125-0_12

2   Related Work

LED Light is a flexible media used in digital art, and information display. Through coding and designing, it metaphorically conveys information like human movement, emotions and attitudes with its aesthetic features, such as light intensity, dynamic and colors. Being related to our work, Gravity of Light [1], a LED hat has been designed to mimic the field with gravity according to human movement. And Situated Apparel [2], a wearable LED display system, has been designed to display dynamic information during the outdoor sport and situated communication. Many researchers and explorations have been done to analyze sociable and emotional communication within public space scenarios, such as Chit Chat Club [3] and Telemurals [4]. Dunne [5] explore areas of significant potential for the development of smart clothing, and identify the design barriers of achieving commercialization of these applications in four major areas: functionality, manufacture, developmental practice, and consumer acceptance. Vega et al. [6] explored body's surface as an interactive platform by integrating technology into beauty products applied directly to one's skin, fingernails and hair.

Based on prior studies and social psychology theory, the emotional identity and resonance can be stimulated by cross-infection and interoperability obtained in communication scenarios. Thus, we designed and published the LightingHair system [7] in CHI 2017 which claimed a basic hair-like lighting device with a little interaction extension. Not much attentions to the visualization, expression and communication.

3   System Description

VisHair system is an upgrade from the LightingHair that contains three parts, a head mounted part, an arm wearable part, and a mobile software process platform. The head mounted part is HairSlice which is used to do the fashion job by displaying the beauty of lights. However, the arm wearable part is SmartBand which response for the interaction with the wearer. Both wearable parts contain sensors, but the main data transferring part is contained in arm wearable part. Mobile phone is playing a critical role in the whole system because of its strong data processing capabilities. Thus, the mobile end is responsible for all the data calculation, pattern recognition and light form generation.

3.1   Interaction Framework

Figure 1 shows the framework of hair decoration and environment. Originally, physical situation, social environment and personal preference are essential keys to people's outlook and hair style. VisHair amplifies the interactions between hair decoration and wearer, external environment through visualization and behavior interaction. The VisHair system has two data inputs (the monitoring data from sensors and the data manually entered from mobile terminal). HairSlice consists full-color LED for output, Arduino [8] for computational processing, and Bluetooth for data transportation.

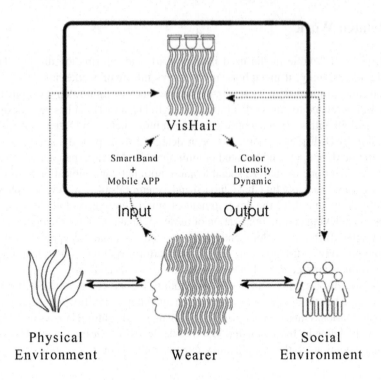

VisHair

SmartBand
+
Mobile APP

Color
Intensity
Dynamic

Input   Output

Physical   Social
Environment   Wearer   Environment

──── Original interaction of human and environment
.... Interactions of VisHair system and environment

Fig. 1. Interaction framework of VisHair

3.2 Hardware

HairSlice. Taking use of optical fiber, it mimics the shape of hair to perform a good visual fusion. HairSlice is basically a unit with a bunch of several optical fibers planted in a Bluetooth data transferring root. Both body-glowing and tip-glowing optical fibers [9] are used in hair slice. They share different LED light source so they can be turned ON/OFF separately according to the mobile APP's command. Each hair slice unit can be attached to wearer's hair with a clip and has its own battery. Full-color LED can display static or dynamic lights with almost all colors. Furthermore, the user can feel the light from fiber's tips and halo without looking directly at light. For other people around, the gorgeous e-fashion is not glaring light pollution. Figure 2(a) and (b) show the constructure of a HairSlice unit. It can communicate with SmartBand and mobile APP through Bluetooth, and display different colors with LED.

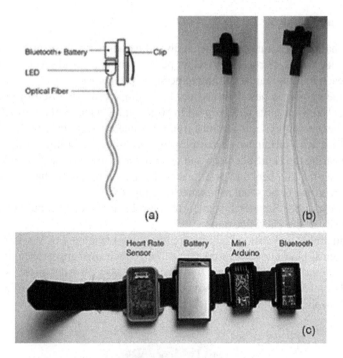

Fig. 2. (a) Constructure of HairSlice (b) Image of HairSlice unit (c) Compositions of SmartBand

SmartBand. Consists of mini Arduino, Bluetooth, heart rate sensor, photosensor, accelerometer, three-axis gyro and battery, it collects data of human movement and heart rate, then communicate with the HairSlice units (see Fig. 2(c)) in realtime.

Currently the whole prototype hardware system is not as small as a perfect wearable device because the modules we use are universal modules which are commonly used in all kinds of smart devices. With integration improvements, we can reduce the band size to a common watch.

3.3 Software

Beyond the data transfer software running on Arduino, VisHair system relies more on the mobile software system. The APP "vishair" actually handles all functions from light effect generation to user interaction recognition. The interface only shows user an input and control entrance, but many things are running behind. What the software handles:

- Separate HairSlice units control.
- User customization input such as color mode customization.
- Wearer heart rate calculation and emotion mode pattern match.
- Wearer arm movement detection and control gesture pattern match.
- Ambient light detection and control pattern match.
- Receiving from other wears' system and response pattern match.

3.4   Wear and Control

For traditional hair decoration, people comb and fix hair with accessories, and observe the appearance with a mirror. For VisHair, people can wear it and set static or dynamic colors for each lighting unit according to personal preference.

When the system is newly turned on, according to the photosensor embodied in SmartBand, HairSlice units will keep off in bright ambient and turn on in dark ambient. It is set to be automatic. User can turn it into manual through the mobile APP named "vishair". Besides, VisHair can also display lighting colors according to digital pictures.

After wearing the HairSlice units and making the connection with mobile APP, the wearer can set the numbers and positions of the units through "vishair". Set color for each unit according to personal preference (see Fig. 4).

While wearing the SmartBand part, arm control is involved to control ON/OFF and effect intensity of the HairSlice units.

Reproducibility and customizability are instincts of fashion. For VisHair, the application of optical fiber allows wearers to customize their own appearance. Besides, the unique appearance of optical fibers with loose end also provides more aesthetics in dynamic. To clearly show how VisHair works, the following content describes it without form customization (Fig. 3).

Fig. 3. Wearing VisHair without restyle

4   Interactive Application Scenarios

Based on the prototype of VisHair, we organized 3 scenario tests for different level functions: self-awareness, affective visualization and social interaction. In each test, there were ten local users. We picked all female users because it is fashion related and hair decoration is very gender oriented. Despite of very few cases, Chinese males cares less about their hair color even if they care much about personal fashion. All users are aged between 17 to 30, not married. Most of them are college students. They wore prototype devices in every test and were given certain tasks to perform.

4.1   Scenario 1: Self-awareness

VisHair is designed to be interactive. Scenario 1 involves HairSlice and "vishair" – the mobile APP. The users were told to accomplish three color switching tasks while wearing HairSlice units. The first two tasks are to pick their two favorite colors for their HairSlice. The third one is to pick a dynamic color pattern for HairSlice (see Fig. 4). After that, they were given 5 min for free play.

Fig. 4. Scenario 1 of lighting control through "vishair" (Color figure online)

All users showed great interests during the color switching tasks. The after-interview proved this phenomena we observed. Even more interesting, 8 users found the "photo match" function which is another type of color switching function according to the photos in your mobile device's album or from your real-time taken. They all enjoyed it and tried with several photos.

4.2 Scenario 2: Affective Visualization

The second scenario test is affective visualization which is to express human's emotion visually with VisHair.

Arousal is a vital element in PAD emotion theory [10]. HRV can reveal people's arousal situation [10]. Since color has a great performance to express affection [11] according to psychological and physiological theories, here we brought dynamic colored lighting to indicate the wearer's arousal situation according to the heart rate detected [12] with the heart rate sensor.

The test mainly involves HairSlice and SmartBand. But user needs "vishair" to switch to the "emotion mode". The users were given images picked from the date-sets of International Affective Picture System (IAPS) [13] which is classified already. All users were navigating through the same images with the same sequence and the same period of time.

The system is set to have green and slow dynamic lighting for low hear rate to express calm. Blue and medium dynamic is for medium heart rate to express sad. Red and fast dynamic is for high heart rate to express happy.

During the test, the dynamic colors shifted between green, blue, and red. The users showed their interests. But only 4 users thought they want to express their emotion with this demonstration-like style. In the after-interview, even those 4 expressed they would only use this mode in particular situations.

Notice the affective cognition with heart rate may not accurate here, and need more experimental data support.

4.3 Scenario 3: Social Interaction

The third scenario test is social interaction which involves HairSlice, SmartBand, and "vishair".

Social interaction means communication between users' systems. Different wearers can contrast a social network. In entertainment scenarios such as party or living concert, different wearers can change colors in VisHair for each other. During the interactive process, such openness experience can help to evolve a game-like, interesting feeling for the wearer who change the color. For whom being changed, he/she can experience surprise and joy. And for others, they will observe and enjoy the color-changing.

Currently the social interaction mode is set to sync modes between two or more friends. We haven't researched deeply into the complex social interaction situations. So we divided users into 5 groups. The first task is one on one sync. Each group has a starter and a joiner. The starter will initiate a friend group. This group can be set open publicly or secretly which means if the joiner needs a password to join or not. The second task is big group sync. 5 groups will be gathered in one room and be synced one by one. The interesting part is in this situation, if the groups happen to have the same light mode and they don't want to sync, the VisHair will bounce to another mode automatically like a bouncing ball.

This test is not about the function test. Just to show if the users are interested about this mode. The observation and the after-interview showed positive feedbacks. All users wanted social interaction with visual expressions. And they like this lighting decoration effects in social interactions. We presume this is because of the user age and occupation. They are too much alike to show the difference. We may achieve huge different feedbacks if we involve different kind of users. We need to research deeper into this field to find more valuable modes in social interaction context.

5 Discussion

We introduce a wearable fashion hair lighting interaction system with three level of functions: a self-customizable hair lighting decoration method, a user-status defined interactive hair lighting decoration method, and a multi-user interactive hair lighting decoration method. We then used three scenarios to test those methods (see Figs. 4, 5 and 6).

Fig. 5. Affective visualization (a) Calm, (b) Sad and (c) Happy (Color figure online)

Fig. 6. Interaction in entertainment scenario

VisHair offers the following advantages: (1) Customizable personal hair decoration with hair-like and energy-saving LED lights. (2) Cool unlimited effect compared to traditional hair dying to increase confidence among people. (3) New visualization and expression method for single user or group of users.

VisHair is also subject to limitations: (1) The decoration effect is now limited in several bunches of HairSlice units because of the limitations of the unit size, the Arduino control capabilities. (2) Some user interaction recognition is not very accurate for some critical application. More sensors and new detection methods should be introduced to improve the accuracy issue.

6   Conclusion and Future Work

Through exploration of different scenarios, it can be seen that bringing digital and intelligent elements into hair decoration provides new functions and aesthetic expressions of hair decoration. Except for the ability of decoration our appearance, it can also become a data collection and display interface.

For future work, we will explore more interactive possibilities, such as interacting with sound or music. Involving and incorporating additional sensors and display. This will bring more applications in entertainment, sport and fashion.

Acknowledgements. The authors thanks all the reviewers for providing valuable insights and suggestions that have helped in substantially improving this paper, as well as all volunteers for general support. This project is supported by the National Natural Science Foundation of China (Grant No. 61332017) and Zhejiang Science and Technology Project (Grant No. 2017C31097).

References

1. Kim, Y., Cho, Y.: SIGCHI extended abstracts: gravity of light. In: CHI 2013 Extended Abstracts on Human Factors in Computing Systems (2013)
2. Tao, Y., et al.: Situated apparel: designing to reinforce affective communication. In: Proceedings of the Ninth International Conference on Tangible, Embedded, and Embodied Interaction, pp. 529–532. ACM, Stanford, California, USA (2015)
3. Karahalios, K.G., Dobson, K.: Chit chat club: bridging virtual and physical space for social interaction. In: 2005 Conference on Human Factors in Computing Systems, CHI 2005, Portland, Oregon, USA, April 2005
4. Karahalios, K., Donath, J.: Telemurals: linking remote spaces with social catalysts. In: Conference on Human Factors in Computing Systems, CHI 2004, Vienna, Austria, April 2004
5. Dunne, L.: Smart clothing in practice: key design barriers to commercialization. Fashion Pract. 2(1), 41–66 (2010)
6. Vega, K., Cunha, M., Fuks, H.: Hairware: conductive hair extensions as a capacitive touch input device. In: Proceedings of the 20th International Conference on Intelligent User Interfaces Companion. ACM, Atlanta, Georgia, USA (2015)
7. Li, B., Zheng, D., Lu, Y., et al.: LightingHair Slice: situated personal wearable fashion interaction system. In: Proceedings of the 2017 CHI Conference Extended Abstracts on Human Factors in Computing Systems, pp. 1824–1828. ACM (2017)
8. Arduino Homepage. https://www.arduino.cc/. Accessed 20 Jan 2018

9. Optical Fiber. https://en.wikipedia.org/wiki/Optical_fiber. Accessed 20 Jan 2018
10. Boehner, K., et al.: How emotion is made and measured. Int. J. Hum. Comput. Stud. **65**(4), 275–291 (2007)
11. Kaya, N., Epps, H.: Relationship between color and emotion: a study of college students. Coll. Student J. **38**(3), 396 (2004)
12. Quintana, D.S., Guastella, A.J., Outhred, T., et al.: Heart rate variability is associated with emotion recognition: direct evidence for a relationship between the autonomic nervous system and social cognition. Int. J. Psychophysiol. **86**(2), 168–172 (2012)
13. International Affective Picture System (IAPS). http://csea.phhp.ufl.edu/media.html. Accessed 20 Jan 2018

Design for Fetal Heartbeat Detection and Monitoring in Pregnancy Care

Biyong Zhang[1,3(✉)], Iuliia Lebedeva[1], Haiqiang Zhang[3], and Jun Hu[1,2]

[1] Department of Industrial Design, Eindhoven University of Technology, Eindhoven, The Netherlands
b.zhang@tue.nl
[2] School of Digital Media, Jiangnan University, Wuxi, China
[3] BOBO Technology, Hangzhou, China

Abstract. The piezoelectric pressure sensor technology has been developed for many years and it shows broad possibilities of using this technology in development of smart wearables for heart rate monitoring. The project goal was to explore the possibility to use the pressure sensor technology in Pregnancy Care. The focus of this project was to come up with concepts of a product that can be used by pregnant women to monitor fetal heartbeat in home-based context, and to explore different ways of representation and visualization of real data.

Keywords: BCG (Ballistocardiograph) · Fetal monitoring · Pregnancy Care
Heartbeat detection

1 Introduction

Findings have confirmed the developing a relationship with the fetus is critical for a successful physical and psychological adjustment to pregnancy and parenthood. Stronger feelings of attachment towards the fetus have been associated with positive health practices of the mother during pregnancy. Mothers with more positive and stronger feelings towards their fetus report more positive feelings towards their infant in the postnatal period [5].

The idea to monitor fetal heartbeat at home-based context is actually not new. For expectant moms and dads, who wish to bond with their unborn baby, the market offers different kinds of dopplers, listening systems and monitors for listening to fetal heartbeat, hiccups and kicks. Most of them can be used already from 10–12 weeks of pregnancy. These devices use a probe to detect the high frequency sound waves produced by the fetal heart using low emission ultrasound technology. Some of the fetal heartbeat listeners offered by the market are connected to the special Apps on a mobile phone, which is actually an interface to use functions of listening to, recording and sharing of the fetal heartbeat. Moreover, some Apps of the devices, such as Modoo and Baby CTG, provide 1-on-1 consulting service from a professional medical team based on monitoring data, what gives the great possibility for expecting mothers to be always in contact with professionals just in case.

© Springer International Publishing AG, part of Springer Nature 2018
N. Streitz and S. Konomi (Eds.): DAPI 2018, LNCS 10921, pp. 156–167, 2018.
https://doi.org/10.1007/978-3-319-91125-0_13

The development of new technologies brings more possibilities to monitor a fetal heartbeat in a user-friendly way. The piezoelectric pressure sensor technology shows broad prospects in the field of the heart rate monitoring [1, 3, 4]. Indeed, some studies have been done for the fetal heart rate diagnostic by using the piezoelectric pressure sensor [6]. Couple of studies describe the ideas of a sensor for fetal heart rate monitoring at home and a wearable system for remote fetal monitoring [2, 7].

However, how a product could be designed combining the new technology and what do the users think of it are still the questions. We introduce several new product concepts and evaluate these concepts with international users from different cultural backgrounds in this project.

2 Concepts Development

The product we are going to develop is supposed to be composed of two main parts:

1. SENSING part: a physical wearable product with the pressure sensor inside to collect the data.
2. ACTUATING part: a product to represent the data (that also could be a physical product or digital representation/visualization).

2.1 Concepts of the SENSING

During the individual brainstorm the concept named 'Smart' maternity pillows was created as the SENSING for collecting the fetal heartbeat data. The idea was based on the existing maternity pillows with the function of 'reading' fetal heartbeat by using the pressure sensor inside.

Two different shapes of the existing maternity pillows C and D shapes were chosen. This choice was made for several reasons. The C pillow nowadays is the most popular maternity pillow that was uniquely designed to follow the natural contour and shape of pregnant woman's body from head to toe, and which is perfect for sleeping and relaxing. The D pillow is compact, portable and versatile pregnancy cushion to support pregnant woman's bump, knees and back. Both pillows are different not only in their shapes and sizes, but also the materials they made from: C pillow – polyester, D pillow – foam. For the both pillows the place for the sensor was chosen by taking into account position of pregnant woman's belly (=approximate position of a fetus) when the women are using the pillows. We assumed these places for the sensor as the best cases to get a better signal.

In addition, we also consider a variant of the D pillow as another option which is called double D shape. As shown in Fig. 1, the D shape pillow is available for one side, while the double D shape pillow is available for both sides.

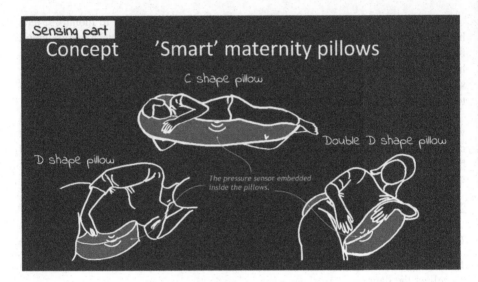

Fig. 1.

2.2   Concepts of the ACTUATING

We wanted to come up with an idea of the product that represents 'sign of life' of a baby and gives to a pregnant woman feeling of the 'connection with a baby', as well as for other family members.

During the Concepts development phase while brainstorming individually several concepts named 'Smart' bracelet, 'Creature' on a phone and 'Live' toy were created as different ideas of a second part of the product as the ACTUATING for visualization and representation of the fetal heartbeat real data.

1. Concept: 'Smart' bracelet

For the first concept as inspiration was a mood board with some existing fancy fitness trackers for women that look like jewelry.

The concept was named as 'Smart' bracelet (Fig. 2). The form of the main part of the bracelet is the shape of a womb with a baby (or an abstract shape of a fetus) inside. The baby on the bracelet has a small heart that supposed to blink when the real heartbeat of a baby detected by the SENSING. If it could be technically possible and we could extract data such as kicks we could also add indicators on the fetal feet to show kicks as well. On the bracelet there are 42 indicators around the womb shape that actually represent 42 weeks of pregnancy. On the bracelet a pregnant woman can see a current week of her pregnancy and how many weeks approximately left before the birth. The inspiration specifically for the last-mentioned feature was the idea of a pregnancy calendar that is used nowadays in the most of the pregnancy Apps. To be able to use this feature on the bracelet, a simple additional App is needed that can store some basic settings and collect data.

After coming up with the concept of the 'Smart' bracelet, some existing ideas of the 'smart' bracelets in Pregnancy Care were found (Fig. 3):

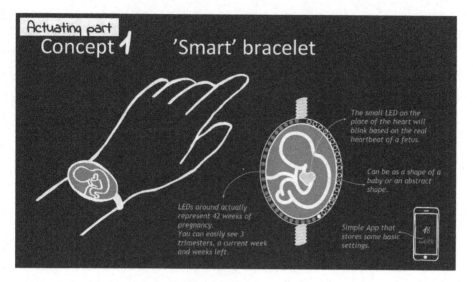

Fig. 2.

- Lisawatch – a bracelet that works as a sensing tool for fetal kicks and the actuating is displayed a mobile phone App (developed in Beijing, China) [8].
- Birthstone – an anti-radiation healthy band smart bracelet for pregnant women.
- Fibo bracelet – a smart bracelet for men to feel kicks of their unborn babies (an idea from Danish startup) [9].

Fig. 3.

2. Concept: 'Creature' on a mobile phone

For the second concept as an inspiration were some beautiful pictures of the body art on pregnant women's bellies. This idea was about the visualization of a 'creature' inside a belly on a mobile phone screen. Moreover, to keep the idea of the visualization to be different over time we were inspired by the idea of the digital game 'tamagotchi' that was so popular in 90s, where creatures in the game grew up during the definite period of time (Fig. 4).

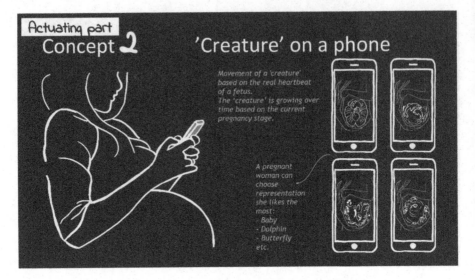

Fig. 4.

The concept was named as 'Creature' on a mobile phone (later on as just Visualization on a mobile phone). The idea was as a visual representation on a mobile phone screen a belly with a 'creature' inside. A pregnant women can chose representation she likes the most of feeling her baby, for example, baby, clam, fish, butterfly, flower, etc. Movements of these 'creatures' supposed to be based on the real heartbeat of a baby – fish is floating, butterfly is moving her wings, flower is moving its petals, etc. The size of the 'creatures' supposed to be changed over time based on a stage of pregnancy, thereby the 'creatures' will grow.

3. Concept: 'Live' toy

For the third concept as an inspiration was a mood board with different kind of pillows and toys of different shapes and forms, some of which have breathing, warming and lighting effects (Fig. 5).

The concept was named as 'Live' toy. It was an idea that actually came out from another idea of having only one pillow that works as the SENSING and the ACTUATING at the same time, for example, a pillow that gives haptic feedback like heartbeat or just can 'breath' based on real heartbeat of a baby.

3 Evaluation

Since the target user group may have multicultural backgrounds, we hope these concepts can be evaluated by the users living in different countries. Therefore, video prototypes were considered to be the best choice for the evaluation. To do that we created and showed to our users a video with the concepts and asked them in the form of an online survey to give their feedback about the ideas. This approach could help us to get already in advance insights from potential users and show more or less if the idea actually looks promising for the market in the future.

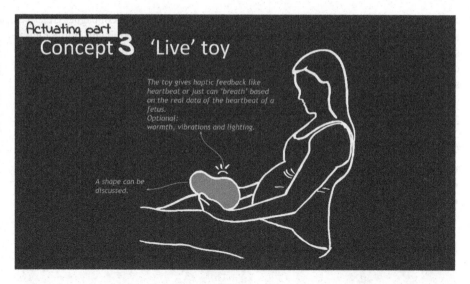

Fig. 5.

3.1   Process

First of all, a video with the concepts was created. The idea was to show in the video the all 3 pillows (C, D and Double D shapes) with an explanation that they are actually 'smart' version of the existing maternity pillows with the pressure sensors embedded inside that help the pillows detect fetal heartbeat. In the video after showing the pillows all 3 ideas of the ACTUATING were shown – 'Smart' bracelet, 'Creature' on a phone and 'Live' toy as they were prepared. The idea of the 'Creature' on a phone for the Online User tests was renamed to a simple Visualization on a mobile phone. Since it was not possible to record a video with the prototypes we made with any pregnant woman in the home context with the pillows, for the video some part of the existing videos of the maternity pillows C, D and Double D shapes were used.

When the video was ready, a short survey was created by using the platform TypeForm. The survey had a link to the video with the concepts and several questions according to the video, such as:

- Would the participants like to have at home a 'Smart' pillow that can 'read' fetal heartbeat?
- Which pillow from the video the participants like the most and would like to use at home?
- Which actuating from the video the participants like the most?

The initial version of the video and questions were prepared in English, then two more versions were prepared in Chinese and Russian languages based on the English version. The both Chinese and Russian versions were as duplicates of the English version with literal translation of the questions. In the Chinese and Russian versions, the same video was used with the same voice-over, but with the subtitles in Chinese and in Russian respectively.

All 3 versions of the Online survey were shared as links within colleagues, relatives and friends and posted in social medias and special forums for pregnant. In the Online survey could participate not only pregnant women, but also women who had just delivered their baby 0–12 month ago, what was mentioned on the main page of the surveys.

3.2 Results

After 3 weeks following amount responses were received:

- English version – 27
- Chinese version – 2
- Russian version – 19

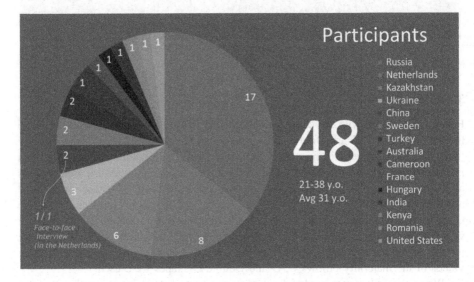

Fig. 6.

In total 48 women from 15 countries at the time of deriving the data were involved in the Online User tests with the age range 21–38 years old in different pregnancy stages and also who had just delivered their baby (Fig. 6):

- 1st Trimester – 4
- 2nd Trimester – 5
- 3rd Trimester – 17
- Gave birth (0–12 month ago) – 22

Many positive expressions from the participants about the ideas presented in the video were received, such as:

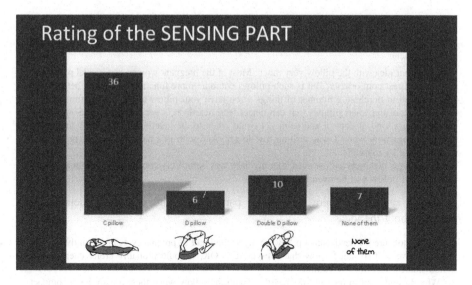

Fig. 7.

"It's a nice idea", "Good idea", "I like everything!", "Nice concept!" "I wished this be exist when I was pregnant!", "It takes away some fear when you don't feel your baby", "I like the idea with fetal heartbeat detection. It would be super nice to know how my baby is doing in my belly".

Couple of the participants pointed that the ideas are good especially for the first pregnancy:

"I think it will be interesting especially during the first pregnancy!", "Really good ideas, especially for those who pregnant first time and don't have experience".

Couple of the women commented that they would prefer to have the sensor, which monitors the fetal heartbeat, not only when using the pillows:

"It would be great if I would have this kind of sensor always with me and not only on a horizontal position only by using the pillow", "It's pity that the sensors only in the pillows. I think that it would be good if you can monitor constantly the heartbeat of a baby. For example, a comfortable belt with the sensors for everyday usage would be good".

29/48 (60%) women mentioned that they would like to have a 'smart' pillow that can detect fetal heartbeat at home. All the participants, regardless of their answer if they would like or would not like to have a 'smart' pillow at home, could make their choice which ideas they like from the video – which pillow and which idea of the visualization/representation.

As a result, the C pillow became a winner from the all pillows presented in the video according to the votes (36 women) (Fig. 7).

Plenty of positive feedback was received about the initial idea about the 'smart' maternity pillows that can detect fetal heartbeat:

"I like that it is integrated in something I already use (the pillow)"
"It's a good idea to create such pillows which can calm down the always worried mommy"

"I love the idea of pregnancy pillow with heartbeat detector!!"
"Awesome idea to use pillows! It's very necessary for a pregnant woman. But the greatest here that using the pillow you can not only rest, but also get a heartbeat of your baby! Very interesting!"
"I like your idea with the pillow very much. Most of the pregnant women use special pillows to sleep and rest comfortably. But if such pillows combine more functions it is even better! You don't need to purchase a number of things - you have your pillow and it is multifunctional"
"The idea of the smart pillows that can detect fetal heartbeat is very interesting! Somehow it gives you a kind of control and calm… I could listen to the heartbeat of my baby and know other things only when I was visiting my doctor. And with this new product I would know everything by myself"
"I'm using C maternity pillow even after my baby was born. Very comfortable. I'm sure that the functional pillow will be even better!"

At the same time there were some participants who expressed their skeptical opinions about the ideas:

"I'm … not sure if I need such a pillow on my second half of pregnancy as I constantly feel my fetus movement so that I know that everything is OK. I would probably prefer cheaper, but non-smart pillow for my comfort"
"Why do you want to measure the heartbeat with the pillow when there are so many compact technologies present in the market? I don't see a reason why I would prefer this one over others. Moreover, it only measures the heartbeat" "I've never felt concern over my fetal heartbeat. I trust my body is doing what it needs to do and I rely on my midwife to tell me otherwise. I think this is an unnecessary item playing into people with stressful personalities"

One of the women expressed her doubts by comparing the 'smart' pillow with a Doppler she currently uses:

"I own a doppler which can be used much earlier than the pillow (I imagine)… I cannot imagine it to be nearly as accurate as a doppler".

Also, different concerns were expressed from the participants about situations if something can be wrong, what we should definitely take into account:

"I would worry if… something goes wrong with technology. This results in stress and that is not a good thing"
"What if something will go wrong with the system and panic will happen? I had a situation when before the labor doctors checked the heartbeat of my baby. Something went wrong with a device, all values were shown not correctly, everyone started to panic"

Different opinions were received about the ideas of the visualization/representation of the fetal heartbeat data. There were participants who liked different ideas:

"I like the idea with the bracelet"
"I prefer the smartphone as a main device to connect to the pillow"

Since in the video very simple prototypes were shown, we can assume that the visualization style might have effect on the opinion of the participants.
Couple of the women seems specifically did not like the visual and representation:

"I don't like the idea of representation as blinking butterfly/fish etc. I'd better prefer to see the fetal heartbeat rate"
"I'd like not to compare my child to an animal (fish or cat or whoever). Baby is a baby. I am waiting for Baby, not for butterfly or a flower"

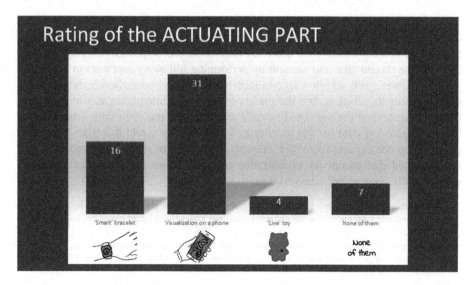

Fig. 8.

"I don't like a toy... Looks like for a kinder garden"

One woman expressed the idea about representation of the fetal heartbeat in the same pillow:

"I think there is enough to have kind of indicator on the pillows C and D shapes looks like a small heart which will be beating based on your fetal heartbeat. And you don't need any additional stuff".

Some of the concerns from the participants about the idea of the 'Smart' bracelet mostly was about the fact that it is an extra thing that they need to buy and wear, or because they just do not like it:

"I would like it to be cost efficient. I won't buy a smart watch just for this case" "I don't really like the smart bracelet. While being pregnant for example I didn't really like anything on my wrists"
"I don't like smart watches"
"I don't wear a watch, and wouldn't want to start wearing one during pregnancy".

Among all ideas the idea of the Visualization on a mobile phone got the most number of votes (31 women) (Fig. 8). Most of the opinions were that it is the best idea:

"I think that the App is the best!", "The app is the best variant!", "For the functional inspection, I think, the mobile would be the best!", "The phone is the most accessible for me", "As about visualization I prefer a mobile phone. Mobile phone is always with me and no needed to buy and carry new devices".

Only 4 women have chosen the 'Live' toy idea. Some of them commented:

"Toy I don't mind because it is something cute and maybe useful for the baby later on?", "The idea of the toy is cute!".

The low number of votes for this idea could be probably because the initial idea could not be shown clear in the video and participants did not get sense that the pillows and the toy actually match each other. Or maybe the prototype was not good enough. This fact we should take into account by performing following user tests in the future.

The women, with whom a face-to-face interview was conducted, mentioned that she liked actually all ideas, but she prefers to have a mobile phone as a main device. But the bracelet and the toy could be only as additional and extra things, because the last ones "give less data for this monitoring". Moreover, she told that from the mobile visualization she expects more "for example, some data or more history record".

It seemed that except for visualization of the heartbeat of a baby in metaphors women really want to see practical data:

"An interesting idea, but there is also needed to show information about the normal heartbeat of a baby, because a pregnant woman can have concerns about if the heartbeat of her baby is too fast or slow"
"And give more advice like... for example, I'm on the 5th month of the pregnancy... on this stage... what range of heartbeat is normal... Give me more detailed inspection and I feel more professional on this device".

One of the comment was about expecting from the ACTUATING a medical suggestion based on collected data:

"For example, the data... some medical suggestion. For example, on the late stage if the heartbeat is really quick or really slow is abnormal... it can pop out some warning or this kind of reminder 'Mother, you should be careful. Maybe you need to visit a doctor or have more rest...' Things that actually help me to protect my baby"

Some women wanted to be able to see more data from a baby and not only heartbeat:

"Would be great if it can detect the hiccups and imitate the different movements also", "Also it would be nice to know if the baby is sleeping or no".

By performing the Online user tests with a video with the concepts we could get preliminary feedback from the potential users if the ideas are actually attractive for them. Of course, for the real user tests women need to try the prototypes in live – check how comfortable the pillows are with the sensor inside, and at the same time test how usable the ACTUATING prototypes.

Overall, the results from the Online User tests are quite positive, which show that the idea of the 'Smart' maternity pillows seem attractive for the potential users. The question is only to see which product as the ACTUATING actually will be the best in the real context of using the pillows, by taking into account not only practical matters, but also possibility of playful and emotional interactions.

4   Conclusion and Recommendations for Future Development

In this project, we come up with the design of a new 'smart' product for pregnant women which consists two parts as the SENSING – a 'Smart' maternity pillow with the pressure sensors embedded to collect the fetal heartbeat data, and as the ACTUATING – several different concepts of representation and visualization of real data such as 'Smart' bracelet, 'Creature' on a phone (Visualization on a mobile phone) and 'Live' toy. Just by using approaches as Prototyping and Online User tests by showing a video with the concepts we could quickly check the ideas with our potential users and get some positive insights and feedback from them. The results show that the main idea of making existing maternity pillows 'smart' by embedding the pressure sensor inside for baby's heartbeat monitoring looks quite attractive for our potential users. The ideas of the 'Creature' on a phone (Visualization on a mobile phone) and 'Smart' bracelet seem more promising for representation and visualization of the real data.

To turn the prototypes into useable devices, a series of technical tests specifically of the SENSING prototypes are needed. Special schemes should be prepared with explanation how to perform the technical tests and how to adapt the inner materials of the pillows if needed in case of trying out to get a better signal.

References

1. Babu, I.: Piezoelectric composites. Design, fabrication and performance analysis. Eindhoven University of Technology (2013)
2. Fanelli, A., Ferrario, M., Piccini, L., et al.: Prototype of a wearable system for remote fetal monitoring during pregnancy. In: 2010 Annual International Conference of the IEEE Engineering in Medicine and Biology Society, EMBC 2010, pp. 5815–5818 (2010)
3. Jose, S., Shambharkar, C., Chunkath, J.: HRV analysis using ballistocardiogram with LabVIEW. In: Proceedings of the International Conference on Computing and Communications Technologies, ICCCT 2015, pp. 128–132 (2015)
4. Karki, J.: Signal conditioning piezoelectric sensors. Application report, Sensors Peterborough NH, 48, pp. 1–6 (2000)
5. Maas, J.: Mother & fetus: the start of a relationship. Tilburg University (2013)
6. Nassit, M., Berbia, H.: On the fetal heart rate diagnostic technologies. In: 2015 10th International Conference on Intelligent Systems: Theories and Applications, SITA 2015 (2015)
7. Sato, H., Yoshimura, K., Nakamoto, H., et al.: 19.2 cm^3 flexible fetal heart rate sensor for improved quality of pregnancy life. In: Proceedings of the 2016 IEEE Biomedical Circuits and Systems Conference, BioCAS 2016, pp. 140–143 (2017)
8. http://www.lisawatch.com
9. http://www.redbookmag.com/body/pregnancy-fertility/news/a48938/fibo-bracelet-men-pregnancy/

Internet of Things and Smart Cities

Collecting Bus Locations by Users: A Crowdsourcing Model to Estimate Operation Status of Bus Transit Service

Kenro Aihara[1,2(✉)], Piao Bin[1], Hajime Imura[3], Atsuhiro Takasu[1,2], and Yuzuru Tanaka[3]

[1] National Institute of Informatics, 2-1-2 Hitotsubashi, Chiyoda-ku, Tokyo 101-8430, Japan
{kenro.aihara,piaobin,takasu}@nii.ac.jp
[2] The Graduate University for Advanced Studies, Hayama, Japan
[3] Hokkaido University, N-13, W-8, Sapporo, Hokkaido 060-8628, Japan
{hajime,tanaka}@meme.hokudai.ac.jp

Abstract. This paper describes a crowdsourcing model to collect bus locations from onboard passengers.

Bus location service, or realtime bus tracking service, is getting more and more general these days. Some models are proposed to build such services. One approach is facilitated every vehicle has a function to position itself with location sensor, such as GPS receiver, and transmits its own location with time to the server. Another is an environmental approach that bus detectors are deployed along the route to detect ids of nearby buses and transmit to the server. These models are well-established and practical. However, it is not easy to install such services especially for small operators because costs on devices and data transmission are relatively high.

This paper proposes that a sustainable model even for small operators to provide bus locations to passengers. The key idea of the proposal is that collecting bus locations is not by bus operators but by onboard passengers. To collect them, a smartphone application of bus tracker is provided to public. The application shows current locations of buses in operation on bus transit services, while it detects nearby buses around users and transmits bus ids with time and location of detection to the service platform. That is, locations of buses are collected by users.

Keywords: Internet of Things · Smart and hybrid cities
Crowdsensing · Crowdsourcing

1 Introduction

This paper describes a crowdsourcing model to collect bus locations from onboard passengers.

Bus location service, or realtime bus tracking service, is getting more and more general these days. Some models are proposed to build such services. One

© Springer International Publishing AG, part of Springer Nature 2018
N. Streitz and S. Konomi (Eds.): DAPI 2018, LNCS 10921, pp. 171–180, 2018.
https://doi.org/10.1007/978-3-319-91125-0_14

approach is facilitated every vehicle has a function to position itself with location sensor, such as GPS receiver, and transmits its own location with time to the server. Another is an environmental approach that bus detectors are deployed along the route to detect ids of nearby buses and transmit to the server. These models are well-established and practical. However, it is not easy to install such services especially for small operators because costs on devices and data transmission are relatively high. The smaller number of buses are scheduled, the more necessary the bus tracker service is.

Therefore, this paper proposes that a sustainable model even for small operators to provide bus locations to passengers.

2   Background

2.1   Crowdsourcing for Civil Problems

The term "crowdsourcing" was described by Howe in [3] and defined that crowdsourcing is the act of taking a task traditionally performed by a designated agent and outsourcing it by making an open call to an undefined but large group of people [4]. This can take the form of peer-production, but is also often undertaken by sole individuals [2].

The concept of smart cities can be viewed as a recognition of the growing importance of digital technologies for a competitive position and a sustainable future [8]. Although the smart city-agenda, which grants ICTs with the task to achieve strategic urban development goals such as improving the life quality of its citizens and creating sustainable growth, has gained a lot of momentum in recent years.

Tools such as smartphones offer the opportunity to facilitate co-creation between citizens and authority. Such tools have the potential to organize and stimulate communication between citizens and authority, and allow citizens to participate in the public domain [1,10]. One example is FixMyStreet[1] that enables citizens to report broken streetlights and potholes [6]. It is important that these approaches will not succeed automatically and social standards like trust, openness, and consideration of mutual interests have to be guaranteed to make citizen engaging in the public domain challenging.

Waze[2] is another crowdsourcing service to collect data of traffic. Even though Waze provides users to traffic information collected from users and route navigation function, it seems not enough to motivate users to get involved in, because recommended routes are not as adequate as car navigation appliances, especially in Japan where such appliances are well-developed.

2.2   Bus Location Services

Route bus system is a fundamental transit service. However, due to a progress of motorization, the number of bus passengers has been gradually decreasing

---

[1] https://www.fixmystreet.com/.
[2] https://www.waze.com/.

especially in suburban areas. As a result, the decline in passengers has led to a decline in unprofitable routes and it is in a vicious circle that accelerates the decline of passengers. To attract more choice passengers to route buses, the transit service must not only have a high level of service in terms of frequency and travel time but also must be reliable [11]. Although such efforts often come at a substantial cost, one inexpensive way to improve unreliability from the user perspective is providing real-time transit information.

A bus location service, or realtime bus tracking service, provides up-to-date bus location and estimated times of arrival at bus stops. Most existing bus location systems (e.g., [5,9]) use onboard location sensors, such as GPS receivers, to perceive the current location and then send it to a server. In these systems, it is necessary to prepare a communication line, such as cellular phone network, and GPS receiver in advance.

Another model is a bus detector installed on the environment side along the route detects the ID of the nearby bus and sends it to the server. Typically, these detectors are installed at the bus stop and detect the passing bus. Detectors installed at the bus stop need a communication line for transmitting data to the server.

Both models have high initial cost of equipment and operational cost of communication, and there is a problem in introducing services.

3 Methodology

The key idea of the proposal is that collecting bus locations is not by bus operators but by onboard passengers. To collect them, a smartphone application of bus tracker is provided to public.

Figure 1 shows the proposed method, compared with existing ones. Typical existing methods are equipped with onboard location sensors, such as a GPS receivers, and transmitters. Every perceived latest location will be sent to the server frequently through a wireless communication line, such as cellular phone. That is, bus operators must prepare such devices and a communication line for each bus vehicle.

On the other hand, in the proposed method, bus operators only install Bluetooth beacons on each bus vehicle. Instead of installing a location sensor on the bus, the proposed method uses a passenger's smartphone and our application. An onboard beacon broadcasts its own identification number nearby. In the case of Bluetooth, its range is usually several tens of meters. When the application on passenger's smartphone detects specific Bluetooth information including UUID and vehicle identification number, it perceives its location and transmit it with the vehicle information to the server.

The application shows current locations of buses in operation on bus transit services, while it detects nearby buses around users and transmits bus IDs with time and location of detection to the service platform. That is, locations of buses are collected by users.

We have been developing a bus tracker application called "Ride around-the-corner (Ride ATC)."

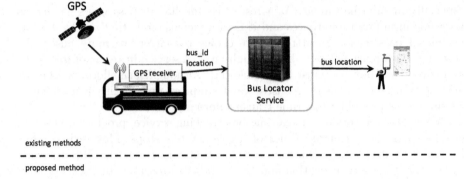

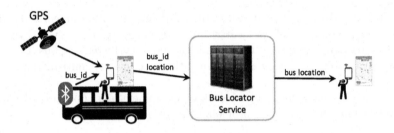

Fig. 1. Comparison of methods

3.1 Onboard Beacon

For enabling mobile applications detect IDs of buses, Bluetooth beacons are deployed on buses. In our preliminary experiment, we set one beacon for each bus vehicle, because the range of Bluetooth signal is usually several tens of meters and that can cover the whole vehicle.

Each beacon broadcasts the common service UUID and its own identification number. For IDs, we use the same major number for bus vehicles and an unique minor number. Ids of buses and relations to the fleet are stored in a database in the server. In addition to IDs of buses, some static information, such as bus routes and timetables, are given to the server database. The system can identify which bus on which route the beacon is on by the correspondence table of major and minor number, vehicle and route in the database.

3.2 Beacon at the Bus Stop

For additional services beyond the bus location, we also set up a beacon at the bus stop. Figure 2 shows an scene where a beacon is installed at a bus stop. A beacon is installed near the base of the column of the bus stop indicated by red circle.

Fig. 2. Beacon at the bus stop (Color figure online)

3.3   Mobile Application

User Functions. The Ride ATC provides users with current locations of buses in operation. It indicates the position of the buses on the map. The user can check it and estimate arrival time of their possible target bus on map beforehand so that it is possible to minimize the waiting time at the bus stop without missing it. The authors, therefore, believe that the application can make the bus operations more reliable and then may be able to be preferred by bus passengers.

Logging Functions. While the user is using the application in both the foreground and the background, the Ride ATC application scans a specific range of Bluetooth IDs. Once it detects an ID nearby, the application obtains location from onboard sensors. The location data with bus IDs and time are collected and pooled in the local data store and then transmitted to the service platform.

On the platform, current positions are updated and estimated by using collected bus IDs with spatiotemporal information and static information in database.

4   Scenario

The service is based on the following scenarios.

4.1   Grasping Bus Location and Estimating Arrival Time

The most typical and basic scenario is to check the bus's current position and estimated time of arrival as already mentioned so that passengers can wait for the bus efficiently.

If at least one passenger who enables the Ride ATC is onboard, the service grasps the current location of the bus. Therefore, at least one user of the Ride ATC gets on a bus, this service gets effective. Conversely, it is not possible to acquire the location information of the bus where there is no user onboard. In other words, the more users want to know the location of the bus, the more practical this service will be. The authors think that this point is very important. People who collect information on the location information of the bus think that motivation for their information gathering will be stronger because it is not a position to cooperate on information unilaterally, but a beneficiary of information.

By the way, do we need at least one user in every section of every vehicle to make this service practical? The authors think that it is not necessary because of some reasons. One is that the signal of the beacon on the bus can be received not only within the bus but also in the vicinity of the outside of the bus (Fig. 3a). For example, in the case where the bus passes by the side of the user walking on the sidewalk, the user can provide the location information of the bus to the service.

As another reason, the system can interpolate and estimate the position in the section in which the data is missing. Obviously, the greater the loss of data becomes, the larger the estimation error becomes. The authors consider that it is possible to estimate with a certain degree of accuracy by considering the usual travel time and the differences from the usual in other sections on this day. Verification of the estimation accuracy of missing data is a future task.

4.2   Grasping Waiting Passengers at the Bus Stop

By placing a beacon at the bus stop in addition to the bus, it is possible to use methods other than bus location (Fig. 3b). One of them is that bus operators can grasp the situation waiting for passengers at the bus stop. There is a possibility to grasp how many passengers got on and off at which bus stop, but nobody has been able to grasp how many passengers are waiting at the bus stop and how many people are waiting. By acquiring the situation where the application continuously detects the beacon ID of a specific bus stop, the above can be obtained. Considering future bus schedule consideration and service improvement, it seems important to become able to grasp the situation which can not be grasped now.

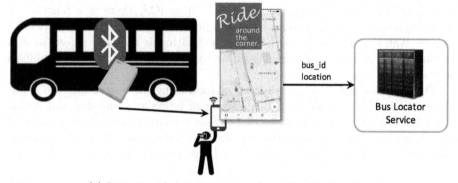

(a) Detecting Onboard Beacons from Outside the Bus

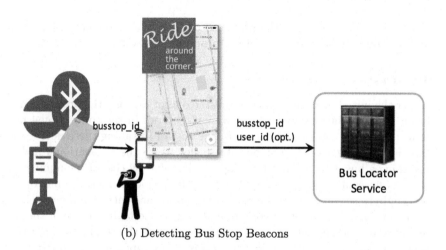

(b) Detecting Bus Stop Beacons

Fig. 3. Variations of detecting beacons

4.3 Notifying Getting On/Off

As another utilization method, use as a so-called "watching service" can be considered. In Japan, it is common that elderly people going to hospitals and children go to school by using public transportation by themselves. It is important to care for these vulnerable people throughout the society, but close relatives such as families are concerned about whether these close relatives are acting as planned safely.

The service called "Anshin Goopas" (safe goopas) is a service to distribute passing information to parent's mobile phone by e-mail when the child passes through the ticket gate at the station using their IC card [7]. Goopas can only deal with passing through ticket gates corresponding to transportation IC cards. Toll machine on the bus is often offline, so this system can not be used on buses.

Meanwhile, in recent smartphone OS such as iOS, there is a function of notifying a specific other account of its own position, such as "Find My Friends" of iOS. Watching functions can be performed with this function as long as it is a relationship allowing permanent position to be grasped, but privacy problems may arise.

On the other hand, in the proposed method using the beacon and the application, it is possible to detect a bus waiting situation at a bus stop and get on and off of a specific user, and to notify the close relative who has been designated in advance. For this purpose, the application needs to be allowed to transmit the user ID along with the beacon ID and position information of the bus and the bus stop.

5   Discussions

Here the authors compare the proposed method with the conventional method and discuss the characteristics of the proposed method.

5.1   Cost

As for the initial introduction cost and the operation cost, the proposed method has a big advantage over the conventional method. In the conventional method of installing gps receiver on each bus, the cost of installing these devices on the bus takes as much as the number of vehicles. With the conventional method of installing a bus detector at a bus stop, the installation cost of the number of bus stops is necessary. On the other hand, in the proposed method, bus operators need only to set beacons for buses and bus stops, and introduction cost is small.

Regarding the operation cost, in addition to the maintenance of the device, in the conventional method, it is necessary to bear the communication cost for collecting data from each device. In contrast, the proposed method requires only the beacon battery, and the cost is relatively very low.

5.2   Accuracy

The accuracy of position information is discussed from two viewpoints. One is data integrity, and the other is density.

Regarding data integrity, the conventional method can basically grasp the movement of all the sections of all vehicles, whereas the proposed method is disadvantageous in that it depends on the number and distribution of users.

As mentioned before, at least one user of the Ride ATC gets on a bus, this service gets effective. The authors consider that it is possible to estimate with a certain degree of accuracy by considering the usual travel time and the differences from the usual in other sections on this day. Verification of the estimation accuracy of missing data is a future task.

The key to this crowdsourced approach is that data providers that enable this service are considered to be more willing to gather information and data by being identical to users who need this service.

On the other hand, regarding the density of data, it is considered that positioning and communication are carried out generally once per minute in the conventional method of installing a GPS receiver on the bus. In the method of installing the detector at the bus stop, since the position of the bus is detected only when the bus approaches the bus stop, its density is smaller and it is impossible to grasp the behavior between bus stops. In the proposed method, the user can continuously measure and transmit the position information while detecting the beacon, and in the current implementation of the Ride ATC, these are performed every second.

5.3 Extended Services

In the conventional method, because it is specialized in collecting and sharing bus location information, it is considered difficult to extend the service beyond utilizing location information. On the other hand, in the case of the beacon installed by the proposed method, as described above, deployment such as watching service to the user and waiting situation at the bus stop, grasping the state of the user and utilization thereof can be considered.

6 Conclusion

This paper describes a crowdsourcing model to collect bus locations from onboard passengers. The model can be installed even to small operators to provide bus locations to passengers.

The authors have been doing preliminary experiments. Under the cooperation of the Hokkaido Chuo Bus, we set up beacons to the bus for the six routes and beacons to the bus stop, and we are proceeding with the operation verification using the developed Ride ATC application. Through experiments, in particular, the authors will clarify the relationship between data integrity and location estimation accuracy and hope to proceed with the verification of the data density at which the proposed method works.

Acknowledgment. The authors would like to thank City of Sapporo, Hokkaido Government, Hokkaido Chuo Bus Co., Ltd. for their cooperation with this research.

Part of this research was supported by "Research and Development on Fundamental and Utilization Technologies for Social Big Data" of the Commissioned Research of National Institute of Information and Communications Technology (NICT), Japan.

References

1. Amichai-Hamburger, Y.: Potential and promise of online volunteering. Comput. Hum. Behav. **24**(2), 544–562 (2008)
2. Howe, J.: Crowdsourcing: a definition. Crowdsourcing: Tracking the Rise of the Amateur (2006)
3. Howe, J.: The rise of crowdsourcing. Wired Mag. **14**(6), 1–4 (2006)

4. Howe, J.: Crowdsourcing: How the Power of the Crowd is Driving the Future of Business. Random House, New York (2008)
5. Kanatani, N., Sasama, T., Kawamura, T., Sugahara, K.: Development of bus location system using smart phones. In: Proceedings of SICE Annual Conference, vol. 2010, pp. 2432–2433 (2010)
6. King, S.F., Brown, P.: Fix my street or else: using the internet to voice local public service concerns. In: Proceedings of the 1st International Conference on Theory and Practice of Electronic Governance, pp. 72–80 (2007)
7. Koyanagi, T., Kobayashi, Y., Miyagi, S., Yamamoto, G.: Agent server for a location-aware personalized notification service. In: Ishida, T., Gasser, L., Nakashima, H. (eds.) MMAS 2004. LNCS (LNAI), vol. 3446, pp. 224–238. Springer, Heidelberg (2005). https://doi.org/10.1007/11512073_17
8. Schuurman, D., Baccarne, B., De Marez, L., Mechant, P.: Smart ideas for smart cities: investigating crowdsourcing for generating and selecting ideas for ICT innovation in a city context. J. Theor. Appl. Electron. Commer. Res. 7(3), 49–62 (2012)
9. Shigihara, I., Arai, A., Saitou, O., Kuwahara, Y., Kamada, M.: A dynamic bus guide based on real-time bus locations - a demonstration plan. In: 2013 16th International Conference on Network-Based Information Systems (NBIS), pp. 436–438 (2013)
10. Stembert, N., Mulder, I.J.: Love your city! An interactive platform empowering citizens to turn the public domain into a participatory domain. In: International Conference Using ICT, Social Media and Mobile Technologies to Foster Self-Organisation in Urban and Neighbourhood Governance (2013)
11. Watkins, K.E., Ferris, B., Borning, A., Rutherford, G.S., Layton, D.: Where is my bus? Impact of mobile real-time information on the perceived and actual wait time of transit riders. Transp. Res. Part A: Policy Pract. 45(8), 839–848 (2011)

Home Automation Internet of Things: Adopted or Diffused?

Badar H. Al Lawati$^{(\boxtimes)}$ and Xiaowen Fang$^{(\boxtimes)}$

School of Computing, College of Computing and Digital Media, DePaul University,
Chicago, IL 60604, USA
ballawat@mail.depaul.edu, XFang@cdm.depaul.edu

Abstract. The term Internet of Things has become very popular over the past few years. Major tech organizations and manufacturers are dedicating big portions of their focus on developing the foundations of the Internet of Things, including IBM, Cisco, Google, and many others. Most companies are developing tools and applications that are targeted to different industries like: home automation, smart cities, manufacturing, logistics, etc. This study is focused on the Home Automation and how the Internet of Things is disrupting the regular "non-smart" homes we once knew. This research is planned to study the effects of the Home Automation devices and tools currently available in the market and measure how adopted "accepted" they are within the general community. We will also measure how much disruption is it causing to the non-smart home appliances and devices industry, and how is the industry is being reshaped to cater for this newly developed market.

Keywords: Internet of Things · Home automation · Smart homes
Technology disruption

1 Introduction

Connecting every object in our lives through a unified network has been the hype at many of the major technology giants over the past few years to allow different devices to communicate with each other on a common ground. Some of them have taken the lead on creating what later became known as the Internet of Things 'IoT'. The entire idea is simply the presence of tens of objects (things) around us like RFID tags, sensors, mobile phones, home appliances, manufacturing equipment, cars, buses, trains, etc. that can through some common platform communicate, interact & cooperate with each other to reach common goals [1]. One important aspect of the IoT is its impact on different everyday-life and behavior of potential users, on the individual side users are expecting to see technology-based enhancement on assisted living, e-health, home automation, life management, etc. [2]. Such enhancement is expected to make lives easier and more proactive; however, it is disrupting a huge industry on both an individual level as well as on an organization & businesses level. This research is planned to study different theories that assess the adoption and acceptance of the Internet-of-Things on an Individual level and propose a framework that can be used for future technologies.

© Springer International Publishing AG, part of Springer Nature 2018
N. Streitz and S. Konomi (Eds.): DAPI 2018, LNCS 10921, pp. 181–190, 2018.
https://doi.org/10.1007/978-3-319-91125-0_15

2   Literature Review

While the Internet of Things (IoT) has the power to change our world, we are still at the beginning of the transformational journey that will revolutionize the way we live and work for the better. In the next few years, we can expect to see incredible advancements being made by tech giants, such as IBM and other companies. Such enhancement is expected to make lives easier and more proactive; however, it is disrupting a huge industry on both an individual level as well as on an organization & businesses level. The IoT was included by the US National Intelligence Council in the list of six "Disruptive Civil Technologies" with potential impacts on US national power. The NIC foresees that *"by 2025 Internet nodes may reside in everyday things – food packages, furniture, paper documents, and more"* [3]. The Origins of the Internet of Things go back to merging two terms: Internet and Things, where the 1st one pushes towards a connected oriented vision of the IoT, while the 2nd one focuses on integrating objects into a common framework [2]. When these terms are put together they semantically create: *"a World-Wide network of interconnected objects uniquely addressable, based on standard communication protocols"* [4]. The ITU had a more extensive vision for the IoT, in their report published in 2005 they stated: *"from anytime, anyplace, connectivity for anyone, we will have the connectivity for anything"* [5].

The Internet of Things is expected to enable things "objects" to become active participants in business, information, & social processes where they would be able to interact and communicate among them-selves by exchanging data and information [6]. In an article by the NY Times [7], Mathew Wood, the general manager of product strategy at Amazon Web Services said: *"The idea is turning the world into a smart object that can be continuously improved, and we couldn't be more excited"*. The concept of the Internet of Things is built on 3 main pillars from an object perspective [8]:

1. Be identifiable (anything identifies itself)
2. To communicate (anything can communicate)
3. To interact (anything interacts)

The Internet of Things Paradigm is a mixture of attributes of 3 different paradigms. The first are the Things Oriented visions, where it is about connecting different things to each other or simply offering a connectivity for different objects to communicate, such paradigm is far beyond the simple RFID tags, NFC, or wireless sensors [2]. The European Commission in their latest definition of the Internet of Things reported: *"Things having identities and virtual personalities operating in smart spaces using intelligent interfaces to connect and communicate within social, environmental, and user contexts"* [4]. On the other hand, the second paradigm is the Internet Oriented visions. According to Gershenfeld et al. [9] the IoT will be integrated with some kind of simplified version of the current Internet Protocol IP, to adapt it to any object and allow these objects to be addressable and reachable from anywhere in the world. Finally, the last paradigm is the Semantic Oriented visions. The idea behind these visions is the number of things "objects" that will connect to the internet in the future will be extremely massive and that will raise issues of how to represent, store, interconnect, search, and organize the information generated by these objects will be very challenging and will require a special IoT storing and communication infrastructure [10]. In their article about how "smart objects" are the backbone behind the Internet of Things concept [11], the researchers define the basics for objects to be considered as smart they would need to:

1. Have a physical embodiment and features
2. Have a minimal set of communications functionalities
3. Possess and unique identifier
4. Associated to at least one name and one address
5. Possess basic computing capabilities
6. May possess means to sense physical phenomena

While Miorandi et al. [8] believes that the Internet of Things in its practical shape should support and enable the following features:

– Devices heterogeneity: The Internet of Things as a technology would be able to connect various kinds of devices if they can communicate on a common interface with other objects "things".
– Scalability: When every object we have is a candidate of being part of the Internet of things many issues raise and must be addressed as early as possible. Naming and addressing, data communication & networking, information management, and service provisioning & management are some of the main ones.
– Ubiquitous data exchange through proximity wireless technologies: Communications limitation and spectrum availability might cause issues when substantial number of things are interconnecting within a certain geographical location.
– Energy-Optimized solutions: Minimizing the energy required for communicating and processing within the "things" is a critical and important aspect.
– Localization and tracking capabilities: Things will connect on low-range frequencies and this would allow physical movement tracking while in range, which would be very beneficial in the logistics & life-cycle management.
– Self-organization capabilities: Networks of the Internet of Things will have to handle hundreds, or thousands of things connected to one or more nodes, and such activity should be managed automatically and autonomously without the need of any human interaction.
– Semantic interoperability and data management: Internet of Things will enable thousands of devices to communicate with each other and for that to happen there must be a standard format of data transmission so various categories of things can understand each other.
– Embedded security and privacy-preserving mechanisms: for humans to trust that things connect to each other and communicate among each other they must have proper security mechanisms and an integrated authentication process before allowing them to communicate.

In their paper about the integration of the Smart Home with Cloud Computing [12] the researchers present the system architecture of the Smart Home that fulfills the requirement of measuring home conditions, processing instrumented data, and has the ability to monitor home appliances. Their system architecture [12] includes those major components:

- Microcontroller-enabled sensors: those sensors measure home conditions, interprets and processes the collected data.
- Microcontroller-enabled actuators: the actuators receives commands transferred by the microcontroller to perform certain actions. Those commands are issued based on the interaction between the microcontroller and Cloud services.
- Database/Data Store: stores data from microcontroller-enabled sensors and Cloud services for data analysis and visualization.
- Server/API layer between the back end and the front end: it would facilitate the received data processing from sensors and storing the data in the database. It also receives different commands from the web client to control the actuators and stores those commands in the database.
- Web application serving as Cloud services: it enables the measurement and visualization of sensor data, and controls devices using a mobile device.

In their paper about classifying the IoT and predicting the future [13] the researchers divide the IoT development into 3 consecutive phases to ultimately reach the perfect IoT vision era, the stages they described are:

- Early stage (1999–2005):
  - This was during the early stages of the idea development of Internet of Things
  - The early outcomes were connecting objects through the RFID transponders through a globally unique Electronic Product Code [14]
- Unit IoT stage (2005–2011):
  - This stage witnessed the decisions made by many governments around the globe to invest into IoT research and development and the agreement that the Internet of Things is going to be a life changer
  - The addition of Sensors on the Internet of Things field added a huge value to the Internet of Things development. Sensors included contact, contactless, and remote sensing methods (sound, light, & electricity sensing)
  - Because industry was leading the development while academic experts were behind, no universal framework of standards was developed at that stage
- Ubiquitous IoT stage (2011-present):
  - This stage will last for at least 35–50 years
  - It could be divided into 3 steps:
    - Step 1 - Industrial IoT: *"Some national standards for industrial IoT will be formulated and cross-field cooperation mechanism will be established. Also, some global industrial standards concerning cross-nation communication, such as global logistics, will emerge at this stage"* [13]
    - Step 2 – National IoT: In this step the national standards of the IoT will be established. These standards along with the regulations will allow countries to internally manage their informational network and resources
    - Step 3 – Global IoT: Cross-national cooperation will be formed, and major changes in people's life styles, ideals, social organization structures, and government functions are expected drastically.

Most of the research conducted on the Internet of Things has focused on the technical issues and consequences of the IoT, but very limited work has been done on the impact of the IoT on the human behavior and interaction. Few researchers have attempted to evaluate the literature of the Home Automation Internet of Things [15] where they evaluated more than 220 articles discussing different aspects of the Internet of Things and they categorized them into 4 different categories:

- Review & Survey Articles: including articles about the applications in intelligent smart homes, and the challenges of IoT based smart homes
- Studies Conducted on IoT apps and their use in smart homes: including articles of evaluation studies, comparative studies, and activities of IoT applications
- Proposals of System design and framework to develop and operate applications: including articles of system design and implementation, module designs and methods, and framework designs
- Report of actual attempts to develop apps

They summarized the conclusions all the reviewed articles and derived 3 major conclusions of the Internet of Things:

1. IoT-based Smart Home Benefits
2. IoT-based Smart Home Challenges
3. IoT-based Smart Home Recommendations

However, almost none of those articles focused on the adoption or behavioral impact and assessment of the Home Automation Internet of Things. There was a mention of user acceptance in one of the articles relating to the healthcare IoT-based Internet of Things, but it was not discussed in details, nor any elaboration on how can we overcome those challenges. As [13] mentioned in their article that academia is trying to catch up with the industry when it comes to the Internet of Things. This is on the main reasons that most the academic research is currently focused on the technical integration and the standardized frameworks of the Internet of Things. Never the less in their paper [16] the researchers created a framework to examine the adoption, usage and impact of the Internet of Things, and created a list of questions that will assess the impact of the Internet of Things on the Individual level, the Organization level, the Industry level, and the Society level. The list of questions they propose on an individual level are:

- Adoption of the IoT by Individuals
  - How will the global proliferation of consumer electronic technologies such as smartphones, wireless devices, and smart wearable devices impact the adoption, usage and impact of the IoT?
  - Who will bear the cost of the IoT-enabled systems? How will costs be shared?
  - What is the availability of easy-to-use individualized big data analytics tools? How will individual use these tools?
  - What will be the impact of the IoT and big data analytics on digital divide issues?
  - To what extend can the dominant current user acceptance theoretical models be used to study the user acceptance of IoT-enabled applications?
- Usage of the IoT by Individuals
  - How will usage of the IoT be influenced by, and influence, views and usage of personal data?

- Will the IoT open up new security vulnerabilities and who will be subjected to these vulnerabilities?
- How will individuals make use of the IoT in their daily lives?
- Impact of the IoT on Individuals
  - What are the primary and secondary costs and benefits of using

Just like any now innovation, adoption & diffusion are very critical to its success or failure. No matter how good the innovation is, it will be considered unsuccessful unless adopted [17]. Decision makers of any new innovation should always keep in mind that maximizing the adoption rate is a key element in the success of the product or service. In order to maximize the adoption of new innovations, stakeholders need to understand the factors that contribute in adoption or diffusion of that innovation. In his paper Weber [18] discuss the security and privacy challenges that faces IoT and a major obstacle IoT is currently facing is the lack of governing security regulations, which in his predictions relied solely on the self-regulations of users until a more global regulations are implemented. This indeed is a major challenge to the adoption of IoT at least on the individual level, however with that fear some people are still widely adopting different IoT based devices in their homes without paying much attention to those security and privacy concerns. In their paper [19] the researchers point out that the importance of the non-technical aspect is becoming more important in the development of the Internet of Things as it adds "a new quality" to the technical aspects. They discuss that the current public debate is wither to accept or reject the Internet of Things, so the dilemma of "security versus freedom" and "comfort versus data privacy" [19]. They then elaborate on how privacy concerns can be a barrier of the adoption of the Internet of Things as those smart objects will collect massive amounts of personal data about every step we make during the day, and even a small data breach would have major consequences. In addition, our lives will be heavily dependent on a steady internet connection, and this might be an obstacle in many regions where the internet is not stable enough during the day. To test the privacy vulnerability on the IoT-based home automation devices, the researchers [20] tested 4 different devices and through a simple observation they were able to infer user behavior from encrypted smart home traffic. This privacy concern would have a big impact on the adoption or rejection of IoT-based devices on the home level.

There are many theories that measure the adoption rate of innovation. One of the widely used theories is the Technology Acceptance Model (TAM) introduced by Davis [21] to assess the user adaptation to technology. Venkatesh and Davis extended this model in [22] to examine the user acceptance of Information technology, "The goal of TAM is to provide an explanation of the determinants of computer acceptance that is general, capable of explaining user behavior across a broad range of end-user computing technologies and user populations, while at the same time being parsimonious and theoretical" [22, 23].

In their original model of measuring IS success, DeLone and McLean [24] evaluated the literature extensively and concluded that there are main 6 categories that represent the level of success in information systems, the categories are:

- System Quality: Measures of the Information Processing System Itself
- Information Quality: Measures of Information System Output
- Information Use: Recipient Consumption of the Output of an Information System

- User Satisfaction: Recipient Response to the Use of the Output of an Information System
- Individual Impact: The Effect of Information on the Behavior of the Recipient
- Organizational Impact: The Effect of Information on Organizational Performance

They describe impact as the most difficult to define in a non-ambiguous context. It could be related to the improvement of performance, as well as an indication of better understanding of the decision context [24]. Then they introduced a success measurement model for IS based on an intensive review of the literature. 10 years later DeLone and McLean [25] revisited the model they introduced, they reviewed the literature over the past years and introduced some changes on the original model to include 6 modified categories, including: Information Quality, System Quality, Service Quality, Use (Intention to Use), User Satisfaction, & Net Benefits. There has been multiple attempts to modify the original and updated models introduced by DeLone and McLean, including the model introduced by Seddon [26], where he introduces extra categories to the original model in order to effectively measure the success of IS on different levels. However, all those related models focus on different elements that might not specifically be applicable in the case of IoT adoption on the individual level.

One of the most successful theories is the Diffusion of Innovations framework introduced by Everett Rogers in 1962, where he defines diffusion as a process in which innovation is communicated through certain channels over time among members of a social system [27]. He explains that there four main elements in the diffusion of new ideas [27]:

1. The innovation: Why do certain innovations spread more quickly than others? While others fail without real adoption of the general public.
2. Communication channels: The process by which participants create and share information with others to reach a mutual understanding.
3. Time: It is involved in 3 different ways:
   a. Innovation-decision Process: *"Is the mental process through which an individual (or other decision- making unit) passes from first knowledge of an innovation to forming an attitude toward the innovation, to a decision to adopt or reject, to implementation of the new idea, and to confirmation of this decision"* [27]
   b. Innovativeness of the adopter: *"Is the degree to which an individual or other unit of adoption is relatively earlier in adopting new ideas than other members of a social system"* [27]
   c. The rate of adoption: *"Is the relative speed with which an innovation is adopted by members of a social system"* [27]
4. The social system (context): It is the set of interrelated units that are engaged in mutually solve problems to accomplish a common goal.

He then defines five main factors that influence adoption of an any new innovation:

- Relative Advantage: The degree to which an innovation is seen as better than the idea, program, or product it replaces.
- Compatibility: How consistent the innovation is with the values, experiences, and needs of the potential adopters.
- Complexity: How difficult the innovation is to understand and/or use.

- Triability: The extent to which the innovation can be tested or experimented with before a commitment to adopt is made.
- Observability: The extent to which the innovation provides tangible results.

In his book, Rogers [28] encourages researchers in the field of diffusion to consider additional attributes that could be important in a specific situation of a specific innovation. He defines 5 major stages that a decision regarding an innovation usually goes through before it is accepted or rejected (Fig. 1):

- The Knowledge Stage: when the individual learns about the existence of innovation and searches for information about the innovation.
- The Persuasion Stage: when an individual form a favorable or unfavorable attitude towards an innovation without directly making a decision about adopting or rejecting the innovation.
- The Decision Stage: when the individual chooses to adopt or reject a specific innovation, however the user would try the innovation before adopting or rejecting it.
- The Implementation Stage: would the innovation be applicable to put in practice? During this stage the innovation could lose some of its features to meet the user's requirements during the implementation.
- The Confirmation Stage: when the individual seeks support for his decision, either by accepting or rejecting the innovation.

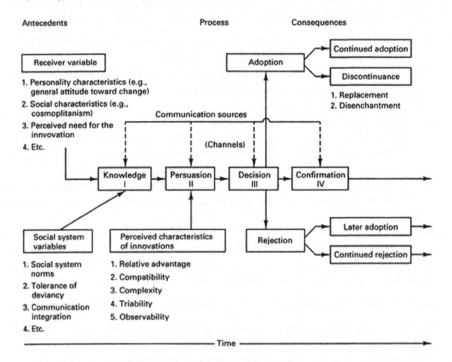

Fig. 1. Conceptual model introduced by Rogers [29]

3   Current Stage

Our objective in this research is to investigate different adoption theories and test their attributes on the Internet-of-Things adoption on the individual level to see which of the theories or mixture of theories is applicable and then introduce a new framework that can be applied on different levels of the Internet-of-things.

We are currently in the 1st stage where we are exploring different theories and preparing for collecting data based on those different theories, the plan is to have the analyzed data ready to be presented at the conference.

References

1. Giusto, D., et al.: The Internet of Things: 20th Tyrrhenian Workshop on Digital Communications. Springer Science & Business Media, New York (2010). https://doi.org/10.1007/978-1-4419-1674-7
2. Atzori, L., Iera, A., Morabito, G.: The internet of things: a survey. Comput. Netw. **54**(15), 2787–2805 (2010)
3. SCB Intelligence: Disruptive Civil Technologies–Six Technologies with Potential Impacts on US Interests out to 2025 CR 2008-07.–34 S., 1 Abb., 6 Tab., 6 Anh. National Intelligence Council, Washington (2008)
4. INFSO D.4: Internet of Things in 2020: A Roadmap for the Future INFSO D.4 Networked Enterprise & RFID and INFSO G.2 Micro & Nanosystems in co-operation with RFID Working Group of the European Technology Platform on Smart Systems Integration (EPOSS). Technical Report (2008). http://www.iot-visitthefuture.eu/fileadmin/documents/researchforeurope/270808_IoT_in_2020_Workshop_Report_V1-1.pdf
5. Strategy and Policy Unit: ITU internet reports 2005: the internet of things. Geneva: International Telecommunication Union (ITU) (2005)
6. Vermesan, O., et al.: Internet of things strategic research roadmap. Internet Things-Glob. Technol. Soc. Trends **1**, 9–52 (2011)
7. Hardy, Q.: Looking Beyond the Internet of Things. New York Times, 1 January 2016
8. Miorandi, D., et al.: Internet of things: vision, applications and research challenges. Ad Hoc Netw. **10**(7), 1497–1516 (2012)
9. Gershenfeld, N., Krikorian, R., Cohen, D.: The internet of things. Sci. Am. **291**(4), 76–81 (2004)
10. Guinard, D., Trifa, V.: Towards the web of things: web mashups for embedded devices. In: Workshop on Mashups, Enterprise Mashups and Lightweight Composition on the Web (MEM 2009), Proceedings of WWW (International World Wide Web Conferences), Madrid, Spain (2009)
11. Kortuem, G., et al.: Smart objects as building blocks for the internet of things. IEEE Internet Comput. **14**(1), 44–51 (2010)
12. Soliman, M., et al.: Smart home: integrating internet of things with web services and cloud computing. In: 2013 IEEE 5th International Conference on Cloud Computing Technology and Science (CloudCom). IEEE (2013)
13. Ning, H., Hu, S.: Technology classification, industry, and education for Future Internet of Things. Int. J. Commun. Syst. **25**(9), 1230–1241 (2012)
14. Huansheng, N.: RFID National Major Projects and National Internet of Things. China Machine Press, Beijing (2012)

15. Alaa, M., et al.: A review of smart home applications based on Internet of Things. J. Netw. Comput. Appl. **97**, 48–65 (2017)
16. Riggins, F.J., Wamba, S.F.: Research directions on the adoption, usage, and impact of the internet of things through the use of big data analytics. In: 2015 48th Hawaii International Conference on System Sciences (HICSS). IEEE (2015)
17. Chigona, W., Licker, P.: Using diffusion of innovations framework to explain communal computing facilities adoption among the urban poor. Inf. Technol. Int. Dev. **4**(3), 57–73 (2008)
18. Weber, R.H.: Internet of things-new security and privacy challenges. Comput. Law Secur. Rev. **26**(1), 23–30 (2010)
19. Mattern, F., Floerkemeier, C.: From the internet of computers to the internet of things. In: Sachs, K., Petrov, I., Guerrero, P. (eds.) From Active Data Management to Event-Based Systems and More. LNCS, vol. 6462, pp. 242–259. Springer, Heidelberg (2010). https://doi.org/10.1007/978-3-642-17226-7_15
20. Apthorpe, N., Reisman, D., Feamster, N.: A smart home is no castle: privacy vulnerabilities of encrypted IoT traffic. arXiv preprint arXiv:1705.06805 (2017)
21. Davis, F.D.: A technology acceptance model for empirically testing new end-user information systems: theory and results. Massachusetts Institute of Technology (1985)
22. Venkatesh, V., Davis, F.D.: A theoretical extension of the technology acceptance model: four longitudinal field studies. Manag. Sci. **46**(2), 186–204 (2000)
23. Davis, F.D.: Perceived usefulness, perceived ease of use, and user acceptance of information technology. MIS Q. **13**(3), 319–340 (1989)
24. DeLone, W.H., McLean, E.R.: Information systems success: the quest for the dependent variable. Inf. Syst. Res. **3**(1), 60–95 (1992)
25. DeLone, W.H., McLean, E.R.: Information systems success revisited. In: 2002 Proceedings of the 35th Annual Hawaii International Conference on System Sciences, HICSS. IEEE (2002)
26. Seddon, P.B.: A respecification and extension of the DeLone and McLean model of IS success. Inf. Syst. Res. **8**(3), 240–253 (1997)
27. Rogers, E.M.: Diffusion of Innovations. Simon and Schuster, New York (2010)
28. Rogers, E.M.: Elements of diffusion. In: Diffusion of Innovations, vol. 5, no. 1.38 (2003)
29. Rogers, E.M.: Diffusion of Innovations, vol. 12. Free Press, New York (1995)

Visualization of Farm Field Information Based on Farm Worker Activity Sensing

Daisaku Arita[1](✉), Yoshiki Hashimoto[2], Atsushi Shimada[2], Hideaki Uchiyama[2], and Rin-ichiro Taniguchi[2]

[1] Faculty of Information Systems, University of Nagasaki, Nagayo, Nagasaki, Japan
arita@sun.ac.jp
[2] Graduate School of Information Science and Electrical Engineering, Kyushu University, Fukuoka, Japan

Abstract. Our research goal is to construct a system to measure farm labor activities in a farm field and visualize farm field information based on the activities. As the first step for the goal, this paper proposes a method to measure harvesting information of farm labors in a tomato greenhouse and to visualize the tomato yield distribution in the greenhouse, we call it a harvesting map, for supporting the farm managers making decisions. A harvesting map shows daily, weekly and monthly tomato yields in small sections into which the tomato greenhouse is divided.

Keywords: Smart agriculture · Farm work information
Action recognition · Position estimation · Wearable sensor

1 Introduction

Farm managers are required to make some decisions when they manage their farm field or work plan. And, farm labors works according to the decisions by the farm managers. For example, a farm manager decides the times when they sow tomato seeds, when they harvest tomato, and when they cut dead leaves of tomato plant. When they make such decisions, information about the plants and the field environment, and so on is required. Recently, sensors for environmental information have been introduced into farm fields and helped farm managers taking decisions.

Although introduction of sensors to greenhouses have been proceeded, the field environmental condition is not spatially uniform even in a greenhouse. Due to the lack of uniformity, there are spatial variations of the tomato yields. A farm manager of a greenhouse conducting our experiments, does not know the spatial variation of the tomato yields.

The purpose of this research is to construct a system that automatically measures harvesting work of farm labors and visualizes the spatial distribution of tomato yields. By providing the information to farm managers, they can grasp the variation in the tomato yields, which leads to cultivation support.

© Springer International Publishing AG, part of Springer Nature 2018
N. Streitz and S. Konomi (Eds.): DAPI 2018, LNCS 10921, pp. 191–202, 2018.
https://doi.org/10.1007/978-3-319-91125-0_16

2   Harvesting Map

A harvesting map is a map which visualizes the spatial distribution of yields in a greenhouse. The objective of generating harvesting maps is to inform farm managers about the farm conditions and to help them decide what farm work should be done.

The greenhouse where we conducted experiments has 21 passages where farm labors walk, and the width of the passage is 1.3[m] (Fig. 1). There are 20 ridges between passages where tomatoes are planted, and the length of a ridge and a passage is 45[m]. In three of the passages, 15 pillars which support the roof of the greenhouse are aligned, and the distance between two adjacent pillars is 3[m].

Each passage is divided into small sections constituting the units for measurement and visualization based on the ridges and pillars (Fig. 1(b)). To identify which section the farm labor works on, we have set the X-axis as the axis along the ridge and the Y-axis as the axis across ridges. The size of one section is 1.3[m] × 3[m], and the number of the section defined in the greenhouse is 336, because there are 21 passages and each passage has 16 sections.

3   Measurement of Farm Work

In this paper, we propose a system which measures the harvesting work to visualize the spatial distribution of tomato yields in the greenhouse. The system measures position and action information of farm labors with smart devices, and visualize the spatial distribution as a harvesting map.

3.1   Position Estimation

In this section, we present a method to estimate the position of a farm labor in a greenhouse. We have placed 150 beacons which broadcast Bluetooth UUID (Universal Unique IDentifier: a 128-bit number used to identify the beacon) and each farm labor has a smartphone that receives these signals for position estimation. Based on the received signals, the system estimates the section where the farm labor is working in every one second.

The method consists of three steps as follows. First, the farm labor's approximate position is estimated from signals broadcast by multiple beacons. Next, the X-position is smoothed with the mode function. The final step is smoothing the Y-position using the map matching technique. Finally, the system obtains a time series of a farm labor $P_n = (x_n, y_n)$, which indicates the position where the farm labor is working at discrete time $n = \frac{t}{T^P}$ and T^P is the sampling interval of the beacon signal reception. The details of the position estimation method are described in [1].

3.2   Action Recognition

The system estimates the time when a farm labor harvests a tomato by recognizing specific actions made by the farm labor. Farm labors harvest tomatoes by repeating four actions listed below.

(a) Ridges, passages, and pillars of the greenhouse.

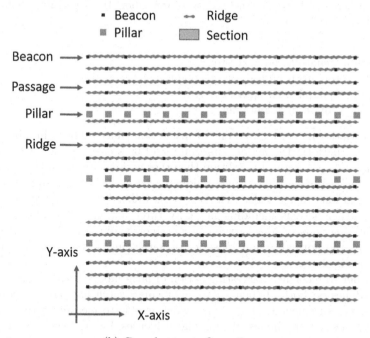

(b) Greenhouse configuration.

Fig. 1. The greenhouse where we conducted experiments.

(a) Snapshot 1.   (b) Snapshot 2.

(c) Snapshot 3.   (d) Snapshot 4.

Fig. 2. A series of harvesting actions of a farm labor. He is putting a tomato in a container with left hand.

1. Search a tomato to be harvested.
2. Pick the tomato from the tomato plant.
3. Cut the stem off with scissors.
4. Put the tomato in a container.

In this experiment, we focused on the 4th action, since all of farm labors in the greenhouse perform the action uniformly, and it is easy to know when a farm labor harvests a tomato. In addition the other actions are difficult to recognize, because the actions are performed uniquely in each farm labor and do not have specific motions to recognize. This action is defined as the harvesting action, and the other actions including not only three actions listed above but also unrepeated actions such as carrying a container, wiping the seat, and so on are defined as the normal action. A series of harvesting action of a farm labor is shown in Fig. 2.

In order to recognize harvesting action of farm labors, farm labors wear two smartwatches on both of their wrists. The smartwatch has an embedded IMU (Inertial Measurement Unit) sensors, which is able to measure a time series of triaxial accelerations and triaxial angular velocities. Figure 3 shows a time series data when the farm labor performed the harvesting action shown in Fig. 2. The farm labor put a tomato in a container with left hand, hence a time series data of the left hand changed more significantly than the right one.

The system classifies all actions in a harvesting work into the harvesting action and the normal action by the acceleration and the angular velocities. To classify actions in a harvesting work, first, raw time series data are smoothed

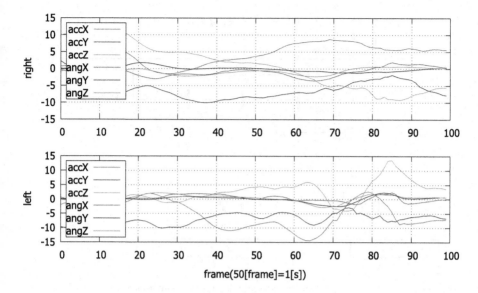

Fig. 3. Acceleration and angular velocities of the right and left wrists and of a farm labor.

because the sensor data include a considerable amount of high-frequency noise in each axis, which hinders high recognition performance. To smooth the raw time series data, we apply a weighted moving average to each of triaxial accelerations and angular velocities.

A feature vector represents a time series of acceleration and angular velocity data in a fixed window size l_w, and, as shown in Fig. 4(a), the window-sized data is divided into multiple sub-windows, each of which is, again, divided into multiple sub-sequences. Here, we represent the number of sub-windows of a window is n_{sw}, the number of sub-sequences in a sub-window is n_{sq}, and the length of a sub-sequence, or the number of frames in a sub-sequence is l_{sq}. Therefore one windows size l_w is defined as $l_w = n_{sw} \times n_{sq} \times l_{sq}$.

Next, a sequence of acceleration and angular velocity data in a sub-sequence is transformed into a single quantized value, where the number of quantization level is five in this study. To achieve the quantization, we have used two representations: one is Symbolic Aggregate approXimation (SAX) [2]; the other is gradient of acceleration and angular velocity [3,4]. In SAX, a sequence is symbolically represented, and, here, the acceleration and angular velocity subsequence is transformed into a single constant value, which is quantized with a small number of quantization levels. The gradient of acceleration and angular velocity is calculated as the angle between the start and end values of the sub-sequence, and it is also quantized by simple thresholding shown in Fig. 4(b). Then, a feature histogram, or a histogram of the quantized data, is calculated in each sub-window as shown in Fig. 4(a). Finally, the histograms generated in all the sub-windows in a window are concatenated to represent the feature vector of the window.

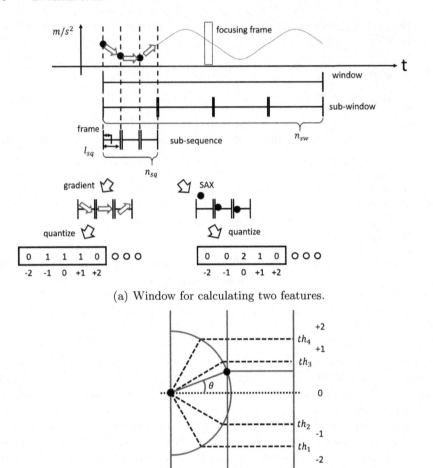

(a) Window for calculating two features.

(b) Features quantized into five levels.

Fig. 4. Diagrammatic depiction of the calculation of a feature vector. To calculate a feature vector of the focusing frame, a fixed window is extracted, and the feature vector is calculated from the triaxial acceleration in the window. In each sub-sequence, two features (SAX and the gradient) are calculated, and in each sub-window, a histogram is created. (a) Two histograms are shown within a single sub-window. Next, eight histograms (four histograms for each SAX and the gradient feature) are created and the histograms are concatenated to represent the feature vector of the window. (b) Shows how feature value is quantized into five levels: for example, the gradient between start and end values is between th_2 and th_3, therefore the gradient value is quantized into "0".

Our goal is to recognize the harvesting actions from the entire time series data acquired by harvesting work. Therefore, the recognition is a two-class discrimination problem: the harvesting actions as a positive class and the normal actions as a negative class. In other words, a one-vs-rest strategy is applied [5], and the classification is performed in Random Forest [6,7] which is one of the

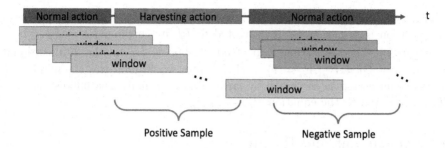

Fig. 5. Windowed data are labeled based on the class labels. Windowed data which overlaps with the harvesting action are labeled as positive samples, and the others are labeled as negative samples.

machine learning method. Here, we extract windowed data, frame by frame, from the entire acceleration and angular velocity sequence of all the harvesting work, and each of windowed data is represented in a feature vector. Windowed data which overlaps with the harvesting action are labeled as positive samples, and the others are labeled as negative samples (Fig. 5). Then Random Forest is trained with the feature vectors of those positive samples and negative samples.

In a testing phase, we extract windowed data as same as train phase, and each of windowed data is represented in a feature vector. When the one-vs-rest strategy is applied, Random Forest produces a time series of a posteriori probability $(0 \leq P_m \leq 1, 0 \leq m < M)$ as the output for each class, in this experiment, for the harvesting action or the normal action within each frame, where m is discrete time $m = \frac{t}{T^A}$ and T^A is the sampling interval of the IMU.

To locate the harvesting actions in the sequence, we have set the following rules.

1. Representative time of each harvesting action is decided by finding, in the sequence, local maximum of P_m which is greater than th_p.
2. If the difference between a representative time and its following one is smaller than $2 \times l_w$ frames, the following one is ignored.
3. Based on the local maximum P_m, a harvesting action A_m is determined, which indicate a farm labor harvests a tomato or not at discrete time m.

3.3   Generating Harvesting Map

To generate a harvesting map, the system measured information about position and action of farm labors according to the method outlined previous subsections respectively. Position information is obtained as $P_n^f = (x_n, y_n)$, and it indicates the section in a greenhouse of a farm labor f at a discrete time n. Action information is obtained as $A_m^f = \{0, 1\}$, and it indicates that the farm labor harvests a tomato $(A_m^f = 1)$ or not $(A_m^f = 0)$ at a discrete time m. To generate a harvesting map, they had to be combined, because these two types of information are obtained separately.

First, the discrete time of position and action information is adjusted based on the time of the action information, in order to know the section P_n^f where a farm labor harvests a tomato with the harvesting action at time m. Therefore position information P_n^f is converted to P_m^f by copying, $P_m^f = P_n^f$, where $n = \lfloor m\frac{T^A}{T^P} \rfloor$. The harvesting map of farm labor f, H_p^f, is the 2-dimensional histogram of $\{p = P_m^f | A_m^f = 1\}$, each bin p of which indicates the number of tomatoes harvested in section p by farm labor f. Finally, the harvesting map H_p is generated by the equation $H_p = \sum_f H_p^f$.

4   Experiment and Result

4.1   Confirming Action Recognition

In order to verify the proposed method on action recognition, time series data of acceleration and angular velocity of a farm labor's both wrists during harvesting work were measured. An experiment was conducted to see whether the time of harvesting action is correctly recognized. Three farm labors' (F1, F2, F3) actions were measured three times, and the data is used for training and recognition. The smartwatch used for the measurement is moto 360 sport, and the measurement time is about 30 to 60 min. The measurement frequency of the smartwatch is 50[Hz]. The parameters in this experiment are used as $T^P = 1[\sec]$, $T^A = 0.02[\sec]$, $n_m = 5$, $n_s = 5$, $l_s = 2$, $th_s = \{-9, -6, -3, -1.5, 0, 1.5, 3, 6, 9\}$, $th_p(F1) = 0.65$, $th_p(F2) = 0.6$, $th_p(F3) = 0.7$.

The results of the action recognition is shown in Table 1. In the experiment, training of Random Forest was carried out with the first day of each farm labor,

Table 1. Result of the action recognition of three farm labors.

Day		F1	F2	F3
1 (Train)	Precision	144/173	139/225	64/81
		0.83	0.62	0.79
	Recall	144/144	139/140	64/64
		1.00	0.99	1.00
	F-measure	0.91	0.76	0.88
2 (Test)	Precision	94/131	16/66	47/76
		0.72	0.24	0.62
	Recall	94/115	16/115	47/54
		0.82	0.14	0.87
	F-measure	0.76	0.18	0.72
3 (Test)	Precision	158/221	84/121	49/79
		0.72	0.69	0.62
	Recall	158/202	84/129	49/100
		0.78	0.65	0.49
	F-measure	0.75	0.67	0.54

and the test was conducted with the first, second and third data. The system can recognize the actions of farm labor F1 with stable accuracy. However, the accuracy of action recognition of farm labor F2 and F3 is not so high, and there seems to be two reasons for this low accuracy.

The first reason is how smartwatches were worn. Farm labors F2 and F3 were wearing their smartwatches over their clothes, therefore the smartwatches

Table 2. Counting the number of harvesting tomatoes.

Day	F1	F2	F3
	Number (man/sys)	Number (man/sys)	Number (man/sys)
1	640/885	160/250	320/144
2	744/963	240/362	-
3	560/672	320/310	160/121
4	480/607	80/147	-
5	448/336	128/133	80/86
6	504/680	104/137	-
7	424/305	-	-
8	184/222	-	-
MAE	187	73	56

(a) Snapshot 1.   (b) Snapshot 2.

(c) Snapshot 3.   (d) Snapshot 4.

Fig. 6. Harvesting action accidentally detected. He took a tomato which is once classified as A quality, and put B quality.

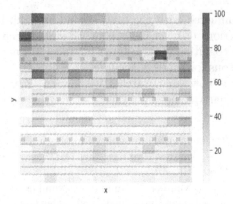

(a) Harvesting map of the first week.

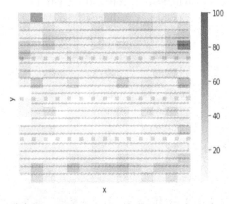

(b) Harvesting map of the second week.

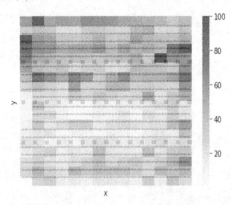

(c) Harvesting map for two weeks.

Fig. 7. Generated harvesting map. (Color figure online)

can roll and slide easily. This makes the action recognition more difficult. On the other hand, farm labor F1 wears a smartwatch directly on his skin, and the position is considered to be stable.

The second reason is re-classification. It is necessary for farm labors to select a container from two containers in which they put each tomato according to the tomato quality. Farm labor F2 and F3 often re-classify a tomato after they put it in a container. This action is much similar to the harvesting action and causes over-recognition of the harvesting action. On the other hand, farm labor F1 rarely re-classifies tomatoes.

4.2   Creating a Harvesting Map

We conducted experiments for two weeks which included position estimation and action recognition, and each week has four working days of harvesting tomato. The results of position estimation is 86% (average of six farm labors to estimate the passage where they were working). The result of action recognition is shown in Table 2. In the table, number means how many tomatoes are harvested by each farm labor, and "man" means the number of tomatoes counted manually and "sys" means the number of tomatoes counted by the proposed system. The results of position estimation and action recognition is not high enough, and it is required to improve the accuracy.

The system combines position and action information into tomato yields information, and visualize them as harvesting maps for two weeks (Fig. 7). The color of the harvesting map shows the number of harvested tomatoes in each section. The spatial distribution of the tomato yields in the greenhouse is confirmed with the harvest maps.

5   Conclusion

This paper proposed a system visualizing the spatial distribution of tomato yields in a greenhouse, and two experiments were conducted. Firstly, a experiment to recognize the harvesting action of three farm labors is conducted. Next, harvesting maps for two weeks are generated based on a experiment to measure harvesting work of three farm labor. By visualizing the number of tomato yields as the harvesting map, it is confirmed that the spatial distribution of tomato yields in the greenhouse.

As for the next task, since the subjects of action recognition were three in this experiment, it is necessary to recognize the action of the remaining one farm labor. The information of the farm labor is necessary to generate a harvesting map for the system, because there usually four farm labors harvest tomatoes. In addition, it is required to calculate the accuracy of the harvesting map, and also to be evaluated by the farm manager. We aim to visualize information obtained by the system as a harvesting map over a long period of time, and to provide these information to farm managers for making decisions.

Acknowledgement. This work was partially supported by JSPS KAKENHI Grant Numbers JP15H01695 and JP17H01768.

We would like to thank Shunsuke Hamachi and his labors, a tomato farm labor in Fukuoka, for their cooperation in obtaining farm work information in his tomato greenhouse.

References

1. Hashimoto, Y., Arita, D., Shimada, A., Okayasu, T., Uchiyama, H., Taniguchi, R.: Farmer position estimation in a tomato plant green house with smart devices. In: Proceedings of International Symposium on Machinery and Mechatronics for Agriculture and Biosystems Engineering, pp. 200–205 (2016)
2. Lin, J., Keogh, E., Lonardi, S., Chiu, B.: A symbolic representation of time series, with implications for streaming algorithms. In: Proceedings of the 8th ACM SIGMOD Workshop on Research Issues in Data Mining and Knowledge Discovery, pp. 2–11. ACM (2003)
3. Zhang, M., Sawchuk, A.A.: Motion primitive-based human activity recognition using a bag-of-features approach. In: Proceedings of the 2nd ACM SIGHIT International Health Informatics Symposium, IHI 2012, pp. 631–640. ACM, New York (2012)
4. Kawahata, R., Shimada, A., Yamashita, T., Uchiyama, H., Taniguchi, R.: Design of a low-false-positive gesture for a wearable device. In: 5th International Conference on Pattern Recognition Applications and Methods, pp. 581–588, February 2016
5. Weston, J., Watkins, C.: Multi-class support vector machines. Technical report, Citeseer (1998)
6. Breiman, L.: Random forests. Mach. Learn. **45**(1), 5–32 (2001)
7. Liaw, A., Wiener, M.: Classification and regression by randomforest. R News **2**(3), 18–22 (2002)

The Use of Live-Prototypes as Proxy Technology in Smart City Living Lab Pilots

Michelle Boonen$^{(\boxtimes)}$ and Bram Lievens$^{(\boxtimes)}$

Imec-SMIT-VUB, Pleinlaan 9, 1050 Brussels, Belgium
{Michelle.boonen,Bram.lievens}@imec.be

Abstract. With the rise of Internet-of-Things (IoT) a new wave of so-called smart technologies and related services have been introduced. When applied within an urban context, they tend to be ubiquitous, enabling a real-time interaction between the city, its environment and users, leading to a new set of human-computer interactions and user experiences. For the design of such technologies and services, researchers are challenged in finding effective methodologies that take into account this complex context of use. Especially in the very early phases of technology design, it can be rather complex to capture accurate user insights and requirements. In this paper, we investigate whether implementing a "live-prototyping tool" can respond to this need. By combining elements from both lo-fi prototyping as well as Proxy Technology Assessment (PTA), we investigated the benefits of an IoT-enabled proxy device as "live-prototyping tool", that can be used during the first stages of development and deployed in the real-life environment of end-users. Results show that the use of such tool enables (HCI) researchers to collect more detailed data, interact more accurately and by so provide quick wins for the design and development process.

Keywords: Proxy Technology Assessment · HCI · User experience
Smart city design · Live-prototype

1 Introduction

Designing smart city services is a challenging and difficult process. First of all, there is the complexity of the urban context that exists out of an interplay of users, diverse types of technologies and other influencing urban factors, resulting in diverse usage contexts. These pose new challenges for designers in creating services and constructing interfaces that consider and simultaneously respond to this. Secondly, as these smart technologies evolve towards more personalized and interconnected tools, interactive modalities representing these novel functionalities in urban environments are needed and must be considered in order to fully explore the potential of new smart urban services [1].

This challenge has been gaining attention in (HCI) research, with various suggestions to tackle these gaps [2, 3]. The problem with existing research is that the solution is often seen in high-fidelity prototypes, due to their advanced interactive modalities and direct interactions. Hence, they demand quite some time in development and are implemented rather late in the design stage when most functionalities are already

© Springer International Publishing AG, part of Springer Nature 2018
N. Streitz and S. Konomi (Eds.): DAPI 2018, LNCS 10921, pp. 203–213, 2018.
https://doi.org/10.1007/978-3-319-91125-0_17

set and fixed. At this later stage, modifications would already imply extra costs in time and money and thus arrive with a high level of reluctance.

Next to this, the development and shaping of these high-fi prototypes is still preferably done in the safe and closed environment of the company or the lab environment. Opting for this design trajectory means often a trade-off against early user testing, currently performed by paper sketches or mock-ups. As more 'smart' and 'personalized' technologies are being used in the urban context, and city services are becoming smart, the involvement of these end-users is becoming of ever higher importance.

In this paper, we present an approach where we combine lo-fi prototyping with the philosophy of PTA, to support the early stage of the design process. This "live-prototyping proxy" seeks to enable researchers to study HCI not only in the very early design stage, but also to provide more realistic and contextual feedback, answering to the challenges referred to in the first two sections. Illustrated by a smart city pilot use case, we will describe the benefits of using live-prototyping proxies for HCI research in the development of complex urban IoT-related services.

We start by addressing current approaches that aim at capturing early and contextual feedback. We will emphasize on the importance and opportunities which early contextual feedback brings, and secondly describe how current early design approaches try to respond to this importance. Thereafter, we proceed by describing our live-prototyping methodology, providing the context and background details that motivated this approach, followed by a case study. Finally, results and our methodology impact on the design process will be discussed and future research directions will be delineated.

2   Early and Contextual User Feedback

In recent years, the importance of involving users in the design process of a technology has grown. In particular, the inclusion of users in product development processes is described as a well-suited approach to increase the "fit-to-market" qualities of an innovation [4, 5] and to ensure smooth integration into users' habit and everyday lives [6, 7]. Different empirical studies have therefore proven the impact of user involvement on product success, and state that this is most successful in the early stages of the product development (idea generation and specification) [8–11].

Early user feedback not only allows effective means for defining user requirements, it also proves to be cost-effective as it lowers risk and unneeded effort in design [11]. At the same time, early user feedback generates early identification and resolution of usability problems [12]. This makes it also time-effective, as it provides researchers with something tangible to start with, and allows clear directions towards the further trajectory of the product. Moreover, it helps in finding and defining end-users of the device, steers engagement along the way and assures the understanding of the product [13].

However, this feedback will be most efficient and reflect reality when captured in the context of use. As Hastreiter et al. [14] point out, "focusing on early development stages, collecting functional requirements from prospective users is not sufficient to develop adequate design solutions. A detailed understanding of the user's task, context, aims and workflow in which the product will be embedded is essential to adapt the design to his needs."

Kjeldskov and Skov [15] indicated already in 2003 that we needed to break with the traditional lab context and techniques. Accordingly, they suggested to evolve towards an expansion of testing mobile technologies that focus on capturing and monitoring contextual data by means of what they call mobile laboratories [16, 17]. Today we see that HCI researchers have adopted this vision. More and more we see approaches where interactive prototyping tools are tested "in-the-wild", in which the design and evaluation process goes beyond the lab environment and performs context-based, mobile interaction design [18]. Testing technologies, devices or services in the context of use provides the consideration of external influences and illustrates how devices and technologies influence users' interaction and experiences, such as e.g. environmental effects [19]. These are valuable insights that cannot be measured in a closed, indoor setting or pre-scripted scenario testing. Also, taking the HCI research approach into an open, urban environment has the advantage to capture different contexts of use [20]. An important element here is serendipity. In normal lab conditions, it is impossible to draft each type of use case scenario and interaction upfront, live testing, in contrary, enables one to discover various, unforeseen types of use.

3   Current Approaches

In various user research domains, there is the growing need for adjusted methodologies and tools that can aid a multidisciplinary team of researchers and designers to collect this early realistic and contextual feedback. In order to support the latter and to overcome existing limitations, we have investigated whether the combination of early lo-fi proto-typing with the philosophy of PTA allows for the implementation and testing of a tool, which can be used to inform further development and involve end-users of smart city services at early stages. This to offer insights to HCI research which will, if not already, be increasingly confronted with the difficult realities that smart urban technologies and services imply.

Different from high-fi, lo-fi prototypes imply raw material such as paper or other sketch-based prototypes and are focused on providing quick iterations and validations of a first drafted design. These are beneficial to capture early user feedback as they are easy to build, modify, use and detect errors with. Examples of such tools are DENIM, SketchiXML or UISKEI [21]. Nevertheless, main points of critique are their lack in interaction, attractiveness and "on-point functionalities", hence missing out on real user experiences and context of use. Over the years this has evolved towards more interactive lo-fi mockups, often simulated by Wizard-Of-Oz techniques, where the underlying system is controlled by the researcher [22, 23]. Although they already offer some kind of interaction, they still remain controlled by the researcher and often imply a low-quality substitute of the real device, with no ability of testing non-functional require-ments (NFRs) like privacy, reliability and operability.

When lo-fi prototypes are not yet available, one can use the Proxy Technology Assessment method to observe the interaction between human and technologies. This method might be less known and comes forth out of the domestication theory [24]. Within this method, (existing) off-the shelf technologies are being used in order to simulate future functionalities of the future device. These are introduced to the user in their daily setting for a certain period of time [25]. The latter derives from the philosophy that the introduction of a technology to an everyday setting is the start of a dynamic process wherein actors, technology and context are exposed to continuous change until they reach an equilibrium and the adoption is more or less stable. Proxy technologies have therefore been used to define social requirements and the place of these technologies in users' household. By doing so, researchers can study the embedded practices these devices evoke, and capture changes in user behavior and social structures and motivations [26].

4 Live-Prototype Technologies

As we present it, the live-prototype tool aims to capture direct user feedback and gain insights on the technology development process. This is based on solid data deriving from the IoT-technologies incorporated in the device. Due to new low-threshold technologies such as 3D-printing, it has become quite fast and easy to develop a proxy as "an ideal proxy". Not only can it already resemble specific design elements, it can also incorporate basic functionalities, combined with real-time monitoring and feedback mechanisms. This latter enables one to capture the contextual parameters in which the interaction occurs. By taking this prototype live in the wild, we can evoke, capture and evaluate the realistic experience of the end-user.

To develop such a live-prototype, some elements are required. First, there should be the ability to work in a multidisciplinary team with developers, designers and user researchers. Second, there ought to be context-aware technologies placed in the device to capture the contextual data, such as e.g. location tracking. Thirdly, users should have the option to provide direct feedback. Applying the experience sampling method is in that sense something that is within reach and favorable. Finally, the prototype should be flexible and adjustable so that an iterative design and testing process can take place.

These "live-prototype proxies", should in the end cover an approach that tests usability, functionality, convenience and ease-of-use, while also covering a more "human actors" approach that evaluates aspects like social context, user experience, value and meaning. Furthermore, this "live-prototype proxy" distinguishes itself with the philosophy that testing in the field can already offer huge value even if there is no fixed idea of the future product. Such live-prototype proxy can be applied to research, to explore, design and shape new interaction devices to enhance products and services in an urban interactive context.

5   Live-Prototype Proxy – Citizen Bike

To demonstrate the use of live-prototyping proxies, we evaluate the Citizen Bike project, a pilot that is part of a larger smart city project in the City of Antwerp, Belgium[1]. This pilot was an experimental set-up that focused on exploring how the cycle experience within a city could be improved with the support of IoT-technologies. Instead of working with a predefined concept, we started from the user experience. How do citizens experience cycling in the city? Are there contextual elements that influence this experience, which are they? What needs do cyclists have? To answer those questions, insights on how and why citizens were cycling were needed. Along with insights to inform the design and shaping process of a potential cycling service. The targeted outcome of this pilot was namely to shape an idea by means of an 'undefined' live-prototype and by so move towards a first enriched and validated proof-of-concept.

For our "live-prototyping" methodology we used the process of Bleumers et al. [25] as a generic guideline, which are (1) the preparation phase, that involves both the preparation of the prototype as the recruitment of the participants (2) the distribution of the proxy device and last (3) the studying of the proxy technology use, via data triangulation. It is important to note that during this process we have made use of different philosophies deriving from both the HCI as the Living Lab world, among them the importance of iteration and the involvement of the quadruple helix.

5.1   The Live-Prototype Proxy

The first step of the preparation phase implied a desk research and an initial ideation session (with prospective end-users). These were set up to gain knowledge on the future technology, its characteristics, its users and the setting for which the technology aimed for. Within these sessions, we focused on defining cycling profiles, identifying existing urban cycling services and collecting insights on general cycling experiences related to the city of Antwerp. Based on these, a set of primary functionalities for the initial live-prototype were defined, with among them location tracking, a gyroscope, an accelerometer and noise sensors. This in order to capture objective data on the participants' cycling context, such as routes, speed, location etc. For the user feedback, two interaction buttons were foreseen.

Instead of using a mixture of off the shelve technologies, as normally used in PTA, we developed our own, dedicated live-prototyping proxy. This resulted in a special 3D printed case, in which the abovementioned sensors were integrated, and which could be mounted on a bicycle. The prototype was designed in such a way that cyclists could use it for at least a week without additional charging. By means of LoRa technology, the data was not only available in real-time, but also no additional connection with the users' smartphone nor the traditional cellular network was required. The latter was important to increase the battery lifespan and to avoid bad coverages.

The design itself was kept deliberately lean and simple so that first of all, these prototypes could be built as quick as possible and no time was lost in design steps (at

---

[1] https://www.imec-int.com/en/cityofthings.

least not in this stage of the pilot) and secondly, so that users could adequately provide feedback on what the proper design should be. For that reason, the interaction buttons we had foreseen (that provided the user with the ability to give any form of signal or feedback) were kept agnostic. They were labelled with * and # so that the meaning could be changed based on the users input. In line with the lean and agile approach and the objective of such live-prototype, only a limited set of devices were created. In total ten devices were produced of which six were distributed to a live test-panel, while the four others were used for internal testing.

5.2 Participants – Recruitment and Intake

For the initial test-pilot, six citizens were recruited with the profile of cycling commuter, varying in age and gender. These citizens were given the assignment to use the prototype for a period of two weeks and to participate in different user feedback sessions, such as an intake workshop, questionnaires and a focus group discussion. For this participation, each citizen received a coupon with the value of 20 euros as incentive.

Fig. 1. Live-prototype proxy mounted on a users' bike

During the first workshop, which we framed as an "intake session", a twofold objective was obtained: first of all, the objective was to learn more about the participants' cycling experience in the city. Second, was to capture the users first feedback on the live-prototyping proxies. For the first we elaborated on the participants' cycling profiles by looking at their habits. We let them draw their city cycling routes on a map and let them evaluate their daily routes. For the second objective, we let the participants experiment themselves with the device, i.e. by turning it on and off, by pushing the buttons etc. First reactions, technical difficulties and additional questions were captured on the spot. This information was of high value as it taught us that e.g. privacy issues, the effect of weather conditions and possible theft of the device were of high concern. The last part of the session consisted of the mounting of the device onto the participants' bicycles, as can be seen in Fig. 1. Being able to perform this with the live-prototypes, we could collect first impressions on the device in the context of use, such as the implications of different bicycle types, the users' knowledge and skills and unforeseen design issues with the mounting kit (e.g. the clickable connection...).

5.3   The Pilot

After the intake, the users were free to use the live-prototype for two weeks in their regular daily life. Within PTA research, this is usually 4 weeks of testing in order to allow the users to get sufficiently acquainted with the technology before being able to optimally experience the different functionalities. In this case, we opted for a two-week testing period for several reasons: first of all, the live-prototype was limited in terms of direct user interaction and feasibility, secondly, an intense feedback interaction loop with the user was foreseen and third, there was the importance of the iterative process.

During these two weeks, the use of the live-prototyping proxy was monitored. This was done via automated logging deriving from the sensor data, which provided high accuracy on the routes cyclists were taking and the input they provided via the buttons. This offered us insights in daily use of the device over time and space, yet also allowed us to identify cycling patterns, with which we could combine other sensor data such as noise, and possibly identify relations as is shown in Fig. 2. In addition, the cyclists were also given the assignment to use the feedback buttons as a way to provide positive or negative experiences while cycling. Along with this, the device automatically registered time and locations.

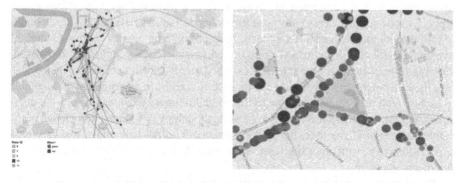

Fig. 2. The live-prototypes provided data on users' mobility (left) and users' cycling experiences compared with different levels of noise in the city (right)

Simultaneously, we used contextual inquiries to provide more qualitative insights on the cycling experiences. We provided a daily survey that questioned participants on the use of the interaction buttons and the underlying experience. This information was later mapped upon the automated location data, deriving from the device. By doing so, we were not only able to point out perceived positive and negative locations across the city, but could also provide additional context, such as a negative experience due to a traffic jam. In addition to this, we had direct interactions with the users through one-on-one phone calls. This in order to check if the assignment was going well and to confront users with their cycling data and 'dropped' experiences.

In the end, having the possibility of combining this information proved to be very valuable. By doing this, we could compare and reveal links with the objective data that we retrieved from the sensors. On one hand this helped us to stimulate users' recollection. For instance, as soon as we confronted one participant with a certain push on the button, she remembered the whole route and could provide more information on why she pushed the button whilst reflecting on her general use. On the other hand, it allowed to obtain a better understanding on the objective data and helped to identify possible technical problems (i.e. if a sensor was not working well).

At the end of the two-week trial period, a closing focus group was held to reflect on the overall practice and experience. By using the logging data along with the information which we required from the survey and the phone calls, we were able to quickly move into specific issues and get more thorough and deeper insights from the discussions. We also used other probing techniques such as drawing the future trajectory of the application to have something more tangible on users' feedback. This offered not only insights on what they liked and disliked but also on the place this technology could have within their cycling patterns.

6   Conclusion

In this paper, we have described and illustrated a new methodology called "live-prototyping", to be used in the very early pre-elementary design stage. By combining elements of lo-fi prototyping with a PTA approach, "live-prototyping proxies" allow researchers to capture early HCI insights and design requirements (both technical as user-based) deriving from contextual user experiences. The latter has the objective to develop lo-fi prototypes in such a way that they can be used in a real-life environment and are able to capture both the contextual elements that might influence the interaction as the interaction and the usage itself. By applying this methodology, we gained knowledge in the contextual needs of the user, the HCI experience with the technology and the users expectations to it, with alongside a set of technical design and architectural insights for future development.

Based upon our experience, we do think that live-prototyping has potential in the early development stage. First of all, it takes the benefits that prototypes offer. But by immediately designing them in such a way that they are tangible with basic functionalities, and moreover can operate in a real-life environment, real experiences can be evoked. This leads to a set of both technology-related and contextual usage insights of the device or service such as the appropriation of the technology, the daily routines, social relations and even non-usage. Second, by capturing user data on a (near) real time basis, experience is being caught in the natural habitat and moment of use. Based upon this data, direct user feedback can be initiated and gathered. By so the issue of a recollection bias can be reduced and more in-depth research questions can be posed. Finally, an additional benefit is the bounding character this live-prototype sets upon developers and user researchers. It allows developers to start with the initial engineering, exploring various technological scenarios without a predefined and fixed track. While at the same time, user researchers can focus on capturing the user needs and insights to steer and input the further development track. By doing so, a solution to the paradox that often exist between those two is provided, along with a structured process that allows sufficient explorative freedom and flexibility.

Nevertheless, the methodology still needs to be further elaborated in order to benefit from its full potential. First, the objective of the live-prototype is above all a mean for collecting proper data and insights. Being able to collect different streams of real-time context and usage data in combination with user feedback, requires the proper analytical tools and processes. Second, the development of such initial live-prototype is a trade-off between what is technologically possible (in terms of functionalities), what is needed, the purpose and the available timing and resources. Therefore, a good framework to decide upon the basic functionalities and the technological options is beneficiary. Third, the live-prototypes still remain lo-fi prototypes with preliminary ideas of functionalities. As a researcher, it is important to know and acknowledge the limitation that comes along with it. Also, towards the user, it is even more important to frame this correctly and set the right expectations. The prototype remains a proxy, something that needs to be further shaped and therefore cannot be considered as a final product. Due to its lo-fi character and thus lack of maturity one should also consider the possibility that these devices are unstable or not performing well. Therefore, a good monitoring along with short testing periods is required with an importance for the iterative and agile development process.

As mentioned, nowadays the design process is being challenged. The context wherein new technologies tend to operate is constantly changing and influenced by actors and other surroundings that are part of this setting. New methods to capture the use-in-context are required. Live-prototyping wants to contribute to this by offering researchers and developers an approach that, enables enriched user interaction research through real-life, contextual inquiry and this at already the very early stages of the design and development process.

References

1. Korsgaard, H., Brynskov, M.: Prototyping a smart city. In: Proceedings of the International Workshop Digital Cities, Munich, Germany, p. 4 (2013)
2. de Sá, M., Carriço, L.: A mobile tool for in-situ prototyping. In: Proceedings of the 11th International Conference on Human-Computer Interaction with Mobile Devices and Services, MobileHCI 2009, No. 20. ACM Press, New York (2009). https://doi.org/10.1145/1613858.1613884
3. de Sá, M., Carriço, L.: Designing and evaluating mobile interaction: challenges and trends. Found. Trends Hum.–Comput. Interact. 4(3), 175–243 (2011). https://doi.org/10.1561/1100000025
4. Reichwald, R., Meyer, A., Engelmann, M., Walcher, D.: Der Kunde als Innovationspartner. Konsumenten integrieren, Flop-Raten reduzieren, Angebote verbessern. Gabler, Wiesbaden (2007)
5. Von Hippel, E.: Democratizing Innovation. The MIT Press, Cambridge (2005)
6. Oudshoorn, N., Pinch, T.: How Users Matter. The Co-construction of Users and Technologies. MIT Press, Cambridge (2003)

7. Barberà-Guillem, R., Campos, N., Biel, S., Erdt, S., Gámez Payá, J., Ganzarain, J., Vidal Cabello, U.: User involvement: how we integrated users into the innovation process and what we learned from it. In: Moritz, E.F. (ed.) Assistive Technologies for the Interaction of the Elderly. ATSC, pp. 33–47. Springer, Cham (2014). https://doi.org/10.1007/978-3-319-00678-9_4

8. Gruner, K.E., Homburg, C.: Does customer interaction enhance new product success? J. Bus. Res. **49**, 1–14 (2000)

9. Hoyer, W.D., Chandy, R., Dorotic, M., Krafft, M., Singh, S.S.: Consumer cocreation in new product development. J. Serv. Res. **13**(3), 283–296 (2010)

10. Witell, L., Gustafsson, A., Johnson, M.D.: The effect of customer information during new product development on profits from goods and services. Eur. J. Mark. **48**(9/10), 1709–1730 (2014)

11. Hoffmann, E.: User Integration in Sustainable Product Development: Organisational Learning Through Boundary-Spanning Processes, 2nd edn. Routledge, New York (2017)

12. Kujala, S.: User involvement: a review of the benefits and challenges. Behav. Inf. Technol. **22**(1), 1–16 (2003)

13. Damodaran, L.: User involvement in the systems design process-a practical guide for users. Behav. Inf. Technol. **15**(6), 363–377 (1996)

14. Hastreiter, I., Krause, S., Schneidermeier, T., Wolff, C.: Developing UX for collaborative mobile prototyping. In: Marcus, A. (ed.) DUXU 2014. LNCS, vol. 8517, pp. 104–114. Springer, Cham (2014). https://doi.org/10.1007/978-3-319-07668-3_11

15. Kjeldskov, J., Skov, M.: Evaluating the usability of a mobile collaborative system: exploring two different laboratory approaches. In: Proceedings of the 4th International Symposium on Collaborative Technologies and Systems, pp. 134–141 (2003)

16. Kjeldskov, J., Graham, C.: A review of mobile HCI research methods. In: Chittaro, L. (ed.) Mobile HCI 2003. LNCS, vol. 2795, pp. 317–335. Springer, Heidelberg (2003). https://doi.org/10.1007/978-3-540-45233-1_23

17. Pedell, S., Graham, C., Kjeldskov, J., Davies, J.: Mobile evaluation: what the data and the metadata told us. In: Proceedings of OzCHI 2003, pp. 96–105 (2003)

18. Jumisko-Pyykkö, S., Vainio, T.: Framing the context of use for mobile HCI. Int. J. Mob. Hum. Comput. Interact. **2**(4), 1–28 (2010)

19. Kim, C.-M., Heo, S., Jeong, K. A., Lim, Y.-K.: Formula one: mobile device supported rapid in-the-wild design and evaluation of interactive prototypes. In: HCI Korea 2016 (2016). https://doi.org/10.17210/hcik.2016.01.333

20. Schmitt, H., Thomassen, J.J.A.: Dynamic representation. Eur. Union Polit. **1**(3), 318–339 (2000). https://doi.org/10.1007/BF01324126

21. Segura, V.C.V.B., Barbosa, S.D.J., Simões, F.P.: UISKEI: a sketch-based prototyping tool for defining and evaluating user interface behavior. In: AVI 2012. ACM, Capri (2012)

22. Claes, S., Slegers, K., Vande Moere, A.: The bicycle barometer. In: Proceedings of the 2016 CHI Conference on Human Factors in Computing Systems - CHI 2016, pp. 5824–5835 (2016)

23. De Sá, M., Churchill, E.F.: Mobile augmented reality: exploring design and prototyping techniques. MobileHCI 2012. ACM, San Francisco (2012)

24. Silverstone, R., Haddon, L.: Design and the domestication of information and communication technologies: technical change and everyday life. In: Communication by Design: the Politics of Information and Communication Technologies, pp. 44–74. Oxford University Press, Oxford (1996)

25. Bleumers, L., Naessens, K., Jacobs, A.: How to approach a many splendoured thing: proxy technology assessment as a methodological praxis to study virtual experience. J. Virtual Worlds Res. **3**(1), 3–24 (2010)
26. Pierson, J., Jacobs, A., Dreessen, K., Van Den Broeck, I., Lievens, B., Van Den Broeck, W.: Walking the interface: uncovering practices through 'proxy technology assessment'. In: Proceedings of EPIC 2006: The Second Annual Ethnographic Praxis in Industry Conference, pp. 40–54. National Association for the Practice of Anthropology, Portland (2006)

Study on Innovative Design of Urban Intelligent Lighting Appliance (UILA) Based on Kansei Engineering

Jianxin Cheng, Junnan Ye[✉], Chaoxiang Yang, Lingyun Yao,
Zhenzhen Ma, and Tengye Li

School of Art Design and Media, ECUST, M. BOX 286, NO. 130 Meilong Road,
Xuhui District, Shanghai 200237, China
13901633292@163.com, yejunnan971108@qq.com,
yangchaoxiang@qq.com, ylyyshly@qq.com,
1057791717@qq.com, onodesign@outlook.com

Abstract. Urban Intelligent Lighting Appliance (UILA) is a technological terminal device of smart city, which is a energy-saving lighting based on urban street LED lamp and achieves the functions of smart city in the environment of big data, including intelligent control, energy-saving lighting, charging of electrical vehicles, information distribution and exchange, intelligent transportation, WIFI, environmental monitoring, audio broadcasting, asking for help with one key and so on.

Kansei engineering aims at the development or improvement of products and services by translating the customer's psychological feelings and needs into the domain of product design, so It's essential to research innovative design of UILA based on kansei engineering.

The purpose of this research is to clarify a method to construct a support system capable of UILA modeling elements that fit the customer's Kansei, and to verify the effectiveness of this method based on Kansei engineering, for the selection of recommended design samples. To accomplish this, this paper analyse the necessity of Kansei engineering applied in the innovative design of UILA and put forward the framework of UILA innovative design based on Kansei engineering of forward quantitative inference. Then it discussed how to build the relationship between emotional images and UILA modeling elements in detail by means of the innovative design of UILA shaping, which will provide a basis for guiding UILA styling innovation and design effect evaluation. In the end, it pointed out that the expansion of applications of Kansei engineering in the field UILA products design have broad prospects and can better meet the users'perceptual needs.

Keywords: Kansei engineering · Urban Intelligent Lighting Appliance (UILA)
Innovative design · Perceptual demand

1 Introduction

With the development of smart city construction around the world, more and more intelligent city research experts, intelligent street lamp industry and related technology research and development departments found that urban street lights can be important

© Springer International Publishing AG, part of Springer Nature 2018
N. Streitz and S. Konomi (Eds.): DAPI 2018, LNCS 10921, pp. 214–222, 2018.
https://doi.org/10.1007/978-3-319-91125-0_18

technological realization terminals for intelligent city project applications. Urban Intelligent Lighting Appliance (UILA) is researched and developed from the intelligent street lights of intelligent city construction projects. Urban Intelligent Lighting Appliance (UILA) is a technological terminal device of smart city, which is a energy-saving lighting based on urban street LED lamp and achieves the functions of smart city in the environment of big data, including intelligent control, energy-saving lighting, charging of electrical vehicles, information distribution and exchange, intelligent transportation, WIFI, environmental monitoring, audio broadcasting, asking for help with one key and so on [1, 2].

Currently, domestic and foreign research works on UILA mainly include: (1) In terms of related technologies and standards, the research works mainly include energy efficient control of intelligent street lights, intelligent monitoring system research and technology development. For example, Wu et al. examined the significance of IoT in the construction process of intelligent city, and built the urban street lights-based IoT basic platform by integrating intelligent sensor technology, power line carrier communication technology, cloud computing technology and other advanced technologies; [3] (2) With a view to system and management, the research works mainly include technological realization and intelligent dynamic management of intelligent urban street lighting system. For example, Elejoste et al. jointly proposed a wireless communication-based portable street light intelligent control system, which enables the dimming control of intelligent street lights by analyzing and deploying the data collected on the light sensors, thus improving the energy efficiency; [4] (3) As to practice and expansion, the research works mainly focus on intelligent control and energy efficiency of urban street lights, Singapore, France, Switzerland and other countries have placed urban street lights under automatic control by exploiting information technology.

Kansei Engineering (KE) is a set of technologies, theories and methods that quantitatively transform user's feelings or intentions towards a product into design elements [5, 6]. It refers to a set of product development technologies that are user-oriented and ergonomics-based, which in turn can turn user's ambiguous Kansei needs and images specifically to the modeling elements of a detailed product design [7]. Generally, it can be divided into forward-inference KE system, backward-inference KE system, and mixed-type KE system [8]. Thus, the principles and methods of KE can be used to accurately capture user's perceptual intention and quickly establish the correlation between Kansei intention and modeling elements, thus providing reference and basis for designers to perform modeling innovative design and evaluation.

At present, most works on UILA are mainly carried out from the perspective of information and communication engineering, or computer science and technology, while few works perform design and evaluation study of UILA from the perspective of product system design, user experience, social psychology, design aesthetics or other Kansei design perspectives. In this paper, research methods for KE are mainly employed to build Kansei semantics space and modeling elements space of UILA, the correlation between Kansei semantics and UILA modeling elements is constructed through cluster analysis, Quantification Theory Type I and other mathematical statistical method, so as to provide a ground for instructing the evaluation of UILA modeling innovation and design effect.

2 Research Process and Method

According to the design flow and method in relation to forward-inference KE, provided with a rigorous and scientific data and process to the extent possible, UILA innovative design framework that is applicable to the product conceptual design phase is constructed, see Fig. 1. Coupled with the design theory and method in relation to product innovative design, an in-depth study of the KE-based UILA modeling innovation design is carried out.

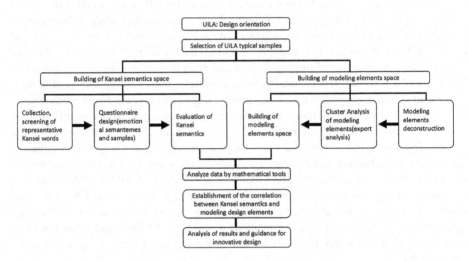

Fig. 1. UILA innovative design framework based on Kansei engineering

2.1 Selection of UILA Typical Samples

84 UILA samples are initially obtained through product brochures, user manuals of similar product, magazines and websites, 20 representative samples (see Table 1) are finally screened by multivariate analysis and cluster analysis. To avoid color factors from impacting the modeling Kansei images of UILA, all representative samples are discolored.

2.2 Building of UILA Kansei Semantics Space

2.2.1 Collection, Screening of Representative Kansei Words

Here, 202 UILA Kansei intention words are acquired through project team brainstorming, related UILA design R&D professionals, manufacturers, product manuals, magazines, websites and other channels, then initially screened, modified and classified using expert method (the expert panel is composed of UILA senior design R&D professionals and industrial design teachers) and referring to the UILA modeling features, 7 pairs of adjectives with clear intention are finally selected. See Table 2.

Table 1. Selected representative sample of UILA

1	2	3	4	5
6	7	8	9	10
11	12	13	14	15
16	17	18	19	20

Table 2. Selected adjective couples

Simple-complicated	Intelligent-non-intelligent
Caring-distant	Fashionable-traditional
Efficient-inefficiency	Convenient-cumbersome
Environmental-wasteful	

2.2.2 Questionnaire Design

7 UILA samples that are finally selected are renumbered using semantic differential method (SD method), then made into 5-level SD scale with the said 7 pairs of Kansei adjectives (see Table 3), which are combined into a questionnaire.

Table 3. SD scale of sample 4

Simple	9	7	5	3	1	Complicated	
Intelligent	9	7	5	3	1	Non-intelligent	
Caring	9	7	5	3	1	Distant	
Fashionable	9	7	5	3	1	Traditional	
Efficient	9	7	5	3	1	Inefficiency	
Convenient	9	7	5	3	1	Cumbersome	
Environmental	9	7	5	3	1	Wasteful	

2.2.3 Evaluation of Kansei Semantics

In this thesis, online evaluation is used. 48 students and teachers of our industrial design program are respondents, in which the ratio of male to female is 1:1, thanks to their active teamwork, all the 48 questionnaires distributed are returned and all are valid. The average value of Kansei semantics evaluation on these UILA samples is obtained through data processing (see Table 4).

2.3 Building of UILA Modeling Elements Space

Relying on the basic principles of morphological analysis, members of the project team invite the UILA R&D professionals to analyze the modeling feature elements of UILA. In the first step, UILA modeling is used as a set of several design elements; next, the modeling is divided into a number of independent design items, i.e.: base, post, ads screen, and LED holder; finally, each design item is subdivided into a number of modeling design elements, for instance, the base can be subdivided into cylinders, geometries, and special shapes. UILA modeling elements space is thus built in this way, see Table 5.

Table 4. Average of emotional semantic evaluation

Sample	1	2	3	...	20
Simple-complicated	6.34	3.56	7.43	...	3.02
Intelligent-non-intelligent	5.46	2.25	4.35	...	4.29
Caring-distant	3.36	3.37	3.66	...	4.82
Fashionable-traditional	7.73	2.44	6.48	...	4.47
Efficient-inefficiency	4.76	1.64	5.37	...	4.29
Convenient-cumbersome	4.65	2.51	2.48	...	3.08
Environmental-wasteful	6.57	2.42	4.33	...	3.02

Table 5. Major modelling elements

Design item (a)	Shape-designing fact(b)
Foundation (a1)	Cylinder b_{11}, Geometric solid b_{12}, Irregular solid b_{13}
Lamp-post (a2)	Cylinder b_{21}, Irregular solid b_{22}
Advertisement screen (a3)	Rectangle b_{31}, Geometric b_{32}, Other b_{33}
LED lamp cap (a4)	Round b_{41}, Square b_{42}, Irregular b_{43}

2.4 Establishment of the Correlation Between Kansei Semantics and Modeling Design Elements

In the course of transform the product Kansei semantics scale into the design elements engineering scale, available methods include multiple linear regression analysis, Quantification Theory Type I, neural network algorithm, rough set analysis and other mathematical statistical methods [9]. Specifically, Quantification Theory Type I is a method used for the factor analysis and prediction problem where all independent variables are qualitative variables and benchmark variables are quantitative variables, that simulates the quantitative change of benchmark variables in the linear expression using explanatory multivariable, and examines the correlation between multiple independent variables and dependent variables to perform the multivariable analysis method of the dependent variables problem prediction [10]. Here, Quantification Theory Type I will be used to establish the correlation between Kansei semantics and UILA modeling elements, when the qualitative data for the modeling design element of the ath design item in the Nth sample is the bth class, then bs = 1; otherwise, bs = 0. Where a is the design item, b is the modeling design element, and bs (a, b) becomes the design response of the bth modeling design element in the ath design item to the Nth sample. Thus, 20 UILA modeling elements are quantified and converted into the quantitative data of 1 and 0, namely the response value for the modeling elements of each sample, so that UILA modeling design elements decomposition coding list is obtained, see Table 6.

And the average value of UILA Kansei semantics evaluation, the response value of modeling elements is taken as the dependent variable, and the independent variable respectively to establish the following multiple linear mathematical prediction model:

Table 6. UILA modeling design elements decomposition coding list

Sample	b_{11}	b_{12}	b_{13}	b_{21}	b_{22}	b_{23}	b_{31}	b_{32}	b_{33}	b_{41}	b_{42}	b_{43}
1	0	1	0	1	0	0	1	0	0	0	1	0
2	0	0	1	1	0	0	1	0	0	1	0	0
3	0	0	1	1	0	0	0	0	1	0	0	1
...	...	...	...	...	...	...	...	...	...	...	...	...
20	0	1	0	1	0	0	1	0	0	0	1	0

$$y = w_{11}b_{11} + w_{12}b_{12} + w_{13}b_{13} + w_{21}b_{21} + w_{22}b_{22} + w_{23}b_{23} + w_{31}b_{31} + w_{32}b_{32}$$
$$+ w_{33}b_{33} + w_{41}b_{41} + w_{42}b_{42} + w_{43}b_{43} + m \qquad (1)$$

In Eq. 1, y is the average value of UILA Kansei semantics evaluation: w_{ij} is the weighting coefficient of each independent variable; b_{ij} is the response value of modeling elements (i is the design item, j is the modeling design element); m is the value of a constant term.

3   Research Result and Analysis

3.1   Research Result

The average value of the evaluation of different Kansei semantic words and the UILA modeling design elements decomposition coding list are analyzed using Quantification Theory Type I analysis tool (Japanese professor Shigenobu Aoki's VBA tool), so as to

Table 7. The QTT-I results of "convenient-cockamamie"

Items	Design elements	CS[a]	PCC[b]
Foundation (a1)	Cylinder b_{11}	0.984	0.525
	Geometric solid b_{12}	−0.141	
	Irregular solid b_{13}	−0.233	
Lamp-post (a2)	Cylinder b_{21}	−0.820	0.854
	Irregular solid b_{23}	1.522	
Advertisement screen (a3)	Rectangle b_{31}	0.505	0.687
	Geometric b_{32}	0.641	
	Other b_{33}	−0.808	
LED lamp cap(a4)	Round b_{41}	−0.610	0.664
	Square b_{42}	−0.391	
	Irregular b_{43}	0.851	
C		3.985	
R = 0.911			
R2 = 0.830			

obtain the corresponding data result. Due to limitation of length, the correlation between UILA Kansei word "convenient- cumbersome" and UILA modeling design element is mainly discussed here, see Table 7.

3.2 Analysis of Results and Guidance for Innovative Design

From the analysis result of Quantification Theory Type I of Kansei word "convenient-cumbersome", R2 = 0.830 > 0.5 has a strong reliability. Other analysis results are given as follows:

Partial correlation coefficient represents the degree of each design item influencing Kansei semantics, the greater value means the greater influence. From Table 7, the partial correlation coefficient of each design item is greater than 0.5, which indicates that each design item has a certain influence on Kansei word "convenient-cumbersome", the degree of such influence can be arranged in a descending order: post > ads screen > LED holder > base. If the design orientation of UILA is "convenient", we can prioritize the convenient modeling design of post.

From the weighting coefficient as shown in Table 7, for Kansei word "convenient-cumbersome", the innovative design of UILA can be cylindrical base, special shaped post, geometric or rectangular ads screen, or special shaped LED holder.

From Table 7, the predictive function of Kansei image words over the correlation between "convenient-cumbersome" and each modeling element of UILA: $y = 0.984b_{11} - 0.141b_{12} - 0.233b_{13} - 0.82b_{21} + 1.522b_{22} + 0.505b_{31} + 0.641b_{32} - 0.808b_{33} - 0.61b_{41} - 0.391b_{42} + 0.851b_{43} + 3.985$ (the coefficient of determination is 0.83); in order to validate the said function, we can reselect the samples, carry out questionnaire survey, perform T-test analysis of the data acquired from the survey and the data calculated by the said predictive function, result shows its significance level is greater than 0.05, there is no significant difference, so this result is reasonable. Similarly, this method can be used to get the predictive function that represents the correlation between other Kansei image words and each modeling element of UILA, which can judge whether the Kansei image communicated by designer through his innovation design scheme is consistent with user's perceived need, so as to provide a ground for the selection of design schemes and the subsequent in-depth design.

4 Conclusion

In this thesis, the quantitative forward-inference KE-based UILA innovative design method is proposed, and coupled with UILA modeling innovative design, the correlation between user's Kansei semantics and UILA modeling elements is established, so as to provide an innovative guidance for UILA modeling design. The proposed research method can be also used to analyze the color, material and other innovative designs of UILA for the aiding of design and the evaluation of design effect, thus aligning Kansei with rationality of UILA product. Therefore, there is a broad potential and prospect if we can extend the applications of KE in UILA product design to make up for the deficiencies of traditional design method.

Funding. This research was supported by master studio project of regional characteristic product research and development for "the belt and road initiatives" supported by Shanghai summit discipline in design (Granted No. DC17013).

References

1. Ye, J., Cheng, J., Yang, C., Zhang, Z., Yang, X., Yao, L.: Research on the construction of the hierarchical classification model of the urban intelligent lighting appliance (UILA) based on user needs. In: Karwowski, W., Ahram, T. (eds.) IHSI 2018. AISC, vol. 722, pp. 315–320. Springer, Cham (2018). https://doi.org/10.1007/978-3-319-73888-8_49
2. Ye, J., Cheng, J., Yang, C., et al.: Construction and application of functional requirement model of the urban intelligent lighting appliance (UILA) based on the users' need. In: Advances in Transdisciplinary Engineering, vol. 5, pp. 925–993 (2017)
3. Wu, G., Huang, Y., Yang, T.: A new perspective of smart city: building the internet of things based on streetlight. Urban. Dev. Stud. **20**(11), 4–7 (2013)
4. Elejoste, P., et al.: Easily deployable streetlight intelligent control system based on wireless communication. In: Bravo, J., López-de-Ipiña, D., Moya, F. (eds.) UCAmI 2012. LNCS, vol. 7656, pp. 334–337. Springer, Heidelberg (2012). https://doi.org/10.1007/978-3-642-35377-2_46
5. Nagamachi, M.: Kansei Engineering and Methodology, pp. 93–99. Kansei Engineering Committee, Tokyo (1997)
6. Nagamachi, M.: Kansei engineering and comfort. Int. J. Ind. Ergon. 79–80 (1997)
7. Zhou, M.: Kansei Engineering. Shanghai Scientific & Technical Publishers, Shanghai (2011)
8. Fan, Y.: Research on the product form image design system based on Kansei engineering and neural network. Lanzhou University of Technology, Lanzhou (2011)
9. Zhang, Z., Huang, K.: Study on innovative design of furniture shaping based on Kansei engineering. J. Cent. South For. Univ. **32**(11), 195–199 (2012)
10. Wang, F.: Research on the prediction of potential accidents of the ordinary arterial highway in mountain area based on the quantification theory. Chang'an University (2016)

UMA-P: Smart Bike Interaction that Adapts to Environment, User Habits and Companions

Jiachun Du[1][✉], Ran Luo[1], Min Zou[1], Yuebo Shen[2], and Ying Yang[1]

[1] Zhejiang University, Hangzhou, China
jiachun_du@foxmail.com
[2] InnoMake Inc., Hangzhou, China

Abstract. In modern transportation system, biking with smart bikes will be a flexible and environmental friendly option for over-crowded mega cities. Aiming at making the biking experience with smart bikes more attractive we create a playful smart bike light UMA-P that forms its own light interaction mode with the metaphor of personality. UMA-P will collect data of the biking condition and perform certain sets of light animations. With the help of UMA-P users are expected to see their smart bikes as a pet that reacts to their biking behavior, biking environment and other smart bikes nearby. A pilot user test is conducted and an increase in acceptance of smart bikes is observed. Our exploration will benefit the human-computer interaction community in designing playful interaction on future transportation which adapts to user behavior and environment.

Keywords: Smart bike · Playful experience · Adaptive interaction
Tangible user interface · Machine personality

1 Introduction

As more and more smart products are being introduced into our daily lives, users are expected to build better connections with them. One of these products is the smart bike. Smart bikes can collect data which helps organizing biking in a more efficient way. However, users call for a more connective interaction to create empathy with the smart bike, instead of just scanning numbers on a screen. This requirement creates an opportunity for adaptive interaction that responds to the user's habits and environment.

After researching how a human gains emotional intelligence and forms his or her personality, a new interaction framework named machine personality is proposed. In this framework, the smart product will try to adjust its interaction mode to adapt to the user's environment and habits. It collects data from the user and their environment to form its own personality gradually. What's more, this product will not only react to the user but also to other smart products that have machine personality for creating a more connective interaction.

This framework will be applied to the interaction product UMA–P on a smart bike. It will collect data from user's biking habits using an accelerometer and the noise of environment using a sound sensor. Based on this data it will form its own machine personality with three different actions, and perform one action with different LEDs as

© Springer International Publishing AG, part of Springer Nature 2018
N. Streitz and S. Konomi (Eds.): DAPI 2018, LNCS 10921, pp. 223–231, 2018.
https://doi.org/10.1007/978-3-319-91125-0_19

a facial expression each time. The user can give feedback on actions under a certain machine personality by touch sensor. UMA-P will try to perform those actions which users have previously given a high score. What's more, it will search for other UMA-P's in the surrounding area and respond to them with different LED animation.

After going through a pilot test with users, this product is expected to give users a more interesting and connective biking experience that encourages them to use the smart bike more often.

Fig. 1. A figure caption is always placed below the illustration. Short captions are centered, while long ones are justified. The macro button chooses the correct format automatically. (Color figure online)

Fig. 2. A figure caption is always placed below the illustration. Short captions are centered, while long ones are justified. The macro button chooses the correct format automatically. (Color figure online)

2 Background

2.1 Robot Expressions for Empathy

One of the workable solutions for social robots to create empathy is partly mimicking human behaviors in an exaggerating way to evoke a playful experience. In this way user can create empathy with social robots without encountering the uncanny valley phenomenon [6]. Keepon [3] and Leonardo [9] showed early prototypes of this mindset with abstract motions and facial expressions that had inner connections with human behaviors. NAO [7] and Jibo [2] have become successful commercial products by providing meaningful responses to human commands in a playful and cute way. These examples show that by abstracting human behavior patterns and performing these as metaphors, social robots can achieve a connective interaction with humans.

2.2 Emotion Intelligence

The definition of emotion intelligence shows it's a response to emotional information. Emotion is considered as the reactions to the external environment, such as threat, cooperation, play, etc. Different reaction signals will bring about different emotional information. The way in which humans respond is known as personality [5]. Neurologists found that emotional information processing is based on reinforcement learning [4]. These findings provide us inspiration of reconstructing emotion on the bike.

2.3 Creating Playful Adaptive Interaction

There are a several related works illustrating adaptation to user habits or environment. Situated Apparel shows how to visualize information with LEDs in order to enhance affective communication. What's interesting was that it could show lights in line with the environment the user had been in [8]. Another work from Kim Baraka and Manuela Veloso gave us an example of how to model different users according to their interaction habits with the robot. By analyzing dynamic user preferences, the robot could divide different users into three groups and present different interactions [1]. These works also integrated the concept of affective computing, which were inspirational to our work.

3 Machine Personality

3.1 Framework

As mentioned above, social robots have been well developed in providing metaphors of human behavior for creating connective interactions. However, when it comes to smart products, different contexts might require new methodologies. The use of some products, for example smart bikes, might be affected by the outdoor environment and by user's habits. Furthermore, social interaction between smart products themselves is not thoroughly considered in traditional frameworks.

To fill these gaps, we developed a new framework called machine personality based on the knowledge of emotional intelligence and forming of human personality. We have a definition of machine personality as following:

The smart product forms its own interaction mode and machine personality based on user's habits and environmental variables during use. This mode will be applied to human-machine interaction and machine-machine interaction with a few actions that meets the user's preference and collects feedback for improving the user's experience.

Here are some explanations of these concepts within the framework:

Action. A concrete interaction under a certain machine personality. One machine personality can have several corresponding actions that have reasonable inner connection. For example if the machine personality is 'irritated' then all the actions will perform red LEDs. Different actions will provide a slightly different red color (See Fig. 3).

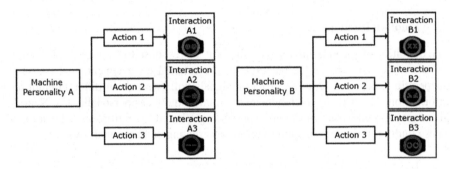

Fig. 3. Each machine personality can have a few actions which are concrete light animations. (Color figure online)

Environmental Variables. The natural variables in the environment such as light, humidity, temperature and noise. By relating environmental variables to the interaction system, the user will better understand the context of machine personality. In our prototype we used sound sensors for judging the noise of the biking environment.

User Habit. The user's preference of using the functional part of the system. This functional part can be related to the interaction but can also be unrelated. For example, the frequency of braking is one user habit of the smart bike.

Companion. Other smart products that have machine personality. More concretely, interaction products that have machine personality will seek whether there are other machine personality products nearby to determine their interaction. We used Wifi modules with specifically coded SSID for this purpose (Fig. 4).

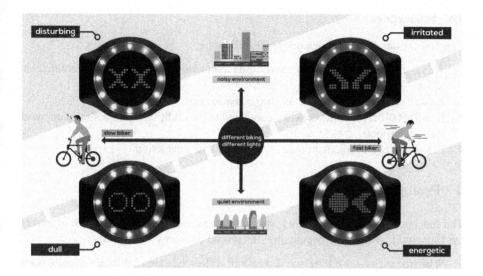

Fig. 4. Relationship between environment, biking pattern and interaction style, 'personality', selection in UMA-P.

3.2 Workflow

The interaction system that integrates machine personality will have three parts – the input system, processor and the output system. The system works as following: (Fig. 5)

1. As the system starts, it will collect data about environmental variables and user habits, which influence the forming of machine personality.
2. The system will pick up a machine personality to be performed later by judging the historical average data of environmental variables and user habits.
3. Next it will seek for companions nearby with the companion sensor.
4. After that an action under the certain machine personality will be selected and performed according to historical data about user feedback and companion numbers.
5. Finally user feedback for this action will be collected and the next loop starts.

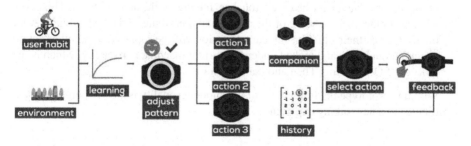

Fig. 5. The work flow of machine personality on UMA-P.

3.3 Innovations

The innovations of this framework are as following:

1. This framework contains human machine interaction and machine to machine interaction.
2. It takes environmental variables into consideration.
3. It utilizes different contexts when compared to the traditional interaction framework for social robots.
4. It doesn't rely on internet connection for a social interaction.

4 Prototype

The concept of machine personality was integrated in our prototype, UMA-P. Based on the framework of machine personality, the prototype works as following:

1. When the user starts biking, the system will collect the environmental variables using a sound sensor and user habits using an accelerometer. It will add this data to the historical data to calculate a new average.
2. The system will compare this new average with the preset threshold and select one of the four machine personalities.
3. Companion sensor, the Wifi, will scan for the companions in the area. The Wifi will get all the SSIDs of devices nearby and counts their specially enciphered SSID.
4. If there is at least one companion around, the system will start interaction between bikes with red LEDs and a heart shaped matrix that represents shyness. If there is no companion around, the system will start actions under a particular machine personality.
5. Each action under a machine personality has a weight according to the historical feedback. The weight will determine the action's possibility of being picked up and performed. The action of UMA-P contains LED animations, color switches and matrix eye expressions. For example, actions under 'irritated' will have red colored and frowning eyes, while 'calm' has white light and plain looking eyes (Figs. 1 and 2).
6. Before the user gives any feedback the system will continuously perform the same action. Users can use the touch sensor on the handle to express his or her appreciation of the action. The longer he or she touches, the higher the action scores. This score will add to the average score of the action and contribute to the new weight. After the user gives their opinion, the current action will be replaced by another action weighted randomly and picked under the current machine personality, which is the process of Q-Learning. Then another loop starts.

With this prototype the framework of machine personality is clearly performed and contributes to a new biking experience (Fig. 6).

Fig. 6. UMA-P in use.

5 User Test

For evaluating the usability and user experience of UMA-P we design a user test conducted in the university. Users are first introduced how UMA-P works according to their biking condition. Then they are asked to set up UMA-P on their smart bike and cycle around the university for half an hour. After that we will have an interview with them and give them a questionnaire to quantify the performance of UMA-P. Users can rate their answers to the questions from 1 (negative feeling) to 7 (positive feeling). The questions are divided in the following categories:

1. The industrial design: We ask users 6 questions about the accessibility of setting up UMA-P (Q1–Q2) and if the design fits their understanding of a smart biking experience (Q3–Q6).
2. The interaction design: We ask users 16 questions about the light animation. Some questions are about if they understand the light interaction in the ring in the eye (Q10–Q12), (Q13–Q16), in the color (Q17–Q19) and in the companion interaction (Q20–Q22). Some other questions are about their acceptance (Q8–Q9) in the light animation on the bike and if it distracts them (Q17–Q19).
3. The biking experience: We ask users 5 questions about their acceptance of seeing smart bike as their pet (Q23–Q26) and if it will encourage more biking (Q27).

In our pilot test, four smart bike users (2 male and 2 female, age 20, 22, 21, 23) were invited to user UMA-P and give their feedbacks. The quantitative results are shown in Fig. 14. Overall users rated 5.1 UMA-P, which was higher than the neutral point (4). This means our prototype was attractive to them in a certain extend. Their opinions on the interaction, however, had a huge difference in light animations. The function of interacting with companions (Q20–Q22), which rated 5.5, was most appealing to them. It showed that users highly valued the fascinating experience of connective interaction with other users. The LED ring interaction (Q13–Q16) rated lowest (4.375) which meant the ring interaction was not initiative in the biking context. For encouraging more biking (Q27), users rated quite high score (5.75) for us. It meant UMA-P did motivate them to have more biking with the smart bike.

In the qualitative data we observed noticed that users were quite amazed by the eye interaction. They thought the eyes made UMA-P more vivid for them to create empathy with. Here are some comments during the interview:

'It's an appealing interaction, especially the eye expression on the bike! Additionally the appearance and colors are corresponding to the smart bike. I can see it bring an intriguing biking to me in the near future.' (Female User Lu)

'The light, as fashionable as the bike, is attractive for young people because it's changing during biking. What surprised me most is UMA-P integrated machine learning and has its own personality, which is surely a new concept. Also it can help me interact with other companions. Feels good! I will definitely use it when it's on the market!' (Male User Xu)

These feedbacks provided an interesting perspective of what users like UMA-P most. They appreciated the fashionable and dynamic light interaction on the bike. They also made use of the information provided by the light animations. The pilot user test also provided us design insights that we need to create a more humanoid interface for users to feel playful during their biking. The element of minimalist design surface, such as LED rings, will not contribute much to the playful aspect. We guessed it was because a simple interface will not lead users to create empathy, just like it is hard to imagine a round stone can speak since it doesn't have a mouth. Creating a 'face' metaphor on the smart bike will be more effective (Fig. 7).

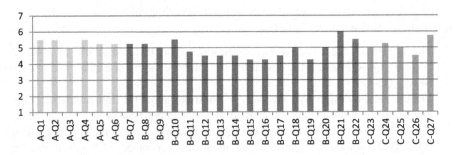

Fig. 7. Quantitative result of questionnaires. A-type questions are in industrial design aspect, B-type questions are in interaction design aspect and C-type questions are in biking experience aspect.

6   Conclusion and Future Work

In this paper we introduced an interactive smart bike light UMA-P for a playful biking experience. With the metaphor of forming personality, UMA-P tries to perform useful biking information of environment and user habits. Also UMA-P is able to automatically response to companions nearby, which fits users' need of social interaction in certain extend. Pilot user test showed users were willing to have more biking with UMA-P and suggested the next design should be more humanoid.

The limitation of the design is the integration on smart bike is not finished. Also the eye animations are not fully developed. We still need a co-creation session with users for better eye animations. Moreover the necessity of using a tangible user interface instead of a phone screen should be discussed since users didn't appreciate LED rings much.

The next step is involving more users for a more quantified and persuasive user test. We want to apply persuasive technology into this product to motivate more use of the smart bike, which calls for more effort in the experiment design and user tests. What's more, we are going to explore how to integrate other into other transportation.

References

1. Baraka, K., Veloso, M.: Adaptive interaction of persistent robots to user temporal preferences. In: Tapus, A., André, E., Martin, J.C., Ferland, F., Ammi, M. (eds.) Social Robotics. LNCS (LNAI), vol. 9388, pp. 61–71. Springer, Cham (2015). https://doi.org/10.1007/978-3-319-25554-5_7
2. Breazeal, C., Faridi, F.: Robot. Google Patents (2016). https://www.google.com/patents/USD746886
3. Kozima, H., Michalowski, M.P., Nakagawa, C.: Keepon. Int. J. Soc. Rob. 1(1), 3–18 (2009)
4. LeDoux, J.E.: Brain mechanisms of emotion and emotional learning. Curr. Opin. Neurobiol. 2(2), 191–197 (1992). https://doi.org/10.1016/0959-4388(92)90011-9
5. Mayer, J.D., Salovey, P., Caruso, D.R.: Emotional intelligence: theory, findings, and implications. Psychol. Inq. 15(3), 197–215 (2004). https://doi.org/10.1207/s15327965pli1503_02
6. Mori, M., MacDorman, K.F., Kageki, N.: The uncanny valley [from the field]. IEEE Rob. Autom. Mag. 19(2), 98–100 (2012)
7. Shamsuddin, S., Ismail, L.I., Yussof, H., Zahari, N.I., Bahari, S., Hashim, H., Jaffar, A.: Humanoid robot NAO: review of control and motion exploration. In: 2011 IEEE International Conference on Control System, Computing and Engineering (ICCSCE), pp. 511–516. IEEE (2011). http://ieeexplore.ieee.org/xpls/abs_all.jsp?arnumber=6190579
8. Tao, Y., Chen, H., Meng, F., Zhang, X., Ying, F., Yao, C.: Situated apparel: designing to reinforce affective communication. In: Proceedings of the Ninth International Conference on Tangible, Embedded, and Embodied Interaction, pp. 529–532. ACM (2015). http://dl.acm.org/citation.cfm?id=2687893
9. Thomaz, A.L., Breazeal, C.: Robot learning via socially guided exploration (2007)

Simulation of Energy Management by Controlling Crowd Behavior

Maiya Hori$^{(\boxtimes)}$, Keita Nakayama, Atsushi Shimada, and Rin-ichiro Taniguchi

Kyushu University, 744, Motooka, Nishi-ku, Fukuoka 819-0395, Japan
{hori,nakayama,atsushi}@limu.ait.kyushu-u.ac.jp, rin@kyudai.jp
http://limu.ait.kyushu-u.ac.jp/

Abstract. We propose a method of energy management aimed at reducing the emission of carbon dioxide by changing people's behavior in small and medium-sized electricity communities. In the conventional energy management system, a power peak is cut and shifted mainly using solar power generation and batteries. In this research, a power peak is cut and shifted by controlling the power demand. The power demand for each facility in small communities is controlled by changing crowd behavior. In experiments, models for predicting power demand according to crowd congestion are constructed for each facility and the accuracies of prediction are verified.

Keywords: Energy management system · Power demand
Crowd behavior

1 Introduction

A cyber-physical system (CPS) analyzes and uses data obtained from the real world. The use of various data and functions allows improvements to the performance of the social system and efficient operation management. In the CPS, a huge amount of real world data is collected and analyzed to construct a virtual world on a computer. Here, it is important to blend information of the physical world with information of the cyber world. The CPS finds the optimal solution by simulating the future world in the constructed virtual world and feeds it back to society. This makes it possible to efficiently solve various urban problems, such as those pertaining to traffic and energy.

CPSs are expected to become a common part of social infrastructure in the energy sector [1]. Because of recent developments in this sector, there is a need to provide a stable energy supply to realize a low-carbon society. A smart grid is a power grid with a communication function and control function; e.g., the grid may use smart meters. The purpose of the smart grid is to optimize the supply-demand balance within a small community. In Japan, a large amount of renewable energy is scheduled for installation by 2020 [2]. Against such a background, analyses and optimization of the energy supply and demand balance are required. Because the supply side has a limited ability to control the

© Springer International Publishing AG, part of Springer Nature 2018
N. Streitz and S. Konomi (Eds.): DAPI 2018, LNCS 10921, pp. 232–241, 2018.
https://doi.org/10.1007/978-3-319-91125-0_20

power demand, attempts to optimize the energy problem have been made on the demand side. For instance, energy management systems optimize a wide variety of energy sources to carry out local production for the local consumption of energy [3].

2 Related Work

In the conventional energy management system, power peaks are cut and shifted mainly using solar power generation and batteries. A reduction in the emission of carbon dioxide can be expected from the optimum operation of batteries according to the prediction technologies of the power demand and photovoltaic power generation using weather information. However, the effect of the reduction of carbon dioxide largely depends on the photovoltaic power generation and battery capacity. It is a problem that the costs of solar panels and battery installation are high. Additionally, it is a problem that power consumption is strongly affected by the behavior of people even if the generation of photovoltaic power is accurately forecast.

Meanwhile, a demand response [4, 5] can be used to manage energy by controlling the electric power demand itself. This method saves electricity by changing the electricity price dynamically. Energy is conserved by setting the electric unit price high when the electric power demand is large. Although a large power saving can be expected depending on the setting of the unit price of electricity, it is not an ideal method because there is a possibility that the living comfort of the user will be sacrificed. Additionally, at institutions where there are many people who are not conscious of electricity charges, such as universities and complex commercial facilities, the energy saving will be small.

The present research therefore attempts to cut and shift the power peak of an entire target area by controlling the congestion of each building without a compulsion to demonstrate a strong energy management effect even for universities and complex commercial facilities. Targets such as universities and compound commercial facilities comprise multiple facilities. Some areas of these targets are sometimes locally crowded and uncomfortable. Meanwhile, there are wide spaces containing only a small number of users, where energy is used inefficiently. We attempt to change crowd behavior to solve these problems. A conventional study [6] showed that the power consumption of each facility depends on the congestion of the facility. It is assumed here that it is possible to control the congestion of each facility any time by presenting information that prompts behavioral change via social networking services or e-mail. In fact, we control the congestion of each facility to level the electric power use. This makes it possible to reduce the emission of carbon dioxide. It is thus conceivable that we can manage energy without the user being consciously aware of the power savings.

3 Proposed Method

The purpose of our research is to realize energy management aimed at reducing the emission of carbon dioxide by changing people's behavior in small and medium-sized electricity communities. We assume that small and medium-sized electricity communities comprise facilities with multiple power demand characteristics. We attempt to cut and shift the power peak of the entire target area by controlling the crowd congestion of each building and thus demonstrate a strong energy management effect even for small and medium-sized electricity communities. Under the above assumption, the power demand is leveled in the following procedure.

1. Crowd congestion in each building is changed by the presentation of information prompting a behavioral change.
   Some areas of targets are sometimes locally crowded and uncomfortable. Meanwhile, there are wide spaces containing only a small number of users, where energy is used inefficiently. We attempt to change crowd behavior to solve these problems. It is assumed here that it is possible to control the congestion of each facility any time by presenting information that prompts a behavior change via social networking services or e-mail. Here, even if congestion changes, it is important that the total number of people does not change.
2. The power consumption of each building changes with the crowd congestion. We here assume that the power demand will change with the change in crowd congestion. A conventional study [6] showed that the power consumption of each facility depends on the congestion of the facility. We control the crowd congestion of each facility to change the power consumption of each building by using this knowledge.
3. The total power demand is leveled by aggregating the power consumption of multiple buildings.
   The goal of the system is to level the total power demand in the community. The changed power consumption of multiple buildings is aggregated. As a result, it is conceivable that we can manage energy without the user being consciously aware of power savings.

Functions necessary for a CPS to level the power demand as mentioned above are listed as follows.

- Acquisition of heterogeneous data and construction of a database
- Construction of a power demand prediction model for each facility
- Creation of presentation information that promotes a behavioral change and realizes the optimum crowd congestion for each facility for energy management

The following sections present the details of each process.

3.1 Acquisition of Heterogeneous Data and Construction of the Database

Various sensors were installed on the campus of a university to acquire heterogeneous data. In the construction of the database, each datum was synchronized with respect to time. In this database, data were normalized and missing

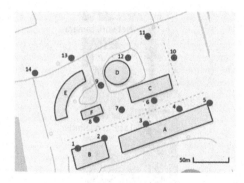

Fig. 1. Target buildings A–F at Ito Campus, Kyushu University. Blue circles indicate the positions of 14 P-sen units. (Color figure online)

data filled in. The experimental environment selected for this study encompasses multiple buildings on the Ito Campus of Kyushu University in Fukuoka, Japan. Students are free to access and stay in these buildings during the day.

Acquisition of Power Consumption Data for Each Facility. There are six targets (buildings A–F) in the central zone of the university campus, as shown in Fig. 1. Power consumption within each building is measured hourly.

Acquisition of Meteorological Data. Each sensor is installed on the roof of a building on the campus and measures temperature, humidity, solar irradiance, wind speed, and wind direction every minute. In addition, the Japan Meteorological Agency publishes various local data, such as temperature, humidity, and solar irradiance data, every hour [7], and we can thus alternatively use data recorded at the position closest to the university. This approach has data redundancy.

Acquisition of Crowd Congestion. Crowd flow data can be measured using a pole-type small sensor node (P-sen) installed at several locations on the campus. Figure 2 shows the appearance of a P-sen, which has a network camera, wireless LAN access point, and range finder. Data for analyzing human behavior can be redundantly acquired using multiple sensors. In this study, crowd flow was measured using only the range finder. This measurement method is not accurate when there is occlusion in the crowd. However, this approach preserves privacy and can measure congestion under various illumination conditions. Figure 1 shows the positions of the 14 P-sens (Nos. 1–14). It is possible to measure the positions of moving objects in the area in front of each P-sen at about 10 Hz. The 14 P-sen units cover the entire area over which people can move in the zone.

Crowd flow data are generated from the acquired moving object information using a Kalman filter [8]. Furthermore, the number of unique users observed per

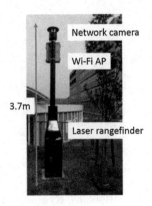

Fig. 2. P-sen unit for crowd flow measurement. In this study, only the range finder was used to measure crowd flow.

minute is calculated from the crowd flow data for each P-sen. In this study, the mean number of unique users per hour is defined as the degree of congestion for each zone. It is possible to estimate the degree of congestion robustly taking this approach, even if there is some short-term data loss.

3.2 Construction of a Power Demand Prediction Model for Each Facility

It is necessary to construct a model to estimate the power consumption when the crowd congestion changes. Because it is known that crowd congestion affects the power consumption of buildings [6], we build a power demand prediction model using this knowledge. We use a vector autoregression (VAR) model as a power demand prediction model. We here explain VAR, which is a technique that can be used to forecast power demand from heterogeneous data. VAR is represented by the model

$$\mathbf{Y_t} = \sum_{m=1}^{M} \mathbf{A_m Y_{t-m}} + \epsilon_t, \tag{1}$$

where the inputs are n kinds of time series data, $\mathbf{Y_t} = (\mathbf{y_{1,t}, y_{2,t}, \cdots, y_{n,t}})$ with M lags. We use Akaike's information criterion (AIC) [9] to determine parameter M, calculated as

$$AIC = -2\ln L + 2k, \tag{2}$$

where L is the maximum likelihood and k is the number of free parameters. The AIC is used to evaluate the goodness of the statistical model maintaining a balance between the fitting of the data and the complexity of the model. The number of lags M is determined so as to minimize the AIC. The constructed VAR model is used in forecasting by inputting n kinds of time series data, $\mathbf{Y_t} = (\mathbf{y_{1,t}, y_{2,t}, \cdots, y_{n,t}})$ with M lags. It is possible to predict the power demand for each building when changing the crowd congestion using these models.

3.3   Creation of Presentation Information that Promotes a Behavioral Change and Realizes Optimum Crowd Congestion for Each Facility in Energy Management

In the case of providing information that promotes behavioral changes, it is ideal to provide the most effective information for leveling energy at the most effective time according to the congestion situation of the facility. However, it is difficult to judge whether the timing and content of the information to be provided are appropriate for leveling energy by simply observing crowd congestion after the presentation of information. For example, even if congestion is temporarily eliminated immediately after information is provided, if the energy is not leveled as a result, the information provided is not appropriate. Conversely, even if congestion increases temporarily after information is provided, if the energy is leveled as a result, the information to be provided is appropriate. In the case of solving the congestion problem of commercial facilities, if the total number of users decreases as a result of congestion mitigation, the presented information is inappropriate on the facility side. In this way, it cannot be decided whether the provided information is appropriate unless the result of how congestion changes in the real world. We therefore determine the content and timing of information to be provided in a reinforcement learning framework for this problem.

Reinforcement learning is a method of learning appropriate behavior in unknown circumstances. The learner in reinforcement learning is called an agent and learns appropriate behavior rules through interaction with the environment. The agent observes the state of the environment and executes an action according to that state. Selecting an action for the state of the environment is called a policy. The action affects the state of the environment, and the environment rewards the agent as a form of behavior evaluation. The objective of reinforcement learning is to seek the optimal policy that finally obtains maximum rewards through the repetition of this process. Reinforcement learning has been particularly successful for game tasks [10,11]. However, in the learning process of reinforcement learning, because agents perform actions through trial and error according to environmental conditions and rewards, they take wrong actions in the early stage of learning in many cases. Although this is not a problem in game tasks, in the case of learning by interaction with the real world as in this research, taking a wrong action may cause confusion in the real world. To solve this problem, we construct a model that is close to the real-world environment as a preliminary stage of the experiment in the real world, and conduct a simulation using the model.

4   Experiments

This paper focuses on the construction of a power demand prediction model for each facility. In this experiment conducted to validate the proposed method, power demand models are constructed by analyzing the acquired heterogeneous data for Ito Campus, Kyushu University. Data were acquired hourly over a period of 6 months from September 8, 2015 to March 8, 2016. Appropriate locations and

Table 1. Mean and standard deviation of the power consumption of each building.

Building	Mean (SD) [kWh]
A	119.50 (±43.51)
B	56.11 (±37.53)
C	56.40 (±29.17)

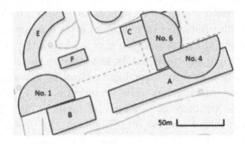

Fig. 3. Congestion information used for constructing power demand models.

periods were selected for the experiment so that there was no long-term data loss that would affect the accuracy of data interpolation. The experimental targets were buildings A, B, and C shown in Fig. 1. Building A has lecture rooms, many of which are used for daytime lectures. Building B is not used for lectures but is made available to students at all times. Building C contains university administration offices and rooms used for lectures. The mean and standard deviation of the power consumption for each building are given in Table 1. The mean power consumption of building A is larger than the mean consumptions of buildings B and C. The standard deviation of the power consumption increases from building C to building B to building A.

To analyze heterogeneous data, congestion information from the P-sens closest to the entrances of the target buildings was used. Specifically, as illustrated in Fig. 3, P-sen 4 was used to forecast the power demand of building A, P-sen 1 was used for building B, and P-sen 6 was used for building C under the assumption that the power demand is affected by the congestion information obtained from these P-sens. It was found in preliminary experiments that this assumption provides good results. Table 2 gives the mean and standard deviation of congestion data acquired by the P-sens. The mean degree of congestion is highest for P-sen 1, the standard deviation of the degree of congestion is highest for P-sen 4, and both the mean and standard deviation are lowest for P-sen 6. We used temperature, humidity, and solar irradiance data for Fukuoka, made available by the Japan Meteorological Agency.

In the analysis, we verified whether a statistically suitable model can be constructed by combining the congestion and meteorological data. We forecast the power demand for each building in a one-sample future. In the analysis, the

Table 2. Means and standard deviations of the congestion data acquired by the P-sens.

P-sen	Mean (SD) [person/minute]
No. 1	0.89 ($\pm$1.28)
No. 4	0.75 ($\pm$1.43)
No. 6	0.20 ($\pm$0.48)

Table 3. Results of the power demand forecast for building A. The mean error is smallest when temperature and congestion information are used. There is a significant difference with respect to all other results.

Factor	Lags M	Error (SD) [kWh]
cong.	168	6.05 ($\pm$4.98)
cong.+temp. (optimal model for building A)	**168**	**5.93 ($\pm$4.84)**
cong.+temp.+sol.	28	6.73 ($\pm$5.62)
cong.+temp.+sol.+hum.	28	6.70 ($\pm$5.61)
temp.	164	6.19 ($\pm$5.04)
temp.+sol.	53	6.68 ($\pm$5.56)
temp.+sol.+hum.	29	6.83 ($\pm$5.77)

Table 4. Results of the power demand forecast for building B. The mean error is smallest when temperature and congestion information are used. There is a significant difference with respect to all other results.

Factor	Lags M	Error (SD) [kWh]
cong.	168	8.33 ($\pm$7.00)
cong.+temp. (optimal model for building B)	**168**	**8.19 ($\pm$6.78)**
cong.+temp.+sol.	51	8.92 ($\pm$7.58)
cong.+temp.+sol.+hum.	27	9.07 ($\pm$7.81)
temp.	168	8.57 ($\pm$7.25)
temp.+sol.	52	9.23 ($\pm$7.93)
temp.+sol.+hum.	29	9.38 ($\pm$8.08)

degree of congestion, temperature, humidity, and solar irradiance were selected to construct the statistical model. The results of the power demand forecasts of buildings A, B, and C are respectively given in Tables 3, 4, and 5. The results obtained without using the congestion data are also shown for comparison.

It was found that for all buildings, the mean difference between the estimation results and actual measurement values was smallest when temperature and congestion data were used. It is important to note here that the parameters constituting the model vary greatly for each building.

Table 5. Results of the power demand forecast for building C. The mean error is smallest when temperature and congestion information are used. There is a significant difference with respect to all other results.

Factor	Lags M	Error (SD) [kWh]
cong.	168	5.98 ($\pm$5.15)
cong.+temp. (optimal model for building C)	**168**	**5.82 ($\pm$5.00)**
cong.+temp.+sol.	29	6.46 ($\pm$5.79)
cong.+temp.+sol.+hum.	29	6.45 ($\pm$5.76)
temp.	162	6.06 ($\pm$5.19)
temp.+sol.	53	6.46 ($\pm$5.74)
temp.+sol.+hum.	29	6.58 ($\pm$5.85)

5   Discussion

The experimental results showed that the power consumption characteristics differ for each building. In particular, the effect of the change in crowd congestion varies from building to building. This means that there is a possibility that the total power consumption will change with a change in crowd congestion. It is thought that this relationship can be used for energy management by changing crowd congestion appropriately. We will determine the content and timing of information to be provided in a reinforcement learning framework.

6   Conclusion

We proposed a method of realizing energy management aimed at reducing the emission of carbon dioxide by changing people's behavior in small and medium-sized electricity communities. We constructed a model with which to estimate the power consumption of each building when the crowd congestion changes. In experiments, we found that the effect of the change in crowd congestion varies from building to building. Future works are to estimate the optimum crowd congestion for energy management and to create presentation information that promotes behavioral changes that realize the estimated optimum crowd congestion.

Acknowledgements. This research was supported by the Japan Science and Technology Agency (JST) through its Center of Innovation: Science and Technology Based Radical Innovation and Entrepreneurship Program (COI STREAM).

References

1. Behl, M., Jain, A., Mangharam, R.: Data-driven modeling, control and tools for cyber-physical energy systems. In: ACM/IEEE International Conference on Cyber-Physical Systems (ICCPS) (2016)
2. Ministry of the Envirnment, Government of Japan. Mid-and long-term roadmap for global warming measures. https://funtoshare.env.go.jp/roadmap/index_en.html
3. Barbato, A., Delfanti, M., Bolchini, C., Geronazzo, A., Quintarelli, E., Olivieri, V., Rottondi, C., Verticale, G.: An energy management framework for optimal demand response in a smart campus. In: International Conference on Green IT Solutions (ICGREEN) (2015)
4. Siano, P.: Demand response and smart grids - a survey. Renew. Sustain. Energy Rev. 30, 461–478 (2013)
5. Deng, R., Yang, Z., Chow, M., Chen, J.: A survey on demand response in smart grids: Mathematical models and approaches. IEEE Trans. Ind. Inform. 11(3), 570–582 (2015)
6. Hori, M., Goto, T., Takano, S., Taniguchi, R.: Power demand forecasting using meteorological data and human congestion information. In IEEE International Conference on Cyber-Physical Systems, Networks, and Applications (CPSNA) (2016)
7. Japan Meteorological Agency. Weather, climate & earthquake information. http://www.jma.go.jp/jma/indexe.html
8. Fod, A., Howard, A., Mataric, M.A.J.: A laser-based people tracker. In: IEEE International Conference on Robotics and Automation (ICRA) (2002)
9. Akaike, H., Nakagawa, T.: Statistical Analysis and Control of Dynamic Systems. Springer, Heidelberg (1988). ISBN 978-90-277-2786-2
10. Mnih, V., Kavukcuoglu, K., Silver, D., Graves, A., Antonoglou, I., Wierstra, D., Riedmiller, M.: Playing Atari with deep reinforcement learning. arXiv preprint arXiv:1312.5602 (2013)
11. Seijen, H., Fatemi, M., Romoff, J., Laroche, R., Barnes, T., Tsang, J.: Hybrid reward architecture for reinforcement learning. In: Advances in Neural Information Processing Systems, pp. 5398–5408 (2017)

Socio-Technical Challenges of Smart Fleet Equipment Management Systems in the Maritime Industry

Jingyi Jiang[1], Guochao Peng[2(✉)], and Fei Xing[2]

[1] Peking University, Haidian, Beijing 100000, China
[2] Sun Yat-sen University, Panyu District, Guangzhou 510000, China
penggch@mail.sysu.edu.cn

Abstract. Fleet management systems have been widely used in the maritime industry. Traditional fleet management systems focus on the whole vessel/ship. With the emergence of the Internet of Things and new smart technologies, smart fleet management systems are now embedded with greater power in comparison with traditional solutions, e.g. can be used to monitor the performance, status and behaviour of not just the whole ship but crucial internal components, such as engines, water treatment equipment, and propellers. However, developing, implementing and operating such new generation of fleet management system may not be straightforward and can encounter a wide range of socio-technical challenges, which have not been adequately explored in the current literature. This paper attempts to fill this knowledge gap by critically discussing these challenges, with practical suggestions drawn.

Keywords: Smart fleet management · Vessel management · Maritime industry
Socio-technical challenges

1 Introduction

Ocean shipping is one of the most economical, secure and environmental-friendly transportation options for delivering large quantities of goods and cargos across different countries and in fact continents [1]. As such, approximately 90% of the world's international trading is completed by using ocean transportation, which covers items of all kinds including important natural resources (e.g. iron ore, coal, oil and gas), semi-manufactured products (e.g. car engines), electronic equipment (e.g. TVs, Fridges, PCs), as well as commodity goods and foods [2, 3]. According to the annual statistical report provided by the United Nations, there were 90,917 commercial vessels in service in the world by Jan 2016, with a combined tonnage of 1.8 billion dwt, implying an average tonnage of around 20 thousand dwt per ship [4].

In order to monitor and manage ships and vessels offshore continuously and properly, fleet management systems have been widely used in the maritime industry. Fleet management is the management of a company's transportation fleet (including cars, vans, trucks, airplanes, helicopters, and ships), and aims to remove or minimize potential

© Springer International Publishing AG, part of Springer Nature 2018
N. Streitz and S. Konomi (Eds.): DAPI 2018, LNCS 10921, pp. 242–252, 2018.
https://doi.org/10.1007/978-3-319-91125-0_21

risks associated with transportation usage, coordination and maintenance, when increasing productivity and reducing overall transportation and staff costs [5]. Maritime fleet management systems generally include a set of functions, like operation monitoring, maintenance planning and management, route management, fuel consumption management, and crew management [5].

Traditionally, maritime fleet management systems focus on the whole vessel/ship. With the emergence of the Internet of Things and new smart technologies (e.g. sensors, cloud computing, big data tools), there is an increasing trend of developing a smarter generation of fleet management systems, which can be used to monitor the performance, status and behaviour of not just the whole ship (in a macro level) but crucial components and equipment inside the ship (in a micro level), such as engines, water treatment equipment, and propellers. However, developing, implementing and operating such smart fleet equipment management systems in the maritime industry will not be straightforward and can encounter a wide range of socio-technical challenges, which have not been sufficiently explored in the current literature. This paper attempts to fill this knowledge gap by drawing on the perspectives of Computer Sciences, Information Systems, Electronic and Electrical Engineering, and Management Sciences. The paper is structured as follows: the next section presents the technical features of smart fleet equipment management systems (SFEM) used in the maritime sector, followed by a discussion of the methodology that involves a desktop study based on the process of a critical literature review. We then present and discuss a range of identified socio-technical challenges associated with SFEM, with practical suggestions and conclusions drawn.

2 Technical Features of Smart Fleet Equipment Management System (SFEM)

Generally speaking, SFEM systems contain three types of functions targeting on key components of the ship [5, 6]: (1) real-time monitoring and diagnosis: to continuously monitor the operational performance of the component, diagnose signs of problems, and identify changes associated with its internal and external conditions; (2) self-control and optimization: based on the results of monitoring and self-diagnosis, the system can make automatic adjustments on the operational settings of the component in relation to environment changes and needs, and so optimize its performance while reducing cost, fuel consumption and pollution; (3) maintenance and repairing: to perform predictive data analysis, generate proactive warnings on repairing and maintenance needs, and support maintenance planning and decision marking of onshore staff. In order to achieve these intended functions with high smartness, SFEMs typically combines the usage of wireless sensors, microprocessors, automatic control systems, cloud computing data storage, software applications, and big data analytics with enhanced user interface [6].

More specifically, and taking the propulsion system as an example, a marine power plant generally consists of a main engine and several auxiliary engines [3]. The main engine generates the power needed for propeller operation and vessel navigation, and auxiliary engines are used to generate additional energy to support the main engine and ensure that there is sufficient power to support all other systems (e.g. heating system, freshwater treatment system) of the ship to perform properly. When an SFEM system is implemented, each engine will be embedded with one or more sensors to collect real-time data about, e.g. the engine's temperature, fuel consumption, power rate, and running condition. There could be many other types of sensors to be deployed into different kinds of ship components for collecting the suitable types of data needed, such as propeller shaft rpm sensor, propeller shaft power sensor, propeller shaft torque sensor, freshwater consumption sensor, ship speed over ground (i.e. GPS speed) sensor, and relative wind speed/direction sensor [4]. In addition, SFEM systems will also rely on telematic and GPS technology to track the offshore location of the vessel (and in fact also related components of the vessel [7].

All these data will then need to be transmitted to the onshore control center by using a stable, reliable and cost-effective channel, namely satellite communication system based on DVB-RCS standard (an acronym for Digital Video Broadcasting - Return Channel via Satellite). By using geostationary satellites, DVB-RCS systems can offer large offshore coverage all over the world, wide band and flexible bandwidth allocation [9]. Together with GSM (global system for mobile)/VOIP (voice over Internet protocol) technologies, crew members onboard can even enjoy the services of web browsing, e-mail, e-banking, and Internet voice call [8].

The real-time data collected from various sensors will be initially processed by a local data server and automatic control devices onboard, to allow the system to perform self-control and self-adjustment on the settings of related ship components. But these data will eventually be transmitted through DVB-RCS technologies to onshore data centers for proper storage, processing and analysis. As a large amount of data will be generated from different components and different ships on a daily basis, these data will need to be centrally stored in onshore data centers by using cloud computing technologies. Cloud computing is a technology that provides a sharing resource pool to store large datasets, while also allowing on-demand access to this shared pool of computing resources (networks, servers, data storage, applications and services) via a network [11, 12].

Further to internal data, ship companies may also retrieve and store external environment data (e.g. water-column data, bathymetry, ocean acoustics, bioluminescence, and tides) from the Naval Oceanographic Office (NAVOCEANO in short) [10] in their cloud data center. These internal and external data with large volume and various formats will be integrated together and analyzed by using machine learning, artificial intelligence and big data analytics tools embedded in SFEM systems, which can thus assist the crew and onshore staff in complex decision making and other knowledge processing tasks. Some very specific analytical functions can be designed and developed in SFEM systems, depending on the actual needs of shipping companies, including: (1) voyage performance analysis and management, such as speed optimization, autopilot improvements, trim and draft optimization; (2) hull condition analysis and management, such as propeller condition management, engine maintenance onboard, auxiliary engine maintenance, boiler maintenance; (3) energy consumption analysis and management; (4) prognostic performance analysis and management, such as fault prediction, trending analysis, alarm prediction for various crucial components [13, 14].

3 Methodology

Although the technical features of SFEM can offer very attractive benefits to shipping companies, implementing, operating and using such systems will not be easy in practical terms. The study presented in this paper aims to identify and explore potential socio-technical challenges associated with the implementation and exploitation of SFEM systems by conducting a desktop study based on the process of a critical literature review. This critical review followed the approach proposed by Saunders et al. [15], and relied on surveying and using secondary sources. Literature search for this critical review consisted of two phases.

Table 1. Journals and databases searched

Journals searched	Database searched
Procedia-Social and Behavioral Sciences	ScienceDirect
Journal of Cleaner Production	Emerald
Communications in Computer and Information Science	IEEE Xplore
Journal of Navigation	Google Scholar
International Journal of Satellite Communications and Networking	Web of Science
Journal of Computer Information Systems	Etc.
IEEE Journal of Oceanic Engineering	
Journal of Manufacturing Technology Management	
Industrial Management & Data Systems	
Journal of Management Information Systems	
Applied Ocean Research	
Etc.	

Table 2. Keywords used for journal and database search at stage one

For journal search	For database search
(searched within: title, abstract and/or full text)	
Smart fleet management system	Challenges "OR" issues "AND" smart fleet management
Fleet equipment management issues	Challenges "OR" issues "AND" fleet equipment management
Ship equipment management challenges	Challenges "OR" issues "AND" ship management
Intelligent fleet management	Challenges "OR" issues "AND" maritime industry
Ship management challenges	Challenges "OR" issues "AND" vessel management
Vessel management issues	Etc.
Etc.	

At the first phase of the critical review, the researchers attempted to retrieve academic articles that are directly related to issues, problems or challenges regarding the development and implementation and usage of SFEM from a number of reputable journals and databases (see Table 1 for details). A set of predefined keywords (e.g. challenges, smart fleet management system, Internet of Things, fleet equipment management, intelligent fleet management systems, vessel, ships, maritime industry) as shown in Table 2 was used in this round of article search. Although this endeavor returned some technical studies on SFEM (e.g. [8, 11, 13]), we were not able to retrieve any relevant articles or in-depth studies on the socio-technical phenomenon under investigation.

As a result, a broader and more extensive literature review was conducted at the second stage. Instead of looking for studies directly about SFEM, this second attempt focused on all related technologies (e.g. sensors, cloud computing, software applications, and big data analytics) covered in fleet management and the difficulties of implementing such kind of technologies (Table 3). Although the same set of academic journals and databases were searched, but an alternative set of search keywords were defined and used (e.g. including new terms like sensors, cloud computing, and big data) to reflect the broader coverage of this round of literature search.

Table 3. Keywords used for journal and database search at stage two

For journal search	For database search
(searched within: title, abstract and/or full text)	
Fleet equipment management issues	Challenges "OR" issues "AND" maritime industry
Vessel management issues	Challenges "OR" issues "AND" sensors in ships
Ship equipment management challenges	Challenges "OR" issues "AND" cloud computing
Sensors deployment issues	Challenges "OR" issues "AND" internet of things
Internet of Things challenges	Challenges "OR" issues "AND" vessel software
Cloud computing issues	Challenges "OR" issues "AND" big data analytics
Vessel software issues	Challenges "OR" issues "AND" shipping big data
Software applications in ships	Challenges "OR" issues "AND" big data fleet management
Big data analytic in maritime industry	Challenges "OR" issues "AND" IT in maritime industry
Big data challenges	Etc.
Information technology in maritime industry	
Etc.	

With much effort, the researchers successfully retrieved and reviewed a good number of valuable literatures. These retrieved articles and materials were systematically analyzed and synthesized, and then used as raw materials to construct arguments for the identification and exploration of socio-technical challenges associated with the development, implementation and usage of SFEM. These challenges are presented and discussed in the next section.

4 Challenges Associated with the Development, Implementation and Usage of SFEM Systems

The results of the critical literature review process identified a range of interrelated socio-technical SFEM challenges, respectively related to system integration, cloud computing, data quality and big data analytics, user resistance, and operational aspects, as detailed below.

System Integration Challenges. Crucial ship components like main engines, auxiliary engines, freshwater treatment equipment, and propellers are generally designed, manufactured and maintained by very different and specialized vendors [16, 17]. As a consequence, a separated SFEM system may often be developed for each of these components and equipment by different vendors, using diverse database models and interfaces, different data formats and possibly totally incompatible architectures [18, 19]. Therefore, integrating these separated SFEM systems together with legacy systems (which can in turn have very different IT architectures and formats) can be a very difficult and costly task [17, 19]. In light of this discussion, and in order to protect their own benefits, component/system vendors may often set up strict system access and data sharing policies, which can present further barriers for cross-system integration [20]. This is particularly true in a cloud environment, where client companies often have limited control on their data stored by third-party cloud vendors and have insufficient freedom and right to customize a cloud application and integrate it with other systems [19, 21, 22]. Such system integration issues will inevitably lead to system fragmentation in the shipping company, through the creation of technological islands, which are very often totally isolated and non-communicable and so leading to poor data quality and potentially misleading data analytical predictions and results [20, 23].

Lack of Control in the Cloud. Traditionally, IT resources (including data, module applications, and database servers) are internally hosted and maintained by user organizations. Accompanied with the emergence of cloud technologies, there is an increasing trend for companies to migrate their internal IT applications and databases into the cloud [24, 25], which allows companies to use these applications and data as on-demand services through a web browser, without physically installing software programs or storing the data in local servers [19, 26]. Such cloud service model enables less hardware investments, as well as less fees and internal hazard for system maintenance and upgrade [11, 12], and is highly suitable for the deployment of SFEM solutions that involve large amount of real-time datasets collected by sensors [25, 26]. However, and in contrast to these attractive benefits, the adoption of cloud technologies can also raise many challenges, uncertainties and problems to shipping companies if they do not plan carefully [12, 19, 27]. The root of these problems lies in the fact that client companies often have less transparency, freedom and rights to control their data and applications in the cloud environment [12, 28]. Further to causing potential system integration problems as discussed above, lack of control and rights can often make client companies suffer from what so called "vendor lock-in" events [22, 28]. A vendor lock-in event refers to the scenario that user companies are not able to change their cloud providers even in the case of service dissatisfaction, due to high cost of moving data from one cloud provider to another and potentially legal traps set up by the original vendor, e.g. cloud providers may claim that they (rather than the client company) are the owner of the data stored [19, 22, 29]. For smart fleet equipment management systems, when cloud vendors are often also shipping component/equipment providers, changing them will be extremely difficult, costly and time-consuming [27].

Challenges on Data Quality and Big Data Analytics. Maintaining high data quality is crucial for the success of any IT applications [30, 31]. However, our extensive review of the literature identified that data quality of SFEM systems can potentially be influenced by a range of factors [21, 29, 32]. Most notably, real-time data of ship components are collected by using a wide range of wireless sensors, but the quality and sensitivity of sensors used by different providers can vary and so may lead to inaccurate measurements [21, 33, 34]. Further to the usage of sensors, some significant operational data (e.g. actual time and place of component repairing) will need to be input by crew members and/or onshore staff, but human errors can occur during the data entry process, especially when there is a lack of suitable training and there is a high level of user resistance [23, 35, 36]. Moreover, the issue of system integration as discussed above can lead to incomplete, redundant, and potentially very fragmented datasets [23, 37]. Poor data quality will inevitably affect the analytical results (such as proactive fault detection, repairing needs prediction and route planning) generated by big data tools of SFEM systems [12, 23, 37]. On the other hand, the practicality, suitability and feasibility of these big data analytical results and predictions can be threatened by real-world conditions, legal restrictions and operational limitations [32, 38]. For instance, when the SFEM system identifies the need of component repairing and makes advanced warning, the vessel may still not be able to reach onshore repairing centers on time [30, 31, 39]. This is not just caused by distance-related reasons, but may also be attributed to the fact that different countries will have specific legislative regulations, custom control systems, and official documentation requirements, which can potentially delay the voyage and so make the vessel miss the best time for component repairing [32, 33, 38].

Sources of User Resistance. The implementation and usage of SFEM systems can have a lot of impacts on both crew members and onshore supporting staff [30, 36]. For crew members, they will be assigned with new responsibilities and tasks for monitoring the performance of crucial shipping components, by using SFEM and new operational processes [40, 41]. This will require crew members to learn a new set of skills in order to use and operate the system effectively [23, 35, 42]. However, crew members may not always be willing to accept such new duties and changes [35, 43]. And the learning process could also be difficult to crew members with higher age and lower education level [23, 35, 44]. Similarly, onshore supporting staff will be assigned with more power and freedom to make important maintenance, repairing and route planning decisions, by considering the analytical results and predictions generated by big data functions of SFEM systems [42, 44, 45]. They may also be required to perform further data analysis on the system, in order to explore the datasets more deeply and generate more in-depth insights [43, 45]. Nevertheless, onshore supporting staff may not always be equipped with the right level of skills, experience and knowledge to play such decision-making and data analysis roles [35, 46]. All of these issues can become potential sources of user resistance, which will not just reduce users' intention/willingness to use the new SFEM system but will often also increase the possibility of human errors and so leading to poor data quality as discussed earlier on [23, 46].

5   Further Discussion and Recommendations

It clearly emerged from our above analysis and discussion that the identified SFEM challenges seem to be interwoven and closely related with each other (e.g. lack of control in the cloud environment can raise problems of system integration, which together with user resistance can lead to poor data quality and affect the results of big data analytics). In order to overcome these interrelated socio-technical challenges, shipping companies need to establish very holistic and thorough system development and implementation strategies, by considering the following recommendations:

Shipping companies need to be very careful when selecting their SFEM system vendors. In particular, they have to make sure that the selected solution can offer high compatibility, and so all legacy and new systems can be integrated easily and seamless. Shipping companies also need to pay specific attention to service agreement with cloud vendors, and need to have a clear understanding about their rights, data ownership, and level of freedom before signing the contract.

In order to minimize potential user resistance, a suitable change management program should be designed and implemented to make sure that all staff concerned are properly trained, know the benefits of the new SFEM systems, and understand the importance of their roles and cooperation. It will also be beneficial to inform, consult and involve users as early as possible in order to improve their level of acceptance toward using the system.

In order to increase the practicality of maintenance and repairing options suggested by big data tools, more flexible plans and collaborative relationships will be needed to be set up with component/system vendors and other shipping companies. For instance, when a component of a vessel breaks down during voyage, it is difficult for onshore support centers to provide immediate help over long distance. But the crew can seek for help from nearby vessels, which may not be from the same shipping company but have the same system vendor and so may be able to offer the needed spare components and even offshore technical support. Such new type of collaborative relationship may also lead to the establishment of new service and business models, and can benefit all parties involved.

6   Conclusions

This paper reviews the technical features of the next generation of vessel fleet management systems, namely smart fleet equipment systems or SFEMs. It also provides a critical analysis and discussion on potential socio-technical challenges associated with the development, implementation and usage of SFEM systems in the maritime industry, together with recommendations. Some important conclusions have been drawn from the study. Specifically, although SFEM relies heavily on advanced information technologies, its success can be affected by a wide range of regional, legal, organizational, operational, analytical, user and vendor-related factors and challenges as identified, explored and discussed in this paper. More importantly, because these factors and challenges will not exist independently and can have very sophisticated interrelationships, they may be very difficult to manage and contain. Overall, it can be concluded that researchers and practitioners should not simply focus on the technical aspects of SFEM, more attention should be paid to socio-technical factors and their interrelationships that can lead to substantial usage problems and even severe technical failures.

References

1. Soner, O., Akyuz, E., Celik, M.: A maritime research concept through establishing ship operational problem solution (Shipos) centre via information technologies integrated with or/ Ms. Procedia-Soc. Behav. Sci. **195**, 2796–2803 (2015)
2. Poulsen, R.T., Johnson, H.: The logic of business vs. the logic of energy management practice: understanding the choices and effects of energy consumption monitoring systems in shipping companies. J. Clean. Prod. **112**, 3785–3797 (2016)
3. Perera, L.P., Mo, B., Kristjánsson, L.A., Jønvik, P.C., Svarda, J.Ø.: Evaluations on ship performance under varying operational conditions. In: ASME 2015 34th International Conference on Ocean, Offshore and Arctic Engineering, OMAE 2015, Proceedings of the International Conference on Offshore Mechanics and Arctic Engineering - OMAE, vol. 7, p. V007T06A060. American Society of Mechanical Engineers (ASME) (2015)
4. United Nations Conference on Trade and Development. http://unctad.org/en/pages/publicationwebflyer.aspx?publicationid=1650. Accessed 4 Nov 2017
5. Joszczuk–Januszewska, J.: Importance of cloud-based maritime fleet management software. In: Mikulski, J. (ed.) TST 2013. CCIS, vol. 395, pp. 450–458. Springer, Heidelberg (2013). https://doi.org/10.1007/978-3-642-41647-7_55
6. Porter, M.E., Heppelmann, J.E.: How smart, connected products are transforming competition. Harv. Bus. Rev. **92**(1–2), 64–88 (2015)
7. Hornby, A.S.: Oxford Advanced Learner's English-Chinese Dictionary, 7th edn. Oxford University Press, Oxford (2009)
8. Lozano, J.L., Corbera, J., de Osés, F.X.M.: Design of a remote monitoring system for high speed craft. J. Navig. **53**(3), 465–471 (2000)
9. Gentile, A., Luglio, M., Manzo, M., Zampognaro, F.: Sensible: IP-layer dynamic bandwidth management for DVB-RCS network subdomains. Int. J. Satell. Commun. Netw. **32**(5), 393–406 (2014)
10. Gathof, J.M., Bassich, J.B.: Recent development in the Naval Oceanographic Office survey operation center. In: MTS/IEEE Conference on Celebrating the Past - Teaming Toward the Future, Oceans Conference Record (IEEE), San Diego, Calif, vol. 1, pp. 417–422. Institute of Electrical and Electronics Engineers Inc. (2003)
11. Thoma, C.: Fleet management on the basis of cloud software. Ship Offshore **3**, 76–77 (2011)
12. Dutta, A., Peng, G.C., Choudhary, A.: Risks in enterprise cloud computing: the perspective of IT experts. J. Comput. Inf. Syst. **53**(4), 39–48 (2013)
13. Beşikçi, E.B., Kececi, T., Arslan, O., Turan, O.: An application of fuzzy-AHP to ship operational energy efficiency measures. Ocean Eng. **121**, 392–402 (2015)

14. Logan, K.P.: Prognostic software agents for machinery health monitoring. In: 2003 IEEE Aerospace Conference, IEEE Aerospace Conference Proceedings, vol. 7, pp. 3213–3225. IEEE Computer Society (2003)
15. Saunders, M., Philip, L., Adrian, T.: Research Methods for Business Students, 5th edn. Prentice Hall Financial Times, Upper Saddle River (2006)
16. Seman, A.J.: Next generation Navy ship automation systems engineering from sensors to systems. In: Proceedings - 2005 International Conference on Systems, Man and Cybernetics Society, vol. 2, pp. 1218–1222. Institute of Electrical and Electronics Engineers Inc. (2005)
17. Luckose, L., Hess, H.L., Johnson, B.K.: Power conditioning system for fuel cells for integration to ships. In: 5th IEEE Vehicle Power and Propulsion Conference, VPPC 2009, pp. 858–864. IEEE Computer Society (2009)
18. Pan, K., Nunes, J.M.B., Peng, G.C.: Risks affecting ERP post-implementation: insights from a large Chinese manufacturing group. J. Manuf. Technol. Manag. **22**(1), 107–130 (2011)
19. Peng, G.C., Gala, C.J.: Cloud ERP: a new dilemma to modern organisations. J. Comput. Inf. Syst. **54**(4), 589–599 (2014)
20. Challita, A., Barber, J., Ykema, J.: Integrating electromagnetic launchers on ships. In: 12th Symposium on Electromagnetic Launch Technology, pp. 495–498. Institute of Electrical and Electronics Engineers Computer Society (2004)
21. Zhao, M., Ma, J.W., Luo, H.L.: Schema of big data service oriented to ocean shipping service integration with WSN. In: International Conference on Computer Science and Environmental Engineering (CSEE 2015), pp. 712–717. Destech Publications, Inc. (2015)
22. Ghazouani, S., Slimani, Y.: A survey on cloud service description. J. Netw. Comput. Appl. **91**, 61–74 (2017)
23. Peng, G.C., Nunes, J.M.B.: Surfacing ERP exploitation risks through a risk ontology. Ind. Manag. Data Syst. **109**(7), 926–942 (2009)
24. Liu, X., Zhang, Q., Wang, S.: Research of ship maintenance management platform based on cloud computing. In: 4th International Conference on Mechatronics, Materials, Chemistry and Computer Engineering (ICMMCCE 2015), vol. 39, pp. 2997–3001. Atlantis Press (2015)
25. Wang, X.V., Xu, X.: Cloud manufacturing in support of sustainability. In: 9th ASME International Manufacturing Science and Engineering Conference (MSEC 2014), vol. 1, p. V001T04A014. American Society Mechanical Engineers (2014)
26. Sidorov, V., Ng, W.K.: Transparent data encryption for data-in-use and data-at-rest in a cloud-based database-as-a-service solution. In: Proceedings - 2015 IEEE World Congress on Services (SERVICES 2015), pp. 221–228. Institute of Electrical and Electronics Engineers Inc. (2015)
27. Padilla Roland, S., Milton Simo, K., Johnson Lester, W.: Impact of service value on satisfaction and repurchase intentions in business-to-business cloud computing. Serv. Sci. **9**(1), 5–13 (2017)
28. De Oliveira, R.R., Martins, R.M., da Silva, S.A.: Impact of the vendor lock-in problem on testing as a service (TaaS). In: Proceedings - 2017 IEEE International Conference on Cloud Engineering, IC2E 2017, pp. 190–196. Institute of Electrical and Electronics Engineers Inc. (2017)
29. Choudhury, P., Sharma, M., Vikas, K.: Service ranking systems for cloud vendors. In: 2011 International Conference on Material Science and Information Technology, MSIT 2011, Advanced Materials Research, vol. 433–440, pp. 3949–3953. Trans Tech Publications (2011)
30. Majewska, K., Mieloszyk, M., Ostachowicz, W.: Experimental method of strain/stress measurements on tall sailing ships using Fibre Bragg Grating sensors. Appl. Ocean Res. **47**(2), 270–283 (2014)

31. Luo, H., Wu, K., Guo, Z.: SID: ship intrusion detection with wireless sensor networks. In: Proceedings of the 31st International Conference on Distributed Computing Systems, ICDCS 2011, pp. 879–888. Institute of Electrical and Electronics Engineers Inc. (2011)

32. Perera, L.P., Mo, B.: Data compression of ship performance and navigation information under deep learning. In: ASME 2016 35th International Conference on Ocean, Offshore and Arctic Engineering, OMAE 2016, Proceedings of the International Conference on Offshore Mechanics and Arctic Engineering – OMAE, vol. 7, p. V007T06A086. American Society of Mechanical Engineers (ASME) (2016)

33. Oh, S., Seo, D., Lee, B.: S3 (Secure Ship-to-Ship) information sharing scheme using ship authentication in the e-Navigation. Int. J. Secur. Appl. **9**(2), 97–109 (2015)

34. Krush, D., Cammin, C., Heynicke, R., Scholl, G., Kaercher, B.: A wireless communication system for energy and environmental monitoring. J. Sens. Sens. Syst. **6**(1), 19–26 (2017)

35. Du Plessis, M.: Re-implementing an individual performance management system as a change intervention at higher education institutions - overcoming staff resistance. In: 7th European Conference on Management Leadership and Governance, pp. 105–115. ACAD Conferences Ltd. (2011)

36. Chow, R., Lamb, M., Charest, G.: Evaluation of current and future crew sizes and compositions: two RCN case studies. Nav. Eng. J. **128**(4), 53–58 (2016)

37. Chaturvedi, S.K., Yang, C.S., Ouchi, K.: Ship recognition by integration of SAR and AIS. J. Navig. **65**(2), 323–337 (2012)

38. Lazakis, I., Dikis, K., Michala, A.L.: Advanced ship systems condition monitoring for enhanced inspection, maintenance and decision making in ship operations. In: 6th Transport Research Arena (TRA 2016), vol. 14, pp. 1679–1688. Elsevier Science BV (2016)

39. Xiong, X., Wei, F., Li, J.: Vibration monitoring system of ships using wireless sensor networks. In: 11th IEEE International Conference on Mechatronics and Automation (ICMA 2014), pp. 90–94. IEEE (2014)

40. Runnerstrom, E.: Human systems integration and shipboard damage control. Nav. Eng. J. **115**(4), 71–79 (2003)

41. van de Merwe, F., Kahler, N., Securius, P.: Crew-centred design of ships - the CyClaDes project. In: 6th Transport Research Arena (TRA 2016), vol. 14, pp. 18–21. Elsevier Science BV (2016)

42. Zhu, L., Hou, M., Li, J.: Crew qualification comprehensive evaluation of shipping enterprise based on multi-level fuzzy evaluation method. In: 2013 International Conference on Materials, Transportation and Environmental Engineering, CMTEE 2013, Advanced Materials Research, vol. 779–780, p. 636+. Trans Tech Publications Ltd. (2013)

43. Sydow, K.R.: Shipboard maintenance: what do Surface Warfare Officers need to know-and when do they need to know it. Nav. Eng. J. **120**(2), 89–98 (2008)

44. Naftanaila, I., Nistor, C.: Strategic importance of human resources recruitment and training for competitiveness and business excellence in maritime transport. In: 4th International Conference on Business Excellence, vol. 2, pp. 26–29. Infomarket Publ House (2009)

45. Sherbaz, S., Duan, W.: Operational options for green ships. J. Mar. Sci. Appl. **11**(3), 335–340 (2012)

46. Baker, C., Krull, R., Snyder, G.: Survey of reduced workload and crewing strategies for ocean patrol vessels. Nav. Eng. J. **113**(2), 29–44 (2001)

Opportunistic Data Exchange Algorithm for Animal Wearable Device Through Active Behavior Against External Stimuli

Keijiro Nakagawa[1](✉), Atsuya Makita[1], Miho Nagasawa[2], Takefumi Kikusui[2], Kaoru Sezaki[1], and Hiroki Kobayashi[1]

[1] Center for Spatial Information Science, The University of Tokyo, Kashiwa, Chiba 277-8568, Japan
{kenakaga,amakita,sezaki,kobayashi}@csis.u-tokyo.ac.jp
[2] Department of Animal Science and Biotechnology, Azabu University, Sagamihara, Kanagawa 252-5201, Japan
{nagasawa,takkiku}@carazabu.com

Abstract. This paper proposes a method of communication wake control for encounters between three or more users of animal wearable communication devices when threatening behavior against an external stimulus is detected. Specifically, it identifies an encounter of three or more contacts using an acceleration sensor attached to an animal, and uses this as a trigger to wake the communication device to transmit and receive data between the devices. In order to evaluate this algorithm, evaluation experiments were conducted using four standard poodles. With the cooperation of veterinary researchers, we established conditions where strangers with cameras passed immediately in front of the dogs' run, in order to provide the threatening behavior used to trigger communication wake control.

Keywords: Animal wearable · Behavior · Animal-Computer Interaction

1 Introduction

The concept of humans and animals wearing sensors to enable the monitoring of their behaviors and the surrounding environment was introduced in the early stages of sensor network research. However, when studying wild animals, there are very limited opportunities to recharge sensor batteries. In order to acquire sensor information, an animal's device must contact a sink node that eventually connects to an external network, and the frequency of these contacts is low. It is therefore crucial to design sensor nodes with longer lifetimes and lower power usage.

More specifically, communication between wireless sensor nodes requires 100 times more power consumption than other operations [1]. Terrestrial mammals inhabiting forests are known to behave differently when they encounter other animals, compared to how they act in other situations [2].

When they encounter a different animal (which can be seen as threatening behavior against external stimulus), the probability is high that the sensor nodes worn by the

© Springer International Publishing AG, part of Springer Nature 2018
N. Streitz and S. Konomi (Eds.): DAPI 2018, LNCS 10921, pp. 253–263, 2018.
https://doi.org/10.1007/978-3-319-91125-0_22

animals are within each other's communication radius. Therefore, by activating the communication capabilities of a sensor node only when numerous animals are present (and putting the sensor node into a sleep state otherwise), it is possible to substantially prolong the lifetime of a sensor node.

This paper discusses the design, development and evaluation of a system to tackle this issue. Firstly, a new experimental system is designed based on observation methodologies in related studies. In addition, the spatial-temporal process of the nonhuman-centric interactions of users is evaluated using quantitative content analysis. Finally, on the basis of the experimental results, the overall findings are discussed, including a description of the possible applications of the system. The remainder of this paper is structured as follows. Section 2 describes the background to this study; Sect. 3 presents the proposed method; Sect. 4 gives details of the evaluation; Sect. 5 presents a detailed discussion; Sect. 6 summarizes directions for future research; and Sect. 7 offers conclusions.

2   Background

2.1   Technical Limitations on Animal Wearable Interfaces

The ecological monitoring of wild animals via ubiquitous sensor networks and mobile phones has already been realized in locations close to urban areas [3] (i.e. close to human societies); however, in wildlife habitats, power and information infrastructure networks are severely limited. More specifically, the profitability of infrastructure services is too low in areas where the number of users is extremely small, for example within the habitats of most wildlife. Furthermore, when setting up a ubiquitous sensor network, a great deal of effort is required in terms of coordinating with national parks and owners, administrative stakeholders, and other stakeholders. In addition, sensors installed outdoors incur very high installation, operational, and environmental costs. Given these limitations, wearable sensors for wildlife are attracting increased research attention.

To retrieve records acquired via sensors, we must recapture these animals (Fig. 1(a)) or use a wearable telemetry transmitter. The habitat within which wild animals can be recaptured and the telecommunication range for telemetry are both very limited, making it difficult to expand the scope of surveys and studies.

When targeting endangered species in Japan, the lifespan for the continuous operation of a compact and lightweight sensor for an animal is typically two years. The weight of the wearable device is limited to approximately 2–5% of the weight of the target animal [4]. Given that many target animals are small-sized terrestrial mammals that are light in weight, it is difficult to install and operate inertial navigation recording devices and the like, as illustrated in Fig. 1(b).

Furthermore, accurate time and position information cannot be expected from the records obtained from the wearable sensor nodes of wild animals. Given the weight limit restrictions, these do not contain an internal clock or an inertial navigation recording device. Satellite positioning and radio clock signals also face difficulties within forests [4], as illustrated in Fig. 1(c).

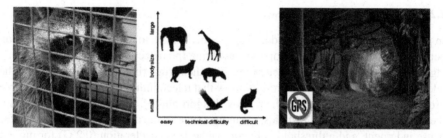

Fig. 1. (a) A wild animal captured in a trap; (b) a diagram showing the relationship between body size and technical difficulty; and (c) illustration that within a forest, GPS and mobile signals typically do not work.

In view of the above, we need a system that minimizes cost and maximizes efficiency in terms of acquiring spatial information, in order to conduct extensive and long-term wildlife surveys in habitats where there are minimal power supply and information infrastructures. There are three key problems here, and it is necessary to simultaneously satisfy all of the conditions summarized below:

- Coverage problem: Wearable sensors are restricted to physically recapturable individuals
- Operational time problem: Wearable sensors are restricted in terms of their operational period of time, since the weight of the wearable device needs to be limited to 2–5% of the animal's body weight
- Reliability problem: Satellite signals face major difficulties within various habitat topographies; thus, there is the problem of obtaining accurate location information for the acquired data.

Our proposal for realizing much longer lifetimes and power savings in sensor nodes by leveraging the ecological interactions of multiple wild animals is, to our knowledge, the first attempt at such an endeavor, and is an innovative system involving HCI. An illustration of this system is given in Fig. 2.

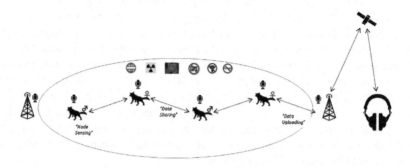

Fig. 2. Proposed sensing system/concept

2.2 Summary of Previous Research

In previous research, as illustrated in Fig. 3, a mechanism to realize telecommunication between two individuals was proposed involving the detection of an encounter by an algorithm using synthesized acceleration, and then triggering the wake control of the telecommunication device. The results show that telecommunication is possible with a probability of about 70% using the proposed algorithm [5]. In the proposed algorithm, the authors focus on two thresholds, meaning a time frame of between one and 10 s for pause judgment, and a threshold value of synthesized acceleration (0.2 G) for motion and pause judgment. However, we regard that it is not considered enough that their thresholds are optimized to each specific animal.

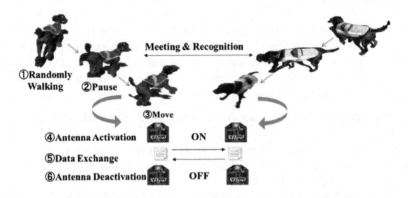

Fig. 3. Animal-to-animal data sharing between two individuals

The reason for this is that these thresholds vary depending on the conditions of the encounter with other animals, and the optimal threshold may differ depending on the species, the individual's physique, age, gender, personality and so on. Indeed, as discussed in previous research [8], the frequency of waking of the communication device varies depending on individual differences even for four individuals. In particular, there is a correlation between body height and sampling rate, and it is necessary to optimize the judgment threshold on the basis of the body height of each individual.

However, it is difficult to optimize the threshold according to body height in a genuinely wild environment, and it is not sufficient to consider only this element. Since it is necessary to determine the body height of each individual in advance, an increase in the number of individuals increases the preparatory labor, and the level of difficulty for local workers also increases, making this impractical. In encounters between individuals, there is also a difference between characteristic quantities of habitual behaviors in encounters with threats and herds of flocks, and existing studies so far have used no concrete definition for encounters between two individuals; it cannot therefore be said that this method has been sufficiently examined.

Since equipment is worn over several years, it is also necessary to consider changes in habitual behavior due to the growth of individuals, and it is necessary to set thresholds corresponding to time-series changes. Thus, dynamic algorithms reflecting these spatial and time-series changes are required.

3   Proposed Method

3.1   Detection Algorithm for Threatening Behavior Against External Stimulus

This paper proposes an algorithm optimization for the wake control of communication equipment in the time of a threatening encounter from the characteristic quantity of synthesized acceleration, as shown in Fig. 4. This algorithm is a preparation stage for a dynamic algorithm corresponding to spatial and time-series changes.

Concerned Behavior   **(1) Move**   **(2) Pause**   **(3) Strenuous Movement**

Fig. 4. Threatening behavior against external stimulus (single individual)

We will propose a method for algorithm optimization that improves the accuracy of waking of communication equipment by accurately determining both commonly seen and threatening behavior, and responding to chronological changes in the future work. The proposed algorithm is as follows:

$$if\,(\Delta G > G')$$
$$\{Call\,for\,pause\colon 0.1\,s \,<\, t \,<\, 1.0\,s\} \tag{1}$$

Where G' is a threshold value for judging threatening behavior. A mechanism for judging the time of intimidating behavior is added to the existing algorithm from the synthesized acceleration, acquired at a frequency of 20 Hz.

When judging threatening behavior using G', the algorithm transitions to a threatening behavior algorithm. In this second algorithm, $G = 0.2$, which is the same threshold used in the motion and pause judgment of the existing algorithm.

The rest time is set to $0.1\,s < t < 1.0\,s$, which means that the judgment interval related to the rest time is set to a tenth of the time of that used in the existing algorithm. Operation during threatening behavior is fierce compared with the commonly seen behavior and it is necessary to optimize the sampling rate according to its operation. In order to clearly separate the sampling rate from the commonly seen behavior, this is set to a tenth of the time.

4   Evaluation

4.1   Experiment

In order to evaluate this algorithm, four evaluation experiments were conducted using the four standard poodles shown in Fig. 5. In order to acquire accurate data during threatening behavior, we carried out an evaluation experiment in the outdoor dog run shown in Fig. 6, using acceleration sensors (MSR145 data logger) supplied by MSR Electronics. The dogs were free to move around without restraint. With the cooperation of veterinary researchers, we set up a situation where strangers passed immediately in front of the dogs' run, in order to provide the threatening behavior used to trigger waking of the communication equipment between two individuals. Evaluation experiments lasting 20 s each were carried out twice, and video recordings were made to evaluate the synthetic acceleration data and habit behavior. Sampling rate of MSR145 data logger in this experiment was 20 Hz as well as previous research [8].

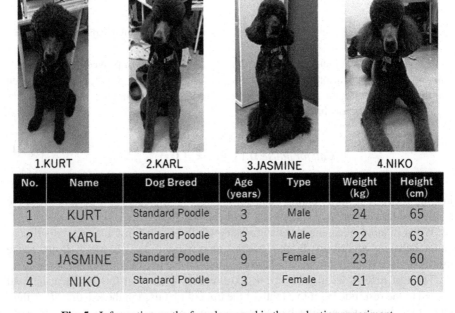

No.	Name	Dog Breed	Age (years)	Type	Weight (kg)	Height (cm)
1	KURT	Standard Poodle	3	Male	24	65
2	KARL	Standard Poodle	3	Male	22	63
3	JASMINE	Standard Poodle	9	Female	23	60
4	NIKO	Standard Poodle	3	Female	21	60

Fig. 5.   Information on the four dogs used in the evaluation experiment.

Fig. 6. The target individuals (four dogs) responding to an external stimulus (camera).

The evaluation method used in this experiment was different from that used in the previous research. In the prior study, we evaluated the success rate of waking of the communication equipment using the features of synthetic acceleration. Video camera recorded to evaluate the synthetic acceleration data and the habit behavior of a target dog when throwing a ball with it. In this study, in order to generate a more accurate evaluation of the time of the threatening behavior, we allowed each animal to continue to encounter other individuals for about 20 s from the start of the experiment, and evaluated the number of times the communication device was woken by each algorithm for one encounter.

4.2 Evaluation

The threatening behavior algorithm was evaluated with respect to the number of times the communication device was woken for $G' = 1.2, 0.8, 0.4$. We acquired synthetic acceleration data from the acceleration sensors attached to (1) KURT, (2) KARL and (3) JASMINE, but could not acquire data from (4) NIKO due to a terminal malfunction. We evaluated the experimental results based on the data from these three animals.

The experimental results presented in Fig. 7 show that number of activations in this proposed algorithm is higher for each threshold compared with the number of existing algorithms. The number of activations in the threatening behavior algorithm $G' = 0.4$ is approximately eleven-point-two-five times higher than in the prior algorithm, indicating that the maximum accuracy is high for all individuals.

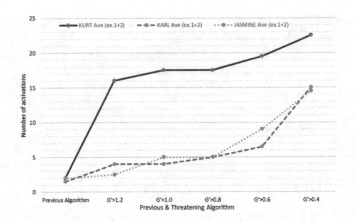

Fig. 7. Experimental results (number of activations vs. each algorithm).

It can therefore be said that threatening behavior when encountering other individuals can be detected more efficiently by our proposed method than by existing algorithms.

5   Discussion

5.1   Improvements to Data Communication Throughput

Using the proposed algorithm, which considerably improves the detection success rate for waking the communication device during threatening behavior, it is possible to consider incorporating the existing method of efficient data transfer into a wireless space. For example, since half-duplex communication and communication with a base station have basically a one-to-one correspondence in the radio space, the waiting time for the next communication is a factor that lowers throughput. IEEE 802.11n/ac implements a frame aggregation method called A-MPDU [9] to reduce waiting time as far as possible and to improve data transfer performance. In the present technology, headers such as carrier sense and acknowledgment (ACK) become unnecessary every communication, by connecting a large number of data transmissions from the base station, and receiving a large amount of data in one frame on the client side. Overhead is reduced for the whole data transfer, enabling more efficient data transfer by this method.

In prior research, for data transmission and reception between two individuals, bidirectional communication based on the order determination using preamble and ACK of data transmission/reception has been assumed; however, insufficient examination of improvements to data transfer throughput has been done. In this study, we narrowed the encounter pattern to include only threatening behavior, and optimized encounter detection, improving the detection rate more than tenfold. In addition, by shortening the stationary time in the algorithm to a tenth of that in the existing algorithm, the duration between the actual encounter and detection of the encounter by the algorithm has improved, extending the data transfer time, and an overall improvement in throughput can be obtained. In addition, throughput can be improved, for example by the use of a frame aggregation method that reduces the overhead due to the ACK, as mentioned above, ensuring stable end-to-end wireless communication and improving the detection rate.

5.2 Power Savings for Animal Wearable Interfaces

Improvements to the throughput of data transfer in inter-individual communication are important for environmental survey methods using wild animals in infrastructure-free environments; however, power savings are also important, and this is always a trade-off with data transfer. Animal wearable devices can only add 2–5% of the weight of the animal, and there are therefore severe restrictions on battery capacity. Since the system operation time depends on the battery life, improvements to battery performance and power savings are important in long-term monitoring over several years that takes spatial and time-series expansion into account. In this research, we focus on power saving, and show that it is possible to efficiently detect events such as encounters.

Beacon technology utilizing Bluetooth or BLE is not a realistic detection method for this system, due to its high power consumption. It is therefore important to improve the efficiency of data transfer while maintaining power savings by operating only the acceleration sensor, which has low power consumption, in order to improve the feasibility of this system. While the proposed method improves the encounter detection rate and improves the data transfer efficiency, power savings are also achieved by operating only the acceleration sensor.

6   Applications

A report published by the International Atomic Energy Agency regarding the Chernobyl nuclear disaster of 1986 [6] stated that it is academically and socially important to conduct ecological studies of the levels and effects of radiation exposure on wild animal populations. Here, long-term and wide-range monitoring is required to understand the effects of such a nuclear accident. For the more recent Fukushima nuclear disaster of 2011, we have little evidence regarding the direct effects of radioactivity on wildlife [7]. As reported in [7], Ishida has begun conducting regular ecological studies of wild animals in the northern Abukuma Mountains, near the site of the Fukushima Daiichi nuclear power plant; high levels of radiation have been detected in these mountains. Ishida aims to place automatic recording devices at over 500 locations and has already collected and analyzed the vocalizations of target wild animals.

When monitoring species in this way, counting the recorded calls of animals is often an effective method, since acoustic communication is used by many types of animals including mammals, birds, amphibians, fish and insects [2]. In addition to visual counts, this method is commonly used to investigate birds and amphibians [2]. An observer listens to calls and identifies species from the recorded data. However, this method has a disadvantage in that the result is affected by the lack of an information and electrical power supply infrastructure.

To address this limitation, wearable sensors can be used for wild animals (Fig. 2). To collect the data recorded by these wearable sensors, it is necessary to recapture the monitored subjects; thus, wearable sensors are limited to collecting data from the recaptured subjects' habitats. To solve the problems with existing systems, the proposed project will develop a system where wild animals are fitted with a wearable sensor, the spatial information in their territory is recorded via their individual actions, information obtained through group actions (with reduced power requirements) is shared, and this shared information is eventually uploaded to the Internet.

7   Conclusion

This paper proposes a method for communication equipment wake control for encounters through active behavior against external stimuli. Specifically, it involves three or more contacts between acceleration sensors attached to animals; each sensor is triggered to wake the communication device to transmit and receive data between the animals' devices when threatening behavior against an external stimulus is detected. In order to evaluate this algorithm, evaluation experiments were conducted using four standard poodles. In order to more accurately evaluate the time of the threatening behavior, we set conditions for continuing to encounter other individuals for about 20 s from the start of the experiment, and evaluated the number of times the communication device was woken by each algorithm in one encounter. With cooperation from veterinary researchers, we set up a condition where strangers passed immediately in front of the dogs' run, in order to generate the threatening behavior used to trigger waking of the communication equipment between two individuals.

Acknowledgments. This study was supported by JSPS Kakenhi via grants 26700015 and 16K12666, MIC Scope via grant 162103107, JST Presto 11012, and the Moritani Scholarship Foundation.

References

1. Shimizu, K., Iwai, M., Sezaki, K.: Social link analysis using wireless beaconing and accelerometer. In: 2013 27th International Conference on Advanced Information Networking and Applications Workshops, pp. 33–38 (2013). https://doi.org/10.1109/waina.2013.141
2. Begon, M., Harper, J.L., Townsend, C.R.: Ecology: Individuals, Populations, and Communities. Blackwell Scientific, Boston (1990)
3. Doniec, M., Detweiler, C., Vasilescu, I., Anderson, D.M., Rus, D.: Autonomous gathering of livestock using a multi-functional sensor network plat-form. In: Proceedings of the 6th Workshop on Hot Topics in Embedded Networked Sensors, Killarney, Ireland, pp. 1–5. ACM (2010)
4. Kobayashi, H., Hiyama, A., Kobayashi, S., Izawa, M., Matsushima, J., Michitaka, H.: Wild theremin: electronic music instrument for remote wildlife observation. Trans. Hum. Interface Soc. **12**(1), 15–22 (2010)

5. Kamma, Y., Sezaki, K., Kobayashi, H.: Poster: spatio-temporal information correction mechanism for wild animal wearable sensors. In: Proceedings of the 14th Annual International Conference on Mobile Systems, Applications, and Services Companion, Singapore, p. 40. ACM (2016)

6. Chernobyl Forum: Expert Group "Environment." and International Atomic Energy Agency. Environmental consequences of the Chernobyl accident and their remediation: twenty years of experience; report of the Chernobyl Forum Expert Group 'Environment'. International Atomic Energy Agency, Vienna (2006)

7. Ishida, K.: Contamination of wild animals: effects on wildlife in high radioactivity areas of the agricultural and forest landscape. In: Nakanishi, T., Tanoi, K. (eds.) Agricultural Implications of the Fukushima Nuclear Accident, pp. 119–129. Springer, Tokyo (2013). https://doi.org/10.1007/978-4-431-54328-2_12

8. Nakagawa, K., Kobayashi, H., Sezaki, K.: Poster: carrier pigeon-like sensing system: animal–computer interface design for opportunistic data exchange interaction for a wildlife monitoring application. In: Proceedings of 5th Augmented Human International Conference 2014, Kobe, Japan, 07–09 March (2014)

9. Skordoulis, D., Chen, H.-H., Stephens, A.P., Liu, C., Jamalipour, A.: IEEE 802.11n mac frame aggregation mechanisms for next-generation high-throughput WLANS. IEEE Wirel. Commun. (2008)

Measuring Scarcity or Balancing Abundance: Some Reflections on Human-Building Interaction Paradigms from an Architectural Perspective

Selena Savic[✉] [iD]

Technical University Vienna, Wiedner Hauptrstrasse 7, 1040 Vienna, Austria
selena.savic@attp.tuwien.ac.at

Abstract. Reyner Banham, author of *The Architecture of the Well Tempered Environment*, described two contrasting approaches to natural resources and architecture: massive structure and power-operated environment. The former, he claimed, is never sufficient on its own: we always needed to also include power-operated infrastructures to make buildings livable.

Few decades later, moved by the oil crises and contemporary pollution concerns, we began to measure building performance and livability by the scarcity of natural reserves of resources. The sense of scarcity became a major drive in development of technologies to measure and reduce energy use.

Parallel to this development, massive structure and power-operated environments conflated in several ways. We can locate smart building development in this lineage of immixture of power-operated environment with massive structure. Rich data collection from sensors and logging of users actions permit to orchestrate, to a certain extent, the co-operation between buildings and their human users.

The discourse on scarcity, however, still haunts the discipline. Scarcity of resources and our attempts to measure them have been a strong drive behind technological developments. This starts to change slowly, with the advances in renewable energy technologies and proliferation of communication networks. By moving away from the scarcity discourse and placing more value on abundance of information, I pertain to address the interplay between user agency and building automation. I discuss three cases of scarcity that can be read in a different key: energy, wireless communication and attention. It is in this way that we can work towards turning mere automation into sophisticated orchestration.

Keywords: Human-building interaction · Infrastructure · Measurement
Scarcity · Abundance

1 On Buildings and Computation

Computational processes regulate temperature, shades, permission to open doors throughout contemporary buildings. If we adopted the lens of Le Corbusier's infamous statement that houses are machines for living in, we could be easily fooled into thinking

© Springer International Publishing AG, part of Springer Nature 2018
N. Streitz and S. Konomi (Eds.): DAPI 2018, LNCS 10921, pp. 264–274, 2018.
https://doi.org/10.1007/978-3-319-91125-0_23

that we should have to simply compare houses to computers. But let's look at it more carefully. Le Corbusier also said that an armchair is a machine for sitting in; the street is a traffic machine; cities are machines too. This generative power of things is what the architect was addressing, not merely comparing elements of a house construction to a machinery: "Important advance can only come from without, from quarter where no question at all arises of such a thing as inextricably locked machinery." [9]

Space, not building is the machine, claimed Hiller [6]. He considered Le Corbusier's use of the word metaphorical, rather than paradigmatical: machine as a metaphor of the style and not of the floor plan. Function is never fully encoded in building form as cultural practices tend to be more complex than the possibilities offered by space. At the same time, the form of the building is a mapping of the behaviour. Buildings are machine-like, they produce functional outcomes through their spatial properties; they are at the same time language-like, embodying and transmitting social information. But they are neither language nor machines. "Buildings are thus probabilistic space machines, able to absorb as well as generate social information through their configuration." [6]. Real space is the continuous space of material objects through which we move; logical space is the discontinuous world of expressive form; building is the point where real space is converted into logical space. Hillier saw the building's social configuration inseparable from its materiality.

In the capacity and capability-attuned discussion on the urban and the three gestalts of architecture-turned-symbolization, Vera Bühlmann summarized Michel Serres' thinking on the machine, which he described as the first gestalt [4]. Machine, a tool, means (Greek) and enabler (Proto-Indo-European) uses energy found in nature, and operates on the principle of the linkage of geometrically continuous circular movements. These machines work with motion, they are rotative machines and as such they are strictly geometrical, constructed from universal forms, and mostly used for transport. They convert energy from one form to another. The most important decision when designing a machine is what this machine is going to do. "A car is always going to move from A to B" [7].

Computers and buildings are coming closer together, in the unavoidable proliferation of sensors and chips that contribute to a space of potentiality constituted by this generic infrastructure. But buildings and computers have a different purpose, they do different things. Buildings are closer to cars, in terms of their specificity of application.

A computer is a universal machine. However, a computer is not a mechanical machine that operates geometrically – it operates through logic, and processes information. What becomes primary when working with computers is the application [7]. The design and development of an application does not use up any particular physical resources (apart from developer's time, and the electricity needed to charge a laptop battery).

Computation and communication networks are capturing and counting predetermined parameters about environment conditions (air temperature and moisture, amount of light, etc.) as well as users actions and interactions with the system (presence, movement, use of certain features). Many of these systems have developed solely with the purpose of optimizing resource use and space management – as Yolande Stengers observed in a text on the imaginaries of the smart home [17]. Scarcity of resources becomes in this way an important driver of technical developments in terms of measuring building performance.

Without pertaining to answer the very large question of "what are the drives of technological development in building industry?", I want to present these two views: scarcity-driven measurement technology on one side and communication-driven infrastructure technology on the other. With the interest in the interplay between user agency and building automation I look at the ways we talk about computation in buildings, particularly about the way automation is dependent on one or the other previously mentioned views. I observe a connection between the discourse on scarcity and a particular approach to interaction design that is concerned with establishing causality between measurement and building use. I propose, on the other hand, to appreciate a discourse in a different key, one that is concerned with capacity and communication, without moralizing on the availability of resources and production.

2   What Buildings Are About: Burning Wood or Making Shelter?

In the first edition of The Architecture of the Well-tempered Environment, Reyner Banham observed two basic methods of exploiting the environmental potential of natural resources, more specifically timber [1]. The first method suggests using wood to construct a shelter from environmental effects (such as wind or rain): a structural solution. The second method suggests using the material as a non-scarce resource to build a fire. He calls the latter the *power-operated solution* [1]. At the time of writing, he already observed a sort of a tipping point between the first, structural method, largely adopted by the Western culture, and the power-operated approach, based on abundance of electricity and water supply. Banham strongly advocated for a proliferation of energy-dependents solutions (Heating, ventilation, and air conditioning or HVAC systems) to achieve indoor comfort.

The first concerns over access to electrical power were caused by newly raised perception of energy as scarce following the fuel crisis of 1973–74 in the United States. As a consequence, the building industry and construction engineers began considering energy efficiency as a design constraint.

In the preface to the second edition of the same book, Banham offers a kind of remedy to the severe criticism his book was met with in the times of 1970s oil crisis [2]. He defended his position towards energy consumption as a progressive argument, one that is made with the assumption energy would not be scarce. He did not set to solve all the problems implied by building electrification and gradual automation. He simply talked about its potentials, from a point where scarcity of resources was not an issue.

The dichotomy in approaches that Banham identified is still important in thinking about building design and energy efficiency. Evaluation of a building's performance developed into an elaborate measurement-driven discipline. Interaction with buildings became significantly more complex and powerful. But the idea of scarcity still haunts some of these discourses.

2.1 Interactive Monocoque

The two polarities: power-operated environments and structural solutions persists in the intellectual divide in terms of the interests in building design. On one side, we have the interest in designing the skin (independent from the structure, preserving the conditions of a power-operated solution inside) and on the other we have the interest in the structure itself. A holistic approach would be, Branko Kolarevic argued in his discussion on performativity of architecture to "avoid the binary choices of skin or structure and to reunify the two by embedding or subsuming the structure into the skin" [8]. In a few words, he suggested that the structure and the skin conflate in a monocoque[1]. In this way, the building is reacting to some environmental condition while at the same time enclosing a controlled environment within it. Even with its relatively small size, Lars Spuybroek's D-tower would be a good example of this approach. And while structure and enclosure become one, what Banham called a "man made climate" [1] they both become a way of making shelter, a massively structural method of environmental management, without much attention to the power provisions.

2.2 Media-Architecture

In the versatile manifestations of media architecture, the interactive skin transformed the static structures into building-events. At night, the city becomes a stage for electrical energy, shifting focus from space to time-based architecture. An observer drawn into this play is no more outside nor inside. Media facades are not operating as shelter – that which is outside is more important than that which is inside.

A large number of public buildings designed in the past 20 years feature some kind of a screen – a matrix of interactive elements, be it LEDs or kinetic elements[2]. The well known BIX facade designed by realities: united for the Kunsthaus Graz embodies the principle of a communication skin. Furthermore, some contemporary examples such as MegaFaces, designed by Asif Khan for Sochi Olympic Games exhibit this communicative property: MegaFaces continuously molded into three-dimensional selfies of visitors to the building. The difference between such media architecture from architecture in general is in it having a screen as an integrated and infrastructural element of the facade. It is a power-operated skin, whose functioning as a shelter is not affected by the flow of electricity.

This focus on the facade is, in a way, another iteration of the old game, massive structure rendered into its dynamic representation. At the same time, it makes a difference: it separates the inside from the outside in a different fashion, where communication takes place outside of the building. Through activities such as the Media Facade Festival

---

[1] Monocoque (single shell) is a term that describes a structural system where loads are supported through an object's external skin. It is used in the aircraft industry to describe the chassis is integral with the body. It is also used in architecture to describe artefacts that are constructed from single pieces of pre-tensed concrete, plastic or laminated wood.

[2] For an overview, consult the Media Architecture Compendium, complied by the Media Architecture Institute, http://catalog.mediaarchitecture.org/.

and other events coordinated by the Connecting Cities network[3] media facades show their infrastructural potentiality, they can perform as a communication network. Media architecture should be thus taken more largely as a potential that is not exhausted with the display of commercials or temporary media art installations.

2.3 Smart Homes

In a recent text, Yolande Strengers made a critical overview of the way the smart home and its agenda were imagined in the past decades and the realities that are unfolding as these become integrated into everyday lives [17]. One of the mainstream visions she identified is the quantified home: a system attuned at capturing and counting, with the aim of changing users' consumption patterns. A key task associated with smart home is meeting better the energy demand: decarbonizing and de-peeking energy systems. The narrative of efficiency springs out of that, where automation is seen as a relief for our everyday chores, with the deceptive neutrality of automated servants. Strengers used these observations to advocate for alternatives, against the control narrative, in which user's agency is the driver of system design. She proposed doing away with the gender-less and utilitarian concept of a universal user; engaging with the eclectic composition of households and their human and nonhuman occupants in a messy way; design for different types of time and for different understandings of productivity and busyness.

One interesting question raised in smart home and smart office scenarios in terms of agency of the user is the personalization of these systems. In a project by Carlo Ratti Associati for Angeli Foundation headquarters, the proposal for Office 3.0 conceptualizes shared space as individually-tailored environmental bubbles, based on indoor position tracking and profiling of users[4]. The smart system they developed instructs heating, lighting and cooling systems to follow occupants around the building and adjust the settings to their preferences.

3 Measuring Efficiency: The Scarcity Paradigm

There are several ways in which interactive technologies and communication infra-structures have been integrated with buildings. Building automation driven by smart applications or by temporary media art installations open new spaces of potentiality for an infrastructural role of these technologies. The discourse on scarcity, however, still haunts the discipline. After the oil crisis, the main driver of smart homes, as Strengers reminded us, was the de-peaking of energy systems. Scarcity of resources and our attempts to measure them have been a strong drive behind technological developments. At the same time, each contemporary episteme is influenced by technology that we have at hand.

---

[3] Connected Cities network is an initiative for exploration of combined effects of media facades in cities, led by Susa Pop of the Public Art Lab, Berlin.

[4] For more details about the project, see https://www.carloratti.com/project/fondazione-agnelli/ (accessed February 20th, 2018).

Banham's call for the use of power-operated solutions in building design and engineering was met with severe criticism. But the 1970s oil crisis that the United States suffered was caused by several foreign policy moves that preceded it. Oil prices did not go up because resources were suddenly replete, they raised because of a political situation in which OPEC[5] members proclaimed an oil embargo on the US. Several crises have passed since, most recent one arguably once more demonstrating that the problem of scarcity is not only localizable in the resources being finite (although they mostly probably are) but also in an artificially created scarcity.

3.1 Scarcity in the Wireless Spectrum

The above discussed principle enabled creation of scarcity in the wireless spectrum. The electromagnetic spectrum is difficult to grasp and we often resort to tangible metaphors of roads or territories when talking about it. Roads can be congested, territories crowded. We tend to say that wireless communication channels are saturated today.

Access to the electromagnetic spectrum is regulated in terms of available frequencies (both licensed and unlicensed), the maximum signal strength permitted, the geographic region over which the license applies and the designated service provided by an operator. Network operators buy rights to use specific frequencies from national regulatory authorities (FCC in the United States, RED in Europe, BAKOM in Switzerland). A relatively small portion of radio is reserved for the unlicensed spectrum[6]. Contemporary wireless communication technologies (Wi-Fi, cellular, Bluetooth, NFC, etc.) make use of the different bands in both licensed and unlicensed spectrum and are based on continuous exchange between networked devices. In this way we are able to both send and receive information over the air.

Spectrum mask – the set of protocols that define different channels and regulate frequency use is provided by the Institute of Electrical and Electronics Engineers (IEEE). This spectrum mask is as an international standard which ensures device interoperability while minimizing interference with devices that share the same frequency range – amongst them microwaves, Bluetooth gadgets, Zigbees, Baby phones and wireless surveillance cameras.

In contemporary discourse on overcrowding, wireless networks are often seen as something scarce, something we need more and more of. This view conflates the capacity of communication equipment to transmit information with efficiency of protocols and techniques to encode this information onto signal. It is the spectrum mask that renders networks scarce. Researcher in cultural and economic aspects of networking technology, Rachel O'Dwyer noted that spectrum policy is broadly emblematic of the prohibitions operating over what she calls the substrate infrastructure [13]. She saw ownership of

---

[5] OPEC stands for: Organization of Petroleum Exporting Countries. It is an organization of 12 oil-producing countries, that control 61 percent of the world's oil exports and hold 80 percent of the world's proven oil reserves.

[6] For a discussion of spectrum management approaches, see: Cave, M., Doyle, C., & Webb, W. (2007). Essentials of modern spectrum management. Cambridge; New York: Cambridge University Press.

infrastructure, which implies both the right to use specific frequency bands and access to telecommunication cables, as a central asset in valorization of wireless communication technologies. Management of interferences through spectrum masks renders unlicensed frequency bands scarce.

3.2 Scarcity of Human Attention

Today, we often talk about scarcity of another resource: human attention. Malcolm McCullough discussed this at length in his book about attention and architectural atmospheres [11]. He claimed that we constantly confront an overabundance of information in the environment, be it the movement of the shadow over a wall (persistent high resolution) or digitally enabled communication networks that drive complex systems of sensors and actuators.

The idea of attention scarcity traces back to Herbert Simon's observation of a counterbalance between information and attention – namely that the abundance of information necessarily leads to the scarcity of attention, consumed by it [16]. Following this line, McCullough set as the combined task of architects and interaction designers (which is delimiting the field of human-building interaction) to reduce information overload to something we can meaningfully consume and process. He observed interaction design as an analog to architecture in terms of organizing flows of people, resources, and ideas [12]. They both address how contexts shape action. With embedded microprocessors and communication networks architecture, he said, acquired a digital layer. The ambient processes of shaping intention through architecture and relating it to opportunities in space through interaction design are driven by the aim to control the flow of information, to emancipate the user from an overabundance of it.

3.3 Scarcity as the Key to Measurement and Causality

The discussions on energy, wireless networks and human attention point to scarcity of resources as the driver of technological developments. When we want to reduce the use of something, we first need to measure it. This is a long used technique in sustainable design and it has been successfully applied to reduce energy use through different kinds of feedback (how much CO_2 consumed, how much money saved) [10]. What we can conceive of measuring is that which we consider needs saving. Once the causal relationship is established between a resource and its environmental impact (such as the use of oil or coal and their CO_2 footprint), it is only a matter of optimizing measurement instruments and finding the best way to incentivize the users to save.

4   The Internet of Everything: Abundance and Balance

The communication paradigm sets itself apart from the production paradigm in which we measure and count resources, products created, labor costs, accumulation of goods and wealth. Going away from the idea of scarcity of resources, it is about emitting, receiving, storing and processing information. What becomes important is the application – the programming of software routines that computers will compute and communicate, and network infrastructure – not as a resource but as a space of potentiality. Hovestadt et al. saw one of the most important properties of the network its virality: the ability to spread information virally. Virality is inseparable from communication: media theorist Jussi Parikka pointed out the decisive role of computer viruses in the generation of novel ideas in the new science of networks – such as viral marketing or experimental vaccine software[7] [14]. He repeated the observation of Fred Cohen – one of the most important names in computer virus defense techniques – in order to secure communication from viruses, one would have to block it entirely. In their discussion on the abundance of energy, Hovestadt et al. propose to imagine this virality applied to energy, and not information.

4.1   Energy Is Essential, but Not Necessarily Scarce

Energy is today central to almost all activities – from working on computers, communicating over wireless devices, cooking and washing, transportation and distribution to money transfers. Without it, nothing goes: no person, no business and no infrastructure. This centrality of energy is too quickly translated into the call to use less of it – simply because of its importance. Questioning the amount of energy we use leads to the question where the energy is coming from. If we observe our fossil fuel resources as finite (or too slowly renewed) then it is clear that is should be saved for as long as possible. However, relying on oil and coal is certainly not the only option and it has been challenged repeatedly in the past 40 years. Numerous other techniques of producing electricity (water, wind, sun) have been invented and practiced. The recent trend for sustainability and self-sufficiency of buildings partly came out of the concerns for finiteness of some of the above-mentioned resources, as well as the environmental impacts electricity production has had on Earth.

While most sustainability advocates see renewable resources (wind, sun, temperature difference) as equally interesting, Hovestadt et al. make it very clear how abundant and independent from Earth's conditions Sun's energy is [7]. And we are already able to capture up to 22% of it with today's mass produced silicon-based solar panels[8]. New technologies and techniques are being developed, such as transparent dye-sensitized cells patented by Michael Grätzel who won a Millenium Prize for this invention, and was able to increase their efficiency up to 19% [3, 5].

In the *Genius Planet*, Hovestadt et al. present a detailed calculation of the amount of solar panels that would be needed to satisfy current world energy needs, based on total solar emissions received per square meter on Earth [7]. That would be, for example, our current road network, which takes up about 10% land surface. Distributing energy's abundance is a question for logistics, a question of making it accessible to everyone.

---

[7] Vaccine is software designed to find and repair problems in a larger number of networked computers, propagating through networks in the same way as viruses do.

[8] See for example the Frauenhofer Photovoltaics Report: https://www.ise.fraunhofer.de/content/dam/ise/de/documents/publications/studies/Photovoltaics-Report.pdf (accessed February 22nd 2018).

The structure is that of the Internet: channeling information (or energy) from where it is to where it is needed. Much to Banham's possible pleasure, Hovestadt et al. recognize the importance of power for operating buildings, in a similar relationship between energy and matter. The difference is that the former advocated burning of fossil fuels, while the latter authors articulated a sophisticated proposal for capturing and sharing of solar energy. Once it is converted to electricity, it becomes universally available.

The challenge we are presented with is, thus, not merely to capture the source of energy and store it (which is a significant challenge still today). It is in communication: how to get the energy from one place to. This is a challenge for the networking infrastructure. It is also a challenge for the way we will relate to it, the way energy will be balanced throughout.

Bühlmann observed that electricity is the only way that energy can be medial, meaning that it can carry information about itself while carrying its own energy [7]. With electricity, it is not only possible to send energy from the source to consumers, but also from one user to the other, networking the distribution. In such an 'intelligent' energy network a device may be used both to provide, store as well as to consume energy. This would be the Internet of energy.

5   Consequences for Human-Building Interaction

Interaction refers to something happening between and among. The first part of the word, *inter-* coming from the verb "to enter" (Proto Indo European) and "entera" (Old Greek for intestines), with the root *en-* meaning in, something that is inside, interior to. Action draws from latin *actio-*, referring to something being put in motion, doing, performing. In order to critically reflect upon new trends in ambient computing or what I analyze here through human-building interaction perspective, we need to see interaction with buildings as something more profound than cause-and-effect reactions between the human users and decisions taken by the infrastructure (turn on the heating, roll down the blinds). It is a question of orchestrating infrastructures.

Mainstream interaction design has largely adopted the disappearing interface metaphor for its goal, epitomized in the study of contemporary trends presented in The Age of Context [15]. At the same time, designers have pointed towards the loss of agency that is inherent in such disappearance. Timo Arnall, whose work consistently explored invisible infrastructures (*Immaterial: Light Painting Wi-Fi*, 2010, *Robot readable world* 2012, *The Internet Machine*, 2014) articulates such concerns in his *No to NoUI* manifesto[9]. Arnall opposed the myth of immateriality and childish mythologies like "the cloud" in favor of design that integrates the actual qualities of the interface and increases our ability to become proficient at using technical systems. He illustrated this discussion with the example of the Nest thermostat interface, which gives out all necessary information to the user while seamlessly "learning" the user's habits. Arnall argues for focusing on legibility and readability instead of seamless invisibility and removal of the interface. Strengers had a similar take on the matter: in her account of alternatives to the

---

[9] The text of the manifesto is available at http://www.elasticspace.com/2013/03/no-to-no-ui (accessed February 20th 2018).

mainstream smart-home vision, she talked about the coordinated home and the DIY home. The fist one is centered on creating increasing degrees of flexibility around different sites of activity and new opportunities for energy to be consumed. The second one is a vision in which users are able to adapt technology to their own needs – be it because it failed to work properly or simply because it allowed certain degrees of freedom to be modified by design. The question becomes how to create enough space for choices to be made on the go by people, rather than predefining the states of these infrastructures in terms of causalities (user not at home: switch heating off). Users attention is not scarce, it can be focused meaningfully on intentional interactions.

5.1 Designing with Abundance

Some design principles can be articulated, that stem out of the perception of energy or communication networks as abundant, and the interest in balancing them.

Rather than interaction design, Hovestadt sees computer and information science and technology directly relevant and somewhat analog to architecture. Architecture and infrastructure engineering coupled through computer science give rise to truly intelligent buildings. This would mean that our homes, our places of work and leisure become, in effect, applications [7]. Application is the potentiality of computational technology. Resources are not being used up and exploited – application is, independent of the hardware on which it runs, about the ability to create potentiality [7]. It is easy to understand this when we think about the fact the computer is not getting heavier from running more software applications. The fundamental shift is in the potentiality of virtuality.

In general, this principle of interaction can be described as orchestration of infrastructures. Matched to our own eyes, brightness of light used to be measured by the size of a candle flame. With the introduction of electrical infrastructure, brightness was determined by the available force of the power turbine and the incandescence of the wire in the bulb [7]. With the invention of different lighting technologies and the normalization of artificial lighting, the question transforms to what kind of light do we want: reading light, relaxing light, at which time of the day, etc. It becomes a question of orchestrating the quality of light.

The non-scarce approach to resources liberates one's thinking from a centralized network paradigm and questions of control: it requires thinking about a proliferation of sources and dispersal of directions, it is a thinking about choices. Rather than deciding to burn wood because it is cold, we look at conditions and states: we ask which, out of many things that can be done, do we want to do when it gets cold.

The interplay between user agency and building automation is then not driven by control and the attempt to decarbonize and de-peek energy consumption, as Strengers identified [17]. Rather, it is driven by a user's emotion, their momentary preference for the kind of ambient and atmosphere they wish to be surrounded with. The discreetness of automated systems (heating, blinds control, management of appliances) can pass into a continuity of an ambient apparatus, whose states and changes are communicated through the energy supply network. This constant communication should be something that a human might want to look at at any point, but does not need to be monitoring. At the same time, the actions of the inhabitant remain discreet – they are not seen as a repetitive pattern. The hypothetical system described here is not attuned at predicting user's behavior but at balancing the momentary tendencies. It is in this way that we can work towards turning mere automation into sophisticated orchestration.

References

1. Banham, R.: The Architecture of the Well-Tempered Environment. Architectural Press, University of Chicago, New York, Chicago (1969)
2. Banham, R.: The Architecture of the Well-Tempered Environment. University of Chicago Press, Chicago (1984)
3. Bi, D., et al.: Facile synthesized organic hole transporting material for perovskite solar cell with efficiency of 19.8%. Nano Energy 23, 138–144 (2016). https://doi.org/10.1016/j.nanoen.2016.03.020
4. Bühlmann, V.: Primary Abundance, Urban Philosophy—Information and The Form of Actuality. In: Metalithikum, I., Hovestadt, L., Bühlmann, V. (eds.) Applied Virtuality Book Series Printed Physics—Metalithikum I, pp. 114–154. Birkhäuser Verlag GmbH, Basel (2013). https://doi.org/10.1007/978-3-7091-1485-8_3
5. Grätzel, M. 2003. Dye-sensitized solar cells. Journal of Photochemistry and Photobiology C: Photochemistry Reviews. 4, 2 (Oct. 2003), 145–153. https://doi.org/10.1016/S1389-5567(03)00026-1
6. Hillier, B.: Space is the Machine. Space Syntax (2007)
7. Hovestadt, L., et al.: Genius Planet Energy Scarcity to Energy Abundance: A Radical Pathway for Creative Professionals and Environmental Active Amateurs. Birkhauser, Basel (2017)
8. Kolarevic, B., Malkawi, A. (eds.): Performative Architecture: Beyond Instrumentality. Routledge, Abingdon (2005)
9. Corbusier, L.: The City of Tomorrow and Its Planning. Dover Publications, Mineola (1987)
10. Lockton, D., et al.: Exploring design patterns for sustainable behaviour. Des. J. 16(4), 431–459 (2013)
11. McCullough, M.: Ambient Commons: Attention in the Age of Embodied Information. The MIT Press, Cambridge (2013)
12. McCullough, M.: Digital Ground: Architecture, Pervasive Computing, and Environmental Knowing. The MIT Press, Cambridge (2004)
13. O'Dwyer, R.: Spectre of the commons: Spectrum regulation in the communism of capital. Ephemera: Theory Polit. Organzation 13(3), 5–34 (2013). Communism of capital?
14. Sampson, T.D., Parikka, J.: Learning from network dysfunctionality: accidents, enterprise, and small worlds of infection. In: Hartley, J., et al. (eds.) A Companion to New Media Dynamics, pp. 450–460. Wiley-Blackwell (2013)
15. Scoble, R., Israel, S.: Age of Context: Mobile, Sensors, Data and the Future of Privacy. Brewster, Chicago (2013)
16. Simon, H.A. (ed.) Designing organizations for an information-rich world. In: Computers, Communications, and the Public Interest. Johns Hopkins Press (1971)
17. Strengers, Y.: Envisioning the smart home: reimagining a smart energy future. digital materialities: design and anthropology. In: Pink, S., et al. (eds.) Bloomsbury Academic (2016)

Design and Development of an Electric Skateboard Controlled Using Weight Sensors

Sai Vinay Sayyapureddi[1], Vishnu Raju Nandyala[1], Akil Komarneni[1],
and Deep Seth[2(✉)]

[1] Mahindra Ecole Centrale, Hyderabad, Telangana 500043, India
{saivinay14170,vishnu14118,akil14089}@mechyd.ac.in
[2] Mechanical Engineering Program, School of Engineering Sciences, Hyderabad, India
sethdeep12@gmail.com

Abstract. Existence of non-electric skateboards in the past few decades which involved a lot of physical effort while riding has now been overthrown with the invention of electric ones. As we moved onto a generation where everything is electric controlled, this paper introduces the skateboard as an electric vehicle based on weight sensing technology. The board is propelled by an electric motor powered by a battery pack and it is designed for easy and fast commuting where the rider just need to lean forward to advance and lean backward to slow down or stop. The proposed board is easy to carry anywhere because of its compatible design and also suitable for off road conditions. As of now we are testing the performance of the board and hoping for satisfactory results.

Keywords: Belt-driven board · Electric skateboard · Robotics
Personal mobility · Weight sensing electric skateboard

1 Introduction

Witnessed as one of the more suitable innovations for this century, origin of these kinds took place in 1975 which was a gasoline powered long board called as the Moto board [9]. Although being non-electric skateboard, this was considered to be first of its kind. But it wasn't until the late 90's an electric skateboard had been produced. Following this there were several attempts made in order to achieve the goal. Gradually showing increase in the interest of people in the market it achieved a good percent increase in success in the late 2000's [12].

Originated from the idea of simplifying the methods of portable commuting [7], it seems to be satisfying the needs of a consumer. Our idea has originated in our university [10, 11, 16] to make the students life less stressful and reduces fatigue [3] in our muscles while commuting between classes. But there is a drawback of this board; Most of the youngsters who are already habituated with the skateboards are finding the rides on these electric boards less comfortable. In order to address this complication, we decided to build a board which gives comprehensive experience to all the users. It is hoped that they will address challenges relating to transport, the environment and human health [5].

© Springer International Publishing AG, part of Springer Nature 2018
N. Streitz and S. Konomi (Eds.): DAPI 2018, LNCS 10921, pp. 275–285, 2018.
https://doi.org/10.1007/978-3-319-91125-0_24

This paper discusses about objective and our approach towards constructing an electronic skateboard. As a part of our approach we began by researching on the boards available [6, 8] in the market and started to implement the best compatible feature into our design to make it more efficient, reliable and affordable. In order to make the previously said things achievable, we have taken some measures in choosing the accessories like battery, sensors, motor, speed controller etc. Although choosing a component and testing their compatibility of them with rest other components seemed to be a little tricky, we had to deal with the construction part of our board in order to make it easily controllable [2] by a normal human being is what we believe makes our board unique.

Moreover, this paper also states our purpose on why we chose a certain component to be suitable in the prototype discussion. Further, since we know that the most important thing is the mechanical transmission, we have given a detailed description on it as said by many of them, 'efficiency gives us more time to spend on becoming efficient' likewise, we believe that our product is efficient and better.

2   Literature Survey

As a part of our research [4] we gathered most of the information on the boards existing in the market. Firstly, we classified those boards into 2 divisions on their type of working i.e. Skateboards based on remote control [1] and boards based on weight sensing. After our observation on few established boards on both of the categories, we have decided to discuss about three boards which could describe all the major features present in rest of the boards. The following details give an understanding on the Electric skateboard.

2.1   Boosted Board

Boosted board is one of the first commercially produced remote controlled skateboards. The board consists of two Brushless motors which along with lithium batteries and some other custom electronics and trucks. It has got different power levels depending on the proficiency of the rider. The higher the level, the more power it produces and more the top speed (Fig. 1).

Fig. 1. Boosted board [13]

Specifications [13]: This board has the motor power of about 2000 W where its top speed is around 20 mph. This is a remote-controlled skateboard, with a range of 6 miles and the time to completely charge the lithium ion battery is close to 2 h. The boards manufactured by this company weighs from 12 to 15 lbs each.

Although the Boosted belt drive system allows it to produce more torque and more responsive, we need to replace their customized belts as they wear out frequently which can be seen as the drawback.

2.2   In Board

Inboard is the electric skateboard which has motors embedded into the wheels. One of its major features include:

Power Shift Swappable Batteries: Inboard is the world's first electric skateboard brand with swappable battery packs. The depleted battery can be recharged inside the board or on its own with a separate charging cable (Fig. 2).

Fig. 2.   In board [14]

Specifications [14]: This remote-controlled skateboard with the specialty of motors embedded in the wheels has a top speed of 24 mph where the battery range is up to 10 miles and has the weight of 17 lbs. The material of the deck is light weight composite and is designed for speed and stability.

But, one of the major drawbacks in Inboard is slow start-up speeds and poor low-end torque hubs.

2.3   Z - Board

The first ever electric skateboard to use weight sensing technology. The skateboard uses footpads as their pressure sensors. The design allows for a more natural coast, allowing on to push the board many miles even after the battery expires. This board includes a belt-driven motor, integrated lights, and of course two pressure pads for your feet to move the board forwards and backwards (Fig. 3).

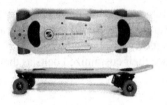

Fig. 3. Z-board [15]

Specifications [15]: Z board has a Brushless DC motor of power 500 W which can achieve a top speed of 20 mph. This skateboard has a high range compared to that of other skateboards available in the market i.e. 16 miles. The time taken to fully charge the board is around 2 h and it uses lithium ion battery. This board weighs around 18 lbs.

Although our initial attempts on building our skateboard were related to boosted and inboard both being remote control, we have later decided to build skateboard based on weight sensing mechanism. Since, by sensing weight difference instead of simply having an acceleration switch like in remote controlled board, it allows the rider to accelerate and decelerate without modifying stance. This weight sensing feature allows for a more intuitive and smooth riding system as well as faster actuation time for acceleration and deceleration. Almost similar to the z board in terms of technique but we have embedded the sensors inside the board instead of having foot pads. The idea of the belt driven mechanism has been taken from boosted board but the pulley system in our board unique compared to the former.

3   Objective

The objective of this project is to successfully build a weight sensing electric skateboard that is completely controlled by the rider's body movements. There are no footpads or remote control involved. The rider just needs to lean forward to advance and lean backward to slow down or stop.

4   Methodology

4.1   System Overview

This board is controlled using load sensors. The input is processed by Arduino and the speed of the board is controlled by VESC. Parallelly, the power is supplied to both the above-mentioned components. The motor transmits the power to the wheels. The block diagram of the system is shown in Fig. 4.

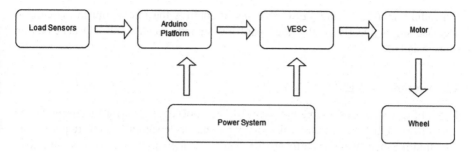

Fig. 4. Overview of the system

4.2   Construction Overview

The entire control system consists of two components: Sensor and Motor control. For the sensor control, Arduino is used to collect data from Force Sensitive resistors and process the analog signal. Secondly for the motor control, Arduino will connect to the motor through VESC. This allows the skateboard to have a steady acceleration and deceleration .

Fig. 5.   RFP-602

Fig. 6.   Arduino Uno

5   Prototype Description

5.1   Sensor Mode

The board has Force sensitive resistors sensors (RFP-602) embedded on the front and back of the deck respectively. Now depending upon the pressure applied by the rider on the deck, the sensor sends the analog value to the A0 or A1 input of the Arduino, depending upon the pressure applied on the front or back of the deck. The sensor calibration was done by taking 5 different levels and thresholds each with a different pressure applied on the sensor in an incremental way. The algorithm written in the Arduino IDE ensures that if the input value crosses a certain value or threshold value, the value is mapped upon to the output value or the output pin which is connected to the VESC.

Depending upon the value VESC receives, it controls the motor rpm to increase or decrease speed linearly so that the board has smooth acceleration and deceleration (Figs. 5 and 6).

5.2 Customized VESC

This VESC has an open source platform (BLDC Tool) especially for Electronic Speed Controllers so that we can customize every parameter depending on our requirements from limiting the power and current to the motor, to safeguard the electronics equipment from heating up and fired. The maximum rpm limit is also set for safe riding and also the regulations of the power modes for up and down hill. This VESC also includes a regenerative braking method which comes into action when brakes are applied, and the VESC stops supplying power to motor and in turn takes the power produced by the motor back to the battery. The VESC we used, is the BLDC speed controller and it is calibrated for the particular motor we used, so that the board achieves a smooth start when starting from complete rest. It has a v4.12 Hardware, Latest v2.18 for Firmware for FOC, 10 awg motor wires w/5.5 mm bullet connectors and 2 mm JST-PH Connectors (Fig. 7).

Fig. 7. VESC

5.3 Battery System

We have used Lithium polymer (Li-Po) rather than Lithium ion (Li-on) battery as they have really high discharge rates and are high in power density. A C-rate is a measure of the rate at which a battery is discharged relative to its maximum capacity. This is a 12 S 3 Ah 45 C battery pack which gives a maximum output of 44.4 V to drive motor and 45 C rating ensures that maximum amount of current is drawn from it which can easily go up to 20+ miles range. Also, a 2.1 A power adapter is used to fully charge the batteries in 5 h safely.

5.4 Long Board

The long board used here is of size 42 in. long and 7-in.-wide making it sufficient spacious to add all equipment in the circuitry. Under the board, near to back axle, all the main components like motor, battery, ESC are arranged. All the components are arranged in a rugged casing for protection from ground. Drive generated by motor will be provided to one of the wheels using belt drive mechanism. Belt drive mechanism creates enough force and torque for application (Figs. 8 and 9).

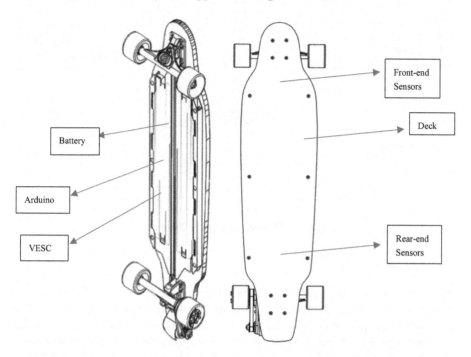

Fig. 8. Back view of the model   **Fig. 9.** Front view of the model

6   Mechanical Transmission/Drive Train

There are few parameters that need to be determined so we can design and build Drivetrain. They are gearing reduction ratio, Motor KV, Battery Voltage, Wheel diameter. These parameters are all related to each other and if one is changed, the top speed of our propulsion system will also change. That is why we determined our desired top speed as 22 mph (36 km/h) then worked backwards to determine the others. The overall design overview of the mechanical drive train is shown in Fig. 10.

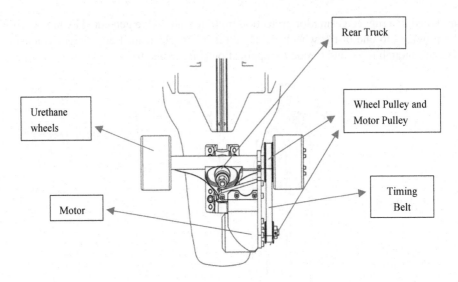

Fig. 10. Detailed view of the drive train.

6.1 Wheels

The preferable wheels for electric skateboards are of 80 mm–90 mm diameter as they have a good ground clearance and can also safely hold the electronic components from touching the ground. We chose to use 80 mm diameter wheels as they have a hollow core that is perfect for passing bolts through & securing the wheel pulley. The size of the wheels also matters a lot. The bigger wheel diameter produces more top speed and less torque whereas, the smaller the wheel diameter results in producing low the top speed and more torque which is required when riding the skateboard uphill. But also considering the ground clearance and acquiring max torque for a given drive train we chose to use 80 mm diameter wheels.

6.2 Gearing Reduction Ratio

The gearing ratio depends upon the motor pulley and the wheel pulley used in the drive train. The reduction ratio is directly proportional to the torque and inversely proportional to the top speed, so more the reduction ratio, the more the torque but less the top speed. But in general, it is recommended to use high reduction ratio to increase torque and considerable motor to achieve top speed. The pulleys we used here are 16 teeth motor pulley (Pinion), 54 teeth wheel pulley (Spur). The pitch of the pulleys we chose is 3 mm which is comparatively less because, the higher the pitch, the more the pulley circumference and less the ground clearance, but also keeping in mind that less the pitch value, less the number of teeth is intact with belt and less the output torque. 3 mm pitch pulleys are fit to satisfy the mentioned constraints.

6.3 Motor KV Rating

The motor we used is a 6355 190 kV rating with a maximum stator size of 55 mm width. The lower the kV rating, the more the torque and less the top speed but as we are powering the motor with 12 S 44.4 V, we could get our desired top speed with more torque. The maximum power and torque this motor can produce is 2500 W and 2.83 Nm respectively which is sufficient for general usage of the board.

6.4 Center Distance

Our next constraint is the center distance 'D_c' which is the distance between the motor pulley and the wheel pulley. It is always best to keep the center distance as low as possible to avoid the mount to flex, bend or snap while braking hard or accelerating quick. A shorter D_c value also means that less leveraging force is being applied onto the motor mounting hardware and also helps in reducing vibrations of the hardware.

6.5 Drive Train and Motor Mounting Plate

The customized mount shown in Fig. 11 did an imperative role to hold the motor to connect with the wheel and transmit the power smoothly.

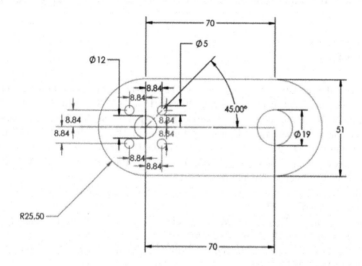

Fig. 11. CAD model of motor mount

7 Working and Discussion

The weight sensing electric skateboard we have built creates an effective interaction between human and machine based on intuitive control. The integrated sensor system allows to quickly accelerate or decelerate depending upon the pressure applied on the deck. The VESC used ensures a smooth speed-up process based on the data from Arduino. The regenerative braking used can conserve battery power and increase range. We opted for a Belt driven motor rather than in-wheel Hub motor as the former has an advantage of high power and also it is better in absorbing shocks while riding on rough roads. So here we have used pulley and belt drive mechanism between motor and the wheel to which drive will be connected. For mechanical parts we manufactured certain parts like Motor Mount, timing belt and pulleys to reduce the overall cost.

8   Conclusion

We have built an Electric Skate board on weight sensing method which needs to be tested on different age groups and diverse road conditions. This weight sensing feature allows for a more intuitive and smooth riding system. In addition, the customized VESC and battery pack allows us to pre-set different maximum speed of the skateboard to meet the purposes for different level of users so that people having no experience can easily learn and ride it. Right now, we are using only one motor to drive one of the rear wheels. Later, we could add another motor to achieve a full rear wheel drive so that it is more powerful and more torque is attained.

The features of this board include low cost, less weight, regenerative braking and easy operation. We want to make it more user friendly improve by taking feedback from the users.

References

1. Romero, C., Cedeno, O., Romero, C.: E-SKATE, University of Central Florida, Department of Computer and Electrical Engineering, Orlando, Florida, U.S.A. EECS (2011)
2. Kalaiyarasu, K., Leelavathi, G., Suganya, M., Vignesh, S., Santhosh, N.: Design and implementation of smart roulette using gesture control. IJSART 2(3), 21–23 (2016)
3. Seth, D., Chablat, D., Bennis, F., Sakka, S., Jubeau, M., Nordez, A.: New dynamic muscle fatigue model to limit musculo-skeletal disorder. In: Proceedings of the Virtual Reality International Conference, Laval, France (2016)
4. Liu, S.F.: Research on prospective innovation design of smart electric vehicle. Adv. Ind. Eng. Manag. 2(2), 63–67 (2013)
5. Hyvönen, K., Repo, P., Lammi, M.: Light electric vehicles: substitution and future uses. Transp. Res. Procedia 19, 258–268 (2016)
6. Prasad, S., Rane, K., Joshi, V.: Electronic utility vehicle: E – board. IJSRD-Int. J. Sci. Res. Dev. 4(02), 1857–1859 (2016)
7. Babey, S.H., Hastert, T.A., Huang, W., Brown, E.R.: Sociodemographic, family, and environmental factors associated with active commuting to school among US adolescents. J. Public Health Policy, 30(1), no. 5 S203–S220 (2016)
8. Jung, U., Youn, S.: The first Korean-made IT convergence electric skateboard. J. Korea Convergence Soc. 8(3), 31–40 (2017). Department of Drone System, Chodang University
9. The History of Snowboarding. The Beginning of Snowboarding: 1982 (2013). http://www.sbhistory.de/hist_in_the_beg.htm#1982
10. Bonham, J., Koth, B.: Universities and the cycling culture. Transp. Res. Part D: Transp. Environ. 15(2), 94–102 (2010)

11. Fang, K.: Skateboarding as a mode of transportation: review of regulations in California cities and college campuses. In: Transportation Research Board 92nd Annual Meeting Transportation Research Board, issue 13-3500 (2013)

12. Németh, J.: Conflict, exclusion, relocation: skateboarding and public space. J. Urban Des. **11**(3), 297–318 (2006)

13. https://boostedboards.com/board/ (2016)

14. https://www.inboardtechnology.com/pages/m1-product-page (2018)

15. https://www.zboardshop.com/pages/2017-zboards (2017)

16. Haworth, N., Schramm, A.: How do level of experience, purpose for riding, and preference for facilities affect location of riding? Transp. Res. Rec.: J. Transp. Res. Board **2247**, 17–23 (2011)

Challenges for Deploying IoT Wearable Medical Devices Among the Ageing Population

Fei Xing[1(✉)], Guochao Peng[1], Tian Liang[1], and Jingyi Jiang[2]

[1] Sun Yat-sen University, Panyu District, Guangzhou 510000, China
xingf5@mail2.sysu.edu.cn, penggch@mail.sysu.edu.cn
[2] Peking University, Haidian, Beijing 100000, China

Abstract. The phenomenon of ageing population is raising substantial pressure to the national health and welfare systems of many countries in the world, and can be a potential threat to social stability and economic development. IoT wearable medical technologies have the potential to aid this struggle, but anecdotal evidence showed that large-scale deployment of IoT wearable devices among the ageing population could be fraught with challenges, which have not been well reported in academic literature. Therefore, this paper aims to address this knowledge gap by reporting on an exploratory study that firstly investigated older people's user requirements towards wearable medical devices and secondly explored potential challenges and difficulties for large-scale deployment of such devices. Five focus groups were conducted to collect insights and opinions respectively from five families (i.e. each contained 1–2 elderly members, accompanied with 2–4 family members who held caring responsibilities). The data collected was analyzed by using a thematic analysis approach. The results showed that elderly people have complicated and diverse user requirements towards IoT wearable medical devices, and that a range of challenges related to hardware providers, caregivers, legal regulations and technical features can affect large-scale deployment of such devices. The paper concluded that these identified user requirements and challenges should be carefully considered by wearable hardware designers, system developers, and service providers if they want their innovative products and services to be accepted and deployed among the ageing population globally.

Keywords: Wearable devices · Healthcare · Ageing population
User requirements · Challenges

1 Introduction

Ageing population as a global grand challenge has received increasing attention from governors, practitioners, academics and the general public worldwide. According to the United Nations, the global share of older people (aged 60 years or over) increased from 9.2% in 1990, to 11.7% in 2013, and will continue to grow and reach 21.1% by 2050. Globally, the number of older people is expected to more than double, from 841 million people in 2013 to more than 2 billion in 2050. In light of this trend, the old-age support ratios (i.e. number of working-age adults per older person in the population) will significantly and continuously fall in the coming decades. This is leading to substantial

© Springer International Publishing AG, part of Springer Nature 2018
N. Streitz and S. Konomi (Eds.): DAPI 2018, LNCS 10921, pp. 286–295, 2018.
https://doi.org/10.1007/978-3-319-91125-0_25

pressure to the national health and welfare systems of many countries, and can be a potential threat to social stability and economic development.

Consequently, there is an imperative need for countries to seek for innovative, reliable and convenient solutions to provide better healthcare services to the ever-increasing ageing population, with less workforce, over distance [1]. The concept of IoT wearable medical devices has thus become increasingly important in recent years. Besides being lightweight and portable, this kind of device allows the provision of health monitoring and caring over distance, and so reduces the burden of commuting that many older adults experienced when visiting a healthcare facility for a regular checkup [2].

However, anecdotal evidence showed that large-scale deployment of IoT wearable devices among the ageing population could be fraught with socio-technical challenges, especially considering that older people have very different health and medical conditions and their caring needs may not be easily satisfied by technological means over distance. In the current literature, a large number of studies about wearable devices focused on the contexts of fitness and leisure (e.g. [3, 4]). There are also other studies, from a developer and technical perspective, that look into functionalities and monitoring capabilities of wearable devices for health and medical purposes (e.g. [5–9]). Nevertheless, there is currently very limited understanding and study on the views of older adults towards using wearable medical devices as well as potential difficulties and challenges for large-scale deployment of such technologies. Therefore, this paper aims to address this knowledge gap by reporting on an exploratory study that aims to answer two research questions:

- What do older people really need from IoT wearable medical devices?
- What are the socio-technical challenges in deploying such devices among the ageing population?

The results derived from this study will be of importance to city governors, service providers, IT practitioners and researchers who are interested in not just the development of IoT wearable medical devices but more significantly in large-scale deployment of such technology among the ageing population. The rest of this paper is structured as follows: the next section presents the research methodology adopted by the research. Subsequently, the findings derived from the study are presented and discussed, followed by a discussion of the implications of the results, with conclusions drawn.

2   Methodology

Owing to the exploratory nature of this study, a qualitative research approach was adopted. Merriam and Tisdell describe qualitative research as studies that interpret people's experiences and behaviors to contribute to knowledge [10]. The researchers initially planned to use interview to collect data in the study. However, it was soon recognized that elderly people may often not have sufficient understanding on novel technologies like wearable medical devices, so normal one-to-one interviews may not lead to the best output. On the other hand, when using wearable medical devices, elderly people may often seek help from their younger family members, especially who have caring responsibilities. Therefore, it was deemed that the views of elder people could be better complemented by the opinions of their family members. These considerations pointed the researchers to select focus group rather than individual interview as a more suitable method of data collection for the study. In particular, a focus group will allow the researchers to involve both elderly people and their family members to have an open and interactive discussion on the issues and phenomena under investigation. It was hoped that the use of focus group could trigger a more in-depth conversation that covers the angles of different relevant stakeholders, and so lead to a richer set of data and findings that may not be easily explored by using other methods [11].

Consequently, five face-to-face focus groups were conducted respectively with five families. As shown in Table 1, each focus group in this study involved a family that contained 1–2 elderly members plus 2–4 younger family members. In order to provide a more comfortable and protective environment for elderly people and their families, all focus groups took place in their respective homes with a pre-booked appointment. Each focus group lasted for 40 min to 1 h, and was recorded by using a digital camera. The resulted transcripts were sent to the corresponding participants to double-check the correctness of the recorded contents.

Table 1. Summary of focus group participants

Family ID	Number of 60 + people	Number of family members	Total
Focus group/family 1	1	2	3
Focus group/family 2	1	2	3
Focus group/family 3	1	2	3
Focus group/family 4	2	4	6
Focus group/family 5	2	2	4

Subsequently, the focus group data was analyzed by using a thematic analysis approach. Thematic analysis is one of the predominant techniques for analyzing qualitative data. Braun and Clarke described it as data-driven inductive approach "for identifying, analysing and reporting patterns (themes) within data" [12]. Following guidelines given by Braun and Clarke, the thematic analysis conducted in this study consisted of five stages, as shown in Table 2 [12].

In order to organize and represent concepts and findings derived from the analysis, a concept map was established. As shown in Fig. 1, irradiating from the center of the map are the three identified categories/themes, which are linked to specific user requirements and deployment challenges raised by the elderly people and family members during the focus groups. This concept map provides the structure for reporting the research findings in the next section.

Table 2. Five stages of the thematic analysis

Phase	Description
1. Getting familiar with the data	The transcripts that resulted from the focus groups and interviews were read multiple times for clarification and a better understanding of the participants
2. Coding the data	Coding the textual data in a systematic fashion across the entire data by using NVivo
3. Connecting codes with themes	Classify codes based on potential themes, collecting and gathering all data have relationships with each potential theme
4. Reviewing themes and developing concept maps	Make sure each theme is identified properly considering relevant coded quotes and the entire data set; integrate concept maps of the analysis
5. Reporting findings	Final analysis of selected quotes, considering of the analysis to the research question, producing a new section to report the findings

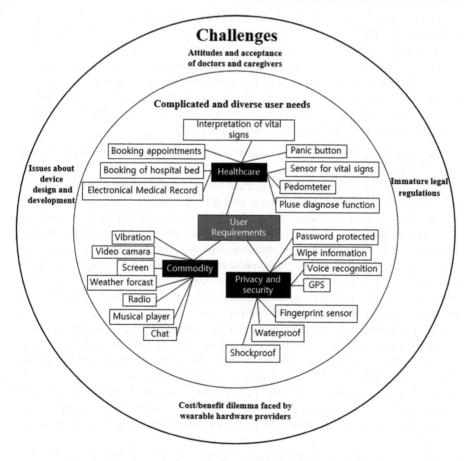

Fig. 1. Concept maps of focus group findings

3   Results and Findings

The results of the focus groups identified that elderly people have complicated and diverse user requirements towards IoT wearable medical devices, and that a range of other challenges related to hardware providers, caregivers, legal regulations and technical features can affect large-scale deployment of such devices, as detailed below.

3.1   Complicated and Diverse User Needs

It emerged from the focus group data that user requirements of elderly people for wearable technologies contain three main categories, namely healthcare, data privacy, and commodity requirements. In terms of healthcare needs, the participated elderly people and their families raised a number of essential hardware and software functions to be ideally included in wearable medical devices, such as:

- Having a panic button exclusively for medical emergencies;
- Having embedded sensors that automatically monitor vital signs (e.g. blood pressure, pulse, heart rate, blood oxygen), measure steps and sleep duration;
- Having additional sensors that can accurately measure and support pulse diagnosis (i.e. a disease measurement method used commonly in traditional Chinese medicine);
- Allowing creation of electronic medical record, booking of hospital beds, booking of medical appointments, interpretation of their vital signs, and medical recommendations and medicine reminders through mobile app.

It is apparent that these types of functions could be particularly useful to elder people with chronic diseases (e.g. Hypertension, High Cholesterol, Diabetes, Ischemic Heart Disease, Dementia, Parkinson's disease, Heart Failure), which do not necessarily require hospitalization but need long-term monitoring and treatment [13, 14].

Further to healthcare requirements, the focus group participants also raised the importance and needs of data privacy protection. Specifically, many participants expressed the fear that personal information collected from wearable medical devices may not be strictly protected and may even be misused by device manufacturers, service providers, and/or caregivers. In other words, device and service providers will need to establish and follow efficient data usage policies to protect data privacy, if they want to gain trust of prospective users and maximize sales.

The third category of identified requirements dealt mainly to commodity and entertainment features (e.g. video camera, chatting tools, social media, location maps, traffic conditions, radio, games) that older adults and their family members will like to have on a wearable device. In fact, the findings showed that older people with or without chronic diseases can often still remain socially active with friends and family members. Previous research also reinforces that older adults with better social connection and interaction tend to have a healthier lifestyle as well as a lower chance of getting depression [15].

By further examining these identified user requirements, it became clear that as physical and psychological conditions of elderly people can vary significantly, their monitoring, caring and entertaining needs can be very complicated and different, and so cannot be easily supported by a universal model of wearable device. In other words, the above identified user requirements and functions will need to be customized to fit the needs of particular individuals in practical terms.

3.2 Issues About Device Design and Development

The complexity and variety of user requirements as discussed above will inevitably raise issues and difficulties when designing and developing wearable medical devices.

In particular, in order to monitor physical variables (e.g. movements, steps, and motion) and various vital signs (e.g. blood pressure, pulse, heart rate, blood oxygen, etc.) of elderly people, different types of sensors will need to be used [16–18]. The ideal solution will be to integrate all the needed sensors into one single device. This was supported by the focus group participants, who stated that they *"want an integrated piece of tool rather than wearing too many different devices" (Focus Group 3)*. This however can lead to severe technical challenges regarding accuracy, stability, battery lifetime, size, and weight of the wearable device. Specifically, when too many sensors need to be embedded into one single device, its internal circuit and structure will become very complicated. When device manufacturers try to reduce and compress the size of the device, its accuracy and stability can often be affected [19, 20]. Faced with these problems, some manufacturers may then try to reduce the size of the device battery in order to leave more space for other crucial components, but this solution can in turn reduce battery lifetime and so lead to inconvenience to the users [16, 19]. Owing to these technical issues, the weight and size of an integrated wearable medical device may not be reduced easily, and so can cause discomfort to elderly people when they wear a relatively large and heavy piece of device on a daily basis [21].

On the other hand, the focus group participants also raised their concerns about how these medical devices may look like and be worn on their body. In fact, many wearable devices for fitness and sport purposes (Fitbit Alta HR, Samsung Gear Fit 2 Pro, Steel HR) are currently designed as a bracelet or watch. But in order to collect more accurate data, wearable medical devices may be designed into different forms. For example, Holter monitor is a well-established piece of wearable healthcare device for monitoring electrocardiography (or ECG) heart activity, and can be particularly useful for elderly people with heart-related diseases [22]. However, these devices require the usage of a series (normally 3–8) of electrodes attached to the user's chest. An elderly person involved in the focus groups cogently stated that *"we are getting old, but we do not want to wear devices that make us look like aliens" (Focus Group 4)*. In other words, the current design of wearable medical devices will need to be carefully reviewed and revised by considering the feeling and opinions of their intended users.

3.3 Cost/Benefit Dilemma Faced by Wearable Hardware Providers

The complicated list of user requirements and associated design and development challenges is leading to a cost/benefit dilemma to wearable device providers. On one hand, the global market of wearable medical devices is getting increasingly competitive. If any device manufacturers want to play successfully in the market, they need to make a greater endeavor to satisfy the identified needs and requirements of the elderly people [23]. Failure in doing so will inevitably reduce use acceptance and diminish the value and usefulness of the developed wearable devices, and so affecting competitive advantages of the product in the market. But on the other hand, overcoming the design and development challenges associated with these user requirements (e.g. especially to have a highly integrated, reliable, stable, light and long-lasting wearable device with all the needed functions) will require very substantial R&D investment. Such high R&D cost can then lead to high selling price of the device, which may not be affordable to many elderly people and their families. From a customer perspective, the focus group participants reinforced that for most wearable medical devices available in the market, "*the affordable ones often did not contain all the functions they need, and the ones that can satisfy their requirements are always far too expensive for them to buy*" *(Focus Group 2)*. This dilemma will inevitably affect large-scale deployment of IoT wearable medical devices. In order to resolve this, device and service providers will need to seek for new business models, which do not simply reply on the selling of the device itself, but allow a cheaper device selling price that can be compounded by add-on service charges in the long run.

3.4   Attitudes and Acceptance of Doctors and Caregivers

IoT wearable medical devices are not just simply monitoring tools. In fact, vital signs and other essential data collected by the device will normally be sent through wireless network to a back-office cloud system, which will process, store and analyze the data and then generate warnings and disease predictions in due course [24]. These analytical results can be used by elderly people and their family members to take proper actions if needed. More importantly, these data and analytical results can be constantly and remotely monitored and reviewed by doctors and medical caregivers to provide necessary treatments to the elderly people. For those with chronic diseases, this type of remote monitoring and caring will be particularly useful and can reduce the need of hospitalization [13, 14].

However, the focus group participants worried that it might not be easy to get involved a large number of doctors and medical caregivers in public hospitals in the caring end of wearable devices. This view has actually also been reported in other studies. Specifically, Kornreich et al. [25] highlighted that doctors and caregivers in hospitals already have a lot of pressure and very tight daily schedules, and so may not be willing to take any additional remote monitoring/caring duties. Kroll et al. [26] echoed that medical professionals might also have concerns about the accuracy, validity and currency of the data collected and sent by wearable devices, and so might not be willing to carry diagnosis and make medical decisions based on these data. The focus group participants added that "*the scenario will become even more complicated when considering the very strict regulations and rules of hospitals, which may not allow doctors to accept and use data supplied by different wearable devices used by elderly people*" *(Focus Group 3)*.

3.5   Immature Legal Regulations

Last but not least, the focus group results showed that elderly people and their family members had serious doubts about current legal regulations associated with the usage of wearable medical devices. For instance, the two elderly people in focus group 5 questioned that *"if we use these wearable devices on a regular basis, but things did not go well, such as, the device did not measure my heart rate accurately and so wrong treatment is provided to me, who should be legally responsible for it"*. In fact, the failure of wearable devices and related services can be caused by a mixture of potential reasons, including hardware issues (e.g. inaccurate and unstable measurements), software flaws (e.g. inadequate data processing and analysis), irresponsible caring professionals (e.g. wrong diagnosis and decisions made by doctors), and even inappropriate user behaviors (e.g. the elderly person does not charge and/or wear the device properly). Consequently, when medical accidents happened to the device users, it could be difficult to identify clearly whether the accident is owing to hardware, software or human reasons. As such, it will be hard to draw a clear answer to tell who the responsible parties are. Because local regulations and legal rules often have not been developed sufficiently to resolve these conflicts, device manufacturers, software developers and medical service providers may try to find excuses to avoid being responsible for the accident. The participants in focus group 1 cogently concluded that *"when a wearable medical device fails, the elderly person who uses it can face severe risk and even become a truly victim"*.

4   Further Discussions and Conclusions

Faced with the global grand challenge of ageing population, the evolution of wearable healthcare technologies has attracted increasing interest from the society. However, the adoption of wearable devices among the ageing population is still in an infancy stage. This paper reported on a study that aimed to explore potential socio-technical challenges affecting large-scale deployment of IoT wearable medical devices. The results showed that elderly people with different health conditions can have very complicated and diverse needs towards the usage of wearable devices. These needs and requirements may not be easily satisfied with current technical constraints. In addition, the findings also showed that elderly people and their family members have many concerns about the current medical and legal systems, which were deemed to be insufficiently prepared to enable large-scale deployment of wearable medical devices in the society.

Overall, it can be concluded that technology is important but not the only determinant for the success of IoT wearable medical devices. In order to realize the benefits promised by these devices and achieve a high level of adoption and penetration rate, device designers, service providers, governors and medical practitioners need to make a stronger endeavor together to resolve the identified socio-technical challenges as well as to provide a better business, medical and legal environment that can support long-term development of the wearable medical device market. Finally, it should be highlighted that as an exploratory study which was limited by time and resources, this research has an apparent weakness. That is, only a limited number of stakeholders were involved in the focus groups of this study. Therefore, further research on this topic is strongly recommended.

References

1. Fan, M., Sun, J., Zhou, B., Chen, M.: The smart health initiative in China: the case of Wuhan. J. Med. Syst. **40**(3), 1–17 (2016)
2. Li, B., Chen, S.: A study of residential condition and satisfaction of the elderly in China. J. Hous. Elderly **25**(1), 72–88 (2011)
3. Fritz, T., Huang, E.M., Murphy, G.C., Zimmermann, T.: Persuasive technology in the real world: a study of long-term use of activity sensing devices for fitness. In: Proceedings of the SIGCHI Conference on Human Factors in Computing Systems, pp. 487–496. ACM (2014)
4. Buttussi, F., Chittaro, L.: MOPET: a context-aware and user-adaptive wearable system for fitness training. Artif. Intell. Med. **42**(2), 153–163 (2008)
5. Zheng, Y.L., et al.: Unobtrusive sensing and wearable devices for health informatics. IEEE Trans. Biomed. Eng. **61**(5), 1538–1554 (2014)
6. Pantelopoulos, A., Bourbakis, N.G.: A survey on wearable sensor-based systems for health monitoring and prognosis. IEEE Trans. Syst. Man Cybern. Part C (Appl. Rev.) **40**(1), 1–12 (2010)
7. Appelboom, G., et al.: Smart wearable body sensors for patient self-assessment and monitoring. Arch. Public Health **72**(1), 28 (2014)
8. Zheng, J., et al.: Emerging wearable medical devices towards personalized healthcare. In: Proceedings of the 8th International Conference on Body, pp. 427–431. ICST (Institute for Computer Sciences, Social-Informatics and Telecommunications Engineering), Networks (2013)
9. Chang, Y.J., Chen, C.H., Lin, L.F., Han, R.P., Huang, W.T., Lee, G.C.: Wireless sensor networks for vital signs monitoring: application in a nursing home. Int. J. Distrib. Sens. **8**(11), 685107 (2012)
10. Merriam, S.B., Tisdell, E.J.: Qualitative Research: A Guide to Design and Implementation. Wiley, Hoboken (2015)
11. Morgan, D.L.: The Focus Group Guidebook. Sage publications, Thousand Oaks (1997)
12. Braun, V., Clarke, V.: Using thematic analysis in psychology. Qual. Res. Psychol. **3**(2), 77–101 (2006)
13. Prince, M.J., et al.: Ageing 2. The burden of disease in older people and implications for health policy and practice. Lancet **385**(9967), 549–562 (2015)
14. Wang, Z., Li, X., Chen, M.: Catastrophic health expenditures and its inequality in elderly households with chronic disease patients in China. Int. J. Equity Health **14**(1), 8 (2015)
15. Moak, Z.B., Agrawal, A.: The association between perceived interpersonal social support and physical and mental health: results from the national epidemiological survey on alcohol and related conditions. J. Public Health **32**(2), 191–201 (2010)
16. Lo, B., Yang, G.Z.: Key technical challenges and current implementations of body sensor networks. In: Proceedings of 2nd International Workshop on Body Sensor Networks (2005)
17. Otto, C., Milenkovic, A., Sanders, C., Jovanov, E.: System architecture of a wireless body area sensor network for ubiquitous health monitoring. J. Mob. Multimedia **1**(4), 307–326 (2006)
18. Baig, M.M., GholamHosseini, H., Moqeem, A.A., Mirza, F., Lindén, M.: A systematic review of wearable patient monitoring systems–current challenges and opportunities for clinical adoption. J. Med. Syst. **41**(7), 115 (2017)

19. Khan, Y., Ostfeld, A.E., Lochner, C.M., Pierre, A., Arias, A.C.: Monitoring of vital signs with flexible and wearable medical devices. Adv. Mater. **28**(22), 4373–4395 (2016)
20. Prasad, D., Chiplunkar, N.N., Nayak, K.P.A.: Trusted ubiquitous healthcare monitoring system for hospital environment. Int. J. Mob. Comput. Multimed. Commun. (IJMCMC) **8**(2), 14–26 (2017)
21. Hung, K., Zhang, Y.T., Tai, B.: Wearable medical devices for tele-home healthcare. In: 26th Annual International Conference of the IEEE Engineering in Medicine and Biology Society, IEMBS 2004, pp. 5384–5387 (2004)
22. Glaros, C., Fotiadis, D.I.: Wearable devices in healthcare. In: Silverman, B.G., Jain, A., Ichalkaranje, A., Jain, L.C. (eds.) Intelligent Paradigms for Healthcare Enterprises Studies in Fuzziness and Soft Computing, vol. 184, pp. 237–264. Springer, Heidelberg (2005). https://doi.org/10.1007/11311966_8
23. Gao, Y., Li, H., Luo, Y.: An empirical study of wearable technology acceptance in healthcare. Ind. Manag. Data Syst. **115**(9), 1704–1723 (2015)
24. Chan, M., Estève, D., Fourniols, J.Y., Escriba, C., Campo, E.: Smart wearable systems: current status and future challenges. Artif. Intell. Med. **56**(3), 137–156 (2012)
25. Kornreich, Y., Vertinsky, I., Potter, P.B.: Consultation and deliberation in China: the making of China's health-care reform. Chin. J. **68**, 176–203 (2012)
26. Kroll, R.R., Boyd, J.G., Maslove, D.M.: Accuracy of a wrist-worn wearable device for monitoring heart rates in hospital inpatients: a prospective observational study. J. Med. Internet Res. **18**(9), e253 (2016)

Practical and Numerical Investigation on a Minimal Design Navigation System of Bats

Yasufumi Yamada[1](✉) ⓘ, Kentaro Ito[2], Ryo Kobayashi[3,4], Shizuko Hiryu[1,5] ⓘ, and Yoshiaki Watanabe[1]

[1] Doshisha University, Kyotanabe, 610-0321, Japan
yasufumi.yamada1@gmail.com
[2] Hosei University, Koganei, 184-0002, Japan
[3] Hiroshima University, Higashi-Hiroshima, 739-8526, Japan
[4] JST CREST, Chiyodaku, Tokyo, 102-0076, Japan
[5] JST PRESTO, Chiyodaku, Tokyo, 102-0076, Japan

Abstract. In this study, to investigate how the behavioral strategy employed by bats contributed to acoustic navigation based on a minimal design sensing, we conducted vehicle experiments and numerical simulation based on a simple algorithm inspired by bats. Especially, a double-pulse scanning method was proposed as a bat-inspired navigation algorithm in which (1) the direction of pulse emission was alternately shifted between the direction of movement and the direction of the nearest obstacle, and (2) the direction of movement was calculated for every double-pulse emission based on integrated information from all echoes detected by double-pulse sensing. To quantify that method, a conventional scanning method was also developed. The conventional scanning method was that (1) the pulse direction was fixed in the direction of travel of the car body and (2) the moving direction was calculated for every pulse emission. As a result of 100 repeated drives with autonomous vehicle equipped with 1 transmitter and 2 receivers in a practical course, the success rate of an obstacle-avoidance drive on a test course improved from 13% for conventional method to 73% with the proposed method. Furthermore, the numerical simulation demonstrated that the proposed method operate the robust path planning by suppressing the localization ambiguity due to interference of multiple echoes. These practical experiments and numerical simulation suggest that bats employed the simple behavioral solution on the operation of acoustic sensing for various problems occurring in the real world.

Keywords: Awareness in distributed, ambient, and pervasive environments
Echolocation · Bats · Autonomous vehicle · Bio-inspired-navigation

1 Introduction

Echolocating bats perceive spatial information using ultrasonic sensing even in the absence of visual information. They emit ultrasound pulses from the nose or mouth and detect the returning echoes with the right and left ears, which can be regarded as the minimum sensor requirement for three-dimensional (3D) spatial sensing. From the view

© Springer International Publishing AG, part of Springer Nature 2018
N. Streitz and S. Konomi (Eds.): DAPI 2018, LNCS 10921, pp. 296–315, 2018.
https://doi.org/10.1007/978-3-319-91125-0_26

point of sensor inputs, echolocation acquires a one-dimensional time-amplitude signals, but since visual sensing acquires two-dimensional images, the raw sensor inputs of echolocation seem to be fewer than those of visual sensing. Nevertheless, bats can achieve robust navigation with a small brain in complex environments, i.e. avoiding randomly located obstacles and flying with other conspecifics [1–4]. Here, the term "cheap design" refers to a concept, based on studies of mobile robots, that entails low calculation cost and simple mechanical design [5, 6]. If the decision-making process of echolocating bats that is used for 3D path planning in real time from low-dimensional acoustic sensor inputs can be modelled with simple mechanical design, it is expected to lead us to create a bat-inspired navigation system supporting cheap design mobile robots.

In order to negotiate a complicated environment using a restricted acoustic field of view with a simple mechanical design, bats may employ not only physiological specialization of their auditory systems [7, 8] but also behavioral strategies [9] of temporal-spatial scanning adapted for the capacity of the scanning range. The dynamics of the relationship between "acoustic gaze" (direction of ultrasound pulses emitted by bats) and bats' flight control has been investigated by using aerial-feeding echolocating bats [10–14]. However, it remains unclear how bats can be operated the temporal-spatial scanning in an intuitive and efficient way. Our motivation is to understand the behavioral usefulness of the bats for the temporal-spatial scanning throughout the development of the autonomous vehicle which can be evaluate in conjunction with practical acoustical sensing problems in real environments.

In this study, we embedded the algorithm inspired by bats in an autonomous vehicle equipped with simple ultrasonic sensors (one transmitter and two receivers). Then, vehicle performance was experimentally investigated in obstacle environment. Finally, the numerical simulation was conducted to quantify that the algorithm inspired by bats was robust to the practical sensing problems.

2   Vehicle Experiment

2.1   Purpose

In a previous study, during the flight in unfamiliar space, we have often observed the double- and triple pulse (a set of two and three pulses emitted with short interval) scanning of bats, the direction of pulse emission of which was alternately shifted between the intended flight direction and the nearby obstacle's direction. Such an alternate shifting of the pulse direction has been confirmed in many bats that fly in various obstacle environments, as shown in Fig. 1. To investigate how selective spatial scanning with multiple pulses contributed to improving the robustness of navigation based on cheap design sensing, a double-pulse scanning method was proposed as a bat-inspired navigation algorithm. In the double-pulse scanning method, (1) the direction of pulse emission was alternately shifted between the direction of movement and the direction of the nearest obstacle, and (2) the direction of movement was calculated for every double-pulse emission based on integrated information from all echoes detected by double-pulse sensing. To quantify the double-pulse scanning method, a conventional scanning method

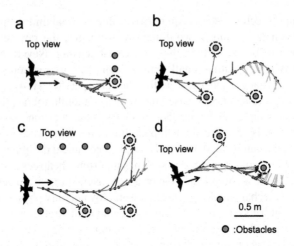

Fig. 1. Examples of pulse direction control by four different individual bats during flight in various obstacle environments. Measurement procedure was described in our previous paper [15]. Each bat was observed only one time (<20 s), focusing on exploratory behavior in an unfamiliar place. Red and blue lines indicate that the pulses were alternately emitted towards the bats' own flight direction (red) and the obstacle direction (blue). Light blue lines indicate any other pulses that the bats' intention could not be estimated. Because the emission pulse was a broad beam, we considered bats to have aimed the pulse emissions towards the target obstacles as long as the pulses were directed towards the dashed-line circles the diameters of which are 16 cm. As a result, all of these aiming pulses were emitted towards the target with an angle deviation within 7 degrees. (Color figure online)

was also developed, in which: (1) the pulse direction was fixed in the direction of travel of the car body and (2) the moving direction was calculated for every pulse emission.

2.2   Vehicle Design

We made a mobile vehicle (30 (H) × 15 (W) × 25 (L) cm), which consisted of three ultrasonic sensor units, one transmitter (MA40S4R; Murata, Kyoto, Japan, ±50° at 6 dB off-axis angles from the centre of the beam direction), two receivers (SPM0404UD5; Knowles, Itasca, IL, USA), two servomotor units, and a central processing unit (Arduino LLC, Somerville, MA, USA; fs = 140 kHz). One of the servomotors controlled the pulse direction from the transmitter and the other servomotor was connected to the right and left front wheels shaft so that the pulse direction could be adjusted independently of the control of the vehicle driving direction.

Our used piezoelectric sensor was difficult to emit a wideband FM signal similar to the bats; hence, the transmitter emitted a short duration tone burst signal that had a frequency of 40 kHz and 2 ms duration. The sound pressure level of the pulse was 103 dB at a distance of 1 m in front of the transmitter. The vehicle was designed to extract echo arrival timings for all echoes detected per emission, ranging from 2 to 30 ms from pulse emission, corresponding to detection distances of 34 cm to 5.1 m (note that the minimum value was set at 2 ms to avoid temporal overlap of emitted pulse and echo). While driving, the echo arrival timings at the right and left receivers (t_{right}, t_{left}) were determined by reading the instant timing when the amplitude value of the echo exceeded the voltage threshold. It should be noted that, when the echoes returning from different objects were temporally overlapped, only the fastest arrival timing was regarded as the echo arrival time, and the arrival times of the subsequent overlapping echoes were ignored. The position of each obstacle was localized using Eqs. (1) and (2) in real time, respectively.

$$r_{obs}(t, n) = \frac{c\left(t_{right}(t, n) + t_{left}(t, n)\right)}{4} \tag{1}$$

$$\theta_{obs}(t, n) = arcsin\frac{c\left(t_{right}(t, n) - t_{left}(t, n)\right)}{d} + \varphi_p \tag{2}$$

where d indicates the distance between the right and left receivers which was set on 8 cm, t indicates the pulse emission timing, n indicates the order in which echoes are detected by each receiver, r_{obs} is the distance from the vehicle to the obstacle, φ_p is the direction of the emission pulse relative to the vehicle driving direction, and θ_{obs} is the direction of the obstacle relative to the vehicle driving direction. Because the echoes arriving at the right and left receivers were paired in time-sequence order to calculate r_{obs} and θ_{obs} using Eqs. (1) and (2), they were sequentially numbered; thus, the n of r_{obs} and θ_{obs} were defined as $r(t, n)$ and $\theta(t, n)$, respectively. Here, the number of all obstacles detected by the pulse emission at time t is defined as $N(t)$ for calculation of the vehicle navigation algorithm.

The vehicle was controlled based on two simple movements: (1) moving straight forward and (2) pivoting in place (without moving forward) to change the driving direction. Figure 2a and b provide schematic diagrams of the control dynamics for moving direction φ_d with the conventional scanning method and double-pulse scanning method, respectively. The timing of the ith pulse emission is defined as t_i. The moving direction φ_d of the conventional scanning method was changed by pivoting after pulse emission, with a response time Δt including both mechanical and echo processing time (Fig. 2a). On the other hand, the moving direction φ_d in the double-pulse scanning method was calculated for every double-pulse emission (Fig. 2b). Then, the vehicle moved straight forward for a duration τ, which was set at 0.6 s in the conventional scanning method and 1.2 s in the double-pulse scanning method. Because the response time Δt (<0.1 s) was sufficiently shorter than τ, we could consider the inter-pulse interval to be 0.6 s for both the conventional and double-pulse scanning methods, with the result that the inter-pivot interval (inter-pivot distance) of the double-pulse scanning method was twice as long as that of the conventional scanning method. The vehicle driving speed was set at ~15 times slower (21 cm/s) than flight speed of R. ferrumequinum nippon during obstacle-avoidance flight. Therefore, the inter-pulse interval of the vehicle was set at 0.6 s, which was approximately 15 times that of the bats' inter-pulse interval.

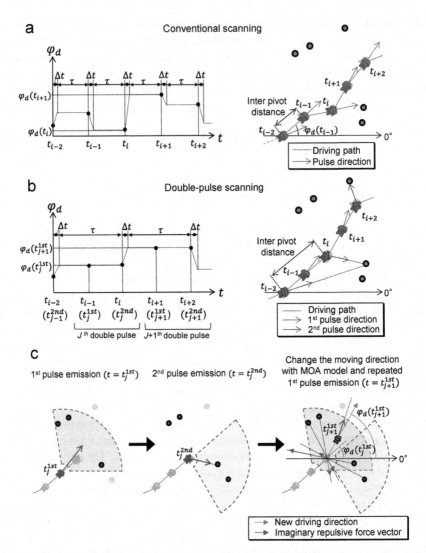

Fig. 2. Comparison of vehicle movement between the conventional scanning system and the double-pulse scanning system. Schematic of temporal change in moving direction φ_d of the vehicle with the conventional scanning (*a*) and double-pulse scanning (*b*). The conventional scanning system repeated the pivot turn in the duration of response time Δt toward the calculated moving direction at every sensing. In contrast, the double-pulse scanning system was set for pivot turns every double-pulse emission. (*c*) Schematic of control law for pulse direction φ_p in the double-pulse scanning system. The 2nd pulse emission was directed towards the nearest obstacle among all obstacles detected by the previous two successive emissions, i.e. the 1st pulse emission of the jth double pulse and the 2nd pulse emission of the $(j-1)^{th}$ double pulse. Then, the direction of the 1st pulse emission of the $(j+1)^{th}$ double pulse, $\varphi_p\left(t_{j+1}^{1st}\right)$, was determined based on the amount of change in the moving direction φ_d between j^{th} and $(j+1)^{th}$ double pulses.

2.3 Vehicle Navigation Algorithm

First, we constructed an obstacle-avoidance model for both the conventional and double-pulse scanning methods to control the vehicle's moving direction using multiple obstacle information (multi-obstacle-avoidance [MOA] model. See Appendix). To explain the MOA model briefly, we determined the moving direction φ_d in the case of the conventional scanning method using the following equation (Fig. 2a):

$$\varphi_d(t_{i+1}) = \arg(e^{i\varphi_d(t_i)} - 2\sum_{n=1}^{N(t_i)} \sqrt{\frac{\alpha}{r(t_i,n)}} \sin\left(arctan\frac{r(t_i,n)}{k}\right)e^{i\theta(t_i,n)}) \tag{3}$$

where $k = 1.3$ m, $\alpha = 0.015625$ m and arg means a function operating on complex numbers (symbol i in the exponents means imaginary unit) which gives the angle from real axis $(=0°)$. The moving direction φ_d was changed after the ith pulse emission. On the other hand, in the case of double-pulse scanning method, after the 2nd pulse emission of the jth double pulse, φ_d could be determined using the following equation (Fig. 2b):

$$\varphi_d\left(t_{j+1}^{1st}\right) = \arg(e^{i\varphi_d(t_j^{1st})} - 2\sum_{n=1}^{N(t_j^{1st})} \sqrt{\frac{\alpha}{r(t_j^{1st},n)}} \sin\left(arctan\frac{k}{r(t_j^{1st},n)}\right)e^{i\theta(t_j^{1st},n)}$$

$$- 2\sum_{n=1}^{N(t_j^{2nd})} \sqrt{\frac{\alpha}{r(t_j^{2nd},n)}} \sin\left(arctan\frac{k}{r(t_j^{2nd},n)}\right)e^{i\theta(t_j^{2nd},n)}. \tag{4}$$

where $k = 1.3$ m and $\alpha = 0.0078125$ m. Thus, the moving direction φ_d in the double-pulse scanning method was calculated using all obstacle information obtained from the 1st and the 2nd pulse emissions. It should be noted that the positions of obstacles detected by the 1st pulse emission were corrected according to the movement of the vehicle to calculate the φ_d. In the double pulse scanning method, the parameter k was set to be the same value as that of the conventional scanning method. However, the parameter α was set to half the value of the conventional scanning method, since the proposed method was subjected to a more repulsive force by double sensing. It was confirmed that the vehicle operate the almost same avoidance path in those proposed method and the conventional scanning method when the obstacle pole placed at 1 m in front of the vehicle.

In the MOA model of both the conventional and double-pulse scanning methods, the moving direction φ_d can be calculated by adding the imaginary attraction force vector of the vehicle's current driving direction and imaginary repulsive force vectors. The imaginary repulsive force produced from each obstacle was determined by the distance $r(t,n)$ and the direction $\theta(t,n)$ $(n = 1,\dots,N(t))$ of the obstacles. Furthermore, by assuming the imaginary width of individual obstacles according to the distance $r(t,n)$, the MOA model calculates the imaginary repulsive force, which is inspired to the concept of monoscopic depth cues of the visual sensing (i.e. the perceived object size changes with distance). As a result, the driving direction can be defined by adding reconstructed imaginary two-dimensional images of surrounding objects that were derived from one-dimensional sound information.

In the conventional scanning method, the pulse direction was fixed in the direction of travel of the car body at all times for every pulse emission (Fig. 2a). In the double-pulse scanning method, the direction of the 1st pulse emission of the $(j + 1)^{th}$ double pulse, $\varphi_p\left(t_{j+1}^{1st}\right)$, was determined by the amount of change in the moving direction between the jth and $(j + 1)^{th}$ double pulses (Fig. 2c).

$$\varphi_p\left(t_{j+1}^{1st}\right) = \varphi_d\left(t_{j+1}^{1st}\right) + \beta\left(\varphi_d\left(t_{j+1}^{1st}\right) - \varphi_d\left(t_j^{1st}\right)\right), \tag{5}$$

where β was set at 0.6. After the vehicle detected the obstacles by the 1st pulse emission, the 2nd pulse emission was directed to the nearest obstacle among all obstacles detected by the previous two successive emissions, i.e. the 1st pulse emission of the $(j + 1)^{th}$ double pulse and the 2nd pulse emission of the jth double pulse. As a result, in the double-pulse scanning method, the direction of pulse emission alternates between the direction of movement and the direction of the nearest obstacle, simulating the movement of bats flying in unfamiliar spaces. Figures 3a and b show flowcharts of the avoidance algorithm based on the MOA model for the conventional scanning and double-pulse scanning methods, respectively. The frequency of decision making for movement direction in the double-pulse scanning method was half that in the conventional scanning method. On the other hand, avoidance direction could be calculated using twice as much obstacle information by spatial integration obtained from double-sensing.

2.4 Experimental Method

An obstacle course was constructed by arranging plastic poles (12 cm diameter) in a 4×2 m driving field. While driving on the obstacle course, obstacle distance and direction localized by the vehicle, and the pulse direction of the transmitted signal, were stored instantly in memory on the vehicle, and then transmitted using wireless serial communication (X-bee; Digi International Inc., Minnetonka, MN, USA) to a personal computer in real-time. In addition, the vehicle driving path and moving direction were measured externally using two digital high-speed video cameras, with the same recording procedure used in the behavioural experiments with bats. The vehicle has a LED light that flashed in synchronization with pulse emission, so that the actual pulse emission timing could also be recorded by these video cameras. The localization errors of $r(t, n)$ and $\theta(t, n)$ $(n = 1, \ldots, N(t))$ were evaluated using the differences between the localized values from the vehicle and the values measured by the external cameras at every pulse emission. Furthermore, the obstacle-avoidance performance of a vehicle was measured to permit comparison between the conventional scanning and double-pulse scanning methods.

For statistical comparisons, a Mann–Whitney U-test and a Student's t-test were used, where appropriate, to test for significant differences in obstacle localization accuracy, the number of detected obstacles, N, and detection rate of the nearest obstacle from the

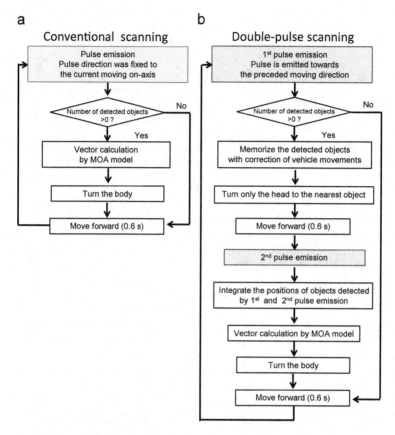

Fig. 3. Schematic diagrams of vehicle navigation algorithms. (*a*) Conventional scanning system. (*b*) Double-pulse scanning system.

vehicle position between the double-pulse scanning method and the conventional scanning method.

2.5   Result of the Vehicle Experiments

Examples of the moving path and pulse direction of the vehicle while driving on the obstacle course are shown in Figs. 4*a* and *b*, respectively. With the conventional scanning method, the vehicle collided with the pole located at the centre of the obstacle course even though the vehicle detected the pole (Fig. 4*a*), whereas the double-pulse scanning method could avoid the pole (Fig. 4*b*). Figures 10*c* and *d* also show vehicle driving paths taken from the first 10 trials in each method. Vehicle collision frequently occurred at the centre pole with the conventional scanning method, but centre pole was avoided with the double-pulse scanning method in all of 10 trials. The total success rates for the 100 obstacle-avoidance trials (i.e. the proportion of trials where the vehicle successfully avoided collisions) on this course were 13% (13/100 trials) for the

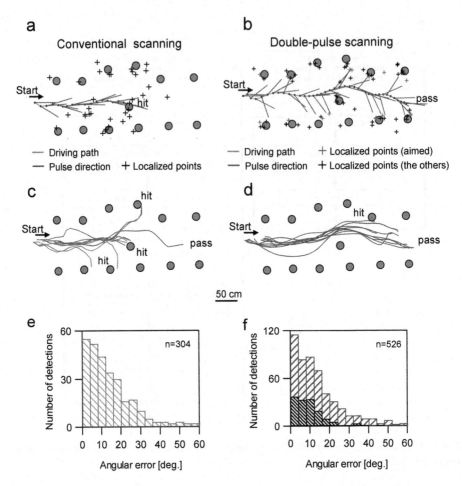

Fig. 4. Demonstration of vehicle navigation during obstacle-avoidance driving. Top views of representative driving trajectories (red line) and pulse directions (blue line) for the conventional scanning system (*a*) and the double-pulse scanning system (*b*). All obstacle positions localized by the vehicle are shown with cross-marks. Red cross-marks in the results of the double pulse scanning system indicate the nearest obstacle positions localized by obstacle-aimed pulse emission. (*d, c*) Top views of driving trajectories for the conventional scanning system (*c*) and double-pulse scanning system (*d*) (10 trials per system). (*e, f*) Distributions of error angle for obstacle detection in the conventional (*e*) and double-pulse scanning systems (*f*). It should be noted that the error angle of the nearest obstacles localized by the obstacle aiming pulse in the double-pulse scanning system was also indicated by a black histogram. (Color figure online)

conventional method and 73% (73/100 trials) for the double-pulse scanning method. The collisions in each method were categorized into two types: collisions with the centre obstacle pole (52% for conventional and 10% for double-pulse) and collisions with the right- and left-side poles (35% for conventional and 17% for double-pulse).

In Fig. 4*a* and *b*, the positions of all obstacles localized by the vehicle are marked with crosses. The localized positions, however, deviated from the actual obstacle positions; the localization error for the first 10 trials was 19 ± 12 cm in the conventional scanning method and 20 ± 12 cm in double-pulse scanning method, a non-significant difference (Mann–Whitney *U*-test, *P* = 0.07). Furthermore, Fig. 4*e* and *f* show the distributions of the angular error of detected obstacles for the 10 trials in Fig. 4*c* and *d*. The angular error of the conventional method was not significantly different from that of the double-pulse scanning method (Mann–Whitney *U*-test, *P* = 0.54). However, in the double-pulse scanning method, the localized position focused by the 2nd pulse emissions of the double pulse directed toward the nearest obstacle (see red cross-marks in Fig. 10*b*) had a significantly lower angular error (see black histogram in Fig. 4*f*, Mann–Whitney *U*-test, *P* < 0.01) and distance error (Mann–Whitney *U*-test, *P* < 0.01) compared with the other localized positions and this was also significantly lower than that of the conventional method (Mann–Whitney *U*-test, *P* < 0.01). These results suggest that obstacle-aimed pulse emission improves the localization accuracy for the target obstacle.

The distributions of the number of obstacles *N* used to calculate moving direction are shown in Fig. 5*a*. The mean *N* was 4.5 ± 1.3 in double-pulse scanning, which was almost twice that in conventional scanning (*N* = 2.0 ± 1.0) owing to the integration of obstacle information obtained from double sensing (Mann–Whitney *U*-test, *P* < 0.01). In the double-pulse scanning method, the angles θ_{obs} of detected obstacles relative to pulse direction were distributed mainly around the centre of the pulse's own acoustic field (Fig. 5*c*), whereas the conventional scanning method tended to detect obstacles to its own right or left off-axis sightline (Fig. 5*b*). Moreover, the detection rate of the nearest obstacle from the vehicle position reached ~80% (334/526) in the double-pulse scanning method, which was significantly higher than that in the conventional scanning method (50%, 186/304, Student's *t*-test, P < 0.05) (Fig. 5*d*).

These findings suggest that the double-pulse scanning method has several practical advantages for obstacles detection, for example, allowing vehicles to drive without losing the nearest obstacle within the acoustic field of view, even when the frequency of decision making with respect to movement direction was reduced by half.

3 Numerical Simulation

3.1 Simulation Situation

In the previous chapter, we experimentally revealed that vehicles with proposed methods improve the robustness of the path planning comparing to those without proposed methods. Although, vehicle experiment has not been revealed certain factors that improve the robustness of path planning. In order to clarify this, the numerical simulation was conducted in the same situation as the vehicle experiment. In particular, obstacle course arrangement, moving speed of simulated vehicle (21 cm/s) and inter-pulse interval (0.6 s) were set in the same way as the vehicle experiment situation.

Furthermore, the obstacle detection range was also estimated to be similar to the practical sensing situation by using the actually measured pulse and receiver directivity

306   Y. Yamada et al.

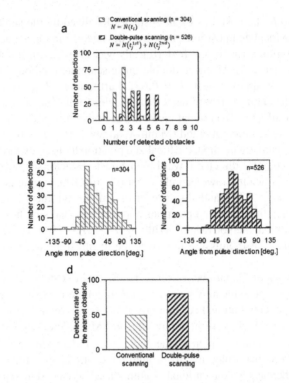

Fig. 5. Comparison of obstacle-detection performance between the conventional and double-pulse scanning systems for the first 10 trials. (*a*) Distributions of the number of obstacles *N* that were used to calculate moving direction in the conventional and double-pulse scanning systems. Distributions of obstacle-detection angle from the pulse direction in the conventional (*b*) and double-pulse scanning system (*c*). (*d*) Comparison of detection rates of the nearest obstacles, according to vehicle coordination, between the conventional and double-pulse scanning systems.

pattern (Fig. 6a and b) and the distance attenuation characteristics of the pulse (Fig. 6c). Those pulse directivity patterns and the distance attenuation characteristics of the pulse were fitted by Gaussian and exponential functions as following equations

$$F\left(r_{obs}(t,n)\right) = k_{f1} + k_{f2} \cdot e^{k_{f3} \cdot r_{obs}(t,n)} + k_{f4} \cdot e^{k_{f5} \cdot r_{obs}(t,n)}, \tag{6}$$

$$G(\theta_{obs}(t,n)) = 1 \bigg/ \left(k_{g1} + k_{g2} \cdot e^{\left(\frac{\theta_{obs}(t,n)}{k_{g3}}\right)^2} \right), \tag{7}$$

where $k_{f1} = 0.012658829$, $k_{f2} = 0.261003066$, $k_{f3} = -3.065341475$, $k_{f4} = 2.441670304$, $k_{f5} = -23.2536802$, $k_{g1} = 0.00658$, $k_{g2} = 1.009079$ and $k_{g3} = 59.94135$. By using Eqs. (6) and (7), from the distance $r_{obs}(t,n)$ and the direction

$\theta_{obs}(t, n)$ of the obstacle, echo strength level $P_e(t, n)$ in each obstacle was estimated by assuming it as total internal reflection with following equation

$$P_e(t,n) = 20log_{10}\big(2F(r_{obs}(t,n)) \cdot G(\theta_{obs}(t,n))\big) \tag{8}$$

where echo strength level $P_e(t, n)$ is respect to the strength of the pulse. When the calculated echo strength level $P_e(t, n)$ was higher than minimum strength level for echo detection (P_{min}), the obstacle was regarded as detected. It should be note that minimum strength level for echo detection P_{min} was determined as -36 dB from the maximum detection range of the actual vehicle in this study. As a result of these estimations, obstacle detection range was reproduced, shown in Fig. 6d, without setting an unreasonable detection range such as a fan shape.

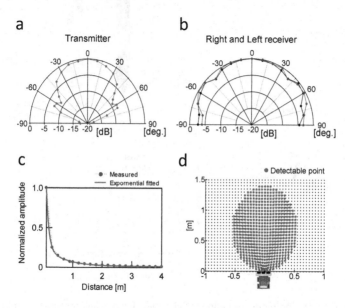

Fig. 6. Detection range estimation based on the actual sensors characteristics. (*a, b*) Directivity pattern of the transmitter (red line), right (blue line) and left receivers (black line) which were measured by using 40 kHz constant frequency sound. (*c*) Distance attenuation characteristic of the propagation sound of 40 kHz. The actual measured distance attenuation pattern (blue line-plots) was fitted by exponential curve-fitting (red line). (*d*) Estimated detectable range (red plots) for the vehicle simulation by using the gauss-fitted directivity pattern of the transmitter and the curve-fitted distance attenuation characteristic. (Color figure online)

3.2   Simulation Method for Ideal and Practical Condition

To quantify the robustness for the sensing ambiguity, the numerical simulation was conducted in different two conditions. The one was the ideal sensing condition which can be localized the detection point to the accurate obstacle position. The other one was the practical sensing condition which included the localization ambiguity (1) due to the interference problem of echoes returned from multiple objects and (2) due to sensing performance of the vehicle.

Echoes interference problem was implemented based on practical sensing problem, in which the subsequent echo was made blinded when that arrives within the duration (2 ms) of the preceding echo. As a fatal problem related to this, echo-pairing mismatching was also implemented when the order of the echo sequence was different between the right and left receivers (Fig. 7a and b). In this paper, Localization error due to the mismatched echo-pairing was defined as ghost localization.

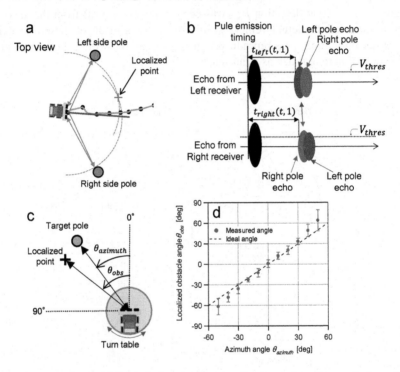

Fig. 7. Actual sensing problems including the ghost localization and sensing resolution reflected in the simulation of the practical condition. (a) Actual case of the ghost localization caused by miss-pairing the multiple echoes reflected from right and left-side poles. (b) Schematic diagram of echo sequence order of the right and left receivers in the situation of (a). Echoes from right receiver were arrived in the order of right side pole and left side pole, whereas the left receiver shows that echoes' order were inversely. (c) Measurement procedure for the directional error of the localized obstacle angle θ_{obs} depending on the azimuth angle of the obstacle $\theta_{azimuth}$ in stationary condition. (d) Average localized angle depending on actual azimuth angle by 100 repeated sensing in each condition. Error bar indicates the standard deviation for 100 localization and dashed line indicates the ideal localized angle for each azimuth angle. (Color figure online)

For embedding the localization ambiguity due to the sensing resolution of the vehicle into the numerical simulation, a characteristic of directional error of localization with respect to the obstacle azimuth angle was measured in stationary condition by using the vehicle (Fig. 7c). As you can see in Fig. 7d, the direction error of localization was increased by increasing the obstacle azimuth angle. By fitting the characteristics of the average and distribution of the direction error to the Lorenz curve, localization ambiguity was embedded into the numerical simulation as following equation

$$\theta_{obs}(t, n) \sim N\left(\mu\big(\theta_{azimuth}(t, n)\big), \sigma\big(\theta_{azimuth}(t, n)\big)^2\right), \tag{9}$$

$$\mu\big(\theta_{azimuth}(t, n)\big) = \theta_{azimuth}(t, n)\left(1 + \frac{k_{\mu1} + k_{\mu2}e^{-\frac{\theta_{azimuth}(t, n) - k_{\mu3}}{k_{\mu4}}^2}}{\big|\theta_{azimuth}(t, n)\big|}\right), \tag{10}$$

$$\sigma\big(\theta_{azimuth}(t, n)\big) = k_{\sigma1} + k_{\sigma2}e^{-\frac{\theta_{azimuth}(t, n) - k_{\sigma3}}{k_{\sigma4}}^2}, \tag{11}$$

where $k_{\mu1} = 156.1898301044632$, $k_{\mu2} = -155.3931174799931$, $k_{\mu3} = -0.2661352979727751$, $k_{\mu4} = 177.4961370454644$, $k_{\sigma1} = 183.209814430525$, $k_{\sigma2} = -179.1180618723616$, $k_{\sigma3} = -3.635825346353006$, $k_{\sigma4} = 234.4054352819113$.

By comparing the specific performance in proposed and conventional methods between the ideal condition and practical sensing condition, influence of the sensing ambiguity was investigated.

3.3   Results of Numerical Simulations

Figure 8a and b shows representative moving path, pulse direction and localized points simulated in ideal sensing condition by using conventional and proposed methods, respectively. As a result of 200 times simulation by changing the initial start position, the total success driving rates were 50% for the conventional method and 58% for the double-pulse scanning method (Fig. 8c). Therefore, the ideal simulation could not reproduce the success rate differences shown in vehicle experiment (13% for conventional and 73% for double-pulse).

On the other hand, for the practical sensing conditions, the localized points tend to be distributed in both scanning methods, which was similar to the vehicle experiments (Fig. 8d and e). As a result of 200 repeated trials at each 8 start position where both scanning methods were successfully operated under ideal conditions, the success rate was 36% for the conventional method whereas 55% for the double-pulse scanning method (Fig. 8f), suggesting that the success driving rate of the conventional method was lower than that of the proposed method, as shown in the vehicle experiment.

Figure 9a shows occurrence probability of ghost localization for every pulse emissions in each scanning method. The mean ghost localization probability was $2 \pm 2\%$ in double-pulse scanning whereas $8 \pm 4\%$ in conventional scanning. Therefore, the double-pulse scanning method suppressed the ghost localization occurrence comparing to the conventional scanning method (Mann–Whitney U-test, $P < 0.01$). Furthermore, an

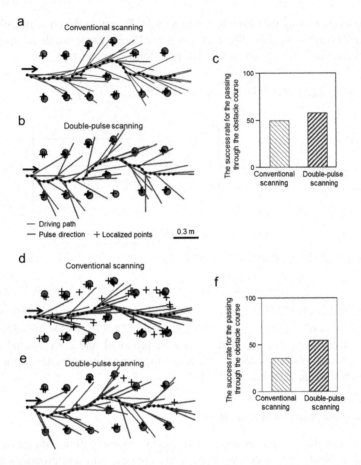

Fig. 8. Simulation of the vehicle navigation during obstacle-avoidance driving in the case of ideal condition and practical condition. Top views of representative driving trajectories (red line), pulse directions (blue line) in the case of ideal condition for the conventional scanning method (*a*) and the double-pulse scanning method (*b*). Note that all obstacle positions localized by the vehicle are shown with cross-marks. (*c*) A comparison of the success rate for the passing through the obstacle course between the conventional and double-pulse scanning methods. In this analysis, 200 times simulations were conducted for each scanning methods by changing the initial start position. Then, extracted 8 starting positions where both scanning methods were successfully operated under ideal conditions, the same analyses were also conducted by the practical condition, which results were shown in (*d, e, f*). (Color figure online)

avoidance direction calculated from accurate obstacle coordinates is defined as an ideal avoidance direction, the directional error of the avoidance direction was also evaluated for each scanning method as shown in Fig. 9*b*. As a result, the directional error of the avoidance direction was $6 \pm 7°$ in the double pulse scanning method whereas $9 \pm 11°$ in conventional method, indicating that the directional error of the double pulse scanning method is smaller than that of conventional methods (Mann–Whitney U-test, $P < 0.01$).

a
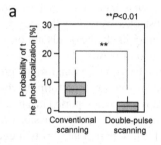

b
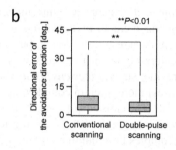

Fig. 9. Comparison of obstacle-detection performance between the conventional and double-pulse scanning methods in the case of practical condition. (*a*) Occurrence probability of the ghost localization for the every sensing in the conventional and double-pulse scanning methods. (*b*) Angular error for the avoidance direction in the conventional and double-pulse scanning methods.

These findings suggest that the double-pulse scanning method is a robust navigation method against external disturbances included in actual acoustic sensing such as the localization ambiguity and the ghost localization due to overlapping echoes.

4   Discussion

In the present study, with reference to our observed behavioral pattern of bats which shifts the direction of the double-pulses between nearby obstacle and moving directions during the obstacle avoidance flight, we constructed a bat-inspired algorithm double-pulse scanning method. As a result, we demonstrated that the behavioral ingenuity exhibited by bats during echolocation also helped minimal designed vehicles to avoid obstacles.

In fact, we found that the double-pulse scanning method improved the avoidance performance of the autonomous vehicle by conducting the practical experiment. In the conventional scanning method, in which the pulse direction was always fixed to the current driving on-axis, the immediate obstacle was often outside of the angle of the detection range when the vehicle changed direction to avoid a previous obstacle. As a result, the detection rate of immediate obstacles was approximately 50% (Fig. 5*d*). In contrast, the double-pulse scanning method, mimicking the bats' behavior, could eliminate such a "blind spot" by keeping the critical obstacle point within the acoustic field of view, which was spatially expanded by double-pulse sensing. This is one of the effects of the integration of spatial information provided by the double-pulse sensing method. Furthermore, the vehicle calculates its own moving direction using not only immediate obstacle information, but also more distant obstacle information: this allows the vehicle to select a more robust avoidance path (Fig. 4*d*).

Moreover, the double-pulse scanning method allows the vehicle to double-count a specific obstacle using two emissions. Since the imaginary repulsive force is calculated using all of the detected obstacles, the double-pulse scanning method gives weights to obstacles that are detected twice to guide the driving direction. This is considered *temporal integration* of obstacle information, which is another advantage of the double-pulse scanning method, as double-counted obstacles were usually located near the driving path. As a result, the double-pulse scanning method extends not only spatially but also temporally its own vehicular acoustic field of view.

In a previous study, *Eptesicus fuscus* was found to produce sonar sound groups (i.e., double pulses) more often in complex environments or when performing complicated tasks [16–18]. The emission of sonar sound groups has been reported in a number of bat species, which suggests that exercising temporal control over emissions helps bats negotiate complex or unfamiliar environments [19]. In particular, it was suggested that the emission of double pulses allows bats to obtain immediate and more detailed surrounding information for planning flight paths [17] or for improving the resolution of an uncertain target's position [16]. Our vehicle demonstration and numerical simulation also supported the idea that multiple pulse emissions with information integration are efficient for complex environment navigation. From the viewpoint of an actual localization problem, large errors of localization have often occurred owing not only to the capability of the sensing resolution, but also to unintended correct combination problems of echo paring which was named ghost localization (Fig. 7a). Our numerical simulations represent that the proposed method suppresses the interference of echoes returning from multiple objects by selecting the pulse direction toward to the targeting obstacle (Fig. 9a). Even in the previous simulation research of the three dimensional localization mechanism of bats, similar results have been reported that adjustment of direction of attention with ear movements is efficient to accurately localize the obstacles positions [20]. Moreover, in our proposed method, even if the interference occurred in one of the double sensing processes, the influence of the localization error due to a mismatch of echo combinations can be reduced by integrating the twice-sensed information that was obtained by scanning at a slightly moved position. As a result of such a localization error reduction, the directional error of the avoidance direction was also suppressed (Fig. 9b). These numerical simulations indicate that the proposed method can be robust path planning against to the localization ambiguity. Though the double-pulse scanning method reduces the frequency of the decision making regarding the direction of movement to half that of the conventional scanning method (Fig. 2), our findings suggest that the integration of information from two emissions is effective; i.e. acoustic detection restricted to only one transmitter and two receivers, demonstrating that the ingenuity inspired by bats has a large effect on simple design sensing.

The recent trend in spatial sensing technology is to increase the number of sensor units so that the whole of the surrounding space can be covered by integrating the spatial information of multiple sensors. On the other hand, the vehicle in the present study has only one transmitter and two receivers. In this study, we demonstrated a method to collect and integrate spatial information regarding the external world inspired by the observation of the echolocating bats. Because the proposed double-pulse sensing uses simple algorithms based on temporally and spatially integrated obstacle information, it can be applied readily to various navigation methods with modest calculation costs. For example, simulation research for the humanoid robot navigation with stereo vision has demonstrated that control of alternate gaze shifting between the direction of movement and the direction of an obstacle is effective to avoid collision against critical obstacles

[21]. Even in the animal research, behavior regarding spatial perception has been studied extensively in visually guided animals through measurements of eye movement (humans) or head angle (flies, birds) [22–24]. With reference to those researches, we can compare gaze control by vision-guided animals with simple acoustic sensing inspired by the bat bio-sonar method. The basis of our idea may provide new insight into not only method for representative ultrasonic sensing relying on cheap and simple methods but also other sensing technologies for spatial perception. We suggest that the processes of decision making and conception observed in higher animals offer new insight into future biomimetic research.

Acknowledgements. This work was supported by JSPS KAKENHI Grant Numbers JP16H06542 (Grant-in-Aid for Scientific Research on Innovative Areas) to SH, and JP17H07242 (Grant-in-Aid for Research Activity Start-up) to YY, and by the Japan Science and Technology Agency PRESTO program to SH.

Appendix: MOA Model

In this appendix, we briefly show our method for determining the direction of movement after echolocation. The basic idea of the MOA model in the case of the conventional scanning method is shown schematically in Fig. 10. After the ith pulse emission at time t_i, the vehicle changes its moving direction, and the new moving direction is determined according to the weighted sum of the vector of the current driving direction and imaginary repulsive force vectors arising from the recognized obstacles. We set the repulsive force from obstacle n, described as the integration of the imaginary pressure $g(r(t_i, n))$ with respect to viewing angle θ from $\theta(t_i, n) - W(r(t_i, n))$ to $\theta(t_i, n) + W(r(t_i, n))$. Thus, the new moving direction $\varphi_d(t_{i+1})$ is described by the following equation:

$$\varphi_d(t_{i+1}) = \arg\left(e^{i\varphi_d(t_i)} - \sum_{n=1}^{N(t_i)} \int_{\theta(t_i,n)-W(r(t_i,n))}^{\theta(t_i,n)+W(r(t_i,n))} g(r(t_i,n)) e^{i\theta} d\theta \right), \tag{12}$$

where $N(t_i)$ indicates the number of recognized objects at $t = t_i$. It should be noted that the positions of the recognized objects are calculated with the echolocation method. The distance factor $g(r(t_i, n))$ and the obstacle window factor $W(r(t_i, n))$ are given by following equations, respectively:

$$g(r(t_i, n)) = \sqrt{\frac{\alpha}{r(t_i, n)}} \tag{13}$$

$$W(r(t_i, n)) = \arctan\left(\frac{r(t_i, n)}{k} \right), \tag{14}$$

where α and k are parameters with length dimensions. By substituting Eqs. (13) and (14), Eq. (12) can be written in a simpler form as Eq. (3). In the double-pulse scanning method, the moving direction was calculated for every double-pulse emission using double sensory information. In this case, Eq. (12) can be written as Eq. (4).

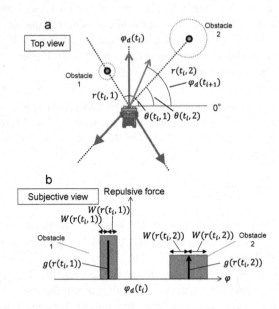

Fig. 10. Schematics of multi-obstacle-avoidance [MOA] model for obstacle avoidance. (*a, b*) Top and subjective views of the schematics of the MOA, respectively. The new moving direction $\varphi_d(t_{i+1})$ was determined according to the weighted sum of the vector of the current driving direction $\varphi_d(t_i)$ and imaginary repulsive force vectors arising from the recognized obstacles.

References

1. Barchi, J.R., Knowles, J.M., Simmons, J.A.: Spatial memory and stereotypy of flight paths by big brown bats in cluttered surroundings. J. Exp. Biol. **216**, 1053–1063 (2013)
2. Griffin, D.R.: Listening in the dark: the acoustic orientation of bats and men (1958)
3. Jen, P.H.-S., Kamada, T.: Analysis of orientation signals emitted by the CF-FM bat, *Pteronotus p. parnellii* and the FM bat, *Eptesicus fuscus* during avoidance of moving and stationary obstacles. J. Comp. Physiol. **148**, 389–398 (1982)
4. Surlykke, A., Ghose, K., Moss, C.F.: Acoustic scanning of natural scenes by echolocation in the big brown bat, *Eptesicus fuscus*. J. Exp. Biol. **212**, 1011–1020 (2009)
5. Iida, F.: Cheap design approach to adaptive behavior: walking and sensing through body dynamics. In: Proceedings of AMAM 2005, p. 15 (2005)
6. Pfeifer, R., Lambrinos, D.: Cheap vision—exploiting ecological niche and morphology. In: Hlaváč, V., Jeffery, K.G., Wiedermann, J. (eds.) SOFSEM 2000. LNCS, vol. 1963, pp. 202–226. Springer, Heidelberg (2000). https://doi.org/10.1007/3-540-44411-4_13
7. Dear, S.P., Simmons, J.A., Fritz, J.: A possible neuronal basis for representation of acoustic scenes in auditory cortex of the big brown bat. Nature **364**, 620–623 (1993)

8. Suga, N.: Amplitude spectrum representation in the Doppler-shifted-CF processing area of the auditory cortex of the mustache bat. Science **196**, 64–67 (1977)

9. Geipel, I., Jung, K., Kalko, E.K.: Perception of silent and motionless prey on vegetation by echolocation in the gleaning bat Micronycteris microtis. In: Proceedings of the Royal Society B, p. 20122830 (2013)

10. Aihara, I., Yamada, Y., Fujioka, E., Hiryu, S.: Nonlinear dynamics in free flight of an echolocating bat. Nonlinear Theory Appl. IEICE **6**, 313–328 (2015)

11. Fujioka, E., Aihara, I., Watanabe, S., Sumiya, M., Hiryu, S., Simmons, J.A., et al.: Rapid shifts of sonar attention by *Pipistrellus abramus* during natural hunting for multiple prey. J. Acoust. Soc. Am. **136**, 3389–3400 (2014)

12. Ghose, K., Horiuchi, T.K., Krishnaprasad, P.S., Moss, C.F.: Echolocating bats use a nearly time-optimal strategy to intercept prey. PLoS Biol. **4**, e108 (2006)

13. Ghose, K., Moss, C.F.: The sonar beam pattern of a flying bat as it tracks tethered insects. J. Acoust. Soc. Am. **114**, 1120–1131 (2003)

14. Ghose, K., Moss, C.F.: Steering by hearing: a bat's acoustic gaze is linked to its flight motor output by a delayed, adaptive linear law. J. Neurosci. **26**, 1704–1710 (2006)

15. Yamada, Y., Hiryu, S., Watanabe, Y.: Species-specific control of acoustic gaze by echolocating bats, *Rhinolophus ferrumequinum nippon* and *Pipistrellus abramus*, during flight. J. Comp. Physiol. A **202**, 791–801 (2016)

16. Kothari, N.B., Wohlgemuth, M.J., Hulgard, K., Surlykke, A., Moss, C.F.: Timing matters: sonar call groups facilitate target localization in bats. Front. Physiol. **5**, 168 (2014)

17. Moss, C.F., Bohn, K., Gilkenson, H., Surlykke, A.: Active listening for spatial orientation in a complex auditory scene. PLoS Biol. **4**, e79 (2006)

18. Warnecke, M., Lee, W.-J., Krishnan, A., Moss, C.F.: Dynamic echo information guides flight in the big brown bat. Front. Behav. Neurosci. **10**, 81 (2016)

19. Moss, C.F., Surlykke, A.: Probing the natural scene by echolocation in bats. Front. Behav. Neurosci. **4**, 33 (2010)

20. Vanderelst, D., Holderied, M.W., Peremans, H.: Sensorimotor model of obstacle avoidance in echolocating bats. PLoS Comput. Biol. **11**, e1004484 (2015)

21. Seara, J.F., Strobl, K.H., Schmidt, G.: Path-dependent gaze control for obstacle avoidance in vision guided humanoid walking. In: Robotics and Automation, pp. 887–892 (2003)

22. Eckmeier, D., Geurten, B.R., Kress, D., Mertes, M., Kern, R., Egelhaaf, M., et al.: Gaze strategy in the free flying zebra finch (*Taeniopygia guttata*). PLoS One **3**, e3956 (2008)

23. Land, M.F., Collett, T.: Chasing behaviour of houseflies (*Fannia canicularis*). J. Comp. Physiol. **89**, 331–357 (1974)

24. Land, M.F., Lee, D.N.: Where we look when we steer. Nature **369**, 742–744 (1994)

Design and Research on Human-Computer Interactive Interface of Navigation Robot in the IOT Mode

Ye Zhang ⓘ, Bingmei Bie, and Rongrong Fu⁽✉⁾ ⓘ

East China University of Science and Technology, No. 130 Meilong Road
Shanghai 200237, China
Misscchina@yeah.net, Muxin789@126.com

Abstract. The display design methods in the background of media convergence is improving gradually, and the navigation robot is applied to the public environment as a new kind of display assistant method, which can better meet visitors' needs and enhance their emotional experience to the exhibition. However, the existing exhibition displaying methods were passive by practical researches, it has blank areas in path planning, which includes the period from visitors generating visiting consciousness to enter the pavilion, visiting process and the time people are out of visiting state but still in the exhibition hall. Based on the problem and existing human-computer interactive interfaces, conduct design and research from the perspective of audience experience. Using the theories of human eye cone cells biological characters and experience design, Internet of thing and the basic design principles of human-computer interactive interface, to complete the human-computer interactive interface design schemes of navigation robot, test the prototypes and by scheme optimization to reach the final result, based on the research and analysis of existing problems. To design an easy to use and user-friendly human-computer interactive interface, and achieve the result which shortened unnecessary time and optimize the visiting path ways of the audience. It solves the problems include unbalanced visitors flow rate, special individual visiting path needs of the visitors and improve people' satisfaction of visiting experience. And hoping it can provide a basic design paradigm and an effective reference for the solution to user navigation problem.

Keywords: Art with new technology · Interaction design
Service design · Navigation robot · IOT

1 Introduction

As one of the display design approaches for public, the navigation robot can effectively enhance the visitors' exhibition experience. And many scholars have studied it, which mainly focus on four aspects: (a) Development trend, which is more intelligence, network and modularization [1, 2]. (b) The problems in path planning of navigation robot, including how to detect and avoiding obstacles, identifying objects, and achieving a better path effectively with the lowest cost, etc [3–6]. (c) Special design of navigation

© Springer International Publishing AG, part of Springer Nature 2018
N. Streitz and S. Konomi (Eds.): DAPI 2018, LNCS 10921, pp. 316–331, 2018.
https://doi.org/10.1007/978-3-319-91125-0_27

robot for the disabled [7, 8]. (d) Improvement in human-machine interaction, including the trend on man-machine collaboration, more attention to the sense of immediacy on interaction methods, accuracy improving, evaluations and so on [9–12]. But those are all about the intrinsic function from the navigation robot aspect, ignoring the connection between visitors and their environment, human factor and special individual needs, and the practical application hasn't met the original design goal as well. Additionally, the visiting process is segmented and the whole navigation process is incomplete, which results in one-way human-computer interaction and asymmetric information exchange process.

This paper is mainly to solve the path planning problem in the period from visitors generating visiting consciousness to the pavilion, visiting process and the time people are out of visiting state but still in the exhibition hall, transforming the original robot oriented navigation behavior into visitor oriented, conducting data capture and analysis to the entire display area with IOT tool, and presenting the information which visitors needs on the human-computer interactive interface. We also did field surveys to several museums and exhibition halls in Shanghai, Hefei, and Nanjing, and finding that the relations in human, exhibits and environment are determined by the result of information exchange in practical visiting process. The fluency of the information exchange is related to effective and real-time data capture of the visitor flow, which is consistent with the IOT concept. For improving the original interactive approach, realizing effective information exchange, enhancing visiting experience and a better navigation effect, the IOT concept is introduced to the design of the navigation robot' human-computer interactive interface.

The remainder of the article is organized as follows. Solutions and four schemes design to the path planning problem in the form of human-computer interactive interface is discussed in section two. In section three, the brief analysis of internal technical system in human-computer interaction is displayed, and proper presentation carrier is filtrated considering the actual situation. And in section four, the schemes in section two are simulated and we conduct prototypes tests with 20 invited samples to simulate interactive experience in real environment, and have schemes optimization based on the tests. Section five concludes the paper.

2   Design and Research on Human-Computer Interactive Interface

Human-computer interaction is an important medium for navigation robot to realize its function, and the visual way is more direct for information dissemination. For the visitor oriented path planning problem of navigation robot, we codify the visitors' real needs to form the function modules for problem solution, and integrate the function modules with IOT to exchange the navigation space information with visitors in the most direct and effective visual interaction way, that is the human-computer interactive interface.

2.1   Research on Path Planning

The navigation behaviors between visitors and navigation robot is actually an information interactive process among people, things and environment, which is lasting and dynamic as well. However, from the preliminary survey data, we found that the visitors are guided only by the set navigation route, and the human-computer interaction is one-way, which is limited to exhibits introduction to visitors by navigation robots. Visitors' unsatisfied navigation needs exist in three periods which is from visitors generating visiting consciousness to enter the pavilion, visiting process and the time people are out of visiting state but still in the exhibition hall. And it appeared to be the visitor oriented path planning problem in the process.

Based on the preliminary investigation, visitors' navigation states of the three periods can be divided into two categories. One is visitors generating visiting consciousness before their entrance and visiting process, their actual psychological need is seeking no repeated routes on their move for visiting purpose. And the other is out of visiting state but still in the hall, their actual psychological need is the exploration and understanding to the surroundings. The influence factor of the two states is exhibition area ambience which concrete expression to visitors flow. And the factor causes visitors' original exhibition route change and negative emotion generating, thus the visitors' needs can be subdivided into three types based on their behavior model and psychological states (the influence factor is the attendance of each viewing area):

(a)   Visitor with specific visit purposes, manifest as preference to certain kinds of exhibits;
(b)   Without specific visit purposes, manifest as some degree of sequenced itinerary;
(c)   Location needs for the exhibition surrounding facilities, such as washrooms, restaurants and so on.
      Then we propose corresponding function modules to meet various demands, which are as follows:
(d)   Optimal path, corresponding (a), providing visitors' exhibition path planning in the shortest time based on the actual human flow and surroundings;
(e)   Interest path, corresponding (b), on the basis of visitors' interest, prioritizing the areas and providing the best path planning;
(f)   For surroundings, corresponding (c), providing nearest and shortest queuing time route planning.

These three function modules shorten and qualify the information exchange between human and surroundings based on the visitor flow of the display area. The key point is realizing information interaction and the settlement of interconnection between objects and objects, people and objects, and people. And the point is consistent with the concept of IOT [13, 14], so we propose it here and conduct research and design based on it.

Compared with traditional ones, the navigation robot in IOT mode will transform from single workstation to whole area collaboration. Here the entire area is divided and numbered, the real-time data of visitor flow of the corresponding area are captured by each on-line navigation robot, then sent back to each robot after processing by service desk. When visitors have navigation demand, classify which function module it belongs to, and then conduct path planning based on the real-time information feedback and stored exhibition hall map. Thus forming a continuous navigation process, extending the navigation range and creating a good visiting experience for visitors.

2.2 Interface Framework Design

Existing interaction modes of traditional navigation robot, including voice and easy visual interaction, are simple, slow and the effect is not obvious. Compared with the modes, the human-computer interactive interface can carry more information and is more intuitive. Using it could better exchange information with visitors, their demands could be received more quickly and the feedback is direct. After introducing the IOT mode, information exchange process is realized by the real-time data capture function of IOT between visitors and surroundings based on the advantages of the original interfaces. Thus visitors could obtain information they need, shorten unnecessary visiting time and get good visiting experience. In this state, the entire exhibition space will be in a dynamic balance, realizing optimal resource allocation to some extent.

The human-computer interactive interface design is based on the function modules for problem solution in 2.1part. Based on the depth of information exchange between users and navigation robots, here we divide the interactive behavior into two levels. The first level is visitors don't have any instructions to the navigation robot, we called shallow interaction mode. In this mode, the human-computer interactive interface is on standby state, and shows color-coded real-time visitor flow of corresponding areas at regular intervals according to the flow size, so the visitors could know flow size at any time; The second level is visitors have deep information exchange with navigation robot, at this point, visitors have strong navigation demand, we called deep interaction mode. Visitors do touch, click and other behaviors to the interactive interface to exchange information with navigation robot and surroundings by function modules. The second level is visitor oriented path planning based on the first, we correspond the function modules to real exhibition and plot function prototype wireframe of the human-computer interactive interface, the function modules are divided or combined to more specific function set (see Fig. 1). Module one and two belong to different directions of route planning, module three is for the surroundings navigation and crystallized into washroom, restaurant and shopping area (here refer to stores like adjacent boutique). Moreover, considering visitors' other needs and helping them learn more about the exhibition, we add emergency call and exhibition features function. Because the solution is realized via interactive interface, the other methods are not detailed here.

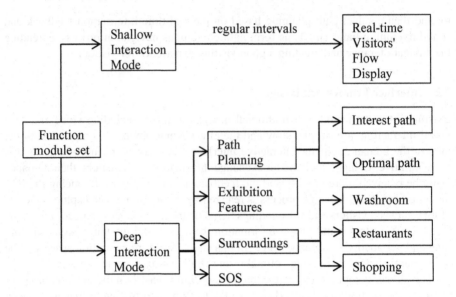

Fig. 1. Function module set of human-computer interactive interface.

2.3   Interface Design and Research on Vision Scheme

Human-computer interactive interface is a medium that people could "see" and exchange information with the outside, its usability, which is determined by two parts, operating system (this one will be showed in section three) and interface visual design, effecting the fluency of information exchange process and then the visitors' navigation experience. Interface visual design includes prototype framework building which is showed in 2.2, and UI design which includes interface layout and visual elements. We do scheme design of human-computer interactive interface based on 2.1part and function module set in 2.2part.

Interface Layout Design. The human-computer interactive interface design system has been completed generally and is advancing to more natural. More natural reflects in layout matching users' operating habits and providing good psychological and physical experience to them. When operating behaviors happen in the human-computer interactive interface, eyes and hands play a leading role. Eyes receive information and then hands do feedback to it, which is related to the eye' attention mechanism. The features of uneven distributed receptor cells in retina lead to attention priority in order when people are watching thing besides factors of the objects themselves [15]. Zeev [16] has proposed the generalized Gabor scheme of image representation in biological and machine vision. The Gabor function is usually used in image processing for edge extraction as a liner filter. And biological experiments have proved it can approximate receptive field function of single cell which can also be called the transfer function of light intensity stimulation as a bionic mathematical model. The Gabor function provided a theory for the layout design of human-computer interactive interface, and Li [17] proposed an optimization method for the layout design of human-computer interactive interface based on it. In this method, human-computer interactive interface is divided into several parts corresponding to the distribution of light-sensitive cells in retina, and then building a partition model to solve the model. It is proved that the optimized interface is better and more natural in practical interaction. Here we adopt the method to the layout design based on the functional solution modules in 2.1 and 2.2 parts.

The screen resolution we choose is 1920 × 1080 and the division chart is divided into five areas by five concentric circles based on the quantity of the function modules. The radiuses are 8.73 mm, 43.75 mm, 79.19 mm, 115.45 mm and 152.87 mm from the centre, and more close to the centre, the visual perception is stronger. Thus we get rough distribution range of the function module set in the interface. And then for more accurate result, we do a complete plan from Fig. 1, getting and numbering the specific function modules (see Fig. 2). The back button is included in the HOME button for the interface frame structure.

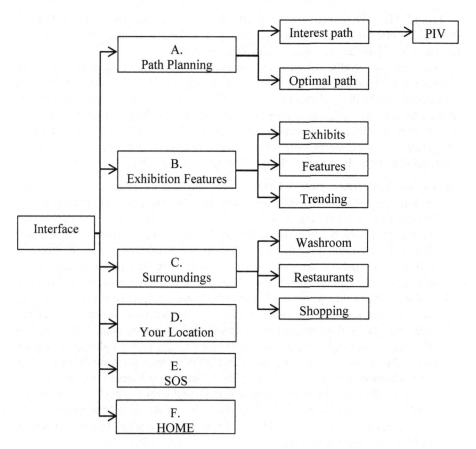

Fig. 2. Specific number function modules of human-computer interaction interface.

The sequence of the specific function modules on priority is based on the importance of the modules by ordering method, details are as follows: after numbering, comparing their importance between every two modules, more important we plus 1 and the less one plus 0, the same plus 0.5, then getting Table 1.

Table 1. The priority numbers of specific function modules.

Intensity (from weak to strong)	Numbers of the modules	Importance
6	D	5
5	A	4.5
4	B	2.5
3	C	2.5
2	E	0.5
1	F	0.5

From Table 1, the sequence of the specific function modules on priority is DABCEF. But the optimized interface layout we got above is still not accurate, so we do a refinement to it based on the sequence for a more accurate result.

We investigate, synthesize and analyze existing layout forms of interaction interface, conclude main kinds of human-computer interactive interface layouts. The existing interfaces could be divided into three categories, including web, software and mobile phone, and what we design and research is belongs to the software category. There are no any interfaces in the same direction we do, so we do comparative research with similar interaction interfaces, and the similar frame structure layouts are put as one kind for later easier refinement of the interface design. The details are as follows:

(a) Layout likes a frame, such as T-type, L-type, etc. This kind has many variants, and is usually applied to the interface with more information and functional sites because of its large coverage. It has clear structure and priorities. But meanwhile, the interface may become crowded visually, which makes visitors' information finding process more difficult. And its background is often darker, so the interface will be easily tedious without good detail treatment. Except for enterprise and forum, it seldom appears in other areas due to compatibility and aesthetic problem;

(b) Full-page. The entire screen is a frame with pictures as design centre likes a poster, and has some text and web links in it as well. Its direct and strong visual effects often lead to comfortable and interface atmosphere impressions. However, it is often used in the website homepage and some enterprise web with special requirements due to its slow loading speed and little contents only. Additionally, one special branch of it has the same simplified frame but belongs to responsive interaction. Its all content included in one screen without scrolling, perfect screen fitting, highly focused and clear levels are the differences from the full-page one.

(c) Header text and classic F-type. This kind is mainly for content display and applied for blogs and login interface.
     Classic F-type is based on human's reading habits, its layout is from up to down, the wide left is for left-aligned information, and the right is related links.

(d) Layout likes Roman numeral III or similar. Simple, clear and with interface atmosphere, which can use more interface space.

(e) Layout with lattice structure. This style is minimalistic and clear with easily controlled breakpoint and good responsive interaction, which not only can display vast content without crowded feeling but also has many details. And different division methods lead to different effects, its popular form is clear large image with clean and logical flowcharts. But we should pay more attention to the distance and size between each part, otherwise, the interface balance will be broke.

Rhee [18] has proposed and tested a theory about efficient digital signage-based online store layout. They found the signage-based online store layout can be divided into three kinds: Tree, pipeline and guiding pathway, and verified the tree kind is better than the others. We find the tree kind is similar to the layout kinds (b), (d) and (e), what we proposed above. Based on 2.1 and 2.2 part, function modules of visitors' demands are not too much and its relatively large vertical extension and visitors aim at getting information they need as quickly as possible in the surroundings, adopting clear layout can attain the design propose better. Thus we apply the layout kinds (b), (d) and (e) for the scheme design.

We superimpose the preliminary layout partition result and the three layout methods respectively from effect, and then choose their intersection parts for twice interface layout refinement of the navigation robot.

Interface Visual Element Design. After getting refined human-computer interactive interface layout in the part of interface layout design, for the preliminary interface scheme design, we will discuss the interface visual element design next. Take the museum as an example, for the existing application area of navigation robot is museum. From user experience perspective, we conduct scheme design on icon and color with aesthetic theories and application features. Details are as follows.

Icon. Icon is one of the most direct and effective information interactive medium in human-computer interactive interface. A good icon should have usability, helping visitors acquire information quickly and decreasing the malfunctions.

According to 2.1 and 2.2 parts, clear and bright style, easy to response is the direction for the design requirements. Here we introduce the concept of quasi flat design which is more nature. Comparing with flat design, it adds the concept of depth and design language of usability and high efficiency, which increases visitors' comprehension to human-computer interactive interface and highlights important information without ruining the whole design atmosphere. This is consistent with our goals.

Additionally, icon shape is also an important factor for interaction experience. The visual attention mechanism of human demonstrates that larger areas, more obvious contour changes and graphics with a certain threshold around the corner are easier to notice. Here we use large icon for main functional modules and simplify other elements on the premise of usability for visitors' good navigation experience. As for the icons with stereotype, keep identity without any changes.

Color. Rational color use can coordinate and even fill the gaps in interface design. In color psychology, light color is soft, dark color is tough, warm color is forward and the cool one is backward. Generally, in case of visual fatigue, interface should use high purity and light color and no than five categories. In large area of interface, gray hue is better. And for the vital function modules, colors like red, blue and green is suggested, but the area shouldn't be too large in case of visual mess. In our scheme design, the application is museum, thus we choose blue and green with little gray for visitors' impression to it.

2.4   Scheme Design of Human-Computer Interactive Interface

As mentioned earlier, we solve the path planning problem of the periods from visitors generating visiting consciousness to the pavilion, visiting process and the time people are out of visiting state but still in the exhibition hall in the IOT mode, and then for the solution presentation, do quadratic sieve from physiology and user experience perspective and analysis of the visual elements to the human-computer interactive interface layout. The following will propose four concrete schemes based on the research results above.

Scheme One. Different size means the function keys' importance, which with larger area will has more attention. The function keys can be moved left or right in a dynamic and interesting interactive approach (see Fig. 3).

Fig. 3. Scheme one of the human-computer interactive interface design.

Scheme Two. Combining layout (b) and (d), having more use of the interface space. Clear and clean design style makes people feel comfortable and broad in visual, the main function keys are designed on the graphic designing principles (see Fig. 4).

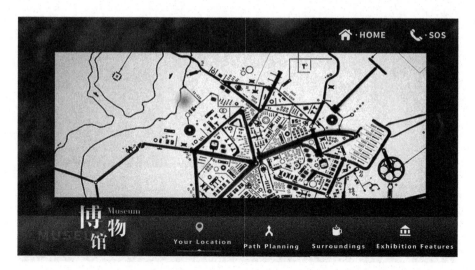

Fig. 4. Scheme two of the human-computer interactive interface design.

Scheme Three and Four. Combining layout (d) and (e), scheme three is free but ordered. Unique shapes could attract visitors while the switching command process may cause uncomfortable feeling (see Fig. 5); Combining layout (b) and (e), direct and strong pictures in visual make people feel comfortable for scheme four. Highly focused interface and clear structures make information finding process more easily (see Fig. 6).

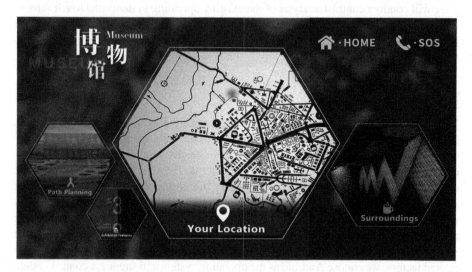

Fig. 5. Scheme three of the human-computer interactive interface design.

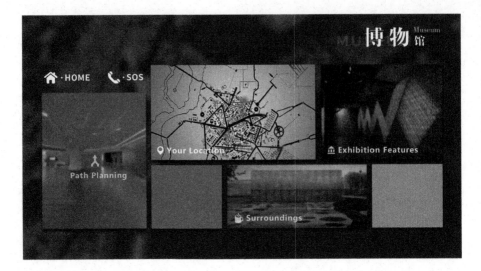

Fig. 6. Scheme four of the human-computer interactive interface design.

3   Operating System of Human-Computer Interactive Interface

We mentioned that operating system can influence visitors' exhibition experience by directly influencing the usability of human-computer interactive interface, and section three will conduct contrast analysis of the existing operating systems and touch screens to conclude a better one for the human-computer interactive interface. We propose corresponding responsive process design and measures for possible system problems as well.

3.1   Control System

WinLOL, Android, Linux and SCM are the existing four easy operating systems. According to the scheme design in section two, the design goals require strong compatibility of controls. SCM cannot satisfy the goals for its simple structure. WinLOL is excluded for its complicated implementing process. Linux has advantages of simple configuration process, less applications and easy submitting procedures of app store, but its development system is closed, with low adaptability of cross-platform and complicated field tests methods. For Android, though the functions are opposite to the Linux and the technology is maturing, its version and applications have mess, which cannot satisfy customers without loyalty. Therefore, considering the design goals, cost and other related factors, we choose Android as the operating system and suggest a control system frame (see Fig. 7).

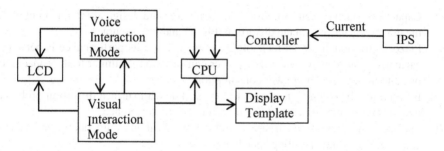

Fig. 7. Control system frame.

In software design, Du [19] has proposed a modularize method for control system which can shorten the reaction time of robots greatly. Thus for enhancing visitors' exhibition experience, we adopt modularize method to divide the whole system into several modules based on Android system, and add feedback and monitoring system as well. When an error occurs, the error module will be monitored, sent and managed quickly, which can reduce the workload of maintenance, shorten the troubleshooting time and is more manageable. And we also propose several solutions to the defects of Android system which are the sluggish phenomenon due to repetitive operations. Details are as follows.

(a) Enhancing system property, using latest Android 7.0 to improve the capacity of data processing.
(b) Clearing cache, which is major causes of sluggish phenomenon. Storing data in cloud regularly and extracting when needed on IOT mode to improve the operating speed.
(c) Frequency reduction in physical way. Besides installing ventilation fan inside the navigation robot, thermal conductivity glue is used to connect the components. The environmental non-toxic thermal conductivity glue has good bond strength, excellent thermal conductivity and superior temperature resistance, which benefits for the performance and service of products.
(d) Setting command orders. For sluggish reduction, execution sequence bases on orders when there are multiple valid commands.

3.2 Touch Screen

As an absolute positioning system and a kind of computer output equipment, touch screen is the simplest and most natural human-computer interactive medium. It has advantages of quick reaction, space saving, easy accessibility and so on. Here we use the touch screen in the scheme design.

The existing touch screens can be classified into six categories [20] as follows:

(a) Vector pressure sensing touch screen technology. For tech hysteresis it is rarely in use now.
(b) Resistive touch screen technology. It is accurate but with high cost and physical limitations, and its surface is easy to scratch.

(c) Capacitive touch screen technology. Its structures and design are rational but with the defects of serious image distortion, PEAD and low accuracy.

(d) Piezoelectric touch screen technology. Low cost and its performance is between capacitive and resistive ones. The power consumption is similar to the capacitive one and no touching no power consumption.

(e) Infrared touch screen technology. Low cost, but with surface distortion problem due to fragile outer frame which can lead to light interference.

(f) Surface acoustic wave touch screen technology. Clear and solid, but water droplets can easily slow the operating speed and even stop it.

We finally adopt IPS based on the analysis to these six touch screens and consideration of the applications for its low cost, relatively high accuracy and linear characteristic.

Based on Sect. 2 and visitors' interactive behavior pattern, we do flow chart of the operating process with IPS (see Fig. 8). The process of operating is as follows: CPU runs, the interface shows visitor flow of the exhibiting area at regular intervals without any touching behaviors. When there is a touching, judge its validity, if it is, then to the navigation process, otherwise, come to the end. Additionally, it only executive one valid command at a time with orders.

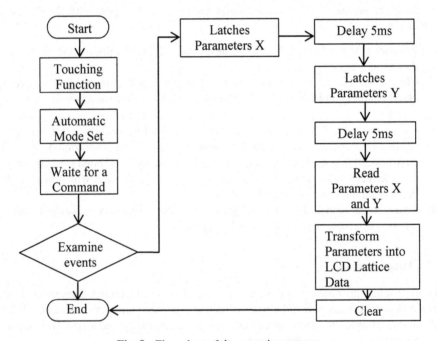

Fig. 8. Flow chart of the operating process.

4   Scheme Optimization and Evaluation

For the optimum scheme and rationality, we conduct simulation to the four preliminary interface schemes in 2.4part for quadratic sieve, and then filtrate with questionnaire. Visitors' experience of the operating process is dynamic, their psychological states cannot be monitored directly, thus here dividing the optimization process into two parts for more practical. In the first part, we simulate the schemes with MockingBot software which is easy and fast for interaction design. And the second part is a questionnaire survey to visitor samples for an optimum.

In July 2017, we choose twenty five samples randomly in Shanghai museum and do questionnaire to the simulation models got in the first part. The samples are required to do online simulation tests to the four schemes and fill the questionnaire. Finally, we get the optimal design scheme from visitors' perspective by the analysis of the questionnaire's results. The questionnaire includes basic information of the samples in anonymous way and their evaluations to the four schemes. Through the analysis to visitors' preference rank of the schemes we can get the final result. There are two influence factors, layout and shape. And the color factor is neglected due to the same color application. The sample selecting method is random, after deviation excluding, the effective sample is twenty, half men and half women, eight students, five enterprise staff and seven professional technicians. For accuracy, here some subjects are multiple choices or unnecessary to select if visitors don't have the will. The specific statistical results are as followed tables from four aspects:

The Table 2 shows people prefer scheme four, and for men, scheme four is better, for women, is the scheme one.

Table 2.   Preferences of schemes.

Schemes	Number of man	Number of women
1	1	5
2	0	1
3	3	1
4	6	4

The Table 3 shows that the layout of scheme four is better, both men and women.

Table 3.   Analysis of layout factor.

Schemes	Number of man	Number of women
1	4	6
2	0	2
3	3	2
4	6	7

We can conclude that the icon shape of scheme three is more popular. Women don't have special preference to the icon shape of the schemes. Although more men like the icon shape of scheme three and four, the figures is close without any reference. Thus for the shape factor, there is no any effect on the design (Table 4).

Table 4. Analysis of shape factor.

Schemes	Number of man	Number of women
1	1	3
2	1	3
3	2	3
4	2	2

And as for the ranks of the schemes preference, scheme four is the first and scheme one follows, here we only select the first one.

We analyze the questionnaire results from four aspects above and get the optimal one. People prefer the Scheme four which is with lattice structure and quasi flat design style, their preference is related to layout greatly compared with other factors. Here the human-computer interaction interface design is for the special application, color is certain, thus is out of the consideration.

5   Conclusion

A visitor oriented solution based on the IOT mode is proposed and presented in human-computer interactive interface form through research and design on the path planning problem. It realized the resource optimization allocation in exhibition hall, made the visitors get path planning before and after their visit, optimized visitors' visiting experience, improved the efficiency and effectiveness of information exchange among human, machine and environment. This paper firstly proposes the concept of visitors oriented path planning in navigation robot based on IOT mode, thus filling the space of this field, and providing research ideas for the user navigation problem in public as well. But for the interesting navigation aspect, visitors' information identification still needs further research.

References

1. Pasztor, A.: Gathering simulation of real robot swarm. Tehnicki vjesnik-technical gazette **21**(5), 1073–1080 (2014)
2. Cifuentes, S., Maria Giron-Sierra, J., Jimenez, J.: Virtual fields and behaviour blending for the coordinated navigation of robot teams. Expert Syst. Appl. **42**(10), 4778–4796 (2015)
3. Arai, Y., Fujii, T., Asama, H.: Local communication-based navigation in a multirobot environment. Aav. Robot. **13**(3), 233–234 (1999)
4. Pala, M., Osati Eraghi, N., Lopez-Colino, F.: HCTNav: a path planning algorithm for low-cost autonomous robot navigation in indoor environments. ISPRS International Journal Of Geo-Information **2**(3), 729–748 (2013)
5. Savkin, A.V.: Hoy, Michael.: Reactive and the shortest path navigation of a wheeled mobile robot in cluttered environments. Robotica **31**, 323–330 (2013)

6. Park, J.-H., Huh, U.-Y.: Path planning for autonomous mobile robot based on safe space. J. Electr. Eng. Technol. **11**(5), 1441–1448 (2016)
7. Lacey, G.J., Rodriguez-Losada, D.: The evolution guido a smart walker for the blind. IEEE Robot. Autom. Mag. **15**(4), 75–83 (2008)
8. Tsui, KM., Flynn K., McHugh, A., Yanco, HA., Kontak, D.: Designing speech-based interfaces for telepresence robots for people with disabilities. In: 2013 IEEE International Conference on Rehabilitation Robotics, Seattle, Washington USA, pp. 1–8. IEEE (2013). https://doi.org/10.1109/icorr.2013.6650399
9. Giovannangeli, C., Gaussier, P.: Interactive teaching for vision-based mobile robots: a sensory-motor approach. IEEE Trans. Syst. Man Cybern. Part A-Syst. Hum. **40**(1), 13–28 (2010)
10. Muhlbauer, Q., Xu, L.: Navigation by natural human-robot interaction. At-automatisierungstechnik **58**(11), 647–656 (2010)
11. Kamei, K., Ikeda, T., Shiomi, M.: Cooperative customer navigation between robots outside and inside a retail shop-an implementation on the ubiquitous market platform. Ann. Telecommun. - Annales des Telecommunications **67**(7–8), 329–340 (2012)
12. Lam, C.-P., Chou, C.-T., Chiang, K.-H.: Human-centered robot navigation-towards a harmoniously human-robot coexisting environment. IEEE Trans. Robot. **27**(1), 99–112 (2011)
13. Wikipedia. http://baike.so.com/doc/5327834-5563006.html. Accessed 03 July 2017
14. Kala, R.: Routing-based navigation of dense mobile robots. Intell. Serv. Robot. **11**(1), 25–39 (2018)
15. Zi, F.: Research on visual attention mechanism and its application of thermal image processing, Xian, China (2005)
16. Porat, M., Zeevi, Y.Y.: The generalized Gabor scheme of image representation in biological and machine vision. IEEE Trans. Pattern Anal. Mach. Intell. **10**(4), 452–468 (1988)
17. Li, Y., Zhang, B., Ding, M.: Optimization design of human machine interaction interface based on visual perception. China Mach. Eng. **27**(16), 2196–2201 (2016)
18. Ijaz, M.F., Tao, W., Rhee, J., Kang, Y.-S., Alfian, G.: Efficient digital signage-based online store layout: an experimental study. Sustainability **8**(6) (2016). https://doi.org/10.3390/su8060511
19. Du, D., Wen, G.-Q., Zhao, J.-Y., Ge, M.-J.: Organize method on platform of machine automation control system. In: Kumar, V., Park, Y.-J., Reddy, B.V., Wu, A.F. (eds.) Achievements in Engineering Science, Applied Mechanics and Materials, vol. 548–549, pp. 1011–1016. Trans Tech Publications, Switzerland (2014). https://doi.org/10.4028/www.scientific.net/AMM.548-549.1011
20. Wikipedia. http://baike.so.com/doc/143593-151716.html. Accessed 18 Oct 2015

Intelligent Environments for Cultural Heritage and Creativity

Collaborative Music Composition Based on Sonic Interaction Design

Mauro Amazonas[1], Victor Vasconcelos[1], Adriano Brandão[1], Gustavo Kienem[1],
Thaís Castro[1(✉)], Bruno Gadelha[1], and Hugo Fuks[2]

[1] Federal University of Amazonas (UFAM), Manaus, AM, Brazil
{mauro.jr,vfv,thais,bruno}@icomp.ufam.edu.br,
abgroovy2@yahoo.com, gustavo_gustavo1@hotmail.com
[2] PUC-Rio, Rio de Janeiro, RJ, Brazil
hugo@inf.puc-rio.br

Abstract. This work proposes a way to create sonic interaction through collaborative composition of spatialized sounds in real time, based on SID (sound interaction design). There is no centralizing figure for the sound designer, and each person may begin a sonic interaction spontaneous and independently, or join an ongoing interaction. Therefore, each person is responsible for the result of his own interaction. Every movement a person makes within the reach of the determined space, the sound is captured and processed and then externalized as feedback in the multichannel sound system, perceived as a unified sound. The concepts and app designed for sonic interaction discussed in this work is intended for use in multidisciplinary contexts, raising important technical challenges. We have devised a design process resulting in four different prototypes, attending to different perspectives. Each prototype had its own experiment.

Keywords: Collaborative music composition · Real time spatialization
Interaction design

1 Introduction

Performing music is a natural collaborative activity. Although there is the possibility of a song being performed by a single interpreter (i.e. singer, guitarist or violinist), usually music performances are within groups, bands or orchestras, where each musician collaborates playing with his instrument and the audience have the perception of hearing all of them as one unified sound. This perception is achieved by the effective communication among different instruments and musicians, coordinated by the maestro.

Technology have been promoted new ways of collaboration regarding music creation and performance. Especially, electroacoustic music, one of the many music facets, dives deeply in the potentialities provided by technology. Since its rising in the end of the years 1940, electroacoustic music shows an intimacy with technology, acousmatic, mixed or derived from electronics in real time, such as Live Electronics [13]. An electroacoustic product is composed by sounds, previously recorded or live performed, later

© Springer International Publishing AG, part of Springer Nature 2018
N. Streitz and S. Konomi (Eds.): DAPI 2018, LNCS 10921, pp. 335–346, 2018.
https://doi.org/10.1007/978-3-319-91125-0_28

treated in a computer and refined musically in order to be part of the final product, may having synthesized sounds or from nature [5].

The artists have been combined emerging technologies with art to produce new music expressions [2]. Simple objects as balls, floaters, microphones and sensors become means for interaction, each of them performing its own characteristic sound, resulting in a composition [8]. Other use of technology in playful, artistic and creative experiences, is obtained when mixing art with technology. Based on Sonic Interaction Design (SID) concepts, some authors [10] have developed interactive sound interfaces using computing vision software, named ReactiVision. According to [12], SID is the study of sound exploration as a means of information exchange, meaning and emotional aspects in interaction. As a result, SID belongs to both domains: interaction design and computational music.

There are also other uses for SID. For example, in movie industry. SID is behind the creation of immersive effects through multiple sound sources. People barely noticed that there is a specific design for the sound and this is the way the sound is presented, involving the audience in a spatialized sound field [4]. Other example of SID, and may be the oldest use, is in videogames.

This work proposes a way of creating sonic interaction through collaborative spatialized sound composition in real time, based on SID. In our proposal, there is not a centralized role for the sound designer, meaning that each person who takes part of the interaction may initiate a spontaneous and independent sonic interaction or may join an ongoing one. Consequently, each person is responsible for the result of his own interaction. In practical terms, every movement a person makes towards the determined space is captured, processed and externalized as a feedback in the multichannel sound system, perceived as a unified sound.

This work's scope relies on electroacoustic music, where collaboration become art as an original source for music composition. Many people play a part in interaction space with their own sounds, bringing up the style and random principle Pierre Boulez [7] to result in music and random collaborative music. All those interaction is processed and spatialized by the system in real time.

2   Method

The spatialization environment for sonic interaction design described in this work was achieved through the evolutionary prototyping approach. In this approach, each prototype is evaluated at a time, having different goals [3]. Altogether, the prototypes are part of the product prototype.

The process of evolutionary prototyping, usually, follow four iterative steps: (i) identification of user basic needs; (ii) development of a working prototype; (iii) implementation and use of the prototype; (iv) revision and enhancement. In the case of this work, this method was chosen for having these different possibilities for testing different technologies and yet result in a product prototype. This was, prototypes are extremely useful in the discussion with the users, being a communication device among members of the development team and an effective way for the designers exploring their design ideas [13].

The product prototype resulted from the evolutionary process was built combining and testing concepts of four different prototypes, according to distinct goals: (1) testing the initial composition idea using simulators, through the simultaneous execution of user sounds which enter and leave the space; (2) same technology behind, but adjustments were made for testing with real users, in real time; (3) using location-based features for detecting users in the space and directing their sounds to the closest speaker; and (4) simulating geolocation with controls for using the prototype in closed spaces.

3 Prototyping for Collaborative Sonic Interaction

According to the evolutionary prototyping approach, as aforementioned, we developed four prototypes for testing different features. Although each one uses a specific technology, they all share resources for spatialized sonic interaction, as an amplified sound system, a delimited space where the interaction happens and a device for initiating the interaction.

The focus of the proposed environment is to foster interaction among people using the sound each person chosen to play and represent herself. Interaction space can be any room or an open space with a delimited area. Speakers must reproduce sounds from people who are intentionally in the interaction delimited space. Once a person leaves the space, the system turns off her corresponding sound automatically. People may enter and leave the interaction space, tuning on and off their sounds, activating and deactivating the speakers in real time. Other feature for the proposed environment is that's when moving around, people are represented by their sounds and the direction of that sounds moves with each person. Furthermore, every composition executed at any moment with individual sounds is recorded and reproduced in real time.

In order to give appropriate support for the aforementioned scenario, some computational resources are needed. The overall architecture of the product prototype is described through a schematic diagram, in Fig. 1, showing which and how those resources are used as well as the environment's dynamic.

According to Fig. 1, there is a server with double functionality, acting as a web server for storing user profiles and an audio server, for processing real time spatialization of users' chosen sounds. Four amplified speakers are connected to the audio server for giving immediate feedback to the interaction space. Router A, which works as an access point, allows the connection between a client app and a server app. Router B, which does not have any kind of connection with the client and server works only as a central point, delimiting the interaction space. This router B radius defines whether a person is within the reach of the interaction space. Whenever the client app is able of detecting router B signal, the sound is reproduced. Otherwise, the sound is interrupted.

Following we present and discuss this environment's evolutionary process, main goals, experimentation and analyses for each one of them.

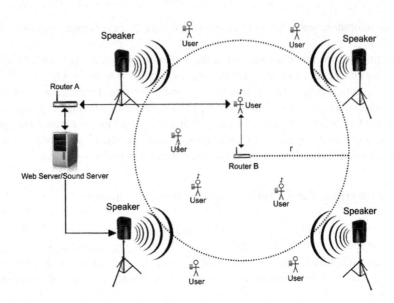

Fig. 1. System's schematic diagram.

3.1 Prototype 1 – Viability

In order to evaluate the viability of an implementation from the server side using Pure-Data [11] it was necessary to develop a concept prototype and carry on a study to check whether PureData were able to deal with many users reproducing different sounds at the same time. PureData proved to be robust enough to deal with many users and sounds ate the same time.

Given that this study had a technical objective and its results would guide this research specific technology adoption, it wasn't necessary to carry out an experiment with users. However, the prototype simulates the interaction space using a simulation software, named TUIO Simulator [15], represented in Fig. 2.

TUIO was adapted for giving support to the most quantity of geometric figures as possible. Each geometric figure represents a person in the interaction space. In addition to that, they can "walk" on the circle in the middle, selecting one of the twenty possible sounds.

The circle in the middle represents the interaction space. When a figure is inside the circle a message is sent to the server's app and the corresponding sound starts to play. When the user leaves the interaction space (removing the figure) other message is sent to the server's app which finishes the sound reproduction.

As the simulation pointed out, it proved viable to adopt PureData as the environment platform. This conclusion came after the successful reproduction (with no overload) of many sounds at the same time. The platform was robust enough to support many possibilities and different quantity of requests.

In this prototype, all users (people) were modeled each one at a time, with the upper limit of fifty. In this way, if it was necessary that more users used the app, each one could be added manually. Although being flexible regarding the number of users, this kind of

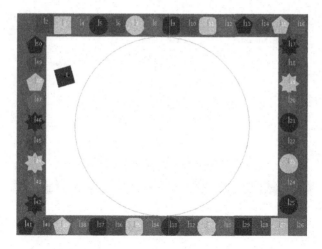

Fig. 2. Virtual interaction on TUIO simulator.

implementation had some flaws, as the one about code's correction. If there were implementation errors, it would be hard to find them because the number of elements on screen was considerably big and complex once PureData has difficulties in dealing with more than 50 objects.

Other critic aspect of this prototype was the use of the TUIO communication protocol. This protocol has a particular syntax to stablish communication between device and server. When using the simulator, the protocol works just fine, but when using it with a mobile device, some problems appeared. As a result, we decided to use the Open Sound Control (OSC) protocol for the next prototype. One instance of this test is available at the internet address: [1].

3.2 Prototype 2 – Mobile

Prototype 2 involved a client application developed for mobile devices for Android. This application is represented in Fig. 3. In this case, an empirical study was conducted with real users, yet without sonic spatialization, for identifying users who were inside or outside the interaction space.

The mobile app, named Compomus (from MUSic COMPOsition), was developed only for Android because the potential users are the educational community from the University of Amazonas, in which almost 80% has a smartphone with Android.

Compomus has three main screens (Fig. 3). Screen (A) is for user's information display, where it's mandatory for the user to register a user name, email and password. Then, it shows screen (B), where the user chooses one of the sounds already stored on the database. It's worth mentioning this sound represents the user in the interaction space. All the sounds are from birds of the Amazon Forest. These samples were used to try recreating the sonic scene of the forest.

Next screen is (C), where the app informs user's id, his status (inside or outside the interaction space) and a button for sound change, which can be pressed anytime.

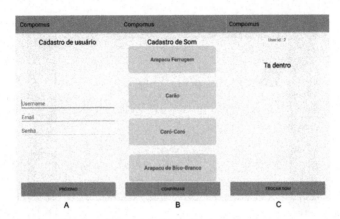

Fig. 3. Prototype 2: compomus.

Empirical Study. According to [6], viability studies must be conducted when using different technologies. For testing the application on both sides, client and server, we decided to recruit real potential users. Still during planning, the questions raised were (i) participants will notice their interaction in the interaction space?; (ii) participants will notice audio feedback from the speakers?; (iii) participants will notice the collaborative composition in real time? Following we present empirical study's elements.

Participants. Ten students enrolled in the Collaborative Systems course volunteered to participate. They were already familiarized with the concepts involved in the use of the prototype but they did not have any knowledge or previous experience with music composition, production or theory.

Location. A pre-defined space in a classroom was reserved for the test. For doing that, the router responsible for propagating the sounds in the middle of the interaction space was configured for this limitation. Only one amplified speaker was used, located in the middle of the interaction space.

Tasks. Participants had six tasks: (1) to install Compomus; (2) To fill the registration form with their information; (3) To select a sound to represent them; (4) To interact freely, in and out the interaction space; (5) To change their sound; and (6) To complete a post-test questionnaire. After task 3, all students had 15 min to complete tasks 4 and 5. After that, they completed task 6.

The three questions (i, ii, iii) that guided this study are about people's awareness, regarding audio, collaboration and interaction. Regarding their overall experience, analyzing the post-test questionnaire, we surprisingly found out that all of them deemed important their participation in the global composition during interaction, being able to have all awareness elements, raised by the questions.

Although their overall experience was good using Compomus, they experienced also some difficulties during their experience. One example was the lack of graphical feed-back because they had to rely only on the sound and the written status. At some point, a student's status wasn't refreshed, he didn't hear his sound and became confused.

One explanation for the synchronization problem reported above is that we noticed a ten seconds delay when Android system look for new networks. The same problem happened when a student left the interaction space and his sound continued to be executed for some time.

With that study, we noticed that the resultant composition of sounds (music) is always different, even when using the same scenario configuration, what puts in evidence the collaborative aspect of this kind of interaction. Other aspect is that besides participants describe their experience as a good one, their interaction was limited only to their entrance and exit. This aspect had to be improved to foster more interaction.

3.3   Prototype 3 – Four Channels Spatialization

Considering the results from the study of prototype 2, server application was totally re-implemented, with a more robust code to increase performance and to become more scalable. It consists of techniques to generate executable codes, sub patches and dynamic patches, solution that drastically decreased the number of graphical elements in screen, as shown in Fig. 4. Besides that, it was added a sonic spatialization support for four channels, using a cross-art quadraphonic panorama technique.

In Compomus, it was implemented a location based feature using GPS technology to automatically direct users' sounds to a speaker. As each user uses the app on his smartphone, data from his smartphone, the app request the data and sends it to the audio server, which interpret the information, performing the real time spatialization.

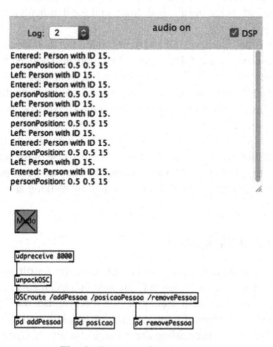

Fig. 4.   Prototype 3: server app.

Empirical Study. Within this new solution, another question was raised: Will the participants notice their own sound being spatialized according to their location in the interactive space? This study consisted of the same elements as the previous one, adding only the complexity of spatialization for the user's point of view and a change in the location. By this means, it was set as follows. Figure 6 shows the test.

Participants. Ten students enrolled in the Collaborative Systems course volunteered to participate. They were already familiarized with the concepts involved in the use of the prototype but they did not have any knowledge or previous experience with music composition, production or theory.

Location. A pre-defined space (for technical restrictions as the size of the cables) in an open space, in a hall of the University of Amazonas. For doing that, the router responsible for propagating the sounds in the middle of the interaction space was configured for this limitation. Four amplified speakers were used, distributed on the corners of the interaction space.

Tasks. Participants had four tasks: (1) To select a sound to represent them; (2) To interact freely, in and out the interaction space; (3) To change their sound; and (4) To complete a post-test questionnaire. All students had 15 min to complete tasks 1, 2 and 3. After that, they completed task 4.

This test was very relevant to the research because it confirmed our assumptions about the imprecision of GPS in smartphones. System's overall performance in the location wasn't as good as it was expected because due to technical limitations, the space was very restricted and for having an upper floor, making it difficult to get more precision from the GPS.

Participants said they could spatialized their sounds and their location correctly, even for a short time. However, many GPS imprecisions were also noticed by the participants, as jumps in location and errors. For instance, a participant was in a spot and the GPS indicated he was on the opposite side. Due to these difficulties, with this technology, the interaction space has to be in a more open space at the University, as in the student hall in the campus entrance (Fig. 5).

Besides problems with GPS students said they had a good experience with spatialization and the felt they were immersive in the space because of the number of speakers and the change in the source of the audio feedback. They also felt powerful for being able to control the source of feedback for their sound by walking around the interaction space.

3.4   Prototype 4 – Closed Spaces

As the client app was well accepted by participants, the fourth prototype consisted mainly on the server's side, including performance enhancements and the swap of the cross-art quadraphonic panorama technique for the Ambisonics [9] technique, that provides more flexibility regarding the increase of speakers and also precision in the virtualization of the sonic source, using the open access library Open Audience.

Fig. 5. Spatialization test with people.

Compomus, was configured in such a way that it could test the new auralization technique and improving sonic spatialization. This way, a new screen (C) was added, as shown in Fig. 6. Screen (C) has a joystick where the participant can direct his sound to wherever he wants as he was walking in the interaction space.

Empirical Study. Different from the previous studies, this one had four new volunteers, non-familiarized with the environment for collaborative sonic interaction, shown in Fig. 8.

Participants. Two teachers and two students volunteered to participate. They were already familiarized with the concepts involved in the use of the prototype but they did not have any knowledge or previous experience with music composition or production. One of them had experience with music theory.

Location. A pre-defined space in an acoustic room, in the Arts Center at the University of Amazonas. For doing that, the router responsible for propagating the sounds in the middle of the interaction space was configured for this limitation. Four amplified speakers were used, distributed on the corners of the interaction space.

Tasks. Participants had four tasks: (1) To select a sound to represent them; (2) To change directions in the interaction space; (3) To identify his own sound among others; and (4) To complete a post-test questionnaire. All students had 15 min to complete tasks 1, 2 and 3. After that, they completed task 4.

Considering the interaction space, a small area in a rehearsal studio was prepared. In this case, router (A), that would delimit the interaction space, wasn't necessary

Fig. 6. Compomus – screen for spatialization.

because participants had the possibilities of coming in and going out of the system whenever they wanted.

As aforementioned, this prototype focus is the spatialization using the Ambisonic auralization technique and the sound spatialization using the library Open AUDIENCE. This empirical study is more about improving the sonic experience than the application itself. For that reason, the test took place in a more confined space and the tasks were slightly different from the ones with the other prototypes (Fig 7).

Fig. 7. Test with prototype 4.

The last task, common to all prototypes, was a post-test questionnaire. This time, participants answered seven questions about their experience with the space, interaction, collaboration and spatialization. One of the participants had some difficulty in the beginning of the interaction using Compomus, due to his smartphone has frozen a few times. Other participants had a good experience with Compomus and with the interaction space as a whole.

Regarding their awareness about the mixture of the different sounds they were aware of each sound and the composition made by each one. About the identification of his own sound, one participant noticed that whenever he directed his sound to one speaker and another participant direct his sound as well, the first sound stopped being performed. It did not happen with other participants.

All of the participants correctly identified their own sounds and with a good precision about the location and they could Interact with each other trying to guess where his sound was.

The mixture of sounds, according to participants statements, did not affect their awareness about their own sound and the other sounds individually. Besides a few problems with spatialization, they had a good experience with the interaction space and they enjoyed the possibility of creating some kind of music composed by individual sounds. In the way, this prototype was conceived, without using GPS technology, it also proved to be possible to take this spontaneous interaction experience to other spaces, where there is much interference with the GPS signal.

4 Conclusion

The concepts and applications projected for the sonic interaction environment discussed in this work resulted from a partnership between researchers from the Informatics Institute and Faculty of Arts, both from the University of Amazonas. This multidisciplinary context raises technical challenges for both areas. From computing point of view, there are challenges about how to provide interaction and make the process transparent for the user, involving sensors, network connections, interaction design, accessibility and user experience. From arts point of view, the challenges are in analyzing the resultant sounds, changing sound perspective from consumer to producer and dealing with sound production with sound production without total control.

In this work, we discussed how sonic spatialization can foster spontaneous collaboration in a pre-defined space, as a museum room, hall in a University campus or even open spaces. In order to get good results, we emphasize that the coworkers in different research areas may achieve interesting results. The spatialization using SID have already been explored in games, cinema, virtual reality, artistic performances and musical performances. The problem is that spatialization is usually pre-recorded in those contexts, what loses a potential for collaboration. For that reason, this work brings innovation by introducing more interaction possibilities for places where people only pass by.

From the evolutionary prototyping used in the research we have some possibilities for extensions and development of the product prototype. Possible improvements for the current environment are: improvements in redundancy of the information received;

studies about tridimensional configurations for speakers, according to the Octonal Cubic model; portability to a structured language as Super Collider, to make this system stand-alone, without the need of the PureData and with the possibility of being embedded in specific software, as indie games, VR apps. Possible improvements for a product proto-type are: improvements in the graphical user interface according to interaction evalua-tion; development of new modules for the sonic spatialization system to get a more precise identification of the sound source; and to changing system's modules and components to be external functions for the PureData environment.

References

1. Amazonas, M.J.B.: https://www.youtube.com/watch?v=913Y3yew5sw. Accessed 01 Oct 2018
2. Blaine, T., Fels, S.: Contexts of collaborative musical experiences. In: Proceedings of the International Conference for New Instruments for Musical Expression (NIME-2003), pp. 129–134 (2003)
3. Carr, M., June V.: Prototyping and software development approaches. Department of Information Systems, City University of Hong Kong, Hong Kong, 319–338 (1997)
4. Costa, N.J.B.: O Surround e a Espacialidade Sonora no Cinema. Dissertação (Mestrado)—Escola de Belas Artes - UFMG (2013)
5. Fritsch, E.F.: Musica Eletrônica - Uma Introdução Ilustrada. Ed. da UFRGS (2008)
6. Shull, F., Carver, J., Travassos, G.: An empirical methodology for introducing software processes. In: CM SIGSOFT Software Engineering Notes (2000)
7. Guberniko, C.: Pierre Boulez e o pensamento musical da segunda metade do século XX: XVI Congresso da Associação Nacional de Pesquisa e pós-graduação em Música- ANPPOM, Brasília (2006)
8. Jensenius, A.R., Voldsund, A.: The music ball project: concept, design, development, performance. In: Proceedings of the International Conference on New Interfaces for Musical Expression (NIME 2012), pp. 300–303 (2012)
9. Lecomte, P., Gauthier, P.-A.: Real-time 3D ambisonics using faust, processing, pure data, and OSC. In: 15th International Conference on Digital Audio Eects (DAFx-15), Trondheim (2015)
10. Nas, E., Lopes, J.: Design de interfaces para experiências lúdicas com novas tecnologias: O caso do software-livre reactivision em interações sonoras. In: Blucher Design Proceedings, pp. 4960–4970 (2016)
11. Puckette, M.: Pure Data. http://www.puredata.info. Accessed 06 Jan 2016
12. Rocchesso, D., Seran, S., Behrendt, F., Bernardini, N., Bresin, R., Eckel, G., Franinovic, K., Hermann, T., Pauletto, S., Susini, P., Visell, Y.: Sonic interaction design: sound, information and experience. In: CHI 2008 Extended Abstracts on Human Factors in Computing Systems, pp. 3969–3972 (2008)
13. Rocha, F.: Questões de Performance em Obras Eletrônicas Mistas. XX Congresso da ANPPOM, Goiânia. ANPPOM (2010)
14. Sharp, H., Rogers, Y., Preece, J.: Design de Interação: além da interação homemcomputador. 3a edição. ed. [S.l.], Bookman (2013)
15. TUIO. http://www.tuio.org. Accessed 09 Oct 2016

A Study on the Virtual Reality of Folk Dance and Print Art - Taking White Crane Dance for Example

Jia-Ming Day[✉], Der-Lor Way, Ke-Jiuan Chen, Weng-Kei Lau, and Su-Chu Hsu

Taipei National University of the Arts, Taipei, Taiwan
Jimmyday2010@gmail.com

Abstract. This research studies on virtual reality (VR) of folk dance and print art, allowing users experience playing White Crane Dance through 3D avatar. White Crane Dance is a small piece of woodcut print of Mazu Festival Celebration made by artist Chih-Shin Lin. Our research team already completed the transition from woodcut prints into animation arts. Step forward, this research intends to develop a set of motion capture detects user action, and drive the corresponding 3D avatar content with preset 3D animation. Head Mounted Display (HMD) of VR combined with Kinect motion capture sensor, allowing the user to view the space environment in addition to the White Crane Dance animation and the user can observe the operation status of 3D avatar.

Keywords: Folk dance · Print art · White Crane Dance · Virtual reality (VR)
Motion capture · Head Mounted Display (HMD)

1 Introduction

United Nations Educational, Scientific and Cultural Organization (UNESCO) have officially announced the folk dance of the Mazu Festival Celebration as "Intangible Cultural Heritage of Humanity" in August 2009 [1]. Among the Mazu Festival Celebration image performance, the woodcut prints by Lin [2] are the most representative images. Our research team already completed the transition from woodcut prints into animation arts, the results have accepted by the Digital Humanities organization in 2014 [3], SIGGRAPH 2015 conference [4] and the HCI International 2017 [5]. The international experts and scholars all agree with the integrated studies of humanities, technology and art, especially the White Crane Dance is about to disappear. In recent years, HMD devices have become more and more compact in appearance and provide an immersive space environment for the viewer. The HMD becomes the ideal development model for this research and provides users with natural interactive experience. In order to develop the VR of folk dance and print art, our team have two major purposes to accomplish in this research. There are:

© Springer International Publishing AG, part of Springer Nature 2018
N. Streitz and S. Konomi (Eds.): DAPI 2018, LNCS 10921, pp. 347–358, 2018.
https://doi.org/10.1007/978-3-319-91125-0_29

White Crane Dance in VR

White Crane Dance is a typical double play performance that consists of two characters, Crane and Fairchild. For viewing White Crane Dance in VR, we have to convert the completed White Crane Dance animation from video to VR format, this process required to overcome the data error when the animation file convert to different platform, we used Unity as VR platform and the finished 3D Max animation was input to unity. Users wearing VR glasses can experience the White Crane Dance, and are free to walk around to watch different perspectives, as the user next to the Crane and Fairchild dance scene. As mentioned in the previous study, the movement of Crane and Fairchild was captured by the folk dances. The character modeling and material are referenced to Chih-Shin Lin's print style. The combination of folk dance and print art makes this VR experience both in folk dance culture and art style.

Interactive Experience of VR

With the interactive and display technology innovation, and gradually be used in various forms of cultural relics collection and education. This research aims to promote the interaction between user and virtual character. With the theme of "White Crane Dance", wet developed the 3D avatar in a VR environment. This research first adopted RGB-D image capture technology, which features easy to carry, without adding any tracker on the body, the new device such as Kinect 2.0 has been able to automatically calculate the shadow interference phenomenon, capture the accuracy and quality significantly improved. To achieve this goal, we required to integrate the motion capture system with the HMD module, detect the user's action and drive the corresponding 3D avatar image content, presented in the user's environment. Through the HMD, the 3D avatar calculated by the foregoing 3D environment is projected onto the user's eyes so that the user can watch both the demo and the played roles. The role of the 3D avatar is the state of operation, allowing users to experience White Crane Dance effect.

2   Literature Research

2.1   Mazu Faith and White Crane Dance

Mazu is a sea god faith centered on the southeastern coast of China. With its worship and praise of Mazu's ethics, good deeds and love as the core. Mazu belief is Taiwan's first world-class heritage of faith, has a history of thousands years. At present, Mazu culture spread to more than 20 countries and regions in the world. Mazu temple is the main place for cultural activities and the customs. Typical folk dance groups are the forms of temple fairs. There are more than 5,000 Mazu temples and more than 200 million believers in the world. Among the folk dance groups, White Crane Dance is an original display in Tainan, south of Taiwan. According to the elder's descriptions, the written materials and the relics, Bao-An Temple in Tainan wanted to escort Kong-Fu God in 1928. The people then got the god's message to protect him by displaying White Crane Master (Fig. 1(a)) as the battle front [6]. White Crane Dance became a significant temple activity of Bao-An Temple (Fig. 1(b)). The story describes a man wearing a mask of fairy, holding the red cloth fairy fan, make-up for Fairchild. Another man is put on the head of the crane disguised as a crane, left and right hands tied wings, you can open and close the wings to swing. Fairchild tease play crane, crane dances with the Fairchild's fan ups and downs, moving parts with both harmonious funny and dynamic rhythm.

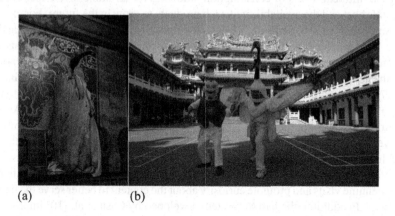

Fig. 1. (a) Statute of White Crane Master, (b) Dancers in front of Bao-An Temple

2.2 Artist Chih-Hsin Lin

Among the Mazu Festival Celebration images performance, the woodcut prints by Chih-Hsin Lin are the most representative images. Lin completed the print of Mazu Festival Celebration in 20 years, has a total length of 408 ft (124 m) (Fig. 2(a)). It is the longest print in the world by a solo artist. Mazu Festival Celebration has been exhibited at home and abroad for its attention by international museums and many academic and research institutions. Lin's print expanded the elements of space and time in the picture by using Chinese scroll style expressions. Through elaborate arrangement of 70 scenes which records the process of the Taiwanese people's most important faith, including the rise of Mazu, the road sign, the lamp, the post, the Mazu head flag, the God of Wealth, White Crane Dance (Fig. 2(b)), rocking boat (peach blossom transition) and the clan array, spring Bulls, Sangu six Po, twelve flower gods, eight will, seven master bye, ... and other dance groups.

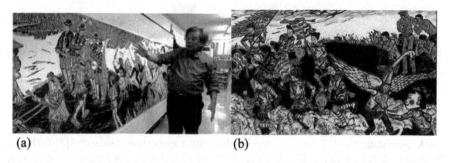

Fig. 2. (a) Lin with his woodcut print (b) White Crane Dance print by Chih-Hsin Lin

2.3 Applications of Virtual Reality (VR)

The evolution of HMD technology has led to the creation and commercialization of devices at different levels of consumption, allowing for an immersive experience at a reasonable cost and the availability of such products to grow in the future. For example, Microsoft's Oculus Rift, Samsung's Gear VR emphasize the combination with handsets, HTC's Vive emphasizes high definition, and Google Cardboard already exists for a solution that is very cheap for converting handsets into the HMD. The application of VR in the field of art and cultural heritage has different purposes. For examples, Gaitatzes et al. [7] put forward the advantages and disadvantages of immersive interactive VR through the application of museums (Fig. 3(a)), Kennedy et al. [8] rebuilt St. Andrews Cathedral (Fig. 3(b)). In the Styliani et al. [9] survey, virtual museums and exhibitions empowered by ARs or authors that mapped different implementations and techniques for such applications investigated VRs. They defined the Virtual Learning Museum as a specific type of museum that provides background, and interest-related content can inspire genuine visits and promote curiosity about the content to better serve the interests of the user. In addition, the RiftArt system developed by Casu et al. [10] improved the learning of art textbooks in a virtual reality manner. As shown in Fig. 3(c), Woodard et al. [11] developed a viable combination of Oculus and Kinect interactive virtual buildings, as shown in Fig. 3(d). In order to overcome the problem of wireless bandwidth transmission, Hao et al. [12] proposed a wireless interactive VR architecture by means of server-side and client-side divisions, as shown in Fig. 3(e).

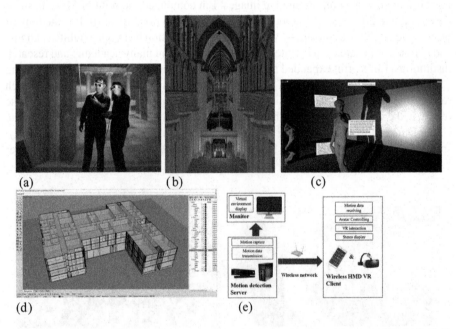

Fig. 3. Applications of VR: (a) interactive VR through the application of museums [7], (b) Rebuilt St. Andrews Cathedral [8], (c) Rift Art art textbooks in a VR [10], (d) Interactive virtual buildings [11], (e) wireless interactive VR architecture [12].

3   Methods

This research is to construct a VR system of White Crane Dance, which is intended to build a prototype of real-time interactive platform after data collection and system integration and development. This system used Unity as integrated platform to import 3D data and connect Kinect motion and output to HTC Vive HMD. The research system architecture is as show in Fig. 4.

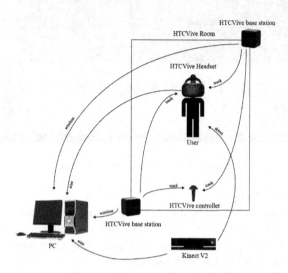

Fig. 4.   System architecture of White Crane Dance VR

1. Integrated original 3D animation

The 3D animation with the texture map imported into Unity, such as the characters, background, skeleton and animation, and Unity was used as the instant interactive platform. The unity animation engine converts the original animation data into real-time interactive data. The original animation made by 3D Max, exported all the data to Unity as FBX file format. In the process we found a loss of the map, so after rebuilt the Material in Unity and re-affixed the model's texture, then used the Bumped Diffuse shader to match the print-style visual effects. Since 3ds Max and Unity had a slight error in the definition of character skeletons, they needed to go into the skeleton of the model and calibrate to fit the skeleton that Unity can use (Fig. 5).

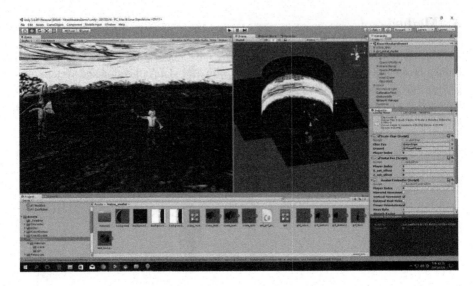

Fig. 5. White Crane Dance in Unity

2. Role Play action design

With Crane Dance is a typical double play, composed of Crane and Fairchild. To achieve the purpose of playing avatar, we designed a role-play action system on the choice of Fairchild or Crane. User can choose to play Crane or Fairchild avatar to imitate the role of practice or interactive with the other.

When choose Crane practice mode, in the HMD would appear two identical virtual Cranes, one is playing Crane animation, and the other Crane as avatar, through the synchronous operation to achieve the purpose of practice, and choose Fairchild practice mode in the same way. On the interactive mode, when choose Crane interactive mode will operate the Crane avatar with the Fairchild animation, and choose Fairchild interactive mode will operate the Fairchild avatar with the Crane animation (Fig. 6).

Fig. 6. White Crane Dance is a typical double play performance

3. Play Menu

In order to achieve the above optional play experience, we created a simple menu that allows users to choose from the beginning to play Crane or Fairchild, to practice or interactive play (Fig. 7). Based on the choice of the following needs to establish the following menu: 1. Crane practice mode, 2. Crane interactive mode, 3. Fairchild practice mode, 4. Fairchild interactive mode. The user used HTC Vive Handle controller to select a character and at the same time sees that the 3D animation played by the character appears in the virtual environment. The user can watch the animation action and imitate learning, select the character and operate the avatar. Due to technical bandwidth constraints, this study is one-person experience and has not been designed to provide both experience and co-performance. The process of creating a menu in Unity was made by script. Create an empty object named Select Avatar, and then create a Button object, and then create a Script Prefab can be generated into the virtual scene. After setting up, click Button to set the click event in On Click (), when finished, click the menu button and generate the user's selected character (Table 1).

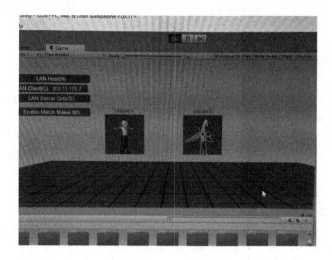

Fig. 7. Interface of avatar

Table 1. Avatar choice

Avatar choice	Avatar and 3D animation characters are displayed in the virtual environment at the same time	
Avatar Mode: Crane Practice	Avatar-Crane	3D animation-Crane
Avatar Mode: Crane Interactive	Avatar-Crane	3D animation-Fairchild
Avatar Mode: Fairchild Practice	Avatar-Fairchild	3D animation-Fairchild
Avatar Mode: Fairchild Interactive	Avatar-Fairchild	3D animation-Crane

4. Action capture and playback

The research previously used the Kinect module to capture the performance of the folk dancers and animates the motion to the 3D animation characters. Now the Kinect was used to capture user actions. Through the Unity integration platform, the 3D animation characters played and the 3D avatar to be instantly driven were presented to user in the environment, as shown in Fig. 8.

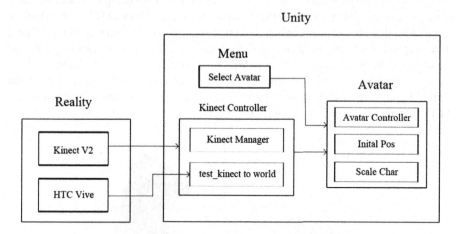

Fig. 8. System framework of Kinect and HTC with Unity

Action Capture

1. Positioning correction with the avatar of user in a virtual space: The Kinect must be placed in front of the user in real space, using one of the HTC Vive handle controllers as a positioning reference point, in front of the Kinect, The handle controller must be within the virtual space set by the HTC Vive optical sensor, otherwise the handle controller can not be sensed and the positioning of virtual space and real space is lost.
2. Import the motion of user (the skeleton has been calibrated) into the virtual scene: When the controller of the handlebar is ready, Kinect can accurately capture the user's motion and then insert the model into the virtual scene. When using a HMD, do some slight adjustment according to visual result.

Playback

1. Animation setup: First create an Animator controller (animation editor) for the White Cane model, and then imported animation data to the model and confirm the numbers of animation is correct or not. Add this Animator controller to the Animator property in Inspector for the Crane Model in the scene.
2. The model in the virtual scene position correction: In order to make the model in the virtual scene to play the animation in the ideal position, in addition to the virtual scene model to do a little coordinate value adjustment, we also set the virtual scene Vive Camera coordinate adjustment, so that the user in the virtual space can feel and sense of space, to match with the sense of reality in the space.

5. Wearing a display technology approach

In this research, the 3D character and avatar calculated by the unity 3D environment is projected onto the eyes of the user through the HMD device so that the user can watch the contents of the space environment at the same time. Experiencing the operated status of the character in 3D of VR. The HMD we used for this project was HTC Vive (Fig. 9), so we had to download a resource bundle named Steam VR from Unity's official resource store, expand it into the project, and then drag an object called CameraRig into the resource bundle Scene, you can temporarily turn off the preset scene camera, and the scene captured by this object (CameraRig) will be the user to watch the picture in the HMD, if you want another point of view to watch an animation within a virtual scene, then adjust the Rotation or Position of the object.

Fig. 9.   White Crane Dance VR system

From Table 2 shows the four avatar mode without background which can reduce the interference of background, the user can easy find the avatar and the other character at the beginning, however, there are still some motion error when do the dance action because the limitation of Kinect sensor. Once user knows how to control the avatar then we can add background back to the environment as show in Fig. 10.

Table 2. Avatar mode without background

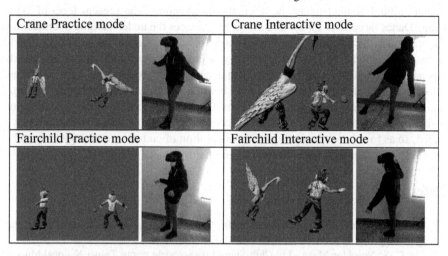

| Crane Practice mode | Crane Interactive mode |
| Fairchild Practice mode | Fairchild Interactive mode |

Fig. 10. White Crane Dance in VR

4 Conclusion

Our research delivers a balance of art and technology in culture creativity. VR and motion capture have become accessible and affordable which makes new media art a new vision. The valued culture materials like print art may preserve in traditional way and folk dance may varnish day by day. In this research, one is a still art showing in museums and the other is a dynamic performance showing on street of temple affairs, both have weak connection in present time. By integrated folk dance and print art with technology become a digital way to represent culture and art. Transform two art styles into a new style and provide an experience of VR is the mission of this research.

We developed a prototype of Mazu faith with Virtual Reality, in order to extend the digital cultural content under the international attention. The present form of White Crane Dance targeted at interactive avatar experiences the understanding of culture and the original data compiled into a virtual reality playing system to preserve folk art with technology. Taiwan's creative and industry oriented integration of technology and the arts are still immature. This research's achievements and experiences will provide and relocate the domestic "Future Museum" builders and hopefully stimulate Taiwan's digital creative transformation. We will stand on the cutting edge of the digital era and demonstrate the possibility of unlimited creativity and new forms of creative value-added, so as to achieve the cross cutting integration of culture, technology and art that are currently under active development in all fields.

References

1. UNESCO: Mazu belief and customs (2009). http://www.unesco.org/culture/ich/index.php?lg=en&pg=00011&RL=00227. Accessed 20 Jan 2013
2. Lin, C.-S.: Poseidon Mazu - Lin Chih-Shin Mazu woodcut prints. Taipei National Museum of History (2010)
3. Day, J.-M., Hsu, S.-C.: Empowering celebrating the Matsu festival: from static woodcut print to animated art. In: DH 2014 Abstracts Proceedings, pp. 449–450 (2014)
4. Day, J.-M., Chen, C.-C., Hsu, S.-C.: White crane dance. In: SIGGRAPH 2015 Dailies Program, Los Angels Convention Center (2015)
5. Day, J.-M., Hsu, S.-C., Chen, C.-C.: White crane dance-transforming woodcut print and folk dance into animation art. In: Yamamoto, S. (ed.) HIMI 2017. LNCS, vol. 10274, pp. 562–571. Springer, Cham (2017). https://doi.org/10.1007/978-3-319-58524-6_45
6. Huang, S.-H.: The Study of Chu-A-Ka White Crane Battle Array in Tainan. National University of Tainan (2009)
7. Gaitatzes, A., Christopoulos, D., Voulgari, A., Roussou, M.: Hellenic cultural heritage through immersive virtual archaeology. In: Proceedings of 6th International Conference on Virtual Systems and Multimedia, Ogaki, Japan, pp. 57–64 (2000)
8. Kennedy, S., Fawcett, R., Miller, A., Dow, L., Sweetman, R., Field, A., Campbell, A., Oliver, I., Mc-Caffery, J., Allison, C.: Exploring canons amp; cathedrals with open virtual worlds: the recreation of St. Andrews Cathedral, St. Andrews day, 1318. In: Digital Heritage International Congress (DigitalHeritage), October 2013, vol. 2, pp. 273–280 (2013)
9. Styliani, S., Fotis, L., Kostas, K., Petros, P.: Virtual museums, a survey and some issues for consideration. J. Cult. Heritage 10(4), 520–528 (2009)
10. Casu, A., Spano, L.D., Sorrentino, F., Scateni, R.: RiftArt: bringing masterpieces in the classroom through immersive virtual reality. In: Smart Tools & Apps for Graphics (2015)
11. Woodard, W., Sukittanon, S.: Interactive virtual building walkthrough using oculus rift and Microsoft Kinect. In: Proceedings of the IEEE SoutheastCon 2015, 9–12 April 2015 - Fort Lauderdale, Florida (2015)
12. Hao, S., Song, W., Huang, K., Xi, Y., Cho, K., Um, K.: An interactive virtual reality system with a wireless head-mounted display. In: Park, J., Jin, H., Jeong, Y.S., Khan, M. (eds.) Advanced Multimedia and Ubiquitous Engineering. LNEE, vol. 393, pp. 203–207. Springer, Singapore (2016). https://doi.org/10.1007/978-981-10-1536-6_27

LIVEJACKET: Wearable Music Experience Device with Multiple Speakers

Satoshi Hashizume[✉], Shinji Sakamoto, Kenta Suzuki, and Yoichi Ochiai

University of Tsukuba, Tsukuba, Japan
pota1401@hotmail.co.jp

Abstract. There are two conventional methods to experience music: listening physically (Live) and listening through digital media. However, there are differences in the quality of the music experience between these listening methods. To improve the quality of music experience and entertainment when listening through digital media, we developed LIVE-JACKET, a jacket capable of vibrotactile presentation and music playback. By simultaneously presenting vibration and sound from 22 multiple speakers attached to a jacket, we created the sensation of being enveloped in sound. Wearers feel like they are singing, which can improve the quality of the music experience. We set five music listening methods, completed experiments, and conducted a questionnaire survey on the music experience. Based on the results, we found that the system we proposed can provide a music experience that cannot be obtained by listening to music through traditional digital methods.

Keywords: Embodied interaction · Wearable · Audio · Haptics

1 Introduction

There are two conventional methods to experience music: listening physically (live) and listening through digital media. The method to listen to music physically is to go to a live venue or concert hall and listen to live performances by bands and orchestras. The method of listening through digital media is to listen to digitized sound through a medium such as a CD or a television. Typically, there are more opportunities to listen to music through digital media.

Live performance not only transmit sounds to the audience, but vibrations and sound pressure are also simultaneously transmitted. Conversely, when listening audio through digital media, it is difficult to feel vibrations and sound pressure on the body through general speakers or headphones. Therefore, the quality of the music experience greatly differs between these two methods. Furthermore, due to the difference in the quality of the music experience, it is hard

---

S. Hashizume and S. Sakamoto have contributed equally to the work.

© Springer International Publishing AG, part of Springer Nature 2018
N. Streitz and S. Konomi (Eds.): DAPI 2018, LNCS 10921, pp. 359–371, 2018.
https://doi.org/10.1007/978-3-319-91125-0_30

to convey the music's excellence through a digital medium. This makes it difficult to utilize digital method in entertainment such as music promotion and performance. Therefore, we thought that we could improve the quality of the music experience and use it for entertainment while listening to music through digital media.

It is believed that vibration that is felt by the body along with sound greatly affects the quality of the music experience. Since sound is air vibrations, especially large sounds and low frequency sounds can not only be heard by the ear but resonate through the body as vibrations. At live venues and concert halls, there are loud sounds and low frequency sounds, so the body feels vibrations strongly. However, general speakers and headphones cannot transmit strong vibrations. Furthermore, to improve entertainment, the listener need to feel as if he or she is enveloped in music, as if he or she was singing. This cannot be experienced by simply listening to music.

We attached speakers to the jacket, thereby creating a LIVEJACKET that presented a vibratory tactile sensation throughout the body, while one could hear the music. It is possible to play high band sounds and feel vibration by using multiple speakers including piezo speakers, full range speakers, and subwoofers. The listener can become more immersed into the music by mixing sounds exclusively for each body part.

This study's contributions are as follows.

- We experimented on methods to listen to music and found that emotions do not change significantly depending on how one listens.
- We found that using the proposed method, LIVEJACKET, improves the music experience compared to other music listening methods.
- The method of listening to music with headphones while vibrating the body also contributed to improving the music experience.

2   Related Work

Vibration tactile technology has already been used for the purpose of improving the quality of music experience. In addition, vibrotactile technology is also used in the field of entertainment such as games and movies. However, there are few studies on tactile presentation technology aimed at both improving music experience and utilizing it in the field of entertainment.

2.1   Improve Music Experience

There has been much research on the relationship between vibration tactile and music experiences [3]. Most of music playing devices that reproduce vibration are chair type devices. A chair-type device presents vibration by attaching transducers to a chair. The Emoti-Chair [7] converted acoustic signals directly into vibration by attaching eight voice coils to a chair. Merchel and Altinsoy [12] vibrated the entire chair and examined the change in the music experience. By individually controlling the sound and vibration to be played back, they clarified that vibration affects the music experience. Nanayakkara et al. [13] developed a chair-type vibratory sensation device for the hearing impaired. Experiments with hearing impaired individuals indicated that the music experience improved. Karam et al. [6] developed a jacket type vibration presentation device. Although no change in emotion was seen, it was observed that changing the vibration according to the music frequency improved the music experience better than adding a certain vibration.

Rovan [14] developed a haptic presentation system as an interface for playing virtual instruments. When playing a virtual musical instrument, vibrations are feedback, so that it feels as though the user is manipulating real instruments. In the research to improve the music experience using vibration tactile, music was played from the external speaker as before, and only vibration was presented from the haptic presentation device. To further improve the music experience, we played not only the vibration but also the music from the tactile presentation device. By playing music from the device as well, it sounds as if wearer is generating sound himself. Wearner feel as if he or she are being enveloped in sound, which leads to an improvement in the music experience.

2.2 Utilization in the Entertainment Field

Vibration tactile presentation devices are used not only in the music field but also in the entertainment field. As observed from the widespread use of 4DX[1], a chair-type vibration presentation system, vibration presentation is an important technique in movie viewing. Lemmens et al. [9] developed a jacket-type upper body vibration tactile presentation device for movie viewing. Dijk [4] has developed a blanket type vibrotactile presentation device for movie viewing with 176 vibrating motors. Mood Glove [11] is a globe type vibration tactile presentation device for viewing movies. It was determined that vibrotactile stimuli at low intensity and low frequency induced a sense of calmness in users, whereas vibrotactile stimuli at low intensity but higher frequency increased excitement. Abdur Rahman et al. [1] developed a wearable device that presents vibrations to correspond with movies published on YouTube.

Vibration tactile sense is also an important technology in gaming. Lindeman et al. [10] developed a vibrotactile presentation device for VR games. Synesthesia Suit [8] has developed a suits-type vibrotactile presentation device specializing in Rez Infinite games. It was used to promote of Rez Infinite. Surround Haptics [5] is a device that creates a sensation as if the vibrating part is moving between the transducers by arranging a plurality of transducers in an array in a chair; this is used to represent movement in the game. Emojacket [2], a jacket type haptic sense presentation device, presented not only vibrotactile presentation but also haptic sense by using air and temperature.

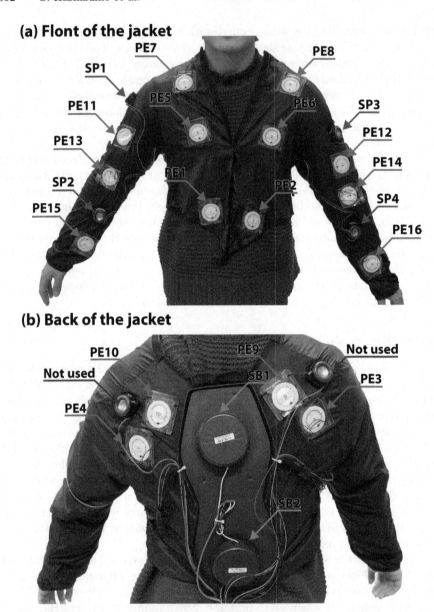

(a) Flont of the jacket

(b) Back of the jacket

Fig. 1. Layout drawing of the speakers to be attached to the jacket.

In the entertainment field there are few cases of using vibration tactile for music listening. We consider that this research will increase the entertainment aspect of the music experience.

3   Implementation

LIVEJACKET consists of a jacket and 22 multiple types of speakers. Since the frequency band that can be played back is different depending on the speaker type, it is possible to reproduce broadband sound and vibration by using multiple speakers. We used 16 piezo speakers "pzBASS B26C" (PE1–16), four full range speakers "NSW 1-205-8A"[2] (SP1–4), and two subwoofers "SUBPAC M2"[3] (SB1 and SB2). We attached six piezo speakers in front of the jacket, three piezo speakers and two full range speakers in the right arm, three piezo speakers and two full range speakers in the left arm, and four piezo speakers and two subwoofers on the back (Fig. 1). Each speaker is connected to the audio interface MOTU 16A[4] that can output 16 channels via an amplifier. The piezo speakers are connected to a compact amplifier, full range speakers are connected to two 5 W amplifiers FOSTEX AP 05, and the subwoofers are connected to the attached dedicated amplifier (Fig. 3). The audio interface is connected to the laptop by a USB cable. Some speakers (PE1 and SB1; PE2 and SB2; PE15, SP1, and SP2; and PE15, SP1, and SP2) are connected to the same channel (Fig. 2).

The vibration and sound presented by LIVEJACKET needs to be dedicated. We split music for each part such as an instrument or a vocal and assigned the divided sound part to each channel of the audio interface using Logic Pro X.

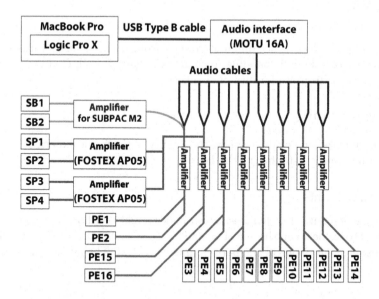

Fig. 2. Block diagram of speakers and amplifiers used for LIVEJACKET.

---

[2] http://www.ari-web.com/aurasound/NSW1-205-8A/index.htm   (last   accessed March 2, 2018. In Japanese).

[3] http://thehand.co.jp/subpac/ (last accessed March 2, 2018. In Japanese).

[4] http://motu.com/products/avb/16a (last accessed March 2, 2018).

Fig. 3. Experiment setup. Subjects wore the LIVEJACKET and listened to music while standing.

Since it is possible to play different sounds from each speaker, various sound designs are possible. It is possible to change the gain of each channel or to send the same sound from a plurality of speakers.

4   Evaluation

We experimented and evaluated how the quality of the music experience changed between five music listening methods.

4.1   Participants

Twelve participants (five females, seven males, eight of whom were members of our laboratory) between the age of 19 and 38 (M = 23.08, SD = 4.82) participated in the experiment. None of the participants were deaf. The average height of the participants was 168.5 cm (SD = 8.54).

4.2   Experimental Design

We prepared five music listening methods and two experimental music methods and compared the quality of the music experience. A questionnaire survey was conducted for each music listening method. Five kinds of music listening methods were prepared as follows. In all listening methods, subjects wore the LIVEJACKET and listened to music while standing (Fig. 3).

Speaker method: A method of listening to music using an external speaker. Subjects listened to music while standing 1.5 m in front of the stereo's external speaker. We played the original, unprocessed sound source on the external speaker.

Headphone method: A method of listening to music using headphones. Subjects wore headphones. We played the original, unprocessed sound source on the headphones.

Speaker with vibration method: A method of listening to music using LIVEJACKET, which was set to present only vibration, and external speakers. We played the original, unprocessed sound source, on the external speakers. We mixed 100 Hz or 200 Hz low pass filtered sound source to each LIVEJACKET speaker and played. We played the sound source for LIVEJACKET and the external speaker simultaneously.

Headphone with vibration method: A method of listening to music using LIVEJACKET, which was set to present only vibration, and headphones. Subjects wore headphones. We played the original, unprocessed sound source on the headphones. We mixed 100 Hz or 200 Hz low pass filtered sound source to each LIVEJACKET speaker and played. We played the sound source for LIVEJACKET and the headphones simultaneously.

LIVEJACKET method: A method of listening to music wearing LIVEJACKET. We mixed each part of the original sound source for each speaker of LIVEJACKET and played.

Two kinds of songs were used in this experiment. To evaluate LIVEJACKET from the entertainment perspective, we selected rock and orchestra, as these music genres are often played at live venues. The song details and the mixing settings are listed below.

M1 - We are (ONE OK ROCK): For rock music, we selected "We are"[5] from ONE OK ROCK, a Japanese band, as rock music. We trimmed M1 from the original to 1 min 18 s. M1 is divided into 12 parts: bass, drums, percussion, rhythm, lead guitar, rhythm guitar, acoustic guitar, synth bass, synthesizer, string, chorus, and lead vocal. Bass and synth bass were output from PE1, PE2, SB1, and SB2. Vocals were output from SP1, SP2, SP3, SP4, PE15, and PE16, which are about the tip of the arm. By being able to hear vocals from the arms, it feels as though wearer are singing. The other parts were mixed so that the sound was reproduced from the whole body. In the experiment, subjects held their arm in front of his or her face like he or she had a microphone so that vocals reproduced from their arms could be heard from the face.

M2 - Symphony No. 5, Op. 67 (Ludwig van Beethoven): We selected Beethoven's Symphony No. 5, Op. 67 for orchestra music. We trimmed M2 from the original song to 58 s. M2 is divided into 12 parts: trombone, trumpet, viola, violin, bassoon, clarinet, oboe, flute, cello, contrabass, horn, and timpani. Each part was associated with each speaker.

---

[5] https://www.youtube.com/watch?v=nU307tV32B0 (last accessed March 2, 2018).

4.3   Procedure

Each participant was briefly informed of the study's purpose and advised that they could abort the study and take a break at any time. Further, they were provided with a consent form to sign and a demographics questionnaire to complete.

Subjects listened to first to M1 then to M2 through the five types of listening methods. The order of five music listening methods was randomly presented to each subject. Both music selections were played once for each listening method.

We used Rousse's circumplex model of emotion [15], a Multidimensional Scaling (MDS) model with two-dimensional interpreted parameters, arousal (weak to strong) and valence (positive to negative), to examine the subjects' emotions after listening to music. Subjects responded to the MDS after listening to music with each listening method. They were asked the following questions, which were based on 7 scale likert scale. At the conclusion, we provided a free description field.

Q1. Did the music feel comfortable? (comfortable - not affected - uncomfortable)

Q2. Did the vibration feel comfortable? (comfortable - not affected - uncomfortable)

Q3. How did you feel the music volume? (big - small)

Q4. Did you feel the music to whole body? (overall - moderate - locally)

Q5. Did you feel as if you were in a live concert venue? (I felt - I did not feel)

Q6. Did you feel wrapped in sound? (wrapped - not wrapped)

Q7. Did you enjoy it? (fun - not fun)

Q8. Did you feel as if you became a singer/conductor? (I felt - I did not feel)

Q9. Did you feel like you were in an audience? (I felt - I did not feel)

Q10. Did you feel the sound pressure? (I felt - I did not feel)

Q11. Were your emotions shaken? (shaken - not shaken)

Q12. Did you want to move your body? (I wanted to move it - I did not)

Q13. Did you want to sing along? Would you like to play in instrument? (I did - I did not)

Q14. Did you want to go to a live venue? (I wanted - I did not)

Q15. Would you recommend this to someone? (I would like to recommend - I did not want to).

4.4   Result

We conducted a statistical test on the questionnaire result using mauchly's sphericity test and sidak for the multiple comparison. We used the SPSS Statistics version 24.

MDS results are shown in the Fig. 4. Significant differences were observed in arousal in M1 ($F(4, 44) = 3.540$, $p < 0.05$). As a result of multiple comparison, the LIVEJACKET method showed higher awareness than the speaker method ($p < 0.05$). Conversely, the valence in M1 did not show any significant difference

Table 1. Result of statistical test on the questionnaire result using multiple comparison in M1.

Question	Test statistic	P-value
Q4	$F(4, 44) = 10.767$	$p < 0.01$
Q5	$F(4, 44) = 5.872$	$p < 0.01$
Q6	$F(4, 44) = 11.614$	$p < 0.01$
Q7	$F(4, 44) = 6.311$	$p < 0.01$
Q8	$F(4, 44) = 7.153$	$p < 0.01$
Q10	$F(4, 44) = 3.979$	$p < 0.01$
Q11	$F(4, 44) = 5.550$	$p < 0.01$
Q13	$F(4, 44) = 2.693$	$p < 0.05$
Q14	$F(4, 44) = 4.005$	$p < 0.01$
Q15	$F(4, 44) = 6.070$	$p < 0.01$

Table 2. Result of statistical test on the questionnaire result using multiple comparison in M2.

Question	Test statistic	P-value
Q4	$F(4, 44) = 7.410$	$p < 0.01$
Q5	$F(4, 44) = 7.002$	$p < 0.01$

$(F(4, 44) = 1.286$, n.s.$)$. In M2, there was no significant difference between arousal and valence (arousal: $F(4, 44) = 3.508$, n.s.; valence: $F(4, 44) = 1.999$, n.s.).

We conducted a statistical test on 15 questions as well as MDS. Only the results on the question items with significant differences are shown in the Fig. 4. Significant differences were found in Q4, Q5, Q6, Q7, Q8, Q10, Q11, Q13, Q14, and Q15 in M1 (Table 1). Significant differences were found in Q4 and Q10 in M2 (Table 2).

The results of the multiple comparison are as shown in the Fig. 4. Characteristic results indicated the following. From the result for Q4 in M1 and M2, we proved that the LIVEJACKET method can create the sensation of music being felt throughout the body. However, the headphone with vibration method also proved to be effective to some extent. According to the result of Q8 in M1, we found that subject could feel as if he or she became a singer by using the LIVEJACKET method, speaker with vibration method and headphone with vibration method more than the speaker method. In Q4, Q5, Q6, Q7, Q8, and Q11 of M1 and Q4 and Q10 of M2, not only the LIVEJACKET method but also the headphone with vibration method showed significant differences.

P1 answered that jacket was heavy and tiring. P3, P4, P5, P10, and P11 answered that it would be better to strengthen the front vibration, not the back. P8 answered that he felt music playing in the back. P2 and P4 answered that the sound quality of LIVEJACKET was bad.

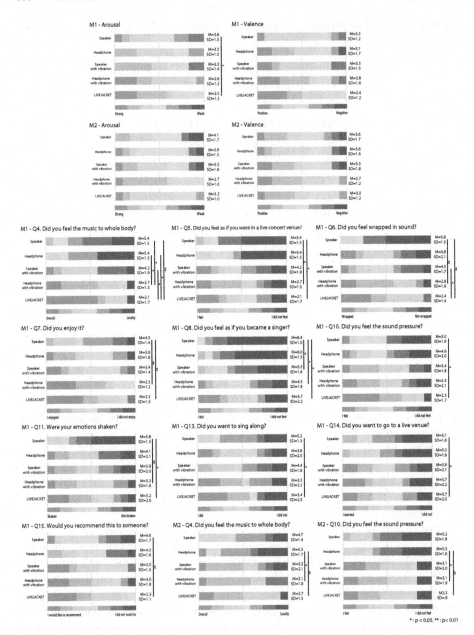

Fig. 4. The result of MDS model of emotion and questions about emotion. Only the result on the questions with significant difference are shown.

5   Discussion

We conducted a questionnaire survey on MDS and music experience in subject experiments. In the MDS evaluation, it was suggested that there was no significant difference in emotions with each music listening method. This indicates that the differences in listening methods do not affect emotions. It is thought that the tune of the song itself subject's affects. The rock music in M1 had higher arousal and valence than M2, which is an orchestral piece.

In the questionnaire survey on the music experience, there were significant differences in many questions. From M1, there were significant differences with 10 questions, however with M2, there were significant differences with only two questions. This is thought to be due to the difference in songs. As P2 and P4 answered, LIVEJACKET has poor sound quality compared to external speakers and headphones. As for an orchestra, which has many kinds of musical instruments and high resolution, sound quality changes greatly depending on the device to be reproduced. Therefore, when playing the orchestra with LIVEJACKET, it is thought that the sound quality decreased more than with external speakers and headphones, which affected the music experience. However, since M1 is a kind of rock music with fewer musical instruments, the influence of difference in sound quality is considered to be small. In the seven questions, significant differences also appeared in the headphone with vibration method in addition to the LIVEJACKET method. This is also considered to be related to sound quality. Compared to the LIVEJACKET speakers, the headphone sound quality is better. Furthermore, the position of the LIVEJACKET loudspeaker is closer to the subject than the external speaker, but similarly the sound source from the headphone is closer to the subject. According to these points, it is considered that the music experience also improved in the headphone with vibration method in which the sound quality was good and the sound source was close to the subject.

A questionnaire survey about the music experience indicated that LIVE-JACKET can provide a new music experience. By wearing the LIVEJACKET, subjects were able to experience music as it would be originally felt in a live venue, such as feeling music throughout the whole body and feeling sound pressure. Furthermore, subjects felt like they became singers. Subjects felt that they wanted to go to a live venue. These experiences were hard to feel when listening to music through conventional digital mediums. From these results, we can consider about how to use LIVE JACKET. For example, we can use LIVEJACKET for entertainment so that wearer can feel the experience of being a singer. The jacket can also be used to promote live participation.

According to the subjects, it would be better to strengthen the vibration in the front side, not just the back side. Because the current system has a subwoofer on the back, the vibration felt in the rear side is strong. However, subjects mostly go to the live venue as an audience, so speakers and musical instruments that generate sound exist in front of the subjects. For that reason, we feel intense vibration on the front body in a live venue. LIVEJACKET vibrates strongly at the back, so they feel the difference between being in a live venue and wearing the LIVEJACKET. This is why they suggested that the front vibration be stronger. To bridge this experience gap, it is necessary to install a speaker that generates intense vibration such as a subwoofer in the front as well as on the back.

6 Conclusion

We developed LIVEJACKET, a jacket capable of vibrotactile presentation and playing music. In this paper, we conducted experiments with five music listening methods to investigate the quality of the music experience. We found that LIVEJACKET creates a higher quality music experience than other listening methods. LIVEJACKET is suitable for music which has fewer instruments. In the discussion, we examined how to utilize LIVEJACKET in promotion and entertainment. To convey more of the music's excellence, we need to raise the quality of the music experience. We believe that LIVE JACKET can fulfill this objective.

Acknowledgement. We would like to thank University of Tsukuba and HAKUHODO Inc. for supporting this work. We are also thankful to all the members of the Digital Nature Group at University of Tsukuba for their discussions and feedback.

References

1. Abdur Rahman, M., Alkhaldi, A., Cha, J., El Saddik, A.: Adding haptic feature to YouTube. In: Proceedings of the 18th ACM International Conference on Multimedia, MM 2010, pp. 1643–1646. ACM, New York (2010)
2. Arafsha, F., Alam, K.M., Saddik, A.E.: EmoJacket: consumer centric wearable affective jacket to enhance emotional immersion. In: 2012 International Conference on Innovations in Information Technology (IIT), pp. 350–355, March 2012
3. Danieau, F., Lecuyer, A., Guillotel, P., Fleureau, J., Mollet, N., Christie, M.: Enhancing audiovisual experience with haptic feedback: a survey on HAV. IEEE Trans. Haptics 6(2), 193–205 (2013)
4. Dijk, E., Weffers, A., De Zeeuw, T.: A tactile actuation blanket to intensify movie experiences with personalised tactile effects, February 2018
5. Israr, A., Kim, S.C., Stec, J., Poupyrev, I.: Surround haptics: tactile feedback for immersive gaming experiences. In: CHI 2012 Extended Abstracts on Human Factors in Computing Systems, CHI EA 2012, pp. 1087–1090. ACM, New York (2012)
6. Karam, M., Russo, F.A., Fels, D.I.: Designing the model human cochlea: an ambient crossmodal audio-tactile display. IEEE Trans. Haptics 2(3), 160–169 (2009)
7. Karam, M., Branje, C., Nespoli, G., Thompson, N., Russo, F.A., Fels, D.I.: The emoti-chair: an interactive tactile music exhibit. In: CHI 2010 Extended Abstracts on Human Factors in Computing Systems, CHI EA 2010, pp. 3069–3074. ACM, New York (2010)
8. Konishi, Y., Hanamitsu, N., Minamizawa, K., Outram, B., Mizuguchi, T., Sato, A.: Synesthesia suit: the full body immersive experience. In: ACM SIGGRAPH 2016 VR Village, SIGGRAPH 2016, p. 20:1. ACM, New York (2016)
9. Lemmens, P., Crompvoets, F., Brokken, D., van den Eerenbeemd, J., de Vries, G.J.: A body-conforming tactile jacket to enrich movie viewing. In: World Haptics 2009 - Third Joint EuroHaptics conference and Symposium on Haptic Interfaces for Virtual Environment and Teleoperator Systems, pp. 7–12, March 2009

10. Lindeman, R.W., Yanagida, Y., Noma, H., Hosaka, K.: Wearable vibrotactile systems for virtual contact and information display. Virtual Real. **9**(2), 203–213 (2006)
11. Mazzoni, A., Bryan-Kinns, N.: Mood Glove: a haptic wearable prototype system to enhance mood music in film. Entertain. Comput. **17**, 9–17 (2016)
12. Merchel, S., Altinsoy, M.E.: The influence of vibrations on musical experience. J. Audio Eng. Soc. **62**(4), 220–234 (2014)
13. Nanayakkara, S., Taylor, E., Wyse, L., Ong, S.H.: An enhanced musical experience for the deaf: design and evaluation of a music display and a haptic chair. In: Proceedings of the SIGCHI Conference on Human Factors in Computing Systems, CHI 2009, pp. 337–346. ACM, New York (2009)
14. Rovan, J., Hayward, V.: Typology of tactile sounds and their synthesis in gesture-driven computer music performance. In: Trends in Gestural Control of Music, pp. 297–320 (2000)
15. Russell, J.A.: A circumplex model of affect. J. Pers. Soc. Psychol. **39**(6), 1161 (1980)

An Interactive Smart Music Toy Design for Children

Shijian Luo[1,2(✉)], Yun Wang[1], Na Xiong[1], Ping Shan[2], and Yexing Zhou[2]

[1] Design Industrial Innovation Center, China Academy of Art, Hangzhou 310024, China
wy_james@126.com, 27006683@qq.com
[2] Department of Industrial Design, Zhejiang University, Hangzhou 310027, China
sjluo@126.com, 403191990@qq.com, 616316889@qq.com

Abstract. With the improvement of social material conditions, children's education has drawn increasing attention. Children's toys enter the field of vision as an important medium for children's education, while the advent of a variety of scientific and technological achievements gave birth to the intelligent trend of children's toys. At the same time, traditional children's music education has many inconveniences, application of scientific and technological achievements is also needed in this education process. It provides a perfect opportunity for children's musical education to be the perfect application scenarios for children's smart toys.

With related market research and targeted user research, a new design idea of interactive smart music toy for children is put forward. The musical instrument type music toy is selected for product design, and designed from three parts: design research, product scheme design and program test. Using the hand wearable product solution, an interactive way was designed that conforms to the natural behavior and psychological cognition of the children, to let children feel the charm of music and enhance children's visual perception and coordination of hand movements ability.

This article uses the methods of desktop research, user interviews and tangible user interfaces design principles to sort out the design characteristics of children's music toys in the market, and draw our design opportunities after analyzing its advantages and disadvantages. Then the target user's needs and product design were taken. Under the theoretical guidance of the tangible user interface, the product's design ideas are improved and the system design of the product is carried out. Finally, the feasibility of the design scheme is verified through user test. The analysis and experimental results show that the design of the interactive children's smart music toy scheme is reasonable and feasible, which can stimulate children's interest in use and enhance the user experience to a certain degree when they carry out music education.

Keywords: Interactive design · Tangible user interface · Smart devices
Music toys · Children's education

© Springer International Publishing AG, part of Springer Nature 2018
N. Streitz and S. Konomi (Eds.): DAPI 2018, LNCS 10921, pp. 372–390, 2018.
https://doi.org/10.1007/978-3-319-91125-0_31

1   Introduction

Childhood is the window of hope in one's life, the best time to build a positive character and develop intelligence [1]. Children's toys have played an important role in the growth of children during their childhood. Toys attract the curiosity and attention of children, bring them joy, and also subtly help enhance their intelligence, physical and social skills. With the rapid development of technology, the functions and forms of children's toys are undergoing tremendous changes, more intelligent toys appear than past times. It can promote two-way interaction between children and toys to accomplish certain tasks better [2, 3]. Moreover, Applications such as speech recognition, human-computer interaction and other technology in smart toys will significantly improve products' market imagination.

With the public demand for spiritual culture gradually growing. More and more people realize that early music education is of great importance to the future development of children. People generally believe that early musical enlightenment education for children can cultivate their musical interests, artistic accomplishments, and even intelligence levels. However, there are many drawbacks in music education nowadays, such as time-laden courses, tedious repetitive exercises, incomprehensible music scores, which can easily destroy children's natural intimacy toward music. Only when children live in beauty, games, conversation, music, fantasy, creative world, can they have enough spiritual life. Without these, he is a withered flower [4, 5].When we are educating our children with music, we should also pay attention to the spirit of entertaining.

This article studies a better interactive smart music toy program for children compared with the traditional instruments program. It based on tangible user interface, through fun interactive design to help children enjoy music and learning happily. Let children be able to perform their musical activities in a free, independent, happy way and full of aesthetic imagination and creativity.

2   Method

2.1   Target Population Analysis and User Interviews

User Interview. The subject of the proposed target population for children aged 4 to 8 years. During the user research phase, the single-person interview method was used to gain insight into the target population.

Identify the Target Respondent. The target population was children aged 4 to 8 years old. Since their thinking and presentation skills were not yet mature, we defined the interviewees as their parents.

Confirm the Interview Form. There are two types of interviews, structured interview and unstructured interview [6]. Considering each child's specific situation, this interview will use unstructured forms of interviews.

Respondents Basic Information. The interview invited 4 parents, and all of them have musical instruments at home. The basic information can be seen in Table 1.

Table 1. Basic information about parents and children interviewed

Code	Identity	Children's gender	Child's age	Parent description (occupation, education and knowledge of music background)
A	Mother	Male	5 years old	Accounting, undergraduate, no music background
B	Mother	Female	8 years old	Housewife, high school, no music background
C	Father	Female	6 years old	Programmer, undergraduate, with music background
D	Mother	Female	7 years old	Clerk, college, no music background

Interview Design. We invited four parents and arranged four one-on-one in-depth interviews, each lasting 45 min, using notes and recordings. The contents and purpose of the interview outline are shown in Table 2.

Table 2. Interview outline and purpose of parents

Interview stage	Time	Content	Purpose
First stage	10 min	Self introduction, the rules described, warm field	Allow respondents to relax and gain trust, paving the way for the smooth progress of the following interviews
Second stage	10 min	Children's basic information; children's normal contact with traditional toys and intelligent toys related	Understand children's basic information, tap children's interest in toys, and motivations and considerations for parents to buy toys
Third phase	15 min	Music toys and musical instruments at home related to the situation	Understand the current use of musical instrument music toys, find our design opportunities
Fourth stage	10 min	Content of home music education, the daily activities of children at home and future plans for music education	Understand the development of children's musical literacy and interest in music; parents' views on music education

Interview Results. Through interviews, we learned a few key points:

1. Limited musical interaction between parents and children.
2. Basically idled musical instruments.
3. High difficulty of playing instrument type music toys.
4. Children soon lose their interest in difficult musical instrument toys.
5. Parents without musical background cannot guide children to play musical toys.
6. Some musical toys are too large.
7. The purpose of parents to buy musical toys is music enlightenment.
8. The factors Parents concerned: safety, informative, playability (how long children will play) and the price factor.
9. Parents most likely to accept the price lower than instruments for musical toys.

User Needs Summary. By studying the relevant children's cognitive and physiological development characteristics, combined with the content of this interview, we summarize the design needs of children's musical toys essentials:

1. Cultivate musical literacy for children.
2. To enhance the fine hand movement, capacity especially for 4–8 ages children.
3. Safe for children. Use soft fabrics or nontoxic materials, such as rubber toys.
4. Good music interaction between parents and children.
5. Easy to learn, even for those without the knowledge of music.
6. A playable toy, have more novelty to play, to attract the curiosity of children.
7. The size of the toy has to be considered, since the request of more living space.

2.2 Tangible User Interface Theory of Product Design

Applications in the Program Design. According to the tangible user interface, we will start from the four levels of their corresponding children's music toys design; they are the physical layer, the behavior layer, the indication layer, and the information layer (see Fig. 1).

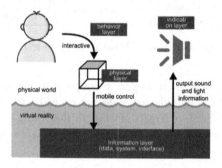

Fig. 1. The relationship between the four layers under the tangible interaction theory

The physical layer refers to the interactive physical interface designed for children; Behavioral layer refers to the interaction between children and products; Instructional layer refers to the need for information guidance and feedback in children's interactions with toys; Information layer refers to the data hidden behind the product information.

Behavior Layer Design. We start with the interaction of people when using instruments and then map their abstraction to the tangible user interface system. Figure 2 shows the hand movements when playing a variety of instruments. We can find that almost all the interaction involves the tap action. In addition, when using the instrument, each finger of a person has a fixed position where it is placed, which shows that while playing the instrument, each human finger has a different but distinct division of labor.

Fig. 2. Hand movements when playing musical instruments

In this subject, we mainly extract that the "tap" is equal to this behavior pattern, mapping to play a musical instrument, and the meaning of each finger should be different, corresponding to a specific pitch, see Fig. 3.

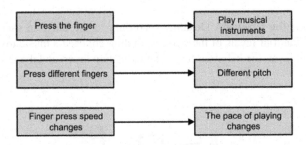

Fig. 3. Tangible user interface behavior mapping and meaning analysis

This means that a child's ten fingers correspond to ten specific tones. Research found that most of the children's songs do not exceed ten scales. As shown in the musical notation of "The Two Tigers" in Fig. 4, the whole song only requires eight scales of G3 to G4 when playing on the piano. Table 3 shows the pitch of each note in this design.

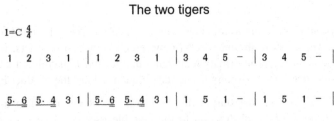

Fig. 4. "The two tigers" notation

Table 3. Left and right fingers corresponding to the note pitch

Finger	Left little finger	Left ring finger	Left middle finger	Left index finger	Left thumb	Right thumb	Right index finger	Right middle finger	Right ring finger	Right little finger
Corresponding note	G3	A3	B3	C4	D4	E4	F4	G4	A4	B4

As for the feasibility analysis of the behavioral layer, we will come to a conclusion by testing the usability of the product after the prototype is completed.

Physical Layer Design. Design of the physical layer needs to consider user survey obtained, including toys to play with greater freedom and occupies less space. Toy manufacturers are trapped in the original shape of the instrument, imitating real instruments for product design. However, if wearable thinking is adopted, the shape of the product can be detached from the traditional form of the instrument.

Indicator Layer Design. Through research, we learn that due to the laciness of children's experiments or parents' weak music theory knowledge, more explicit information is needed.

Beautiful music must include rhythm and melody. We disassemble a song. Each note corresponds to a light signal. The rhythmic changes and the length of the note are translated into flashing and the continuous lighting of small lights. Each finger corresponds to a small light; tap of each finger controls a note. When the corresponding light is on, children tap their fingers; the toy senses the signal and emits the corresponding pitch of the finger.

We numbered the small light from the little finger to the thumb of the left hand to Led1–Led5, and the thumbs to the little finger of the right hand numbered Led6–Led10 respectively. Figure 5 shows the changes of the small light signals corresponding to the second and third beats of the children's song "two tigers".

The second beat

Time (s)	2~2.5	2.5~3	3~3.5	3.5~4
Corresponding light	Led 4	Led 5	Led 6	Led 4

The third beat

Time (s)	4~4.5	4.5~5	5~6
Corresponding light	Led 6	Led 7	Led 8

Fig. 5. LED signals corresponding to "two tigers"

In order to ensure sufficient freedom, the user can also choose to turn off the small light indicator mode, enter the free play mode.

Information Layer Design. The information layer includes: information data of the related melody stored in the system; sound signals generated; and an intelligent system. There are two main requirements for the information layer: (1) More song storage than hard disk does. (2) Parents' needs to record children's performance.

The entire music toy contains a hardware system, the physical layer. A fixed number of songs are loaded on the hardware system. The hardware system has its own playback module that can still sound without connecting the phone. And a software system, parents can use the online music library to download music on their phones and update to the hardware system through Bluetooth. The system also has a special song-recording page. When the phone and the hardware are connected, the song-recording page can be opened, sound can be received and played on phone. Some animation effects will also accompany the phone's recording page.

Product System Design Framework and Functional Requirements. The design points corresponding to the four levels described above can be integrated into a complete system design, as shown in Fig. 6.

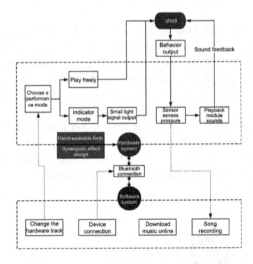

Fig. 6. System design framework of product

The system is mainly divided into two parts of hardware system and software system, including hardware functions are:

1. Express melody by light signals, guide children use the corresponding fingers.
2. Each finger corresponds to a note, different notes correspond to different colors.
3. The sensor detects the action of pressing the finger of the child and the sounding module outputs the corresponding note.
4. Light indication mode or free play mode can be chosen on hardware.

The main function of the software system is:

1. Change hardware built-in music library.
2. Download music from the Internet to the phone.
3. After connection, music can be played and recorded through the phone.
4. Stores the recorded song.

The whole system is designed to allow children to integrate into the game through simple, natural interactions. At the same time, the entire toy design adopts the wearable form to break the inherent shape of the musical instrument music toy and enhance the portability and openness of the toy.

3   The Experimental Description

3.1   Hardware System Concept Design

The design of the hardware part of the product adopts the wearable solution of the hand, which has the characteristics of large degree of freedom under the scene, small size of the product and easy to use. Children wear a glove shape toy, which can physically emit notes of ten different pitches by fingers tapping to create a complete piece of children's music, and the toy can also indicate the child to use the corresponding finger through a light signal of ten LEDs (Fig. 7).

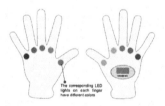

Fig. 7.   Hardware concept design (front view) (Color figure online)

Figure 7 is the main view of the concept of toy design, corresponding to the back part of the hand. From the figure we can see the back of the glove, the back of the hand installed ten LED small lights, and the color of LED lights using audio-visual synesthesia design principle, each corresponding to the LED lights emitted by different colors, respectively corresponding to ten colors from deep blue to deep red.

Figure 8 is the rear view of the toy, which corresponds to the palm position. The pressure sensor is installed on the corresponding fingertip part of the toy. When the sensor detects the pressure signal, it will be transmitted to the motherboard to receive the signal and then control the sound-emitting module to issue the corresponding note.

Fig. 8. Hardware concept design (rear view)

Hardware Prototype System Principle. Through previous research, we started developing product prototypes with original capabilities based on previous design concepts for the first phase of product testing.

The basic working principle of the hardware system (Fig. 9):

1. Both hand prototypes are connected by Bluetooth and share one sound module.
2. Light up and light up time written in advance according to a specific track, the length of time a light is lit is related to the beat length of a note.
3. Pressure film sensor continuously detects pressure changes between the fingers. When the SCM found that the pressure value is greater than the critical value, it controls the voice playback module to play the corresponding note and make a sound through the speaker.

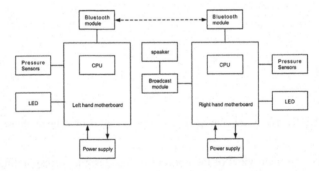

Fig. 9. The hardware system working principle diagram

Motherboard and Sensor Selection

(1) Motherboard

We choose the Blunonano controller (model DFR0296) as the master for this prototyping, which compatible with the Arduino development platform. Motherboard's small size, only 53 × 19 × 12 mm, comes with integrated Bluetooth 4.0 module, which can achieve the interconnection between the two controllers, and has a strong Bluetooth communication capabilities, ideal for the current prototype development needs.

(2) Pressure sensor

Since we are using a hand-wearable product solution, we consider a flexible pressure sensor. The RFP603 Flexible Film Pressure Sensor is a resistive pressure sensor that measures both static and dynamic pressure at any contact surface and converts the pressure applied to the sensor's sensing area into a resistive signal. Then according to the calibration curve of the force and resistance to obtain the change of pressure exerted by the external force, the greater the pressure, the smaller the resistance of the sensor output. For the hand press estimation, we selected the range of 100 g to 2 kg.

(3) Broadcast module

The YS-M3D5 voice-playing module can support up to 32 kinds of voice playing. The user can copy the voice to be played back to the TF card in advance and rename the file according to certain naming rules, and then correspondingly play port grounding, which can complete the playback. The module's maximum supply voltage is 5 V, speaker power up to 3 W, impedance 4 to 8 Ω.

Hardware Prototype Design and Implementation. The entire hardware prototype is divided into four areas, namely: motherboard area, LED light area, pressure sensing area and sounding area.

Motherboard area: This area is programmed Blunonano controller, it includes four main functions: 1. control the light and dark of the small light in a set time sequence; 2. judge the analog input signals of several pressure sensors and identify them; 3. Transform the analog input signal into a digital output signal and transmit it to the playback module; 4. achieve the motherboard signal interconnection of left and right gloves through the built-in Bluetooth 4.0 module.

Led small light area: Motherboard control small lights light and dark in rhythmic order, as a guide. This area is composed of LED chip light and 220 Ω resistor.

Pressure Sensing Area: This area incorporates the RFP603 flexible membrane pressure sensor, 1 MΩ resistor, and a current-stabilizing diode. Logic Flow: When the pressure sensor receives the pressure signal, the structure will generate a voltage pulse signal of

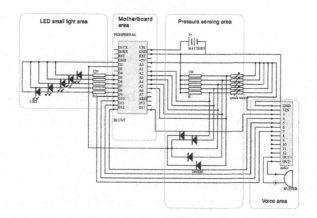

Fig. 10. Hardware prototype design circuit

about 4.5 V. The signal is input to the motherboard's external interrupt judgment port D2. The motherboard judges whether it enters the interrupt function or not, and also ensures that the signal. It is accepted by the different analog input pins of the motherboard for the logic judgment of the motherboard (Fig. 10).

Sound area: Sounding area: the YS-M3D5 voice playback module accepts low-level signals from the motherboard output, play the corresponding notes stored in TF card, through a speaker or headset to be sound.

Figure 11 shows the status of the right half of the hardware integrated into the breadboard, including the Blunonano controller (Appendix 1) which records the sensor control program and the song indication program, the light emitting diode, the pressure Film sensor and playback module. Since the speaker is not soldered to the playback module, the headset is temporarily used as the note output.

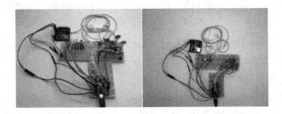

Fig. 11. Hardware prototypes built on breadboard

We then integrated the pressure sensor with a cotton child glove and replaced the small light with a patch LED light, sewn to the back of the glove (Fig. 12). This is the final build of the prototype hardware prototype; the prototype will be used for user testing.

Fig. 12. Hardware prototype (right hand) integrated into children's gloves

3.2   Software System Design Analysis and Design Implementation

Considering the software and toys versatility, the software part of the system will be developed based on the mobile phone side (mainly IOS and Android). Unlike hardware systems, users of software systems are parents. Its main function is to provide background support to hardware systems so that parents can change tracks in hardware through software systems or record songs played by children.

The entire software system design process can be divided into four steps: software requirements analysis; task flow design; page layout design; page visual design.

Software System Requirements Analysis and Information Architecture. Before entering the page design, we need to first clear the page needs. Specifically, the main functions of the page need to be designed according to requirements, so as to classify the functions of the software and form the information architecture of the software. Information architecture can make the structure of the software becomes clear, allowing users to find the information they want in a certain information planning more easily.

According to the user needs for software systems in previous study, we finished the product information architecture. The main structure of the entire APP can be divided into three parts: online music library, music library management, and personal center.

The main function of the online music library is to allow users to browse songs on the Internet and download them to their mobile phones. Music library management includes two major functions: track management and software song recording. Track Management: The user can delete, add, etc. to the music list, and then synchronize the list to the hardware device. Software Song Recording: The user can select songs in the list and perform song recording. The personal center features mainly include user personal information management, download music and recording music management and device connection management.

Software System Page Interaction Design

1. Device connection process and page design

It's the design instructions for the device Bluetooth connectivity page.

There are two entrances to the device connection. One is that when first time use, the software will remind the user to make a Bluetooth connection; the other is to enter the Bluetooth connection page from the device management of the personal center.

Here is the final Bluetooth connection process interactive wireframe (Fig. 13) after the software system and hardware flow chart of Bluetooth connection.

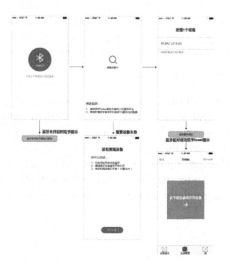

Fig. 13. Bluetooth connection interactive wire diagram

2. Discover music page design

According to the Fig. 14, the design of the entire APP uses the bottom-tabbed navigation. In the bottom of the APP integrated "Discover Music", "Music Management" and "I" three labels. The advantage of this navigation mode is that the entrance is flattened and the navigation control occupies a large area, so can be easily clicked. The page structure is suitable for switching frequently between functions.

The Discover Music page corresponds to the online library section of the information architecture. The main function of this page is to allow the user to find the desired song within the software (Fig. 14).

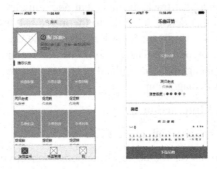

Fig. 14. Found music page wireframe

Under the "Discover Music" tab, users can download songs in three ways. The first is to search by the search box at the top of the page for accurate searches; the second is to view the system's selection of popular children's songs through the Top Songs module; and the third is to recommend songs to users based on their preferences.

After the user clicks the song, it will enter the detail page of the song, which shows information such as author, difficulty of playing, notation and so on. The user can click the download button on the bottom to download the song to mobile phone.

3. Music management page design (Fig. 15)

The middle label at the bottom is song management. When switching to this tab, a song list shows the list of songs that will be synchronized to the hardware device, different from the song downloaded by the user. The user can swipe left and right with his finger to switch between the songs in the song list. Users can also enter the new page through the "Manage" button in the upper left corner and delete or add tracks from the song list. After returning to the main interface, click on the synchronization library button in the upper right corner, to complete the software and hardware synchronization of music.

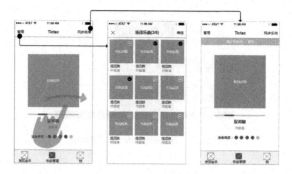

Fig. 15. Music management page design

4. Song recording page (Fig. 16)

In the music management page, tap the song to enter the song details page. There is a "start recording" button at the bottom of the page. If the software and hardware have been completed Bluetooth connectivity, the button is activated. Click to enter the recording page, once started recording, the page will play animation to match the children's play, enhance the interaction. If the Bluetooth is not connected, the button is grayed out. When the user clicks, "toast" will prompt to complete the Bluetooth connection before recording.

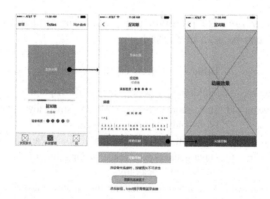

Fig. 16. Song recording process and page design

5. Software system page visual design

After completing the design of the interactive page, we started to visualize the software system. Since our system targeted at young parents now, the whole page is designed in a flat style, making the page look simple and bright in color choice, showing youthful vigor. The overall effect of the page is shown in Fig. 17.

Fig. 17. System interface design

3.3 Product Design System Testing

Target Hardware Prototype Test. In this prototype test, we will invite children aged 4 to 6 years to use the hardware prototypes we developed to find out product design deficiencies in order to improve the hardware design. This test will use observation to collect test information.

The main purpose of the test is to invite children of the target age to use prototypes of the products, observe and collect the problems encountered by the children during the testing process, and find out the optimization direction of the products.

The testing process focuses on two dimensions:

1. Observe the children's interest in the prototype function during the game.
2. The availability of problems encountered in the process of children's games.

Subjects' Basic Situation. The prototype test invited four children to be tested, and the basic information can be seen in Table 4.

Table 4. Subjects-based information

Code	Gender	Age	Children's basic information description
A	Male	6 years old	Have more experience playing smart toys, like to play iPhones, iPods and other smart devices
B	Female	7 years old	Like doll toys, six months of piano learning experience
C	Male	5 years old	Have general experience playing smart toys, contact more assembled blocks toys
D	Female	8 years old	Like plush toys, having instruments musical toys at home

Experimental Design. Before the start of the experiment, teach the children how to use the music gloves and let them put on gloves to adapt for a moment. After the test starts, tell them the specific game task is: When the small light is on, press the corresponding finger.

The test set three procedures:

Program 1: Control the small light on the prototype glove, starting from the little finger on the left hand to the little finger on the right hand turn on, and each lamp illuminates for one second;

Program 2: Performing according to the notation of "Two Tigers," but slowing down the overall rhythm and controlling the duration of one note per second;

Program 3: Speed up the "two tigers" music notes playback speed; each note playback time is shortened to 0.5 s;

Each of the above three programs requires the subject to perform three times.

Test Results. Figure 18 shows the scene of the game after children wear the prototype toy.

Fig. 18. Children wear a toy prototype to play the game

By observing the test of the four subjects, the author recorded the test cases. In this test, we obviously found that girls are very concerned about the shape of the product; boys are more concerned about the novelty of playing. Due to the rough prototype and the low degree of freedom in space, children have a greater impediment to carrying out their tasks. However, we still find some product usability problems, such as:

1. The current toy light instruction is punctate, at the root of the finger. This has a certain degree of difficulty for children, it means easy to press the wrong finger. In later product enhancements, increasing the light cue area may be considered and the location requires some closer to the fingertips.
2. In addition, the current use of the membrane pressure sensor range is 100 g–2 kg. Sometimes there will be miscarriage of justice when young children press. We should consider using a more accurate pressure sensor.
3. In order to minimize the interference of children on the gloves, the product finger part of the material should be used more lightly and soft material.

However, the children under test and their parents endorsed the product concept and interaction of this test, so we will continue to improve the product design based on the test results.

Software System Usability Testing. We used Axure to make the previous interactive interface prototyped as an interactive interface and recruited users for page usability testing. Process of the test: task setting, user recruiting, user test, and problem analysis.

Task Design. We designed two usability-testing tasks:

1. Instruct the user to complete the software and hardware system device connection through the app.
2. After completing the device connection, instruct the user to manage the song and synchronize the song to the hardware device.

User Recruitment. The test recruited 4 young parents for usability testing, all of whom have extensive experience in smart product use and are proficient in using smart phones and computers. During the test, we will use the observation method to record the user's operation, for some improper operation, we will ask them the reason after the test.

Test Result Analysis. In this test, the user could independently complete the task, and the task duration of the two tasks was between 1 and 3 min, indicating that the product basically achieves the level of availability. However, some ease-of-use problems were still found in the testing process and need to be iteratively improved in later designs. See Table 5 for details.

Table 5. Usability testing summaries and analysis

Number	Problem Description	Problem pages	Solution
1	The "Device Connection" entry has too deep color; the "Unconnected" status of the device is too weak and hidden in the personal center.		Placing device connection status Prompts on the music management page, and to be connected to the device on the current page.
2	At present, the synchronized music function requires two independent steps; the whole process is a bit cumbersome.		Make the music management and synchronized music two functions into one process.
3	The "Music Management" page is used more frequently than "Discover Music", but it stay in the latter music tab when the APP is turned on, and requires Manual switching.		Put higher frequency "music management "on the first tab.

Software System Page Optimization

(1) Equipment connection process optimization

At the top of the music management page, a description of the connection status of the device is added. The user can connect and disconnect the device on the music management page without having to switch to the personal center (Fig. 19).

Fig. 19. Device connection flow optimization

(2) Merging music management and song synchronization process

After the merging process, the user can click the Synchronize to Hardware to complete the song update after finishing the management of the music list. If the device is not connected, the management button cannot be clicked (Fig. 20).

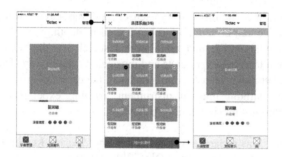

Fig. 20. Music management process optimization

(3) The bottom tab bar changes

With the "Find Music" tab position to be replaced, "Music Management" tab has been moved to the first tab position. On the home page of the app, the style is shown in the tab bar at the bottom of the page shown in Fig. 21.

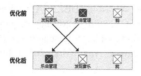

Fig. 21. Bottom tab label position change

4 Discussions

This article introduces a smart music educational toy designed for children, conducted scene analysis and system design research, analyzed and summarized the impact mechanism and potential contradiction of children's music learning. According to the theory of tangible user interface, this paper constructs a smart prototype, implements the hardware prototype of each module, and illustrates the key technologies of the software modules used. Finally, the prototype of mobile terminal is introduced and tested. The results are summarized and analyzed.

The subject has achieved three research goals: combining the research and analysis of products and users, refining the design features and principles of children's music toys; summarizing the design methods and principles of tangible user interface theory to guide the design of children's smart toys. The design of toys provides new ideas and methods. Based on the theoretical guidance, the design and development of children's musical toys are designed to design a musical toy that accords with children's habits, enhances the interest of children's games, cultivates musical qualities and promotes children's cognitive development.

In this paper, the stability of the sensor and the circuit has great room for improvement, which can continually to be studied in depth.

There is no quantitative and qualitative research on the relationship between musical instrument learning experience and musical toy familiarity. This analysis needs to learn the correlation between operating data and the error rate from a large number of children with or without musical instrument learning experience, thus providing guidance for children's music learning behavior.

Acknowledgement. This research was supported by the Zhejiang Key Laboratory of Healthy Smart Kitchen Integrating System Project (No. 2014E10014).

References

1. Pangelinan, M.M., Zhang, G., Vanmeter, J.W., et al.: Beyond age and gender: relationships between cortical and subcortical brain volume and cognitive-motor abilities in school-age children. Neuroimage **54**(4), 3093–3100 (2010)
2. Hornecker, E., Buur, J.: Getting a grip on tangible interaction: a framework on physical space and social interaction. In: Conference on Human Factors in Computing Systems, CHI 2006, Montréal, Québec, Canada, pp. 437–446. DBLP, April 2006
3. Cagiltay, K., Kara, N., Aydin, C.C.: Smart toy based learning. In: Spector, J., Merrill, M., Elen, J., Bishop, M. (eds.) Handbook of Research on Educational Communications and Technology, pp. 703–711. Springer, New York (2014). https://doi.org/10.1007/978-1-4614-3185-5_56
4. Piper, B., Ishii, H.: PegBlocks: a learning aid for the elementary classroom. In: CHI 2002 Extended Abstracts on Human Factors in Computing Systems, pp. 686–687. ACM (2002)
5. Grissmer, D., Grimm, K.J., Aiyer, S.M., et al.: Fine motor skills and early comprehension of the world: two new school readiness indicators. Dev. Psychol. **46**(5), 1008–1017 (2010)
6. Cameron, C.E., Brock, L.L., Murrah, W.M., et al.: Fine motor skills and executive function both contribute to kindergarten achievement. Child Dev. **83**(4), 1229–1244 (2012)

Robotic Stand-Up Comedy: State-of-the-Art

Anton Nijholt[1,2(✉)] [ID]

[1] University of Twente, Enschede, The Netherlands
anijholt@cs.utwente.nl
[2] Imagineering Institute, Iskandar, Malaysia

Abstract. Humanoid and social robots have to perform in socially acceptable ways. They interact with humans and support humans in their needs and their activities. Stand-up comedy is an extreme form of human-human and human-audience interaction. It can be mild, but often it goes beyond what is socially accepted in verbal and nonverbal behavior and expressed opinions. But it makes people laugh and we can ask whether this can be done by robots and what we can learn from it for other ways of robot-human or robot audience interaction. In this paper we confine ourselves to a survey of developments in robotic stand-up comedy. We hope that this survey helps to stimulate research in this area and identify topics of more general interest in robot-human interaction.

Keywords: Humor · Social robots · Stand-up comedy · Human-robot interaction
Audience responses · Verbal interaction · Nonverbal interaction

1 Introduction

Humor is an essential part of our social interactions with others. We use humor in our interactions with others. We appreciate humor generated by others. We are aware of humorous events in our environment. We have a sense of humor and also we want our partner and friends to have a sense of humor. We have favorite TV comedy series, comic strips, cartoons and comedians.

We can make a distinction between intentional and unintentional humor. In the case of intentional humor we can make a distinction between spontaneous humor and prepared humor. Spontaneous humor is created real-time, based upon what is happening at that moment and what is perceived by those who are present. Spontaneous humor can be a response to events happening in a physical environment, including conversational and imagined events. Prepared humor can be a joke, an anecdote, a humorous text, a cartoon, an animation or a prank. Of course TV comedy series, stage comedies and comedy movies are also examples of media that use prepared humor.

Stand-up comedy contains both prepared and, to a lesser extent, spontaneous humor. There is interaction between the stand-up comedian and his or her audience. Timing of actions (gestures, bodily movements, facial expressions) and speech (prosody) are not only functions of the prepared humor, but also functions of the feedback (laughter, applause, gestures, bodily movements, attention, gaze, et cetera) provided by the audience.

© Springer International Publishing AG, part of Springer Nature 2018
N. Streitz and S. Konomi (Eds.): DAPI 2018, LNCS 10921, pp. 391–410, 2018.
https://doi.org/10.1007/978-3-319-91125-0_32

1.1 Introducing Humor

Humor is a well-known research area in philosophy, psychology and linguistics. The role of humor and laughter was already discussed in writings of the Greek philosophers Plato and Aristotle, and the Roman orator Cicero. Well-known 18th and 19th Century English, German and French philosophers developed thoughts about what causes amusement and what makes people laugh. Wit and absurdness, intentional and unintentional humor, but also aesthetics, moral and social issues became part of their attempts to characterize 'the comics'. Obviously, at that time rough humor and jokes were present in daily life, but they received less attention than wit, word play and other forms of upper class humor (e.g., in the literature or in theatrical performances) that required some intellectual effort. Sigmund Freud investigated jokes from a point of view of relief of tension that has been built up because of being obliged to follow social conventions in real life. In jokes 'naughty' issues can be addressed we don't usually introduce in social and polite conversations.

Irony, sarcasm and, more generally, non-literal language use became research issues in 20th Century linguistics. Computational linguistics and artificial intelligent (AI) approaches to language humor followed. Victor Raskin in his book "Semantic Mechanisms of Humor" [1], based on his earlier work in the 1970s, introduced a theory of joke analysis. Refinements followed in later years. In 1989 Douglas Hofstadter and his students organized a first workshop on 'Humor and Cognition'. In this workshop we see, apart from Raskin's work, the first computational modelling approaches to humor. The focus in these linguistic and artificial intelligence approaches was on finding conditions that make incongruities humorous and in later years on finding knowledge representation schemes that in addition to model the structure of a joke, model the knowledge that is required to understand the joke. The latter turned out to be the main problem of designing a usable formal model of jokes and of artificial intelligence in general. Modelling all common-sense and world knowledge, reasoning about this knowledge and finding associations between concepts, and exploring different forms of instantiations of concepts turned out to be an unreachable goal.

In 1996 we introduced the term 'computational humor' when we organized the first International Workshop on Computational Humor [2]. In this workshop we collected approaches to verbal humor that gave rise to an expectation that an algorithmic approach to humor could be successful. This workshop was followed by two other workshops [3, 4]. In these latter workshops there was interest to investigate the relation between humor and emotion, to investigate machine learning approaches to humor, and to investigate the role of humor engineering for smart environments. These environments have interconnected embedded sensors and actuators and the question arises whether their smartness can be used to generate humorous events. For smart robots, whether they act autonomously or are controlled through the Internet (of Things), the same question can be asked.

1.2 Smart Robots and Humor

Social robots can be made to know about their environment, their interaction partners, and the tasks they have to perform. Unfortunately, knowledge that is modelled is (very) limited, restricted to a very limited domain, and robot behavior based on that limited knowledge can go wrong. But, nowadays AI is less science fiction than it used to be. We will meet such robots in our daily environments.

The first robots appeared in the literature in a theatre play [5].[1] Robots, as they appear in the literature, on stage or in movies are infamous because of their lack of sense of humor, and not being able to understand and express emotions. We can see that in the behavior of Commander Data, a robot in the Star Trek television series and feature films. Despite Data's enormous computational abilities humor and emotions are beyond his reach.

Human-Robot Interaction is now a well-established area of research. Many research papers have addressed the role of humor in human-robot interaction research. However, research does not really address humor modelling. Rather it addresses how to provide a robot with delivery skills or how people experience being addressed by a robot that is telling jokes. Does it make the robot more human-like or do people prefer a humorous robot above a non-humorous robot are research questions that are asked.

We should mention that in human-computer interaction research there is much interest in embodied virtual agents. This is a related research area. Natural communication with embodied virtual agents require that these agents have intelligence and have affective and conversational skills, including having the correct facial expressions, gestures and bodily movements when interacting with a user. Hence, similar models can be used for embodied virtual agents and social robots. Chatbot research, where the bots are not necessarily embodied, is another research area related to social robotics research.

1.3 About This Paper

The main focus of this paper is on robots that have been designed to perform stand-up comedy. These robots need to know about how to deliver humorous content to an audience: how to tell jokes, make witty remarks, and how to adapt their joke telling and timing on audience responses. In order to do so we can learn from humor research, virtual agents research, human-robotic interaction research, speech and natural language processing research, and research on nonverbal interaction. It should look like the robot understands the humorous content and the reactions of its audience. The robotic stand-up comedian should be believable. We can ask that a performing robot is also the creator of the humorous content it is delivering. Deciding about delivering prepared 'witty' remarks because of audience reactions seems to be a feasible aim. Maybe not that different from what is done by a human stand-up comedian.

In the next section, Sect. 2, we discuss some background and related research. We mention some relevant humor theories, various ways a robot can be equipped with a

---

[1] Probably Čapek was inspired by the Prague legend of the Golem, a creature that was created from mud that changed into iron and that was made alive to protect Jewish people by Rabbi Judith Löw in the 16th Century.

sense of humor, joke telling by robots, aspects of nonverbal and physical humor and unintentional humor. There are different senses of humor. Social robots may require a particular type of humor sense or maybe it should depend on its task or it should adapt to the sense of humor of its user, its users, or its audience. Nevertheless, the assumption is that social and performing robots have facial expressions and can make gestures or have other means to display affect with a similar effect on their users, partners, or audiences. Section 3 is on robot actors in comedy and play. Section 4 gives a state-of-the art survey of current activities of robotic stand-up comedy. Some conclusions can be found in Sect. 5, this paper's final section.

2   Background and Related Research

In this section we have observations on humor theories and on humorous human-human and human-robot interaction. Since in this paper we are interested in robotic stand-up comedy, there is a bias in our observations to delivering humor rather than on analyzing, understanding or creating humor. Nevertheless, we need to have some knowledge of humor in order to implement humor in the interaction skills of social and stand-up comedy robots. What makes an anecdote, a joke, a story, a product, a cartoon, an animation, or a situation humorous? We can fully script a robot to deliver a particular humorous content with appropriate speech, facial expressions and gestures. The humorous content should be in the comic script, where, when and how the humor should be delivered. The comic script needs to be transformed to a robot script that tells the robot or a backstage controller of the robot how the humorous content should be delivered using detailed instructions on robot movements, speech, timing, et cetera. In an ideal situation this translation should be done automatically. This requires understanding of the comic script, it requires models of humor and models of verbal and nonverbal behavior related to the delivery of humor. Humor research should make it possible to reduce the human effort to translate a comic script into a robot behavioral script.

But clearly, we can also ask whether we can have the robot design a comic script, for example, design a joke. Or improvise and spontaneously compose a humorous act or a witticism when an interaction and situation makes that possible. As will be clear from the next subsections, we cannot expect that to happen in the next decades. But of course, progress can be made.

2.1   Theories on Humor

As mentioned in the introduction of this paper, philosophers, psychologists and linguists have tried to identify the characteristics of humor. What makes us distinguish between humor and non-humor? Various humor theories have been introduced. Some of them emphasize the function of humor rather than trying to analyse why a particular object (event, situation, product, text, cartoon, animation, …) gives rise to amusement and, maybe, laughter.

Usually a distinction is made between the reasons between why appreciate humor (superiority considerations), the functions of humor (its positive effect on our psychological state) and cognitive state changes (perceiving and resolving incongruities). Hence, there are three complimentary viewpoints.

From the superiority point of view we experience amusement and maybe start laughing laugh because we are not the butt of a joke, a prank, or whatever humorous event. Rather we laugh about the misfortune of others. This superiority viewpoint can be found in the writings of the British philosopher Thomas Hobbes (1588–1679), but it can also be deduced those of Greek philosophers such as Plato and Aristotle. In [6] an attempt is made to explain all humor from this particular point of view. The relief perspective is usually attributed to Herbert Spencer (1820–1903) and Sigmund Freud (1856–1939). It emphasizes that due to social conventions we build up tension and humor, in particular jokes that have content we don't dare to talk about in daily conversations, releases us from that tension. Finally, the incongruity point of view emphasizes that many situations (displayed in text or in reality) can be interpreted in different ways. Slight differences in interpretations are not humorous. Opposing interpretations can be humorous. Making the successful shift from one interpretation (a stereotypical one) to a correct one (it should be far from being stereotypical) is what leads to comic amusement. This incongruity point of view has been discussed explicitly in writings of 18th Century British philosophers and writers such as Mark Akenson (1721–1770), James Beattie (1735–1803) and more famous philosophers such as Immanuel Kant (1724–1804), Arthur Schopenhauer (1788–1860) and Henri Bergson (1859–1941). Although the superiority and the relief perspective remained, in current humor research the emphasis is on incongruity. It allows us to analyze why texts or events are humorous. Victor Raskin [1] used this perspective to build a theory of joke analysis and understanding.

A stand-up comedian is not necessarily aware of these theories. For talented comedians intuition and experience are more important than humor theories and how to adhere to them. But this is not something we can expect from a robotic stand-up comedian. A robot stand-up comedian should be equipped with computational models, maybe obtained through machine learning, that tells him or her what is humorous and what is not. It is hard to imagine a stand-up comedian who does not understand the humorous effect of the content he or she is delivering. Maybe we can nevertheless imagine a robot or virtual agent simulating such a comedian in a performance where there are jokes and maybe even witty remarks and interaction with the audience, without any understanding about the content that is delivered.

Humorous content can be scripted in such a way that its deliverance by an artificial agent leads to a believable performance. The timing of humor delivery depends on audience feedback, but this feedback can be measured and can be made input for the agent interacting with the audience and make its performance dependent on this feedback. The creation of humorous content is not that 'easy'. A stand-up comedian can have text writers, but when attending a performance we 'believe' that the humor that is presented to us is coming from the comedian's creative mind and sense of humor. Design guides for creating stand-up comedy humor or sit-comedy humor are available. Superiority and relief theory aspects can guide the intentional creation of humor. Make others ridiculous (superiority) or introduce taboo topics. But the audience has to be surprised, misled and amused by verbal and nonverbal incongruities and incongruities in physical acts, events, and situations.

2.2 Humor in Human-Robot Interaction: Global Observations

We use the term humor in a wide sense. But there are different styles of humor. For example, in [7] eight styles are distinguished and discussed: sarcasm, cynicism, satire, irony, fun, humor, nonsense and wit. In the narrow sense humor is more about having a positive attitude towards incongruities, imperfections and human shortcomings. Human-Robot Interaction research is concerned with natural, that is human-human-like, interaction between social robots and their users. There have been many investigations and attempts to translate human-human interaction characteristics into what is expected by human users in human-robot interaction. These investigations include the use of humor. Instead of aiming at comprehensive human-like humor in human-robot interaction it is also possible to accept that social robots can be given or will develop an own sense and style of humor, just as individuals, families, professions, cultures, age groups, and social classes can have different preferences for humor. Humor in human-robot interaction research usually assumes that the robot should have a friendly attitude towards its users, so, no use of sarcasm, cynicism, satire or irony.

In this section we provide a global view on research on humor in human-robot interaction. Obviously, this research assumes face-to-face interactions between human and robot. That is different from human-audience or the interaction between a comedy robot and its audience. However, humor in the form of jokes, anecdotes, and witty comments are studied in humor-robot interaction and the results of this research can be used in modelling stand-up comedian research as well.

Rather than creating or adapting humorous content, the research on humor in human-robot interaction is usually about how to tell a joke and how to, as a reaction to a joke or humorous event, to display laughter in a robot or in a virtual embodied agent. Displaying laughter and distinguishing between various kinds of laughter and reasons of laughter is part of current-day research on virtual embodied agent. They are more easy to control than physical agents such as robots.

Current research on the use of humor in human-robot interaction is very limited. We can distinguish the following approaches.

- We can give robots artificial intelligence that makes them aware of and understand their environment. They need to understand humans. It requires human-level intelligence and a further development of interaction technology in such a way that it can replace the human senses by artificial speech and language processing, vision, taste, smell, and touch experiences for the social robot. Despite progress in modelling multi-sensory interactions and experiences, the research results don't allow us to be optimistic about modelling human humor intelligence where all these senses and intelligence have been given a place. Obviously, nothing wrong with continuing research in these areas. Humor, until now, is not really a research topic here.
- We can implement the telling of a joke in a social robot. We have a prepared joke, it can be annotated with instructions about intonation, speech rate and pauses, and

annotations can also instruct the robot to perform the gestures and facial expressions that are needed to deliver the joke in a human-like way. Obviously, we can have research that attempts to generate these instructions automatically from a joke text. In that case we have some simulated understanding of the joke and how it should be presented by a robot or a virtual agent. This does not require all the artificial intelligence and multi-sensory perception mentioned in the preceding approach. Annotating text with instructions how to turn it into verbal and nonverbal behavior of artificial agents (virtual embodied agents, robotic agents) is the research area of intelligent virtual agents and affective computing. Results of these areas are now slowly becoming part of social robotic research. Of course, the physical embodiment of social robots introduces lots of other interesting research questions. From the point of humor we can mention that there is limited research on verbal and nonverbal performance of joke telling. In addition there is research on different ways of laughing in nonverbal speech research and how to implement them in virtual agents.

- There is also ongoing research on whether people prefer a robot that makes humorous remarks during social or task-oriented interaction above a robot that performs its task without using task-oriented or general humor. How and when should a robotic receptionist use humor in its interactions with visitors? In this research it is often the case that humans are asked to interact with a virtual representation of a robot, rather than have real interaction with the robot that includes humor in interaction. There are findings that tell us (often in Wizard of Oz interactions) that robots that seem to display a sense of humor are more appreciated and are considered to be more human-like than robots that do not use humor in their interaction with their partners. However, the experiments that lead to such a conclusion mainly concern the use of humor in some task-oriented applications rather than daily conversations we can have with colleagues, friends or family members.

- Less research is available on when and why a robot would like to perform a physical funny act or engage in physical humorous activity that also involves human partners. This is different from research on verbal and nonverbal behavior where we expect to communicate with a robot to have a social conversation, to have it perform a particular task in which we are interested, or ask for some support and collaboration that require physical tasks. Can we use AI to make our robots design pranks or involve them in performing (digital) pranks?

- Finally we should mention unintentional humor. There is humor when people make errors, don't understand technology or are absent-minded. Social robots can fail in what they are supposed to do either by shortcomings in their algorithms or by bugs. Both can have serious consequences, but it is also the case that due to shortcomings, bugs, and non-anticipated human use of such digital technology humorous situations will occur. There is intentional humor evoking smiles and laughter when we tell a joke or make a witty remark. In daily life there are many more reasons to smile and laugh, and, of course, these reasons should become topic of research.

2.3 Human-Robot Joke Telling and Conversation

We can have a look at how in research on human-robot interaction how these above mentioned issues are addressed. In the following paragraphs we survey the existing literature.

In order to investigate the effect of the use of humor in human-robot interaction it is often the case that this is done without using a real, physical robot. Online surveys or Wizard of Oz experiments are more usual. Also, the experiments are usually based on the effect that is obtained when a robot tells a joke. Hence, the investigations are usually about the use of humor by a robot in a human-robot conversation. How does the use of humor support the conversation? Does it increase or interaction enjoyment, our appreciation of how the robot performs its task? Does it enhance sociality? Moreover, is there a difference in humor appreciation when the humor is presented by a human or robot and is that also dependent on the humor style or type of joke?

The questions that we ask here are relevant both for humans interacting with physical robots and humans interacting with virtual agents in general and animated virtual agents in particular. Humor that is presented using speech requires humor-related nonverbal speech features (prosody, timing) or laughter, further embodiment requires the adding of nonverbal and humor-related interaction features such as facial expressions, gestures and whole body movements. Nowadays we have control languages and not yet fully developed models that can be used to generate appropriate nonverbal speech, nonverbal expressions and bodily movements. Implementing such features in animated virtual agents is a more doable task than it is for physical robots. Further development to physical robots also requires that other features need to be taking into account. For example, movements from body, limbs and head, three-dimensional physical appearance, proximity, and physical contact, as far as they related to delivering humorous content or receiving humorous content. Obviously, apart from the questions mentioned above we can have a focus on research dealing with the modelling and implementing the issues that are related to make the steps from text to speech, from speech to virtual and animated embodiment, and from virtual embodiment to physical embodiment. This will not be done here.

Classification of responses to a joking robot where humor was elicited through canned jokes and conversational humor appears in [8, 9]. The possible enhancement of sociality in robots using different kinds of humor (wit, dry humor, corny jokes, self-depreciation) has been the topic of the experiments reported in [10]. Whether likability depends on the humor style is also investigated in [11]. They distinguish between the effect of Schadenfreude humor versus self-irony humor, where in their investigations they have two robots where one laughs at another robot (Schadenfreude), or where a robot laughs at itself (self-irony). In [12] we have also a situation where more than one robot is involved in a humor experiment. Here the main aim is to see whether jokes are more funny when they are presented by a robot rather than presented as text. But to make it more interesting, what differences in joke rating funniness will appear when one robot tells a joke and there is one more robot present that responses with either laughter or booing? While in [12] we have a question about a possible difference between joke delivery by text or robot, in [13] there is investigation whether there is difference in appreciation when a joke is delivered by a human or robot. In [14] types of jokes (disparaging or non-disparaging) are part of these investigations in appreciation of humor in human-robot interaction. Detailed investigations on user perception of task enjoyment through different combinations of voice pitch and language cues (humor and empathy) can be found in [15].

2.4 Nonverbal and Physical Humor for Robots

Although there is a lot of research on modelling of nonverbal interaction behavior of humans and also of that of animated virtual agents (see for example the proceedings of the yearly Intelligent Virtual Agents conferences), similar efforts, making use of research in these two areas, cannot yet be found in human-robot interaction, let alone modelling intended humor in humorous human-robot interaction. A humanoid robot needs, among many other things, a model that allows it to understand human nonverbal behavior and a model that allows it to generate appropriate nonverbal behavior. An overview of verbal and nonverbal aspects of human-robot interaction is presented on [16]. Most humor research focuses on textual humor (written jokes, wordplay, wit as it appears in anecdotes, humor in longer texts), so it is no surprise to see few papers published on nonverbal aspects of humor delivery. Some observations on joke performance are discussed in [17], but they rather focus on whether humor theories should take into account the role of the performance.

Another example is [18], but here the focus is on timing of joke telling (discussing pauses and speech rate only) and the conclusion is that there is no convincing theory of timing available. Automatic selection of gestures that are appropriate to use when telling a joke or a short story is discussed in [19]. Exploring different verbal and nonverbal behaviors and study the effect on the perception of funniness is discussed in [20]. In human-human interaction entrainment (synchrony) occurs between conversational partners. This entrainment shows in the face (expressions, gaze), gestures and other bodily expressions. Mimicry is an example of this entrainment [21]. This behavioral entrainment also occurs between the teller and the responder to a joke [22]. If a robot is listening to a joke it should act in synchrony with the human joke teller. If the robot is delivering a joke, it should be aware of distortions in this entrainment and treat them as signals that the responder is not understanding the joke narrative or not interested in it, and then adapt to that situation.

Laughter has received more attention than nonverbal physical behavior. Obviously, here we don't mean the interest of philosophers investigating the sources and the functions of laughter, rather we look at research that aims at recognizing different kinds of laughter and also the artificial production of laughter. Humanoid robots need to distinguish between different kinds of laughter (laugh classification) and need to be able to produce different kinds of laughter [23]. Detection and recognition of laughter in the context of human-robot interaction is reported in [24]. Perceived naturalness of laughter in humanoid robots is discussed in [25]. Clearly, a laughing robot should also express its laughing with changes in facial expressions, head and body movements.

When a humanoid robot can move around and can perform various tasks or acts it can become part of humorous events or be active in creating humorous events in physical space. An entertainment robot that moves around or robots that guide visitors in a museum environment or travelers in an airport can detect or comment on changes in the environment in a humorous way. Observations on the kind of global responses an entertainment robot draws in a public environment can be found in [26]. In [27] experiments with a serving robot, delivering objects to its owner, are reported. It can move around, it has whole body movements and in the experiment tasks are performed in a straightforward or humorous way. Questions that are addressed are about the effect of humor in the perceived interaction quality and in the evaluation of some other humor-related characteristics of the robot.

2.5   Unintentionally Performed Humorous Acts by Physical Robots

Robots do not have to be designed to be humorous in order to make people laugh. There are YouTube compilations of robot failures that should be considered humorous. They include robots that fall while they climbing stairs, or a robot dog that slips on a banana skin. And unlike the BBC aired Robot Wars (a robot combat competition) and the high-tech RoboCup for autonomous robotic footballers, there are also contests for idiotic and crappy robots. These contests have some rules but, for example in the 'Bacarobo' comedy contest, the most important thing is that their stupidity should make the audience and the judges laugh. In [28] it is mentioned that the robots, the contestants, the announcer, the judges and the audience together create a 'clown's theatre'. This Bacarobo contest started in 2007 and 2008 in Tokyo, but later it was organized in other countries too. The same happened with the 'Hebocon' contest for dummy robots in which the robots have to follow some Sumo rules. The most stupid robot wins a prize. Robots that will be laughed at because of their imperfect (and too robotic) behavior have also been designed by Simone Giertz[2]. These robots are not humanoid and although their behavior evokes laughter they cannot be compared with human stand-up comedians.

3   Robots in Comedy

Robots have been welcomed as 'actors' in movies. It is interesting to look at robots displaying humorous behavior in movies. This is not the topic of this paper. In stage plays we can also see a development from just clumsy robots moving in a mechanical way and having no sense of humor, to robots that become intelligent and have a sense of humor. The latter is often seen as a distinguishing distinction between humans and robots. In Čapek's play we had, as was the case in early movies, human actors impersonating robots. Robots (or androids) also appear in plays of the English playwright and director Alan Ayckbourn. An extremely clumsy automatic child-minder called NAN 300F and played by actresses appears in his comedy 'Henceforward' (1987). Robots from that NAN series had some teething problems such as putting a baby in a microwave oven, not realizing that the kitchen had been changed by the mother. In Ayckbourn's comedy 'Comic Potential' (1998) robot JC-F31-triple 3, also known as "Jacie

---

[2]   https://en.wikipedia.org/wiki/Simone_Giertz.

Triplethree" has a sense of humor and through its exposure to human behavior learns about emotions. In later years we see real robots appearing on stage, but their behavior is pre-programmed or tele-operated.

In virtual and physical worlds we can look at developments that allow going from fully hand-crafted scripted animation of agent behavior and interaction capabilities to animation that is based on the availability of models that describe non-verbal speech, facial expressions, body language and eye gaze behavior and use such models to generate appropriate behavior without detailed instructions from a script. Although such models are being developed in human-computer interaction research they are not yet used to fill in details of nonverbal behavior of robots automatically. In robot theatre acts and interactions between actors are scripted and usually a robot actor is remotely controlled. In robot theatre we can make a distinction between theatre where there is no or hardly need for the actors to be aware of the audience and theatre were the authors need to be aware of the audience responses. This latter is of course the case when there is explicit interaction with the audience (interactive theatre) or where the actors adapt their timing, their nonverbal behavior, or even their choice of next actions to the audience response.

We mention a few robotic theater projects that illustrate these points. It/I is an inter-active pantomime play [29] for a human actor and a computer-controlled computer-graphics actor projected on a stage screen. The human actor is tracked by cameras and this information helps in synchronizing the joint activity in the performance. The play was performed six times for a total audience of about 500 people. Cynthia Breazael [30] exhibited an interactive theater installation at the 2002 SIGGRAPH Emerging Tech-nologies Exhibit in San Antonio. implemented an interactive installation with a terrarium as stage. Hence, the main performer was not a humanoid robot but an anemone that, using the installation's computer vision, was aware of audience activity and changed its behavior accordingly, for example, becoming afraid when someone came too close to the terrarium. Breazael's observations were more general: "In the future; we may see more elaborate versions of interactive robot theatre in theme parks, museums, and store-front windows. Someday, there may even be fanciful robotic characters on Broadway performing with human actors on an intelligent stage." A step in this direction can be found in [31]. Here the stage has already three interactive robots. The narrator has a latex face that allows the display of facial expressions, the other actors have wooden mask faces. They perform a traditional Korean Hahoe play. There is computer vision, speech synthesis and recognition that allows the audience to interact in a chatbot-like way with the actors. In [32] we find a stage performance with two human actors and a robotic desk lamp. The lamp has pre-programmed gestures and sequences that are trig-gered by a human operator and, together with 'eye gaze' movements, adapted to the timing of the human performers.

The Robot Theater Project, a collaborative research project of Oriza Hirata and Hiroshi Ishiguro, started in 2008 and is ongoing. In this project robots are used as actors in theat-rical performances, among them a version of Anton Chekhov's "Three Sisters", where Irina (Ikumi), the youngest sister turns out to be an android. Irina's role is played by a tele-operated Robovie robot, operated by engineers from backstage. Ishiguro's robot Gemi-noid F became actress in a short play, titled "Sayônara" in 2010. In 2015 she appeared in a feature film with the same title. The Robot Theater Project is discussed in [33]. This reference also includes a detailed discussion on the issues that play a role when aiming at natural and believable human-robot interaction and in particular interaction between a robot actor and human actors on stage as perceived by an audience. This discussion includes observations on scripted dialogues, synchrony, movements and gaze, anthropomorphism, appearance and the 'uncanny valley'.

Plays including robot actors have also been performed in the Robotic Theater of the Copernicus Science Centre in Warsaw. One of the plays, "Prince Ferrix and Princess Crystal" (see Fig. 1) had a scenario based on one of the stories in "Tales of the Robots", a book by Polish author Stanislaw Lem. Plays were performed using the programmable RoboThespian humanoid robots. A RoboThespian robot makes gestures, has facial expressions and a speech engine. It has computer vision to analyze the audience and individual faces, and it can receive audio information from various microphones.

Fig. 1. RoboThespian Actors. Photo by A. Kozak, Copernicus Science Center

As mentioned earlier, there are applications where a robot actor or a remote controller 'just' has to follow a script in order to have humorous content delivered in an appropriate way. But who is responsible for the humorous content? Most humor research is concerned with the analysis of jokes. There is some research on the automatic creation of puns. There is only very preliminary research on the automatic creation of humorous events. Such research could lead to automatic or computer-assisted creation of humorous content in a comic script or the spontaneous creation of humor in a particular situation. For completeness we want to mention some research that can illustrate this point of view.

Planning comic events in which virtual characters are involved has been topic of research in various papers. Can we automatically create cartoons [34, 35], humorous storytelling [36], or Mr. Bean like sketches [37, 38]? Stand-up comedy can be considered as a limited form of comic theatre. This research can help in designing events during stand-up comedy where props, sidekicks and audience play an important role. Admittedly, there is a long way to go from a computer assisting in the human, manual, creation of a script for a stand-up comedy performance to the spontaneous and real-time creation of humorous events. In virtual or digitally enhanced real world environments virtual, robotic and 'real' humans have to cooperate in order to create humorous events. This cooperation can be fully controlled by the script of the desired performance or it can allow non-scripted spontaneous humorous interactions when the artificial actors (whether they are virtual or physical) have an algorithmic sense of humor. Scripts that guide virtual agents in comic activities can as well be used to guide robotic agents or a mix of virtual, robotic, and human agents.

Comedy can be designed both for virtual characters and physical robots. The underlying models for their comic behavior can be the same, but it is more easy to implement humorous nonverbal behavior and acts in a virtual web-based world than in a physical robot-inhabited real world. In addition to humorous behavior and acts in virtual and physical worlds we can have an augmented reality point of view where real-world events are augmented with virtual information and events that make them humorous. This can take the form of simple textual comments or even a virtual character that is introduced to play a role in the event. No examples of this research point of view are available yet.

4   Robots as Stand-Up Comedians

We already mentioned silent comic movie and stage play actors who display robot-like behavior or act as robots, humorous from a Bergsonian point of view. There are also stand-up comedians who have imitated robots in their voice and their movements and sometimes in their simulated failures to act human-like. Among the robot imitators we have Mike Michaels[3] as Mr. Zed the 'Human Robot', David Kirk Taylor[4] as the 'Mechanical Magician, both from the nineteen nineties, and Alex Muhangi[5] as the 'Robot Stand-up Comedian'. But now, rather than having human stand-up comedians impersonate robots we can look at robots impersonating human stand-up comedians. We cannot yet expect to experience a robot-equivalent of Lenny Bruce or Eddie Murphy. But some research that goes into the direction of replacing them with artificial stand-up comedians is done.

In the first subsection we will look at investigations into comic duos on stage, where one or both comedians are played by robots or virtual agents. This is more an area where we can expect that the performers need to be aware of the audience responses to their acts. In the second subsection we survey some of the research projects that aim at developing humanoid robots as stand-up comedians and adapt their performance to audience responses.

4.1   Comic Stand-Up Duo Performances

Comic dialogues are performed as stage acts, in circuses between the whiteface and auguste clowns and in movies, e.g. the famous 'Who's On First' skit by Abbott and Costello. Manzai is a popular form of comic dialogue in Japan. It has a long tradition in Japan, but it is also a form of comic dialogue that appears in other cultures as well and we can find it wherever a comic duo performs, whether it is in a circus, on stage, or a in movie. It is also called the 'Double Act', or the 'Straight and Wise Man' act. Usually the characters have opposite personalities in order to make the duo more comical. Similar

---

[3] https://www.youtube.com/watch?v=-pxFyiWwZTE.

[4] https://www.youtube.com/watch?v=H0FBGrtAicY.

[5] https://www.youtube.com/watch?v=oMsveYEEUEQ.

'Straight and Wise Man' acts can be performed by a ventriloquist and his puppet, a human comedian and a robot (or virtual agent), or by two robots.

In Japan the two comical characters play the roles of Boke, usually the more extrovert person who expresses superficial opinions about his experiences, and Tsukkomi who usually has disdainful comments on Boke's stories and behavior, and sometimes hits him on the head to correct him. In addition to nonverbal speech behavior (timing, utterance speed, and intonation) there are issues of appropriate nonverbal behavior (gestures, facial expressions, body movements), coordination and personality characteristics that need to be addressed. In [39] an interactive comedy system is introduced where the human plays the role of the Boke and the system the role of Tsukkomi. In this case the system uses speech and emotion recognition (the latter from speech) and speech output and facial animation of a virtual Tsukkomi is generated. Output phrases are selected from a database.

Since then other Manzai duos have been introduced, where usually we have the Boke and the Tsukkomi represented as physical human-like robots and users as by-standers or audience [40]. Hence, rather than give the humans an interactive role, the display of the robots' conversations should be considered as a passive social medium, comparable to watching television. In [40] two humanoid "Robovie" robots took the roles of Manzai comedians. Robots were provided with script written in a scripting language designed for this purpose. Interesting also is the work presented in [41], based on results presented in many of their previous papers, where dialogue scripts for Boke and Tsukkomi (see Fig. 2) are automatically generated from web news. Keywords suggested by the audience let's the system retrieve a news article from the web which is then transformed into a Manzai scenario consisting of humorous dialogues and misunderstandings and performed in real time.

Fig. 2. Two Manzai robots (Reprinted by permission from Springer Nature [41])

"Kobian" is a life-sized humanoid robot with an expressional face and gestures. It can detect and recognize laughter using microphones for recording sound and computer vision for detecting laughter movements [24]. Laughter elicitation is done by providing Kobian with skits based on Manzai comedy techniques, such as funny behavior (e.g., exaggeration), funny context (e.g. do unexpected things), and funny character (e.g., imitation and self-deprecating humor) [42]. The research is meant for application in nursing environments for mood improvement.

The Yoshimoto Robotics Laboratory has as motto "Making Robots To Make You Smile." They have various entertainment and healthcare applications for the humanoid Pepper robot, among them human-robot comic dialogue, where the human is the 'straight man'. Pepper's voice, timing and movements are controlled behind the stage. The humor focuses on Pepper's own robotic characteristics and capabilities.[6]

4.2   Humanoid Robots as Stand-Up Comedians

There are not that many examples where humanoid robots act as stand-alone stand-up comedians. In a Manzai context they can have a robotic or human partner and especially with a human partner, whether in a Manzai context or a context where the robot is a sidekick of a human comedian, imperfections in a robot's behavior can be made part of the act. A script that tells the robot where, when, and what to do does not exclude the possibility that there is adaptation to an audience's response or that there is explicit interaction with the audience, although it may be in an Eliza-like way.

Stand-up comedy is about fun. We first look at a fun application where digital technology is used to capture the nonverbal behavior of stand-up comedians and translate it to similar behavior of an avatar (embodied virtual agent) impersonating the comedian. In this 2011 Kinect Comedy Fest the Kinect device was used to capture the movements of performing stand-up comedians and translate them into those of their virtual representation. In this case there was not really a scientific aim. Nevertheless, an approach where comedians' nonverbal behavior are captured allow the analysis of such behavior and the results are useful when generating such nonverbal behavior on an avatar (embodied virtual agent).

There are not that many examples of robots that act as stand-up comedians. In the previous sections we met robots that have been programmed to tell a joke, displaying appropriate scripted nonverbal behavior, but also attempts to generate such behavior from a joke or short story text. In research on Manzai simulations with two robot performers the audience watches the performance just as it watches TV. On stage, serving an audience, it is more natural to have at least one human performer interacting with a robotic performer. One of the Manzai partners can be robotic, a robot can play the role of a sidekick, a human performer can play the role of a puppeteer. These human-robot interactions certainly assume the presence of an audience and performers, including the robotic performer, being aware of the audience and the audience responses to the humorous interactions on stage.

In the previous section we already mentioned some research projects where audience responses have impact on the interaction behavior of human and robotic conversational partners on stage. Although presented as a robotic stand-up comedian by Heather Knight [43, 44], her robot companion is a sidekick that needs her scripted guidance to initiate a scripted witty remark or to tell a joke. However, her Nao robot does some audience tracking. The Nao robot has access to a database of pre-scripted jokes. The jokes have attributes, have they been used before, what interaction do they allow, are they appropriate, et cetera. These attributes make up an audience model that shows the audience's

---

[6] https://asia.nikkei.com/Business/Trends/Pepper-gives-comedy-a-mechanical-twist.

appreciation of these features, using this appreciation in order to choose a next joke to tell, and updating this model with the audience's appreciation of this next joke. Audience's appreciation was measured using audio (amount, intensity, and length of laughter and applause) and vision. Audience members could show their approval or disapproval by raising red (not funny) or green (funny) feedback cards during the performance.

A more 'natural' robotic stand-up comedian was introduced in the Robot Comedy Lab [45, 46]. The RoboThespian robot comedian performed during two evenings for a live audience (see Fig. 3). Its performance was preceded by the performance of two human comedians. The robot's gestural and gaze behavior was based on observations of stand-up performances of two professional comedians. Four performative gestures were introduced: a "Welcome" gesture, a reprise gesture, a pointing gesture and a applause elicitation gesture. The robot received input from microphones and an audience tracking system. The latter allowed the robot to track individual faces and to focus on individual audience members. Moreover, the vision system used facial expression recognition for identifying the "Happy", "Sad", "Angry", and "Surprised" emotions. Audio-visual recordings allowed the study of the effect of the robot's gaze behavior and its performative gestures on the audience responses.

Fig. 3. A robotic stand-up comedian [45] (Photo by Toby Harris)

5   Conclusions

In this paper we surveyed research attempts to have humanoid robots perform as stand-up comedians. We mentioned, sometimes implicitly, research challenges. On the one hand we can ask that the robot comedian fully simulates the behavior and funniness of a human stand-up comedian. On the other hand, human stand-up comedians have different styles and why shouldn't be there a style appreciated by a human audience that should be called a robotic style of stand-up comedy?

Robots can perform in movies, TV series, or on-stage plays with human and other robot actors. In our examples in this paper we have scripted dialogues that allow adapting to particular audience responses or planned interactions. A few times we mentioned that results of humor research should make it possible to reduce human efforts in translating a comic script into a robot behaviour script or even to design a comic script. It has been mentioned that humor is 'AI-complete'. This is a notion from complexity theory and theoretical computer science, meaning that when we have models (and associated algorithms) for humor understanding and generation, this is only possible when we have such models and algorithms that allow a computer to behave like a human being. In the various subsections of Sect. 2 we have made clear what the problems are that need to be addressed in order to have a computer or robot or virtual agent or smart environment to be able to process humor. In Sect. 3 we looked at instances of robots appearing in theatre performances. Section 4 introduced robots as stand-up comedians. Human support of stand-up comedy was also discussed. Human support varied from having a robot tele-operated by a backstage engineer, having a robot comedian's scripted behavior integrated with a human performer, and having such behavior adapted by being aware of an audience response to the displayed humor or humorous interactions.

There is more to stand-up comedy than the various aspects that have been mentioned in this paper and for which attempts have been made to model them in a comic robot-audience interaction. There are numerous books on stand-up comedy with attractive titles such as "Step by Step to...", "Zen and the Art of...", "Get Started in...", et cetera, and several theses have been written about stand-up comedy, for example [47], or more recently [48].

We certainly are far away from robots that have autonomous humorous behavior. But there are attempts to have them act in humorous ways, to have them display joke-telling behavior and to have them become aware of audience appreciation. Let's conclude with mentioning that in 2017 Disney Enterprises filed a patent application for huggable humanoid robots (Patent Number: US20170095925 A1 Soft body robot for physical interaction with humans). They can be used to replace the character actors at Disneyland. Maybe that is a start to have robots acting in real world environments and intentionally creating humorous acts in interaction with an audience.

Acknowledgements. This paper finds its origin in an "Artificial Intelligence and Comedy" meeting with stand-up comedians, comedy writers and AI and humor researchers. The meeting took place in St. Peter's College in Oxford on November 25th, 2017. I'm grateful to organizer and comedy writer Charlie Skelton for inviting me and allowing me to present.

References

1. Raskin, V.: Semantic Mechanisms of Humor. Studies in Linguistics and Philosophy. Springer Science & Business Media, New York (1984)
2. Hulstijn, J., Nijholt, A. (eds.): Computational humor: automatic interpretation and generation of verbal humor. In: Proceedings Twente Workshop on Language Technology 12 (TWLT12). University of Twente, The Netherlands (1996)
3. Stock, O., Strapparava, C., Nijholt, A. (eds.): The April fools' day workshop on computational humour. In: Proceedings Twente Workshop on Language Technology 20 (TWLT20). University of Twente, The Netherlands (2002)
4. Nijholt, A. (ed.). Computational humor 2012. In: Proceedings 3rd International Workshop on Computational Humor. CTIT Workshop Proceedings WP12-02. Centre for Telematics and Information Technology, Enschede, Netherlands (2012)

5. Čapek, K.: R.U.R. (Rossum´s Universal Robots). Kolektivní drama o vstupní komedii atřech dějstvích. 1920. eBook #13083, Project Gutenberg (2004)
6. Gruner, C.R.: The Game of Humor: A Comprehensive Theory of Why We Laugh. Transaction Publishers, New Brunswick (1997)
7. Ruch, W., Heintz, S., Platt, T., Wagner, L., Proyer, R.T.: Broadening humor: comic styles differentially tap into temperament, character, and ability. Front. Psychol. 9(6), 1–18 (2018)
8. Bechade, L., Duplessis, G.D., Devillers, L.: Empirical study of humor support in social human-robot interaction. In: Streitz, N., Markopoulos, P. (eds.) DAPI 2016. LNCS, vol. 9749, pp. 305–316. Springer, Cham (2016). https://doi.org/10.1007/978-3-319-39862-4_28
9. Bechade, L., Devillers, L.: Detection of humor appreciation from emotional and paralinguistic clues in social human-robot interaction. In: Joshi, A., Balkrishan, D.K., Dalvi, G., Winckler, M. (eds.) Adjunct Conference Proceedings Interact 2017, pp. 215–227. Industrial Design Centre, Indian Institute of Technology, Bombay (2017)
10. Kahn Jr. P.H., Ruckert, J.H., Kanda, T., Ishiguro, H., Gary, H.E., Shen, S.: No joking aside - using humor to establish sociality in HRI. In: ACM/IEEE International Conference on Human-Robot Interaction, pp. 188–189. ACM, New York (2014)
11. Mirnig, N., Stadler, S., Stollnberger, G., Giuliani, M., Tscheligi, M.: Robot humor: how self-irony and schadenfreude influence people's rating of robot likability. In: 25th IEEE International Symposium on Robot and Human Interactive Communication (RO-MAN), pp. 166–171. IEEE, New York (2016)
12. Sjöbergh, J., Araki, K.: A complete and modestly funny system for generating and performing Japanese stand-up comedy. In: Coling 2008: Companion volume – Posters and Demonstrations, pp. 111–114. ACL, Stroudsburg (2008)
13. Sjöbergh, J., Araki, K.: Robots make things funnier. In: Hattori, H., Kawamura, T., Idé, T., Yokoo, M., Murakami, Y. (eds.) JSAI 2008. LNCS (LNAI), vol. 5447, pp. 306–313. Springer, Heidelberg (2009). https://doi.org/10.1007/978-3-642-00609-8_27
14. Tay, B.T.C., Low, S.L., Ko, K.H., Park, T.: Types of humor that robots can play. Comput. Hum. Behav. 60(C), 19–28 (2016)
15. Niculescu, A., van Dijk, B., Nijholt, A.: Making social robots more attractive: the effects of voice pitch, humor and empathy. Int. J. Soc. Robot. 5(2), 171–191 (2013)
16. Mavridis, N.: A review of verbal and non-verbal human–robot interactive communication. Robot. Auton. Syst. 63(Part 1), 22–35 (2015)
17. Norrick, N.R.: A theory of humor in interaction. J. Literary Theory 3(2), 261–284 (2009)
18. Attardo, S., Pickering, L.: Timing in the performance of jokes. Humor 24(2), 233–250 (2011)
19. Hasegawa, D., Sjöbergh, J., Rzepka, R., Arak, K.: Automatically choosing appropriate gestures for jokes. In: AAAI Conference on Artificial Intelligence and Interactive Digital Entertainment, pp. 40–45. AAAI, Menlo Park (2009)
20. Mirnig, N., Stollnberger, G., Giuliani, M., Tscheligi, M.: Elements of humor: how humans perceive verbal and non-verbal aspects of humorous robot behavior. In: Proceedings of the Companion of the 2017 ACM/IEEE International Conference on Human-Robot Interaction (HRI 2017), pp. 211–212. ACM, New York (2017)
21. Sun, X., Lichtenauer, J., Valstar, M., Nijholt, A., Pantic, M.: A multimodal database for mimicry analysis. In: D'Mello, S., Graesser, A., Schuller, B., Martin, J.-C. (eds.) ACII 2011. LNCS, vol. 6974, pp. 367–376. Springer, Heidelberg (2011). https://doi.org/10.1007/978-3-642-24600-5_40
22. Schmidt, R.C., Nie, L., Franco, A., Richardson, M.J.: Bodily synchronization underlying joke telling. Front. Hum. Neurosci. 8(63), 1–13 (2014)

23. Truong, K., Heylen, D., Trouvain, J., Campbell, N. (eds.): Proceedings of the 4th Interdisciplinary Workshop on Laughter and other Non-verbal Vocalisations in Speech. University of Twente, Enschede, The Netherlands (2015)
24. Cosentino, S., Kishi, T., Zecca, M., Sessa, S., Bartolomeo, L., Hashimoto, K., Nozawa, T., Takanishi, A.: Human-humanoid robot social interaction: laughter. In: IEEE International Conference on Robotics and Biomimetics (ROBIO), pp. 1396–1401. IEEE, New York (2013)
25. Becker-Asano, C., Kanda, T., Ishi, C., Ishiguro, H.: Studying laughter combined with two humanoid robots. AI Soc **26**(3), 291–300 (2010)
26. Aaltonen, I., Arvola, A., Heikkilä, P., Lammi, H.: Hello pepper, may i tickle you? Children's and adults' responses to an entertainment robot at a shopping mall. In: Proceedings of the Companion of the 2017 ACM/IEEE International Conference on Human-Robot Interaction (HRI 2017), pp. 53–54. ACM, New York (2017)
27. Wendt, C.S., Berg, G.: Nonverbal humor as a new dimension of HRI. In: Proceedings 18th IEEE International Symposium on Robot and Human Interactive Communication, pp. 183–188. IEEE, New York (2009)
28. Sone, Y.: Double acts: human-robot performance in Japan's Bacarobo theatre. In: Emeljanow, V., Arrighi, G. (eds.) A World of Popular Entertainments, pp. 40–51. Cambridge Scholars Publishing, Newcastle upon Tyne (2012)
29. Pinhanez, C.S., Bobick, A.F.: It/I: an experiment towards interactive theatrical performances. In: CHI 1998 Conference Summary on Human Factors in Computing Systems (CHI 1998), pp. 333–334. ACM, New York (1998)
30. Breazeal, C. Interactive robot theatre. In: Proceedings. IEEE/RSJ International Conference on Intelligent Robots and Systems (IROS 2003). IEEE, New York (2003)
31. Perkowski, M., Sasao, T., Kim, J.-H., Lukac, M., Allen, J., Gebauer, S.: Hahoe KAIST robot theatre: learning rules of interactive robot behavior as a multiple-valued logic synthesis problem. In: Proceedings of the 35th International Symposium on Multiple-Valued Logic (ISMVL 2005), pp. 236–248. IEEE, New York (2005)
32. Hoffman, G., Kubat, R., Breazeal, C.: A Hybrid Control System for Puppeteering a Live Robotic Stage Actor. In: Proceedings of the 17th IEEE International Symposium on Robot and Human Interactive Communication, pp. 354–359. IEEE, New York (2008)
33. Bono, M., Maiolino, P., Lefebvre, A., Mastrogiovanni, F., Ishiguro, H.: Challenges for robots acting on a stage. In: Nakatsu, R., Rauterberg, M., Ciancarini, P. (eds.) Handbook of Digital Games and Entertainment Technologies. LNCS, pp. 935–977. Springer, Singapore (2017). https://doi.org/10.1007/978-981-4560-50-4_62
34. Cavazza, M., Charles, F., Mead, S.J.: Planning characters' behaviour in interactive storytelling. planning characters' behaviour in interactive storytelling. Comput. Anim. Virtual Worlds **13**(2), 121–131 (2002)
35. Cavazza, M., Charles, F., Mead, S.J.: Intelligent virtual actors that plan … to fail. In: Butz, A., Krüger, A., Olivier, P. (eds.) SG 2003. LNCS, vol. 2733, pp. 151–161. Springer, Heidelberg (2003). https://doi.org/10.1007/3-540-37620-8_15
36. Carvalho, A., Brisson, A., Paiva, A.: Laugh to me! implementing emotional escalation on autonomous agents for creating a comic sketch. In: Oyarzun, D., Peinado, F., Young, R.M., Elizalde, A., Méndez, G. (eds.) ICIDS 2012. LNCS, vol. 7648, pp. 162–173. Springer, Heidelberg (2012). https://doi.org/10.1007/978-3-642-34851-8_16
37. Thawonmas, R., Tanaka, K., Hassaku, H.: Extended hierarchical task network planning for interactive comedy. In: Lee, J., Barley, M. (eds.) PRIMA 2003. LNCS (LNAI), vol. 2891, pp. 205–213. Springer, Heidelberg (2003). https://doi.org/10.1007/978-3-540-39896-7_18

38. Thawonmas, R., Hassaku, H., Tanaka, K.: Mimicry: another approach for interactive comedy. In: 4th annual European GAME-ON Conference (GAME-ON 2003) on Simulation and AI in Computer Games, London, UK, pp. 47–52 (2003)

39. Tosa, N., Nakatsu, R.: Interactive comedy: laughter as the next intelligence system. In: International Symposium on Micromechatronics and Human Science, pp. 135–138. IEEE Press, New York (2002)

40. Hayashi, K., Kanda, T., Miyashita, T., Hagita, N.: Robot Manzai - robots conversation as a passive social medium. In: 5th IEEE-RAS International Conference on Humanoid Robots, pp. 456–462. IEEE Press, New York (2005)

41. Umetani, T., Nadamoto, A., Kitamura, T.: Manzai robots: entertainment robots as passive media based on autocreated Manzai scripts from web news articles. In: Nakatsu, R., Rauterberg, M., Ciancarini, P. (eds.) Handbook of Digital Games and Entertainment Technologies. LNCS (LNAI), pp. 1041–1068. Springer, Singapore (2017). https://doi.org/10.1007/978-981-4560-50-4_61

42. Kishi, T., Endo, N., Nozawa, T., Otani, T., Cosentino, S., Zecca, M., Hashimoto, K., Takanish, A.: Bipedal humanoid robot that makes humans laugh with use of the method of comedy and affects their psychological state actively. In: 2014 IEEE International Conference on Robotics & Automation, pp. 1965–1970. IEEE, New York (2014)

43. Knight, H.: A savvy robot standup comic: online learning through audience tracking. In: Workshop paper. ACM TEI (2010)

44. Knight, H.: Eight lessons learned about nonverbal interactions through robot theater. In: Mutlu, B., Bartneck, C., Ham, J., Evers, V., Kanda, T. (eds.) Third International Conference International Conference on Social Robotics (ICSR 2011). LNCS, vol. 7072, pp. 42–51. Springer, Cham (2011)

45. Katevas, K., Healey, P.G.T., Harris, M.T.: Robot comedy lab: experimenting with the social dynamics of live performance. Front. Psychol. **6**, 1253 (2015)

46. Katevas, K., Healey, P., Harris, M.: Robot stand-up: engineering a comic performance. In: Proceedings 2014 IEEE-RAS International Conference on Humanoid Robots (Humanoids 2014), Madrid, Spain, pp. 1–3 (2014)

47. Rutter, J.: Stand-up as Interaction: performance and audience in comedy venues. Ph.D. thesis, University of Salford (1997)

48. Říčný, B.: A Look behind the Curtains of Stand-Up Comedy: Psychology in Stand-Up Comedy. University of Olomouc, Olomouc (2014)

Study on the Digital Expansion
of Chinese Static Works of Art

Jin Sheng[✉] and Ziqiao Wang[✉]

School of Media Arts and Communication of Nanjing University of the Arts,
Nanjing, China
nysmsj@163.com, 549950413@qq.com

Abstract. The development of digital technology broadens the expression space for the recreation of static works of art, and blurs the boundary between static art and dynamic art. The recreation of static works of art from the perspectives of form, content and spirit of digital expansion is also an international research topic today. As one of the four ancient civilizations in the world, China boasts a splendid cultural history, together with various graceful static works of art that have been handed down, most of which are collected by major museums. In this regard, it is necessary to bring vitality and vigor to the static works of art in a bid to meet the development of times. From the perspective of digital art, this paper adopts digital techniques to carry out extension research on different static works of art respectively, and finally transforms the theoretical research into concrete social practice achievements with the aim of making a contribution to the succession, protection and development of static works of art in different regions.

Keywords: Static art · Digitization · Secondary creation · Expansions

1 Introduction

With the rapid development of the digital media industry in China, the concept of consumers has started to shift from a passive media recipient to a participant who actively employs various media tools. A large number of consumers use the platform under the digital media industry for consumption and entertainment. The use of media tools has become part of their life. Besides, the platform effect of digital media is explosive for the brand promotion of enterprises. Enterprises can rapidly establish a huge consumer group through utilizing the network communication of the platform. With little investment and quick response, it is the best result that every enterprise seeks.

In this regard, the Human-Computer Interaction (HCI) connecting consumers and the platform system is particularly important. HCI refers to the information exchange process between people and computers though a certain kind of dialogue and interactive way to complete a certain task. Sensing method is the key to interaction. One of the most exciting technological achievements in the 21st century is the somatosensory technology that makes the visual perception of artificial intelligence a reality. Characterized by the same three-dimensional stereoscopic vision as humans, such technology can distinguish different objects and recognize different behaviors of the human body, like the human

© Springer International Publishing AG, part of Springer Nature 2018
N. Streitz and S. Konomi (Eds.): DAPI 2018, LNCS 10921, pp. 411–427, 2018.
https://doi.org/10.1007/978-3-319-91125-0_33

eyes. Also, it can observe the actions of each person and understand the meanings of each action in a constantly changing environment in real time.

The digital expansion of Chinese static works of art is accompanied by the development of the digital media technologies. When using digital media technology for artistic creation, artistic expression and artistic development, it not only introduces the digital means into the static artistic creation to present the dynamic effect; instead, it can conduct secondary creation created with various types of artistic activities and even give rise to plenty of distinctive new art forms. Hence, digital expansion has a strong creative and development space.

2 The Classification and Characteristics of Chinese Static Works of Arts

Chinese static works of art refer to plastic arts such as calligraphy, paintings, sculptures and installations. As to the classification, works of art can be divided into: Ornamental works of art and practical works of art. Here, ornamental works of art refer to those independent works for people's appreciation, such as calligraphy, paintings, sculptures and installations; the practical works of art refer to the combination of the content of works of art and the object with the use value [1]. By virtue of the artistic taste of works of art, objects boast the ornamental value and the practical value such as ceramics, furniture, lamps and etc. This paper still focuses on the ornamental works of art.

2.1 Creation Classification of Chinese Static Works of Art

Secondary Expansion and Creation of Protection and Inheritance of the Collected Works of Art. Chinese static works of art that have become collections of museums or art galleries feature a long history and a large range of circulation. A large majority of works are preserved in storehouses, especially the easily-damaged calligraphy and Chinese paintings, and seldom put for exhibition. From the point of view of protection and inheritance, it is the highlighted embodiment of the artistic value of such works. After digitally collecting this kind of works, the secondary creation will dominate.

Diverse Art Creation Showing the Themes of Chinese Traditional Culture. There is also a kind of work of art which demonstrates traditional Chinese culture through the use of diverse techniques for direct creation. On the basis of preserving the traits of traditional culture, the contemporary expression of spiritual content is realized through modern digital art techniques.

2.2 The Form Classification of Chinese Static Works of Art

From the form of works, they can be divided into four categories: calligraphy, painting, sculpture and installation. Normally, calligraphy and painting in China manifest in print media, while the sculptures and installation works can only be realized through the use of stereoscopic media. In Chinese static works of art, calligraphy, painting, sculpture, installation and other plastic arts all embody the harmonious thoughts of man and nature, man and society, and man and man.

2.3 The Characteristics of Chinese Static Works of Art

The Characteristics of Calligraphy. Calligraphy is a Chinese writing art with a long history. Such artistic expression of characters deeply influenced the neighboring countries and regions which were edified by Chinese culture. Calligraphy also refers to the writing rules of a language. To write characters according to the characteristics and meaning of words, style, technique of writing, structure and art of composition so as to make them works of art rich in aesthetic perception.

The Main Characteristics of Creation Subject. The basic elements of calligraphy are lines and lines serve as the trajectories of points. Calligraphy appears as a flowing directional and non-repetitive writing process. Also, the creative process and creative results generate simultaneously without any possibility of duplication and production.

The specific writing rules of Chinese. Provisions concerning the order and the sequence of strokes have been established, that is, the writing process should be of consistency in terms of time, which is extended by the single character to the whole article. It is necessary to pay attention to the overall coordination.

Handwritings and patterns represent the full connotation of the time attribute in calligraphy. The creation process of calligraphy is a special process in which time drives space-that is, cause of actions drives vision.

To Appreciate the Characteristics of Creation Subject. Calligraphy gives the impression of a passage of time because each character is read in a specific sentence or textual structure, that is, there is an order in which a literary concept is obtained. Second, each character forms a different form of space compositions and styles in the writing of conjunctions. Such space must produce a continuous rhythm, creating a rhythm sequence of visual relationship and time extension featuring time lapse and internal logical relationship.

Appreciation of calligraphic works makes it easier for people to trace back to their creative process than other artistic appreciation. Appreciators seek to experience the creation mentality from the resulting calligraphic works.

The Characteristics of Paintings. The painting here mainly refers to the paintings on the shelf. Paper, cloth, wood, glass, lacquer or other surfaces may be used as the carriers for paintings, which are filled with certain thought or ideas expressed by conformity, graphics, composition and other contents.

Chinese painting includes Gongbi (traditional realistic painting), Xieyi (free-sketch style painting) and the combination of these two. As to three different forms of expression, Gongbi is characterized by fine brushwork and color rendering of layers. Focusing on details, such painting uses extremely delicate brush strokes to depict objects; Xieyi depicts the shape and spirit of objects with concise, bold and splashed ink to express the painter's feelings. In terms of performance objects, Xieyi painting adopts generalization and exaggeration methods, together with rich associations. Though with simple lines, it demonstrates a far-reaching artistic conception with a certain expressive force. It boasts a high degree of generalization and a subtle conception of using the few to defeat the many. Also, with accurate lines and proficient skills, the author may precisely express his idea [1].

The fundamental difference between painting and other categories of art is the planarity of works. From the perspective of appreciation, the art of painting has the following main features:

Creating Three-Dimensional Space on Two-Dimensional Space. On the two-dimensional space, painting makes use of light and shadow, and image structure to express the concave-convex relationship and the three-dimensional illusion of objects, allowing people to visually perceiving the volume, material and space of objects. Also, it uses sizes of objects, shadowing relationship, perspective changes and color changes, genuine and sham, to create profound spatial effect.

Realistic and Reproductive Paintings and Subjective and Expressive Paintings. Realistic and reproductive painting may achieve an ultra-realistic effect, allowing people to feel the vividness of the painted objects. Although realistic and reproductive paintings have not valued by people with the emerging of Chinese Xieyi paintings and modern western paintings, the effect pictures of commercial advertisement, industrial design and architectural design still embody such characteristic of painting.

Contrary to reproductive painting, subjective and expressive painting focuses on the subjective world of self-expression. It can not only show the subjective state of mind and philosophy, but also depict fantasy and dream. Its artistic charm lies in the originality of forms, the novelty of techniques, and the intense and formal beauty of shapes.

Artistic Beauty of Different Kinds of Paintings. A variety of paintings, due to different kinds of tool materials and techniques and other factors, form their own unique characteristics. Chinese Xieyi painting uses the water absorption trait of Chinese art paper and the artistic effect of masstone and pays attention to the dynamic beauty of profound and powerful lines. It uses ink in a changeable and dense manner, creating lively spirit and charm. Oil painting stresses on the beauty of colors in a vigorous, dense, rich and harmonious manner. Prints focus on "carven aroma", "wooden aroma" and printed beauty. Watercolors focus on the artistic beauty formed by water, color and lines in a crisp, elegant and moist manner.

Composition is the Basis of Painting. Composition organizes the art language of painting, making it a perfect painting. Composition is the basis of the art of painting to express the author's idea and demonstrate the form of beauty.

The Characteristics of Sculptures. Sculpture is a plastic art which uses certain materials and methods to produce three-dimensional images. Its production methods include carving, molding, heaping, pasting, welding, knocking, composing and so on, also known as the three kinds of creation methods of carving, engraving and plastic in general. Sculpture refers to the visual and touchable artistic images created with a variety of plastic materials (such as gypsum, resin, clay, etc.) or carved, carved hard materials (such as wood, stone, metal, jade, onyx, etc.) so as to reflect the social life and to express the artist's aesthetic experience, aesthetic emotion and aesthetic ideal.

The birth and development of sculptures are closely related to the production activities of mankind. Meanwhile, they are directly affected by the social ideologies of religions and philosophies in various periods. The sculpture inheritance of the past generations has become, in a certain sense, the history of human images. The characteristics of sculpture are as follows: Static, visual and touchable three-dimensional objects reflect reality through the visual spatial images created by sculptures, which is considered to be the most typical plastic art, static art and space art. With the development of technology and the change of people's concept, three-dimensional, visual and static forms in modern art have broken through and develop into multidimensional temporal and spatial forms.

The Characteristics of Installation Art. Installation art refers to an art form in which artists artistically and effectively select, use, transform and combine the material and cultural entities that people have or have not consumed in daily life in a particular space-time environment to produce new and rich spiritual and cultural connotation of individuals or groups. Simply put, installation art, is a comprehensive display art of "venue + material + emotion" [2].

Integrity. Installation art is an integration designed and created by artists based on the interior and exterior location and space of a given exhibition site. Just as a movie theater cannot show two movies at the same time, the integrity of the installation requires a corresponding independent space and could not be interrupted by other works in both visual, auditory and other aspects.

Participation. Involvement and participation of the audience is an integral part of installation art. Installation art is an extension of people's life experience. The environment created by installation art is to tolerate, urge or even force them from passive perceptions to active perceptions in a defined space. Such perceptions require audiences to use all their senses in addition to positive thinking and physical involvement: vision, hearing, touch, smell, and even taste.

Openness. Free from the limitations of artistic class, installation art may freely integrate any means such as painting, sculpture, architecture, music, drama, poetry, prose, film, television, sound recording, video recording and photography. It can be said to be an open art.

Variability. Installation art is a variable art. Artists can change the combination during the exhibition, increase, decrease or recombine during the exhibition at other places.

3 New Thoughts of Digital Creation of Chinese Static Works of Art

3.1 Existing Problems and Solutions to Chinese Static Works of Art

Intensified Homogenization Trend of Content and Form. A large majority of collected static works of art are merely used for display, and the promoting digital printing is gradually becoming homogeneous. As people's attention focus on the promotion and dissemination instead of recreation of works, these popular contents and forms are only intended to increase part of the economic value. They fail to realize the artistic value of the original works. In this regard, it is necessary for them to clarify the characteristics of each work of art and give full play to the unique charm of the secondary creation. Also, attention should be paid to innovation based on the existing formal contents.

Single Creative Approach Lacking of Spirit of the Times. In creating the themes of traditional Chinese culture, multiple creative approaches are relatively old-fashioned, and the single creation approach still remains the same like that in the last century. Although it features strong modeling ability and skillful techniques, its outdated concepts cannot adapt to the development of the times. Hence, in the process of creating works of art, on the basis of preserving the traditional cultural traits, the contemporary expression of spiritual content can only be achieved through modern digital art.

Solutions to Chinese Static Works of Art. When Chinese static works of art are combined with technology, though they seem like unrelated, it is actually the trend of artistic development. The emergence, development and application of new technologies and new forms will inevitably give rise to plenty of problems. However, new technologies and new forms cannot be rejected accordingly, which cannot measure up to the laws in the global scheme of things. We find problems in practice and should constantly solve the problems in practice. In view of the homogenization trend of the application of static works of art in domestic collections, the innovation awareness of art should be enhanced. In the early stages of the project, it will prepare sufficient materials and conduct inspection to give more practical chances to new ideas. This is the way out for the Chinese static works of art.

3.2 New Thoughts on Digital Creation of Chinese Static Works of Art

To avoid the homogenization phenomenon of the application and development of the collected static works of art, it is necessary to employ the technical means of digital media to realize innovation. Digital creation is the creation of digital work of arts that came into being in the fifth media era. Digitization mainly includes digital collection, digital interaction and digital presentation of work of arts. The digitization of static works of art breaks the limitation of time and space, and is characterized by cross-media, cross-screen, openness and mobility. As long as people enter the network system, they can participate in the creation of painting art according to their own life experiences and personal interests, and modify, supplement, and create painting works in various ways.

Thoughts of Secondary Creation of Protection and Inheritance. The collected static works of art may undergo secondary creation from the perspective of protection and inheritance. Such kind of artistic creation is conducted based on the digitization of the original works. Digital creation may be carried out through means of conversion based on the material, technique, form and content of different works of art.

Material Conversion. To select materials in the original works among the existing static works of art for digital conversion and to change the material expression of the original works. Meanwhile, the digital content also enhances the interaction and entertainment of the works (Fig. 1).

Fig. 1. *Moonlight on the Lake* of Sheng Jin, Zhang Gaojie, Zhang Peng and Zhu Chunhui

Technique Conversion. Techniques may also be converted in terms of paintings, such as Chinese painting techniques for oil painting or watercolor techniques. The conversion of these techniques is also based on digitization. The powerful digital technology can change the style and technique of its works, make unobstructed conversion among different techniques, and increase the artistic diversification of static works of art.

Form Conversion. The collected static works of art may conduct multiple forms of conversion from plane to three-dimensional, and from static to dynamic, such as painting to animated or digital images, or sculpture to dynamic sculpture. Conversion of digital forms is conducive to the promotion and dissemination of works of art on the Internet (Fig. 2).

Content Conversion. Among the Chinese static art collections, many of the works have a long history but are easily damaged. After digital collection, they can be restored and re-created, which not only protects the style of the original works, but also expands the contents, integrates the mainstream cultures of different stages, inherits and carries forward the spirit of Chinese traditional culture.

Creation Thoughts of Diverse Works of Art. From the perspective of protection and inheritance, the collection of static works of art can be created in multiple manner. Such kind of artistic creation is implemented in combination with digital technology based on the material, technology, performance and concept and different works.

Fig. 2. Experimental animation of *Kong Xiang* of Ma Chao

Material Synthesis. For works of art being created, creation can be done from the perspective of the comprehensive utilization of materials. It is not only a comprehensive manifestation of solid materials, but also an expression of idea of the works through the use of different materials in the virtual digital world.

Technology Synthesis. Technology synthesis is to employ a variety of digitized technical software and hardware tools in the creation of works of art, and takes into account the expression of the digital virtual level on the basis of the real physical level so as to achieve the dual effect of physical creation and digital creation, laying a solid foundation for future communication.

Expression Synthesis. The creation of works of art can also be realized in multiple manners in terms of artistic expression. As to expression mode, from plane to three-dimensional and from realistic to virtual; as to expression methods, from concretization to abstraction and from perceptual expression to rational decoration; as to methods of artistic expression, comprehensive use of methods of artistic expression can maximize the realization of the artistic spirit and content.

Concept Synthesis. Concept synthesis is the collision of various spirits at the level of artistic thought. It represents the core values of art and the soul of artists. It is not only the blending of Eastern and Western cultures but also the comprehensive expression of traditional concepts and contemporary experiments, popular aesthetic and elegant art.

Through the above comprehensive expression from the material level to the spiritual level, it broadens the thought of art creation and guides the creation of works of art in the future. Meanwhile, it has also established the development trend of works of art from static state to dynamic state.

4   The Digital Expansion of Chinese Static Works of Art

4.1   The Digital Expansion of Calligraphy

The Digital Simulation of the Content of Calligraphy. The traditional Chinese calligraphy is a peculiar art form in Chinese culture, and China's major museums have certain amount of the calligraphic masterpieces handed down from the past dynasties. However, they are seldom exhibited in front of us for the protection of cultural relics, which limits the popularization of the traditional culture to some degree. Nevertheless, this problem is solved by the emergence of highly simulative digital technology and the replicating method of the digital simulation. HR-scanning or photo processing takes the photos of the calligraphic works first; then image processing software corrects them and their colors; finally, the digital technology is applied to print the original effect on Chinese art paper, silk and other materials. This technology is able to not only carry on the limited circulation with the value of collection, but also popularize the traditional culture through the Internet.

The Digital Presentation of the Calligraphic Form. In calligraphic works, common forms are all written on the traditional Chinese calligraphy and painting materials before being mounted for exhibition, or sculpted on the surface of materials like wood, stone or pottery. With the continuous improvement of digital technology, artistic methods, such as digital media, animation, interaction and virtual reality have been improving, and the calligraphic works, whose immersive interaction characteristic enriches the presentation of calligraphic art, is able to be exhibited dynamically.

The so-called dynamization of calligraphic works is to apply the animation techniques into strokes, ink color, structure and meaning of the calligraphy to perform dynamically, and the artistic glamor presented by such moving process is what the traditional pattern of the 2D cannot reveal. The final presentation format can be both an image installation and a digital water curtain, and the spread of the image is the trend of the modern information society's development (Fig. 3).

Fig. 3. The exhibition of digital calligraphy

4.2 The Digital Expansion of Paintings

The Dynamic Shift of Traditional Paintings. In May, 2010, Shanghai World Expo exhibited the 100-m long *Riverside Scene at Qingming Festival*, which is a dynamic version based on the *Riverside Scene at Qingming Festival* of Zhang Zeduan in Song Dynasty. It was an exhibition that used the expressive form of animation in digital art to dynamically perform the traditional painting. The painting was 128 m in length and 6.5 m in height, and the cycle of role animation was 4 min. The effect of daytime and nighttime took 2 min each, in which 691 characters appeared in the daytime and 377 at night. Numerous roles dynamically enhanced the visual effect of the picture, which caused a sensation in the Expo and opened a new era for the digital dynamic transformation of traditional painting.

The Digital Enhancement of Modern Painting. The development of digital technology promotes the contemporary painters' idea of combing their works with such technology, which expands the creative thinking of the artists and brings in numerous new works. The painting-oriented method improves the visual motion with strengthening images, it not only breaks the limitations of graphic painting, but also extends the paintings.

The Spatial Creation of Virtual Paintings. VR painting is creating painting in the VR world by using the computer's 3D space system and a handle to position space, thus it has a strong sense of space. It allows artists to paint in a virtual world, solves the problem of perspective in 2D painting, and enables them to arbitrarily express the concept of art. Its unprecedented modifiability changes the unitary presentation in 2D painting (Fig. 4).

Fig. 4. Google's 3D painting *Tilt Brush* (Source: http://www.frontop.cn/about/302071.htm)

4.3   The Digital Expansion of Sculptures

The quiet and harmonious beauty in traditional sculpture is the audiences' primary aesthetic feeling, and the innovation of art should develop in accordance with its time. When sculptures meet digital technology, a dynamic sculpture changes people's visual experience of the traditional sculpture. The development of modern technology can make the aforesaid become real. When creating sculptures, mechanical installations and digital technology are assembled together; with images and sounds, the static sculptures can become the "living sculptures" which are dynamic and able to express the main idea.

The other one is based on the original static sculpture but using projective and sound technology to create a visual dynamic sense. With the development of HCI and the expansion of sculpture's creative language, the dynamic sculpture with creative thinking will bring new vitality and new experience of pleasure to the traditional museum (Fig. 5).

Fig. 5. The digital sculpture in museum (Source: http://fashion.163.com/16/0312/16/BHVJ7RU T00264MK3.html)

4.4 The Digital Expansion of Installation Art

Art galleries, whether at home or abroad, pay more and more attention to the exhibition of installation art. Various types of installation art employ artistic spirit to some public spaces when expressing the theme in a novel way. These works, following the innovation of digital technology, develop into multiple forms such as interactive and image installations, playing an important cultural role in public space.

The Creation of Interactive Installation Works. The creation of the interactive installation consists of two parts: innovation and technology. The former part is the thought expression of the artist's thought through the connotation and expression of the work, while the latter part is using modern electronic induction technology, mechanical transmission technology and computer digital control to achieve HCI, therefore, the key point of mastering the positioning and technical implementation of artistic creation is to master the starting point of creating an interactive installation.

In terms of conception, light and shadow, shape, voice and other forms should be taken into consideration. Technically, it is the same for light intensity and color, shadow change, continuous pictures, sound changes, distance and so on. Creative works must be able to infect the pleasures of the audiences' various sensory organs in order to achieve the creative art effects. These works are not only considered as a simple patchwork, but also requires the ability to process and exchange information; an artist's job is to stimulate the understanding and judging ability of the work itself. Hence, the way to express the works should be an artistic expression which is consistent with creativity theme and make the works achieve the interaction between the artifacts and the audiences.

The creation processes of the interactive installation: ① To propose the creating conception of the works; ② To determine the way of collecting information; ③ To determine the way of performance; ④ To draw the structure and configuration of the interactive installation of works of art; ⑤ To integrate a database and program; ⑥ To display the interactive works. Through these processes, we will achieve the interactive function of the installation art and communication and appreciation between the audiences and the works in an interactive way (Fig. 6).

Fig. 6. The installation work

The Creation of Image Installation Art. The creation of the works of the image installation work is also the work creation consisting of two parts: the installation and the image, which are combined to express certain artistic conceptions. The content of the image can be both animated and a real video shoot. These digital contents should be compromised with installation. It is not only the dynamic extension of the work, but also the organic part of the installation. The two are indispensable.

During the creation process, the first step is to determine a theme. Any public exhibiting area should have a text outline to establish the theme, in which the installation art is used to strengthen the atmosphere and effect, and it must be created according to the theme. Some installations are the architectural space structure to restore a historical period, and the content of an image is exaggerating the atmosphere of rendering the space crossing. These works, of which the content and form should be mainly realistic, appear as the protagonists of the main exhibiting area. If the installation work is just used as the decoration to increase interest, they should appear as the supporting actor in the area and their content and form should be mainly freehand.

These image installations can also increase interactive technology and becomes an interactive video installation. This kind of installation will be more common in the future (Fig. 7).

Fig. 7. The work *The Source*

5   The Digital Expansion Value of Chinese Static Works of Art

5.1   The Artistic Value of Digital Expansion

The Visual Angle of Art and Aesthetics is Widened. The digital expansion of Chinese static works of art broadens the view from the perspective of art and aesthetics. Employing digitalization in the creation of works of art not only achieves the artistic effect of the real works through modeling, colors, and materials of the art entities, but also builds a virtual world of art. Such form of combining art and reality expands our aesthetic perspective. As for the single exhibition of works of art, it can also be exhibited from various perspectives. Digital art enables the interactive communication between the works and the audiences, while the atmosphere of the virtual scene and the processing of the sound effect as if the works were telling the artistic creation process. The art of virtual reality can deconstruct the works of art from all directions and show the thinking process of the whole art creation from the ideological content to the technical realization. The virtual performance of these works of art also gives us a brand-new visual sense. Besides, from the perspective of artistic creation and aesthetics, the digital art recreation of works of art also embodies the expansion of the form and content in the largest degree. Therefore, the digital expansion of static art work unceasingly extends art aesthetics.

The Artistic Creative Thinking is Widened. The digitalization of static works of art largely helps the expansion of artistic and creative thinking; the expansion of creative thinking from the perspective of art is to break the outdated, break through mediocrity and create new ideas. With digital methods, dynamic exhibition bestows wings to artistic creative thinking, breaking the traditional of static 2D way, and seeking a common ground while reserving differences in the organic combination of multiple thinking forms. From a one-way thinking to a multidirectional stereoscopic and dynamic thinking has been the developing trend of the thinking mode of the static works of art. The multi-directional and multi-polar artistic creative thinking lay the ideological basis for the improvement of the static works of art, bringing innovative ideas for further artistic creation, therefore, the digital expansion of the static works of art broadened the field of creative thinking.

The Means of Artistic Creation are Enriched. The digital expansion of static art work has various presentations in the methods of art creation. Firstly, the shape of the work changes the definition of the original works and extends the form of the work with digitalization, transforming the invariable form into the changeable dynamic works. Secondly, in terms of vision, the controllable changes of light and special materials are used to change the color of the work's interface, and such change enables organic interaction with the audiences. The third is the digital expression of images and sounds. The various expressions of interactive images, interactive voice and interaction installations not only enrich the artistic effects of static works of art, but also give audiences a new participatory experience, thus maximizing the social efficiency. Besides, the digital expansion also provides the creation of static works of art with rich and colorful ways of expression, guaranteeing the extension of artistic creation and accelerating the economic transformation of artistic value.

5.2   The Economic Value of Digital Expansion

By thoroughly playing the unique advantages and economic value, digital expansion organically integrates static works of art with tourism, culture and other industries, promoting the development of cultural undertakings and stimulating the promotion of regional soft power and continuous economic development. It is a kind of regional economic developing model.

The economic meaning of the digital expansion of the static works of art has two aspects. On the one hand, the art economy is an economic form that is able to develop in combination with the cultural art and tourism industry; on the other hand, it is a regional economic development model promoting the economic prosperity and development of the whole region through the economic spread and proliferation of the art museum.

The Complementarity of Works of Art' Economy is Strengthened. The economy of works of art and the career of art museum are benign interaction and functional complement. The economic growth of works of art is conducive to the display of the art museums' functions. It is the trend of art development that closely combines career with industry. Generally, art museum is a unit with the nature of public welfare, and the economy has no direct relation to the main body of the art museum, however, the two are closely related and indispensable.

The Indirection of Works of Art Economy is Strengthened. The economic contribution of the art museum itself is not the main aspect, and its economy is mainly presented in its indirect economic value. Specifically, art museums can give full play to the economic and social benefits through the following two aspects. The promotion effect of art museums is an important connection in the field of art communication, and the digitalization of static works further enhances the disseminative function of the works' artistic value. The exhibition of the art museum also plays a guiding role in the sale of the derivatives of static works of art. Digital extension provides the possibility for the creation of art derivatives.

The Fusion of Works of Art is Strengthened. Art Gallery can be the soul, cohesion and bond for the development of regional art economy. Being a source and prerequisite for the economic development of the art gallery, the quality of works of art determines the direction and characteristics of the art gallery's economic development, and it gathers popularity and forms a high-quality cultural atmosphere. The economy of works of art is more reflected in the fusion of regional economy, which includes promoting the development of tourism and cultural industry, realizing the diversification and composite of industrial content, and improving regional soft power, etc.

6   Conclusion

The digital expansion of Chinese static works of art is accompanied with the development and expansion of digital media technology. When employing the digital media technology to create, present and expand artistically, it not only introduces the digital method in the creation of static art to achieve a dynamic effect, but also enables a second creation in various types of artistic activities, hoping to create distinctive new art forms and new values.

This paper, starting from the classification of Chinese static works of art, analyzes the artistic characteristics, advantages and disadvantages respectively, puts forward new ideas for the way to achieve digital art creation, and launches digital expansion from the perspectives of four typical works of calligraphy, painting, sculpture and installation, providing a method and theoretical basis for the digital expansion of the Chinese static works of art. It then expounds the value presentation of the expansion of Chinese static works of art from the perspective of value, thus opening up a new mode which has great room for improvement for the redevelopment of Chinese static works of art. It is hoped that the future development of science and technology, and the transformation of public awareness can be further improved, and thus being beneficial for the inheritance, protection and development of static works of art in other regional cultures.

References

1. Zhu, Y., Qian, C.: The Appreciation of Practical Aesthetics and Aesthetic. Chongqing University Press, Chongqing (2015). (in Chinese)
2. Yuan, Y.: A Brief Discussion on Kohei Nawa: The Art and Installation Artists of the Installation. Chinese Times, Nanjing (2015). (in Chinese)

Case Study of AR Field Museum
for Activating Local Communities

Tomohiro Tanikawa[✉], Junichi Nakano, Takuji Narumi, and Michitaka Hirose

The University of Tokyo, 7-3-1 Hongo Bunkyo-ku, Tokyo, Japan
{tani,jnakano,narumi,hirose}@springer.com

Abstract. In this research and development, we use virtual reality and Augmented Reality (AR) technology which is experiential media accompanying physicality as social value of space resources (buildings, townships, townscape) with historical and cultural values. It is aimed to communicate to the subjects inside and outside the region by using visualization and experience and further combining with the method of community design to find the possibility of active utilization.

Specifically, we will use VR/AR technology to (1) realize the system of preserving and sharing space resources of the region, (2) research of sharing and transferring historical and cultural values, (3) community activities Research on the motivation improvement method of society, society, society, and society.

Keywords: Augmented Reality · Digital museum · Mobile device
Public exhibition

1 Introduction

In Bunkyo Ward, Tokyo, where many spatial resources with historical and cultural values (buildings, towns, townscapes) are accumulated, the conservation and utilization of them is a problem. However, as its social value is unclear, there are present situations where it is lost or not fully utilized. For example, it is said that Higuchi Ichiba passed and the sento which is said to have been established in the middle of the Meiji era, due to the aging of the facilities and the physical condition of the management, was abandoned in September 2015, being missed in the area, the style of the Miya. A certain building was dismantled and rebuilt into an apartment (Figs. 1 and 2).

In this research and development, we use virtual reality and Augmented Reality (AR) technology which is experiential media accompanying physicality as social value of space resources (buildings, townships, townscape) with historical and cultural values. It is aimed to communicate to the subjects inside and outside the region by finding visualization and feasibility, further combining with the method of community design, and finding the possibility of active utilization. The AR/VR content emphasizes spatial consistency and has an effect of conveying an accurate correspondence relationship between the past space reproduced from the live-action video image and the current real space. Therefore, changes in places, buildings and exhibits by the times are easy to

© Springer International Publishing AG, part of Springer Nature 2018
N. Streitz and S. Konomi (Eds.): DAPI 2018, LNCS 10921, pp. 428–438, 2018.
https://doi.org/10.1007/978-3-319-91125-0_34

convey, visualization of the importance of the target spatial resources and visualization and transmission of the impact on the community due to loss are expected to be possible.

The authors have already carried out activities in collaboration with local construction companies, shopping districts, NPOs, local governments (Bunkyo Ward, and District Culture Resource Center), and the space resources with historical and cultural values (buildings and towns. It is expected that it will contribute to revitalizing and creating community activities and shopping street activities, utilizing the cityscape), and contributing to the development of sightseeing town planning.

In response to the above objectives, the authors conducted a study on (1) the preservation and sharing system of space resources in the region using VR/AR technology, (2) research on sharing and transferring historical and cultural values, (3) Research on improvement method of motivation of community activities, targeting three points, and conducting research and development.

In this paper, we introduce our case study of AR Field Museum for activating local communities .

2   Realization of a System for Archiving and Sharing Space Resources in the Region

In this research, in order to realize a history/cultural VR/AR experience that can be used sustainably in a general urban area, VR/AR experiences of the form that the viewer experiences using individual mobile terminals. We propose a system and carry out long-term demonstration mainly around Kikusaka neighborhood in Bunkyo Ward. Figure 3

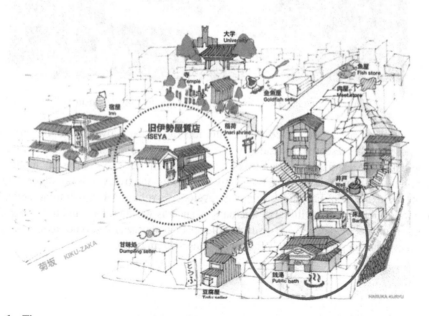

Fig. 1. There are many space resources with historical and cultural values in Bunkyo Ward, Tokyo

Fig. 2. Spatial resources are being lost one by one. "Kikusui-yu"

shows the concept of a field-trial exhibition by personal-owned mobile terminals proposed in this research. Instead of visiting the museum and borrowing the terminal to appreciate the exhibition as before, distribute the exhibition system as an application that runs on the mobile terminal owned by the viewer, and freely. It is possible to appreciate the exhibition. For this reason, we developed a robust AR registration method in outdoor public spaces with large fluctuations such as weather, date and time, targeting various unspecified age groups, sustainable space resources that do not require special markers and support staff AR/VR experiencing system to do.

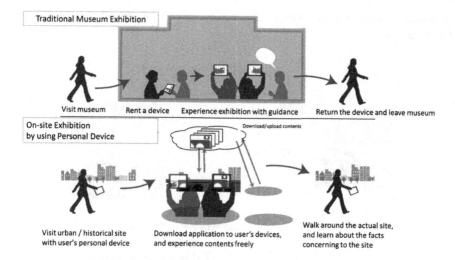

Fig. 3. The concept of AR Field Museum by using individual mobile terminals

The outline of our proposed system is as follows:

1. Users visit the exhibition location. They install the appropriate application onto their own mobile device either on-site or in advance.
2. They look for the point where a photograph of a past scene was taken by holding their mobile device toward the present scene.
3. The application compares the device camera image to the reference scene image taken in advance, and calculates the device position and orientation.
4. If the application determines that the user is standing at the correct point and facing the proper direction, it renders the whole-sky image area of the past scene generated using photographic materials.
5. By moving their devices around, users can see the past scene in the direction they are facing through the screen of the device. They can also easily compare the present scene to the past scene by changing the transparency of the device camera image.

3 Research on Sharing and Transmission Technology of Historical and Cultural Values

In this research, we also constructed a mechanism to collect and share AR/VR content by collective intelligent approach. In the area AR system "mobile cloud type remembrance window" developed for mobile terminals, we introduced a platform that allows users to participate in content creation as well as appreciation by incorporating elements of UGC (User-Generated Containment) 1). In creating AR contents, historical images such as past photos superimposed on the actual landscape are required. In order to gather historical images from many users, we created a system that can post historical images in web pages and applications, and created a system that can be shared by all users (Figs. 4 and 5). With this platform, it became feasible to realize a mechanism for enriching contents by using photos of memories owned by users and pictures with high historical value.

Fig. 4. Crowd-Cloud Window to the Past

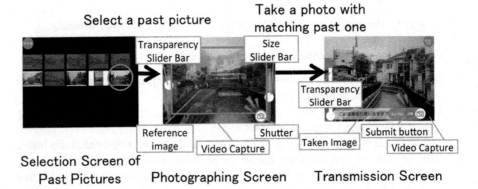

Fig. 5. Application to capture and collect current pictures at estimated photographed positions by users.

We presented a crowdsourcing system that constructs a database for AR contents by user generation and applied it in "Window to the Past," which runs on personal mobile devices. In "Window to the Past," the system designers had to prepare the contents by themselves, so there were only a limited number of contents. We overcame this problem by implementing a system in which many users can participate in creating contents by crowdsourcing. This will extend "Window to the Past" to a larger area with more data created by many users.

We proposed a crowdsourcing system in which users identify the location of the past pictures and capture the current reference pictures. This system helps users generate contents for "Window to the Past" with enjoyment. The database contains current reference pictures of the past pictures, GPS information of the locations, and annotation of the pictures. Our proposed system is realized as a smartphone and a tablet device application. Users explore the spots where old photos were captured on behalf of the designer. They only need to take photos at the correct position and angle where the semi-transparent past image matches the background, and then they can easily add a series of necessary information for "Window to the Past" to our database. We integrate "Window to the Past" and this crowdsourcing database construction system into one application named "Crowd-Cloud Window to the Past."

Through our experiment, we evaluated this proposed crowdsourcing system. The results showed that users who knew a bit about the photographed place in the past picture were able to identify the locations and take photos there. In most uploaded pictures, the distance from the photographed place to the correct location was within 10 m. Moreover, all photos were taken at approximately the same camera angle, which could be sufficiently used as the reference images for "Window to the Past." If the appearance of the uploaded images was significantly different from the corresponding past pictures such as in Pattern 2, they were unable to judge accurately because there was very little information for making a decision. Moreover, users were unable to evaluate the correctness of the present pictures accurately if the appearance of the images was significantly different from the corresponding past ones. We should incorporate functions to judge the accuracy of the pictures.

In addition, we distributed this application, "Crowd-Cloud Window to the Past" through the Internet. We held workshops using this application in cooperation with many local communities and evaluated the interest and feasibility of this application. Here, we found that this application was slightly complex and time-consuming, but it had many interesting and acceptable aspects. For example, our application for looking for photographed positions provides users with entertainment, like games. Although we should sophisticate its user interface and user-motivating design, these results suggest that the proposed system could work well in gathering valuable user-generated contents to provide a richer AR experience.

In addition, we aim to extract the semantic importance of AR/VR contents for sharing and communicating historical and cultural values, and to construct a presentation interface and curation system at AR/VR experience based on its importance. So far, research on AR/VR technology has been focusing on reproducibility and spatial consistency

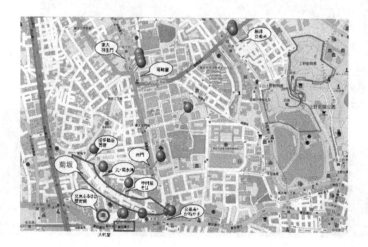

Fig. 6. One participant of our workshop registered

focusing on spatial resolution and three-dimensional accuracy, and semantic contents such as editing historical images. We have not dealt with the technology concerning it. For this reason, at the time of experiencing AR/VR contents, the user does not know what to experience from the degree of freedom, and it is currently impossible to share or communicate value only through AR/VR.

For that reason, weighting is given to the importance of spatial resources registered as images and images with semantics, and we are developing technologies to support experiences. In video materials, there is an attempt to generate content that allows the user to intuitively understand the information of exhibits appropriately by appropriately selecting and selecting portions with high historical value. We appropriately reflect the adjustment by the curation, dynamically adapt to the user's appreciation behavior, present the video, and make it easier to grasp the contents of the whole contents.

Moreover, by asking the user to register language information such as voice at the time of experiencing, the evaluation of the importance of the registered contents is performed by the speech recognition and analysis by the oral history approach, and based on the importance thereof, the user's. We adapted the method to induce appreciation behavior and shared important information.

Fig. 7. Meeting to hear the memories of Hongo 2017

Specifically, as various historical buildings and shops in Bunkyo-ku and Hongo are lost, recently we have talked to people who kept Hongo's "Kioku" such as ryokan and old shop owner, We held a meeting to think about what is the likeness (Fig. 6). As a guest speaker, President of the Imperial Ryokan's Feng Ming Library, also a well-established tea ceremony Bonna maiden, cafe tea shop owner shop owner, calling Oshima and shopkeepers who had been operating but stopped Chinese restaurant for many years, calling for Oral History's I listened (Fig. 7). The results are converted into data as audio and moving images, and are shared with social science researchers.

4　Study on Motivation Improvement Method of Regional Activities

By giving a sense of connecting the landscape of the long-lasting landscape to the future through the history exhibition of the area using the system constructed in Sects. 2 and 3, it is aggressive from the people who know the form of the neighborhood residents etc. We demonstrated and evaluated whether it is possible to revitalize the region while gaining participation. We held a regional experience workshop, evaluated whether we could register old photographs of elderly persons themselves, and brushed up the system while giving feedback.

This project is a "Cultural Resource Conference" (http: // tohbun (http: // tohbun)), organized by volunteers of experts and practitioners in various fields such as the Cabinet Office, Ministry of Land, Infrastructure and Transport, Agency for Cultural Affairs,.jp/) Hongo Project Team, through the kick-off symposium etc., we are deepening the introduction and understanding of the preservation of cultural resources to the residents of Hongo area. At this symposium, exhibitions and event announcements of Hongo's cultural resource materials collected so far (comments from users, recorded videos, pictures, etc., sent to Kikusui hot water disposal) were made on site. After that, we talked about the history and feelings about Hongo's Kioku and shared it, centering on Professor Tanigawa, Associate Professor Tanigawa, Mr. Hosomi Matsushita, others related to cultural resource conservation and utilization. A workshop was held with the theme of utilizing the cultural resources of Hongo, and all the participants gave free ideas on future activities and adopted it as guidelines for future activities (Fig. 8) .

Fig. 8. Kick-off symposium of Hongo Project Team

Fig. 9. Healthy town development festa in Bunkyo & Taito Ward

Fig. 10. Koto Ward AR tournament event tour

Efforts from a health point of view also started. Through regional science town planning, healthy community making festa in Bunkyo and Taito, I was able to ascertain how we can induce local streets walking around the place where old pictures were taken (Fig. 9). We also conducted demonstration experiments to see if it could actually be applied from the viewpoint of sightseeing. We organized an event tour around the Shenzhen during the 1964 Tokyo Olympics hosted by the Koto Ward Tourism Association. Applicants were responsible for building the AR system and customizing the contents, asking the Koto Ward guide meeting today to guide the guide and photograph preparation. Participants were publicly offered by Koto Ward newsletter, and there were a large number of 36 people, including 62 people, for 15 people. Participants got a very memorable remark about the city and got a comment from the guide that they understood the value as a new cultural resource of Shenzhen well (Fig. 10). We have already decided to carry out the second tour of the guided tour next year, we are currently in talks on the concrete contents of the tour, and it is deploying more than originally assumed.

5 Conclusion

The proposed method consists of building an AR system that can be operated sustainably and in a long-term space in public space and daily space, low cost such as content in a wide range, affinity to the environment, low labor cost and maintenance cost, environmental change, disturbance. It is possible to realize robustness to fool proof etc., autonomous development of AR content through user participation mediaization.

In addition, AR contents that can actually enjoy going out with fields of daily human activities as a field are already causing great influence on real economy economy, effect and market size is large. In addition, by creating and communicating AR contents closely tied to the area by themselves, revitalization of visiting behavior and promotion of participation in residents themselves are not limited to transient, but sustainable and autonomous. It can be a phenomenon.

This research applies this knowledge to the framework of community participation of experiencers themselves, making it possible to design social roles and activities of elderly people using ICT. It is also expected to have a great ripple effect on other museums from the viewpoint of collection, preservation and transmission of knowledge and experience of elderly people lost and materials and materials. Not only for museum use but also for the research and development of a wide range of fields related to aging, robust AR presentation method with high usability is desired, so the collection and sharing of regional contents achieved in this research and development. Exhibition technology is expected to have a large ripple effect.

Acknowledgement. This research and development work was supported by the MIC/SCOPE #162303009.

References

1. Narumi, T., Hayashi, O., Kasada, K., Yamazaki, M., Tanikawa, T., Hirose, M.: Digital diorama: AR exhibition system to convey background information for museums. In: Shumaker, R. (ed.) VMR 2011. LNCS, vol. 6773, pp. 76–86. Springer, Heidelberg (2011). https://doi.org/10.1007/978-3-642-22021-0_10
2. Shumaker, R. (ed.): VMR 2011. LNCS, vol. 6773. Springer, Heidelberg (2011). https://doi.org/10.1007/978-3-642-22021-0
3. Tanikawa, T., Narumi, T., Hirose, M.: Mixed reality digital museum project. In: Yamamoto, S. (ed.) HIMI 2013. LNCS, vol. 8018, pp. 248–257. Springer, Heidelberg (2013). https://doi.org/10.1007/978-3-642-39226-9_28
4. Arakawa, T., Kasada, K., Narumi, T., Tanikawa, T., Hirose, M.: Reliving video experiences with mobile devices. In: 2012 18th International Conference on, Virtual Systems and Multimedia (VSMM), pp. 581–584. IEEE (2012)

5. Nakasugi, H., Yamauchi, Y.: Past viewer: development of wearable learning system for history education. In: 2002 Proceedings of the International Conference on Computers in Education, pp. 1311–1312. IEEE (2002)
6. Nakano, J., Narumi, T., Tanikawa, T., Hirose, M.: Implementation of on-site virtual time machine for mobile devices. In: 2015 Virtual Reality (VR). IEEE (2015)
7. Manseibashi Reminiscent Window: On-Site AR Exhibition System 361
8. Uchiyama, S., Takemoto, K., Satoh, K., Yamamoto, H., Tamura, H.: MR platform: a basic body on which mixed reality applications are built. In: Proceedings of the 1st International Symposium on Mixed and Augmented Reality, p. 246. IEEE Computer Society (2002)
9. Chen, S.E.: Quicktime VR: an image-based approach to virtual environment navigation. In: Proceedings of the 22nd Annual Conference on Computer Graphics and Interactive Techniques, pp. 29–38. ACM (1995)
10. Microsoft image composite editor. http://research.microsoft.com/en-us/um/redmond/groups/ivm/ICE/
11. Imura, J., Kasada, K., Narumi, T., Tanikawa, T., Hirose, M.: Paper reliving past scene experience system by inducing a video-camera operator's motion with overlaying a video-sequence onto real environment. ITE Trans. Media Technol. Appl. 2(3), 225–235 (2014)

VR Games and the Dissemination
of Cultural Heritage

Lie Zhang[1(✉)], Weiying Qi[2], Kun Zhao[3], Liang Wang[3],
Xingdong Tan[4], and Lin Jiao[5]

[1] Department of Information Art & Design, Tsinghua University, Beijing 100084, China
zhlie@tsinghua.edu.cn
[2] Henan Police College, Zhengzhou 450046, China
qiwy266@qq.com
[3] Emperor Qinshihuang's Mausoleum Site Museum, Xi'an 710600, China
513419331@qq.com
[4] EZ360 Infotech Co., Ltd., Beijing 100041, China
tanxingdong@ez360.cn
[5] Luxun Academy of Fine Arts, Shenyang 110004, China
jljlgo@163.com

Abstract. Known as the Eighth Wonder of the World, the Emperor Qingshihuang's Mausoleum and Terracotta Warriors contain rich information and unique value in the field of history, culture, military, science and technology and so on, highlight the core values of Chinese civilization, and have become an epitome of Chinese history and culture. In recent years, with the rapid development of technologies such as augmented reality (AR), virtual reality (VR), video analysis based on indoor high-precision positioning, big data, mobile Internet and wearable interactive terminal etc., there are great opportunities and development space for the innovation and dissemination of cultural heritage. In this context, the Emperor Qingshihuang's Mausoleum in China, in collaboration with relevant scientific research units, developed the VR Terracotta Warriors Serious Games which is part of research series on Key Technologies of the Smart Museum for the Audience. The VR games combines the live experience of the audience, using 360° panorama shooting, 3D modeling, virtual reality, intelligent question-answering technology to design this games. From the real scene to the virtual scene, the audience can experience a wonderful journey through time and space, and learn the history and culture of Qinshihuang's Mausoleum. This game allows the audience have a deep experience. Through the combination of cultural heritage and VR games, this paper tries to explore new technologies to promote the interactive dissemination of cultural heritage, as well as the effective ways to promote the further prosperity of cultural tourism market.

Keywords: Cultural heritage · VR game · Virtual reality
The Emperor Qingshihuang's Mausoleum · Terracotta warriors

© Springer International Publishing AG, part of Springer Nature 2018
N. Streitz and S. Konomi (Eds.): DAPI 2018, LNCS 10921, pp. 439–451, 2018.
https://doi.org/10.1007/978-3-319-91125-0_35

1   Introduction

Emperor Qinshihuang's Mausoleum is the tomb of the first Chinese emperor Yingzheng (259–210 B.C.), a world famous cultural heritage and tourist destination. It is one of the largest, most peculiar and rich imperial tombs in the world. It fully displays the technical and artistic ability of the ancient Chinese working people more than 2000 years ago. It is the pride and treasure of the Chinese nation. The mausoleum of the First Emperor of Qin Dynasty contains rich information and unique value of history, culture, military, science and technology, but at the same time it has many unsolved riddles, and it is also a rich source of historical literature and anecdote.

The Terracotta Warriors Pits was discovered in 1974 and are known as "the Eighth Wonder of the World" and "one of the great discoveries in the archaeological history of the 20th century" [1]. The three terracotta warrior pits are arranged in a zigzag pattern with a total area of over 20,000 m². There are more than 7000 terracotta figures and real size terracotta horse statues which are have high artistic value.

The terracotta warriors and horses have an important position in the history of Chinese culture heritage, which reflect the political, military and social development and change from the Warring Sates period to the Qin dynasty. The terracotta warriors have huge model, neat organization, its shape and arrangement imitated the choreography of the army at that time, which showed the history of "The king of Qin conquered other six countries, and became the only king of the whole China". Therefore terracotta warriors and horses are symbols of the power and martial arts of the Qin dynasty. The shape of the terracotta warriors and horses used the extraordinary artistic techniques, vivid model, accurate proportion, rich and colorful clay to depict different identity, personalities and spirits. The terracotta warriors and horses have unique value of learning in the history of architecture, costumes especially the history of emperor tomb system which reflect realistic social life and the cultural traits of the Qing dynasty [2]. In addition, the unearthed cultural relics of the Qin Terracotta Warriors Pits are greatly changed the people awareness of science and technology level of the Qin dynasty.

With the rapid development of technologies such as augmented reality (AR), virtual reality (VR), indoor high-precision positioning video analysis, big data, mobile Internet and wearable interactive terminal, it has brought huge change in the way people get their public cultural resources. At the same time, it also has brought great opportunities and development for the spread of the cultural heritage of innovation and the development of cultural tourism. Based on this background, the Chinese museum of Emperor Qingshihuang's Mausoleum has joint relevant scientific research units to develop a serious VR terracotta warriors game which toward to audience's a series of wisdom museum in the cooperation of the key technology research. This VR games use the world famous "the Eighth Wonder of the World" of the Terra Cotta Warriors pit as the background, Combined with the audience's experience in the spot using technology such as the 360-degree panoramic camera, three-dimension modeling, virtual reality, intelligent questions etc. This game led the audience to learn the history and culture knowledge. With the emerging science and technology and creative development, this game will promote the further prosperity of cultural tourism market.

2   Related Work

With the rapid development of VR technology, in recent years, many museums at home and abroad have launched virtual tours of online museum based on the online virtual museum, enabling users from all over the world to visit the museum online and watch the important cultural relics in the museum through the Internet and the mobile Internet. For example, the British Museum and Google Street View have cooperated to make users use Google Street View online to visit the museum of the scene, and have a closer look at the museum exhibits [3] (see Fig. 1).

Fig. 1. British museum online virtual tour

Although the experience of wearing VR glasses has appear in many games, the application in the museum is not very common. In April 2016, the Capital Museum in Beijing introduced a virtual tour of VR during the exhibition of Fu Hao tomb [4], according to the use of the guide supplied by the museum, attendance can view the tomb of Fu Hao in 360° and experience different excavation layer after wearing VR glasses (see Fig. 2). Virtual reality brings a strong sense of immersion to the audiences, enabling the audiences to experience the historical environment. This bring a brand-new cultural experience to the audience.

Fig. 2. Capital museum VR visiting scene

On June 30, 2017, the EZ360 Company developed a "Van Gogh Virtual Reality Art Exhibition" for Changsha museum [5]. The Exhibition set up a "windmill town" VR cycling program, with the help of virtual wearable devices, the audience can enter Van Gogh's town, roaming in the Van Gogh's tulip country – Holland. This Virtual Reality Art Exhibition allow the audiences trace the footsteps of the artistic and explore Van Gogh' artistic inspiration (see Fig. 3).

Fig. 3. Scene of the Van Gogh virtual reality art exhibition at the Changsha museum

3 VR Terracotta Army Culture-Oriented Travel Game Design

3.1 The Raise of the Question

With technologies of virtual visual and interactive such as VR, AR, MR began to enter people vision, there is a growing demand for the sense of reality, immersion, and interaction of the visual experience. Through the analyze of surveys from audiences of the museum of Emperor Qingshihuang's Mausoleum, and backstage data analysis of APPs such as Yi You Terracotta Warriors and Horses which was launched by the museum over the past two years, and by video identification, mobile phone technology and equipment such as high precision indoor positioning, QR code the statistical analysis of the data and information collected at the museum, we found that the audiences has a great desires to know further about the story behind the cultural relics, and hope to have a closer contact with the Terracotta Warriors. Audiences hope to be able to enter to the Number One Terracotta Warriors Pit, and they even hope the Terra Cotta Warriors could "be alive" and interact with the audiences. Due to the realistic conditions and the safety of cultural relics, these hopes are impossible to be realized during the normal tour, and the audience can only stand outside the fences of the Terracotta Warriors pits. At the same time, through the devices such as the website, APP, VR devices, they could achieve a certain effect in the depth of the content and immersive, but as to lack of experience of "Being Present", it is difficult for viewers to achieve the ideal effect about the continuous attention of this kind of information and user viscosity.

The perception of the body and the surrounding space are the most basic cognitive activity of human beings, unlike the pure digital study, we emphasize the organic combination of numbers and space. As Norberg Schulz said, "The reason why man is interested in space is the root of existence" [6]. In space, we get the perception of the surrounding world through the body, and connect ourselves to the surrounding world, together constitute the perception of the world, and acquire the initial understanding of the world, namely, "beauty is physical and in deep space" by Melo Ponti [7].

In order to achieve a more comprehensive and in-depth tour experience effect, this project build a virtual world of the Terracotta Warriors. The design make full use of the site of cultural heritage, in combination with VR, integrated the "virtual" with "reality". We hope the audiences could get more intense sensory experience by and more profound understanding and cognition by interactive devices when they visit at the scene, and learn the history with modern technology to experience the Terracotta Warriors with zero distance of the story which happened more than 2000 years ago.

3.2 Function of Framework

The Emperor Qingshihuang's Mausoleum and Terracotta Warriors have abundant cultural heritage resources and profound historical and cultural knowledge, in order to meet the audiences' needs of understanding the Terracotta Warriors, and to spread the cultural content of the Emperor Qingshihuang's Mausoleum and Terracotta Warriors profoundly, this paper selects some representative of cultural heritage and cultural knowledge, and use the technologists such as the acquisition of three-dimension data, information on the field data fitting, three-dimension modeling technology, and make use of virtual reality, artificial intelligence technology to develop a set of field real virtual scene roaming and the series of little game in fictitious space with the combination of VR interaction system (see Fig. 4). The system based on the using of the real site of the three dimensional space and the Terracotta Warriors three-dimension data of cultural relics, and related knowledge and history which uncovered by the institute of archaeology. Such as the color of the Terra Cotta Warriors, the ancient military system, the ancient chariots and horses system, knowledge of ancient weapons etc. Using people's preference of the story of "crossing" and "treasure hunt" situation, let the audience wear VR glasses at the scene of the ruins, to feel the Terracotta Warriors Pit grand momentum and to see the full clear image of cultural relics. At the same time, they can also cross the time and space at the scene, and go back to thousands of years ago to find more interesting knowledge and detail. This system can bring the audience a full range of profound experience.

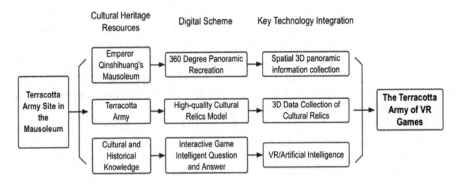

Fig. 4. VR terracotta warriors culture-oriented travel game design framework

The design has the following main points:

1. Conversion of real space and virtual scene. VR Terra Cotta Warriors were designed according to the pattern of the present experience. Using the real experience of the scene and the space experience to give the audiences more intense immersion and the presence experience by using VR technology.
2. Role interaction. The audiences participate in the interactive games with Terra cotta Warriors, resurrect Terracotta Warriors by granting weapons to them. The audiences can have video intelligent Q&A with Terracotta Warriors, virtual hand stitching and repair the damaged of cultural relics and so on. Participating in interactive games with a specific identity, let the audience have a strong sense of participation and identity. Gain knowledge and experience through interaction.
3. Serious game. Rigorous historical and cultural knowledge and archaeological discoveries are the basis of game scenes, props and plot design. The game tries to achieve a better balance between sensory experience and cultural heritage spread education. In setting up the mysterious atmosphere and situation to arouse the audience's desire to explore, with a strong sensory experience to attract the continuous

attention of the audience, and at the same time, put the rich cultural and archaeological information throughout the whole process, stimulating the audience's knowledge exploration desire, to acquire the satisfaction of absorbing knowledge and pleasure.

3.3 Main Development Process and Content

Data Acquisition. It is the first step to transform the live scene of emperor Qinshihuang's Emperor Mausoleum museum into online digital information. The information of the museums and cultural relics includes panoramic three-dimension and rich media information. A spherical panorama is used in the collection of scenes, and a panoramic photograph is taken every 5–10 m (see Fig. 5). After turning a cycle content can be restored in the VR glasses in the museum site 360°. For the collection of cultural relics information, it mainly adopts the 3D modeling which bases on photography technology and the modeling of 3DS Max. Because of the low cost of 3D modeling which base on photography, there is no harm to cultural relics, therefore, most of data collections use this method. Through the calculation of the real scene and the image sequence of the object, the position of each photo in the space is matched, and the special modeling tool is used to create the three-dimensional model with the texture.

Fig. 5. Panoramic view of the No. 1 site of terracotta warriors

Design of the Game Content. Design of VR Terra Cotta Warriors games regard audiences as the center, to the greatest extent possible to meet the audiences' need to get close and interact with the warriors, to learn more about the depth of understanding of cultural, and to the real scene and the virtual world seamless switching, roaming in the virtual world with the first calling, make and design of interesting quizzes, etc. The main structure of the game is as follows (see Fig. 6).

Visit the real site of mausoleum and Terracotta Army site

↓

From the real scene of No .1 site to the underground world

↓

Participate in the Terracotta Army related fun intelligence games
in the underground world. Answer correctly and pass to next level

1. Virtual Archaeology: coloring the Terracotta Army, stitching the bronze chariots and horses	2. Military practice: finding the right weapons, practicing archery	3. intelligent answer and communication with Terracotta Army: understanding the Terracotta Army of Emperor Qin Shihuan history

↓

Complete the final stage of
the game and return to the
real world

Fig. 6. VR terracotta warriors culture-oriented travel game structure

Virtual Tour of the Site. To satisfy the audience needs of having an interactive experience with the Terracotta warriors, VR-terracotta tour interactive equipment was deployed in the museum scene. The VR game can be experienced after visit the Terracotta Warriors pits. After wearing the VR glasses, the audience will firstly watch a scene constructed by the real photos of Emperor Qin Shihuang's mausoleum, the VR scene and the scene have the matching spatial scale, direction and shape matching, giving the audience a strong sense of reality (see Fig. 7).

Fig. 7. Terracotta warriors site VR tour

In this scene, the audience can feel the real museum space when they head down or look around by wearing glasses. As the audience moves forward, the objects on both sides of the scene move back while the contents in front of the eyes are constantly approaching. Through scene switching, VR glasses display the whole scene of the Emperor Mausoleum Museum, including the Terracotta Warriors No. 1 pit, the No. 2 pit, the No. 3 pit, and the Emperor of Qin Shihuang mausoleum.

Visitors can stand outside the fence to see the pit of the terracotta warriors. However, when the audience chooses the corresponding icon according to the on-screen instructions, the audience can enter the pit bottom of the terracotta army and interact with the terracotta warriors in close proximity (see Figs. 8 and 9). This is a completely impossible in the real world tour, which is easily realized in VR.

Fig. 8. Terracotta warriors No. 1 site VR tour

Fig. 9. Close look at terracotta warriors No. 1 site VR tour

From Reality to Virtual Time Travel. When the audience reaches the designated terra-cotta warriors in No. 1 pit, there will be ripples in the screen, which prompts the audience to enter the virtual scene into the ground (see Fig. 10). The VR Terracotta Warriors are designed according to the pattern of the presence experience, and the virtual space-time is seamlessly accessed through VR which give the audiences real scene feeling and the space experience, giving the audience more intense immersion feeling and the presence experience

Fig. 10. VR tour of the ripple effect

Fig. 11. VR tour into the underground world

With the swaying of the ripple, the audience go into the Virtual World of Terracotta Warriors. There is a series of interactive games waiting for the audience to pass (see Fig. 11). The audience can return to the world after completing all the tasks. However, the audience can stop the game at any time and return to the real world.

Knowledge of VR Game Creation. According to the historical data of the Mausoleum of the Qin Emperor, this paper has constructed a virtual underground world which is in line with the historical facts of Terracotta Warriors. In the underground world, the audience can understand the color of terracotta warriors, weapons, as well as bronze chariots and horses of the terracotta warriors. This part of the game experience content mainly "virtual archaeology", "the sword of the sword" and "Terracotta Warriors".

In the underground world, the viewer can pick up the torches on the ground and light the small torches on both sides of the tunnel. The audiences in the underground world can rotate back and forth and can also get the corresponding content of feedback. Although this is the three-dimensional modeling of virtual content, but one can still have a strong sense of immersion. The audience can walk in the tunnel, watch the tips given on the tunnel walls, according to the prompts, if the audience answers to questions about the Terracotta Warriors, then the gate of the figurines will open, and the audience would see the terracotta warriors and horses scattered in the underground world.

In the experience of virtual archaeology, the audience can color the Terracotta Warriors. The Terracotta warriors were originally colored, but exposure in the air made their bright colors fade away. Audiences need to accurately paint the terracotta warriors with corresponding colors, such as black hair, pink faces, black or brown eyes, and different colors on the armors.

The audience can also perform the task of splicing copper chariots. Emperor Qinshihuang mausoleum has the largest and most complete bronze chariots and horses which are great for the study of Chinese ancient chariots and horses system, sculpture art and refining technology, etc. They have the extremely important historical value. During the underground virtual tour, the audience can assemble the main components of the bronze

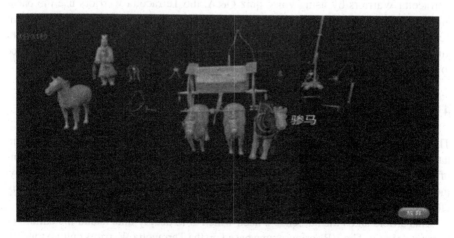

Fig. 12. VR tour into the underground world

wheel and canopy according to the order in which the bronze chariot was assembled by the Qin dynasty (see Fig. 12). When the audience successfully completed the task of the bronze chariot and horses, they can stand on the bronze chariot and ride on the battlefield of ancient times.

In the "sword dance" section, the audience needs to find the correct weapon for the terracotta warriors. Thousands of terracotta warriors belong to different categories and grades including spears and halberds, tomahawk, Shu, beryllium, bows, crossbows [8]. The audience needs to find their corresponding weapons for the terracotta warriors. When the audience finds the weapon correctly, the terracotta warriors will be activated and wield their weapons (see Fig. 13).

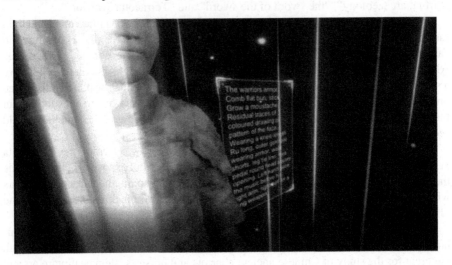

Fig. 13. Find weapons for the terracotta warriors in the underground world

In the process of underground road in the world, the audience can also talk with the Terracotta Warriors by using voice quiz Q&A, the Terracotta warriors use the background of large data, real-time answer audience questions by voice. The speech intelligent question answering system helps the audience to understand the ancient history knowledge, but also can give the audience through the authentic hint, helps the audience to pass quickly back to the ground.

4   Conclusion

The Mausoleum of the Qin Emperor and Terracotta Army is an outstanding representative of Chinese culture heritage. But under the restrictions of reality and safety reasons of cultural relics, the audience cannot be allowed to contact with Terracotta Army, therefore it is difficult to disseminate the brilliant history and culture of Qin Dynasty effectively.

This article takes the audience's need which is to deeply understand the culture of terracotta Army. The VR serious game based on the Terracotta Warriors culture tourism was developed for this purpose. The rigorous historical and cultural knowledge and archaeological evidences are the basis of the game designs including scenes, props and plot. The game tries to achieve a better balance between the sensory experience and the cultural heritage dissemination and education. While setting up mysterious atmosphere and situations along with a strong sense experience stimulating the audience's desire to explore and attracting the audience's attention, the game will enrich the cultural and archaeological information. The game will stimulate the audience's desire for knowledge and allow them explore the Mausoleum of the Qin Emperor and Terracotta Army pits with pleasure.

Acknowledgement. This article was supported by the Ministry of Science and Technology of People's Republic of China Fund Project in Cultural Relics Protection Inheritance and Innovation of Technology Application and Demonstration (Grant No. 2015BAK01B00) and the subproject Four Project in Research and Demonstration of Key Technology of the Audience's Smart Museum in Mobile Internet Environment (Grant No. 2015BAK01B04) and the National Social Science Fund Project in Arts-Development Status and Construction of Interaction Design Discipline (Ministry of Culture 13CB113).

References

1. http://www.bmy.com.cn/2015new/contents/463/18357.html
2. Zhao, Z.: Terracotta Army: Chinese civilization spirit identification. Sanqin Metropolis Daily, 05 March 2015
3. http://www.britishmuseum.org/with_google.aspx
4. http://www.sootoo.com/content/662346.shtml
5. http://hunan.ifeng.com/a/20170630/5785364_0.shtml
6. (Norway) Norberg Schulz: Existence. Space. Architecture. Yin Peitong. Translation. China Architecture Industry Press, Beijing, June 1990
7. Morris Melo Ponti's phenomenology of perception. Jiang Zhihui transl. The Commercial Press, Beijing (2001)
8. Qin Shihuang Terracotta Army Museum: World Heritage Series: Mausoleum of the First Qin Emperor and Terracotta Army. World Book Inc., Beijing (2008)

Thinking Transformation of Traditional Animation Creation Based on the Virtual Reality Presentation

Yue Zhou[✉] and Yunpeng Xu[✉]

Academy of Design Art, Shenyang Jianzhu University, Shenyang, China
824497078@qq.com, 1965621076@qq.com

Abstract. With to the advent of the new media era and the promotion of virtual reality technology, the thinking pattern of traditional animation creation is no longer completely appropriate for the need of social development. Both the animation's artistic context and its communicational mode have undergone profound changes. Based on the connotation of animation creation and the comprehensive influence of the new media's form and environment, this paper analyzes the existing theoretical foundation of creation and the analysis of the characteristics of virtual reality technology, and studies how traditional animation in the period of new media representation can make use of virtual reality to realize the idea innovation and the transformation of creative thinking, and explore the shift of creative thinking and the way of describing stories from the perspectives of subject, script, scene, usage of lens, viewpoint selection, transfer mode, etc. The paper also indicates how to seize the scale of interaction and the communication of the subject.

Keywords: Virtual reality · Traditional animation creation
Thought of traditional animation

1 Introduction

When traditional animation, film and television gradually can not meet people's requirements for visual experience, technical innovation is inevitable. Virtual reality technology was born at a time when it was urgent to address the growing visual experience of people. "Demand Promoting and Technology Driving" is the ubiquitous rule for every kind of technology to develop, including the virtual reality technology.

The application of VR to the animation field is still at the exploratory stage. Comparing the current stage with the traditional animation creation, there are still significant differences in the presenting effect. how to undertake and carry out the thinking in the future development of VR animation are the difficulties which needs to be solve with research and discussions.

2 The Meaning of the Traditional Animation Creation

The Animator's Survival Kit says: "Animation is a special form of art, its soul is above but comes from reality. It can turn life's 'dare not' into 'dare'......" [1], it is animation creation that employs various manifestations to exaggerate the true story

© Springer International Publishing AG, part of Springer Nature 2018
N. Streitz and S. Konomi (Eds.): DAPI 2018, LNCS 10921, pp. 452–466, 2018.
https://doi.org/10.1007/978-3-319-91125-0_36

and present it to the audiences, letting them accept what the creator wants to express joy more easily.

2.1 The Formation and Development of Traditional Animation

Chinese traditional animation creation has various forms and themes. From artistry to cultural connotations, it owns a position in the world's field of animation creation, sets a good example and has a great impact on other countries' animation creation.

From 1920s to 1980s, Chinese traditional animation creation entered the first peak. At that time, the themes and elements of animation creation became the basis of Chinese animation characteristics by exploring and introducing the traditional Chinese art and culture. The former animation creators began to widely absorb the pith of Chinese traditional folk art, dramatically integrating the expressive methods such as paper cutting, opera, puppet, shadow puppet, paper folding and Chinese Brush Painting into the field of animation's art creation. The combination between the element of traditional art culture and animation creation is not only in accordance with the tastes of the people at home and abroad, but also opened up a new way for carrying forward Chinese traditional culture and folk art.

Various excellent animations made at that time also became the classic works of Chinese traditional animation in the memory of a generation of Chinese people and set a firm basis for the following creation. Later on, with the development of the society, the themes and contents of the animated works also become increasingly various, the expressive form of animation art is more diversified, the manifestation of animation art is more diversified, and the domestic animation creators are gradually exploring more possibilities.

2.2 The Characteristics of Traditional Animation

Continuity and Long-Term. Chinese traditional culture is board and profound, and the development of animation has formed the features of Chinese characteristics. The themes of Chinese traditional animation are largely derived from chapter novels, operas, legends and folk stories, which makes it possible to divide a subject into numerous plots and be coherent with long-term and continuous characteristics.

Combining Policy and Marketization. China attaches great significance to the development of cultural soft power; traditional animation, being the carrier of art and culture, it has a large cultural influence globally, and the national promoting policy is one of the positive factors for the development of Chinese traditional animation. Meanwhile, the huge demand in domestic animation industry is the fountain of the creation of traditional animation industry, and satisfying the need of the market's diversification is the primary goal of Chinese traditional animation creation. Therefore, its market's characteristics and industry condition are the fruit of the interplay between policy and market.

Containing Profound Educational Significance. The main audience of animation is teenagers, and traditional animation's guiding effect of spreading idea and social values is not negligible. Chinese traditional animation's theme usually delivers the Chinese traditional virtues, and pursues higher core cultural values.

2.3   The Creative Thought for Composition of Traditional Animation

The creative thought for the composition of traditional animation is through the whole producing process, and is reflected respectively in each stage:

During the general designing stage, in accordance with the social demands and combining with the market research, the animation creators make plan, draft a script, get inspiration from the story and social news and establish the theme and spiritual orientation of the works. The general story is roughly formed during this stage, and the creators all want to render the correct value and interest to the audiences through the works.

During the designing and producing stage, the creators combine their own artistic accumulation and apply color modeling elements with distinctive style and artistic features from numerous traditional art cultures by absorbing and extracting into the design of role and scene. By combining the theoretical basis of audio-visual language, the creators then make storyboards, which reflect the rhythmic cohesion of each link in the script and strengthen the artistic atmosphere of the picture and the infectivity of the role emotion.

During the actual creating stage, the primarily main job is the in-betweens of the original painting and coloring. From the traditional Chinese Brush Painting to the contemporary advanced paperless animation, the creators both pursue the distinctive style of work and explore expressive methods which are more diverse. With the development of creating techniques, more excellent animation works emerge and present a striking artistic effect, bringing us the enjoyment of beauty.

During the post-production stage, edition is conducted according to the director's anticipation and the design of the storyboards; a good edition applies montage to greatly improve the artistic expression, and the integration of sound, soundtrack and sound effect invigorate the works, enhancing the rhythmicity and infectivity of the story from the level of auditory sense.

3   The New Trend of Animation's Development Drove by New Media

Nowadays, being the main communicational means of the information age, new media has replaced many traditional ones. As New Media Literacy puts it, Microblog, blog, online video, online forum, SMS, etc., as the new media emerging in people's life, their practicality and maneuverability is more suitable for existing in the contemporary world when compared with the traditional medium [2].

3.1   The Concept of New Media

New media is the technique and Internet is supported by the digital technique and is mainly characterized by interactivity. They are the media of interaction and the tool and means of two-way information dissemination, such as new material, image and artistic language. It is also represented by new organizations responsible for collecting, distributing and distributing information such as micro-blog, WeChat, social media, and video website. New media is from computers or relies on computer circulation, including URLs, human-machine interface, virtual world, virtual reality, multimedia, electronic games, electronic animation, digital video, movie effects, network movies, interactive computer equipment, etc.

3.2 The Speculative Process of Animation Creation Triggered by New Media

The history of animation's development is firstly the history of media's development. Every progress of the media and the birth of every kind of new media are both the opportunity and challenge of animation, leading to the innovation of idea and thinking pattern.

Animation art is the sheer thought in the creator's mind before its creation, what the animation can do is toward the creator's imaginary world to exhibit the fanciful imagination. The technical support is needed to find a powerful exit beyond the reality and construct a world which parallels the world we live in. The proper intervention of new media is able to make the perspective of the imaginary world credible and enable the audiences to combine the true image with the imaginary figure. The estrangement of the two disappear, and the world mix together and form a new entity. The audiences can be provided with a brand-new perspective.

3.3 The Contextual Relation Between the Formation of New Media and the Development of Animation

Artistic context always refers to the environment produced in the creation of art, and the outcome surrounded by the work and influenced by the art producer, art intermediary and art appreciator in a certain social context; in the three contextual structures including the context of art production, the social context of art, and the text of art, the development of contemporary art is apparently impacted by both the advanced technique in the production chain and the social customs and the appreciators' increasing experience appeal, unceasingly forming the new contextual relationship of animation in the VR age.

New Media Gives Birth to New Ideas. The emerging of new media enables dynamic images and audio to dominate most of our leisure time; the shaped political idea and the social behavior change the structure of our daily life. New media culture also offers many people assistance to mold the world-wide popular views and the most profound value. The affinity between the animation art and the new media reveals that the new medium affects the reality and the future of the independent animation. The new media will have a significant impact on the animation itself when its culture fully affects our cultural life.

New Media Gives Birth to New Structure. New media rebuilds the relations between the virtual and real reality. Synthetic technology constantly refreshes the boundaries to surpass reality, while new media's intermediation and the virtual digital information provide a large amount of fragmentary information to the publishers and recipients. It runs in a semantic web, each of which can be referenced to each other, linked by hypertext, nevertheless, the molding and thinking mode of culture or artistic concept are remolded by the media. With its emergence, the specific media such as electronic screen, mobile phone surface and streaming media reacting to the animation art as content, also change the structural performance of animation.

New Media Changes the Public's Accepting Ways. The most obvious change of new media to our life is the change of our ways to accept information. Today's media are fully linked; the traditional, new, and especially the mobile media make our daily life medialized all the day. Closely linked with the media, animation constantly relates other old and new media; the public create their feeling in animation image text, the animated object he or she accepts is no longer the object from the creator, but the image text from the works interacting between the recipients.

4 The Experiential Characteristics of Virtual Reality in the New Media

Virtual Reality (VR for short) is a technology which is able to create an interactive three-dimensional virtual world with multi-sense and multi-source information fusion. Through such multi-sensory and interactive method, the user can feel an immersive feeling [3]. Virtual reality technology, being the strongest technology of immersive interactive experience in the new media, has been unparalleled in the 2016 of the year of virtual reality.

4.1 Browsing Flow Experience

Virtual reality technology is the lifelike three-dimensional images created by computer according to human's physiological and psychological characteristics of vision and hearing. Putting on the interactive equipment such as helmet indicator and data glove, the user is able to be immersed in a virtual environment and become a member. While moving the head, the images in the virtual environment will change accordingly; objects can move with the hand's motion when picked up, meanwhile, three-dimensional simulation sound can be heard. In the virtual environment, user feels that everything is so lifelike and there is an immersive feeling. Such kind of experience enables the audiences to enter the animation scene with a strong sense of presence to immerse in.

4.2 Conductive Interactive Experience

Human-machine interaction in virtual reality system is nearly like a natural interaction. The user is able to interact not only with the keyboards and the mouse, but also via special helmet, data glove and other sensing devices. The computer can adjust the image and sound presented by the system according to the motion of the user's head, hand, eye, language, and body. The user can test or operate objects in a virtual environment through their natural skills such as their own language, physical movement, or action. This experience can enable viewers to selectively track multiple scenes, observe scene props, thus enhancing the interaction experience between the audience and the scenes.

4.3   Sublime Interactive Experience

Virtual reality technology should have a broad imaginable space to expand the scope of human cognition. It can not only reproduce the real environment, but can also create an objective environment that does not exist or ever happen. As the virtual reality system is installed with visual, auditory, touch, and dynamic sensing and reaction devices, the user can thus obtain visual, auditory, tactile, dynamic, and other perceptions in the virtual environment. The sense perception of their arrangement and reorganization breaks the limitations of previous experience, making the sense of the senses magnified and extended indefinitely. This experience enables the audiences watching movies with technical services provided by the cinema to get more sublimation sensory experience, the audiences and the characters in the movie are able to experience the same feeling, which is the so-called empathy.

5   The Advantage of Introducing VR Technology in Animation

5.1   VR the Progressive Choice of VR Animation's Interactive Level

With the development of the technology and the improvement of people's material civilization and living standard, the characteristics of the traditional two-dimensional animation cannot meet with the audiences' needs; a growing number of audiences attach more importance to the presentation and emotional communication, hoping they themselves could be integrated into the animation and communicate with the characters.

The application of VR technology in animation creation has changed the current animation greatly. The application of such technology to construct 3D virtual animated image with the equipment creating real spatial sense allows the audiences to directly participate in the plot and interact with the characters. While appreciating the animation, the audience is allowed to not only get better visual and psychological satisfaction, but also have new recognition and thinking to art; it is more beneficial to the further development and progress of animation.

VR technology is a technology which is built upon the simulation technology and is more real. It not only extends the audiences' sense, but also enables people to obtain other senses from other ways besides the physical sensory organs and perceive the images beyond the reality via image medium [4].

Currently, VR animation's interaction has achieved three levels:

Simple interaction: The primary way to perform a panoramic view is still relatively simple. Through panoramic photographic equipment's 360-degree rotation and moving shooting, the audiences can fully observe the virtual space exhibited, having a sense of involvement to achieve the most basic visual level of interaction.

Complex interaction: The more profound interactive participation needs to be realized by three-dimensional virtual animated images. Setting a virtual camera to lead the audiences to participate in the exploration of the virtual space screen, and then achieve displacement interaction. Such VR animation is more focused on guiding the audiences to actively observe and discover through rich details.

Creative interaction: The more complex VR animation may involve the development of applications, it is able to achieve the effect where the audiences participate in and choose the development of plot, making the audiences more role-oriented and more involved in the development. The three levels of VR interaction provide them with an increasing sense of immersion and interactive experience in accordance with the degree of active participation.

5.2   The Multiple Choices of VR Animation's Recreational Perception

VR technology can be interpreted as that the VR builds a world and an environment with the help of the computer and some peripheral induction equipment. It is not a consciousness, nor a real existence, but a new existence in the world. It has the dual characteristics of dependence and transcendence with the reality, closing the distance between the reality and the virtual world.

People not only perceive the animation's effect by watching and hearing, but also by desiring to have more feelings of participation to let the taste, touch and every part of the body perceive the rhythm of the plot development of the animation and know when to tense, when to relax, when to enjoy and when to be sad...the audience hopes to link more sensory organs with the virtual worlds in animation to feel the sunshine, the clear river and the wonderful terrain. Hoping to perceive the world in the animated story is possible and personally experience the information of the animated kingdom. People are born with a desire to control and in animated story to be able to flexibly master the time and space of the animation. We also hope for excitement while flying through the jungle with Tarzan and the enjoyment of feeling the agility every time when climbing vines.

People's perception of all things in the world comes from the inductive organs, which are mainly divided into visual, auditory, tactile, smell and taste. Due to their physiological characteristics, the environment and things around them are mainly induced by vision and hearing. According to scientific researches, vision occupies about 80% of human's perception of the objective world; today, most of us use vision to realize virtual reality and augmented reality. Visual deception is closely related to the audiences' physiological responses such as the plot that roller coaster makes people afraid; the use of VR technology to display content enables the human brain's perception of picture to be upgraded to another level of time and space, thus making the emotional interaction between audience and animation becomes deeper.

The freshness and experience of VR animation can also catch the curious audience. Through the virtual space created by the creator, it can create the immersive sense of immersion to quickly mobilize the audience's emotion and participation, attract the audience's attention in a short time, let the audience devote themselves to VR works, and enhance the interest and entertainment of the works.

6   The Display of Virtual Reality (VR) Boosting the Revolution of the Creative Thinking in Traditional Animation

There are differences between the VR animation and the traditional animation. For those who make animation, VR makes the animation become more active compared with traditional passive animation. It could endow the animation with the playful and interactive features through different methods, such as getting into the character. The design of the scripts, characters, scenes and plots should be attached to the features of the VR technology which include interaction, immersion and multi perception in the creation of VR animation.

6.1   The Selection of the Subject and the Content

The main difference between the animated cartoon and other forms of film and television art is that the former needs infinite imagination and is not limited by real and objective rules and shapes. The display of imagination in animation cannot be compared by other traditional film and television forms. This imagination could be amplified and externalized to a larger degree based on the application of the VR technology. Creators could make use of this new technology to experience things that are invisible and unachievable in the real world and make their unrestrained minds be more figurative and authentic to be perceived.

Specifically, creators could conceive with a more open mind instead of being restrained by the perceived environment of the material world in their animation production, in which their imagination and inspiration could be fully presented. The interaction provided by the VR technology enables the audience to be immersed in the story and to actually experience the scenes of the script and interact with the characters, which brings up a new feeling. Undoubtedly, this would spark the creators' inspiration and help reflect the personal features an artist and the differentiation and non-substitutability of each artwork.

Although, currently, the development of the VR technology is likely to display all audiovisual feelings, the films that are more interactive should particularly stress on the content which is more recreational, intellectual and enjoyable or which features exotic culture and pays more attention to travelling in the selection of the subject, as the audience would gain more sensory stimuli and immersive experiences. Nevertheless, horror should be avoided because VR features the enlarged sensory stimuli due to the difficulty in distinguishing between genuine and fake, and the deep immersion.

Based on the authentic news documented by BBC, the film is produced by Aardman Animations can be regarded as the continual exploration of BBC for VR potential for future medium. One of the most famous works of Aardman Studio is the stop-motion Claymation *Wallace & Gromit*. *We Wait* is the initiative attempt at the immersive story description. The familiar Claymation of the Aardman team gives the immersive film a unique and great experience. *We Wait* highlights the loss, fear, anticipation and excitement of homeless refugees when they try to go across the sea to Europe. The team uses motion capture devices and figures out the best way to depict all the characters in the limited conditions of the project (Fig. 1).

Fig. 1. The VR animated short film *We Wait* (Source: http://www.sohu.com/a/121681470_505777)

6.2   The Organization of the Clue in the Script

Different from the "narrative" display of traditional animation, VR animation tends to the actively "discovering" and "exploring" audience. Therefore, the nonlinear narrative method could be considered by the creators in writing the script. Meanwhile, they could take into account the interactive plots which endow the story with immersion and participation. The audience could observe or even explore from multi aspects.

The overall development of the story is guided by the shooting scripts and the nonlinear structure is combined with narration. Details which could be excavated by the audience are added to extend the story through exploration. Differentiating from the continuity of the traditional animation, the information points in VR, such as props, motion, light, color and sound, are adopted to attract the audience's attention and then move the plot.

Audience participation determines the structure of the script in writing. It can be divided into several types, such as one with various moving plots with a similar ending, one with various moving plots with various endings, and one with one moving plot with various endings.

In the VR world, height and walk are free. Linear and nonlinear structures are combined to avoid the excessive freedom and low attention of the audience to plots. The plots will be distinguished as primary and secondary. Although, the plots are different, they will guide the audience into the main plot, which will make the film more interesting and bring rich experiences to the audience.

It describes the story of a girl who accompanies her father, a musician who composes the song *No Wrong Way Home*. The scene of the story is in a car and it plays from the perspective of the passenger. *Pearl* is multi-structural. There are several trigger points in the plot which may produce different endings. Its screen time ranges from five minutes to seven minutes (Fig. 2).

Fig. 2. VR animation *Pearl* – The first VR animation nominated for an Oscar (Source: http://www.sohu.com/a/128967067_223570)

6.3 The Spatial Arrangement of the Scene

In traditional two-dimensional (2D) animation, the display of the space is finished by simulating the three-dimensional (3D) things in the 2D way. 3D animation is able to present a relatively authentic world, but it is fundamentally a 2D display mode. It only displays a 2D plane set up by the author, while the audience cannot perceive from other perspectives and dimensions. Therefore, more attention is paid in displaying the space and dimension in designing the scene of VR animation. The VR technology is adopted to strengthen the sense of reality in the 3D model, break the spatiotemporal limit and bring the actual 3D feeling to the audience.

In designing the scene, each detail of the VR animation should be elaborately designed, there should be a clear distinction between the primary and the secondary, and the virtuality and reality should be combined, compared with the scene designing of the traditional animation. There must be no dead angle at 360 degrees for all objects in the scene. All the directions must be accurate compared to the former behavior that only the part which is shot is prepared.

The leading role Henry is a hedgehog that yearns for friendship. His aggressive appearance makes him fairly annoyed. He is lonely and has no friends. The audience is supposed to be involved in and holds the birthday party with him. The good immersion provided by the delicate scene and the shape design of the character enables the audience to experience a totally different feeling with that on screen in this short story (Fig. 3).

Fig. 3. The scene design of VR animation *Henry* (Source: http://www.sohu.com/a/130034086_ 285313)

6.4   The Control of the Rhythm and Keynote

A clear distinction between VR animation and the traditional animation is the display and control of the rhythm of the story. The director takes absolute control of the rhythm of the story and largely uses montage in editing and cutting in the traditional animation. The sentiment and attention of the audience fully depend on the design of the atmosphere of the story by the director. However, the audience owns the dominant right in VR animation where their participation in the virtual world is further enhanced. It is necessary to start with more details, such as lens switch and the combination of music and sound effect, to highlight the rhythm of VR animation. The treatment should be more natural and subtle so that it seems to be actively uncovered by the audience. It is important to seize the function of details about the stimulation of the mental feelings of the audience and finish the guide of the rhythm of the audience's sentiments insensibly, which could increase the immersion of the work and the participation of the audience.

At present, the way to control the stimulation degree of the audience in response to details is a research difficulty. Faced with different events or objects, individual response degree of the audience is determined by the age, experiences, life experience, interests, focuses and other aspects. It might be an alternative to design various details to guide the audience.

It tells the story of a little girl Ella who goes out wearing her new sunglasses. It rains as long as she puts on the sunglasses and the rain stops if she takes off the sunglasses. It is a VR short film which involves many interactive elements. The time the audience spends on focusing on a certain part of the story would affect the content they watch. For instance, there are two lovers who are drinking in front of the bar. The longer time audience watch them, the more they get drunk (Fig. 4).

Fig. 4. The VR animated short film *Rain or Shine* (Source: http://www.sohu.com/a/128967067_223570)

6.5   Setting of the Observation

In the current traditional animation, the conversion of viewpoint is a narrative practice, which is more conducive to the audience to perceive the message conveyed by the works from multiple levels as of objective ones and subjective ones. The VR animation presents in an entire environment, with no concept of field of view, so the audience as the first-person point of view are under no limits. Audiences do not know where they ought to look at, nor do creators know where to let them look. No editing, no storyboard. Therefore, it is most likely for the audience to lose the key details of the story simply by turning around. Of course, we can design guiding factors like sound, light, color, and video into it which requires the designer of VR animation to carry multiple levels of design thinking.

In the VR animation, the audiences often act as active participants, keeping up with the plot. Therefore, the character design can be made in a richer form, so that the character's style and image can be more distinctive, better fitting the script and plot design. Taking into account the audience's self-recognition and their own conditions like height, environment, and actions, which can be used to guide the plot. Because the participants may vary in observation speed and degree of exploration, there shouldn't be too much plots at the same time, or the audiences would lose the focus, narrative clues, and the continuity of plot.

The background of the story is that two aspiring aliens are bent on ruling the earth and trying to destroy anyone who stops them. But when they came to Earth they met two cute rabbits, and the player's character was one of two rabbits (Fig. 5).

Fig. 5. VR Animated Short Film "Invasion" (Source: http://www.sohu.com/a/128967067_223570)

6.6 Transition Design

In traditional animations, it is necessary for the director to use the lens for the narration of the story. The occurrence of the story needs transition between the scenes. Generally, the audience does not care about the relationship between the characters and the beginning of the next scene, which solely relies on the clipping by the creators to present for the audience. The common traditional transitional methods include: fade in and fade out, cut to, fold change, dark fade out and so on.

Although the VR animation is the active plot participation by the audience, it is difficult to avoid the story transition to promote the story line. In VR animation transition, the audience's sense of involvement can easily be interrupted, thus the transition needs careful consideration to look smoothly, focusing on creating the feelings of the audience, otherwise, their attention would be diverted elsewhere. For example, the audience's attention is concentrated on the main line of this scene when suddenly, behind him, there is a sound, and the audience's attention will be attracted by the voice, and hence the realization of the transition is done. By enlarging the scope of the focus to show a scene, and through narrowing, we can eliminate the surrounding scenes. In this way, we have achieved a transition mode of superposition (Fig. 6).

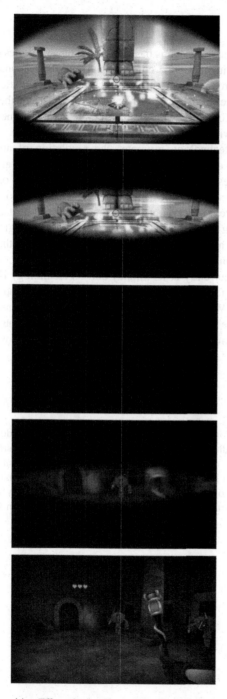

Fig. 6. The Blinked Transition Effects in the Case of *Tomb of the Golems* (Source: https://www.zhihu.com/question/40002907#answer-29107251)

7 Conclusion

Traditional animation at this stage is based on some basic theories of film and television art. In the VR field, it breaks the conventional two-dimensional observation mode, creating great breakthroughs in the means and methods of artistic expression. The VR animation performance needs to be reformed on the basis of the traditional film and television art theory, combined with the unique interaction, immersion and conception of the technology of virtual reality.

The progress of technology promotes the revolution of art. The new medium generates new context of the development of animation art. VR animation can give full play to the advantages of virtual reality. From the selection of theme content, the organization of script cues, arrangement of scene space, master of the basic tempo, and setting of the audience's observation to design of transition, it can change the traditional creative thinking and implement a disruptive innovation, giving the animation art new expressive forms and infectious capabilities, so as to meet the audience's growing aesthetic experience and interaction needs.

VR animation is currently at its infancy and its technology is immature. Relevant research of academic theories needs continuous exploration and reform based on the traditional animation. With the development and application of more advanced devices and technologies, the front-projected holographic display augmented reality can combine with VR animation, it is believed that one day we can walk in a "real" dream hall.

References

1. Richard, W.: Animators' Survival Handbook. Faber & Faber, London (2002)
2. Huang, C.: New Medium Quality: Theory Guide. Intellectual Property Press, Beijing (2012)
3. Liu, Q.: New Ideas of Virtual Reality Technology Development Inspiring New Media Animation Creational Methods. Times Education, Chengdu (2016). (in Chinese)
4. Wang, S.: Research of Application of Virtual Reality Technology in Animation Creation. Popular Culture & Arts Publishing House, Shijiazhuang (2016). (in Chinese)

Author Index

Printed in the United States
By Bookmasters